HUMAN RIGHTS AT WORK

Should workers ever lose their job because of their political views or affiliations? Should female employees be entitled to wear a headscarf in the workplace for religious reasons? Can it ever be right for an employer to dismiss someone for personal activities undertaken in their leisure time? What restrictions, if any, should be placed on the right to strike?

Engagingly written, this innovative new textbook provides an entry point for exploring these and other topical issues, enabling students to analyse the applicability of human rights to disputes between employers and workers in the UK. It offers an original perspective on the traditional topics of employment law as well as looking in greater depth at new issues, such as employees' use of social media or the enforcement of human rights in the gig economy.

Uniquely, the book considers the most important international Conventions that are relevant for the law in the UK, especially the European Convention on Human Rights, the European Social Charter, Conventions of the International Labour Organisation, and the Charter of Fundamental Rights of the European Union.

A central question that each of the chapters addresses is whether UK employment law is compatible with human rights law. Each chapter discusses all the key cases drawn from various jurisdictions, including the Court of Justice of the European Union and the European Court of Human Rights.

Written by a stellar team of authors, this textbook is an invaluable teaching aid for both postgraduate and undergraduate students studying employment law, human rights, human resource management, and industrial relations.

Human Rights at Work

Reimagining Employment Law

Alan Bogg
Hugh Collins
ACL Davies
Virginia Mantouvalou

·HART·
OXFORD · LONDON · NEW YORK · NEW DELHI · SYDNEY

HART PUBLISHING

Bloomsbury Publishing Plc

Kemp House, Chawley Park, Cumnor Hill, Oxford, OX2 9PH, UK

1385 Broadway, New York, NY 10018, USA

29 Earlsfort Terrace, Dublin 2, Ireland

HART PUBLISHING, the Hart/Stag logo, BLOOMSBURY and the Diana logo are
trademarks of Bloomsbury Publishing Plc

First published in Great Britain 2024

Copyright © Alan Bogg, Hugh Collins, ACL Davies and Virginia Mantouvalou, 2024

Alan Bogg, Hugh Collins, ACL Davies and Virginia Mantouvalou have asserted their right under the Copyright,
Designs and Patents Act 1988 to be identified as Authors of this work.

All rights reserved. No part of this publication may be reproduced or transmitted in any form or by any means, electronic or
mechanical, including photocopying, recording, or any information storage or retrieval system,
without prior permission in writing from the publishers.

While every care has been taken to ensure the accuracy of this work, no responsibility for loss or damage occasioned to
any person acting or refraining from action as a result of any statement in it can be
accepted by the authors, editors or publishers.

All UK Government legislation and other public sector information used in the work is Crown Copyright ©.
All House of Lords and House of Commons information used in the work is Parliamentary Copyright ©.
This information is reused under the terms of the Open Government Licence v3.0 (http://www.
nationalarchives.gov.uk/doc/open-government-licence/version/3) except where otherwise stated.

All Eur-lex material used in the work is © European Union,
http://eur-lex.europa.eu/, 1998–2024.

A catalogue record for this book is available from the British Library.

A catalogue record for this book is available from the Library of Congress.

Library of Congress Control Number: 2024940203

ISBN: PB: 978-1-50993-874-2
ePDF: 978-1-50993-873-5
ePub: 978-1-50993-875-9

Typeset by Compuscript Ltd, Shannon
Printed and bound in Great Britain by CPI Group (UK) Ltd, Croydon CR0 4YY

To find out more about our authors and books visit www.hartpublishing.co.uk.
Here you will find extracts, author information, details of forthcoming events
and the option to sign up for our newsletters.

Preface

All four of us have written extensively about human rights issues in the workplace: on the justifications for thinking about (some) labour rights as human rights, on the usefulness of human rights standards as benchmarks against which to evaluate domestic law, on interpretive strategies for labour rights in human rights instruments, and on the practical utility of human rights arguments in strategic litigation, among other themes. Our interests range widely across core labour law topics such as collective rights, domestic work, forced labour, privacy, dismissal and working time. It therefore seemed appropriate and timely to draw our collective expertise together into a single volume, in which we aim to provide scholars and students alike with a critical overview and analysis of the field.

Our interest in human rights at work has also informed our teaching. We all teach courses on this theme in our respective universities – Bristol, LSE, Oxford and UCL – and have, at times, taught together. We would like to express our thanks to our colleagues and to generations of students who have sharpened our thinking and tested our assumptions. We hope that this book will help future cohorts to engage more fully with the challenges of ensuring that the rights of working people are respected.

We would like to thank colleagues at Hart Publishing for their enthusiastic support for the project, their patience during the writing process and their efficiency in getting the book into print.

Alan would like to acknowledge his mum, Jean, with love and gratitude. She died while this book was being completed. She was a single mum engaged in precarious employment, first as a mill worker, then cleaner, retiring finally in social care. Her life as a working class woman animates many of the concerns considered in the pages of this book.

Contents

Preface v
Authors' Bios xi
List of Abbreviations xiii
Table of Cases xv
Table of Legislation (UK) xxiii
Table of EU Materials xxvii
Table of National Legislation xxxi
Table of European and International Materials xxxiii
Table of UK Other Materials xxxvii

1. Introduction 1
   1. In the Beginning … 1
   2. Collective Laissez-Faire and Human Rights 2
   3. Labour Rights as Human Rights? 4
   4. Human Rights as a Threat to Collective Values? 5
   5. The Role of States: Negative and Positive Obligations 6
   6. The Role of Courts: Human Rights and Constitutional Limits 8
   7. The Future of Human Rights at Work? AI, Algorithms, Climate Crisis 10
   8. The Case for 'Human Rights at Work' 11

2. Sources of Rights at Work 13
   1. UK Law and the Human Rights Act 1998 13
   2. Council of Europe: European Convention on Human Rights and the European Social Charter 16
   3. Law of the European Union 20
   4. The International Labour Organization 23

3. Human Rights and Personal Scope 28
   1. The Basic Problem of Personal Scope 28
   2. Employment Status and Human Rights: The Position under General Employment Law 29
   3. Employment Status and Human Rights: Addressing the Gaps Using the ECHR and HRA 1998 35
   4. Personal Scope and Human Rights under EU Law 42
   5. Conclusion 47

4. Right to Equal Treatment and Equal Opportunity 48
   1. The Universality of Human Rights 48
   2. Article 14 ECHR 50

	3.	Positive Rights for Women 54
	4.	Age Discrimination and the Right to Work... 59
	5.	Disability Discrimination 61
	6.	Challenging Exclusion – Migrant Workers.. 63
5.	Freedom of Association... 66
	1.	Freedom of Association: Sources of Protection and the Integrated Approach............ 67
	2.	The Right to Organise as a Fundamental Human Right............................... 68
	3.	Blacklisting and Human Rights... 75
	4.	The Closed Shop 77
	5.	Trade Union Autonomy and Human Rights 81
	6.	Conclusion 85
6.	Human Rights and Worker Voice 86
	1.	Industrial Democracy, Worker Voice, and Human Rights........................... 86
	2.	Sources of Legal Protection: ILO and EU 89
	3.	Trade Union Recognition and Collective Bargaining 92
	4.	The EU Social Model: From Consultation to Collective Bargaining?...... 99
	5.	Conclusion 109
7.	The Right to Strike 110
	1.	The Moral and Political Foundations of a Human Right to Strike 110
	2.	The Right to Strike as a Human Right: Sources of Legal Protection...... 112
	3.	The Right to Strike at the Individual Level.. 116
	4.	The Right to Strike at the Collective Level.. 122
	5.	The Right to Strike in EU Law: Free Movement vs The Right to Strike......... 129
	6.	The Right to Strike in UK Labour Law: Right or Immunity?................... 131
8.	The Right to Work... 133
	1.	The Right to Work in International Human Rights Law........................... 135
	2.	Can Certain Jobs be Prohibited? 139
	3.	Regulatory Exclusions from Jobs and Work Sectors 141
	4.	Employers' Controls Over Access to Work 144
	5.	Prison Labour... 144
	6.	Welfare-to-Work 146
	7.	Conclusion 150
9.	Migration, Slavery, Servitude, Forced Labour and Human Trafficking........... 151
	1.	Labour Migration... 152
	2.	Agricultural Work and Seasonal Visas 153
	3.	Domestic Labour and the UK Overseas Domestic Worker Visa 156
	4.	Undocumented Workers... 158
	5.	Slavery, Servitude, Forced and Compulsory Labour.................................. 160
	6.	UK Modern Slavery Act 2015 163
	7.	Conclusion 165

Contents

10. The Right to Fair Pay 166
    1. Three Interpretations of the Right to Fair Pay 166
    2. Collective Bargaining 168
    3. A Living Wage 170
    4. Fairness within Organisations 175
    5. Conclusion 182

11. The Right to Reasonable Limitation of Working Hours 183
    1. Introduction 183
    2. Sources and Themes 183
    3. Weekly Working Time 186
    4. Paid Annual Leave 191
    5. Rights to Leave for Family Reasons 193
    6. Rights Relating to the Organisation of Working Time 196
    7. Conclusion 198

12. Business, Supply Chains and Human Rights 199
    1. Background 199
    2. Self-Regulation by MNCs 201
    3. Home State Initiatives 204
    4. International Initiatives 209
    5. Conclusion 213

13. The Right to Private Life at Work 214
    1. Private life at work 215
    2. Workplace Monitoring and Surveillance 216
    3. Blurred Boundaries 219
    4. Data Protection 225
    5. Testing 227
    6. Conclusion 228

14. Private Life Away from Work 229
    1. Dismissal and the Right to Private Life 230
    2. Spatial Isolation and Private Life 232
    3. Relevant Factors and Criteria 233
    4. Sexual Intimacy: None of the Employer's Business 236
    5. Criminal Convictions 238
    6. Employers' Reputation 240
    7. Reconceptualising Privacy: A Sharp Line for Life Away from Work 240
    8. Conclusion 241

15. Freedom of Expression Connected to the Performance of Work 242
    1. Tension between Freedom and Contractual Terms 243
    2. Valuable Speech and Abuse 247
    3. Trade Union Activities 248
    4. Whistle-blowing 252
    5. Academic Freedom 257
    6. Conclusion 259

16. Freedom of Expression Outside Work ... 261
1. Private Life and Social Media ... 262
2. Freedom of Belief ... 264
3. Unfair Dismissal and Freedom of Expression ... 268
4. Legitimate Interests of Employers ... 271
5. Political Speech ... 273
6. Offensive Speech and Hate Speech ... 275
7. Conclusion ... 277

17. Freedom to Manifest a Religion ... 279
1. Religious and other beliefs ... 280
2. Framing of Claims ... 282
3. Working Hours ... 285
4. Dress Codes ... 286
5. 'Conscientious Objection' to Providing a Particular Service ... 289
6. Expressing Religious Views ... 290
7. Religious Organisations as Employers ... 292
8. Conclusion ... 294

18. The Right to Protection against Unjustified Dismissal ... 295
1. Why is Protection against Unjustified Dismissal Important? ... 295
2. The Missing Right ... 297
3. The Right to Work ... 299
4. The Right to Respect for Private Life ... 300
5. Justified Grounds of Dismissal for Fault under the ILO Convention ... 304
6. Justified Grounds of Dismissal for Reasons of Business Reorganisation ... 305
7. Fair Procedure Prior to Termination of Employment ... 307
8. Exclusions ... 308
9. Conclusion ... 309

19. Human Rights as the Justification for Labour Law ... 310
1. The Implicit Agenda ... 310
2. The Formal Qualities of Human Rights ... 312
3. Human Rights or Fundamental Rights? ... 314
4. Two Conceptions of the Interests Protected by Human Rights ... 315
5. Are Labour Rights Human Rights? ... 317
6. Should All Labour Rights be Regarded as Human Rights? ... 319
7. Public and Private Law ... 320
8. Subordination in Employment ... 322
9. Radical Critics of Human Rights ... 323
10. The Moral Justification of Labour Law ... 325

Index ... 327

Authors' Bios

Alan Bogg, MA, DPhil, Professor of Labour Law, University of Bristol, Barrister, Old Square Chambers and Emeritus Fellow, Hertford College, Oxford

Hugh Collins, FBA, MA, BCL, LLM, LLD, Cassel Professor of Commercial Law, London School of Economics, and Emeritus Vinerian Professor of English Law, All Souls College, Oxford

ACL Davies, MA, DPhil, FBA, Professor of Law and Public Policy, Faculty of Law, University of Oxford, and Fellow of Brasenose College, Oxford

Virginia Mantouvalou, LLM in Human Rights, PhD, Professor of Human Rights and Labour Law, University College London, Faculty of Laws, and Co-Director of the UCL Institute for Human Rights

List of Abbreviations

ARD	Acquired Rights Directive
AWB	Agricultural Wages Board
CA	Court of Appeal
CAC	Central Arbitration Committee
CCAS	Conference Committee on the Application of Standards
CEACR	Committee of Experts on the Application of Conventions and Recommendations
CEDAW	Convention on the Elimination of All Forms of Discrimination against Women
CESCR	Committee on Economic, Social and Cultural Rights
CFA	Committee on Freedom of Association
CJEU	Court of Justice of the European Union
CRPD	United Nations Convention on the Rights of Persons with Disabilities
CRD	Collective Redundancies Directive
CSDDD	Corporate Sustainability Due Diligence Directive
DPA 2018	Data Protection Act 2018
EAT	Employment Appeal Tribunal
ECHR	European Convention on Human Rights
ECJ	European Court of Justice
ECSR	European Committee of Social Rights
ECtHR	European Court of Human Rights
EEA	European Economic Area
EEC	European Economic Community
ERA 1996	Employment Rights Act 1996
ESC	European Social Charter
ET	Employment Tribunal
ETD	Equal Treatment Directive
ETI	Ethical Trading Initiative
ETUC	European Trade Union Confederation
EU	European Union
EUCFR	EU Charter of Fundamental Rights
EWC	European Works Council
GB	ILO Governing Body
GC	Grand Chamber
GOR	genuine occupational requirement
I&C	Information and Consultation
HRA 1998	Human Rights Act 1998
HRC	UN Human Rights Committee
HRDD	human rights due diligence
ICCPR	International Covenant on Civil and Political Rights
ICESCR	International Covenant on Economic, Social and Cultural Rights
ICJ	International Court of Justice
ILC	International Labour Conference
ILO	International Labour Organization

MNC	multinational company
MNE	multinational enterprise
MSA 2015	Modern Slavery Act 2015
NCP	National Contact Point
NMW	National Minimum Wage
ODW	Overseas Domestic Worker visa
OECD	Organisation for Economic Co-operation and Development
PrWD	Pregnant Workers Directive
SNB	Special Negotiating Body
TEU	Treaty on European Union
TFEU	Treaty on the Functioning of the European Union
TULRCA 1992	Trade Union and Labour Relations (Consolidation) Act 1992
UDHR	Universal Declaration of Human Rights
UKIM	United Kingdom Independent Mechanism
UKSC	United Kingdom Supreme Court
WTD	Working Time Directive

Table of Cases

A, B and C v Ireland [2010] ECHR 2032, (2011) 53 EHRR 13.. 231
Abdul Ahad Ganai And Ors v Ut of J&K & Ors, 26 December, 2022, High Ct of Jammu & Kashmir and Ladakh at Srinagar.. 171
Abrahamsson v Fogelqvist (Case C-407/98) EU:C:2000:367, [2000] ECR I-5539............................... 52
Achbita v G4S Secure Solutions (Case C-157/15) NV EU:C:2017:203, [2017] 3 CMLR 21 .... 283, 287
Advisory Opinion (OC-18/03), Legal Condition and Rights of Undocumented Migrant Workers, 17 September 2003, Inter-American Ct of Human Rights... 41, 165
AEK ry v Fujitsu Siemens Computers Oy (Case C-44/08) [2010] ICR 444 102
AGET Iraklis (Case C-201/15) EU:C:2016:972, [2017] 2 CMLR 32 .... 21, 103
Ahmad v United Kingdom (1982) 4 EHRR 126............ 286
Airey v Ireland (A/32) (1980) 2 EHRR 305 18
Albany International BV (Case C-67/96) EU:C:1999:430, [1999] ECR I-5751 106
Alemo-Herron v Parkwood Leisure Ltd (Case C-426/11) EU:C:2013:521, [2014] 1 CMLR 21 .... 21, 106
Allen v Hounga [2014] UKSC 47, [2014] ICR 847 63
Allonby v Accrington and Rossendale College (Case C-256/01) EU:C:2004:18, [2004] ECR I-873..... 43
ALM Medical Services Ltd v Bladon [2002] EWCA Civ 1085, [2002] ICR 1444, CA..................................... 256
American Cyanamid Co v Ethicon Ltd [1975] AC 396, HL 128
A-MV v Finland, [2017] ECHR 273, (2018) 66 EHRR 22... 231
Andrle v Czech Republic [2011] ECHR 326, (2015) 60 EHRR 14... 52
Antovic and Mirkovic v Montenegro [2017] ECHR 1068, CE:ECHR:2017:1128............................. 219
Appeal No 08-41.359, Cour de cassation, Social Chamber, 4 June 2009, France..................................... 308
Appeal No 11-25580, Supreme Ct, Social Chamber, 26 March 2013, France... 308
Archibald v Fife Council [2004] UKHL 32, [2004] ICR 954... 138
Arrowsmith v UK (1981) 3 EHRR 218, Commission... 281
ASLEF v UK (11002/05) [2007] ECHR 184, (2007) 45 EHRR 34.. 82–3, 84, 85
Association de Médiation Sociale v Hichem Laboubi (Case C-176/12) ECLI:EU:C:2014:2, [2014] ICR 411... 307

Associated Newspapers Ltd v Wilson; Associated British Ports v Palmer [1995] 2 AC 454, HL................. 72
Association de mediation sociale v Union locale des syndicats CGT (Case C-176/12) EU:C:2014:2, [2014] IRLR 310, [2014] 2 CMLR 41............. 46, 91, 106
Association of Academics v Iceland (App No 2451/16) Admissibility decision of 15 May 2018 19
Association of Civil Servants and Union for Collective Bargaining v Germany [2022] ECHR 543, ECLI:CE:ECHR:2022:0705 ....81, 94, 116, 131
Attorney General of Canada v Frederick James Tobin 2008 FC 740, 329 FTR 279, 16 June 2008, Federal Ct (Canada).. 239
Autoclenz Ltd v Belcher [2011] UKSC 41, [2011] ICR 1157... 32, 33, 174
Axel Springer v Germany [2012] ECHR 227, (2012) 55 EHRR 6, 32 BHRC 493, [2012] EMLR 15.. 271
Azam v Ofqual, [2015] 3 WLUK 560, 19 March 2015, EAT... 251
Azmi v Kirklees MBC [2007] ICR 1154, EAT............... 288
Bah v United Kingdom [2011] ECHR 1448, (2012) 54 EHRR 21... 64
Baka v Hungary [2016] ECHR 568, (2017) 64 EHRR 6, Grand Chamber.. 313
Bank Mellat v HM Treasury (No 2) [2013] UKSC 39, [2014] AC 700.. 267
Barbulescu v Romania [2017] ECHR 742 (Press Release)... 217–8, 223, 225, 228, 231
Barbulescu v Romania [2017] ECHR 754, [2017] IRLR 1032... 17, 291
Barclays Bank Plc v Various Claimants [2020] UKSC 13, [2020] AC 973.. 207
Baris v Turkey, (App No 66828/16), 27 January 2020.. 119, 120
Bass Taverns Ltd v Burgess [1995] IRLR 596, CA 251
Belgian Linguistics Case (No 2), (App Nos 1474/62 et al), Merits, 23 July 1968.............................. 51
Besse v Reach CPA Inc, 2023 BCCRT 27, Canada 219
Betriebsrat der Ruhrlandklinik gGmbH v Ruhrlandklinik GmbH (Case C-216/15) EU:C:2016:883, [2017] 2 CMLR 13 45
BVerfG 1 BvL 7/16 (05.11.2019), German Constitutional Ct 147
Bigaeva v Greece [2011] ECHR 2164..................... 143, 303
Blantyre Netting Co v Chidzulo (MSCA Civil Appeal 17 of 1995) [1996] MWSC 1 (Malawi) 305
Botham v Ministry of Defence [2011] UKSC 58, [2012] ICR 201... 299

Bougnaoui v Micropole SA (Case C-188/15) EU:C:2017:204, [2017] 3 CMLR 22 287
Bowater v NW London Hospitals NHS Trust [2011] EWCA Civ 63, [2011] IRLR 331 244–5
Boychuck v H J Symons Holdings Ltd [1977] IRLR 395, EAT 245
Brincat and Others v Malta [2014] ECHR 836 7
British Airways Engine Overhaul Ltd v Francis [1981] ICR 278, EAT 251
British Gurkha Welfare Society v UK (2017) 64 EHRR 11 59
Brough v UK, App No 52962/11, Admissibility Decision of 30 August 2016 .... 76, 303
Byrne Bros v Baird [2002] ICR 667, EAT 31
Çam v Turkey (51500/08) [2016] ECHR 206 52
Campagnano v Italy (App No 77955/01), (2009) 48 EHRR 43, [2006] ECHR 241 142
Campbell v MGN Ltd [2004] UKHL 22, [2004] 2 AC 457 .... 233, 322
Campbell and Cosans v United Kingdom (1982) 4 EHRR 293 .... 265, 281
Carrington and others v Therm-A-Stor Ltd [1983] ICR 208, CA 73
Case of the Tailors of Habits &c of Ipswich (1614) Michaelmas Term, 12 James 1, Coke's Reports, Vol 11, 53a (KB) 144
Cave v The Open University, 5 May 2023, ET 281
Cengiz and Others v Turkey [2015] ECHR 1052 264
Centrum voor Gelijkheid van Kansen en voor Racismebestrijding v Firma Feryn NV (Case C-54/07) EU:C:2008:397, [2008] ECR I-5187 287
Chandler v Cape Plc [2012] EWCA Civ 525, [2012] 1 WLR 3111 207
Chandra Bhavan Boarding and Lodging v State of Mysore and Anr, 29 September 1969, 1970 AIR 2042, 1970 SCR (2) 600, Sup Ct of India 171
Chant v Aquaboats Ltd [1978] ICR 643, EAT 73, 251
Chappell v UK (1988) 10 EHRR CD 510 280
Cheall v United Kingdom (No 10550/83), Comm Dec 13.5.85, DR 42/178 83
Chesterton Global Ltd v Nurmohamed [2017] EWCA Civ 979, [2018] ICR 731 255
CHEZ (Case C-83/14) EU:C:2015:480, [2016] 1 CMLR 14 286
Chowdury v Greece App No 21884/15, Judgment of 30 March 2017 [2017] ECHR 300, ECLI:CE:ECHR:2017:0330 .... 7, 153, 161–2
CJD v Royal Bank of Scotland [2013] CSIH 86, [2014] IRLR 25 239
Clyde & Co LLP v Bates van Winkelhof [2014] UKSC 32, [2014] ICR 730 .... 31, 32, 33
CN v UK, App No 4239/08, Judgment of 13 November 2012 161
CN v UK (4239/08) [2010] ECHR 380 224
Confederation of Swedish Enterprise v Sweden (Collective Complaint no 12/2002) 79
Commission v Germany (Case C-271/08) EU:C:2010:426 130–1
Commission v Italy Case (C-32/02) ECLI:EU:C: 2003:555, [2003] ECR I-12063 44
Commission v UK (Case C-383/92) [1994] ECR I-2479 102

Commotion Ltd v Rutty [2006] ICR 290, [2006] IRLR 171, EAT 197
Copland v UK [2007] ECHR 253, (2007) 45 EHRR 37 216
Copsey v WBB Devon Clays Ltd [2005] EWCA Civ 932, [2005] ICR 1789 .... 270, 283, 285
Cornwall CC v Prater [2006] EWCA Civ 102, [2006] IRLR 362 .... 30, 33
Cox v Ministry of Justice [2016] UKSC 10, [2016] AC 660 175
Crisp v Apple Retail (UK) Ltd, ET/1500258/11, 5 August 2011 .... 232, 263
CW v UK [1993] ECHR 69, (1993) 16 EHRR CD44, Commission 281
Danilenkov v Russia (Application No 67336/01) [2009] ECHR 1243, (2014) 58 EHRR 19 .... 70, 77, 116, 117, 120, 121
Danosa v LKB Lizings SIA (Case C-232/09) EU:C:2010:674, [2011] 2 CMLR 2 43
De Wilde v Netherlands (2023) 76 EHRR SE4 281
Demir and Baykara v Turkey (34503/97) [2008] ECHR 1345, (2009) 48 EHRR 54, [2009] IRLR 766, Grand Chamber 8, 18, 19, 27, 94, 95, 168, 306
Denisov v Ukraine, App No 76639/11, [2018] ECHR 1061, Judgment of 25 September 2018, Grand Chamber 42, 216, 237, 270, 302, 303
Denmark v Parliament and Council (Case C-19/23) (case in progress) 108
DH v Czech Republic No 57325/00 [2007] ECHR 922, (2008) 47 EHRR 3, 13 November 2007 51
Dilek v Turkey, App No 74611/01 and others, 17 July 2007 .... 116, 117
Dixon v West Ella Developments Ltd [1978] ICR 856, EAT 73
DP & JC v United Kingdom, 38719/97, Judgment of 10 October 2002, [2002] ECHR 633, (2003) 36 EHRR 14 7
Drew v St Edmundsbury Borough Council [1980] ICR 513, [10980] IRLR 459, EAT 74
Dudgeon v UK [1981] ECHR 5, (1981) 4 EHRR 149 .... 236, 237
Duport Steels Ltd v Sirs [1980] 1 WLR 142, HL 123
E Ivor Hughes Educational Foundation v Morris [2015] IRLR 696, EAT 102
EB v France (43546/02) [2007] ECHR 211, Grand Chamber 53
Ebrahimian v France (App No 64846/11), [2015] ECHR 1041, 26 November 2015 288
EDF Energy Powerlink Ltd v National Union of Rail, Maritime and Transport Workers [2009] EWHC 2852 (QB), [2010] IRLR 114 125
Edwards v Chesterfield Royal Hospital NHS Foundation Trust [2011] UKSC 58, [2012] ICR 201 .... 42, 299, 300
Edwards v SOGAT [1971] Ch 354, CA 84
ETF v Schuerings (Case T-107/11) P EU:T:2013:624 297
Egenberger v Evangelisches Werk fur Diakonie und Entwicklung eV (Case C-414/16) EU:C: 2018:257, [2019] 1 CMLR 9 292–3
EI v SC Brink's Cash Solutions SRL (Case C-496/22) ECLI EU:C:2023:741 102

Table of Cases

Eiger Securities LLP v Korshunova [2017] ICR 561, EAT 255
Ellis v Parmagan Ltd (unreported, 2 February 2014), ET 265
Emel Boyraz v Turkey [2014] ECHR 1344, [2015] IRLR 164 .... 54, 300
Enderby v Frenchay Health Authority (Case C-127/92) [1993] ECR I-5535, [1994] ICR 112, ECJ 178
Enerji Yapi-Yol Sen v Turkey (68959/01) [2009] ECHR 2251 114
Erbakan v Turkey (App No 59405/00), Judgment of 6 July 2006 277
Esterman v NALGO [1974] ICR 625, ChD 84
Eugen Schmidberger Internationale Transporte Planzuge v Austria (Case C-112/00) EU:C:2003:333, [2003] ECR I-5659 131
Eweida and others (Chaplin, Ladele and McFarlane) v UK [2013] ECHR 37, (2013) 57 EHRR 8, 34 BHRC 519 .... 52, 196, 235, 280, 282–3, 284, 285, 287, 288, 289
Express Newspapers Ltd v McShane [1980] AC 672, HL 123
Faramus v Film Artistes' Association [1964] AC 925, HL 83
Faure v Australia, Comm 1036/2001, UN Doc A/61/40, Vol II at 97 (HRC 2005) 148
Federación de Servicios de Comisiones Obreras v Deutsche Bank SAE (Case C-55/18) ECLI:EU:C:2019:402 190
Fenoll v Centre d'aide par le travail 'La Jouvene' (Case C-316/13) EU:C:2015:200, [2016] IRLR 67 45–6
Fernandez Martinez v Spain [2014] ECHR 615, Grand Chamber 235–6, 301–2
Fernández Martínez v Spain (2015) 60 EHRR 3 .... 293, 294
FKJ v RVT [2023] EWHC 3 (KB), [2023] 1 WLUK 21 220–1
Florindo de Almeida Vasconcelos Gramaxo v Portugal [2022] ECHR 1073, ECLI:CE:ECHR:2022:1213 222
FNV Kunsten Informatie en Media v Netherlands (Case C-413/13) EU:C:2014:2411, [2015] 4 CMLR 1 .... 43, 107, 129
Forstater v CGD Europe, ET 2200909/2019, 18 December 2019; UKEAT/0105/20/JOJ, [2022] ICR 1, EAT 265–6, 281
Fredrick Ouma v Spectre International Ltd [2013] eKLR, Kenya 179
Fuchs v Land Hessen (Case C-159/10) EU:C:2011:508, [2011] 3 CMLR 47 60
Fuentes Bobo v Spain [2000] ECHR 96, (2001) 31 EHRR 50, Grand Chamber 246
Game Retail Ltd v Laws, [2014] Info TLR 369, UKEAT/0188/14/DA, 3 November 2014, 2014 WL 6862769 276
Gan Menachem Hendon Ltd v De Groen [2019] ICR 1023, EAT 293
Garamukanwa v UK (70573/17) [2019] ECHR 445, [2019] IRLR 853 221
Georgiev (Social policy) ECLI:EU:C:2010:699, [2010] EUECJ C-250/09, [2011] 2 CMLR 7 61

Ghaidan v Godin-Mendoza [2004] UKHL 30, [2004] 2 AC 557, HL 14–15
Gibbins v British Council, 2200088/2017, 3 November 2017, ET 261, 262, 263, 264, 271, 272, 275
Gilham v Ministry of Justice [2019] UKSC 44, [2019] ICR 1655 .... 38–9, 254
Grainger Plc v Nicholson [2009] UKEAT 0219_09_0311, [2010] ICR 360, EAT 265, 281, 282
Grange v Abellio London Ltd [2017] ICR 287, [2017] IRLR 108, EAT 188
Gray v Mulberry Co (Design) Ltd [2019] EWCA Civ 1720, [2020] ICR 715 283
Greek General Confederation of Labour (GSEE) v Greece, Complaint No 111/2014, decision on the merits of 23 March 2017 172
Grimmark v Sweden (43726/17) [2020] IRLR 554, ECHR 289
Guja v Moldova [2008] ECHR 144, (2011) 53 EHRR 16 (Grand Chamber) 253
Guja v Moldova (No 2) [2018] ECHR 206, ECLI:CE:ECHR:2018:0227 253
Guevara Díaz v Costa Rica, judgment of 22 June 2022, Series C, No 453 (Inter-American Ct of Human Rights) 138
Gustafsson v Sweden [1996] ECHR 20, (1996) 22 EHRR 409 81
Halford v UK [1997] ECHR 32, (1997) 24 EHRR 523 216
Hall v Woolston Hall Leisure Ltd [2001] 1 WLR 225, [2000] 4 All ER 787, CA 39
Heinisch v Germany [2011] ECHR 1175, [2011] IRLR 922, ECtHR 254, 256
Higgs v Farmor's School [2023] EAT 89, [2023] ICR 1072 .... 266, 267, 284, 291, 292
Hill v Governing Body of Great Tey Primary School [2013] ICR 691, [2013] IRLR 274, [2013] UKEAT 0237_12_2901 .... 16, 246–7, 269
Hizb Ut-Tahrir and others v Germany (31098/08) [2012] ECHR 1045 277
Hode and Abdi v United Kingdom [2012] ECHR 1871, (2013) 56 EHRR 27 64
Hoffmann v South African Airways (CCT 17/00) 28 September 2000 .... 61, 238
Holship Case. See Norwegian Confederation of Trade Unions (LO) v Norway
Hoppen and Trade Union of AB Amber Grid Employees v Lithuania [2023] ECHR 46, ECLI:CE:ECHR:2023:0117 71
Hörnfeldt v Posten Meddelande AB (Case C-141/11) ECLI:EU:C:2012:421 60
Horváth and Kiss v Hungary [2013] ECHR 92, (2013) 57 EHRR 31 52
Hospital Medical Group Ltd v Westwood [2012] EWCA Civ 1005, [2013] ICR 415 32
Hounga v Allen [2014] UKSC 47, [2014] ICR 847 .... 39–40, 158–9
Humpert and Others v Germany [2023] ECHR 1008, Grand Chamber 128
Hungary v European Parliament: Re The Posted Workers Directive [2021] 2 CMLR 9 130
IB v Greece, App No 552/10, [2013] ECHR 908, Judgment of 3 October 2013 .... 17, 61, 238, 303

Iceland Frozen Foods Ltd v Jones [1983]
ICR 17, [1982] IRLR 439, EAT 230, 268
Independent Workers Union of Great Britain v
Central Arbitration Committee and another
(Deliveroo) [2023] UKSC 43, [2024]
ICR 189.. 34, 36, 37, 38, 97, 98
Internationale Handelsgesellschaft, decision
of 29 May 1974, BVerfGE 37................................... 21
Internationale Handelsgesellschaft mbH v
Einfuhr- und Vorratsstelle fur Getreide und
Futtermittel (Case 11/70) EU:C:1970:114,
[1970] ECR 1125.. 9, 21
International Transport Workers' Federation v
Viking Line ABP (Case C-438/05) EU:C:2007:772,
[2007] ECR I-10779 .... 9, 22, 129, 130, 131
IX v WABE ev (Case C-804/18) EU:C:
2021:594, [2022] ICR 190........................ 282, 284, 287–8
Jet2.com Ltd v Denby [2018] ICR 597,
[2018] IRLR 417, UKEAT/0070/17/LA 72
Jivraj v Hashwani [2011] UKSC 40,
[2011] WLR 1872 34–5
JK v TP SA (Case C-356/21) EU:C:2023:9,
[2023] 3 CMLR 8 43
Johanssen v Norway (No 13537/88), Comm
Dec 7.5.90 83
K v Installux, ECLI:EN:CCASS:2022:SO00945,
Cour de Cassation, Chambre Sociale,
21 Septembre 2022... 248
Karacay v Turkey (App No 6615/03),
27 March 2007 116
Karlsson v Sweden (App No 12356/86),
8 September 1988... 293
Khadija Ismayilova v Azerbaijan [2019] ECHR 11,
ECLI:CE:ECHR:2019:0110 223
King v Sash Window Workshop Ltd (Case C-214/16)
EU:C:2017:914, [2018] ICR 693, [2018]
2 CMLR 10 .... 22, 192
Kiobel v Royal Dutch Petroleum Co 569 US 108
(2013) 206
Kiyutin v Russia [2011] ECHR 439, (2011)
53 EHRR 26 61
KMC v Hungary (19544/11) [2012]
ECHR 1563 307–8
Kopke v Germany (420/07) [2010] ECHR 1725 219
Kostal UK Ltd v Dunkley [2021] UKSC 47,
[2022] ICR 434.. 98–9
Kreuziger v Land Berlin (Case C-619/16)
EU:C:2018:872, [2019] 1 CMLR 34 192
Kücükdeveci v Swedex GmbH & Co KG
(Case C-555/07) [2010] ECR I-365 106
Kyriakides v Cyprus (App No 39058/05),
[2008] ECHR 1087, 16 October 2008 304
Lacatus v Switzerland (App No 14065/15),
[2021] ECHR 37, Judgment of 19 January 2021 141
Landeshauptstadt Kiel v Jaeger (Case C-151/02)
EU:C:2003:437, [2003] ECR I-8389.......................... 189
Laval un Partneri Ltd v Svenska
Byggnadsarbetareforbundet (Case C-341/05)
EU:C:2007:809, [2007] ECR I-11767 .... 9, 22, 129, 131
Lawrence v Regent Office Care Ltd (Case C-320/00)
[2002] ECR I-7325... 179
Lawrence v Secretary of State for Justice,
ET/3401016/2016, 23 March 2017, ET 232
Lawrie-Blum v Land Baden Württemberg
(Case 66/85) [1986] ECR 2121................................... 43
Laws v London Chronicle (Indicator Newspapers)
Ltd [1959] 1 WLR 698, [1959] 2 All ER 285, CA 86
Leander v Sweden [1987] ECHR 4, (1987)
9 EHRR 433.. 215
LF v SCRL (Case C-344/20) EU:C:2022:774,
[2023] ICR 133... 282, 287
Libert v France (588/13) [2018] ECHR 185 221–2
Ligebehandlingsnaevnet v HK/Danmark
(Case C-587/20) EU:C:2022:419, [2022]
3 CMLR 31 43
Lingens v Austria [1986] ECHR 7, (1986) 8
EHRR 407.. 242, 269
Lochner v New York 198 US 45 (1905) S Ct US 325
Lockwood v Department of Work and Pensions
[2013] EWCA Civ 1195, [2014] ICR 1257 59
Lommers v Minister van Landbouw, Natuurbeheer
en Visserij (Case C-476/99) EU:C:2002:183,
[2002] ECR I-2891 55
London & Birmingham Railway Ltd v Associated
Society of Locomotive Engineers and Firemen;
Serco Ltd v National Union of Rail, Maritime &
Transport Workers [2011] EWCA Civ 226,
[2011] ICR 848... 124–5
London Borough of Hammersmith and Fulham v
Keable [2021] UKEAT 2019-733, [2022] IRLR 4 270
London Underground Ltd v Edwards (No 2)
[1999] ICR 494, [1998] IRLR 364, CA..................... 286
Lopez Ribalda v Spain (Nos 1874/13 and
8567/13) [2019] ECHR 752, Grand Chamber........... 219
Lustig-Prean and Beckett v United Kingdom [1999]
ECHR 71, (2000) 29 EHRR 548 236
Lyon v St James Press Ltd [1976] ICR 413, EAT 73, 251
M Samzun v Ms de Wee, 1 July 2008,
Appeal No F 07-44.124 Cour de cassation,
Social Chamber.. 308
Mackereth v Department for Work and Pensions
[2022] EAT 99, [2022] ICR 1609............................. 267
Madsen v Denmark (58341/00) [2002] ECHR 855 227
Mahmoud and Malik v Bank of Credit and Commerce
International SA [1998] AC 20, HL 16, 299
Mandla v Dowell Lee [1983] 2 AC 548, [1983]
ICR 385, HL 288
Mangold v Helm (Case C-144/04) EU:C:2005:709,
[2005] ECR I-9981 22
Manole v Romania (App No 46551/06), [2015]
ECHR 575, Judgment of 16 June 2015........................ 36
Marckx v Belgium [1979] ECHR 2, (1979) 2
EHRR 330... 17
Markin v Russia [2012] ECHR 514, (2013) 56
EHRR 8 (Grand Chamber) 53, 55–6
Marschall v Land Nordrhein-Westfalen
(Case C-409/95) EU:C:1997:533, [1997]
ECR I-6363 52
Mason v Huddersfield Giants Ltd 2014 WL
3925309, 15 July 2014 240
Mason v Huddersfield Giants Ltd [2013]
EWHC 2869 (QB), [2013] 7 WLUK 453 272
Mateescu v Romania (App No 1944/10),
[2014] ECHR 37.. 142
Mathewson v RB Wilson Dental Laboratories [1988]
IRLR 512, EAT... 230

Max-Planck-Gesellschaft zur Förderung der Wissenschaften eV v Shimizu (C-684/16) EU:C:2018:874, [2019] 1 CMLR 35 192
Mba v Merton LBC [2013] EWCA Civ 1562, [2014] ICR 357... 283, 286
McClintock v Department of Constitutional Affairs [2008] IRLR 29, EAT......................... 265
Melike v Turkey [2021] ECHR 511, ECLI:CE:ECHR:2021:0615... 275
Mercury Communications Ltd v Scott-Garner [1984] Ch 37, [1984] ICR 74, CA................................ 123
Metrobus Ltd v Unite the Union [2009] EWCA Civ 829, [2010] ICR 173 126
Metropolitan Church of Bessarabia v Moldova [2001] ECHR 860, (2002) 35 EHRR 13 281
Mikkelsen v Danmols Inventar A/S (Case 105/84) EU:C:1985:331, [1985] ECR 2639 44
Mikulic v Croatia (53176/99) [2002] ECHR 27, [2002] 1 FCR 720... 231
Miles v Wakefield Metropolitan District Council [1987] AC 539, [1987] IRLR 193, HL 118
Miller v Interserve Industrial Services Ltd [2013] ICR 445, EAT... 71
Miroļubovs v Latvia, App No 798/05, 15 September 2009... 293
MM v United Kingdom (24029/07) [2012] ECHR 1906.. 226
Mono Car Styling SA v Odemis (Case C-12/08) EU:C:2009:466, [2009] ECR I-6653 102
Morgan v Fry [1968] 2 QB 710, [1968] 3 WLR 506, CA... 117
Morris v Metrolink Ratp Dev Ltd [2018] EWCA Civ 1358, [2019] ICR 90..................................... 251
Mruke v Khan [2018] EWCA Civ 280, [2018] ICR 1146.. 64
Mustafa Erdogan v Turkey (Application Nos 346/04 and 39779/04) [2014] ECHR 530 259
Nagle v Feilden [1966] 2 QB 633, [1966] 1 All ER 689, CA 83, 144
National Union of Belgian Police v Belgium (A/9) [1975] ECHR 2, (1979) 1 EHRR 578 .... 18, 68
National Union of Professional Foster Carers (NUPFC) v Certification Officer [2021] EWCA Civ 548, [2021] ICR 1397, CA; [2020] ICR 607, EAT 36–7, 38
National Union of Rail, Maritime and Transport Workers v United Kingdom [2014] ECHR 551 (8 April 2014).. 19
National Union of Rail, Maritime and Transport Workers v United Kingdom (RMT v United Kingdom) (Application no 31045/10), (2015) 60 EHRR 10, [2014] ECHR 366, 37 BHRC 145, [2014] IRLR 467..115, 116, 121, 123, 125, 128
Niemietz v Germany [1992] ECHR 80, (1992) 16 EHRR 97.. 216, 231, 233
Norwegian Confederation of Trade Unions (LO) v Norway (45487/17) (2021) 73 EHRR 16 130
NUGSAT v Albury Brothers Ltd [1979] ICR 84, CA........ 95
Nursing and Midwifery Council v Somerville [2022] EWCA Civ 229, [2022] ICR 755.............................. 33
NVH v Minister for Justice and Equality [2017] IESC 35, [2018] 1 IR 246 (30 May 2017)................ 133–4

OBG Ltd v Allan [2007] UKHL 21, [2008] 1 AC 1......... 123
O'Brien v Ministry of Justice (Case C-393/10) EU:C:2012:110, [2012] 2 CMLR 25 45
Obst v Germany, App No 425/03; Schuth v Germany, App No 1620/03, judgments of 23 September 2010.. 234–5, 272
Ognevenko v Russia (Appn No 44873/09), [2018] ECHR 950, (2019) 69 EHRR 9, [2019] IRLR 195.. 19, 115, 119
Okedina v Chikale [2019] EWCA Civ 1393, [2019] ICR 1635.. 40, 63, 159
O'Kelly v Trusthouse Forte Plc [1984] QB 90, CA... 31, 33
Okpabi v Royal Dutch Shell Plc [2021] UKSC 3, [2021] 1 WLR 1294 207
Oleksandr Volkov v Ukraine (21722/11) [2011] ECHR 1871... 301
Omega Spielhallen- und Automatenaufstellungs GmbH v Bundesstadt Bonn (Case C-36/02) EU:C:2004:614, [2004] ECR I-9609 .... 9, 21
O'Neill v Governors of St Thomas More Roman Catholic Voluntary Aided Upper School [1997] ICR 33, EAT.. 293
Onu v Akwiwu [2016] UKSC 31, [2016] ICR 756 64
Opinion 2/13 EU:C:2014:2454, [2015] 2 CMLR 21........ 22
Oyatsi v Judicial Service Commission (Petition E111 of 2021) [2022] KEELRC 3 (KLR) (10 March 2022), Kenya 179
Özpınar v Turkey (App No 20999/04), [2010] ECHR 2268, 19 October 2010 .... 233, 301, 303
Page v NHS Trust Development Authority [2021] EWCA Civ 255, [2021] ICR 941 .... 266, 291
Pajić v Croatia (68453/13) [2016] ECHR 203 64
Palomo Sanchez v Spain [2011] ECHR 1319, [2011] IRLR 934, Grand Chamber 73, 249–50, 251, 252
Patel v Mirza [2016] UKSC 42, [2017] AC 467 40
Pay v Lancashire Probation Service [2004] ICR 187, EAT.. 231
Pay v UK [2008] ECHR 1007, (2009) 48 EHRR SE2, [2009] IRLR 139 .... 222, 236–7, 238
Peck v UK [2003] ECHR 44, (2003) 36 EHRR 41 232
Pemberton v Inwood [2018] EWCA Civ 564, [2018] ICR 1291.. 293
Peters v Netherlands (App No 21132/93), (1994) 77A DR 75.. 227
Pichon and Sajous v France (App No 49853/99), [2001] ECHR 898, 2 October 2001 289
Pimm v Sodexo Justice Services Ltd and Secretary of State for Justice (Intervener) Case 3312375/2019, EAT 175
Pimlico Plumbers Ltd v Smith [2018] UKSC 29, [2018] ICR 1511... 30, 174
Pitkevich v Russia (App No 47936/99), 8 February 2001, ECtHR 290
Polkey v A E Dayton Services Ltd [1988] ICR 142, HL.. 307
Post Office v Union of Post Office Workers [1974] ICR 378, HL 73
Pretty v UK [2002] ECHR 427, (2002) 35 EHRR 1... 215, 231
Prigge v Deutsche Lufthansa AG (Case C-447/09) EU:C:2011:573, [2011] IRLR 1052........................... 59

R (BECTU) v Secretary of State for Trade and
    Industry (Case C-173/99) EU:C:2001:356,
    [2001] ECR I-4881 .... 46, 191
R (Boots Management Services Ltd) v Central
    Arbitration Committee [2017] EWCA Civ 66,
    [2017] IRLR 355 97
R (Countryside Alliance) v A-G [2007] UKHL 52,
    [2008] 1 AC 719 241
R (Independent Workers Union of Great Britain) v
    Central Arbitration Committee [2021]
    EWCA Civ 260, [2021] ICR 729 97
R (Independent Workers' Union of Great Britain) v
    Secretary of State for Work and Pensions [2020]
    EWHC 3050 (Admin), [2021] ICR 372 44–5
R (Limbuela) v Secretary of State for the Home
    Department [2005] UKHL 66, [2006] 1 AC 396 164
R (on the application of G) v Governors of X School
    [2011] UKSC 30, [2012] 1 AC 167 307
R (on the application of Johnson and Others) v
    Secretary of State for Work and Pensions [2019]
    EWHC 23 (Admin), [2019] ACD 38 148
R (on the application of P and others) v
    Secretary of State for Justice and others
    [2019] UKSC 3, [2020] AC 185 226
R (on the application of Reilly and Anor) v
    Secretary of State for Work and Pensions [2013]
    UKSC 68, [2014] AC 453, [2013] 3 WLR 1276 148
R (on the application of UNISON) v Lord
    Chancellor [2017] UKSC 51, [2020] AC 869,
    [2017] ICR 1037 .... 34, 42
R (on the application of Williamson) v Secretary
    of State for Education and Employment [2005]
    UKHL 15, [2005] 2 AC 246, HL 265
R (SG) v Secretary of State for Work and Pensions
    [2015] UKSC 16, [2015] 1 WLR 1449 58
R (T) v Chief Constable of Greater Manchester Police
    (Liberty intervening); R (B) v Secretary of State
    for the Home Department (Liberty intervening)
    [2014] UKSC 35, [2015] AC 49 226
R (Wright) v Secretary of State for Health [2009]
    UKHL 3, [2009] AC 739, [2009] 2 WLR 267 143
R v Central Independent Television plc [1994]
    Fam 192, [1995] 1 FCR 521, CA 247
R v National Police Chief's Council [2020] EWCA
    Civ 1348, [2021] ICR 425 226
R v Rogers [2007] UKHL 8, [2007] 2 AC 62 64
R v Secretary of State for Employment, ex parte
    Seymour Smith [2012] UKHL 12, [2000]
    ICR 244 274
R v Secretary of State for the Home Department
    ex parte Davis (25 April 1994, unreported) 175
R v Secretary of State for the Home Department
    ex parte Simms [1999] UKHL 33, [2000] 2 AC 115 41
Rantsev v Cyprus and Russia [2010] ECHR 22,
    (2010) 51 EHRR 1 .... 7, 162, 164
Ready Mixed Concrete (South East) Ltd v
    Minister of Pensions and National Insurance
    [1968] 2 QB 497, [1968] 2 WLR 775, QBD 30, 196
Redfearn v United Kingdom (App No 47335/06),
    [2012] ECHR 1878, (2013) 57 EHRR 2,
    6 November 2012 .... 41–2, 274, 291–2
Regents for the University of California v Bakke
    438 US 265 (1978) 258

'Relating to Certain Aspects of the Laws on the
    Use of Languages in Education in Belgium' v
    Belgium [1968] ECHR 3, (1979-80) 1 EHRR 252 313
Republic of South Africa v Grootboom,
    (Case No CCT 11/00), 2000 (11) BCLR 1169 316
Robinson-Steele v RD Retail Services Ltd
    (Case C-131/04) EU:C:2006:177, [2006]
    ECR I-2531 .... 22, 192
Roca Alvarez v Sesa Start Espana ETT SA
    (Case C-104/09) EU:C:2010:561, [2011] 1
    CMLR 28 55
Rookes v Barnard [1964] AC 1129, [1964]
    2 WLR 269, HL 123
Royal Parks Ltd v Boohene & Ors [2023]
    EAT 69, [2024] IRLR 18 (5 May 2023);
    reversing sub nom Boohene & Ors v Royal Parks
    Ltd (ET Cases 2202211/2020, 2204440/2020 &
    2205570/2020), ET 179
Ruling on wages of officers of the system of the
    internal service [2009] LTCC 29; Case No
    14/07-17/08-25/08-39/08 (11 December 2009),
    Lithuania 179
Rustamova v Governing Body of Calder High School,
    UKEAT/0284/11/ZT, [2013] 11 WLUK 382,
    14 Nov 2013 244
S (Identity: Restrictions on Publication), Re [2004]
    UKHL 47, [2005] 1 AC 593 314
Salgueiro da Silva Mouta v Portugal (33290/96)
    [1999] ECHR 176, 31 EHRR 47 50
Sanders v Kingston (No 1) [2005] EWHC 1145
    (Admin), [2005] BLGR 719 248
SAS v France (43835/11) [2014] ECHR 695,
    (2015) 60 EHRR 11 .... 9, 280, 284, 288
Saunders v Scottish National Camps Association Ltd
    [1980] IRLR 174, EAT; [1981] IRLR 277,
    Ct of Sess 230
Schmidt and Dahlstrom v Sweden (A/21),
    (1979-80) 1 EHRR 637 .... 18, 68
Schuitemaker v the Netherlands (App No 15906/08),
    admissibility decision of 4 May 2010 147
Schüth v Germany (App No 1620/03), (2011)
    52 EHRR 32, 23 September 2010 .... 282, 293,
                                                                                  294, 303
Secretary of State for Justice v Windle [2016]
    EWCA Civ 459, [2016] ICR 721 33
Secretary of State for Business and Trade v
    Mercer [2024] UKSC 12, [2024] 4
    WLUK 161 .... 74, 120–2
Secretary of State for Employment v ASLEF
    (No 2) [1972] 2 QB 455, [1972] ICR 19, CA 118
Sejdić and Finci v Bosnia and Herzegovina
    (Application Nos 27996/06 and 34836/06) [2009]
    ECHR 2122, 28 BHRC 201 52
Seldon v Clarkson Wright & Jakes [2012] UKSC 16,
    [2012] ICR 716, [2012] IRLR 590 .... 60, 305
Serco Ltd v National Union of Rail, Maritime &
    Transport Workers [2011] EWCA Civ 226,
    [2011] ICR 848 15
Sidabras and Dziautas v Lithuania (Nos 55480/00
    and 59330/00) [2004] ECHR 395, (2004) 42
    EHRR 104, 27 July 2004 .... 19, 50–1, 54,
                                                                                60, 141–2, 143,
                                                                          149, 233, 301, 304

Sidabras and Dziautas v Lithuania (50421/08 and 56213/08) [2015] ECHR 674......................................216
Siliadin v France (73316/01) [2005] ECHR 545, (2006) 43 EHRR 287..7, 17, 19, 57, 160–1, 164, 224
Sim v Rotherham Metropolitan Borough Council [1987] Ch 216, [1986] ICR 897, ChD........................118
SIMAP v Conselleria de Sanidad y Consumo de la Generalidad Valenciana (Case C-303/98) EU:C:2000:528, [2000] ECR I-7963......................189
Simmons v Hoover Ltd [1977] QB 284, [1977] ICR 61, EAT...117
Simunic v Croatia (App No 20373/17), Admissibility Decision of 22 January 2019.................277
Sindicatul 'Pastoral Cel Bun' v Romania (2330/09) (2014) 58 EHRR 10, [2014] IRLR 49, Grand Chamber...29, 36, 120
Slaight Communication Inc v Ron Davidson, 4 May 1989, [1989] 1 SCR 1038, Supreme Ct, Canada........300
SM v Croatia (App No 60561/14), (2021) 72 EHRR 1, 25 June 2020, Grand Chamber....................162
Smith v Carillion (JM) Ltd [2015] EWCA Civ 209, [2015] IRLR 467...33–4
Smith v Churchills Stairlifts plc [2005] EWCA Civ 1220, [2006] ICR 524.....................................62
Smith v Hayle Town Council [1978] ICR 996, CA..........72
Smith v Trafford Housing Trust [2012] EWHC 3221 (Ch), [2013] IRLR 86.............................16, 245, 268, 273, 278, 290–1, 322
Smith v UK (App No 54357/15), Admissibility Decision of 28 March 2017.................................76–7, 303
Smith and Grady v United Kingdom (Application Nos 33985/96 and 33986/96) [1999] ECHR 72, (2000) EHRR 493...236, 240
Sorensen (52562/99) and Rasmussen (52620/99) v Denmark (2008) 46 EHRR 29, 20 BHRC 258.........80–1
Specht v Land Berlin (Case C-501/12) EU:C:2014:2005, [2014] ICR 966.................................108
Speciality Care v Pachela [1996] IRLR 248, EAT.............74
Spiller v FJ Wallis Ltd [1975] IRLR 362, IT...................230
Stadt Wuppertal v Bauer (Case C-569/16) EU:C:2018:871, [2019] 1 CMLR 36.............................191
Stec and others v United Kingdom (65731/01) [2006] ECHR 1162, (2006) 43 EHRR 47, Grand Chamber..53
Stedman v United Kingdom (29107/95) (1997) 23 EHRR CD168, Commission...........................196, 285
Straume v Latvia (59402/14) [2022] ECHR 409, [2022] IRLR 802..70, 251
Stringer v Revenue and Customs Commissioners (Case C-520/06) EU:C:2009:18, [2009] ECR I-179...192
Students for Fair Admissions v Harvard, 600 US 181 (2023)..258
Stummer v Austria (37452/02) (2012) 54 EHRR 11, Grand Chamber...146
Sullivan v Isle of Wight Council [2024] EAT 3, [2024] ICR 561, [2024] IRLR 350...................................39
Swedish Engine Drivers' Union v Sweden (A/20) (1979-80) 1 EHRR 617, [1978] ECC 1......................93
Swedish Trade Union Confederation (LO) v Sweden (ECSR 85/2012) (2015) 60 EHRR SE7.......................130
Sweezy v New Hampshire 354 US 234 (1957)...............258

Szima v Hungary (29723/11) [2013] IRLR 59, [2012] ECHR 1788..270
Talmon v the Netherlands (30300/96) [1997] ECHR 207..147
Tek Gida Is Sendikasi v Turkey (35009/05) [2017] ECHR 318, CE:ECHR:2017:0404.......................71
Thlimmenos v Greece (34369/97) [2000] ECHR 162, (2000) 31 EHRR 411.....................................51, 53, 239, 240
Tower Boot Co Ltd v Jones [1997] ICR 254, CA............268
Turner v East Midland Trains Ltd [2012] EWCA Civ 1470, [2013] ICR 525.......................270, 283, 304
Uber BV v Aslam [2021] UKSC 5, [2021] ICR 657.....................................32–3, 34, 174, 186, 189
Union Syndicale Solidaires Isère v Premier Ministre (Case C-428/09) EU:C:2010:612, [2011] 1 CMLR 38...44
Unite the Union v United Kingdom (App No 65397/13) [2016] ECHR 1150, [2017] IRLR 438, (2016) EHRR SE7, 3 May 2016..........................19, 94, 95
United Kingdom v Council (Working Time Directive) (Case C-84/94) [1996] ECR I-5755......................184, 189
Van der Mussele v Belgium (8919/80) [1983] ECHR 13, (1984) 6 EHRR 163.................................148
Van Droogenbroeck v Belgium (7906/77) [1982] ECHR 3, (1982) 4 EHRR 443.................................146
Vedanta Resources Plc v Lungowe [2019] UKSC 20, [2020] AC 1045..207
Ville de Nivelles v Matzak (Case C-518/15) EU:C:2018:82, [2018] 2 CMLR 37........................46, 189
Vogt v Germany (17851/91) [1996] ECHR 34, Grand Chamber...246, 273
Von Hannover v Germany (59320/00) [2004] ECHR 294, (2005) 40 EHRR 1.......................216, 232–3
W v Essex County Council [1999] Fam 90, [1998] 3 WLR 534, CA..38
Wackenheim v France, Communication No 854/1999: France. 26/07/2002 CCPR/C/75/D/854/1999............139
Wandsworth London Borough Council v Vining [2017] EWCA Civ 1092, [2018] ICR 499....37–8, 103, 302–3, 306
Wasteney v East London NHS Foundation Trust [2016] ICR 643, EAT..290
Webb v London Underground Ltd, 3306438/2021, 2 February 2023, ET....................................246, 276, 277
Wignall v British Gas Corporation [1984] ICR 716, EAT..73
William Hill Organisation Ltd v Tucker [1999] ICR 291, CA...134
Williams v British Airways Plc (Case C-155/10) EU:C:2011:588, [2012] ICR 847, [2012] 1 CMLR 23..23, 192
Williams v Compair Maxam Ltd [1982] ICR 156, EAT...306
Wilson and Palmer, National Union of Journalists and Others v United Kingdom (2002) 35 EHRR 523, [2002] IRLR 568..................................7, 17, 18, 70, 71, 73, 74, 75, 82, 83, 93, 95, 98, 121
Wiluzynski v Tower Hamlets [1989] ICR 493, [1989] IRLR 258, CA...118
X v Austria (8278/78) [1979] ECHR 6, (1979) 18 DR 154...227
X v Switzerland (App No 7865/17) [1979] ECHR 10, 1 January 1978..293

X v UK [1981] ECHR 9, (1982) 4 EHRR 126,
    Commission Decision, 12 March 1981 .... 196, 285
X v Y [2004] EWCA Civ 662, [2004] ICR 1634,
    [2004] IRLR 624 .... 15, 231, 237, 238, 268
Yakut Republican Trade Union Federation
    v Russia (29582/09) [2021] ECHR 1033,
    ECLI:CE:ECHR:2021:1207 175
Young, James and Webster v UK, App Nos
    7601/76, 7806/77, Series A no. 44, [1981]
    ECHR 4, Judgment of 13 August 1981 .... 6, 80, 83
Zemmour v France (63539/19) [2022] ECHR 1130,
    ECLI:CE:ECHR:2022:1220 277
Zoletic v Azerbaijan (20116/12) [2021] ECHR 789,
    ECLI:CE:ECHR:2021:1007 161

Table of Legislation (UK)

Abortion Act 1967
   s 4 289
Asylum and Immigration (Treatment of Claimants)
   Act 2004
   s 4 163
Benefit Cap (Housing Benefit) Regulations 2012
   (SI 2012/2994) 58
Contracts (Rights of Third Parties) Act 1999
   s 1 208
   s 1(2) 208
Coroners and Justice Act 2009
   s 71 163
Crime and Disorder Act 1998
   s 66ZA 226
Data Protection Act 1998 76
Data Protection Act 2018 225
   s 10 227
   s 45(1) 221
Education Reform Act 1988
   s 202(2)(a) 258
Employment Relations Act 1999 (Blacklists)
   Regulations 2010 76
Employment Relations Act 2004 .... 71, 74, 85, 98
Employment Relations (Flexible Working)
   Act 2023
   s 1 196
Employment Rights Act 1996 .... 13, 14, 15,
                                               230, 258, 274
   Pt II, ss 13–27 166
   s 1 23
   ss 13–27 166
   s 43B 255
   s 43B(1)(a)–(f) 255
   s 43C 256
   s 43F 256
   s 43G 256
   s 43G(1)(a)–(e) 256
   s 43G(2)(a)–(c) 256
   s 43G(3) 256
   s 43H 256
   s 43J 257
   s 43K(1) 254
   s 43K(1)(a)(i), (ii) 254
   s 43K(1)(b) 254
   s 49(6A) 257
   s 76 195
   ss 80F-80I 196
   s 80F 197, 286
   s 80G 197
   s 86 305
   s 94 9

   s 94(1) 230, 295
   s 98 .... 230, 275
   s 98(1), (2) 230
   s 98(4) 15, 230, 268, 304
   s 108(1) 41, 274
   s 108(3) 309
   s 108(4) 42, 274
   s 119 .... 295, 305
   s 123 305
   s 123(6A) 257
   s 135 295
   s 162 59
   s 203(1) 33
   s 230(3) 174, 254
   s 230(3)(b) 31, 254
Employment Rights (Amendment, Revocation
   and Transitional Provision) Regulations 2023
   (SI 2023/1426) 192
   Pt 3 190
Equal Pay Act 1971 178
Equality Act 2010 .... 13, 14, 42, 49, 50, 63, 64,
                                  84, 144, 178, 179, 248, 257,
                                  262, 264, 267, 274, 291
   s 4 281
   s 9(1) 64
   s 10 .... 264, 267
   s 10(1) 281
   s 10(2) 281
   s 13 264
   s 19 .... 52, 283
   s 19(2)(b) 283
   s 20 .... 62, 138, 196
   s 26(1) 267
   s 41 179
   s 57 84
   s 109 268
   ss 158-159 52
   Sch 9 293
      Pt 1 (paras 1–6) 51
      para 2 293
      para 2(1) 293
      para 2(5), (6) 293
      para 3 293
Equality Act 2010 (Amendment) Regulations 2023
   (SI 2023/1425) 23
European Union (Withdrawal) Act 2018
   s 5(4) 23
   s 5(A2) 22
   s 6 23
Flexible Working (Amendment) Regulations 2023
   (SI 2023/1328) 196

Foreign Prison-Made Goods Act 1897	168
Gender Recognition Act 2004	266
Health and Safety at Work Act 1974	
s 51	224
Higher Education (Freedom of Speech) Act 2023	259
s 1	259
s 4	259
Higher Education Research Act 2017	259
Pt A1	259
Pt A7	259
Human Fertilisation and Embryology Act 1990	
s 38	289
Human Rights Act 1998	3, 4, 7, 9, 10, 13, 14, 15, 16, 28, 29, 33, 35, 36, 38, 120, 131, 230, 231
s 1	14
s 3	9, 14, 15, 16, 36, 37, 38, 39, 41, 72, 74, 103, 120, 122, 230, 268, 283
s 4	9, 74, 120, 122
s 6	14, 15, 122, 230
s 6(1)	230, 268
s 7	14, 283
Immigration Act 2016	40, 158, 159
s 34	34, 39, 63
s 35	39
Industrial Relations Act 1971	3
Information and Consultation of Employees Regulations 2004 (SI 2004/3426)	106
reg 2	88
Maternity and Parental Leave etc Regulations 1999 (SI 1999/3312)	
regs 13–16	185
regs 13–16A	195
reg 13(1)	195
Modern Slavery Act 2015	152, 160, 163, 164, 205
Pt 5	164
s 1	163
s 1(2)	163
s 1(5)	163
s 2	163
s 2(2)	163
s 8	164
s 54	204
s 54(4)(b)	205
s 54(11)	204
National Minimum Wage Act 1998	33, 170, 172
s 45	175
s 54	174
National Minimum Wage Regulations 2015 (SI 2015/621)	172
reg 57(3)	57, 173
National Minimum Wage (Amendment) (No 2) Regulations 2024 (SI 2024/432)	174
Nationality and Borders Act 2022	
Pt 5	164
s 65	164
Police Act 1997	
s 113A	226
s 113B	226
Prison Rules – Prison Service Order 4460	
Annex B	175
Proceeds of Crime Act 2002	159
Protection of Freedoms Act 2012	
ss 109, 110	163
Public Interest Disclosure Act 1998	253, 257
Public Interest Disclosure (Prescribed Persons) Order 2014 (SI 2014/2418)	256
Rehabilitation of Offenders Act 1974	226
Rehabilitation of Offenders Act 1974 (Exceptions) Order 1975 (SI 1975/1023)	226
Sexual Offences Act 1956	
s 13	229
Sexual Offences Act 1967	229
Sexual Offences Act 2003	
ss 57–59	163
Strikes (Minimum Service Levels) Act 2023	126, 127, 128
Strikes (Minimum Service Levels: Border Security) Regulations 2023 (SI 2023/1353)	127, 128
Trade Union Act 2016	110, 126
Trade Union and Labour Relations (Consolidation) Act 1992	13, 14, 35, 36, 37, 38, 69, 71, 72, 74, 79, 82, 85, 98, 126, 127
s 1	35, 36
s 3	124
s 20	119, 124
s 20(2)	124
s 21	124
s 22	128, 129
s 64(1)	85
s 65	84
s 65(2)(a)	85
s 137	35, 71, 72, 74, 78, 79
s 137(1)	144
s 140	74
s 144	79
s 145	79
s 145A	71, 72, 73, 74, 75, 79
s 145A(1)(d)	79
s 145A(2), (3)	75
s 145B	74, 98, 99
s 145B(4)	74
s 145D	98
s 145D(1)	72
s 146	71, 72, 73, 74, 75, 79, 120, 121, 122, 251
s 146(1)(c)	79
s 146(2)	69
s 146(3)	79
s 148(1)	72
s 149(2)	75
s 152	35, 71, 72, 73, 74, 75, 79, 251
s 152(1)(c)	79
s 152(2A)	74
s 152(3)	79
s 156	79
s 160	79
s 161	79, 252
s 174	84
s 174(2)(b)	84
s 174(2)(d)	84
s 174(3), (4)	84
s 174(4C)	84

s 174(4G)(a)	84
s 174(4G)(c)	84
s 174(4H)	84
s 188	102, 103
s 188(1)	306
s 189	102
s 199	307
s 203	127
s 219	119, 120, 123
s 221	129
s 222	79
s 224	123
s 225	123
s 226	124
s 226(2)(a)(iia)	125
s 226(2C)	125
s 226A	125
s 226A(2)(c)	125
s 226A(2G)	125
s 226B	124
s 227	124
s 227(1)	124
ss 229, 230	124
s 231A	125
s 232A	124
s 232B	124
s 234	125
s 234A	125, 126
s 234B	126
s 234C	126
s 234C(6)	126
s 234C(8)	126
s 234E	126
s 234E(2)	127
s 237	119, 120
s 237(2)	119
s 238	119, 120
s 238A	119, 120, 127
s 238A(1)	119
s 238A(3)	119
s 238A(5)	119
s 240	126
s 244(1)	123
s 280	103
s 296(1)	36
Sch A1	36, 95, 96, 97, 98, 109
para 10	96
para 18	96
para 22(3), (4)	96
para 29	96
para 35	96
para 36(1)(a), (b)	96
Trade Union Recognition (Method of Collective Bargaining) Order 2000 (SI 2000/1300)	96
Trade Union Reform and Employment Rights Act 1993	
s 14	84
UK General Data Protection Regulation	225
Art 10	226
Unfair Dismissal and Statement of Reasons for Dismissal (Variation of Qualifying Period) Order 2012 (SI 2012/989)	274
Universal Credit Regulations 2013 (SI 2013/976)	148
Vagrancy Act 1824	
s 3	140
Workers (Predictable Terms and Conditions) Act 2023	23, 198
s 80IC(1)(c)	198
Working Time Regulations 1998 (SI 1998/1833)	
reg 2	186
reg 11	188
reg 12	188

Table of EU Materials

Charter of Fundamental Rights of the European Union – adopted in 2001, amended: (OJ 2012/C 326/2); [2012] OJ C326/391 ...... 3, 9, 13, 20, 21, 23, 129, 133, 137, 152, 170, 287, 316
- Art 5(3) 160
- Art 7 ...... 215, 231
- Art 8 ...... 215, 231
- Art 12 99
- Art 13 257
- Art 14 287
- Art 15 138
- Art 15 152
- Art 15(1) 60, 138
- Art 15(2), (3) 152
- Art 16 ...... 21, 103, 284, 287
- Art 21 282
- Art 27 ...... 21, 91, 99, 106, 307
- Art 28 99
- Art 30 ...... 29, 297
- Art 31 ...... 29, 185, 191
- Art 31(2) 46, 191
- Art 51 21
- Art 52(3) 21, 99

Community Charter of the Fundamental Social Rights of Workers – 10 December 1989, EEC 3, 80, 191, 297
- point 11 80
- points 17, 18 91

Council of Europe Committee of Ministers – Resolution CM/ResChS(2017)9; Complaint No 111/2014 172

Council of Europe Convention on Action against Trafficking in Human Beings 160

Council of Europe Criminal Law Convention on Corruption of 4 November 1999 253
- Art 22 253

Directive 75/129/EEC on the approximation of the laws of the Member States relating to collective redundancies [1975] OJ L48/29 91

Directive 77/187/EEC on the approximation of the laws of the Member States relating to the safeguarding of employees' rights in the event of transfers of undertakings (as amended by Directive 98/50/EC and consolidated in Directive 2001/23/EC) [1977] OJ L61/26 ...... 21, 44, 101

Directive 80/987/EEC of 20 October 1980 on the approximation of the laws of the Member States relating to the protection of employees in the event of the insolvency of their employer [1980] OJ L283/23 101

Directive 92/85/EEC of 19 October 1992 on the introduction of measures to encourage improvements in the safety and health at work of pregnant workers and workers who have recently given birth or are breastfeeding [1992] OJ L348/1 ...... 43, 44, 193
- Art 8 193
- Art 10 193

Directive 93/104/EC of 23 November 1993 concerning certain aspects of the organization of working time [1993] OJ L307/18 184

Directive 94/45/EC of 22 September 1994 on the establishment of a European Works Council or a procedure in Community-scale undertakings and Community-scale groups of undertakings for the purposes of informing and consulting employees [1994] OJ L254/64 ...... 92, 103

Directive 1996/34/EC of 3 June 1996 concerning the framework agreement on parental leave [1996] OJ L145/4 100

Directive 96/71/EC of 16 December 1996 concerning the posting of workers in the framework of the provision of services [1997] OJ L18/1 (as amended, 2018) 20, 129

Directive 97/81/EC of 15 December 1997 concerning the Framework Agreement on part-time work concluded by UNICE, CEEP and the ETUC [1998] OJ L14/9 ...... 45, 100

Directive 98/50/EC of 29 June 1998 amending Directive 77/187/EEC on the approximation of the laws of the Member States relating to the safeguarding of employees' rights in the event of transfers of undertakings, businesses or parts of businesses [1998] OJ L201/88 101

Directive 98/59 of 20 July 1998 on the approximation of the laws of the Member States relating to collective redundancies [1998] OJ 225/16 ...... 44, 91, 101, 102, 103, 104, 105, 306, 307
- Art 2.1 ...... 101, 102
- Art 2.2 102
- Art 2.3 102

Directive 1999/70/EC of 28 June 1999 concerning the framework agreement on fixed-term work concluded by ETUC, UNICE and CEEP [1999] OJ L175/43 100

Directive 2000/78/EC of 27 November 2000 establishing a general framework for equal treatment in employment and occupation [2000] OJ L303/16 ...... 43, 44, 49, 59, 60, 282, 283, 305

Art 1 .... 49, 282
Art 3 44
Art 4 59
Art 4(1) 292, 293
Art 4(2) 292
Art 6(1)(a) 59
Directive 2001/23/EC of 12 March 2001 on the
 approximation of the laws of the Member States
 relating to the safeguarding of employees' rights
 in the event of transfers of undertakings,
 businesses or parts of undertakings or businesses
 [2001] OJ L82/16 101
  Art 2(1)(d) 45
  Art 7 92
Directive 2002/14 of the European Parliament
 and of the Council of 11 March 2002 establishing
 a general framework for informing and consulting
 employees in the European Community [2002]
 OJ L80/29 .... 92, 105, 106
  Art 3 .... 46, 105
  Art 4(2)(a)–(c) 105
Directive 2003/88/EC of the European Parliament
 and of the Council of 4 November 2003 concerning
 certain aspects of the organisation of working
 time [2003] OJ L299/9 .... 22, 44, 46, 101,
                                                    184, 187, 190, 191
  Art 3 .... 187, 188
  Art 4 188
  Art 5 188
  Art 6 187
  Art 7 191
  Art 7(2) 192
  Art 13 196
  Arts 16, 17 187
  Art 18(1)(b) 187
  Art 19 187
  Art 22 187
Directive 2006/54/EC of 5 July 2006 on the
 implementation of the principle of equal
 opportunities and equal treatment of men and
 women in matters of employment and occupation
 (recast) [2006] OJ L204/23 178
Directive 2008/94/EC of 22 October 2008 on the
 protection of employees in the event of the
 insolvency of their employer (Codified version)
 [2008] OJ L283/36 101
Directive 2009/38/EC of 6 May 2009 on the
 establishment of a European Works Council
 or a procedure in Community-scale undertakings
 and Community-scale groups of undertakings
 for the purposes of informing and consulting
 employees (recast) [2009] OJ L122/28 .... 92, 103,
                                                             104, 105
  Art 1(3), (4) 104
  Art 2 103
  Art 2(1)(g) 104
  Art 5 104
  Art 5(1) 103
  Art 6 104
  Art 7 104
  Annex 1
    para 1(a) 104
    paras 2, 3 104
Directive 2010/18/EU of 8 March 2010 on the
 application of the revised Framework Agreement
 on parental leave concluded between
 BUSINESSEUROPE, UEAPME, CEEP and
 the ETUC and repealing Directive 96/34/EC
 [2010] OJ L68/13 .... 55, 100
Directive 2011/36/EU of the European Parliament
 and of the Council of 5 April 2011 on preventing
 and combating trafficking in human beings and
 protecting its victims [2011] OJ L101/1 .... 5, 160
Directive 2013/36/EU of 26 June 2013 on access to
 the activity of credit institutions and the prudential
 supervision of credit institutions and investment
 firms, amending Directive 2002/87/EC and repealing
 Directives 2006/48/EC and 2006/49/EC [2013]
 OJ L176/338 181
Directive 2018/957 of 28 June 2018 amending
 Directive 96/71/EC concerning the posting of
 workers in the framework of the provision of
 services [2018] OJ L173/16 130
Directive 2019/878/EU of 20 May 2019 amending
 Directive 2013/36/EU as regards exempted entities,
 financial holding companies, mixed financial
 holding companies, remuneration, supervisory
 measures and powers and capital conservation
 measures [2019] OJ L150/253 181
Directive 2019/1152 of 20 June 2019 on transparent
 and predictable working conditions in the
 European Union [2019] OJ L186/105 ..... 23, 197
  Art 10 197
  Art 10(3) 197
  Art 12 198
Directive 2019/1158/EU of 20 June 2019 on
 work-life balance for parents and carers [2019]
 OJ L188/79 .... 100, 194
  Art 4 194
  Art 5 195
  Art 5(6) 195
  Art 8 195
  Art 9 196
Directive (EU) 2019/1937 of the European
 Parliament and of the Council of 23 October
 2019 on the protection of persons who report
 breaches of Union law [2019] OJ L305/17 ..... 205, 253
  Art 4 254
Directive (EU) 2022/2041 of 19 October 2022
 on adequate minimum wages in the European
 Union [2022] OJ L275/33 .... 20, 23, 45, 89, 100,
                                                106, 107, 108, 172, 185
  Preamble, para 28 172
  Art 2 45
  Art 4(1) 108
  Art 4(1)(a)–(d) 107, 108
  Art 4(2) 108
  Art 7 107
Proposed Directive Corporate Sustainability
 Due Diligence Directive (CSDDD) 205, 208, 209, 213
  Arts 4–11 206
  Arts 7, 8 .... 208, 209
  Art 12 209
  Arts 17–20 206
  Art 22 .... 208, 209
  Art 22(1) 208

Art 22(5)	209
Annex	205
European Pillar of Social Rights	20, 101
Principle 6	106
Principle 8	101
Framework Agreement on Stress at Work (2004)	101
Framework Agreement on Harassment and Violence at Work (2007)	101
Proposed Directive on Platform Work	43, 46, 107, 226-7
Chapter III	226
Art 4	46
Art 4(2)(a)–(e)	47
Regulation (EU) 2016/679 of the European Parliament and of the Council of 27 April 2016 on the protection of natural persons with regard to the processing of personal data and on the free movement of such data, and repealing Directive 95/46/EC (General Data Protection Regulation) [2016] OJ L119/1	225
Art 9(2)	227
TEU	
Art 6(2)	22
Art 6(3)	21
Treaty on the Functioning of the European Union	
Art 45 TFEU	143, 152
Art 49 TFEU	103
Art 153 TFEU	20, 44, 100
Art 153(1)(b)	107
Art 153(5)	20, 100, 107, 108, 130, 172
Art 154	100, 104
Art 155 TFEU	20, 100
Art 157 TFEU	43
Treaty on the Functioning of the European Union (Consolidated) 01/03/2020	
Art 157(1)	178
Treaty of Rome	
Art 118a EEC	184
Art 119 EEC	20

Table of National Legislation

France

Code du Travail
   Art L 1233-5 303
   Art L 2281-1 247
Constitution 1946
   preamble 134
Constitution 1958 134
Declaration of the Rights of Man 1789 48
Ordonnance n° 2017-1718 du 20 décembre 2017
   Art 1 303

India

Constitution
   Art 43 171

Ireland

Constitution 133

Kenya

Constitution 179

Lithuania

Law on the Evaluation of the USSR State Security Committee and the Present Activities of Permanent Employees of the Organisation 1998 142

Netherlands

Work and Social Assistance Act 147

Norway

Transparency Act 2021 205
   ss 4–7 205

New Zealand

Prostitution Reform Act
   s 3(a)–(b) 140

United States

Alien Tort Statute (US) 1789, 28 USC §1350
   (2012) 206
Civil Rights Act 1964 49
False Claims Act, 31 USC
   ss 3729, 3730(h) 257
Genetic Information Nondiscrimination Act 2008
   Title II 228
Whistleblower Protection Act 1989 255
19 US Codes §1307 (s 307 Tariff Act 1930) 168
Oregon – City of Portland (Charter, Code and Policies) ARB-LIC-5 Pay Ratio Surtax 181

Table of European and International Materials

African Charter of Human and Peoples' Rights 141
   Arts 2, 3 141
   Arts 5–7 141
   Art 12 141
   Art 18 141
American Bar Association
   ABA Model Contract Clauses 203, 209
   Model Contract Clauses to Protect Workers in
      International Supply Chains, Version 2.0 209
Charter of the Organisation of American States
   Art 45(b) 173
Committee on Economic, Social and Cultural
   Rights (CESCR) General Comments
   General Comment No 3 136
      para 9 136
   General Comment No 18 2005 .... 136, 149
      para 1 136
      para 7 .... 136, 149
      para 8 136
      para 23 144
      para 26 136
Council of Europe, European Committee of
   Social Rights
   Conclusion I (First supervision cycle, 1969–70,
      Denmark, Germany, Italy, Ireland, Sweden,
      Norway, United Kingdom) 137
   Conclusions XVI-I, Netherlands (Netherlands,
      Antilles and Aruba) 137
   Conclusions 2004-1, Bulgaria 137
Council of Europe Parliamentary Assembly
   Resolution 2300: Improving the Protection
      of Whistle-blowers All Over Europe
      (1 October 2019) 253
      para 1 252
      para 5 252
European Committee of Social Rights
   Conclusions II, Statement of Interpretation
      on Article 1(2) 138
   Conclusions XIII-1 France – Article 6(4) 117
   Conclusions XVI-1, Germany 146
   Conclusions XVI-1 (2002), Austria 299
   Conclusions XVI-2 (2003) United Kingdom 172
   Conclusions XXII-3 – United Kingdom –
      Article 4.1 (2023) 172
   Conclusions XVIII-I (2007) France 172
   Conclusions 2008, Azerbaijan 299
   Conclusions 2010 France – Article 6(4) 117
   Conclusions 2012, General Introduction,
      Statement of Interpretation of Article 1
      para 2 146

ECSR Conclusions 2012, Statement of
   Interpretation, Article 1(2) 150
Conclusions 2019 – Montenegro – Article 7–5 174
Conclusions 2020 – Albania 224
Conclusions 2020 – Malta (2020) 2020_
   def_MLT_24_EN 305, 309
European Convention on Human Rights
   (Convention for the Protection of Human
   Rights and Fundamental Freedoms (1950)) 3, 4, 7,
      8, 9, 12, 13, 14, 15, 16, 17,
      18, 19, 28, 29, 35, 41, 49, 50,
      51, 53, 61, 64, 67, 68, 69, 73,
      75, 76, 80, 94, 97, 113, 114,
      133, 135, 141, 142, 147, 149,
      152, 162, 215, 217, 218, 230,
      234, 236, 238, 246, 247, 249,
      250, 251, 252, 257, 258, 268,
      270, 271, 273, 274, 277, 299,
      300, 301, 303, 312, 316, 322
   Art 1 .... 7, 17
   Arts 2–12 14
   Art 2 .... 7, 17
   Art 3 .... 139, 164, 313
   Art 4 .... 7, 12, 14, 17, 19,
      138, 145, 146, 147, 148, 160,
      161, 162, 163, 164, 224, 313
   Art 4(3) 147
   Art 4(3)(a) 146
   Art 5 145
   Art 6 .... 14, 143, 302, 307, 308
   Art 8 .... 7, 14, 17, 19, 41, 42,
      53, 54, 60, 61, 64, 75, 76,
      142, 143, 215, 216, 218,
      222, 223, 226, 227, 231,
      232, 233, 234, 235, 237,
      238, 240, 263, 268, 271,
      276, 291, 292, 294, 301,
      302, 303, 304, 309
   Art 8(1) 215, 231, 237, 300, 302
   Art 8(2) 215, 227, 231, 300
   Art 9 .... 14, 19, 52, 239, 262,
      264, 265, 266, 279, 280,
      281, 282, 283, 284, 285,
      286, 291, 293
   Art 9(1) 279
   Art 9(2) 264, 279
   Art 10 .... 14, 17, 19, 32, 38, 41, 42,
      73, 113, 242, 250, 252, 253, 254,
      255, 258, 259, 262, 264, 267, 269,
      273, 274, 275, 276, 281, 290, 292, 294

Art 10(1)	242, 248, 269
Art 10(2)	242, 243, 246, 247, 248, 269, 273, 277
Art 11	6, 7, 8, 10, 14, 15, 17, 18, 19, 27, 29, 36, 37, 38, 41, 68, 70, 71, 72, 73, 74, 75, 76, 77, 80, 81, 82, 83, 85, 89, 92, 93, 94, 95, 96, 97, 98, 99, 103, 109, 114, 115, 116, 117, 118, 119, 120, 121, 122, 126, 128, 130, 144, 248, 250, 252, 273, 274, 292, 306
Art 11(1)	67, 168
Art 11(2)	36, 37, 75, 81, 93, 103, 112, 115, 121, 130
Art 11(3)	5, 76, 303
Art 14	14, 38, 39, 48, 49, 50, 51, 52, 53, 54, 59, 60, 61, 64, 70, 75, 76, 142, 143, 238, 239, 254, 286, 301
Art 17	277, 281, 282
Art 35	17
Art 35(1)	17
Art 35(2)(b)	17
Art 35(3)	76
Art 35(3)(a)	17
Art 35(3)(b)	17, 303
Art 35(3)(c)	76
Protocols	17, 53, 76
Protocol 1	53
Art 1	271
Art 2	281, 287
Arts 1–3	14
Protocol 12	53
Art 1	53
Art 2	54
Protocol 13	
Art 1	14
European Model Clauses (third draft)	209
European Prison Rules	
Art 26(1)	144–5
European Social Charter 1961	1, 4, 6, 8, 9, 13, 17, 18, 19, 21, 67, 68, 79, 80, 82, 91, 93, 114, 115, 117, 135, 171, 172, 184, 185, 297
Art 1	17
Art 2	17
Art 2.1	186, 187
Art 2.3	184, 191
Art 2.5	188
Art 4	170, 172, 175
Art 4.1	167, 172
Art 4.2–4.4	167
Art 4.5–4.6	168
Art 5	17, 67, 79, 80, 82
Art 6	17, 67, 90, 91, 114
Art 8.1	193
Art 8.2	193
Art 8.3	193
Art 14	17
Art 19	17
European Social Charter (Revised) 1996 (in force 1999)	17, 137, 184, 185, 191, 193, 298
Art 1	150
Art 1(1)	137, 138
Art 1(2)	137, 138, 142, 144, 146, 149, 150
Art 1(3)–(4)	137
Art 2	137
Art 2(1)	186, 187
Art 2(3)	184, 191
Art 2(5)	188
Art 3	137
Art 4	137, 170
Art 6(4)	117, 131
Art 7.5	174
Art 8	185, 193
Art 21	91
Art 24	253, 297, 304, 305, 307, 308, 309
Art 27	185, 194
Art 27.1	194
Art 27.2, 27.3	195
Appendix	253
ESC Collective Complaints Protocol 1998	18, 135
European Social Security Code	150
Group of Experts on Action against Trafficking in Human Beings (GRETA) Second Report on Spain, 2018 para	90
OECD Guidelines for Multinational Enterprises on Responsible Business Conduct (1976, as amended; revised 2023)	201, 205, 210, 211
p 28 para 2	210
p 29 para 6	210
Treaty of Versailles 1919	1, 311, 315
Pt XIII	23
Universal Declaration of Human Rights 1948	1, 8, 12, 48, 135, 171, 206, 297, 299, 312, 318
Art 1	48
Art 2	48, 49
Art 7	1
Art 12	215, 231
Art 20	1
Art 22	1
Art 23	1, 167, 318
Art 23(1)	135, 167
Art 23(2)	167, 175
Art 23(3)	167, 170
Art 23(4)	167
Art 24	1, 184, 318, 320
Art 25	171
Art 25(1)	316
United Nations Convention against Transnational Organised Crime	
Protocol to Prevent, Suppress and Punish Trafficking in Persons, especially Women and Children ('Palermo Protocol')	160
UN Convention on the Elimination of All Forms of Discrimination against Women New York, 18 December 1979	50, 54, 55
Art 5	55
Art 9	55

Art 11	55
Art 15	55
UN Convention on the Rights of the Child	58
UN Convention on the Rights of Persons with Disabilities (12 December 2006)	61
Art 27	63, 138
Art 27(h)	62
Art 27(i)	62
Optional Protocol	61
UN Global Compact	201, 202, 203, 211
UN Guiding Principles on Business and Human Rights (2011)	208, 210, 211, 212
principle 1	211
principle 2	211
principle 11	211
principle 12	211
principle 17	211, 212
principle 22	211, 212
principle 25	211
UN Human Rights Council – Updated Draft Legally Binding Instrument to Regulate, in International Human Rights Law, the Activities of Transnational Corporations and Other Business Enterprises (July 2023)	212, 213
Art 6.2	212
Art 8	212
UN International Covenant on Civil and Political Rights 1966, 999 UNTS 171	18, 139, 148, 206
Art 2(1)	48
Art 8	148
Art 17	215, 231
Art 26	49, 139
UN International Covenant on Economic, Social and Cultural Rights Adopted and opened for signature, ratification and accession by General Assembly resolution 2200A (XXI) of 16 December 1966, 993 UNTS 3 (ICESCR)	1, 8, 18, 135, 136, 170, 206, 297
Art 2(2)	48
Arts 6–8	136
Art 6	1, 135, 144, 149
Art 6(2)	136
Art 7	1, 135, 170, 175, 191
Art 7(d)	184, 186
Art 8	1, 135
Art 9	1
Art 10(2)	193
Optional Protocol	18, 135
Vienna Convention on the Law of Treaties of 1969	19
Art 31(1)	19

International Labour Organization

Declaration of Philadelphia 1944 (concerning the aims and purposes of the International Labour Organisation, The General Conference of the International Labour Organization, Twenty-sixth Session in Philadelphia, 10 May 1944)	23, 67, 89, 167, 181, 311
Art I(b)	249
Art III(e)	89, 167
Declaration on Fundamental Principles and Rights at Work 1998 (amended 2022)	25, 68, 89, 160, 201, 202, 205, 210, 211, 213, 319, 320
Draft ILO Multilateral Framework on Labour Migration	157
ILO Constitution 1919	25
Preamble	23
Article 33	25
Article 37	8, 25, 114
ILO Conventions	24
Convention No 1, Hours of Work (Industry) Convention, 1919	183, 186
Convention No 14, Weekly Rest (Industry) Convention, 1921	188
Forced Labour Convention No 29 1930	145, 146, 149, 160
Art 2(1)	145
Art 2(2)	145
Art 2(2)(c)	145
Art 4(3)(a)	145
Convention No 30, Hours of Work (Commerce and Offices) Convention, 1930	186
Convention No 47, Forty-Hour Week Convention, 1935	
Art 1	187
Convention No 87 on freedom of association, 1948	25, 68, 79, 108, 113, 114
Art 2	82
Art 3.1	113
Art 3.2	113
Art 8	82
Convention No 95 Protection of Wages Convention, 1949	166
Convention No 98 Right to Organise and Collective Bargaining Convention 1949	68, 79, 89, 108, 113
Art 1	69, 113, 117
Art 1.1	69
Art 1.2(a), (b)	69, 79
Art 3	69
Art 4	90
Convention No 102 Social Security Convention 1952	149
Convention No 105 Abolition of Forced Labour Convention 1957	160
Convention No 106 Weekly Rest (Commerce and Offices) Convention, 1957	188
Convention No 111 on Discrimination (Employment and Occupation) 1958	142
Convention No 131 Minimum Wage Fixing Convention, 1970	
Art 3	171
Convention No 135 concerning Protection and Facilities to be Afforded to Workers' Representatives in the Undertaking 1971	69
Art 1	69, 252
Convention No 154 Collective Bargaining Convention (1981)	
Art 5	90
Convention No 158 Concerning Termination of Employment at the Initiative of the Employer (1982)	297, 298, 299, 304, 305, 307, 308, 309
Art 2	308, 309
Art 2(1)	308
Art 2(2)	308
Art 2(2)(b)	308

Art 2(5) 308
Art 4 .... 298, 304, 307
Art 5 .... 253, 304
Art 6 304
Art 7 307
Art 8 305
Art 9(3) 306
Arts 10–12 305
Art 13 306
Convention No 159 Vocational Rehabilitation
 and Employment (Disabled Persons)
 Convention, 1983 138
Convention No 182 Worst Forms of Child
 Labour Convention, 1999 (No 182) 26
Art 3 26
Convention No 187 Promotional Framework for
 Occupational Safety and Health Convention,
 2006 (No 187) 26
Convention No 189 Domestic Workers
 Convention, 2011 (No 189) 26, 56–7, 156, 224
Art 6 56
Art 9 57
Art 9(c) 57

Art 10 57
Art 11 57
Art 14 57
Convention No 190 Violence and Harassment
 Convention 2019 26
ILO Forced Labour Protocol (2014) 160
ILO, Tripartite Declaration of Principles concerning
 Multinational Enterprises and Social Policy
 (1977, as amended) 201
ILO
Termination of Employment Recommendation,
 1982 (No 166) 298, 305
Arts 7–12 307
Freedom of Association – Compilation of Decisions
 of the Committee on Freedom of Association,
 Sixth Edition, 2018
 para 77 6
 para 799 125
 paras 805–10 124
 para 815 120
 para 840 126
Freedom of Association and Collective Bargaining,
 81st session, 1994, para 38 6

Table of UK Other Materials

ACAS Code of Practice 1, Code of Practice on Disciplinary and Grievance Procedures (2015), issued under TULRCA 1992, s 199 307
Department for Business and Trade, Minimum Service Levels: updated Code of Practice on Reasonable Steps (November 2023) 127
    para 21 127
Department for Education, Minimum Service Levels in Education (November 2023) 127
Ethical Trading Initiative 202
    ETI Base Code
        para 4.1, 4.2 203
General Medical Council
    Good Medical Practice (2024)
        para 21 290
    Personal Beliefs and Medical Practice (2013) 290
Home Office, Border Security: Minimum Service Levels during Strike Action (November 2023) 127
Immigration Rules 156, 157

Appendix Overseas Domestic Worker – Updated 5 October 2023 157
Appendix Domestic Worker who is a Victim of Modern Slavery – Updated 31 January 2024 157
Appendix Temporary Work – Seasonal Worker, 2016 154
Magna Carta 314
Prudential Regulation Authority of the Bank of England
    CP15/22 – Remuneration: Ratio between fixed and variable components of total remuneration ('bonus cap') (19/12/2022) 181
Bank of England
    PS9/23 – Remuneration: Ratio between fixed and variable components of total remuneration ('bonus cap') 181
PRA policy statement 9/23 181
FCA policy statement 23/15 181
Prudential Regulation Authority Rulebook
    Remuneration – r 15.9(3) 181

1

Introduction

1.	In the Beginning …	6.	The Role of Courts: Human Rights and Constitutional Limits
2.	Collective Laissez-Faire and Human Rights	7.	The Future of Human Rights at Work? AI, Algorithms, Climate Crisis
3.	Labour Rights as Human Rights?		
4.	Human Rights as a Threat to Collective Values?	8.	The Case for 'Human Rights at Work'
5.	The Role of States: Negative and Positive Obligations		

1. In the Beginning …

The foundations for this book were laid three quarters of a century ago in the Universal Declaration of Human Rights 1948 (UDHR). Proclaiming a new moral order based on individual dignity, liberty and rights, the UDHR included not only rights to liberty, equality, and security, but also some labour rights including the right to work, the right to just conditions of work and favourable remuneration, and the right to form and join trade unions.[1] The UDHR was the first international treaty to describe the rights of workers as human rights. The Treaty of Versailles 1919, which established a system for promulgating and enforcing minimum labour standards through the International Labour Office, used the language of standards and principles, not fundamental or human rights (except perhaps in the case of the right to form trade unions). The UDHR transformed many of those international labour standards into abstract human rights, which were subsequently elaborated in the UN International Covenant on Economic, Social and Cultural Rights (ICESCR),[2] the European Social Charter 1961 (ESC), and other international treaties. The idea that protective employment law rights are grounded in human rights or fundamental legal rights proved especially attractive to those concerned that the economic system of market capitalism tends to drive down labour standards and incentivise management practices that treat workers like machines, not human beings. Although the idea that labour law (or employment law or work law) is grounded in human rights was conceived in 1948, we believe that this book is the first attempt to provide a systematic academic treatise on labour law that is a detailed articulation of a collection of the human rights recognised in international law.

---

[1] Articles 7, 20, 22, 23, 24.
[2] Articles 6–9.

2. Collective Laissez-Faire and Human Rights

As the foundations were being laid for international human rights law in 1948, Otto Kahn-Freund was starting to develop his influential account of British labour law through the concept of 'collective laissez-faire'. The main elements of collective laissez-faire were set out in a series of essays in the 1950s.[3] According to Kahn-Freund, British labour law had developed mainly by way of 'industrial autonomy'.[4] It was an account that emphasised the limits of the law in labour relations, and this was reflected in two main features. The first feature concerned the legal relationship between employers and individual employees. In post-war Britain, terms and conditions of employment were mainly negotiated and enforced through collective bargaining between employers and trade unions. Unlike many other countries with labour codes and specialist labour courts, there was very little direct legal regulation of the contract of employment. The second feature concerned the legal relationships between employers, trade unions, and the state. There was very little direct legal support for collective bargaining, for example through a statutory duty to bargain. Instead, governments used indirect supports to promote collective bargaining, through administrative interventions, extending the normative effects of representative collective agreements, or providing substitute mechanisms to set wages where collective bargaining was weak.[5] These indirect mechanisms were less intrusive on the autonomy of the collective parties, and this preserved a wide degree of bargaining freedom. Collective laissez-faire was a description of the role of law in British industrial relations, an exercise in industrial sociology. Yet this description also fitted neatly with the liberal values of the British state and industrial civil society. This liberalism had evident attractions for Kahn-Freund, a labour court judge and scholar who had fled Germany in 1933 as a Jewish refugee.[6]

There was little space in this classical account of collective laissez-faire for strong legal protection of human rights at work. Partly, this was simply because there was not much 'employment law' as we would recognise it today, and so nothing for human rights law to latch onto. It also reflects deeper reservations about the role of courts in labour law during the post-war period. Of course, human rights can be protected in different ways and by a range of public institutions: they are not simply the concern of courts. Yet courts have always occupied an important position in protecting human rights in constitutions, not least because these rights often protect minority groups who are vulnerable to bias or neglect in majoritarian democracies. During the formative period of British labour law, workers and trade unions developed a distrust of courts.[7] The courts had been most active in developing repressive common law liabilities for trade unions, through doctrines such as restraint of trade or the economic torts, and Parliament intervened periodically through 'negative' statutes to exclude (or negate) those common law doctrines.[8]

The period for a 'pure' form of collective laissez-faire was relatively short-lived.[9] In the 1960s and 1970s, the limitations of the voluntary model were recognised by governments. Collective

---

[3] See O Kahn-Freund, 'Legal Framework' in A Flanders and HA Clegg (eds), *The System of Industrial Relations in Great Britain* (Blackwell, 1954).
[4] A Bogg, *The Democratic Aspects of Trade Union Recognition* (Hart, 2009) ch 1.
[5] KD Ewing, 'The State and Industrial Relations: "Collective Laissez-Faire" Revisited' (1998) 5 *Historical Studies in Industrial Relations* 1.
[6] M Freedland, 'Otto Kahn-Freund (1900–1979)' in J Beatson and R Zimmermann (eds), *Jurists Uprooted: German-Speaking Émigré Lawyers in Twentieth Century Britain* (OUP, 2004) 299.
[7] A Flanders, 'The Tradition of Voluntarism' (1974) 12 *British Journal of Industrial Relations* 352.
[8] Kahn-Freund, 'Legal Framework', above n 5, 44.
[9] PL Davies and M Freedland, *Labour Legislation and Public Policy* (OUP, 1993) ch 1.

bargaining did not provide universal coverage for workers but was instead clustered in 'male' sectors such as manufacturing and mining. For example, it was estimated that in 1967 only 50 per cent of manual workers and 30 per cent of white-collar workers were trade union members.[10] There were far lower levels of unionisation among women workers. This created the familiar democratic danger that well-represented interests of the majority might override the interests of minority groups within the trade union. Worse still, many workers had no union representation at all.

From the 1970s, a range of individual employment rights were enacted in legislation. Unfair dismissal protections were introduced in the Industrial Relations Act 1971, and subsequently re-enacted when that legislation was repealed. Other employment rights included protection against unfair deductions from wages, rights to time off work, and redundancy payments, a minimum wage and regulation of hours of work. There were also important statutory interventions on equal pay, sex discrimination, maternity leave and pay, and race discrimination. The enactment (or repeal) of these rights formed a significant part of the programmes of political parties seeking election. This growth of a 'floor of rights' that applied to most employees was justified in different ways, but in general it was regarded as a necessary safeguard for the interests of workers, especially where unionisation was weak or absent. The existence of these legislated employment rights was always precarious, however, in the sense that a new government, particularly a neoliberal government, might decide to reduce costs to employers by abolishing or curtailing those rights.

From about 2000 onwards, it was more frequently asserted that many of these employment law rights were grounded in more fundamental rights, such as human rights law or constitutional rights. In the European Union, the first sign of this development was the declaration by all Member States of the Community Charter of the Fundamental Social Rights of Workers.[11] This foreshadowed the enactment of the Charter of Fundamental Rights of the European Union as a binding treaty obligation.[12] The Charter identified a number of fundamental rights of workers that should always be respected in EU law. At about the same time, the Human Rights Act 1998 (HRA 1998) in the UK enabled employees to rely on human rights in the European Convention on Human Rights (ECHR) for the interpretation of domestic law in their claims for employment rights. These developments and others supported the idea that many employment law rights were not simply legislation that might be enacted or repealed according to the electoral success of political parties, but they were articulations of a higher law of fundamental rights that could be discovered in international and transnational Conventions on human rights. This higher law created a barrier to the repeal or exclusion of workers' rights. To take advantage of this added layer of protection for employment rights, workers and trade unions were increasingly attracted to litigation in courts to defend those fundamental rights against hostile governments and unsympathetic judicial decisions. Workers and trade unions looked to the EU and the Council of Europe to protect their fundamental human rights from legislative restriction. In this way, the emergence of 'human rights at work' as an essential foundation for labour law was rooted in the economic struggle of workers for emancipation. It was not an idea merely cooked up in a textbook or a seminar room.

---

[10] ibid 46.
[11] 10 December 1989, of the European Economic Community.
[12] Originally adopted in 2001, but subsequently amended: OJ C326, 26.10.2012, p 391.

3. Labour Rights as Human Rights?

Labour rights are rights that relate to the role of being a worker. Some labour rights are exercised individually and others collectively. They can include a right to work in a job freely chosen, a right to fair working conditions, a right to a just wage, a right to privacy, a right to be protected from arbitrary and unjustified dismissal, a right to belong to and be represented by a trade union and a right to strike. Even though this definition of labour rights may appear uncontroversial, the question whether labour rights are human rights has been a matter of controversy in labour law scholarship.[13] Some argue that labour rights are human rights and that they should be classified and protected in law as such. An important implication of this is that labour rights should enjoy strong legal protection and resist trade-offs. Others take the view that it is wrong to understand labour rights as human rights. On this view, workers' rights are all about collective solidarity, rather than individual autonomy, dignity and other such values that are central in human rights theory and law.

If we look at the question more closely, though, we see that there are three different ways in which we can approach it.[14] First, we can take a positivistic approach, according to which a group of rights are human rights insofar as certain treaties, constitutions and other legal documents recognise them as such. On this analysis, in order to consider whether labour rights are human rights, we need to look at human rights law. Labour rights that are incorporated in human rights documents are rightly described as human rights. Those that are not included therein are not human rights. One of the difficulties with this analysis is that different human rights documents contain distinct lists of rights. They also have different monitoring and enforcement mechanisms. For this reason, the question of which labour rights can be viewed as human rights will depend on the legal order that we assess. If we take the HRA 1998, which incorporates the ECHR in domestic law, we will come up with a short list of labour rights that are human rights, at least at first glance. The ECHR prohibits slavery, servitude, forced and compulsory labour, and protects the right to form and join a trade union for the protection of workers' interests. If we take the Council of Europe more broadly as a starting point, we will have a long list of labour rights that are also human rights, consisting not only of the rights that we have in the ECHR but also those that we find in the ESC, such as the right to work, the right to strike and the right to just working conditions.

A second way in which the question of whether labour rights are human rights is approached is an instrumental one that turns on the consequences of using strategies, such as litigation or civil society action, which promote labour rights as human rights. This is the most common way in which labour law scholars analyse the issue, and has its roots in the Marxian tradition. On this analysis, '[t]he imperative to present [workers'] claims as human rights comes from the desire to utilise the potentially powerful legal methods of securing advantage to pursue their claims, and also from the perceived need to respond to employers' willingness to use these arguments

---

[13] See, for example, V Leary, 'The Paradox of Workers' Rights as Human Rights' in L Compa and S Diamond (eds), *Human Rights, Labor Rights, and International Trade* (University of Pennsylvania Press, 1996) 22; P Alston (ed), *Labour Rights as Human Rights* (Oxford, OUP, 2005); K Kolben, 'Labour Rights as Human Rights?' (2010) 50 *Virginia Journal of International Law* 449; J Youngdahl, 'Solidarity First: Labor Rights are Not the Same as Human Rights', *New Labor Forum* 18(1) 31–37 (Winter 2009); L Compa, 'Solidarity And Human Rights: A Response to Youngdahl', *New Labor Forum* 18(1) 38–45 (Winter 2009); G Mundlak, 'Human Rights and Labor Rights: Why Don't the Two Tracks Meet?' (2012) 34 *Comparative Labor Law and Policy Journal* 217; H Collins, 'Theories of Rights as Justifications for Labour Law' in G Davidov and B Langille (eds), *The Idea of Labour Law* (Oxford, OUP, 2011) 137.

[14] V Mantouvalou, 'Are Labour Rights Human Rights?' (2012) 3 *European Labour Law Journal* 106.

and tools themselves.'[15] If these legal strategies are successful, the question is answered in the affirmative and the character of labour rights as human rights is endorsed and celebrated; if not, scepticism is expressed.[16] There are challenges with this analysis too. For instance, the success of a litigation strategy should not only be assessed by focusing on a victory or defeat in court. Litigation can have a number of significant implications, which are much harder to measure.[17]

A third approach to the question whether labour rights are human rights is a normative one. It examines what a human right is, and assesses, given this definition, whether certain labour rights should be classified as human rights.[18] Depending on the theoretical foundations that are described as foundations of labour rights, different lists of labour rights as human rights will emerge. We can take the prohibition of exploitation as a central foundational value of labour rights as human rights, for instance, because exploitative treatment may violate human dignity, agency or freedom. We would then need to define exploitation. If we take a Marxian approach to exploitation as a foundation,[19] we might develop a long list of labour rights that should be viewed as human rights. If we take a narrow definition of exploitation, such as the one that we find in the law of human trafficking, we will come up with a very short list of labour rights as human rights.[20] The theoretical justification of labour rights as human rights has normative implications.[21]

That there are different ways to approach the question whether labour rights are human rights does not mean that the three lines of thinking are not interconnected. An answer to the question of foundations can help determine the material scope of labour rights. The question of strategic human rights litigation only arises because we find labour rights in human rights instruments. The connections are many. However, it is important to appreciate that we have these three different ways of thinking in order to be clear on their interactions and further implications.

4. Human Rights as a Threat to Collective Values?

Some express concerns about a human rights turn in the protection of workers' rights. On this view, human rights are viewed as individual rights, while workers' interests can only be effective when exercised collectively, in solidarity with others.[22] This feature is said to distinguish labour rights from human rights that are individual and are typically also exercised individually. This is an important point to consider and address. Indeed, for instance, in the past in the European

---

[15] C Fenwick and T Novitz, 'Conclusion: Regulating to Protect Workers' Human Rights' in C Fenwick and T Novitz (eds), *Human Rights at Work: Perspectives on Law and Regulation* (Oxford, Hart Publishing, 2010) 587–88.

[16] See, for instance, K Ewing and J Hendy, 'The Dramatic Implications of Demir and Baykara' (2010) 39 *Industrial Law Journal* 2; KD Ewing and J Hendy, 'Article 11(3) of the European Convention on Human Rights' [2017] EHRLR 356.

[17] See the discussion in M Dias-Abey, 'Mobilizing for Recognition: Indie Unions, Migrant Workers, and Strategic Equality Act Litigation' (2022) 38 *International Journal of Comparative Labour Law and Industrial Relations* 137. On the effects of strategic human rights litigation, see H Duffy, *Strategic Human Rights Litigation – Understanding and Maximising Impact* (Oxford, Hart, 2018) ch 4.

[18] See J Atkinson, 'Human Rights as Foundations for Labour Law' in H Collins, G Lester and V Mantouvalou (eds), *Philosophical Foundations of Labour Law* (Oxford, Oxford University Press, 2018) 122; P Gilabert, 'Labor Human Rights and Human Dignity' (2016) 42 *Philosophy and Social Criticism* 171. See further chapter 19.

[19] See, for instance, John Roemer, 'Should Marxists Be Interested in Exploitation?' in K Nielsen and R Ware (eds), *Exploitation* (Humanities Press International, 1997) 94.

[20] Directive 2011/36/EU of the European Parliament and of the Council of 5 April 2011 on preventing and combating trafficking in human beings and protecting its victims.

[21] See particularly chapter 19.

[22] See, for instance, Youngdahl, above n 13.

human rights law system, the European Court of Human Rights (ECtHR) was reluctant to protect trade union rights, whilst it was willing to recognise the rights of individuals who refused to be trade union members under Article 11 that protects the right to form and join trade unions. This occurred in a line of cases on 'closed shop' arrangements, namely arrangements of compulsory union membership.[23] The decisions of the ECtHR in these cases led scholars to argue that 'from a trade union point of view, Article 11 was showing a debit balance'.[24]

However, the distinction between individual and collective rights is exaggerated. Human rights instruments protect several collective labour rights, such as the right to unionise, collective bargaining and strike. It is true that some human rights monitoring mechanisms, such as the ECtHR, involve individual applications primarily, and the decisions of courts and other monitoring bodies address these individual cases. However, applications are also submitted by trade unions and other civil society organisations, and not just by individual workers. Moreover, mechanisms, such as the European Committee of Social Rights, monitoring compliance with the ESC, examine collective complaints and state reports. Human rights, in other words, are not only about individual interests, nor are they only exercised individually. As West has noted, 'rights could as readily be grounded in a view of our nature that both respects our individuality and also gives full recognition to our social nature'.[25] They protect collective interests and can be raised by workers' organisations before the relevant monitoring mechanisms. It is also important to note that advocates of labour rights as human rights do not support the view that workers and their organisations should limit their activities to litigation and other legal routes. Different strategies have to be pursued simultaneously to promote workers' interests effectively.

It is also important to appreciate that it is impossible to separate collective labour rights from other human rights. The International Labour Organization (ILO) itself has underlined that trade union rights cannot be effectively protected without strong protection of civil and political rights. For example, in a 1970 Resolution on trade union rights and civil liberties, it emphasised the value of freedom of expression for trade union rights, 'in particular freedom to hold opinions without interference and to seek, receive and impart information and ideas through any media and regardless of frontiers'.[26] In an ILO Report of 1994, it was said that an 'essential aspect of trade-union rights is the right to express opinions through the press or otherwise. The full exercise of trade-union rights calls for a free flow of information, opinions and ideas, and workers, employers and their organisations should enjoy freedom of opinion and expression at their meetings, in their publications, and in the course of their other activities.'[27] Moreover, human rights defenders who are killed or have disappeared are often trade union leaders.[28] Collective trade union rights, in other words, are inextricably linked to individual civil and political rights.

5. The Role of States: Negative and Positive Obligations

A further issue to consider when examining human rights at work involves the role of states. In international human rights law, states typically have obligations to refrain from

---

[23] *Young, James and Webster v UK*, App Nos 7601/76, 7806/77, Judgment of 13 August 1981. See further chapter 5.
[24] K Ewing, 'The Implications of Wilson and Palmer' (2003) 32 *Industrial Law Journal* 1.
[25] R West, *Re-imagining Justice* (Aldershot, Ashgate, 2003) 86.
[26] ILO, Freedom of Association – Compilation of Decisions of the Committee on Freedom of Association, Sixth Edition, 2018, para 77.
[27] International Labour Conference, Freedom of Association and Collective Bargaining, 81st session, 1994, para 38.
[28] See Amnesty International, 'Deadly but Preventable Attacks: Killings and Enforced Disappearances of those Who Defend Human Rights', ACT 30/7270/2017 (2017), 13.

wronging individuals. This is enshrined in fundamental protections that we find in this body of rules that was born out of the necessity to stop the atrocities of the 20th century by holding the authorities accountable for their conduct. In addition, international human rights law recognises positive obligations of state authorities to put in place an institutional machinery that makes rights effective, to guarantee that people have a remedy for violations of their rights, to provide goods and services to satisfy rights, and to promote rights by bringing changes to public consciousness.[29] Most human rights treaties impose obligations on state authorities (not directly on private employers) to guarantee the rights in question. On this basis, state action that breaches workers' rights may give rise to human rights violations.

Over the years, courts and other monitoring bodies have developed a range of positive obligations under human rights law.[30] The basis for these in the ECHR system is Article 1, which provides that states have a duty 'to secure to everyone within their jurisdiction' the rights of the Convention. These consist in obligations to develop an effective legislative and administrative framework, to have effective procedures and take operational measures.[31] For instance, in a case that involved workers' health and safety and protection from harm caused by asbestos in the workplace, the Court ruled that the Government of Malta did not legislate or take any measures necessary to ensure that the applicants were protected from and informed about the risk posed to their health and life.[32] It ruled that Malta violated the right to life (Article 2) and the right to private life (Article 8). In a case involving the exploitation of a migrant domestic worker, the Court ruled that France violated its positive obligation to criminalise the worst forms of labour exploitation and violated Article 4 of the ECHR (the prohibition of servitude, forced and compulsory labour).[33] In relation to trafficking for sexual exploitation under Article 4, it further explained that having legislation in place is not sufficient: states also have to take positive operational measures in order to give effect to the rights under the Convention.[34] On trade union rights, the Court ruled that by permitting employers to give financial incentives to induce workers to surrender these rights, the UK did not meet its positive obligations to secure workers' rights under Article 11.[35]

In all these cases, it is important to appreciate that for a breach of the Convention to arise, the Court must find that the authorities knew or 'ought to have known' of the complaints in question. The 'know or ought to have known' formulation has been developed by the Strasbourg Court to assign responsibility to the state for wrongs in the private sphere.[36] For instance, in a case of undocumented migrant workers in agriculture, who were exploited and ill-treated by their private employer, the Court found that the Greek authorities 'were aware, or ought to have been aware' of this ill-treatment, and did not take positive measures to protect the workers.[37] The authorities therefore violated the ECHR. Positive obligations arise

---

[29] P Alston and R Goodman, *International Human Rights* (Oxford, OUP, 2013) 182–85.
[30] See generally V Stoyanova, *Positive Obligations under the European Convention on Human Rights* (Oxford, OUP, 2023). At domestic level in the UK, the Human Rights Act 1998 recognises indirect horizontal effect to Convention rights. See chapter 2.
[31] Stoyanova, ibid ch 7.
[32] *Brincat and Others v Malta* [2014] ECHR 836.
[33] *Siliadin v France* [2005] ECHR 545.
[34] *Rantsev v Cyprus and Russia* [2010] ECHR 22. On positive obligations under Article 4, see M Jovanovic, *State Responsibility for 'Modern Slavery' in Human Rights Law: A Right Not to Be Trafficked?* (Oxford, OUP, 2023).
[35] *Wilson, National Union of Journalists and Others v United Kingdom* (2002) 35 EHRR 523.
[36] For instance, see the reasoning of the Court in *DP and JC v United Kingdom*, Judgment of 10 October 2002, [2002] ECHR, paras 111–12.
[37] *Chowdury v Greece* [2017] ECHR 300.

under almost all provisions of the ECHR, and have played a central role in the development of human rights in the workplace, where the violations at stake mostly occur in private employment relationships.

6. The Role of Courts: Human Rights and Constitutional Limits

Many of the sources of workers' rights we will consider in this book do not involve courts at all. There is no court attached to the UDHR or the ICESCR, for example, but rather committees with the power to interpret the instrument and comment on the practices of signatory states. The same is true of the ILO. Although there is a power to refer a dispute about the interpretation of a Convention to the International Court of Justice (ICJ),[38] a power which has recently been exercised in relation to the right to strike, this rarely occurs, and, in practice, most interpretation of ILO materials is offered by the Committee of Experts or the Committee on Freedom of Association.[39] Although these interpretations do not emerge from the same procedure as a court decision – a particular dispute with arguments presented on both sides, and a judgment to be made – they are always worth considering, as expert pronouncements on how the instrument in question should be understood.

But some of this book will be concerned with the decisions of courts. At the regional level, we will encounter the ECtHR, which interprets the ECHR. The right of individual petition to the Court, compulsory for all signatory states since 1998, has transformed its role, by giving it a substantial docket of cases through which it can develop its interpretation of the Convention. Several characteristics of the Court are worth noting. First, its approach to the interpretation of the Convention evolves over time. For example, it held in *Demir* that the right to bargain collectively and to conclude collective agreements did constitute 'an inherent element' of Article 11, reversing earlier case law in which it had held that signatory states had a choice about how to enable trade unions to protect their members' interests under Article 11.[40] Second, and relatedly, the Court often adopts what has been termed an 'integrated approach' to the interpretation of Convention rights.[41] In the context of employment rights, this involves using materials from other sources, notably the ESC and the ILO, in order to flesh out the content of those rights. This is also a contrast with an earlier approach in which the Court tended to treat social rights as a matter for the ESC and its institutions. The integrated approach is, again, evident in *Demir*, where the Court relies heavily on ESC and ILO materials in order to understand the crucial role of collective bargaining in the activities of trade unions.[42] This is controversial from a traditional international law perspective, where considerable emphasis is placed on the idea that states only incur obligations when they consent. For example, Turkey objected to the use of ILO materials in *Demir* because it had not ratified the relevant conventions, and was in effect being forced to comply with them by the 'back door'.[43] However, an obvious advantage of the integrated approach is its acknowledgement of the fact that human

---

[38] ILO Constitution, Article 37.
[39] ILO Press Release (11 November 2023), www.ilo.org/global/about-the-ilo/newsroom/news/WCMS_901633/lang--en/index.htm.
[40] *Demir and Baykara v Turkey* (2009) 48 EHRR 54, [140]–[146]; [153].
[41] V Mantouvalou, 'Labour Rights in the European Convention on Human Rights: An Intellectual Justification for an Integrated Approach to Interpretation' (2013) 13 *Human Rights Law Review* 529.
[42] eg *Demir*, above n 40, [147]–[151].
[43] For the Court's discussion, see *Demir*, above n 40, [85]–[86].

rights are intended to have a universal quality, so there should be substantial common ground in the way in which particular rights are interpreted across different systems.

A third point to note about the ECtHR is that, as a supranational court, it applies a 'margin of appreciation' in many of its decisions. This is the idea that national authorities (which may be the legislature or the courts, depending on the circumstances) have some discretion to decide how to implement Convention rights within their particular situation. The Court's use of this concept is often controversial because, for rights advocates, it is disappointing to reach the stage of receiving a judgment from the Court, only to find that it has 'avoided' making a detailed ruling. One example, discussed more fully in chapter 17, is the Court's respect for the French tradition of secularism in its rulings on whether it is legitimate for employers to ban religious clothing at work.[44] Another, discussed in chapter 7, is the decision in *RMT* that the UK's complete ban on secondary strikes (where workers take strike action to support other workers in a dispute) was within the margin of appreciation, despite being contrary to ESC and ILO norms and out of line with the practice in other signatory states.[45]

Another court we will encounter at various points in the book is the Court of Justice of the European Union (CJEU). The CJEU decides questions of EU law, typically on a reference for a preliminary ruling from a national court. It is for the national court to apply that ruling to the facts and to reach a decision on the case before it. It can also be called upon to decide other questions, such as whether a directive is within the EU's competence or whether a Member State has implemented EU law correctly. The Court is not an expert human rights court, but over time it has developed an important jurisprudence on fundamental rights – responding to Member States' concerns that (due to the doctrine of supremacy) EU law overrode fundamental rights protections contained in their national constitutions.[46] It now interprets and applies the EU Charter of Fundamental Rights, which has formed part of the treaty architecture of the EU since 2009. The Court's role in promoting market integration within the EU can sometimes cause it to reason in ways which seem surprising from a human rights perspective, as the *Viking* and *Laval* cases, explored in chapter 7, illustrate.[47]

Last but not least, we will encounter domestic courts as interpreters of human rights law, particularly (given the authors' expertise) in the UK. Perhaps the courts' most obvious role is as interpreters of the many employment law statutes which give effect to the rights of working people, such as the right not to be unfairly dismissed, in detail.[48] Before the UK's exit from the EU, courts in the UK were bound to follow the decisions of the CJEU, and were encouraged to give full effect to certain important labour rights – such as the right to paid annual leave – via this route.[49] Another way to give effect to human rights in court is through the HRA 1998, which creates an obligation under s 3 to interpret the law in accordance with Convention rights as far as it possible to do so, and the power to issue a declaration of incompatibility under s 4. One issue with this is that it skews human rights protection in domestic law away from economic and social rights and towards civil and political rights, just because of the content of the ECHR. However, a more profound problem is that the courts seem somewhat reluctant to use human

---

[44] *SAS v France* (2015) 60 EHRR 11.
[45] *National Union of Rail, Maritime and Transport Workers v United Kingdom* (2015) 60 EHRR 10.
[46] Case 11/70 *Internationale Handelsgesellschaft mbH v Einfuhr- und Vorratsstelle fur Getreide und Futtermittel* EU:C:1970:114, [1970] ECR 1125; Case C-36/02 *Omega Spielhallen- und Automatenaufstellungs GmbH v Bundesstadt Bonn* EU:C:2004:614, [2004] ECR I-9609.
[47] Case C-438/05 *International Transport Workers' Federation v Viking Line ABP* EU:C:2007:772, [2007] ECR I-10779; Case C-341/05 *Laval un Partneri Ltd v Svenska Byggnadsarbetareforbundet* EU:C:2007:809, [2007] ECR I-11767.
[48] Employment Rights Act 1996, s 94.
[49] See chapter 11.

rights arguments to upset what they see as a delicate 'balance' between competing interests in the employment sphere. We will encounter several examples of this in the context of Article 11.[50] The HRA itself also builds in an important limit on the courts' powers: they cannot strike down a statute if it infringes Convention rights. Thus, while the courts have an important role to play, the protection of employment rights in domestic law always involves a combination of legislative and judicial action.

7. The Future of Human Rights at Work? AI, Algorithms, Climate Crisis

Predicting the future is a risky business, since it is so easy to be proved wrong. But there are at least three important developments on the horizon which are likely to have serious implications from the perspective of human rights at work: the increasing role of algorithms as management tools in the workplace, the potential for artificial intelligence (AI) to replace human workers, and the need to change current patterns of production to address climate change. We examine each, very briefly, in turn.

Anyone familiar with the basics of employment law will be aware of the challenges posed by the gig economy, and the uncertainties surrounding the employment status of working people whose work is provided via an online platform.[51] As the courts and legislatures catch up with these challenges, a new and potentially more pervasive issue is emerging: algorithmic management. This involves the use of technological tools to direct the activities of workers and monitor their performance, and it can be applied in any form of work, not just platform work.[52] One problem with algorithmic management is that it can lead to considerable work intensification, as work tasks are broken down into smaller component parts and relentlessly allocated to workers to complete, with penalties if deadlines are not met. This can reduce job satisfaction and cause stress, by limiting workers' discretion and ability to manage their own time. Another problem is that algorithms are not transparent to ordinary working people, so it may be difficult to tell if they are operating in an unfair or discriminatory way. For example, a hiring algorithm might replicate existing biases within a workplace by only selecting applicants with similar backgrounds to existing employees. Privacy, equality and working time rights, among others, will need to be invoked and adapted to meet these new challenges.

Perhaps a more profound challenge is that of AI and automation. There is a long history of technological developments (machines, cars, computers, email and so on) posing a threat to jobs. In practice, while some jobs have become redundant, most have changed or adapted, and the overall level of employment has not been affected. Indeed, technological changes have often enabled workers to become more productive by doing more with their time. But some predictions suggest that a very high percentage of jobs are under threat from AI.[53] For example, computers may be able to scan a huge volume of case law much more quickly and efficiently than a human lawyer in order to identify the applicable legal principles. Perhaps the most immediate challenge here is to develop strong rights on termination of employment, if large numbers of people are to be made redundant. Some have advocated for the introduction of a 'universal basic income' so

---

[50] See chapters 5, 6 and 7.
[51] See chapter 3.
[52] See A Aloisi and V De Stefano, *Your Boss is an Algorithm: Artificial Intelligence, Platform Work and Labour* (Hart, 2022); J Adams-Prassl et al (eds) (2023) 14 *European Labour Law Journal*, special issue on algorithmic management.
[53] For a sensible assessment, see L Nedelkoska and G Quintini, *Automation, Skills Use and Training* (OECD, 2018).

that people have something to fall back on in the event of mass unemployment, but this raises interesting questions about the right to work as a source of fulfilment, not just earnings.[54] An effective policy response might also require closer attention to the way that work is distributed between working people.[55]

Another significant challenge is the need to address climate change. This will require some big changes in polluting sectors such as the extractive industries and transport, though it may also create new jobs, for example, in renewable energy.[56] From a labour rights perspective, the most immediate issue is engaging with workers and helping those facing redundancy to acquire new skills and to transition to 'green' jobs. However, climate change also poses a more profound threat to an economic system built on 'productivism': the idea that people's wealth will gradually increase as we produce and consume more and more over time.[57] An effective response to climate change probably requires people to cut back on their consumption: to limit waste, reuse and recycle, and to buy fewer things overall. This does not fit the existing economic model and may require substantial political change well beyond the scope of employment rights.

8. The Case for 'Human Rights at Work'

We hope to have persuaded our readers that there is a strong case for an academic textbook on 'human rights at work'. The most basic justification is that the province of employment rights, commonly known as employment law, is co-extensive with human rights. Dismissal, equality, wages, working time, time off rights, information and consultation, industrial action, and collective bargaining are all encompassed by human rights laws. General concepts of employment law, such as personal scope, are increasingly influenced by the human rights character of these statutory rights. Whether someone is a worker, and entitled to employment law protections, must be sensitive to the human rights basis of the statutory right. Indeed, you would now struggle to find an area of employment law that does not engage human rights. It would require significant intellectual effort to disentangle employment law from human rights law and to still provide a coherent account of the law without using the grammar of human rights.

The position of the employer as a bearer of power, and the familiar risks of abuse of power, also makes the human rights paradigm especially relevant to employment law. Historically, human rights were focused on the vertical relationship between the state and the citizen. It was but a small step to extend these human rights into horizontal relationships that entailed significant inequalities. The employment contract stands out from most other private law relationships in this respect. Employer prerogatives can affect fundamental civil liberties such as freedom of expression, privacy, and freedom of religion in employees' non-work lives as much as in their work lives. A concern for human rights can maintain that crucial boundary between work and life.

Human rights also have an important role to play in protecting those who are especially vulnerable to serious exploitation, such as migrant workers, workers with protected characteristics, and precarious workers. In the 1990s, a textbook on employment law could proceed without any

---

[54] See chapter 8.
[55] For a more sophisticated discussion, see C Estlund, *Automation Anxiety: Why and How to Save Work* (OUP, 2021).
[56] See the European Green Deal: https://commission.europa.eu/strategy-and-policy/priorities-2019-2024/european-green-deal_en.
[57] For discussion, see K Arabadjieva et al (eds) (2023) 3/4 *International Journal of Comparative Labour Law and Industrial Relations*, special issue on The Labour-Environment Nexus – Exploring New Frontiers in Labour Law.

reference to Article 4 ECHR and issues around 'modern slavery' and trafficking. Today, a failure to address this topic would, in our view, be a very significant omission.

Human rights have undoubtedly enriched employment law, and they have revitalised its worker-protective purposes. Human rights law has provided powerful legal techniques to prevent abuse of power, and it has galvanised workers to organise against exploitation and injustice. This has been critical during periods when the political discourse on employment has been reduced to calculations of economic efficiency. What economists call 'burdens on business', moral and legal philosophers might describe as the duties that are correlative to workers' fundamental human rights. Modes of reasoning that are closely linked to human rights, such as proportionality, are now integral to the employment law canon. It might even be said that employment law is becoming a form of applied human rights law. In all these respects, the framers of the 1948 Declaration should be proud of their legacy for workers in the 21st century.

2

Sources of Rights at Work

1. **UK law and the Human Rights Act 1998**
2. **Council of Europe: European Convention on Human Rights and the European Social Charter**
3. **Law of the European Union**
4. **The International Labour Organization**

This chapter introduces the various sources of human rights that may benefit workers. We consider both legally enforceable rights and rights that comprise internationally recognised labour standards where compliance is monitored by international bodies other than courts. Our focus in this chapter is on those sources of rights that are most likely to influence the legal position in the United Kingdom (UK). In subsequent chapters we also describe occasionally other sources of labour rights that may serve as comparisons or inspirations for legal reasoning. These include national constitutions, international conventions, and reports of international bodies such as the United Nations and the Council of Europe.

The chapter is divided into four broad sections: (1) UK domestic law including the Human Rights Act 1998; (2) The Council of Europe and the European Convention of Human Rights and the European Social Charter (3); Law of the European Union (EU) including its Treaties and the Charter of Fundamental Rights of the European Union; (4) International Labour Rights developed by the International Labour Organization of the United Nations (ILO).

1. UK Law and the Human Rights Act 1998

In the absence of a written constitution containing legally protected fundamental rights in the UK, the human rights of workers are secured to some extent by the principles of the common law developed by the judges through precedent, but to a much greater extent by Parliamentary statutes. Of these many statutes, four statutes are especially important for fundamental rights at work. The Employment Rights Act 1996 (ERA 1996), as amended from time to time, contains many protections for individual employees, such as rights against unfair dismissal and rights in connection with maternity leave and pay. The Trade Union and Labour Relations (Consolidation) Act 1992 (TULRCA 1992), as amended, contains rights in connection with membership of trade unions, collective bargaining, and industrial action. The Equality Act 2010 consolidates the laws against discrimination on prohibited grounds such as sex and race. As the UK has a 'dualist' approach to international law, conventions on international human rights are not directly enforceable through domestic courts. But the Human Rights Act 1998 (HRA 1998) provides a mechanism for the enforcement in domestic courts of the main rights included in the European Convention on Human Rights (ECHR).[1]

For most workers, the normal route for enforcing their labour rights is to commence a claim before an employment tribunal (ET). These tribunals are inexpensive, accessible, and relatively informal courts that hear claims brought by individual workers. Normally ETs rather than ordinary courts have exclusive jurisdiction over claims for employment rights. It is possible to challenge a decision of an ET by claiming before the Employment Appeal Tribunal (EAT) that the tribunal made an error of law in its judgment. In turn, it is possible to appeal the question of whether there was an error of law to the English Court of Appeal (or the Scots Court of Session), and then to the United Kingdom Supreme Court (UKSC). In this book we focus on the decisions of the EAT and the higher courts of appeal, because the decisions of ETs are not regarded as setting binding precedents, though sometimes they provide useful illustrations of issues. Under the HRA 1998, however, the legal process for bringing claims to vindicate rights at work differs in several important respects. To understand the reasoning in many of the cases considered in this book, it is necessary to appreciate the Act's special features.

The HRA 1998 facilitates the protection of the principal rights contained in the ECHR.[2] These include rights against slavery and forced labour (Article 4), the right to a fair trial (Article 6), the right to respect for private life (Article 8), freedom of religion and belief (Article 9), freedom of expression (Article 10), and freedom of association including the right to join a trade union (Article 11). Section 6 of the HRA 1998 declares that it is unlawful for a public authority to act in a way that does not comply with Convention rights. Section 7 of the HRA 1998 enables individuals to bring direct actions in the ordinary courts against public authorities for such unlawful acts. Usually, such claims will comprise a judicial review of the decision or action of a public authority on the ground that it was unlawful because it was incompatible with a Convention right contrary to s 6 of the HRA 1998. In some cases, employees in the public sector may be able to use s 7 to vindicate Convention rights, but this avenue is only possible when their employer's action involves the exercise of a public function rather than a private act such as entering or terminating a contract of employment.

Of far greater importance for most employees' claims is the interpretive obligation under s 3 of the HRA 1998:

> So far as it is possible to do so, primary legislation and subordinate legislation must be read and given effect in a way which is compatible with the Convention rights.

This provision gives what is known as 'indirect horizontal effect' to the Convention rights in ordinary labour relations. It is 'indirect' because Convention rights can only be used as a tool for interpreting existing rights under domestic law. The provision is 'horizontal' because it applies to relations between ordinary people and corporations. Section 3 requires courts and tribunals to interpret legislation such as the ERA 1996, TULRCA 1992 and the Equality Act 2010 in a way that is consistent with the requirements of the rights in the ECHR. The decision of the House of Lords in *Ghaidan v Godin-Mendoza* shows that the interpretive obligation imposed by s 3 is extremely strong:

---

[1] See, generally, KD Ewing, 'The Human Rights Act and Labour Law' (1998) 27 *Industrial Law Journal* 275; ACL Davies, 'Workers' Human Rights in English Law' in C Fenwick and T Novitz (eds), *Human Rights at Work – Perspectives on Law and Regulation* (Oxford, Hart, 2010); V Mantouvalou, 'The Human Rights Act and Labour Law at 20' in A Bogg, A Young and J Rowbottom (eds), *The Constitution of Social Democracy: Essays in Honour of Keith Ewing* (Oxford, Hart, 2020).

[2] The Convention rights included by s 1 of the HRA 1998 are Articles 2–12 and 14 of the ECHR, Articles 1–3 of the First Protocol, and Article 1 of the Thirteenth Protocol.

The mere fact the language under consideration is inconsistent with a Convention-compliant meaning does not of itself make a Convention-compliant interpretation under section 3 impossible. Section 3 enables language to be interpreted restrictively or expansively. But section 3 goes further than this. It is also apt to require a court to read in words which change the meaning of the enacted legislation, so as to make it Convention-compliant. In other words, the intention of Parliament in enacting section 3 was that, to an extent bounded only by what is 'possible', a court can modify the meaning, and hence the effect, of primary and secondary legislation. Parliament, however, cannot have intended that in the discharge of this extended interpretative function the courts should adopt a meaning inconsistent with a fundamental feature of legislation. That would be to cross the constitutional boundary section 3 seeks to demarcate and preserve.[3]

The strong indirect effect produced by s 3 of the HRA 1998 on statutory labour law was accepted by the Court of Appeal in *X v Y*.[4] The case concerned a claim for unfair dismissal brought against a private sector employer. The Court of Appeal acknowledged that a court or tribunal must interpret domestic legislation such as the ERA 1996 in a manner that is compliant with the Convention rights, taking into account the interpretation placed on those rights by the European Court of Human Rights (ECtHR). It follows that, in making the determination of whether a dismissal was unfair, a tribunal should develop a conception of fairness that complies with Convention rights. Thus, in principle, both public and private sector employees can rely upon the Convention rights contained in the HRA 1998 as a source for the interpretation of domestic legislation to ensure its conformity with Convention rights. In general, therefore, a dismissal involving an unjustified interference with an employee's Convention right is likely to be regarded as an unfair dismissal.

The core question in *X v Y* was how to formulate the open textured statutory standard of reasonableness that governs claims for unfair dismissal.[5] The interpretive obligation of s 3 can also be applied to technical rules that apparently give little scope for interpretation. For example, the laws that require trade unions to ballot their members prior to calling industrial action are detailed, elaborate, and costly to comply with. Small inadvertent mistakes have often provided employers with the opportunity to seek an injunction against industrial action, thereby stopping strike action in its tracks. This highly technical interpretation of the balloting rules was rejected by the Court of Appeal in *Serco v RMT*.[6] Accepting that Article 11 of the ECHR had been interpreted by the ECtHR to provide general protection for the right to strike, Elias LJ held that in balancing the rights of the parties, the Court should give equal weight to the workers' right to strike, so that small, inadvertent, and insignificant mistakes committed by the trade union during the balloting process should not be regarded as invalidating it and rendering the strike unlawful.

The duty to interpret the law so that it complies with the Convention rights also applies to cases where courts and tribunals apply judge-made common law. This result is achieved by s 6 of the HRA 1998, which states that the legal duty on public authorities to act in ways that are compatible with Convention rights applies to courts and tribunals. The Convention rights have the potential therefore to influence the interpretation of the common law of the contract of employment, including its implied terms and the common law rules on wrongful dismissal.[7] The requirement that courts should act compatibly with Convention rights requires them, if possible,

---

[3] [2004] UKHL 30, [2004] 2 AC 557, HL, per Lord Nicholls.
[4] [2004] EWCA Civ 662, [2004] ICR 1634, CA.
[5] ERA 1996, s 98(4).
[6] *Serco Ltd v National Union of Rail, Maritime & Transport Workers* [2011] EWCA Civ 226, [2011] ICR 848.
[7] H Collins and V Mantouvalou, 'Human Rights and the Contract of Employment' in M Freedland (Gen ed), *The Contract of Employment* (Oxford, OUP, 2016) 188.

to interpret terms of contracts in a manner that respects an employee's human rights such as freedom of expression.[8]

This statutory duty not to act in a way that is incompatible with Convention rights does not apply directly to employers. Nevertheless, it is arguable that employers that ride roughshod over their employees' Convention rights might not only be in breach of their employees' statutory rights such as the right not to be unfairly dismissed, but also be in breach of express or implied terms of the contract of employment.[9] The common law recognises that employers are under a duty to perform the contract in good faith (or not to act in a way that destroys mutual trust and confidence).[10] It has been suggested that it would be a breach of this good faith duty to infringe Convention rights without a strong justification.[11] Alternatively, it has been argued that an implied mutual obligation not to violate Convention rights is a shared intention between the parties not to undermine the dignity and autonomy of employees as people.[12]

Although the potential of the HRA 1998 to structure and influence the legal analysis of claims for employment rights is considerable, especially in the light of the interpretive obligation in s 3, it is surprising how little impact the Act has had so far on the reasoning of courts and tribunals. It is frequently the case that human rights dimensions of cases are simply not considered at all. Lawyers appear to be more comfortable relying solely on domestic legislation rather than invoking the ECHR as a tool of interpretation. As Philippa Collins has argued, it is possible that the human rights perspective is ignored because claims for the inviolability of human rights at work challenge the normal assumption of the common law of the contract of employment that employees should submit themselves loyally and obediently to the authority of employers.[13] To ignore the relevance of Convention rights is surely a failing on the part of courts and tribunals to comply with their statutory duty to ensure that their decisions are compatible those rights. When an employer's action has interfered with an employee's Convention rights, the better approach is for the court or tribunal to assess whether the action was justified on grounds such as being necessary to protect the rights of others, including the right of the employer to conduct its business without undue interference.[14]

2. Council of Europe: European Convention on Human Rights and the European Social Charter

The Convention for the Protection of Human Rights and Fundamental Freedoms (1950), now known as the European Convention on Human Rights (ECHR), is a very influential human rights document. It was drafted in the aftermath of the Second World War in order to respond to the atrocities of the War, and came into force in 1953 under the auspices of the Council of Europe, Europe's leading human rights organisation. The UK was the first country to sign the

---

[8] *Smith v Trafford Housing Trust* [2012] EWHC 3221 (Ch), [2013] IRLR 86.
[9] J Atkinson, 'Implied Terms and Human Rights in the Contract of Employment' (2019) 48 *Industrial Law Journal* 515.
[10] *Mahmoud and Malik v Bank of Credit and Commerce International SA* [1998] AC 20.
[11] Bob Hepple, 'Human Rights and the Contract of Employment' (1998) 8 *Amicus Curia* 19; M Freedland, *The Personal Employment Contract* (OUP, 2003) 162.
[12] H Collins and V Mantouvalou, 'Human Rights and the Contract of Employment' in Mark Freedland (Gen ed), *The Contract of Employment* (OUP, 2016) 188, 205–06.
[13] P Collins, *Putting Human Rights to Work* (OUP, 2022) ch 6.
[14] eg *Hill v Governing Body of Great Tey Primary School* [2013] ICR 691, [2013] IRLR 274, [2013] UKEAT 0237_12_2901.

ECHR in 1950, and the British MP and lawyer David Maxwell-Fyfe was one of its main drafters. In 1966, the UK accepted the jurisdiction of the European Court of Human Rights (ECtHR or Court) to hear individual complaints. As a result, individuals, groups, NGOs or companies within the UK's jurisdiction have a right to submit an application to the ECtHR for alleged violations. This is subject to admissibility conditions set out in Article 35 of the ECHR. These include the condition that domestic remedies have been exhausted;[15] that the same issue has not already been examined by the ECtHR or another international procedure or investigation;[16] that the claim is not manifestly ill-founded,[17] and that the applicant has suffered a 'significant disadvantage, unless respect for human rights as defined in the Convention and the Protocols thereto requires an examination of the application on the merits'.[18]

The ECHR primarily guarantees civil and political rights, such as the right to life (Article 2), the right to privacy (Article 8), and freedom of expression (Article 10), but it also includes two labour rights: the right to form and join a trade union (Article 11) and the prohibition of slavery, servitude, forced and compulsory labour (Article 4). Even though labour rights are not the primary focus of the ECHR, the ECtHR has developed detailed and influential case law on workers' rights over the decades.[19] Complaints before the ECtHR are against states, not against employers. However, the ECtHR has developed a doctrine of positive obligations on the basis of Article 1 of the ECHR, which provides that states 'shall secure to everyone within their jurisdiction the rights and freedoms defined in … [the] Convention'. In this context, the Court has recognised that the authorities have to protect individuals from violations of their rights by other private entities, including employers, by legislating and enforcing the law.[20] A series of important labour law cases have examined positive obligations in the employment relation.[21]

The European Social Charter (ESC or Charter), adopted in 1961, is the counterpart of the Convention in the area of economic and social rights, and has been ratified by the UK.[22] The ESC protects rights such as the right to work (Article 1), the right to just conditions of work (Article 2), the right to organise (Article 5), the right to benefit from social welfare services (Article 14) and the right of migrant workers to protection and assistance (Article 19). States are permitted to accept only some of the Charter rights. Using this provision, for instance, the UK has not accepted Articles 5 and 6 on the rights to organise, bargain collectively, and to strike. The revised version of the European Social Charter 1996, which entered into force in 1999 and is gradually replacing the 1961 document, contains several new social rights and keeps labour rights as its centrepiece. The UK has not ratified the Revised Charter. The ESC is monitored by the European Committee of Social Rights (ECSR or Committee). The Charter contains reporting

---

[15] ECHR, Article 35(1).
[16] ECHR, Article 35(2)(b).
[17] ECHR, Article 35(3)(a).
[18] ECHR, Article 35(3)(b). On this admissibility criterion, see D Shelton, 'Significantly Disadvantaged? Shrinking Access to the European Court of Human Rights' (2016) 16 *Human Rights Law Review* 303.
[19] For an overview, see F Dorssemont, K Lorcher and I Schomann (eds), *The European Convention on Human Rights and the Employment Relation* (Oxford, Hart, 2014).
[20] See D Spielmann, 'The European Convention on Human Rights – The European Court of Human Rights' in D Oliver and J Fedtke (eds), *Human Rights and the Private Sphere* (London, Routledge, 2007) 427; A Mowbray, *The Development of Positive Obligations under the European Convention on Human Rights by the European Court of Human Rights* (Oxford, Hart, 2004). On this, see also the landmark *Marckx v Belgium* (1979) 2 EHRR 330.
[21] See, for instance, *Wilson, National Union of Journalists and Others v United Kingdom*, ECHR (2002) 35 EHRR 523; *Siliadin v France* [2005] ECHR 545; *IB v Greece*, App No 552/10, Judgment of 3 October 2013; *Barbulescu v Romania* [2017] ECHR 754, [2017] IRLR 1032.
[22] See further C O'Cinneide, 'The European Social Charter and the UK: Why It Matters' (2018) 29 *King's Law Journal* 275; KD Ewing, 'Social Rights and Human Rights: Britain and the Social Charter – The Conservative Legacy' (2000) *European Human Rights Law Review* 91.

obligations, and the ECSR assesses states' compliance in its Conclusions. The reporting mechanism extends periodically even to Charter rights that have not been accepted. The 1998 Collective Complaints Protocol recognises a right to submit complaints for non-compliance of a contracting state with the Charter for some international organisations of employers and employees, national representative organisations of employers and employees, and some international non-governmental organisations.[23] The UK has not signed the Collective Complaints Protocol. The ECSR has developed extensive principles on the employment relation, labour, and social rights more broadly.[24]

As we can see, in line with other human rights documents adopted during that period, such as the UN International Covenant on Civil and Political Rights and the International Covenant on Economic, Social and Cultural Rights, the Council of Europe separated civil and political rights, on the one hand, from economic and social rights, on the other. This divide was initially endorsed by the ECtHR and the (now defunct) European Commission of Human Rights. For about three decades, the ECtHR was reluctant to examine social rights questions, when these were brought under Convention provisions. If social rights materials, such as materials of the ESC, were brought to their attention in support of a claim under the Convention, the Court and Commission viewed their inclusion in a separate document as a reason to reject the application under the Convention. When applicants alleged that Article 11 of the ECHR (the right to form and join a trade union), for instance, encompasses a right to strike, the claim was rejected.[25] The Commission and Court created what was called a 'ceiling effect';[26] the ceiling being, in this context, the ESC and the ILO. Claims that referred to the ESC were 'being used ingeniously as a source of restraint', as Ewing observed,[27] rather than a source of inspiration as to the interpretation of Convention provisions.

However, from *Wilson and Palmer* in 2002, the Court adopted what has become known as an 'integrated approach to interpretation'.[28] It was described as an *integrated* approach, because it integrates certain socio-economic rights into a civil and political rights document. This integrated approach characterises the work of the International Labour Organization (see below) more generally and has also been described as a 'holistic approach'.[29] Applied to the ECHR, it means that certain social and labour rights are essential elements of the Convention, and should therefore be protected as such. Instead of rejecting claims that could be viewed as grounded on social rights, the Court started to integrate them in the scope of the ECHR, in order to make Convention rights 'practical and effective' rather than 'theoretical and illusory'.[30] In the area of labour rights, the adoption of the integrated approach is found in

---

[23] TA Novitz, 'Are Social Rights Necessarily Collective Rights? A Critical Analysis of the Collective Complaints Protocol to the European Social Charter' (2002) 1 *European Human Rights Law Review* 50.

[24] See N Bruun, K Lorcher, I Schoemann and S Clauwaert (eds) *The European Social Charter and the Employment Relation* (Oxford, Hart, 2017).

[25] *Schmidt and Dahlstrom v Sweden* A 21; 1 EHRR 637. See also *National Union of Belgian Police v Belgium* A 19; 1 EHRR 578.

[26] C Scott, 'Reaching Beyond (Without Abandoning) the Category of "Economic, Social and Cultural Rights"' (1999) 21 *Human Rights Quarterly* 633 at 638–39.

[27] K Ewing, 'The Implications of Wilson and Palmer' (2003) 32 *Industrial Law Journal*, 1, 3.

[28] See the discussion in V Mantouvalou, 'Labour Rights in the European Convention on Human Rights: An Intellectual Justification for an Integrated Approach to Interpretation' (2013) 13 *Human Rights Law Review* 529. See also K Ewing and J Hendy, 'The Dramatic Implications of *Demir and Baykara*' (2010) 39 *ILJ* 2; T Teklè, 'The Contribution of the ILO's International Labour Standards System to the European Court of Human Rights' Jurisprudence in the Field of Non-Discrimination' (2020) 49 *Industrial Law Journal* 86.

[29] VA Leary, 'The Paradox of Workers' Rights as Human Rights' in L Compa and SF Diamond (eds), *Human Rights, Labor Rights and International Trade* (University of Pennsylvania Press, 1996) 22 at 40.

[30] On the principle that rights have to be practical and effective, see *Airey v Ireland* (1980) 2 EHRR 305.

several fields where the Court took cognisance of social and labour rights materials of other international bodies that expanded the scope of the Convention.[31] In a significant break with its past stance, the integrated approach brought social and labour rights a step closer to civil and political rights.

The integrated approach to interpretation was best analysed by the Court itself in the Grand Chamber case under Article 11, *Demir and Baykara v Turkey*.[32] The Grand Chamber was clear: 'the Court has never considered the provisions of the Convention as the sole framework of reference'[33] for its interpretation. According to the rules of interpretation found in the Vienna Convention on the Law of Treaties of 1969, a treaty ought to be interpreted according to its object and purpose.[34] The object and purpose of a document that protects human rights is to make these rights practical and effective, not theoretical and illusory.[35] The interpretation of the Convention must also take account of other rules of international law,[36] and be read as a 'living' document in light of 'present-day conditions'.[37] Several materials can serve to elucidate the content of the Convention, both from other international organisations and from the Council of Europe itself, in other words.

The *Demir and Baykara* case was celebrated by Ewing and Hendy as 'epoch-making' for being a 'decision in which social and economic rights have been fused permanently with civil and political rights, in a process that is potentially nothing less than a socialization of civil and political rights'.[38] Indeed, materials of the ESC and the ILO are frequently invoked and sometimes endorsed by the ECtHR as it seeks to establish a European or international consensus on difficult legal, social and political questions. However, they are not permanently fused, as reliance on other bodies' materials is one step among many other considerations that form part of the reasoning of the Court.[39] In particular, where the Convention permits states to try to justify a proportionate interference with rights, as is the case with Articles 8–11, the ECtHR grants states a 'margin of appreciation' in their assessment of whether the interference with a Convention right was proportionate in all the circumstances. This margin of appreciation can accommodate differences in values between member states without, of course, derogating from the core elements of a Convention right.

---

[31] *Sidabras and Dziautas v Lithuania* (2004) 42 EHRR 104. For analysis of the case and discussion of the integrated approach, see V Mantouvalou, 'Work and Private Life: *Sidabras and Dziautas v Lithuania*' (2005) 30 *European Law Review* 573. *Siliadin v France* (2006) 43 EHRR 287. See V Mantouvalou, 'Servitude and Forced Labour in the 21st Century: The Human Rights of Domestic Workers' (2006) 35 *Industrial Law Journal* 395; H Cullen, '*Siliadin v France*: Positive Obligations Under Article 4 of the European Convention on Human Rights' (2006) 6 *Human Rights Law Review* 585.
[32] *Demir and Baykara v Turkey* (2009) 48 EHRR 54.
[33] ibid [65].
[34] Vienna Convention on the Law of Treaties, Article 31(1).
[35] *Demir and Baykara*, above n 32, [66]. Further on the interpretation of the ECHR, see George Letsas, 'Strasbourg's Interpretive Ethic: Lessons for the International Lawyer' (2010) 21 *European Journal of International Law* 509.
[36] *Demir and Baykara*, above n 32, [67].
[37] ibid [68].
[38] KD Ewing and J Hendy, 'The Dramatic Implications of Demir and Baykara' (2010) 39 *Industrial Law Journal* 2, 47.
[39] See, for instance, *National Union of Rail, Maritime and Transport Workers v United Kingdom* [2014] ECHR 551; *Unite the Union v United Kingdom* [2016] ECHR 1150, [2017] IRLR 438; *Ognevenko v Russia* (2019) 69 EHRR 9; and *Association of Academics v Iceland*, App No 2451/16, Admissibility decision of 15 May 2018. See further the discussion in T Novitz, 'Protecting the Right to Strike in the ILO and the European Court of Human Rights: The Significance of Appn No 44873/09 Ognevenko v Russia', UK Labour Law Blog, 8 April 2019; K Arabadjieva, 'Worker Empowerment, Collective Labour Rights and Article 11 of the European Convention on Human Rights' (2022) 22 *Human Rights Law Review*.

3. Law of the European Union

Although the European Union did not begin life as an organisation concerned with human rights, it has become a much more important actor in this sphere as the years have gone by.[40] There are three main strands of EU human rights activity to consider, each of which intersects with the other two: political engagement, through rights-focused programmes such as the European Pillar of Social Rights; legislative engagement, principally through directives giving effect to rights and through the EU Charter of Fundamental Rights; and judicial engagement when rights are at issue in a case before the Court of Justice. We examine each strand in turn, before explaining the ongoing relevance of EU law within the UK after the UK's exit from the EU.

It is often noted that the only right for working people in the original Treaty of Rome was the right to equal pay for men and women,[41] and that this right was included largely for economic reasons rather than out of genuine concern for equality.[42] However, as the EU's competences have expanded over time and it has developed as a political as well as an economic union, rights have become much more prominent. Workers' rights in particular have often been invoked to give a 'human face' to the EU and to garner political support by showing that European integration can bring broader benefits to ordinary working people.[43] A recent example is the European Pillar of Social Rights.[44] This political statement of rights does not have legal effects in itself, but helps to set the direction for legislative action at EU level.

Most of the detail of EU employment law has been developed through the enactment of directives, either through the usual legislative process or through the social dialogue,[45] which must then be implemented by the Member States. The EU has competence to legislate in most areas of employment law, with the important exceptions of pay, freedom of association and the right to strike,[46] though it interprets these exclusions narrowly, as the recent Directive on Adequate Minimum Wages illustrates.[47] Some directives have arisen out of the policy programmes discussed above; others out of a concern to mitigate the adverse impacts of the EU internal market on working people.[48] Later chapters will explore in detail directives on equality, working time, and information and consultation of employees, among other topics. This is important because, although there is a tendency to focus on human rights instruments as the main route to protecting rights, detailed legislative initiatives are often more effective in helping workers to realise their rights in practice.

The EU Charter of Fundamental Rights is the EU's formal human rights instrument.[49] It was first adopted as a political pronouncement in 2000, then became part of the Treaties in 2009.

---

[40] We assume that the reader is familiar with the basic principles of EU law.
[41] Article 119 EEC.
[42] See J Kenner, *EU Employment Law* (Hart, 2002) 4.
[43] Though some policy initiatives relating to labour markets, such as flexicurity, have proved more controversial: Commission, *Towards Common Principles of Flexicurity: More and Better Jobs Through Flexibility and Security* (COM(2007) 359 final), and for discussion, see ACL Davies, 'Job Security and Flexicurity' in A Bogg, C Costello and ACL Davies (eds), *Research Handbook on EU Labour Law* (Cheltenham, Elgar, 2016).
[44] Commission, *The European Pillar of Social Rights Action Plan* (2021), and see S Garben, 'The European Pillar of Social Rights: An Assessment of Its Meaning and Significance' (2019) 21 *Cambridge Yearbook of European Legal Studies* 101.
[45] Article 155 TFEU.
[46] Article 153 TFEU, with exclusions in Article 153(5).
[47] Directive 2022/2041/EU on adequate minimum wages in the European Union. The argument is that the exclusion of pay only covers wage-setting at EU level, not measures with indirect impact on wages. For discussion, see L Ratti, 'The Sword and the Shield: The Directive on Adequate Minimum Wages in the EU' (2023) 52 *Industrial Law Journal* 477.
[48] eg Directive 96/71/EC concerning the posting of workers in the framework of the provision of services (as amended, 2018).
[49] Charter of Fundamental Rights of the European Union (OJ 2012/C 326/02).

From the perspective of workers' rights, the Charter offers a comprehensive statement, incorporating civil and political rights from the ECHR (to be interpreted in the light of the ECtHR's rulings[50]), and a number of economic and social rights found in the European Social Charter and in EU law itself, particularly under the 'solidarity' heading. There are two important limitations on the Charter. First, many of the rights, such as the right to be consulted, are framed in terms of existing EU and national legislation.[51] While their recognition in the Charter serves to highlight their importance, this approach to drafting does not give the rights much independent content beyond existing legislation. This limits their ability to shape legal developments. Second, the rights in the Charter are applicable to the EU institutions and to the Member States when they are implementing EU law, but they do not give rise to any new competences.[52] Thus, it is not possible to base new workers' rights legislation directly on the Charter. The EU's legislative competence must still be found in the Treaties.

A controversial element of the Charter is the recognition, in Article 16, of the freedom to run a business. This has been invoked to limit workers' rights. For example, in *Alemo-Herron v Parkwood Leisure Ltd*, workers who had been transferred from the public sector to a private employer under the Acquired Rights Directive argued that they should continue to benefit from the public sector collective agreement which had been applicable to their contracts of employment.[53] The transferee argued that this would interfere with its Article 16 freedom to run a business, not least because, as a private employer, it could not participate in public sector collective bargaining. The Court accepted the transferee's argument. While there are arguments on both sides on the facts in *Alemo-Herron* itself, the concern is that the recognition of the employer's freedom to run a business as a right simply converts all cases into a 'clash of rights' in which the judges must decide which right should prevail. In the absence of Article 16, the courts would, of course, recognise the employer's concerns, but the reasoning structure would be different: workers would invoke their rights, and the employer's arguments would be considered as potentially legitimate reasons for limiting those rights. This reasoning structure might be thought to be a better reflection of the imbalance of power between workers and their employer.

A third important strand of EU engagement with workers' rights is through the Court of Justice. The Court began to recognise fundamental rights – not just pertaining to workers – when national courts questioned the supremacy of EU law.[54] Under the doctrine of supremacy, EU law prevails over national law, even high-status national law, such as Member States' constitutions. The German Constitutional Court, in particular, was sceptical of this idea, noting that the fundamental rights protected in the German Constitution would not receive equivalent protection in EU law, where – at the time – no legally-binding rights instrument existed.[55] The Court of Justice therefore began to recognise rights from the ECHR – to which all Member States are signatories – and from the 'common constitutional traditions' of the Member States themselves.[56] Since the incorporation of the EU Charter into the Treaty architecture, discussed above, the Court has been able to re-base much of its rights jurisprudence on the Charter.

---

[50] ibid Article 52(3).
[51] ibid Article 27.
[52] ibid Article 51.
[53] Case C-426/11 *Alemo-Herron v Parkwood Leisure Ltd* EU:C:2013:521, [2014] 1 CMLR 21, and see J Prassl, 'Freedom of Contract as a General Principle of EU law? Transfers of Undertakings and the Protection of Employer Rights in EU Labour Law' (2013) 42 *ILJ* 434. See also Case C-201/15 *AGET Iraklis* EU:C:2016:972, [2017] 2 CMLR 32.
[54] Case 11/70 *Internationale Handelsgesellschaft mbH v Einfuhr- und Vorratsstelle fur Getreide und Futtermittel* EU:C:1970:114, [1970] ECR 1125; Case C-36/02 *Omega Spielhallen- und Automatenaufstellungs GmbH v Bundesstadt Bonn* EU:C:2004:614, [2004] ECR I-9609.
[55] *Internationale Handelsgesellschaft*, decision of 29 May 1974, BVerfGE 37. The issue remains controversial.
[56] An approach now codified in Article 6(3) TEU.

In broad terms, the Court has used rights reasoning in two main ways. First, and perhaps most straightforwardly, the Court often recognises that a provision in a directive or another EU instrument is intended to implement a right, and has interpreted it with a view to giving effect to that right. For example, the right to paid annual leave in the Working Time Directive is regarded by the Court as a 'fundamental social right' of workers.[57] This has led it to interpret the right quite strongly, for example, in ruling that 'rolled-up' holiday pay discouraged workers from exercising their right to take leave,[58] or that a worker denied paid leave over many years, because their employer had regarded them as ineligible, could claim back-pay in full when their employment came to an end.[59] In some cases, the Court has used the fundamental nature of the rights involved to overcome technical limitations on the applicability of EU law, such as the absence of horizontal direct effect for directives. For example, in *Mangold*, the Court encouraged the disapplication of national legislation facilitating the use of fixed-term contracts for older workers, on the basis of a general principle of EU law against age discrimination.[60]

Second, the Court has considered whether rights can be invoked defensively, to limit the application of other norms of EU law. The best-known examples of this in the employment context are the *Viking* and *Laval* cases, where trade unions' exercise of their right to strike came into conflict with the exercise by a firm of its freedom of establishment (in *Viking*) and its freedom to provide services across national borders (in *Laval*).[61] These decisions generated a large critical literature, discussed more fully in chapter 7, because although the Court recognised the right to strike, which was a significant move in itself prior to the Charter, it did not prioritise that right over the economic freedoms found in EU law, or even give the two sources equal weight.[62] While some saw this as a simple reflection of the structure of the Treaties, others regarded it as a clear example of the EU's economic focus at the expense of social rights.

It is also worth noting that the EU Charter was accompanied by a proposal that the EU should itself accede to the ECHR.[63] The Court of Justice effectively blocked the accession process by issuing an opinion critical of the plan.[64] Its main concern was that the autonomy of EU law was insufficiently protected. As cases like *Viking* and *Laval* demonstrate, the most challenging situations are those in which there is a clash between a Convention right and a fundamental principle of EU law. In these scenarios, it is difficult to determine which of the two courts should have the final say.

A final question to address is our decision, as scholars based in the UK, to include EU law in this book now that the UK is no longer a Member State. One obvious reason for this choice is that most EU law and EU-derived law in force prior to the UK's exit from the EU has been preserved by statute as 'assimilated law'.[65] This means that the law governing a number of important employment rights – around equality or working time, for example – has an EU origin, and it is therefore important to understand specific provisions in their proper historical context. Although some of this legislation could be repealed in the future, there has so far been little appetite for this and

---

[57] eg Case C-131/04 *Robinson-Steele v RD Retail Services Ltd* EU:C:2006:177, [2006] ECR I-2531, [48].
[58] ibid.
[59] Case C-214/16 *King v Sash Window Workshop Ltd* EU:C:2017:914, [2018] 2 CMLR 10.
[60] Case C-144/04 *Mangold v Helm* EU:C:2005:709, [2005] ECR I-9981.
[61] Case C-438/05 *International Transport Workers' Federation v Viking Line ABP* EU:C:2007:772, [2007] ECR I-10779; Case C-341/05 *Laval un Partneri Ltd v Svenska Byggnadsarbetareforbundet* EU:C:2007:809, [2007] ECR I-11767.
[62] eg ACL Davies, 'One Step Forward, Two Steps Back? The *Viking* and *Laval* Cases in the ECJ' (2008) 37 *Industrial Law Journal* 126; S Weatherill, '*Viking* and *Laval*: The EU Internal Market Perspective' in M Freedland and J Prassl (eds), *Viking, Laval and Beyond* (Hart, 2014).
[63] Article 6(2) TEU.
[64] Opinion 2/13 EU:C:2014:2454, [2015] 2 CMLR 21.
[65] European Union (Withdrawal) Act 2018, s 5(A2) as amended.

widespread deregulation might jeopardise the UK's ongoing trading relationship with the EU.[66] Any divergence seems likely to be gradual, as new EU directives are enacted to which the UK will no longer be subject, and as the UK courts are no longer bound to follow decisions of the Court of Justice of the European Union (CJEU). From a human rights perspective, a point of particular significance is that the EU Charter was not preserved as a part of domestic law.[67] Since it applied to the EU institutions and to the Member States when implementing EU law, it was thought not to be relevant to the UK once it had ceased to be a Member State. This will make it more difficult for domestic courts to develop strongly rights-based interpretations of EU law in some areas, such as paid annual leave, though, in practice, domestic courts seemed to be reluctant to do this without prompting from the CJEU in any event. For example, it took many referrals to the CJEU to establish the straightforward proposition that annual leave should be paid at the worker's normal rate.[68] Thus, it seems likely that the real impact on domestic law will be felt because of the loss of the CJEU's influence, which was mostly, though by no means always, worker-protective and rights-focused, rather than the loss of the Charter itself. Finally, it is worth noting that the EU remains an important source of new ideas in the field of labour rights, a recent example being the Directive on Adequate Minimum Wages.[69] New EU developments are interesting subjects of study in themselves, and may sometimes influence policy in the UK. For example, although the UK is not subject to the Transparent and Predictable Working Conditions Directive,[70] it has extended the right to a written statement to workers as well as employees,[71] and has legislated for a right to request a more predictable contract.[72]

4. The International Labour Organization

The International Labour Organization (ILO) was founded in 1919 in the negotiation of the peace settlement following the First World War. The Preamble to the 1919 Constitution, which became Part XIII of the Treaty of Versailles, declared that 'whereas universal and lasting peace can be established only if it is based upon social justice'. To this end, the Preamble set out the ILO's mission to ensure the improvement of conditions of labour so as to eradicate hardship and injustice. Looking back at the original 1919 Preamble, many of the labour conditions listed would be viewed today as fundamental human rights: a maximum working day and week, an 'adequate living wage', the 'protection of the interests of workers when employed in countries other than their own', the 'principle of equal remuneration for work of equal value', and freedom of association. In 1944, the Declaration of Philadelphia broadened the constitutional remit of the ILO, and this strengthened its focus on social justice and fundamental rights at work. In particular, the fundamental principles affirmed that 'freedom of expression and of association are essential to sustained progress'. In 1946 the ILO became a specialised agency of the United Nations. Today, its membership stands at 185 member states.[73]

---

[66] For example, the Equality Act 2010 (Amendment) Regulations 2023 (SI 2023/1425) preserve a number of important elements of equality law derived from the Court of Justice's case law which would no longer be binding on domestic courts under the European Union (Withdrawal) Act 2018, s 6 (as amended).
[67] European Union (Withdrawal) Act 2018, s 5(4).
[68] eg Case C-155/10 *Williams v British Airways Plc* EU:C:2011:588, [2012] 1 CMLR 23.
[69] Above n 47.
[70] Directive 2019/1152 on transparent and predictable working conditions.
[71] Employment Rights Act 1996, s 1, as amended in 2019.
[72] Workers (Predictable Terms and Conditions) Act 2023.
[73] G Ryder, 'The International Labour Organization: The Next 100 Years' (2015) 57 *Journal of Industrial Relations* 748, 750.

The ILO is a tripartite organisation. This is reflected in its constitutional structure. The formulation and adoption of labour standards depends upon the International Labour Conference (ILC). The membership of the ILC is based upon the principle that each member state delegation consists of a worker representative, an employer representative, and two government representatives. The adoption of a 'Convention' by the ILC depends upon a two-thirds majority by the ILC delegates. The Convention is the main legal instrument used to implement labour standards. Like any international treaty, it must be ratified by a member state to be legally binding. The ILO may also adopt 'Recommendations' which are not binding instruments but provide guidance to member states. The ILO Governing Body (GB), which is like the 'Executive' in the ILO's decision-making structure, is also tripartite. The GB is constitutionally important because it sets the agenda for the ILC. Its members are elected by each of the constituent groups in a ratio of 2:1:1, with government representatives again having the dominant voice. The tripartite structure of the ILO has meant that freedom of association and the right to collective bargaining have always been central to constitutional obligations of member states. Freedom of association has been the most constitutionally visible of the human rights protected by the ILO, from 1919 through to the present day.

The main focus of the ILO is on standard-setting and the supervision of labour standards in member states. The ILO has adopted Conventions across the entire range of employment law: wages, working time, equality at work, forced labour, child labour, labour inspection, employment policy, vocational training, occupational health and safety, employment security, and the protection of specific occupational groups such as in the maritime sector.[74] The supervision of these labour standards occurs mainly through the ILO's committees rather than through a court. While standard-setting is a very important aspect of the ILO's work, the ILO also promotes social justice and human rights in other ways too. The ILO provides technical assistance to member states to help them improve laws and practices so that they better align with labour standards. It also engages in and supports labour market research. This includes the commissioning and publication of reports on areas of current interest and concern, such as Covid-19 or platform work. ILOSTAT compiles and publishes labour market statistics across the entire area of work, labour supply, labour standards, and poverty and inequality in the labour market.[75] These aspects of the ILO's work are vital in supporting standard-setting. It addresses the problem that member states might be respecting human rights in the 'law on the books' but less so in the daily lives of real workers.[76]

The supervisory and enforcement mechanisms of the ILO are channelled through the main ILO committees. There are two main types. The first is based on cyclical reporting obligations by member states. The second is triggered by specific complaints of violations.

The first main mechanism is through a reporting cycle which requires governments to submit reports at regular intervals on their national laws and practices relating to ratified Conventions. These reports must be submitted to the relevant worker and employer representatives, and they may provide their comments on the report to the Committee of Experts on the Application of Conventions and Recommendations (CEACR). These reports are then considered by the CEACR. Unlike many other ILO institutions, CEACR is not a tripartite committee. Its membership consists of 20 eminent jurists who provide an expert and impartial assessment of the application of

---

[74] The ILO has an excellent website that explains its activities and its main decision-making institutions. An up-to-date list of instruments is set out here: www.ilo.org/global/standards/subjects-covered-by-international-labour-standards/lang--en/index.htm.

[75] https://ilostat.ilo.org.

[76] For discussion, see B Hepple, *Labour Laws and Global Trade* (Oxford, Hart, 2005) 47.

relevant Conventions. The CEACR publishes a General Report on an annual basis which collates its observations and provides a General Survey on a specific subject. These reports are considered by the Conference Committee on the Application of Standards (CCAS), a tripartite standing committee of the ILC. In serious cases, CCAS invites government representations, it can issue conclusions, and recommend technical assistance to support member states in achieving compliance. Even in serious cases, the emphasis is on moral persuasion rather than coercive sanctions. The procedures are focused strongly on engagement, dialogue, and promoting compliance.[77]

The second main mechanism is triggered by complaints of violations. There are a number of such mechanisms, but here we shall focus on the Committee on Freedom of Association (CFA). The CFA was established in 1951 and it was empowered to investigate complaints about the violation of freedom of association. This special procedure reflected the importance of freedom of association as a human right in the ILO Constitution. The CFA is a tripartite committee which investigates complaints by any of the tripartite constituents against a member state. It is not necessary for the state to have ratified a Convention in this context, because freedom of association is a constitutional obligation inherent in ILO membership. Even though the involvement of the CFA is triggered by a complaint, its approach is still focused on dialogue with the government concerned. It can issue a report and recommendations to rectify any violations. This may also involve the provision of technical assistance. As with the cyclical supervision of reports, the CFA avoids the more traditional legal techniques of shaming and censure and prefers a consensual approach to resolving disputes.

What is particularly striking to a lawyer is the apparent absence of courts in the ILO supervision machinery. Article 37 of the ILO Constitution provides that 'any question or dispute relating to the interpretation of this Constitution or of any subsequent Convention ... shall be referred for decision to the International Court of Justice'. This provision has rarely been invoked.[78] However, Article 37 has recently been triggered by the ILO GB on 10 November 2023. This referral has arisen out of an ongoing internal dispute about the derivation of the right to strike by CEACR from the core freedom of association Convention, Convention 87. Although this CEACR interpretation is longstanding, it has been contested vigorously by the Employers' group.[79] This dispute around the right to strike reveals the limitations of a dialogue approach where there is a fundamental and intractable disagreement between the tripartite members. It is not helped by the fact that there is not a clear textual basis for the right to strike in C87. It remains to be seen if triggering Article 37 for an authoritative resolution by the ICJ supports the protection of human rights. The ICJ is not a labour court, and it does not have the expertise of CEACR. However, the impasse on the right to strike probably meant that the Article 37 reference was inevitable in this specific context.

The human rights focus of the ILO's work on standard-setting has intensified since the late 1990s. This is reflected in constitutional developments at the organisation. The ILO's Declaration on Fundamental Principles and Rights at Work 1998 focused on a core set of binding constitutional duties for member states. In its original form, it focused on four fundamental principles: freedom of association and the right to bargain collectively; the elimination of all forms of forced or compulsory labour; the effective abolition of child labour; and the elimination

---

[77] In cases of persistent refusal to comply with the recommendations of a Commission of Inquiry, Article 33 of the ILO Constitution makes provision for 'such action as it may deem wise and expedient to secure compliance therewith'. This has only been invoked once, against Myanmar, for its systematic use of forced labour.
[78] Hepple, above n 76.
[79] For a full account of the background, see C La Hovary, 'Showdown at the ILO? A Historical Perspective on the Employers' Group's 2012 Challenge to the Right to Strike' (2013) 42 *Industrial Law Journal* 338.

of discrimination. Within each of these fundamental human rights, there are fundamental Conventions which member states are also encouraged to ratify. In 2022, the ILO added a safe and healthy working environment to its list of fundamental rights with special constitutional significance. Even within this fundamental core of human rights, some recent Conventions aim at eliminating the most serious human rights abuses. For example, the Worst Forms of Child Labour Convention, 1999 (No 182) focuses on the most serious forms of the practice in its defining scope in Article 3. Given the ILO's global mission, and its membership of 185 states, this identification of a universal floor of basic human rights and the prioritisation of the worst abuses makes sense.

There has been a lively debate about the merits of this constitutional shift to a narrow set of core human rights.[80] On the one hand, it enables the ILO to target its scarce resources on the worst forms of exploitation in global labour markets. It is difficult to disagree that dangerous and unsafe work, or forced work, or child trafficking, represent some of the gravest human rights abuses in the world of work. It might be better to target the worst abuses, and eliminate those, before spreading resources to other Conventions such as vocational leave or employment agencies. On the other hand, the designation of matters as non-fundamental is always likely to be controversial. These rankings often reflect compromises negotiated within the politics of the organisation, rather than reflecting deliberation or moral argument. For example, the right to fair and just working conditions (including working time and wages regulation) and the right not to be unjustifiably dismissed would both rank highly on most labour lawyers' list of their 'top' human rights at work. However, they do not count as fundamental in the ILO's constitutional structure.

What does the future hold for the ILO's protection of human rights at work? The first challenge is for the ILO to maintain the relevance of its standard-setting to the rapidly evolving world of work. Many of its recent instruments have addressed key challenges, such as the regulation of the informal economy,[81] violence and harassment at work,[82] and domestic workers.[83] Before the ink has dried on ILO instruments, labour markets throw up new human rights problems. In the years ahead, privacy and technology at work,[84] algorithmic management, and platform work, would all benefit from binding human rights instruments.

The second challenge is the form and technique of ILO instruments. There has been a move away from the detailed specification of standards to more 'reflexive' approaches that encourage the adoption of national policies. For example, the Promotional Framework for Occupational Safety and Health Convention, 2006 (No 187) is framed around national policies and a national programme implemented through regular monitoring and benchmarking by relevant national authorities. This right to safe and healthy work, closely connected with the human right to life and bodily integrity, is a fundamental human right. Is this reflexive approach, based around procedural implementation, appropriate to provide effective guarantees that the right will be respected? We should not assume that more definitional detail is necessarily better. The involvement

---

[80] See BA Langille, 'Core Labour Rights – The True Story (Reply to Alston)' (2005) 16 *European Journal of International Law* 409; and P Alston, '"Core Labour Standards" and the Transformation of the International Labour Rights Regime' (2004) 15 *European Journal of International Law* 457.

[81] Transition from the Informal to the Formal Economy Recommendation, 2015 (No 204).

[82] Violence and Harassment Convention, 2019 (No 190).

[83] Domestic Workers Convention, 2011 (No 189). For discussion, see E Albin and V Mantouvalou, 'The ILO Convention on Domestic Workers: From the Shadows to the Light' (2012) 41 *Industrial Law Journal* 67.

[84] See the discussion of G Standing, 'The International Labour Organization' (2010) 15 *New Political Economy* 307, 316.

of the social partners, and robust protection of freedom of association, is likely to be critical to the success of these new reflexive strategies of implementation.

The final challenge is enforcement. Given the lack of coercive teeth in the ILO, does this undermine its effectiveness as a human rights defender? This overlooks the importance of ILO decisions in other legal regimes that do have stronger enforcement techniques. The 'integrated approach' to adjudication has meant that the ECtHR has often used ILO standards to justify its interpretation of human rights under the Convention. In *Demir v Turkey*, for example, the recognition of the right to bargain collectively under Article 11 was supported by ILO materials.[85] These different legal orders are in dialogue with each other, and developments in 'soft' legal orders can influence legal developments in other legal orders with stronger enforcement mechanisms.

---

[85] *Demir and Baykara v Turkey* (2009) 28 EHRR 54.

3

Human Rights and Personal Scope

1. The Basic Problem of Personal Scope
2. Employment Status and Human Rights: The Position under General Employment Law
3. Employment Status and Human Rights: Addressing the Gaps Using the ECHR and HRA 1998
4. Personal Scope and Human Rights under EU Law
5. Conclusion

1. The Basic Problem of Personal Scope

The personal scope of employment rights is probably the most fundamental legal issue in employment law. Statutory employment rights are distributed to a specific category of employment contract, such as 'employee' or 'worker', and this represents the boundary of worker-protective employment law. Outside of this boundary, individuals must look after their own interests through contractual negotiation. The task of the tribunal is to identify the nature of the parties' agreement and to decide which side of the boundary it should be placed: is this an employee/worker relationship, or is it a fully independent contractor providing services to a customer or client as a business undertaking? Even if employment status can be established, there may be other barriers such as qualifying periods of continuous employment or the employer's illegality defence to employment claims.

Personal scope and employment status is so challenging for the law because it is usually the employer that drafts the contract. It will often be a standard form written contract, drafted by lawyers and presented to the worker on a take-it-or-leave-it basis. The very thing that justifies the statutory protection in the first place, inequality of bargaining power, also allows an employer the contractual freedom to manipulate the law's protective boundary. That is because the contract terms can be designed so as to avoid employment status. It is the most basic regulatory dilemma of employment law.

It is not immediately obvious what any of this has to do with human rights law. After all, if human rights are simply those rights we have in virtue of being human, then no question of boundaries should ever arise.[1] They are rights for everyone. It has been argued that there should be a presumption of universal coverage where human rights are at stake since human rights are universal entitlements, and that any departure from universal entitlement must be

---

[1] J Gardner, '"Simply in Virtue of Being Human": The Whos and Whys of Human Rights' (2008) 2 *Journal of Ethics and Social Philosophy* 1.

justified in accordance with strict criteria of proportionality.[2] Moreover, examining the existing employment law categories of employee and worker, it has been suggested that they should be interpreted as inclusively as possible, rather than discarded, and any exclusions must be justified accordingly.[3] This suggests that there is a presumption in favour of employment status where Convention rights are at stake.[4]

In this chapter, we consider this gap between employment law's traditional categories of employee/worker and the broader approach of human rights law. At the outset, the position under human rights law is not entirely 'universal' in its approach. Some human rights are expressed as rights for 'everyone', but by no means all. For example, fundamental trade union rights under Article 11 of the European Convention on Human Rights (ECHR) seem to be restricted to those in an 'employment relationship': they are not rights for 'everyone'.[5] Many of the rights in the 'Solidarity Chapter' of the EU Charter of Fundamental Rights, such as protection from unjustified dismissal (Article 30) or the right to fair and just working conditions (Article 31) are rights for 'every worker'. Certain kinds of limitation on personal scope also flow from the substantive content of specific human rights. For example, the right to bargain collectively presupposes negotiation about terms and conditions of *employment*. In turn, this presupposes an employer. This envisages some necessary limits on personal scope of right-holders such that they are *in* employment and have terms and conditions that are capable of being negotiated in collective agreements.[6] The same would be true of protection from unjustified dismissal, which presupposes a 'dismissal' and hence some kind of employment contract capable of being terminated by a 'dismissal'. The principle of universality of human rights, in other words, is a moral principle, and its legal implications need further exploration.

For these reasons, the 'universal scope' position in employment law has yet to gain much acceptance in the courts. Instead, human rights law has been more successful in modifying existing boundaries and limitations so that they operate more inclusively in human rights claims. In what follows, we first examine the basic legal definitions of employee and worker in UK law. In practice, these categories have been developed by the courts so as to include many of the most precarious workers within their scope. In section 3, we consider the potential role of the ECHR/Human Rights Act 1998 (HRA 1998) in addressing gaps in employment law's normal categories of personal scope. In section 4, the contribution of EU law to the inclusive protection of human rights is assessed. At the current time, the moral principle of universality tends to operate remedially in respect of the standard legal rules on personal scope.

2. Employment Status and Human Rights: The Position under General Employment Law

The starting point for employment status and the 'personal scope' of human rights is to consider the current law on access to statutory entitlements under general employment protection

---

[2] H Collins and V Mantouvalou, 'Human Rights and the Contract of Employment' in M Freedland and others (eds), *The Contract of Employment* (Oxford, OUP, 2016) 188, 198–200; see also P Collins, *Putting Human Rights to Work: Labour Law, the ECHR, and the Employment Relation* (Oxford, OUP, 2022) 101.
[3] J Atkinson, 'Employment Status and Human Rights: An Emerging Approach' (2023) 86 *Modern Law Review* 1166.
[4] ibid 1195.
[5] *Sindicatul 'Pastoral Cel Bun' v Romania* [2014] IRLR 49, GC.
[6] A Bogg and M Ford, 'Employment Status and Trade Union Rights: Applying Occam's Razor' (2022) 51 *ILJ* 717, 728–29.

statutes. This 'patchwork' of employment protection statutes still provides the basic legal protection for human rights at work.[7] These statutory entitlements, such as the right not to be unfairly dismissed, whistleblowing protections, or trade union rights, are not universal in scope. The relevant legal protections are based in employment legislation. Like any other statutory employment rights in employment law, they are limited to those working under personal employment contracts. The first question to be addressed is whether the general employment law tests for employment status are suitable human rights protections. Or is a different legal approach needed for human rights claims against an employer?

Before answering that, it is important to recognise that there is no single legal category of personal work contract in UK employment law. There are multiple employment status categories that vary depending upon the statutory right being claimed. Some statutory rights are limited to the narrowest category, the 'employee', such as unfair dismissal protections or statutory consultation rights on collective redundancies and transfers of undertakings.[8] These rights may be restricted in other ways too, such as two years' continuous employment as a qualifying requirement for a general unfair dismissal claim. These statutory entitlements correspond with some important human rights, such as the right not to be unfairly dismissed or the right to information and consultation. Increasingly, however, many statutory employment rights extend to the wider and more inclusive statutory category of 'worker'.[9] These include most trade union rights, whistleblowing protections, equality laws, and working time and minimum wage entitlements. They are usually 'day 1' rights without a qualifying period of employment. In this section, we will consider whether those in need of human rights protections at work are able to receive them under the ordinary employment law tests.

It is helpful to start with the foundational concept of UK employment law, the 'employee'. Historically, UK employment law was organised around a basic binary divide between the 'employee' and the self-employed independent contractor. This was a model of 'winner takes all'. Generally speaking, employee status provided the gateway into all statutory protections, whereas independent contractors received none. 'Employee' is a common law category based upon the 'contract of service' or 'contract of employment'. The courts developed strict contractual criteria for defining this category, although the rules and principles have evolved through judicial development. The current legal test encompasses a range of factors: (i) there must be a contract; (ii) there must be a sufficient right of contractual control and a minimum threshold of subordination;[10] (iii) an obligation that the work be undertaken personally by the employee which is inconsistent with a wide power for the individual to delegate their work to a 'substitute';[11] (iv) a requirement of 'mutuality of obligation', so that the employer is under a minimum duty to offer work and the employee is under a duty to accept offers of work;[12] (v) that the overall terms of the work contract are consistent with a contract of employment, examining multiple factors such as tax arrangements, sick pay, provision of uniforms and work materials, and the distribution of economic risks.

This binary divide was dysfunctional because the employee definition tended to exclude many individuals who were in need of statutory protections. It favoured those who worked in

---

[7] P Collins, above n 2, 81.
[8] The employee category is a common law category. For more detailed discussion, see Z Adams and others, *Deakin and Morris' Labour Law*, 7th edn (Hart, 2021) 108–11.
[9] G Davidov, 'Who is a Worker?' (2005) 34 *ILJ* 57.
[10] *Ready Mixed Concrete (South East) Ltd v Minister of Pensions and National Insurance* [1968] 2 QB 497.
[11] *Pimlico Plumbers Ltd v Smith* [2018] UKSC 29.
[12] For sensible judicial reflections on mutuality, see *Cornwall CC v Prater* [2006] IRLR 362, CA. This case is discussed in ACL Davies, 'Casual Workers and Continuity of Employment' (2006) 35 *ILJ* 196.

'standard' employment that was full-time, long-term, working directly for a single employer, and on an open-ended contract. It struggled to accommodate a growing number of workers in 'atypical' or 'non-standard' work such as casual work, part-time and fixed-term work, freelancers, agency workers, and those providing work through personal service companies.[13] In more recent times, these problems of precarious employment have magnified in contexts of 'gig work'.[14]

These excluded workers were often very precarious and more vulnerable to exploitation than 'standard' employees in secure employment. The exclusionary effects of the legal definition of employee meant that the more precarious the work arrangements, the more likely it was that the individual would be classified as an independent contractor. This result could often be achieved by the employer drafting the written contract and allocating the economic risk of unavailability of work onto the weaker party. This meant that the employer could effectively 'contract out' of human rights protections by capitalising on its bargaining power. The exclusion from statutory protections then intensified the worker's vulnerability. This was vividly described as the 'paradox of precarity' by Freedland.[15]

Some of the most controversial examples of unjustified exclusion from employees' statutory protections were human rights cases. The case of *O' Kelly v Trusthouse Forte Plc* demonstrates the inadequacies of the employee category as a basis for human rights protections.[16] The claimants worked as regular casuals for banqueting events at a luxury hotel on Park Lane in London. They were trade union members and their union was seeking recognition from Trusthouse Forte Plc. Following a union request for a meeting, the claimants were informed by the employer that their services were unlikely to be needed. The case appeared to involve a fundamental violation of their freedom of association. The claimants brought proceedings for unfair dismissal for trade union reasons. While there was no qualifying period of employment for trade union dismissals, the Industrial Tribunal concluded that they were not employees. The principal basis for this finding was the absence of 'mutuality of obligation', and the lack of an overarching umbrella contract spanning the discrete engagements at banqueting events. The majority in the Court of Appeal (Sir John Donaldson MR and Fox LJ) took the view that the absence of an overall contract meant that the waiters could only be independent contractors while they were working. This meant that they were unprotected from trade union dismissal under the relevant legislation at the time, which required them to be employees. Yet 'casuals' employed precariously under insecure contracts are precisely the kind of workers most in need of freedom of association protections at work.

To remedy the under-inclusiveness of the common law contract of employment, many employment rights now extend to the broader statutory category of 'worker'. The statutory purpose of this category was to be wider and more inclusive than employee.[17] It is defined in slightly different ways under different statutes though these categories tend to be regarded as co-extensive in scope by the courts.[18] The main type of 'worker' (known as the 'limb (b) worker') is defined in s 230(3)(b)

---

[13] H Collins, 'Independent Contractors and the Challenge of Vertical Disintegration to Employment Protection Laws' (1990) 10 *OJLS* 353.
[14] J Prassl, *Humans as a Service: The Promise and Perils of Work in the Gig Economy* (OUP, 2018).
[15] M Freedland, *The Contract of Employment and the Paradoxes of Precarity*, Oxford Legal Studies Research Paper, No 37/2016.
[16] *O' Kelly v Trusthouse Forte Plc* [1984] QB 90, CA. The case is discussed in ACL Davies, 'O' Kelly v Trusthouse Forte PLC: A Landmark of Legalism' in J Adams-Prassl, A Bogg and ACL Davies (eds), *Landmark Cases in Labour Law* (Hart, 2022) ch 8.
[17] See *Byrne Bros v Baird* [2002] ICR 667, EAT, which described limb (b) as 'lowering the passmark' for workers and so extending the boundary of protection.
[18] *Clyde & Co LLP and another v Bates van Winkelhof* [2014] UKSC 32, [31]–[32].

of the Employment Rights Act 1996 (ERA 1996) as an individual who has entered into or works under 'any other contract, whether express or implied and (if it is express) whether oral or in writing, whereby the individual undertakes to do or perform personally any work or services for another party to the contract whose status is not by virtue of the contract that of a client or customer of any profession or business undertaking carried on by the individual'.

This statutory definition has three elements. There must be (i) a contract where one party undertakes work for the other party to the contract; (ii) the worker must undertake to do or perform 'any' of the work personally; and (iii) the status of the party receiving the work must not be as a 'client or customer' to the other party providing the work as a 'profession or business undertaking'. This includes some self-employed workers within its scope. Does this broader category align better with the human rights basis of 'limb (b) worker' statutory claims?

The matter was considered in *Clyde & Co LLP and another v Bates van Winkelhof*.[19] The Supreme Court analysed the personal scope of whistleblowing protections and whether the worker definition extended to a solicitor member of a Limited Liability Partnership. Lady Hale emphasised the importance of applying the statutory words to the work arrangements, and not being distracted by the addition of 'mystery ingredients' such as subordination.[20] While subordination would often be a relevant factor in applying the statutory definition to the work arrangements, it was not a substitute for the statutory language. It was possible to meet the statutory definition even where the individual worked with a high degree of professional autonomy in circumstances where she was integrated into the other party's business, rather than operating a business undertaking on her own account.[21] Since the generally inclusive statutory definition of worker meant that she was protected, Lady Hale did not consider it necessary to consider the claimant's freedom of expression under Article 10 ECHR.[22] *Bates van Winkelhof* highlights how the standard employment law test can be sufficient in ensuring access to human rights protections (and in fact Lady Hale expressed some reservations about achieving this result through the state's positive obligations under Article 10 had the claimant not been protected under the legislation).[23]

Perhaps the most fundamental difficulty with these different employment status tests is their dependence on 'contract'. This effectively leaves the weaker party vulnerable to 'contracting out' of statutory protections through the use of standard form written contracts that seek to exclude employment status. In *Autoclenz Ltd v Belcher*, Lord Clarke emphasised the importance of identifying the 'true agreement', which may diverge from the written documentation drafted by the employer.[24] This 'purposive' approach allowed the tribunal to consider the working practices as a basis for identifying the 'true agreement', particularly in circumstances where the written terms were a smokescreen designed to avoid the statutory protections that ought to apply.[25] The 'true agreement' approach in *Autoclenz* heralded a new kind of interpretive approach to employee and worker. It favoured the inclusion of those who had a substantive need of legal protection, even where the written documentation might suggest otherwise.[26]

In the landmark judgment of *Uber BV and others v Aslam and others*, the worker status of precarious passenger hire drivers in the gig economy was considered by the Supreme Court.[27]

---

[19] ibid.
[20] ibid [39].
[21] *Hospital Medical Group Ltd v Westwood* [2012] EWCA Civ 1005, [2013] ICR 415.
[22] *Bates van Winkelhof*, above n 18, [41]–[46].
[23] ibid [44].
[24] [2011] UKSC 41.
[25] ibid [35].
[26] A Bogg, 'Sham Self-Employment in the Supreme Court' (2012) 41 *ILJ* 328.
[27] [2021] UKSC 5.

The extensive written documentation portrayed the drivers as independent businesses contracting directly with passengers, with Uber operating simply as a commercial intermediary. Despite the elaborate contractual presentation, the Supreme Court had little difficulty in finding that the work arrangements displayed many of the features that justified the statutory protections. These included intensive surveillance and disciplinary control over contractual performance, the inability of individual drivers to influence contractual terms, and Uber's setting of the payment rate. Applying the statutory test, they were 'workers' entitled to the relevant statutory protections. Lord Leggatt emphasised that tribunals should adopt a 'purposive' and 'realistic' approach to the employment status enquiry. The relevant 'purpose' was the statutory purpose of protecting workers, which must include the purpose of protecting their human rights.[28] This was an exercise in statutory interpretation, not contractual interpretation.[29] The 'realistic' approach emphasises that courts must scrutinise the real working practices as a basis for identifying the 'true agreement'. This requires a worldly-wise approach to the relevant evidence. The statutory interpretation approach was further supported by the restrictions on 'contracting out' of employment protections, which extended to 'indirect' forms of contracting out such as insertion of terms with the 'object' of avoiding statutory protections.[30] As Lord Leggatt explained,

> It is the very fact that an employer is often in a position to dictate such contract terms and that the individual performing the work has little or no ability to influence those terms that gives rise to the need for statutory protection in the first place. The efficacy of such protection would be seriously undermined if the putative employer could by the way in which the relationship is characterised in the written contract determine, even prima facie, whether or not the other party is to be classified as a worker. Laws such as the National Minimum Wage Act were manifestly enacted to protect those whom Parliament considers to be in need of protection and not just those who are designated by their employer as qualifying for it.[31]

In cases like *Autoclenz*, *Bates van Winkelhof*, and *Uber*, the purposive application of the general employment law tests meant that the claimants were included within the personal scope of their statutory human rights' claims. Over the last 20 years, the courts have developed the contractual tests so as to reduce their exclusionary effects. For example, 'mutuality of obligation' is now a much less significant barrier to employment status as a result of worker-protective judgments.[32] As a result, it is very unlikely that *O' Kelly v Trusthouse Forte Plc* would be decided in the same way today. Indeed, in *Bates van Winkelhof*, Lady Hale seemed to suggest that the general employment law test for limb (b) worker offered more reliable protection than relying directly on the HRA 1998.

While the employment law tests have certainly improved in matching the legal protections to the workers who need them, especially post-*Autoclenz*, a distinctive human rights approach is still needed. There are five main areas of concern with the current employment law approach.

The first difficulty is the requirement of a contract across all employment status categories. This can have exclusionary effects in triangular work arrangements involving agency, end-user, and worker. In *Smith v Carillion (JM) Ltd*, for example, the end-user had provided information about

---

[28] ibid [71].
[29] ibid [69].
[30] ibid [80]; ERA 1996, s 203(1).
[31] ibid [76].
[32] See *Prater*, above n 12. Mutuality will now rarely be a difficulty where an individual is actually present and working in a discrete contractual engagement. It has now been dispensed with as an independent requirement for 'limb (b) worker': *Nursing and Midwifery Council v Somerville* [2022] EWCA Civ 229. The absence of 'mutuality' between contractual engagements may nevertheless still be evidentially relevant to issues of control and subordination while an individual is working: *Secretary of State for Justice v Windle* [2016] EWCA Civ 459.

the claimant to a third party maintaining an anti-union blacklist, the Consulting Association.[33] His claim for trade union detriment against the end-user failed because there was no contract between him and the end-user; hence he could not satisfy the employment status threshold. The Court of Appeal refused to imply a contract because it was not necessary to do so.[34] The barrier of contract can also be a problem for those working without any kind of contract, such as volunteers and unpaid interns, who may be especially vulnerable to abuse.[35]

The second difficulty is where the barrier to enforcement results from the operation of legal rules other than employment status. For example, the statutory requirement of a qualifying period of continuous employment for unfair dismissal cannot easily be sidestepped by a court through purposive interpretation. It operates as a jurisdictional bar to the legal claim. The illegality doctrine may also operate to block a statutory claim if the claim arises in a work situation where the worker has committed a criminal offence. This often arises in contexts of irregular migration where working without a visa may be a criminal offence. The worker may be exposed to very serious exploitation, even though they have committed a criminal offence.[36] These contexts of irregular migration are often associated with very serious human rights abuses.[37]

The third problem is the restriction of certain rights like unfair dismissal protection to the narrow category of employees. Given the recognition in *Uber* that workers and employees encounter similar problems of subordination and dependence, this would support a single category of employment status for human rights protections. If unfair dismissal protection is a human right, denying it to workers seems arbitrary.[38] Given their common needs and contractual vulnerabilities, it is very difficult to justify the differential allocation of legal rights to employees and workers in a principled way.

The fourth problem is the continuing difficulties with certain definitional requirements of employment status. As we have seen, the problem of 'mutuality of obligation' is now less important as a result of judicial development of the law. However, the personal work requirement continues to pose a serious obstacle to many claimants in human rights contexts. In *Independent Workers Union of Great Britain v Central Arbitration Committee and another (Deliveroo)*, the insertion of a wide substitution clause into the written contracts of delivery riders negated the personal work obligation.[39] Given the finding at first instance that the substitution clauses were not 'shams', the Supreme Court accepted that the riders could not be 'workers'. This meant that they were excluded from the collective bargaining legislation. It is not clear why fundamental human rights protections should be defeated by a substitution clause in an employment contract. In *Deliveroo*, the issue of personal work was fatal to their claims, but the relevance of this specific requirement to their need for collective bargaining protection is unclear.

Finally, some of the factors that justify employment protections do not necessarily translate easily into justifications for human rights protections. In *Jivraj v Hashwani*, for example, the Supreme Court considered the personal scope of anti-discrimination provisions under the

---

[33] *Smith v Carillion (JM) Ltd* [2015] EWCA Civ 209, [2015] IRLR 467.

[34] For an argument that the Court should have applied a lower threshold for contractual implication in a human rights claim, see A Bogg, 'The Common Law Constitution at Work: R (on the application of UNISON) v Lord Chancellor' (2018) 81 *Modern Law Review* 509, 524.

[35] Atkinson, above n 3, 1187.

[36] The crime of illegal working was introduced in the Immigration Act 2016, s 34: see ACL Davies, 'The Immigration Act 2016' (2016) 45 *ILJ* 431.

[37] N Sedacca, 'Migrant Work, Gender and the Hostile Environment: A Human Rights Analysis' (2024) *ILJ* (forthcoming).

[38] On unfair dismissal as a human right, see chapter 18.

[39] [2023] UKSC 43.

extended category of 'employment under ... a contract personally to do any work'.[40] The case essentially arose out of a commercial dispute focused on the appointment of a commercial arbitrator. It was not an employment claim by the frustrated arbitrator himself. It concerned the enforceability of an arbitration clause specifying a religious qualification for the arbitrator, as agreed by the parties in their commercial joint venture. The arbitrator did not satisfy the religious qualification as he was not a member of the Ismaili community. The Supreme Court regarded the arbitrator as outside the personal scope of the religious discrimination provisions because arbitration lacked the necessary element of subordination. Indeed, the arbitrator must be completely independent of the control of the appointing commercial parties; otherwise they cannot discharge their arbitral responsibilities. This was the antithesis of subordination and control by an employer.

The *Jivraj* judgment sparked a lively academic debate. Academic supporters of *Jivraj* highlighted similarities in the justifications for employment rights and equality rights, which supported the subordination requirement.[41] Academic critics of *Jivraj* regarded the fundamental human right to non-discrimination as requiring a much broader personal scope.[42] The specific facts in *Jivraj*, and the distinctiveness of religious discrimination, may have concealed some of the difficulties with the judgment. For example, would the reaction to it have been the same if the joint venture had prohibited the appointment of an arbitrator on grounds of sex or race?

There may sometimes be situations where the purposive protection of human rights guarantees requires a broader approach to personal scope than the purposive protection of labour standards.[43] While subordination is clearly relevant in justifying many employment law protections, it may be less relevant to the protection of human rights. For example, the fundamental human right to non-discrimination might demand a broader and more inclusive scope. It is not clear why the presence of subordination should matter to protection from, say, wrongful discrimination or sexual harassment. Respect for those rights is simply an aspect of respect for everyone's dignity in the labour market, regardless of their subordination to an employer.

For these reasons, there will sometimes be a need to go beyond the standard employment law tests to ensure that personal scope and human rights guarantees are aligned. In the next section, we consider how far the ECHR and the HRA 1998 can respond to these gaps in personal scope.

3. Employment Status and Human Rights: Addressing the Gaps Using the ECHR and HRA 1998

Employment Status and Freedom of Association

Most trade union rights under the Trade Union and Labour Relations (Consolidation) Act 1992 (TULRCA 1992) extend to the worker category.[44] For example, the basic statutory definition of a 'trade union' in s 1 of TULRCA 1992 is an organisation 'which consists wholly or mainly of

---

[40] [2011] UKSC 40, [2011] WLR 1872.
[41] C McCrudden, 'Two Views of Subordination: The Personal Scope of Employment Discrimination Law in Jivraj v Haswani' (2012) 41 *ILJ* 30.
[42] M Freedland and N Kountouris, 'Employment Equality and Personal Work Relations – A Critique of Jivraj v Hashwani' (2012) 41 *ILJ* 56.
[43] For further discussion, see Atkinson, above n 3, 1184–85.
[44] Some TULRCA 1992 rights are still restricted to the narrower category of 'employee', such as the dismissal protections under s 152 and access to employment under s 137.

workers'. The main legal protections from detriment and inducements are rights for workers, and the protected trade union grounds (trade union membership, activities of an independent trade union, and use of union services) depend upon a nexus with an independent 'trade union' as defined by s 1.

'Worker' is defined broadly for the purposes of TULRCA 1992 in s 296(1) as an individual who works under 'any other contract whereby he undertakes to do or perform personally any work or services for another party to the contract who is not a professional client of his'. In some cases, however, the worker category has not been broad enough to include those who need trade union protection. For example, foster carers were unable to get their trade union 'listed' by the Certification Officer because the courts had determined in an earlier case that they did not work under a 'contract'.[45] The effect of this non-listing was that the National Union of Professional Foster Carers (NUPFC) was then unable to apply for 'recognition' for collective bargaining under the statutory recognition procedure in Sch A1. In another case, Deliveroo Riders did not satisfy the statutory definition of worker because a wide substitution clause had been inserted into their written contracts by the employer.[46] According to the Central Arbitration Committee, this substitution clause was not a sham and there was credible evidence that it had been exercised by some riders without penalty or disapproval. This meant that the delivery riders failed to satisfy the personal work obligation under the statutory definition. Despite the exclusion of foster carers and delivery riders from the worker category, they displayed many of the typical economic vulnerabilities that justified trade union protections. They earned a living through their labour, and were unable to exert any significant individual influence over their contracts. Foster carers were subject to significant oversight and the potential for disciplinary procedures.

In both cases, the affected unions challenged the exclusions using Article 11 ECHR and the HRA 1998. The leading ECtHR case on the personal scope of trade union rights under Article 11 is the Grand Chamber decision in *Sindicatul 'Pastoral Cel Bun' v Romania*.[47] It concerned the right to form a trade union of priests in the Romanian Orthodox Church. Interestingly, the Court did not adopt the wider argument that trade union rights applied to 'everyone'. Instead, the Court applied the narrower indicative criteria of an 'employment relationship' as set out in ILO Employment Relationship Recommendation 198 (2006) to assess the employment situation of the priests. It concluded that, notwithstanding certain special features pertaining to a religious vocation, the remuneration and employment duties of priests were consistent with an 'employment relationship'. For this reason, they were within the personal scope of the right to form a trade union under Article 11.[48]

In *NUPFC* and *Deliveroo*, the question was whether the claimants were within the scope of an ILO 'employment relationship'. If they were, their exclusion from the TULRCA 1992 definition of worker would be an interference with their Article 11 trade union rights. The Court would then need to consider if the exclusion was justified under Article 11(2). If it could not be justified, the Court would be required to interpret the concept of worker 'as far as possible' to ensure compatibility under s 3 of the HRA 1998.

In *NUPFC*, the Court of Appeal concluded that foster carers were in an 'employment relationship' despite the apparent absence of a contract for foster carers under domestic law.

---

[45] *National Union of Professional Foster Carers v Certification Officer* [2020] ICR 607 (*NUPFC*).
[46] *Independent Workers Union of Great Britain v Central Arbitration Committee and another* [2023] UKSC 43 (*Deliveroo*).
[47] [2014] IRLR 49.
[48] Where self-employed individuals do not satisfy the criteria of an 'employment relationship' and do not qualify for special trade union freedoms, their general associative freedom to form and act through a non-trade union association is protected under Article 11: see *Manole v Romania*, App No 46551/06, Judgment of 16 June 2015.

The remuneration of foster carers, coupled with extensive supervision and disciplinary control, were all indicative factors pointing towards an 'employment relationship'. 'Contract' should not be elevated to a conclusive factor. Instead, the Court took an overall view of the work arrangements based on the primacy of facts and a contextual assessment of those indicative features. The exclusion of foster carers could not be justified under Article 11(2). There was nothing about their occupational role supporting a restriction on their right to form a trade union. Consequently, the Court 'read down' the statute so that foster carers without a contract were included within the worker definition for the purpose of listing a trade union under TULRCA 1992.

In *Deliveroo*, by contrast, the Supreme Court reached the opposite view of the Article 11 rights of Deliveroo riders. The ILO Recommendation identifies personal work as a relevant indicative factor in identifying an 'employment relationship'. According to the Supreme Court, 'a broad power of substitution is, on its face, totally inconsistent with the existence of an obligation to provide personal service which is essential to the existence of an employment relationship within article 11'.[49] There is nothing in the Recommendation to suggest that personal work is 'essential', though. Like 'contract', it is an indicative factor. Where there are other factors pointing to dependence and subordination, however, there should be a presumption of an employment relationship under the ILO instrument. This appears to have been overlooked by the Supreme Court.

Some commentators have highlighted a tension between *NUPFC* and *Deliveroo*, because the CAC in *Deliveroo* appeared to treat personal work as a conclusive factor despite other features pointing in favour of an 'employment relationship'.[50] In *NUPFC*, by contrast, 'contract' was treated only as a relevant factor in the broader contextual enquiry. Foster carers and delivery riders share many social and economic vulnerabilities, and both need trade union protection. It is an odd result that only one of these groups is included within an 'employment relationship' when applying the same instrument.

A slightly different legal approach to Article 11 rights can be seen in *Wandsworth London Borough Council v Vining*.[51] This concerned the scope of the occupational exclusion of those employed in 'police service' and whether it extended to parks constables who had been made redundant. If the parks constables fell within the 'police service' category, this meant that they were excluded from the redundancy consultation procedure in TULRCA 1992. The Court of Appeal concluded that the exclusion of the parks constables and their trade union representatives from the redundancy consultation procedures violated Article 11. Consultation over redundancies was closely connected to the fundamental right to collective bargaining protected by Article 11.[52] Since the United Kingdom was under a positive obligation to ensure the effective enjoyment of those rights, any exclusion of particular classes of workers from the coverage of the legislative scheme required justification. Since no such justification was offered for the exclusion of parks constables in this case, the Court of Appeal concluded that the parks police ought to be included within the scope of redundancy consultation.[53] This was achieved through s 3 interpretation. In contrast with *NUPFC* and *Deliveroo*, there was no consideration of whether parks constables were in an 'employment relationship'. This enquiry was no doubt avoided because it was accepted that the parks constables were employees. The reasoning was

---

[49] *Deliveroo*, above n 46, [69].
[50] A Bogg and M Ford, 'Employment Status and Trade Union Rights: Applying Occam's Razor' (2022) 51 *ILJ* 717.
[51] [2017] EWCA Civ 1092, [2018] ICR 499.
[52] ibid [63].
[53] ibid [75].

focused more straightforwardly on the simple equality-based issue whether their occupational exclusion could be justified.

Overall, human rights arguments have made an important but modest contribution in extending personal scope for freedom of association and trade union rights in UK law. This reflects the ECtHR's own caution in pursuing an 'employment relationship' approach under Article 11. A number of points can be made.

The first issue is that in many of these cases, a better legal approach may have been to address the gaps in the general legal definition of worker directly, rather than through the HRA 1998. For example, the legal authority that foster carers do not work under a contract because of the extent to which the incidents of their arrangements are regulated by statute seems very dubious.[54] Similarly, the only statutory requirement for the personal work obligation is that the worker undertakes to do 'any' of the work or services personally. Can it really be said that a rider undertakes to do *no* work personally when engaged by Deliveroo?

The second issue is the impact of the s 3 interpretative duty. Although the s 3 interpretative obligation is very strong in its effects, requiring a compliant interpretation 'as far as it is possible to do so', it is also limited in scope. In *NUPFC*, for example, the Court of Appeal emphasised that its inclusive interpretation did not extend beyond 'listing' to other TULRCA 1992 rights.[55] The worker definition would need to be considered on an incremental basis for other Article 11 rights under TULRCA 1992. This means that foster carers would have to start new litigation to establish, for example, that they are protected from detriment for trade union reasons. This means that s 3 provides a precise surgical response to an existing gap, but it is unlikely to lead to broader structural change.

The third issue is that the HRA 1998 techniques seem to work best where there is a clearly defined occupational exclusion. In *Vining* and *NUPFC*, for example, the foster carers and parks constables represented occupational groups with clear boundaries. This made it easier for the court to apply an equality-style analysis to consider their exclusion from Article 11 rights. In *Deliveroo*, by contrast, the relevant occupational group was much more diffuse and the broader legal and economic consequences of a s 3 interpretation more uncertain.

Employment Status, Article 14, and Status-Based Discrimination

These cases support the view that there is an underlying norm of equality in the distribution of human rights. Unless a specific occupational exclusion from a general employment status category can be justified, then it ought to be treated as included within the scope of the right. A powerful legal technique for challenging unjustified exclusions from statutory employment rights is Article 14 ECHR that prohibits discrimination in the enjoyment of Convention rights. This technique was central to *Gilham v Ministry of Justice*.[56] The case involved the exclusion of judges from statutory whistleblowing protections. These whistleblowing protections were undoubtedly within the ambit of Article 10 and its protection of freedom of expression. In these circumstances, Article 14 requires that the 'enjoyment of the rights and freedoms ... shall be secured without discrimination on any ground'. The Supreme Court had to consider whether the occupational exclusion was based on some 'other status' within Article 14 and, if so, if the difference in treatment was a proportionate means of achieving a legitimate aim. Lady Hale concluded

---

[54] *W v Essex County Council* [2001] 2 AC 592.
[55] *NUPFC*, above n 45, [131].
[56] [2019] UKSC 44.

that this was a relevant 'status' and that there was no justification for the exclusion. Since the Government had identified no legitimate aim at all for the exclusion, it was not possible to evaluate its proportionality.[57] Lady Hale also doubted whether the very deferential standard, that the socio-economic policy must be 'manifestly without reasonable foundation' for it to be outside Parliament's margin of discretion, was appropriate here.[58] Accordingly, the Supreme Court 'read down' the statutory provision using s 3 of the HRA 1998 to include holders of judicial office within its scope.

For Atkinson, this approach might be used to challenge a range of labour market statuses with exclusionary effects: 'having a particular type of working arrangement, whether being self-employed, an agency worker, zero-hours contractor, or live-in domestic worker, should be a protected status under Article 14.'[59] It is certainly true that 'other status' has been interpreted broadly by the courts, though it does have limits. For example, in *Sullivan v Isle of Wight Council*, the EAT concluded that a job applicant could not use Article 14 to secure whistleblowing protections because she was not in an analogous position to those already in employment; and the issue of job applicant as a 'status' was also unclear.[60] This Article 14 technique probably works best where there is a clearly defined status-based group because this means that the court's consideration of proportionality will be more focused. Where statuses are defined more broadly, the expertise and legitimacy of the court could be more strained when it is considering if a labour market exclusion is proportionate.

The Illegality Doctrine and Human Rights

In what circumstances should those who have committed a criminal offence while working be entitled to enforce their human rights in court? This general question often arises in the context of migrants working without a right to work. It may also arise where the Revenue has been defrauded of income tax or national insurance, for example because of 'cash in hand' payments.

The undocumented migrant worker may now be committing a criminal offence of illegal working under the offence introduced by s 34 of the Immigration Act 2016.[61] If workers' human rights are violated during a period of illegal employment, can they still enforce those rights against the employer? This question is central to the illegality doctrine. This doctrine can bar the enforcement of legal claims where they are closely connected to the criminal conduct. Illegality can sometimes conjure up images of unscrupulous criminals benefiting from their crime and then using public resources to enforce their rights. In the employment context, illegality often arises in the context of highly precarious work which may even involve serious exploitation, poverty pay, or even 'modern slavery'.

In *Hounga v Allen*, the Supreme Court considered the illegality doctrine within the context of a race discrimination claim by a trafficked migrant worker.[62] For the purposes of illegality, discrimination claims are categorised as statutory torts.[63] She was working illegally and was very likely

---

[57] ibid [37].
[58] ibid [34]–[35].
[59] Atkinson, above n 3, 1191.
[60] *Sullivan v Isle of Wight Council* [2024] EAT 3.
[61] This legislation also introduced a parallel offence of employing an illegal worker in s 35. In many contexts of undocumented work, both employer and worker may be committing criminal offences in respect of the same work arrangement.
[62] [2014] UKSC 47.
[63] See also *Hall v Woolston Hall Leisure Ltd* [2001] 1 WLR 225, where the Court recognised the right not to be discriminated against because of sex as a human right protected through a statutory tort.

to have committed a criminal offence by working in breach of her visa conditions. The Supreme Court proposed a 'balancing' approach to illegality, weighing the public policy reasons in favour of barring her claim against the public policy reasons in favour of upholding it. While the public policy reasons barring her claim (such as deterring criminal conduct) were held to 'scarcely exist',[64] the public policy protecting victims of trafficking was given decisive weight in this case. This countervailing public policy category provided a way of reflecting the strong importance of protecting fundamental human rights.[65] This balancing approach in *Hounga* was further developed in *Patel v Mirza*,[66] which added a requirement of 'proportionality' as a third element in the balancing exercise. This was not an employment case, but it is relevant to employment law because illegality is a general doctrine applying across the full range of legal claims.[67] This judgment meant that the court should consider whether the law was being applied with a due sense of proportionality where the first two factors in the *Patel* 'trio' supported barring the claim.

There are two main ways in which the illegality doctrine can have legal effects on human rights' claims in employment. The first way is through 'common law illegality'. This is based upon a discretionary enquiry by the court, applying public policy factors to assess whether the *Patel* 'trio' would support barring the legal claim. It is potentially relevant to tort claims (such as discrimination and harassment) and contract claims (such as working time protections, unfair and wrongful dismissal, minimum wage). These statutory rights could all be viewed as implementing human rights of workers. While there is still uncertainty about the relevance of the human rights claims in the public policy balancing exercise, such claims are often viewed as having special significance in the legal system. This could be reflected in a public policy that supports the enforcement of fundamental human rights. This could be encompassed by the second element of the *Patel* trio. To maintain the 'integrity of the legal system', a court should be slow to conclude that human rights claims are barred by illegality. A court might also conclude that the denial of enforcement of human rights will usually be disproportionate, given the moral weight of such claims, engaging the third element of the *Patel* trio.

The second way is through 'statutory illegality'. Here, the contract is expressly or impliedly prohibited by the statutory offence that criminalises conduct. Imagine an offence criminalising the supply of a poison. A court may take the view that a contract for the sale of that poison should also be treated as prohibited, even if the supply offence does not spell this out. If the contract is prohibited by the statutory offence, any statutory claims (such as unfair dismissal or minimum wage) based on that contract must also be extinguished. The critical difference between common law and statutory illegality is that the effects of the illegality on the claimant's legal rights are determined by the statute itself in statutory illegality. The role of the court is simply to give effect to parliamentary intention. In *Okedina v Chikale*, Underhill LJ emphasised that a court should be slow to conclude that a contract is impliedly prohibited, and it should only do so where it is necessary and in clear cases.[68] On the facts in *Okedina*, where the claimant herself was innocent and the employer had committed the criminal offence, there was no implied prohibition. It is less clear what might happen in other cases where the claimant has committed the criminal offence. This is likely to be more common given the illegal working offence in the Immigration Act 2016.

---

[64] *Hounga*, above n 62, [45].
[65] A Bogg and S Green, 'Rights Are Not Just for the Virtuous: What Hounga Means for the Illegality Defence in the Discrimination Torts' (2015) 44 *Industrial Law Journal* 101.
[66] [2016] UKSC 42.
[67] S Green and A Bogg (eds), *Illegality after Patel v Mirza* (Hart, 2018).
[68] [2019] EWCA Civ 1393, [46] and [50]. A Bogg, '*Okedina v Chikale* and Contract Illegality: New Dawn or False Dawn?' (2020) 49 *ILJ* 258.

Since implied prohibition depends upon statutory interpretation, it is possible that s 3 of the HRA 1998 could be engaged where Convention rights are being claimed. For example, if the claimant's Article 8 rights are engaged in a dismissal, the court would construe the scope of implied prohibition 'so far as it is possible to do so' to respect Convention rights. In situations where the human right is not protected under the ECHR, but under other treaties to which the UK is a signatory, statutory interpretation might be guided by the 'legality principle' in *ex parte Simms*.[69] According to Lord Hoffmann, the principle of legality embodies a strong presumption that human rights are not to be overridden except where there is clear and express language or by necessary implication. These techniques of statutory interpretation would ensure that the implied prohibition of statutory human rights claims was limited to circumstances where it was strictly necessary to do so.

Human rights arguments have not yet been developed fully in the context of the complex law on illegality, but it is an area that is ripe for productive engagement between private law and human rights.[70]

Qualifying Periods of Employment and the ECHR

The law on unfair dismissal is based upon a fundamental distinction between automatically unfair reasons for dismissal and potentially fair reasons for dismissal. The first category is protected as 'day 1' rights. This reflects a legislative assessment that dismissal for such reasons, which include retaliation for enforcing statutory rights or acting as a workplace representative, is a serious abuse of managerial power. The second category of ordinary unfair dismissal, where dismissals can potentially be justified by an employer, is subject to a qualifying period of continuous employment of two years.[71] This qualifying period has varied during the unfair dismissal legislation. It has reflected a range of considerations and legislative priorities, such as encouraging employers to hire new employees or linking access to rights to desert, loyalty, and long-term commitment.

In *Redfearn v United Kingdom*, the applicant was dismissed from his employment as a bus driver following his election as a local councillor for the British National Party (BNP).[72] The BNP is a far right political party that propagates views on immigration widely considered as offensive. It is not however an unlawful political party. The bus company, Serco, operated in an area of Bradford providing services to Asian service users. The continued employment of Redfearn was a serious concern to the company given the local community it served. Discrimination rights are 'day 1' rights, but each of his claims for race and philosophical belief discrimination failed. He was unable to bring an unfair dismissal claim because he did not have the requisite period of continuous employment.

In Strasbourg, the ECtHR focused on the infringement of Article 11 (freedom of association) examined in the light of Article 10 (freedom of expression). This combination of Convention rights is powerful. Political expression and association are fundamental to a pluralistic democracy based upon toleration. While the BNP supports views that are shocking and disturbing to many people, it is not an unlawful political association. According to a majority of the Court,

---

[69] *R v Secretary of State for the Home Department ex parte Simms* [1999] UKHL 33, [2000] 2 AC 115.
[70] See, particularly, Inter-American Court of Human Rights, *Legal Condition and Rights of Undocumented Migrant Workers*, Advisory Opinion OC-18/03, 17 September 2003.
[71] ERA 1996, s 108(1).
[72] App No 47335/06, Judgment of 6 November 2012. See H Collins and V Mantouvalou, '*Redfearn v UK*: Political Association and Dismissal' (2013) 76 *Modern Law Review* 909.

the exclusion of the unfair dismissal claim because of the qualifying period limitation could not be justified in this case. Since UK law already provided for various exceptions to this limitation, such as automatically unfair reasons which were 'day 1' rights, there ought to have been an exception in this case. It did not follow that his dismissal should be treated as automatically unfair. It might be possible to justify the dismissal under the proportionality standard. It was necessary to give the claimant access to a court in order to challenge the lawfulness of the dismissal in accordance with proportionality. In this way, *Redfearn* can also be understood as engaging the fundamental right of access to a court, itself recognised as a fundamental common law right.[73] Following the judgment in *Redfearn*, the Government removed the continuity requirement where the dismissal relates to an employee's political opinions or affiliation.[74] This means that the lawfulness of such political dismissals can be challenged from day 1, though they are not automatically unfair.

Does *Redfearn* have wider implications for other types of human rights dismissals implemented before the qualifying period of employment has been reached? Many such dismissals would already be covered from day 1 by the existing category of automatically unfair reasons or the Equality Act 2010. However, there are still some significant gaps. For example, consider an employee who is dismissed for gross misconduct based upon a false allegation of theft. The decision was supported by an inadequate investigation into the alleged wrongdoing and a biased disciplinary hearing. This situation is very likely to engage Article 8 given the very serious consequences for the employee's reputation and wider social connections.[75] It is also very unlikely that the common law would provide real and effective protection to the employee because of the severe restrictions on stigma damages in wrongful dismissal claims.[76] There are also potential gaps where an employee is dismissed for non-political expression on social media which engages Article 10.[77] The provision of 'day 1' access for disciplinary misconduct dismissals and 'free speech' dismissals would require radical revision of the current statutory framework. It might even leave the two-year threshold as the exception rather than the rule. The complete removal of the threshold would have the advantage of protecting those in short-term or casual employment, who are often the most precarious and disadvantaged workers in need of human rights' protection.

4. Personal Scope and Human Rights under EU Law

We turn now to the approach of EU law to questions of personal scope, particularly where human rights are at stake.[78] EU law uses a mix of approaches: an 'autonomous' EU definition of worker in some contexts, and discretion for the Member States to use their own concepts in others. Over time, the EU has applied its own definition more widely, and restricted the scope of

---

[73] *R (on the application of UNISON) v Lord Chancellor* [2017] UKSC 51.
[74] ERA 1996, s 108(4).
[75] *Denisov v Ukraine*, App No 76639/11, Judgment of 25 September 2018, discussed in chapter 18.
[76] *Edwards v Chesterfield Royal Hospital NHS Foundation Trust* [2011] UKSC 58.
[77] On this topic, see chapter 16.
[78] There is an excellent literature on this issue: see S Giubboni, 'Being a worker in EU law' (2018) 9 *European Labour Law Journal* 223; N Kountouris, 'The Concept of "Worker" in European Labour Law: Fragmentation, Autonomy and Scope' (2018) 47 *Industrial Law Journal* 192; E Menegatti, 'The Evolving Concept of "worker" in EU law' (2019) 12 *Italian Labour Law e-Journal* 71; A Sagan, 'The classification as "worker" under EU law' (2019) 10 *European Labour Law Journal* 353.

Member States' discretion, particularly when a Member State is seeking to exclude some people from protection without a proper justification. The Court's approach is less explicitly focused on human rights, though it is strongly purposive, concerned with ensuring that worker-protective directives do in fact include the people they were intended to help. This is usually indirectly protective of workers' rights. We conclude with a brief examination of the proposed Directive on Platform Work, which addresses employment status questions in a sector which, as we have already seen, often gives rise to significant difficulties.[79]

The 'Autonomous' Concept of Worker

The 'autonomous' concept of worker in EU law developed in the context of the internal market. Under the Treaty, 'workers' have the right to 'freedom of movement': to go to another EU Member State to look for work or take up employment. Since this right is EU-wide, it was considered necessary to have a single definition. This was developed in the *Lawrie-Blum* case, in which it was held that 'the essential feature of an employment relationship … is that for a certain period of time a person performs services for and under the direction of another person in return for which he receives remuneration'.[80] It is worth noting that one of the central purposes of this definition is to distinguish workers from 'economically inactive' people, who have lesser rights under EU citizenship rules.

Despite arising in a very particular context, the *Lawrie-Blum* definition is usually cited whenever the CJEU needs to define the term 'worker'. For example, it was used in *Allonby* as the starting-point for the definition of worker for the purposes of the right to equal pay for men and women under Article 157 TFEU.[81] However, the Court has developed the definition over time so that it is no longer so heavily focused on a blunt assessment of whether the relationship is one of subordination. First, in *Allonby* itself, the Court held that the exclusion of self-employed people from equal pay law applied only to those who were *genuinely* self-employed, regardless of their classification in national law.[82] This approach has been applied widely across a number of different contexts.[83] Second, the Court has applied the subordination requirement flexibly. For example, in *Danosa*, a pregnancy discrimination claim, the court held that a company director could still be regarded as a worker under the test because she was answerable in various ways, including to shareholders.[84] The Court has also begun to move away from *Lawrie-Blum* in particular contexts, notably equality law,[85] making it clear that a range of different definitions is in operation.[86]

Until recently, the Court's jurisprudence has followed the familiar pattern of excluding genuinely self-employed people from the scope of labour rights protection. However, the legitimacy of this boundary is open to question for 'solo' self-employed people with limited bargaining power. In *JK*, the Court held that a self-employed person who was refused further assignments by the employer was covered by Directive 2000/78, the Framework Directive on Equality.[87]

---

[79] Commission, *Proposal for a Directive on improving working conditions in platform work* (COM(2021) 762 final).
[80] Case 66/85 *Lawrie-Blum v Land Baden Württemberg* [1986] ECR 2121, [17].
[81] Case C-256/01 *Allonby v Accrington and Rossendale College* EU:C:2004:18, [2004] ECR I-873.
[82] ibid [71].
[83] eg Case C-413/13 *FNV Kunsten Informatie en Media v Netherlands* EU:C:2014:2411, [2015] 4 CMLR 1.
[84] Case C-232/09 *Danosa v LKB Lizings SIA* EU:C:2010:674, [2011] 2 CMLR 2, dealing with Directive 92/85, the Pregnant Workers Directive.
[85] See Case C-587/20 *Ligebehandlingsnaevnet v HK/Danmark* EU:C:2022:419, [2022] 3 CMLR 31.
[86] *Allonby*, above n 81, [63].
[87] Case C-356/21 *JK v TP SA* EU:C:2023:9, [2023] 3 CMLR 8, and see A Aloisi, 'J.K. v TP S.A. and the "Universal" Scope of EU Anti-Discrimination Law at Work: A Paradigm Shift?' (2023) 52 *ILJ* 977.

This Directive is not based on Article 153 TFEU and states that it applies to the conditions of access to 'employment, self-employment and occupation' for 'all persons'.[88] It remains to be seen whether this approach will remain confined to equality law (given the Court's particular textual reasoning) or whether it will extend across labour rights more generally, given that there may be strong reasons for giving some self-employed people access to other labour rights, such as the right to conclude collective agreements.[89]

Personal Scope and Directives

In broad terms, directives take three different approaches to the definition of worker: no definition at all, definition by reference to national law, and definition by reference to both national and EU law. We offer some examples of each.

The CJEU's approach to directives with no definition of worker has changed radically over time. In the early case of *Danmols Inventar*, concerning the original Acquired Rights Directive, it was held that the Directive – which was silent on the definition of employee – was intended as a partial harmonisation measure and therefore applied only to people classified as employees within national law.[90] However, while this approach was followed for a number of years, the Court has gradually departed from it and replaced it instead with the autonomous definition derived from *Lawrie-Blum*. This shift began with a group of cases concerning the Working Time Directive (WTD) and the Pregnant Workers Directive (PrWD).[91] For example, in *Union Syndicale Solidaires Isère*, it was held that the concept of worker in the WTD 'may not be interpreted differently according to the law of Member States but has an autonomous meaning specific to European Union law' and must be defined in accordance with the definition in *Lawrie-Blum*.[92] It is possible that the Court's reasoning was influenced by the health and safety basis of these directives and the fundamental nature of the rights at stake, but later cases have made clear the Court's complete reversal of its original position.[93] This is because the *Lawrie-Blum* approach has also been used in relation to the Collective Redundancies Directive, which protects worker voice in much the same way as the Acquired Rights Directive at issue in *Danmols Inventar*.[94] Of course, it is arguable that the Court is justified in applying an autonomous definition based on the text: if a directive is silent on the definition of worker, there is no particular reason to assume that national definitions should apply. However, it may be that this is what the Member States in fact assumed would happen, before the Court developed its more interventionist approach.

The Court's use of the autonomous definition, with particular reference to workers' rights, has also had important implications for domestic law. In *R (IWGB) v Secretary of State for Work and Pensions*, a trade union representing gig economy workers brought a successful judicial review challenge of the UK's implementation of two aspects of the EU directives on health and safety, dealing with the right to leave an unsafe workplace, and the right to be provided with personal protective equipment.[95] The case was prompted by the Covid-19 pandemic, in which these two

---

[88] Directive 2000/78, Article 3.
[89] A point recognised in EU competition law guidance. See Commission, *Guidelines on the application of Union competition law to collective agreements regarding the working conditions of solo self-employed persons* (2022/C 374/02).
[90] Case 105/84 *Mikkelsen v Danmols Inventar A/S* EU:C:1985:331, [1985] ECR 2639, dealing with Directive 77/187.
[91] Directive 2003/88 and Directive 92/85 respectively.
[92] Case C-428/09 *Union Syndicale Solidaires Isère v Premier Ministre* EU:C:2010:612, [2011] 1 CMLR 38, [28].
[93] Kountouris, above n 78, 202–04.
[94] eg Case C-32/02 *Commission v Italy* ECLI:EU:C:2003:555, [2003] ECR I-12063, dealing with Directive 98/59.
[95] *R (Independent Workers' Union of Great Britain) v Secretary of State for Work and Pensions* [2020] EWHC 3050 (Admin), [2021] ICR 372.

rights were of particular importance. The Administrative Court held that the relevant EU provisions applied to people who met the autonomous EU definition of worker. The UK had failed to implement them correctly because it had confined them to people with contracts of employment. The judge noted that the health and safety purpose would be 'undermined by a narrow interpretation of the term "worker"'.[96]

A number of other directives do make express reference to national law when defining their scope of application. A classic formulation is: '"employee" shall mean any person who, in the Member State concerned, is protected as an employee under national employment law'.[97] Although this appears to give discretion to the Member States, the Court has held in a number of cases that this discretion is not unlimited, and the exclusion of particular groups or types of worker from the scope of protection may amount to a failure properly to implement the relevant directive.[98] For example, in *O'Brien*, a part-time judge who was paid fees rather than a salary sought to challenge his exclusion from the judicial pension scheme.[99] In domestic law, he was classified as an 'office-holder' rather than a worker, so the question arose whether he could rely on the Directive on Part-Time Work to bring his claim.[100] The CJEU held that judges could be excluded from the worker definition 'only if the relationship between judges and the Ministry of Justice is, by its nature, substantially different from that between employers and their employees falling, according to national law, within the category of workers'.[101] Although this was for the national court to determine, the guidance provided by the Court gave a strong steer that the judge should be treated as a worker.

A third approach, found in some more recent directives, is to use a hybrid formulation referring to national and EU law. The recent Directive on Adequate Minimum Wages is a good example. Article 2 provides:

> This Directive applies to workers in the Union who have an employment contract or employment relationship as defined by law, collective agreements or practice in force in each Member State, with consideration to the case-law of the Court of Justice.[102]

This is an important acknowledgement by the Member States and EU institutions of the Court's role in constraining Member States' discretion when defining the personal scope of particular labour rights, and can be seen as giving greater legitimacy to the Court's approach.

The influence of human rights arguments over the Court's decisions on personal scope is not as explicit as one might expect, but there is certainly a strongly purposive element to its approach. This, in turn, can often be linked to the fact that workers' rights are at stake, because the purpose of the directive under consideration is to protect workers' rights. The exclusion of particular groups of workers from protection also raises more basic issues of fairness where there is no clear justification for the exclusion. One of the clearer examples of this is *Fenoll*.[103] The claimant in that case worked at a 'work rehabilitation centre' for people with intellectual

---

[96] ibid [82]. The argument made in this case is, of course, no longer possible in domestic law after the UK's exit from the EU.
[97] Council Directive 2001/23/EC, Article 2(1)(d) (transfers of undertakings).
[98] See also Case C-216/15 *Betriebsrat der Ruhrlandklinik gGmbH v Ruhrlandklinik GmbH* EU:C:2016:883, [2017] 2 CMLR 13.
[99] Case C-393/10 *O'Brien v Ministry of Justice* EU:C:2012:110, [2012] 2 CMLR 25.
[100] Directive 97/81.
[101] Above n 91, [51].
[102] Directive (EU) 2022/2041 on adequate minimum wages in the European Union.
[103] Case C-316/13 *Fenoll v Centre d'aide par le travail 'La Jouvene'* EU:C:2015:200, [2016] IRLR 67.

disabilities. He left his position after a period of ill health and sought a payment in lieu of his accrued annual leave. He could not claim this under French law because he was not classified as a 'worker'. However, the Court held that a person employed at a 'work rehabilitation centre' was, in principle, capable of being classified as a worker, provided that their activities formed part of the 'normal labour market', a matter for the national court to determine. The claimant's case rested on both the WTD and Article 31(2) of the Charter, and also raised (unacknowledged) issues of disability discrimination.[104] However, it is important to acknowledge that not all cases extending the definition of worker have referred to the Charter or been strongly purposive in approach. For example, *Matzak*, a case concerning the working time of a volunteer firefighter, made no such references, though it took a radical approach to the definition of worker by opening up the possibility of including volunteers.[105]

Other Limitations

The Court's role in ensuring that directives are properly implemented has proved useful in challenging other kinds of limitations imposed by Member States on access to employment rights, which typically have a disproportionate impact on workers with non-standard working arrangements. Two examples will illustrate the point.

In the *BECTU* case, a trade union challenged the UK's use of a qualifying period when implementing the Working Time Directive.[106] This provided that a worker would not become entitled to paid annual leave until they had worked for 13 weeks for the same employer. This meant that workers with short-term, casual working arrangements would rarely get access to this right. The CJEU held that the UK had failed to implement the Directive, which did not make any provision for qualifying periods. In the collective context, consultation rights – such as those in the Information and Consultation Directive – only apply to larger firms.[107] However, Member States have been found to have failed to implement the Directive correctly where they have artificially excluded workers with particular types of contract from the calculation of a firm's size.[108]

The Platform Work Directive

At the time of writing, the EU has reached agreement on the Platform Work Directive, though the final text has not yet been published.[109] One of the issues the Directive seeks to tackle is the 'misclassification' of platform workers. The Commission has explained this as a rights issue because, as we saw above, attempts by platforms to present their workers as self-employed denies them access to rights afforded only to workers or employees in national law.

Article 4 of the Directive (as originally proposed by the Commission) put in place a presumption that there was an employment relationship between platform workers and platforms. Under the Commission's original draft, the presumption applied to a 'contractual relationship'

---

[104] See M Bell, 'Disability, Rehabilitation and the Status of Worker in EU Law: Fenoll' (2016) 53 *Common Market Law Review* 197.
[105] Case C-518/15 *Ville de Nivelles v Matzak* EU:C:2018:82, [2018] 2 CMLR 37, on which see Sagan, above n 78.
[106] Case C-173/99 *R (BECTU) v Secretary of State for Trade and Industry* EU:C:2001:356, [2001] ECR I-4881.
[107] Directive 2002/14/EC, Article 3.
[108] Case C-176/12 *Association de mediation sociale v Union locale des syndicats CGT* EU:C:2014:2, [2014] 2 CMLR 41.
[109] Above n 79.

between a platform and a worker where the platform 'controls … the performance of work'. This latter concept was defined in Article 4(2) in the following terms:

> Controlling the performance of work within the meaning of paragraph 1 shall be understood as fulfilling at least two of the following:
> (a)   effectively determining, or setting upper limits for the level of remuneration;
> (b)   requiring the person performing platform work to respect specific binding rules with regard to appearance, conduct towards the recipient of the service or performance of the work;
> (c)   supervising the performance of work or verifying the quality of the results of the work including by electronic means;
> (d)   effectively restricting the freedom, including through sanctions, to organise one's work, in particular the discretion to choose one's working hours or periods of absence, to accept or to refuse tasks or to use subcontractors or substitutes;
> (e)   effectively restricting the possibility to build a client base or to perform work for any third party.

Where these conditions were met, the presumption would apply, and it would be for the platform to rebut that presumption should it wish to do so. Under the agreed draft, it seems that Member States will still be obliged to create a presumption of worker status, but the conditions for doing so will be left largely to the Member States' discretion, having regard to the case law of the CJEU. This means that the precise approach to platform worker status will vary as between the Member States, and there will be less extensive harmonisation than the Commission originally envisaged.

The obvious advantage of using a presumption is that it brings about a subtle shift in the balance of power between the platform, as alleged employer, and the worker. However, much will turn on the precise formulation of the indicators which bring the presumption into play, and how easy they are for platforms to avoid whilst still providing an appropriate service. For example, platforms providing a taxi service are putting workers into direct contact with consumers and probably need to exercise a high degree of control in order to ensure consumer trust and fulfil licensing obligations. Other platforms – commercial delivery services, for example – may be able to relax their control over people working on their platforms, by placing more risk on the consumer, and thus avoid triggering any presumption. A further issue is, of course, that the problems of misclassification, while prevalent in platform work, are by no means confined to this sector.

5. Conclusion

Human rights arguments have reshaped the personal scope of employment rights in important ways. The general legal definitions of 'employee' and 'limb (b) worker' have been developed using a 'purposive' approach, and this is sensitive to the purpose(s) of the rights being claimed. The boundaries of worker protection are now applied less formalistically and more inclusively after judgments like *Uber*. This has also been reflected in developments in EU law.

Where individuals have been excluded from statutory protections, because of an occupational restriction, illegality, or a qualifying period of employment, human rights arguments provide an important legal technique to challenge those exclusions. Even where litigation is not successful, the requirement that an exclusion be justified contributes to transparent and effective governance. It means that legislators must reflect on whether there are good reasons for exclusions, and whether there might be less restrictive alternatives available to them.

Exclusions from existing coverage must be justified, as we saw in this chapter. The interaction between human rights and employment law is likely to be constructive and dynamic for the foreseeable future.

4

Right to Equal Treatment and Equal Opportunity

1.	The Universality of Human Rights	5.	Disability Discrimination
2.	Article 14 ECHR	6.	Challenging Exclusion – Migrant Workers
3.	Positive Rights for Women		
4.	Age Discrimination and the Right to Work		

1. The Universality of Human Rights

Everyone is entitled to respect for their human rights. We possess those rights simply by virtue of being human, not as the result of our citizenship or group membership. Since the 20th century, formal declarations of rights proclaim that 'everyone' is entitled to the rights contained in the document. Article 1 of the Universal Declaration of Human Rights 1948 states: 'All human beings are born free and equal in dignity and rights.' The text was amended to replace 'all men' (as in the French Declaration of the Rights of Man 1789) with 'all human beings' to make the universality of human rights abundantly clear.

Yet the very next Article introduced what appears to be a superfluous statement about equality. Article 2 states:

> Everyone is entitled to all the rights and freedoms set forth in this Declaration, without distinction of any kind, such as race, colour, sex, language, religion, political or other opinion, national or social origin, property, birth or other status. Furthermore, no distinction shall be made on the basis of the political, jurisdictional or international status of the country or territory to which a person belongs, whether it be independent, trust, non-self-governing or under any other limitation of sovereignty.

Why was such a provision regarded as necessary? The history of colonialism, racial segregation, slavery, and the subordination of women provided abundant instances of how privileged groups had insisted that only they possessed fundamental rights. Since Greek and Roman times, powerful states and empires also insisted that only citizens enjoyed fundamental rights, and citizenship was only accorded the privileged few.[1] Given this context, for the Universal Declaration to be acceptable to all member states of the new United Nations, it needed to spell out that the era of human rights could not tolerate discrimination of any kind. We find similar provisions in many other international conventions, such as Article 14 of the European Convention on Human Rights (ECHR).[2]

---

[1] The rights of migrants remain an issue today, as we discuss further below.
[2] See also Article 2(1) International Covenant on Civil and Political Rights 1966, 999 UNTS 171; and Article 2(2) International Covenant on Economic, Social and Cultural Rights 1996, 993 UNTS 3.

From a legal point of view, however, the question is whether this affirmation in Article 2 that human rights are enjoyed equally adds anything to declarations of human rights that apply to everyone. For instance, if there is a right to freedom from slavery and forced labour, does it add anything to say that everyone has the right without distinction or discrimination?

Moreover, the development of anti-discrimination laws in the second half of the 20th century appears to add to the redundancy of an equality provision in the protection of human rights. Since the outlawing of race and sex discrimination by the Civil Rights Act of 1964 in the USA, most states have enacted laws that prohibit discrimination in important aspects of political and economic life, including employment. The prohibitions now apply to a much larger number of protected characteristics or statuses. For example, in the European Union and the UK, as well as prohibitions against sex and race discrimination, the EU Directive 2000/78 laid down 'a general framework for combating discrimination on the grounds of religion or belief, disability, age or sexual orientation as regards employment and occupation'.[3] Once implemented in national laws, these anti-discrimination provisions provide directly enforceable rights for workers against their employers. Many countries also use government agencies to monitor compliance and to assist in the enforcement of these laws. These national equality laws, such as the Equality Act 2010 in the UK, therefore provide powerful protection against discrimination that often renders any appeal to human rights law unnecessary.[4]

Nevertheless, the difference of approach towards unjustifiable discrimination in human rights law permits it to challenge prejudicial actions against disadvantaged groups that may fall outside both discrimination laws, such as the Equality Act 2010, and the normal protection for human rights afforded by the other rights protected in international instruments, such as the ECHR. The first part of this chapter focuses on the different approach provided by human rights law to that existing in national and international anti-discrimination laws. Focusing on Article 14 ECHR, four important differences are highlighted: (1) the unlimited scope of protected characteristics in human rights law; (2) the possibility of justifying direct discrimination to accommodate difference; (3) the absence of the need to establish group disadvantage; and (4), more controversially, the expansion of the scope of the protected human rights themselves in the interpretation of the Convention.

The third section of this chapter examines the application of human rights to women. Under the influence of feminist movements in the 1970s, it was questioned whether the content of human rights documents sufficiently included rights that were important from the perspective of women. Although the equality clause ruled out negative discrimination against women, it was argued that women deserved separate treatment by granting them a special set of positive rights. Many of these rights were connected to reproductive capacity. They included freedom of marriage, a right to control family planning, and additional rights during pregnancy, child birth, and child rearing. Employment laws based on those human rights might include rights to maternity leave and maternity pay. Two further aspects of human rights for women are of particular concern to the law of work. First, there are some types of jobs that are overwhelmingly performed by women, such as sex work and domestic service, where women are particularly vulnerable to exploitation and the denial of their human rights. Second, the law of human rights needs to address any special problems encountered by women who perform unpaid work at home such

---

[3] Council Directive 2000/78/EC of 27 November 2000 establishing a general framework for equal treatment in employment and occupation [2000] OJ L303/16, Article 1.
[4] The exception is Article 26 ICCPR that provides a free-standing right to be free of discrimination on the normal protected grounds including 'other status' without any restriction on the context. The UK is bound by Article 26 in international law, but the right is not justiciable.

as cleaning, cooking, and caring for children rather than taking paid work outside. Together, all these special measures with respect to women's human rights represent a transformative agenda that seeks to reconstruct gender relations so that women enjoy both formal and substantive equality in society.[5] Many of the measures that help to achieve this agenda through human rights law were brought together in the UN Convention on the Elimination of All Forms of Discrimination against Women 1979 (CEDAW).

The final three sections of this chapter address the distinctive issues that arise in cases of the application of human rights law to instances of discrimination on the grounds of age, disability and migration status, three grounds that are of particular importance in the context of work. We suggest that the more individualistic approach of human rights law may be more open to the claims of individuals who wish to keep working past a retirement age set by their employer, and works well with the unique needs of each disabled person. However, it is more difficult to use equality law or human rights law to tackle different treatment of workers based on their migration status, despite the intimate connections between migration status, nationality and race.

2. Article 14 ECHR[6]

Article 14 of the ECHR provides:

> The enjoyment of the rights and freedoms set forth in this Convention shall be secured without discrimination on any ground such as sex, race, colour, language, religion, political or other opinion, national or social origin, association with a national minority, property, birth or other status.

(1) The Unlimited Scope of Protected Characteristics in Human Rights Law

We have noted that laws against discrimination such as the Equality Act 2010 list the characteristics or statuses that are protected against detrimental treatment. The protection is also limited to certain contexts such as employment, housing, public services, and education. In contrast, Article 14 is not confined by a fixed list of protected characteristics or a limited range of contexts. The phrase 'other status' can include any status or characteristic that the ECtHR decides is one that is subject to prejudicial disadvantageous treatment. In a case that concluded that Article 14 included sexual orientation, the Court declared that the list of protected characteristics is 'illustrative not exhaustive'.[7]

Unfortunately, governments and powerful groups have fertile imaginations when devising categories of groups of people who will be treated in prejudicial ways. Examples in the political rhetoric of modern times of such groups whose human rights are in jeopardy include 'terrorists', 'fundamentalists', 'illegal migrants', 'aliens', transgender and intersex people, and people with severe mental health disorders. Article 14 enables the Court to scrutinise the creation of new groups of people who are discriminated against in their enjoyment of rights. In *Sidabras v Lithuania*,[8] for example, the legislation in the newly independent state recovering from control by the USSR purported to exclude former KGB employees from not only public sector jobs but

---

[5] S Fredman, 'Substantive Equality Revisited' (2016) 14 *International Journal of Constitutional Law* 712.
[6] S Fredman, 'Emerging from the Shadows: Substantive Equality and Article 14 of the European Convention on Human Rights' (2016) 16 *Human Rights Law Review* 273.
[7] *Salgueiro da Silva Mouta v Portugal* [1999] ECHR 176.
[8] *Sidabras and Dziautas v Lithuania* [2004] ECHR 395.

also most good jobs in the private sector. The ECtHR accepted that such a classification based on employment by the KGB could be impugned under Article 14.

(2) The Possibility of Justifying Direct and Indirect Discrimination to Accommodate Difference

The concept of discrimination is not defined in Article 14. In EU and UK laws against discrimination, a distinction is drawn between 'direct' and 'indirect' discrimination. Although this distinction is not always straightforward to analyse and apply,[9] the gist is that in cases of direct discrimination the protected characteristic or status is the ground for the decision that puts the victim at a disadvantage, whereas in cases of indirect discrimination the rule or practice that is being challenged is on its face neutral and avoids mention of protected characteristics, but the effect of the rule or practice is to place a particular group at a disadvantage compared to others. The principal legal difference between the two kinds of discrimination is that it is extremely hard to justify direct discrimination, whereas indirect discrimination can be justified if it is a proportionate means of pursuing a legitimate aim.[10]

In contrast, under Article 14 ECHR, the test of proportionality is used to determine whether or not there is the kind of discrimination that the Convention should prohibit. Grounds of distinction between persons can be impugned if they have no objective and reasonable justification. The ground of distinction must pursue a legitimate aim in a reasonable relationship of proportionality between the means employed at the aim sought to be realised.[11] In *Sidabras v Lithuania*, for example, although the Court found that the discriminatory measure pursued the legitimate aims of the protection of national security, public order, the economic well-being of the country and the rights and freedoms of others, it concluded that the width of the ban on access to employment was disproportionate.[12]

Similar to the concept of indirect discrimination, the grounds of distinction that can be impugned under Article 14 ECHR include rules and practices that do not on their face appear to lack a legitimate aim, but have a disproportionate adverse effect in practice.[13] In *Thlimmenos v Greece*,[14] the applicant was denied admission to the accountancy profession on account of a rule that excluded all those with a criminal conviction. His conviction had arisen due to his conscientious objection on religious grounds to performing military service. The blanket rule regarding exclusion for criminal convictions served a legitimate aim in general, but in this instance violated Article 14 because without an objective and reasonable justification it failed to treat differently persons whose situations were significantly different.

Because direct discrimination cannot usually be justified, anti-discrimination legislation traditionally blocks positive discrimination in favour of disadvantaged groups. If an employer decides to achieve a better gender balance in the workforce by exclusively hiring suitably qualified women, this decision would almost certainly be regarded as direct discrimination on grounds of

---

[9] K Lippert-Rasmussen, *Born Free and Equal: A Philosophical Inquiry into the Nature of Discrimination* (Oxford, OUP, 2013) 65; H Collins and T Khaitan, 'Indirect Discrimination Law: Controversies and Critical Questions' in H Collins and T Khaitan (eds), *Foundations of Indirect Discrimination Law* (Oxford, Hart Publishing, 2018) 1, 17–25.
[10] Direct discrimination typically contains an exception for 'genuine occupational qualifications': eg Equality Act 2010, Sch 9, Pt 1.
[11] *Belgian Linguistics Case (No 2)*, App Nos 1474/62 et al, Merits, 23 July 1968.
[12] *Sidabras and Dziautas v Lithuania* [2004] ECHR 395, [56]–[60].
[13] *DH v Czech Republic* [2007] ECHR 922 (school tests applied to everyone, but which put Roma children at a particular disadvantage).
[14] *Thlimmenos v Greece* (2000) 31 EHRR 411.

sex against men. Modern anti-discrimination legislation often carves out exceptions for affirmative action, but these can be difficult to invoke in practice because they go against the grain of 'treating likes alike' and tend therefore to be interpreted narrowly by the courts.[15] Under Article 14, however, the test of proportionality may be more accommodating. In some cases, the Court has accepted that positive measures taken by a state to support an under-represented group are pursuing a legitimate aim in a proportionate way. For example, in *Andrle v Czech Republic*, the Court upheld a scheme which allowed women who had taken a career break to raise children to take their state pension earlier than men, in order to rectify the financial hardship this usually generated, at least until the historical inequalities between men and women in the country had been rectified.[16] Indeed, the Court has gone so far as to say in *Sejdić and Finci v Bosnia and Herzegovina* that 'in certain circumstances a failure to attempt to correct inequality through different treatment may, without an objective and reasonable justification, give rise to a breach of' Article 14.[17] This has been used to support positive obligations to provide reasonable accommodation for people with disabilities[18] and to provide extra support for children who had suffered past educational disadvantage as a result of race discrimination.[19]

(3) No Requirement of Group Disadvantage

Traditional formulations of indirect discrimination focus on the idea of 'group disadvantage': the facially-neutral rule puts members of a particular group (including the claimant) at a particular disadvantage compared with other people who do not share the same characteristics.[20] This requirement has proved problematic in cases relating to religion or belief discrimination in particular, because even if an individual identifies with a religious group, some of their beliefs may be special to them. A human rights approach may help to avoid this.

For example, the claimant in *Eweida v UK*[21] was a Coptic Christian who chose to wear a small crucifix. Her employer had a dress code which prohibited visible jewellery. She was sent home without pay for refusing to comply with the dress code. Her discrimination claim in English law failed, because the Court of Appeal held that she could not demonstrate group disadvantage: it was not part of the Christian faith to wear a visible crucifix, nor had any other employees objected to the rule. The Court of Appeal also held that even if there was indirect discrimination, the dress code was justifiable as a proportionate means of pursuing a legitimate aim. On an application to the ECHR, the Court decided the case solely under Article 9. It held that there was an interference with the right to manifest a religion and that the dress code was disproportionate, a finding that was supported in part by the fact that the employer had already amended the rule under pressure from adverse publicity and had permitted Eweida to return to work. The claim under Article 9 ECHR did not require demonstration of a group disadvantage. It was sufficient that Eweida wanted to manifest her religious beliefs by wearing a crucifix even if no-one else in her religion wished to do so. In short, indirectly discriminatory interference with a Convention right can be established without any requirement of proof of group disadvantage.

---

[15] Equality Act 2010, ss 158–159; Case C-409/95 *Marschall v Land Nordrhein-Westfalen* EU:C:1997:533, [1997] ECR I-6363; Case C-407/98 *Abrahamsson v Fogelqvist* EU:C:2000:367, [2000] ECR I-5539.
[16] *Andrle v Czech Republic* [2011] ECHR 326.
[17] *Sejdić and Finci v Bosnia and Herzegovina* [2009] ECHR 2122, [44].
[18] *Çam v Turkey* [2016] ECHR 206.
[19] *Horváth and Kiss v Hungary* [2013] ECHR 92.
[20] Equality Act 2010, s 19.
[21] *Eweida and others v UK* [2013] ECHR 37, [2013] IRLR 231.

(4) The Expansion of the Scope of the Human Rights Themselves in the Interpretation of the Convention

Many claims that invoke Article 14 point to an interference with a Convention right and then complain that the justification put forward by the state for the interference should not be permitted because it involves discriminatory treatment. For example, in *Stec v UK*,[22] the applicant complained of sex discrimination in her entitlement to an industrial injuries benefit following an accident at work. The benefit was discontinued when she reached the state retirement age of 60, though if she had been a man she would have continued to have received it till age 65 which was the state pension age for men. A legally enforceable entitlement to a welfare benefit is regarded as a possession under Protocol 1 to the Convention. The Grand Chamber held, however, that although discrimination on grounds of sex always requires strong justification, in this case the exclusion was justified as it served a legitimate aim in a proportionate manner. The aim of the welfare benefit was to replace lost earnings from work, which would no longer be required once a state pension was paid. Although this reasoning is not entirely convincing as the industrial injury benefit was 'earnings-related' whereas the state pension was a fixed amount, the case shows how Article 14 can be used to challenge unjustifiable discrimination in welfare benefits.

More significantly, Article 14 may also be invoked in cases even where there is no proof of a *breach* of a Convention right. As the Court frequently states, 'For Article 14 to become applicable it suffices that the facts of a case fall within the ambit of another substantive provision of the Convention or its Protocols.'[23]

The 'ambit' of a right can include rights contained in national legislation that are derived from or seek to implement a Convention right, even though they may not be required by the Convention right. Statutory rights within the ambit of a Convention right must comply with Article 14, so that any discrimination in the application of those rights must be justified. For example, in *EB v France*,[24] the claimant argued that she had been discriminated against on grounds of sexual orientation when seeking to adopt a child. Although Article 8 does not require states to grant a right to adopt, the Court held that the French statutory right to adopt fell within the general scope of Article 8 and should therefore not be applied in a discriminatory manner. It was therefore contrary to Article 14, taken together with Article 8, to deny the right to adopt on the ground of sexual orientation. Similarly, in *Markin v Russia*,[25] the applicant worked in the military as a radio intelligence operator, a job also performed by women. Following a divorce on the birth of his third child, he was made legally responsible for caring for his three children. He claimed the same parental rights as those enjoyed by women in the military and all civilian parents. The ECtHR held that the denial of parenting rights was a violation of Article 14, read in conjunction with Article 8. Although a right to parental leave was not guaranteed by Article 8, parental leave was a way of securing respect for private life and the family, so that legislation that implemented a right to parental leave must not discriminate in access to the right.

The Council of Europe agreed a new protocol to the Convention, Protocol 12, that confirms this principle of forbidding discrimination in the application of any legal rights granted under national law.[26] The UK has not ratified this Protocol, but in practice it appears to add little to Article 14 as it has been interpreted.

---

[22] *Stec and others v United Kingdom* [2006] ECHR 1162 (Grand Chamber).
[23] *Thlimmenos v Greece* (2000) 31 EHRR 411.
[24] *EB v France* [2007] ECHR 211 (Grand Chamber).
[25] *Markin v Russia* (2013) 56 EHRR 8, [2012] ECHR 514 (Grand Chamber).
[26] Protocol 12, Article 1: '1. The enjoyment of any right set forth by law shall be secured without discrimination on any ground such as sex, race, colour, language, religion, political or other opinion, national or social origin, association

In the context of work, *Sidabras v Lithuania* illustrates the breadth of the concept of the 'ambit' of a Convention right. The requirement of respect for private life in Article 8 does not on its face protect workers from exclusion from certain kinds of jobs or from dismissal. Yet the case fell within the ambit of Article 8 because the Court considered that a far-reaching ban on taking up private sector employment does affect private life.[27] The ban affected the applicants' ability to develop relationships with the outside world to a very significant degree and created serious difficulties for them in terms of earning their living, with obvious repercussions on the enjoyment of their private lives. The social stigma resulting from the application of the law also damaged their personal lives. Although it is arguable that subsequent decisions of the Court have expanded the scope of Article 8 so that some dismissals are within its scope,[28] it was sufficient in *Sidabras* to find that the dismissals and ban on employment adversely affected the applicants' private lives. Once the claim fell within the ambit of Article 8, the case could be decided under Article 14 as an instance of disproportionate discrimination.

3. Positive Rights for Women

The case for special protection for the rights of women in paid work arises in part from the persistent disadvantage they experience in most countries. A pattern of structural injustice is evidenced by the continuing (though reducing) gender pay gap, the segregation of women into lower paid and precarious or part-time jobs, and impediments to career progression and other disadvantages linked to motherhood. National equality legislation provides strong protection for women against disadvantage in the labour market, though measures such as equal pay laws have never expunged the gender pay gap.[29] Sex discrimination at work is also likely to be contrary to Article 14 taken in conjunction with Article 8, because exclusion from jobs or dismissal on discriminatory grounds is likely to be regarded as an infringement of private life. In *Emel Boyraz v Turkey*,[30] for instance, a woman was initially refused a job as a security guard and then later dismissed from it after nearly three years of satisfactory service on the ground that the job was restricted to people with military experience, which in Turkey was only possible for men to acquire. The ECtHR concluded that the exclusion and dismissal were within the ambit of interference with her private life and that the ground for the employer's actions was discriminatory contrary to Article 14 because it lacked a legitimate aim. The mere fact that security officers had to work on night shifts and in rural areas and might be required to use firearms and physical force under certain conditions could not in itself justify the difference in treatment between men and women.

(1) CEDAW

After three decades of deliberation by the United Nations Commission on the status of women, in 1979 the Convention on the Elimination of All Forms of Discrimination against Women (CEDAW) was adopted by the United Nations General Assembly.[31] The Convention focuses

---

with a national minority, property, birth or other status. 2. No one shall be discriminated against by any public authority on any ground such as those mentioned in paragraph 1.'

[27] *Sidabras and Dziautas v Lithuania* [2004] ECHR 395, [47]–[49].
[28] See chapter 18.
[29] See European Commission, 'The Gender Pay Gap Situation in the EU': https://commission.europa.eu/strategy-and-policy/policies/justice-and-fundamental-rights/gender-equality/equal-pay/gender-pay-gap-situation-eu_en.
[30] *Emel Boyraz v Turkey* [2014] ECHR 1344, [2015] IRLR 164.
[31] United Nations General Assembly, Convention on the Elimination of All Forms of Discrimination against Women, New York, 18 December 1979.

on three dimensions of the situation of women: their legal status, reproductive rights, and the impact of cultural factors on gender relations.

On legal status, the Convention guarantees women the right to vote, to hold public office, and to exercise public functions. It provides for the independent nationality of women regardless of their marital status.[32] The Convention not only asserts the right to work and prohibits discrimination in employment,[33] but also insists that in both civil and business matters all instruments aimed at restricting women's legal capacity 'shall be deemed null and void'.[34]

Unlike other human rights documents, CEDAW raises women's reproductive rights to the status of human rights by including protection against dismissal for pregnancy and maternity and a right to paid maternity leave, and it exhorts states to develop a network of child-care facilities.[35] Article 5 further encourages states to recognise the common responsibility of men and women in the upbringing and development of their children, and for that purpose to provide the necessary social services that would enable parents to combine family obligations with work responsibilities.

The enforcement mechanism of the Convention is that a Committee of representatives of signatory states makes any reports on the progress of those countries towards realising the goals of the Convention. Apart from the USA and Iran, most member states of the United Nations, including the United Kingdom, have ratified and acceded to the Convention.

In practice, much of the necessary legislation to enforce these positive rights for women has been led by the European Union. Its legislation has often been driven by agreements between the social partners. For example, Council Directive 2010/18/EU that entitles both men and women workers to an individual, non-transferable right to parental leave on the birth of a child was the product of a Framework Agreement between BUSINESSEUROPE, UEAPME, CEEP and the ETUC.[36]

As Fredman explains, one of the significant challenges now facing the EU is in ensuring that positive rights for women in connection with pregnancy and parenthood do not become discriminatory by reinforcing stereotypes about women's primary responsibility for childcare.[37] This is a tricky issue to navigate. On the one hand, providing special support to women in connection with childcare may help to advance equality in the workplace by acknowledging the fact that this responsibility still falls disproportionately on many women. On the other hand, if childcare rights are provided mainly to women, there is no incentive for men to take a greater share of responsibility. For example, in *Lommers*, the CJEU upheld a Dutch scheme which provided access to nursery places for female civil servants but not male civil servants (subject to some exceptions), as a means of addressing the under-representation of women in the workplace.[38] This sought to improve women's access to good jobs by acknowledging that inadequate childcare is often a barrier to labour market participation. However, if policies like this are continued indefinitely, they perpetuate the assumption that childcare is a matter for women. In later cases, such as *Roca Alvarez*, the CJEU has begun to allow men to claim entitlement to parental leave rights previously reserved to women.[39] In *Markin*, discussed above, the ECtHR adopted a

---

[32] Article 9.
[33] Article 11.
[34] Article 15.
[35] Article 11.
[36] Council Directive 2010/18/EU of 8 March 2010 on the application of the revised Framework Agreement on parental leave concluded between BUSINESSEUROPE, UEAPME, CEEP and the ETUC and repealing Directive 96/34/EC.
[37] S Fredman, 'Reversing Roles: Bringing Men into the Frame' (2014) 10 *Int'l J L Context* 442.
[38] Case C-476/99 *Lommers v Minister van Landbouw, Natuurbeheer en Visserij* EU:C:2002:183, [2002] ECR I-2891.
[39] Case C-104/09 *Roca Alvarez v Sesa Start Espana ETT SA* EU:C:2010:561, [2011] 1 CMLR 28.

similar approach, noting that both men and women were equally able to provide parental care for children and should be treated equally in matters of leave.[40] On this basis, while women may need some positive rights in connection with pregnancy itself,[41] true substantive equality is best achieved by keeping these rights relatively limited, and ensuring that all parents have access to leave to enable them to provide childcare.

(2) Sex Work

In many countries, prostitution and other kinds of sex work is predominantly performed by women. National laws often criminalise this kind of work or make it subject to legal restrictions. Working at the boundaries of the law, these women are often vulnerable to exploitation, trafficking, and forced labour, as discussed in chapter 9. Whether women should have a right to perform sex work at all is discussed in the context of the right to work in chapter 8.

(3) Domestic Work

Another form of work performed predominantly by women, which may therefore be in need of special regulation, is domestic work.[42] This form of work has particular characteristics which make sectoral regulation appropriate. First, it is performed in private homes. This means that the workers depend on their employer for accommodation and meals as well as work and pay. It also makes them 'invisible' and harder for trade unions, NGOs and others to access. Employers may argue that any inspection of the working environment by the state interferes with their private life. Second, because it is the same kind of work that family members often do for free, there is sometimes a suggestion that it is not 'real' or skilled work. This may lead to claims that it need not be paid, or need not be paid very well. Third, a high proportion of domestic workers are migrants. This makes them additionally vulnerable because they may not be familiar with the language or legal system of the country in which they are working, making it difficult for them to assert their rights. Employers may be able to use their migration status to threaten them, for example, by confiscating their passports or telling them that they do not have the right to be in the country (whether or not this is true) and will be deported if they complain. Some visas for domestic workers are tied to a particular job, removing one of the simplest protections against exploitation: the ability to resign and look for other work.

The ILO Convention on Domestic Workers addresses a number of these issues.[43] First, taking a broadly-framed human rights approach, it requires signatory states to ensure that the basic human rights of domestic workers are respected. These include rights to decent working conditions[44] and to privacy,[45] breaking down the distinction between economic and social rights on the one hand, and civil and political rights on the other.[46] Second, recognising that domestic work is 'work', the Convention requires states to ensure that domestic workers receive equal

---

[40] *Markin*, above n 25.
[41] Though see Fredman, above n 37, 450–51, for competing views on this point.
[42] E Albin and V Mantouvalou, 'The ILO Convention on Domestic Workers: From the Shadows to the Light' (2012) 41 *Industrial Law Journal* 67; L Addati, U Cattaneo, V Esquivel and I Valarino, *Care work and care jobs for the future of decent work* (International Labour Office – Geneva: ILO, 2018).
[43] ILO Domestic Workers Convention and Recommendation, 2011, available at: http://www.ilo.org/ilc/ILCSessions/100thSession/reports/provisional-records/WCMS_157836/lang--en/index.htm.
[44] ibid Article 6.
[45] ibid.
[46] Albin and Mantouvalou, above n 42.

treatment with other kinds of workers in matters such as minimum wages and social security.[47] States, including the UK, often exclude domestic workers from various statutory employment rights, so this is an important means of improving their protection.[48] Third, the Convention addresses some of the common abuses found in the sector. For example, it requires that domestic workers should be allowed to keep their travel documents,[49] and that they should have a minimum weekly rest period which may be spent away from the home in which they work.[50]

The Convention was welcomed as an innovative measure which recognised the special characteristics of domestic work, whilst also promoting equal treatment with other kinds of work. However, with only 36 ratifications so far, there is some way to go before the Convention establishes itself as the standard for the treatment of domestic workers worldwide.[51] The ECtHR has also been active in the field of domestic work, dealing with a number of cases in which domestic workers were held in conditions amounting to forced labour, to be discussed in chapter 9.[52] However, this approach focuses only on the very worst forms of abuse. While this is important, it does not secure decent work for domestic workers in a more general sense.

(4) Unpaid Work at Home and the Social Minimum

Employment law does not apply to unpaid work at home. By this we do not mean domestic work, discussed above, but work performed within the family context by family members. This might include tasks such as cooking, cleaning, washing clothes, household administration and looking after children or elderly relatives. This is clearly 'work', and would be paid if it were carried out by someone outside the family. Despite many advances in equality in the labour market, women still take a disproportionate share of these tasks in heterosexual couple families even when both partners also engage in paid work.[53] And, of course, many women perform these tasks in place of labour market participation.

The unequal distribution of unpaid work at home has three main consequences. First, it impoverishes women, who are not paid for all of their labour.[54] The amount of time available for work is finite, but women miss out on economic opportunities by swapping some or all of their paid work time for unpaid time. This work in the home makes an important contribution to the economy, in the sense that it enables some family members (usually men) to participate freely in the labour market, unencumbered by domestic responsibilities. However, capitalist systems do not acknowledge this contribution, with any money earned being treated, prima facie at least, as the property of the man rather than the couple. Second, it limits women's capacity to participate equally in the paid workforce. For example, a woman who needs to collect her children from school may be constrained as to where she can take a job and how many hours she can work. She may be forced to take a job below her skill level, with less pay, in order to make life manageable. Third, it limits men's participation in family life. While it might be argued that men could simply choose to work fewer hours and do more unpaid work in the home, a vicious

---

[47] Above n 43, Articles 11 and 14.
[48] eg National Minimum Wage Regulations 2015 (SI 2015/621), reg 57(3), now repealed: cf chapter 10.
[49] Above n 43, Article 9(c).
[50] ibid Articles 9 and 10.
[51] See www.ilo.org/dyn/normlex/en/f?p=1000:11300:0::NO:11300:P11300_INSTRUMENT_ID:2551460.
[52] eg *Siliadin v France* (2006) 43 EHRR 16.
[53] For an overview, taking into account the impact of the pandemic, see M Foley and R Cooper, 'Workplace Gender Equality in the Post-Pandemic Era: Where to Next?' (2021) 63 *Journal of Industrial Relations* 463.
[54] See World Economic Forum, *Global Gender Gap Report 2023* (20 June 2023).

circle can develop in which they feel under pressure to earn more money to make up for their partner's loss of earnings from paid work.

One possible solution to this set of problems (often advocated by 1970s feminists under the label 'full commodification'[55]) might be to convert as much unpaid work in the home as possible into paid work, by hiring other people to do it. Some wealthy families in nations of the Global North may be able to hire cooks, cleaners and nannies to perform domestic tasks while both partners work. However, this is clearly not affordable for most people. It is also potentially problematic from a discrimination perspective.[56] As we noted above, many domestic workers are migrants from the Global South whose work is badly paid and poorly valued (in part, because of a perception that it should be provided by a family member for free). The more equal labour market participation of a few privileged women may be being facilitated by the creation of poor-quality jobs for vulnerable women.

More realistic solutions probably require a multi-faceted approach, with many options falling outside the purview of labour law. One obvious strategy is to make use of the social security system to recognise women's contribution to the economy via unpaid work. Arguably, the UK's child benefit system performs this function to some extent, by providing families with a payment per child. However, this is now subject to the 'benefit cap', introduced in 2012, which places an upper limit on the amount of money a non-working household may receive in benefits.[57] This disproportionately affects women, since most non-working households are headed by a single parent, usually a woman.[58] However, the Supreme Court held, by a majority, that although it was indirectly discriminatory, it was justified as a legitimate measure to encourage people into work and to reduce welfare spending.[59] A particular problem for social security systems in supporting women is that they often fail to acknowledge their specific needs.[60] Historically, social security regimes assumed that most households would consist of a male breadwinner, with the female partner providing unpaid work in the home. More modern attempts to capture rights to social security have failed to break away from this paradigm. For example, Lamarche[61] criticises the ILO Recommendation on social security for its focus on contributory benefits.[62] It emphasises the importance of getting women into formal work so that they can contribute to (and thus receive benefits from) the system. But this ignores the situation of women who either do not work at all, or work in the informal sector. Any contributions-based system is problematic from a gender perspective because of the likelihood that women will have significant periods of time with no contributions while they are taking breaks from the labour market to engage in unpaid work in the home.

From a labour law perspective, probably the most important contributions can be made in two ways. First, the various leave entitlements noted above, such as maternity, paternity and parental leave, should be designed in ways which are as equal as possible as between couples. Making some

---

[55] For discussion, see J Williams, *Unbending Gender: Why Family and Work Conflict and What to Do about It* (OUP, 2001), ch 2.
[56] J Fudge, 'Feminist Reflections on the Scope of Labour Law: Domestic Work, Social Reproduction, and Jurisdiction' (2014) 22 *Feminist Legal Studies* 1.
[57] Benefit Cap (Housing Benefit) Regulations 2012 (SI 2012/2994).
[58] S Palmer, 'The "Benefit Cap" Scheme and the UN Convention on the Rights of the Child' (2016) 75 *Cambridge Law Journal* 34.
[59] *R (SG) v Secretary of State for Work and Pensions* [2015] UKSC 16, [2015] 1 WLR 1449.
[60] CESCR, 'Statement on social protection floors: an essential element of the right to social security and of the sustainable development goals' (E/C.12/54/3, 6 March 2015), para 9.
[61] L Lamarche, 'Unpacking the ILO's Social Protection Floor Recommendation from a Women's Rights Perspective', in B Goldblatt and L Lamarche (eds), *Women's Rights to Social Security and Social Protection* (Oxford, Hart 2014).
[62] ILO Social Protection Floors Recommendation, 2012 (No 202).

leave available only to men and attaching proper pay to the leave may be helpful here. Second, it may be helpful to consider the organisation of working time more generally. Since the Covid-19 pandemic, there has been much greater recognition of the possibility of working flexible hours or from home, but the law still falls far short of, for example, a right to do any job on a part-time basis. Ensuring that both partners in a couple have as much flexibility as possible to manage their time for both paid and unpaid work might also contribute to a shift in culture.

4. Age Discrimination and the Right to Work

The EU Framework Directive 2000/78 on discrimination in employment includes age discrimination as a protected characteristic. Although age is not explicitly mentioned in Article 14 ECHR, it has been found to fall within the category of 'other status' in a number of cases.[63] Inevitably EU law recognises that much age discrimination in connection with work is justifiable, and the ECtHR has so far refused to equate age discrimination with discrimination on other grounds.[64] This reflects the prevalence of age discrimination in the labour market, some of which is clearly justified. For example, school age children can be excluded from most forms of employment in order to protect their wellbeing and educational opportunities. However, it is less clear whether the differential treatment of age discrimination is, itself, defensible.[65]

This differential treatment arises on two levels. First, the Directive itself provides, in Article 6(1)(a), a broad basis for governments and employers to justify age discrimination in employment:

> [D]ifferences of treatment on grounds of age shall not constitute discrimination, if, within the context of national law, they are objectively and reasonably justified by a legitimate aim, including legitimate employment policy, labour market and vocational training objectives, and if the means of achieving that aim are appropriate and necessary.

This allows direct age discrimination – the use of age as a criterion for decision-making – to be justified.

Second, it is arguable that the CJEU (and other courts) subject age discrimination claims to less searching scrutiny. For example, an upper age limit for airline pilots has been found to be a genuine and determining occupational requirement under Article 4 of the Directive, provided that it is set at the 'right' age.[66] This is so even though age in this context is being used as a proxy for the worker's capacity to perform their job in a safe and reliable way. While this is clearly vital for aviation safety, it is hard to imagine a proxy being allowed in any other kind of discrimination. For example, an employer would be expected to determine whether a woman could carry out a job requiring heavy lifting rather than stating that only men could apply. Similarly, younger workers are often treated differently in matters such as the National Minimum Wage (NMW) or redundancy pay. The NMW has two age-related rates in addition to the main adult rate (18–20, under 18)[67] and the calculation of redundancy pay is linked to the age of the employee, so that a person who has worked for the same length of time for the employer will receive a different amount depending on whether they are under 22, 22–41, or 41 or older.[68]

---

[63] eg *British Gurkha Welfare Society v UK* (2017) 64 EHRR 11, [88].
[64] ibid.
[65] S Goosey, 'Is Age Discrimination a Less Serious Form of Discrimination?' (2019) 39 *Legal Studies* 533.
[66] Case C-447/09 *Prigge v Deutsche Lufthansa AG* EU:C:2011:573, [2011] IRLR 1052.
[67] www.gov.uk/national-minimum-wage-rates.
[68] Employment Rights Act 1996, s 162, and see *Lockwood v Department of Work and Pensions* [2013] EWCA Civ 1195, [2014] ICR 1257 for an unsuccessful challenge to age-related rates in the Civil Service redundancy scheme.

Various justifications are offered for these rules, such as young people's lack of experience or financial responsibilities, but once again, these are proxies. Although it is true that a younger worker will not normally have extensive financial responsibilities, some young workers do have a family to support.

The EU Directive is silent on the question whether compulsory retirement ages are permissible in general terms. Some countries grant employers the right to dismiss employees at a fixed age such as 67, or a similar age that often coincides with the age at which state pensions are payable. Other countries permit employers to rely upon a contract term that terminates even permanent jobs at a fixed age. In the UK such a contractual term is valid and provides an effective defence against claims for unfair dismissal if it is justified as part of a coherent human resources policy.[69] For example, an employer may want to use a fixed retirement age in order to create opportunities for hiring and promoting junior employees and to avoid painful performance management procedures that older workers may find demeaning.[70] The age of compulsory retirement needs to be chosen so that it achieves such legitimate purposes as intergenerational balance without unnecessarily disadvantaging older workers by, for instance, forcing them to retire when they are still performing the job extremely well and are not blocking the progression of junior employees. It should be noted, however, that evidence to support the alleged benefits of compulsory retirement ages is weak. In practice, younger workers cannot always substitute for older, more experienced workers, and there is evidence that rates of employment for younger and older people rise and fall together rather than younger workers replacing older workers.[71] More generally, as people live longer, older workers may need to continue working in order to enjoy an adequate income.

A compulsory retirement age also raises the question whether it amounts to an unjustifiable interference with the right to work. Although older workers are not excluded from the labour market entirely, because some employers may hire them post-retirement, almost certainly compulsory retirement will bring their career to a halt and may force them to seek work outside their chosen profession or vocation. The right to engage in work is recognised in Article 15(1) of the Charter of Fundamental Rights of the EU. As we saw above in *Sidabras*, the right to work can also be protected under Article 8 ECHR where a person is excluded from most jobs or a career of their choice without adequate justification.[72] The CJEU has held that provided a compulsory retirement age does not have the effect of excluding a person entirely from the labour market, the interference with the right to work is justified if the compulsory retirement age is based on legitimate labour market and human resources policies, such as a fair intergenerational distribution of jobs, and is a proportionate measure.[73] Furthermore, the fact that compulsory retirement may cause some degree of economic hardship to the dismissed employee is not a sufficient ground for regarding the policy as unjustified.[74]

Would the ECtHR similarly conclude that a compulsory retirement age is not an interference with Article 14 taken in conjunction with Article 8? Although the two senior European courts try for reasons of comity to reach similar results, the focus of the EU Directive on labour market considerations such as creating job opportunities for younger workers fits uneasily within the

---

[69] *Seldon v Clarkson Wright & Jakes* [2012] UKSC 16, [2012] ICR 716.
[70] ibid; Case C-159/10 *Fuchs v Land Hessen* EU:C:2011:508, [2011] 3 CMLR 47.
[71] E Dewhurst, 'Intergenerational Balance, Mandatory Retirement and Age Discrimination in Europe: How can the ECJ Better Support National Courts in Finding a Balance Between the Generations?' (2013) 5 *Common Market Law Review* 1333.
[72] *Sidabras*, above n 8.
[73] Case C-141/11 *Hörnfeldt v Posten Meddelande AB* ECLI:EU:C:2012:421.
[74] ibid.

framework of the ECHR. Assuming that the court decided in a case that there was an interference in private life caused by a mandatory retirement age, perhaps because the effect of the termination was to deprive a person of the chance to pursue their chosen occupation or because it removed a person from contact with their circle of friends, the question would be whether the dismissal served a legitimate aim in a proportionate way. Would labour market considerations such as tackling high levels of youth unemployment count as a legitimate aim, and, if so, would the Court be as ready as the CJEU to conclude that the measure was proportionate? For example, the CJEU rejected a challenge to a compulsory retirement age of 68 for university professors in Bulgaria, even though the rule would prevent them for ever pursuing their career, on the ground that the rule might serve a legitimate purpose of opening up the limited number of jobs to junior staff.[75] The ECtHR hearing the same case might conclude that this discriminatory interference with the right to work contrary to Article 14 read in conjunction with Article 8 was not proportionate because dismissal caused a serious loss to the elderly professor that was hard to justify as a measure designed to protect the rights of others. As we have seen in other chapters, the ECtHR is more likely to favour the rights of the individual over broader social considerations.[76]

5. Disability Discrimination

Although it is not listed in Article 14, disability has been recognised by the ECtHR as a status that may be a ground for prejudicial discrimination. In *IB v Greece*,[77] the applicant had been dismissed from his job when his co-workers refused to work with him on hearing that he was HIV positive, even though it was explained to them that they were not at risk of contracting the disease. This dismissal was regarded as an interference with the right to respect for private life in Article 8 because the stigma of the dismissal might damage many aspects of his life (though in fact he had quickly obtained a different job). Article 14 was applicable, following *Kiyutin v Russia*,[78] which held that a person's health status, including such conditions as HIV infection, should be covered – either as a form of disability or in the same way as a disability – by the term 'other status' in the text of Article 14 of the Convention.

The UK has ratified and acceded to the UN Convention on the Rights of Persons with Disabilities (CRPD). Under the Convention there is a UN Committee state reporting system and, under an Optional Protocol, the possibility of individual complaints to the Committee if all domestic remedies have been exhausted. The United Kingdom Independent Mechanism (UKIM) is tasked by law with promoting, protecting and monitoring implementation of the CRPD across the UK. Its reports reveal how UK laws and social services fall short of the needs of disabled people and the standards of the Convention.[79] For instance, employment rates for disabled people across the UK remain lower than employment rates of non-disabled people (53% compared to 82%); and disabled workers generally earn significantly less than non-disabled workers, and this gap has widened over time.[80]

---

[75] *Georgiev (Social policy)* ECLI:EU:C:2010:699, [2010] EUECJ C-250/09, [2011] 2 CMLR 7.
[76] eg closed shop in chapter 5.
[77] *IB v Greece*, App No 552/10, Judgment of 3 October 2013. See also the South African case: *Hoffmann v South African Airways* (CCT 17/00) of 28 September 2000.
[78] *Kiyutin v Russia* (2011) 53 EHRR 26.
[79] UK Independent Mechanism, *Seven Years On: disabled people's rights to independent living, employment and standard of living in the UK*, August 2023.
[80] Department of Work and Pensions (2023), Official Statistics: Employment of disabled people in 2022.

As we have already seen in relation to women's rights, a basic right to equal treatment with a comparator is often insufficient to achieve genuine substantive equality. The same is true of disability: equal treatment with a non-disabled person is not helpful where the needs of a disabled person are different. The Convention reflects this by means of two important features of Article 27: in paragraph (i), the duty to ensure that reasonable accommodation is provided to persons with disabilities in the workplace, and, more generally, in paragraph (h), the permissibility of affirmative action in favour of disabled persons to support equality of opportunity. We will examine each in turn.

In English law, the first of these duties is expressed in statute as the duty to make reasonable adjustments under s 20 of the Equality Act 2010. This is a threefold duty: to take reasonable steps to avoid a 'substantial disadvantage' caused to a disabled person by a provision, criterion or practice, or by a physical feature of the workplace, or to take steps to provide an auxiliary aid where a disabled person would be put at a disadvantage without it. In the employment context, this duty is reactive. In other words, it applies only when the employer has a disabled job applicant or worker. This contrasts with the anticipatory duty applicable to public services and public functions, which requires the provider to take steps to make their service accessible even if there is no specific disabled person seeking to use the service at the time.[81] To illustrate the contrast, an employer is only under a duty to take (reasonable) steps to make its premises accessible if a person with physical impairments works there, whereas the provider of a public bus service must have wheelchair ramps available. This is not uncontroversial: if workplaces were required to meet certain basic standards of accessibility, there would be no need for (at least some) disabled workers to ask for reasonable accommodation. This might go some way towards tackling the disability employment gap.

Of course, it is important to bear in mind that, even with improved accessibility across the board, we would still need the reasonable accommodation duty in order to address the specific needs of each disabled person. This is one of the advantages of the current approach: its ability to focus on the individual. For example, although autism is a relatively common condition, the needs of people with autism vary considerably and there is no 'one size fits all' set of adjustments for all workers with the condition. The employer is only subject to the duty where it knows or can reasonably be expected to know that the person is disabled and is likely to be put at a substantial disadvantage, as explained above. While this is fair to employers, who cannot be expected to deal with issues of which they have no knowledge, it may sometimes present a dilemma for a person whose disability is not apparent and who may be reluctant to disclose it.

In English law, one important qualification to the duty is the 'reasonableness' element. This allows an employer to decline to make an adjustment on various grounds, including cost, practicality and the effectiveness of the adjustment. A smaller employer may not have to make the same adjustments as a larger employer. But the availability of public funding, for example, via the government's Access to Work scheme, may make an otherwise unaffordable adjustment possible, even for a smaller firm. Importantly, the reasonableness of the adjustment is an objective matter for the tribunal to determine.[82] It is not confined to assessing the reasonableness of the approach taken by the employer. Despite this, there is less case law on the duty to make reasonable adjustments than one might expect. It seems likely that this is because challenging the employer's decision through a tribunal (particularly whilst still employed) is too daunting for many potential claimants. This may be another factor in the disability employment gap.

---

[81] A Lawson and M Orchard, 'The Anticipatory Reasonable Adjustment Duty: Removing the Blockages?' (2021) 80 *Cambridge Law Journal* 308.

[82] *Smith v Churchills Stairlifts plc* [2005] EWCA Civ 1220, [2006] ICR 524.

Another important feature of Article 27 CRPD, which is replicated in English law, is that protection for disabled people is not required to be symmetrical. Whereas race discrimination law protects all racial groups, not just minority groups, disability discrimination law does not protect people with no disability. This means that non-disabled people cannot challenge an employer's support for – or even preference for – a disabled person. This insulates measures designed to accommodate people with disabilities from challenge.

6. Challenging Exclusion – Migrant Workers

One of the difficulties with the law as it currently stands is its capacity to exclude certain groups of people from the scope of protection in a way that is, in itself, arguably discriminatory. We saw above that unpaid work in the home, carried out predominantly by women, falls entirely outside the scope of employment law. But it can be difficult to use equality law or human rights law to challenge structural problems of this kind. We conclude the chapter with another example of structural inequality: the law's treatment of migrant workers.

In most cases, migrants do have access (in principle at least) to all the rights the law offers to employees or workers (depending on how they are classified). However, there are a number of legal and practical problems. One is that many migrant workers are tied to a particular employer and job by means of their visa.[83] This limits their ability to exercise one of the simplest routes to getting better protection: resigning and finding another job. That work should be freely chosen is an important aspect of both the right to work and the freedom from forced labour. Even where migrants do have the right to change jobs, this is often quite constrained, for example, because they must find a new job within a short period of time. Another issue is that migrant workers – particularly those in the UK for a short time – may not be able to access labour law enforcement through the tribunal system. For example, even if the individual is able to find out about their rights and bring a claim, which is unlikely in itself, the hearing may take place many months after they have returned to their home country.[84] Finally, migrants are more likely than UK national workers to be affected by the rules on illegality. This is because it is an offence to work without the correct migration status.[85] So-called illegal working might arise for a variety of different reasons, many not the fault of the worker themselves, ranging from deliberate trafficking to innocent errors on the part of the employer. Where it applies, the doctrine of illegality may prevent the worker from bringing claims, though the courts do now use a public policy test to determine when it should be invoked which may be more protective of workers.[86]

Is it possible to use human rights law or equality law to challenge any of these examples of unequal treatment? The Equality Act 2010 includes nationality and national origins in its

---

[83] See chapter 9.
[84] Official statistics on this issue are difficult to obtain, but it is believed that the average wait for a hearing is about one year: M Machell, 'Employment tribunal delays increase 60% since 2010', HR Magazine (24 August 2023).
[85] Immigration Act 2016, s 34.
[86] *Allen v Hounga* [2014] UKSC 47, [2014] ICR 847; *Okedina v Chikale* [2019] EWCA Civ 1393, [2019] ICR 1635. For detailed analysis, see A Bogg and S Green, 'Rights are not just for the Virtuous: What *Hounga* Means for the Illegality Defence in the Discrimination Torts' (2015) 44 *Industrial Law Journal* 101; A Bogg, '*Okedina v Chikale* and Contract Illegality: New Dawn or False Dawn?' (2020) 49 *Industrial Law Journal* 258.

definition of race for the purposes of equality law.[87] In *R v Rogers*, albeit in the very different context of a criminal conviction, the House of Lords held that 'foreigners' could constitute a race under this definition, even in the most general terms.[88] However, the courts have drawn a distinction between nationality and immigration status, even though there is a clear connection between the two. In *Onu v Akwiwu*, a Nigerian domestic worker was subjected to harsh treatment by her employer, including low pay, insufficient rest breaks and the confiscation of her passport.[89] The tribunal found as a fact that she had been treated less favourably than the employer would have treated a person who was not a migrant worker. The question before the Supreme Court was whether this amounted to race discrimination based on nationality. Baroness Hale accepted that immigration status was a 'function' of nationality, in the sense that British nationals were not subject to immigration rules whereas non-British nationals were. However, she found that the particular reason for the claimant's treatment was that she was particularly vulnerable as the holder of an overseas domestic worker visa under the rules obtaining at that time. Other non-British nationals, for example, those with the right to work in the UK, would not have been treated so badly. Thus, the treatment was on grounds of 'immigration status' – which Parliament had not included in the Equality Act 2010 – and not 'nationality' – which it had. The claim for race discrimination thus failed.

Does Article 14 ECHR offer any help in this context? 'Immigration status' has been accepted as falling within the concept of 'other status' for the purposes of Article 14, even though it is a legal status rather than a personal one.[90] Refugee status is even more clearly within Article 14, since it is not chosen.[91] Most of the Court's case law so far has been concerned with migrants' rights in relation to family reunification, housing or education for their children. The first two are particularly interesting because Article 8 does not give a right to family reunification or housing, but the Court has held that these matters fall within the 'ambit' of Article 8, as explored above, so national rules must not therefore be discriminatory under Article 14. Thus, in *Pajić v Croatia*, it was held to be discriminatory to deny family reunification rights to partners in same-sex couples.[92] However, the Court's scrutiny is more light-touch in some of these cases. For example, in *Bah*, a refusal to give priority to a homeless asylum-seeker in the allocation of social housing was held to be justified even though it discriminated on grounds of migration status.[93] The Court accepted that the state had a wide margin of appreciation when the proportionality test was applied to cases involving the allocation of scarce state resources, and that distinctions based on migration status were easier to justify than distinctions based on personal characteristics.

These cases suggest that there may be some scope for challenges to the unfair treatment of migrant workers based on Article 14. For example, a specific exclusion of migrant workers from a particular employment right might be open to challenge. However, there are two major obstacles to claims of this type. First, it would be necessary to prove that a particular employment right was either protected by the Convention itself or fell within the 'ambit' of another right. The limitation of the Convention to civil and political rights is a particular sticking-point here.

---

[87] Equality Act 2010, s 9(1).
[88] *R v Rogers* [2007] UKHL 8, [2007] 2 AC 62.
[89] *Onu v Akwiwu* [2016] UKSC 31, [2016] ICR 756. See also *Mruke v Khan* [2018] EWCA Civ 280, [2018] ICR 1146.
[90] *Hode and Abdi v United Kingdom* (2013) 56 EHRR 27.
[91] ibid.
[92] *Pajić v Croatia* [2016] ECHR 203.
[93] *Bah v United Kingdom* (2012) 54 EHRR 21.

Second, it is relatively unusual to find express exclusions for migrant workers. Instead, there may be exclusions which have a disproportionate impact on migrant workers (such as the exclusion of domestic workers from certain types of protection[94]) or exclusions which are practical rather than legal in nature, as outlined above. This adds another hurdle in terms of proving that the exclusion is on the grounds of immigration status. Again, then, while the rights perspective helps us to critique the legal position, it does not translate quite so readily into plausible legal claims for migrant workers.

---

[94] Above n 49.

5

Freedom of Association

1.	Freedom of Association: Sources of Protection and the Integrated Approach	4.	The Closed Shop
2.	The Right to Organise as a Fundamental Human Right	5.	Trade Union Autonomy and Human Rights
3.	Blacklisting and Human Rights	6.	Conclusion

In 2009, it emerged that many workers, particularly in the construction industry, were blacklisted. Blacklisting is the practice of compiling information on individuals regarding their trade union membership and activities, and sharing this information with employers and employment agencies so as to enable them to discriminate against those blacklisted in obtaining a job or in their treatment at work. The information serves as a reason to dismiss and systematically deny employment to workers who are viewed as 'trouble-makers'. It was revealed to be a widespread practice in the construction industry.[1] Many blacklisted workers were repeatedly dismissed and not hired to work for long periods of time. These workers' descriptions of the practice of blacklisting and its effects serve to illustrate its gravity. A blacklisted bricklayer described it as follows:

> The Blacklist is an economic, social and political prison. I have served a life sentence and other workers continue to be imprisoned. In cases like my own, the Blacklist effectively takes the form of house arrest because of its effect on a person's social life. My wife was also deeply affected and badly scarred. More often than not, she was forced to financially support me, and our two children, on her low wage as a care worker. This has had a devastating effect on our standard of living. To her great credit my wife supported me and our family unstintingly. She held us together when things got really tough – which it did quite often. We kept our dignity intact and just managed to keep our heads above water by almost completely sacrificing our social life. My wife had to take out loans, which we could not afford, since my credit rating was zero due to very long spells of unemployment. All of this is the direct result of the building employers deliberately using the Blacklist, time and again, to deny me the right to work and to earn a living.[2]

That people's lives are destroyed for the sole reason that they exercise the right to organise in a trade union may appear shocking. Is freedom of association not a basic human right of workers and an essential means to counteract the inequality of bargaining power at work through trade union activity? What does it mean when we say that workers have freedom of association and the right to organise in a trade union if it does not prohibit blacklisting?

---

[1] The description of the problem of blacklisting is based on the discussion in H Collins, K Ewing and A McColgan, *Labour Law*, 2nd edn (Cambridge, CUP, 2019) 483 ff.
[2] ibid 455.

This chapter will consider the right to organise and the extent to which it provides effective legal protection to workers from trade union discrimination at work. While blacklisting is one of the most serious examples of this, because it involves the coordinated repression of trade union membership and activities by employers acting in collusion, trade union discrimination can occur in many forms. If freedom of association means anything of substance for workers, it must surely encompass basic legal protections from employer victimisation for union membership, activities, and use of union services.

It is also important to consider other challenges that raise different kinds of conflict between individual and collective freedoms. For example, is there a right *not* to join a trade union? The 'closed shop' was an arrangement whereby employers and trade unions agreed to enforce union membership requirements. A worker might object to trade union membership for conscientious reasons, for example because of their religious or political beliefs. If closed shops are widespread, they may also be systematically prevented from earning a living when they act in accordance with their conscience and refuse to join. This may be analogous to our blacklisting problem. If we are concerned to protect union members and activists from discrimination at work, should human rights law protect non-unionists from discrimination to the same extent?

Finally, to what extent should trade unions themselves be allowed to discriminate against applicants and trade union members? Trade unions also have their own independent rights to freedom of association, and this can lead to a clash of rights between the trade union and its members. The answer to this conflict will often depend upon the grounds of discrimination. Discrimination by trade unions because of sex or race should be challenged. Otherwise, unjustified barriers to equal pay would be entrenched and the equal participation of citizens in paid employment would be impeded. But what about political discrimination by trade unions against activists on the Far Right seeking to infiltrate the union? Where there is a fundamental clash of political ideologies, it might be appropriate to strike a different balance between the competing rights of trade unions and members. If individual workers can conscientiously object to the closed shop for political reasons, perhaps trade unions themselves can conscientiously object to compelled association with those whose political views are antithetical to the union's objectives.

1. Freedom of Association: Sources of Protection and the Integrated Approach

Such is the importance of freedom of association for workers that immediately after the statement that 'labour is not a commodity', the International Labour Organization (ILO) Declaration of Philadelphia of 1944 proclaimed that freedom of association, together with freedom of expression, 'are essential to sustained progress'. Respect for freedom of association has long been a fundamental constitutional obligation inherent in ILO membership. Freedom of association is also explicitly protected in several other human rights documents. Article 11(1) of the European Convention on Human Rights (ECHR) provides as follows: 'Everyone has the right to freedom of peaceful assembly and to freedom of association with others, including the right to form and to join trade unions for the protection of his interests.' The provision does not explicitly protect other collective labour rights, which were instead included in the counterpart of the Convention in the area of social rights, the European Social Charter (ESC). Article 5 of the ESC protects the right to organise and Article 6 the right to collective bargaining, including a right to strike.[3]

---

[3] Articles 5 and 6 of the European Social Charter.

Freedom of association and the right to organise is also protected in ILO Convention, 1948 (No 87). ILO Convention, 1949 (No 98) protects freedom of association and collective bargaining. These are fundamental ILO Conventions with constitutional significance. Freedom of association and the right to collective bargaining is also protected in the ILO Declaration on Fundamental Principles and Rights at Work, adopted in 1998 and amended in 2022. There is widespread international convergence on the idea that freedom of association in trade unions is a fundamental human right.

The main question that the ECtHR had to address from early on in the case law was what more concrete components Article 11 protects. In the early years, the Court was very reluctant to read social rights into Article 11. For instance, in a line of cases that were decided in the 1970s, 1980s and 1990s, looking at trade union rights, it repeatedly ruled that when a right can be classified as social and is protected in the ESC or in instruments of the ILO, it ought to be excluded from the scope of the ECHR. When applicants alleged that Article 11 encompasses a right to strike, for instance, the claim was rejected.[4] Similarly, the right to consultation and the right to collective bargaining were not regarded as essential components of Article 11 in the early case law of the Court.[5]

What was striking in this context was that at the same time as the ECtHR was reluctant to protect trade union rights, it was willing to recognise the rights of individuals who refused to be trade union members. This occurred in a line of cases on 'closed shop' arrangements, namely arrangements that effectively enforced compulsory union membership.[6] The decisions of the ECtHR in these cases led scholars to argue that it showed a greater interest in individual autonomy rather than collective solidarity.[7]

The picture has changed in more recent years, when courts and other bodies applied an 'integrated approach' to the interpretation of civil and political rights.[8] This is an interpretive technique whereby bodies protecting civil and political rights take note of economic and social rights materials. In the context of Article 11, the Court started to integrate social and labour rights in the material scope of Article 11, looking at the content of social and labour rights treaties as a source of inspiration rather than just using them to exclude rights from the scope of the Convention. It had already used the 'integrated approach' in relation to the 'closed shop' and the right to disassociate. It was now doing so to support the development of positive trade union rights, such as the right to collective bargaining and the strong protection of trade union activities. However, the use of the 'integrated approach' has not been applied consistently by the ECtHR. There are also cases where Article 11 deviates from ILO and ESC standards on trade union freedoms, such as the prohibition of secondary strike action.[9]

2. The Right to Organise as a Fundamental Human Right

ILO and ECHR Standards

The most basic element of trade union freedom of association is the right to organise. The victimisation of trade unionists by employers is one of the most serious violations of freedom of

---

[4] *Schmidt and Dahlstrom v Sweden* A 21; 1 EHRR 637.
[5] *National Union of Belgian Police v Belgium* A 19; 1 EHRR 578.
[6] *Young, James and Webster v UK* [1981] ECHR 4.
[7] T Novitz, *International and European Protection of the Right to Strike* (Oxford, OUP, 2003) 238. See also K Ewing, 'The Implications of Wilson and Palmer' (2003) 32 *ILJ* 1 at 4.
[8] See further chapter 2. See also V Mantouvalou, 'Labour Rights in the European Convention on Human Rights: An Intellectual Justification for an Integrated Approach to Interpretation' (2013) 13 *Human Rights Law Review* 529.
[9] See further chapter 7.

association. If workers can be dismissed or penalised by employers for their trade union membership or activities, this is likely to have a serious chilling effect on unionisation in the workplace. These concerns are even stronger where trade union representatives have been victimised or dismissed by the employer.[10] Under both the ILO and ECHR, states are under a positive duty to provide workers with real and effective protection from anti-union discrimination. The effective protection of this right to organise provides the basic foundation for trade union representation, collective bargaining, and the right to strike. The right to organise is at the fundamental core of freedom of association. Without it, the foundation for everything else that trade unions do in the workplace is very shaky indeed.

The main provision of international law on the right to organise is Article 1 of ILO Convention 98 concerning the application of the Principles of the Right to Organise and Collective Bargaining (1949). This provides that:

1. Workers shall enjoy adequate protection against acts of anti-union discrimination in respect of their employment.
2. Such protection shall apply more particularly in respect of acts calculated to–
    (a) make the employment of a worker subject to the condition that he shall not join a union or shall relinquish trade union membership;
    (b) cause the dismissal or otherwise prejudice a worker by reason of union membership or because of participation in union activities outside working hours or, with the consent of the employer, within working hours.'

In Article 3, the Convention also emphasises the importance of measures 'for the purpose of *ensuring* respect for the right to organise' (emphasis added). This means that it is not enough to guarantee the rights on paper. They must be backed by effective and accessible procedures and strong remedies. The ILO also puts a strong emphasis on the protection of worker representatives from victimisation.[11] The victimisation of trade union representatives can have a particularly damaging impact on the union's ability to represent workers.

The text of C98 Article 1 indicates a broad scope for legal protection. There are two aspects to this. The first is its coverage of the many different forms of workplace victimisation, such as refusal of employment, dismissal, and other forms of detriment like denials of promotion, suspension, or disciplinary warnings ('or otherwise prejudice a worker'). The second is its protection of union membership *and* participation in union activities. Some of the basic legal definitions in the Trade Union and Labour Relations (Consolidation) Act 1992 (TULCRA 1992), such as the definition of 'appropriate time' for protected trade union activities,[12] reflect the structure of C98 Article 1(2)(b). As we shall see, there are also some important differences in the domestic legal model of the right to organise under TULRCA 1992 when compared with C98.

The ILO Committee on Freedom of Association (CFA) has developed an extensive set of principles to give effect to the relevant ILO conventions. It has stated that 'anti-union discrimination is one of the most serious violations of freedom of association, as it may jeopardize the very existence of trade unions'.[13] Given its status as one of the most serious violations, the Committee has

---

[10] A Bogg and KD Ewing, *The Political Attack on Workplace Representation* (Liverpool, Institute of Employment Rights, 2013).
[11] See, for example, ILO Convention No 135 on Workers' Representatives, 1971, especially Article 1.
[12] s 146(2).
[13] Digest of decisions and principles of the Freedom of Association Committee of the Governing Body of the ILO (2018) 1072.

also emphasised the importance of an effective procedural framework for securing redress. From an ILO perspective, access to justice is fundamental to the right to organise. The legal framework should provide redress for workers alleging discrimination that is impartial, inexpensive, and prompt.[14]

In recent times, the ECtHR has been very active in developing the right to organise under Article 11. This has been supported by its use of the 'integrated approach', using the ILO materials to support a purposive and dynamic interpretation of Article 11. The ILO's emphasis on access to justice has also been an important feature of the ECtHR's case law. The leading case is *Danilenkov and others v Russia*.[15] This involved a broad pattern of anti-union victimisation against union members in the Kaliningrad seaport. There were different forms of victimisation, including adverse work allocation decisions, reduction of earnings, the oppressive use of workplace safety tests to make employment more difficult for trade unionists, and eventually mass redundancies. The affected workers had found it difficult to secure adequate redress in the Russian courts. According to the ECtHR, 'States are required under Articles 11 and 14 of the Convention to set up a judicial system that ensures real and effective protection against anti-union discrimination.'[16] In *Danilenkov*, national law did not ensure this protection because it was based on criminal liability. The evidential burden to prove discriminatory intent beyond reasonable doubt meant that anti-union discrimination was difficult to challenge in court. The initiative to prosecute was also with state agencies rather than individual victims. 'Real and effective' protection required civil recourse that could be pursued by the victims themselves, and subject to the less stringent evidential and procedural rules in the civil courts.

The ECtHR has taken a strong approach to individual discrimination wrongs under Article 11, reflecting the gravity of such violations. Five specific features of this approach should be emphasised. First, protection is not restricted to union membership, but it also includes trade union activities and being represented by the trade union.[17] Secondly, the ECtHR has emphasised that even 'minimal sanctions dissuade trade union members from freely engaging in their activities'.[18] It therefore extends beyond the most serious forms of interference such as dismissal. In *Wilson v UK*, a legal framework that permitted the use of financial offers to induce trade union members to opt out of collective bargaining was found to be a violation of Article 11.[19] Thirdly, the court has recognised that the trade union's Article 11 rights may be engaged independently where individual workers are subjected to discrimination for their membership and activities. This is because there is a strong overlap between the trade union's rights and the rights of its members. An attack on one is effectively an attack on both of them because their rights are complementary under Article 11.[20] This could mean that the union itself should have independent standing to enforce the law and seek its own remedies and redress. Fourthly, where a *prima facie* case of discrimination has been established on the facts, the burden of proof should then shift to the

---

[14] See the CFA principles set out by the ECtHR in *Danilenkov v Russia* [2009] ECHR 1243, [107]–[108].
[15] ibid.
[16] ibid [124].
[17] Trade union activities under Article 11 has been interpreted broadly to include acts and speech necessary to support the occupational interests of trade union members: see *Straume v Latvia* [2022] IRLR 802, [91]–[93]. The protection of union members from being deterred or penalised for seeking union representation was established in *Wilson v UK* [2002] IRLR 568.
[18] *Straume*, above n 17, [92].
[19] *Wilson and Palmer, National Union of Journalists and others v UK* (2002) 35 EHRR 523.
[20] On the complementarity of group rights and individual rights in the trade union context, see A Bogg and KD Ewing, 'A (Muted) Voice at Work? Collective Bargaining in the Supreme Court of Canada' (2012) 33 *Comparative Labor Law and Policy Journal* 379.

employer to prove innocent intent.[21] Otherwise, discrimination would be very difficult to prove. Finally, the remedies must be proportionate and dissuasive. In *Tek Gida Is Sendikasi v Turkey*, mass dismissals, which resulted in financial compensation for wrongful dismissal equivalent to a year's wages, did not ensure robust remedial protection for trade union discrimination.[22] The union had effectively been removed from the workplace and its representative role extinguished by the dismissals. Modest levels of financial compensation for wrongful dismissal had allowed the employer effectively to buy itself out of its legal obligations. The remedy of reinstatement would have provided a stronger remedial response, and any financial remedies would need to be set at a high enough level to have a deterrent effect on employers.[23] This might require punitive damages, for example.

The Right to Organise in UK Law

The statutory implementation of the right to organise in UK law is set out in TULRCA 1992. It was amended by the Employment Relations Act 2004 (ERA 2004) following the ECtHR judgment in *Wilson*. The 2004 amendments went further than was required by that judgment, and sought to ensure that UK law was more generally compatible with Article 11. TULRCA 1992 provides an extensive set of legal protections for the right to organise.

The statutory rights in TULRCA 1992 extend across the full range of discriminatory actions (and, where appropriate, failures to act) that might be engaged in by employers victimising workers for trade union reasons This includes access to employment (s 137), inducements consisting in 'offers' (s 145A), detriment (which includes both acts and deliberate failures to act) (s 146), and dismissal (s 152). Trade union dismissals are automatically unfair and an employee qualifies for protection from day 1 of employment. Inducements through offers were introduced in 2004. This was because *Wilson* involved financial offers to workers to induce them to forgo union representation.

There are three main protected trade union grounds in these statutory provisions. These are trade union membership (which also includes the right not to be a trade union member); taking part in the activities of an independent union at an appropriate time, which is either time outside the worker's working hours or time within working hours in accordance with agreed arrangements or consent by the employer; and making use of trade union services at an appropriate time.

Refusal of employment (s 137) is restricted to trade union membership. It is also restricted to employees. There seems to be no good reason for these restrictions, and it is odd that s 137 was not aligned with the other statutory provisions in 2004. Inducements (s 145A), detriment (s 146) and dismissal (s 152) cover all three grounds. The use of union services was added in 2004 to respond to the judgment in *Wilson*, where offers had related to the service of union representation rather than the individual's union membership or their own trade union activities.

The provisions are based on a 'discrimination law' model. We might even think of them as a species of direct discrimination for trade union reasons. Liability therefore depends upon the mental state of the discriminator, the employer. Under s 137, the refusal of employment must be 'because' of union membership. There is no liability if union membership is not the *reason* for refusal.[24] Under s 145A, it must be the 'sole or main purpose' of the offer to induce the worker

---

[21] *Hoppen and Trade Union of AB Amber Grid Employees v Lithuania* [2023] ECHR 46, [230].
[22] *Tek Gida Is Sendikasi v Turkey* [2017] ECHR 318.
[23] ibid [55]–[56].
[24] *Miller v Interserve Industrial Services Ltd* [2013] ICR 445.

not to be or seek to become a union member, to take part in the activities of an independent trade union, or to make use of trade union services. Finally, s 152 makes it automatically unfair to dismiss an employee where the 'reason for it (or, if more than one, the principal reason)' was membership, activities, or union services.

As the Article 11 jurisprudence makes clear, real and effective protection means that there should be provision for shifting the burden of proof where there is a *prima facie* case of discrimination. Otherwise, proving the employer's state of mind would be a serious obstacle to practical enforceability of the right to organise. For refusal of employment cases, the burden of proof is on the employee. For detriment claims under s 146, s 148(1) provides that it 'shall be for the employer to show what was the sole or main purpose for which he acted or failed to act'. For inducement claims under s 145A, s145D(1) provides that it 'shall be for the employer to show what was his sole or main purpose in making the offer.' For trade union dismissals, the position on burden of proof is complicated and depends upon whether the employee has sufficient continuity of employment to qualify for an ordinary unfair dismissal claim (two years). Where they do not have requisite continuity, the burden is on the employee to demonstrate the 'automatically unfair' exception applies to them.[25] Where the employee would otherwise qualify for ordinary unfair dismissal, the burden is on the employer to prove the reason for dismissal. In practice, proof can be tricky where the employer can point to alternative credible reasons for its conduct that do not relate to protected trade union grounds.

Trade Union Membership

The protection of trade union membership is the most fundamental thread running through TULRCA 1992. It is particularly important for refusals of employment under s 137 because it is the only protected trade union ground. Historically, the English courts adopted a narrow view of 'union membership' as the mere fact of holding a union card.[26] Such discrimination is likely to be rare because most employers object to what trade unions *do* on behalf of their members. They do not object to union membership as such. In *Jet2.com Ltd v Denby*, the EAT considered the scope of union membership by reference to Article 11.[27] The applicant, a pilot, left an anti-union company and then subsequently applied to return a few years later. His application was rejected. He alleged that this was because of the employer's animosity to trade union representation, and its hostility to the applicant's involvement in trade union activities during his previous period of employment. Judge Eady QC favoured a purposive construction of union membership under s 137. This meant that there was a natural overlap of trade union membership and activities in s 137, because these activities were simply the external manifestation of trade union membership.

This purposive interpretation was also supported by s 3 of the Human Rights Act 1998 (HRA 1998) and Article 11. This is because a narrow interpretation of union membership under s 137 might otherwise leave a gap in protection of the right to join a trade union for the protection of the applicant's interests. On the facts in *Jet2.com Ltd*, the ET had been entitled to find that the refusal to employ him was because of his union membership, purposively construed. This will generally include the activities and services that are integral to trade union membership. This is particularly important for precarious workers on short-term and intermittent casual contracts, often working in the gig economy, where refusals of employment might be the most effective tool

---

[25] *Smith v Hayle Town Council* [1978] ICR 996, CA.
[26] *Associated Newspapers Ltd v Wilson; Associated British Ports v Palmer* [1995] 2 AC 454, HL.
[27] UKEAT/0070/17/LA.

of discrimination by an employer. In the other statutory provisions, such as s 146, s 145A or s 152, the interpretive onus on union membership is less pressing because of the additional grounds of union activities and use of union services.

Taking Part in the Activities of an Independent Trade Union

The protection of union activities is crucial to supporting trade union functions in the workplace. Union activities has been interpreted broadly by the courts. It includes activities such as recruitment of new union members,[28] writing for union literature,[29] and representing members in the workplace,[30] attending union meetings, and campaigning for union recognition. There are some specific features of the current law that warrant particular attention from a human rights perspective.

First, a trade union official is likely to be protected in a broader range of activities than an ordinary union member. This is because it will be easier for a trade union official acting within the scope of the union's authority to demonstrate that they are participating in the activities of an independent trade union.[31] Under the ILO and ECHR, trade union officials are given particularly strong legal protection because the victimisation of them represents a direct attack on the union itself. This can sometimes mean that trade union members fall outside the scope of protection where they are deemed to be acting in a personal capacity. For example, in *Chant v Aquaboats Ltd*, the organisation of a health and safety petition by a union member was held not to be protected because the member was not acting in an official trade union capacity.[32]

Secondly, there is a distinction between individual activities, which are protected, and the acts of a trade union itself, which are not. In *Carrington and others v Therm-A-Stor Ltd*, a group of employees were made redundant in response to the union's recognition request.[33] The selection of employees for redundancy was not related to anything they had done as individuals. The employer was responding to the union's acts, which the Court treated as severable from those of the individual employees. It is difficult to regard this approach as compatible with the right to organise. The rights of individuals and trade unions are complementary aspects of freedom of association, as judgments like *Wilson* demonstrate. What happened in *Carrington* is very naturally described as discrimination because of trade union activity.

Thirdly, legal protection is excluded where the behaviour is found to be wholly unreasonable, extraneous, or malicious.[34] This might include threatening or offensive conduct, for example. In these circumstances, the employer could argue that the reason for adverse treatment is the wrongful conduct rather than the protected activities of the independent trade union. While this restriction makes sense, it needs to be applied carefully when considering offensive or robust expression in the workplace. The protection of freedom of expression under Article 10 is relevant to the protection of trade union activity under Article 11.[35]

Finally, while strike action is treated as protected trade union activity under Article 11, it is currently unprotected under the s 146 detriment provision. While industrial action would seem

---

[28] *Lyon and Another v St James Press Ltd* [1976] ICR 413, EAT.
[29] *Wignall v British Gas Corporation* [1984] ICR 716, EAT.
[30] *Post Office v Union of Post Office Workers and anor* [1974] ICR 378, HL.
[31] *Dixon and anor v West Ella Developments Ltd* [1978] ICR 856, EAT.
[32] [1978] ICR 643, EAT.
[33] [1983] ICR 208, CA.
[34] *Lyon*, above n 28.
[35] For an example of this interaction, see *Palomo Sanchez and others v Spain* [2011] ECHR 1319, [2011] IRLR 934.

to be included within the ordinary and natural meaning of the activities of an independent trade union,[36] it would not be at an 'appropriate time' because the worker is meant to be working. This means that striking employees are unprotected from detriment short of dismissal even where the strike is official and lawful. The Supreme Court has now issued a declaration of incompatibility under s 4 of the HRA 1998 because the legislation currently provides no protection at all from detriment where workers are engaged in lawful industrial action.[37] This lacuna was held to be a violation of Article 11. The Supreme Court considered that it would not be appropriate to interpret the legislation to render it compatible with Article 11 under s 3 of the HRA 1998. This would lead the Court into the realm of controversial policy choices, and it would cross the important constitutional line between interpreting and legislating.

Use of Trade Union Services

Following the *Wilson* judgment, the ERA 2004 added use of union services to the protected trade union grounds under s 145A, s 146 and s 152. This reflected the fact that the basis of the discrimination in *Wilson*, withholding pay rises from workers, was attributable to union representation rather than their union membership. While some older cases treated membership as including use of union services,[38] the explicit inclusion of this in TULRCA 1992 put the matter beyond doubt.

Trade union services is defined as 'services made available to the employee by an independent trade union by virtue of his membership of the union' (s 152(2A)). This will certainly include using union representation during grievance and disciplinary hearings. However, this excludes collective bargaining as a union service because of s 145B(4), which states that 'having terms of employment determined by collective agreement shall not be regarded for the purposes of section 145A (or section 146 or 152) as making use of a trade union service'. This means that collective bargaining is addressed solely through s 145B, which is focused exclusively on inducements (or offers). This is an odd exclusion because it appears to mean that workers are protected from financial offers, but they can be dismissed or subjected to a detriment for insisting that their terms are set by a collective agreement. This is not compatible with Article 11, which must be read as protecting workers from the more coercive forms of discrimination which strike at the very substance of freedom of association. In these circumstances, the courts are likely to adopt a broader interpretation of union membership using s 3 of the HRA 1998 to close the gap in legal protection.

Remedies

The remedies under TULRCA 1992 are limited in two main ways: they are primarily financial; and they are primarily individual remedies. Under s 137 (refusal of employment because of union membership), the remedies are a declaration, recommendation that the respondent reduce the adverse effect of the conduct on the individual complainant, and compensation (s 140). This compensation may include injury to feelings. The compensation is also subject to the same maximum cap applied to the compensatory award for unfair dismissal. For detriment claims

---

[36] *Drew v St Edmundsbury Borough Council* [1980] ICR 513.
[37] *Secretary of State for Business and Trade v Mercer* [2024] UKSC 12. This decision will be considered in more detail in chapter 7 on the right to strike.
[38] *Speciality Care v Pachela* [1996] IRLR 248, EAT.

under s 146, there is no statutory cap on compensation, and 'loss' may include stress and injury to feelings (s 149(2)). For inducements under s 145A, the tribunal must make a declaration to this effect and must make an award currently set at £5,128 (s 145A(2)–(3)). Under s 152, the main remedy in practice is compensation, and this is subject to the same principles as an ordinary unfair dismissal claim. Significantly, this includes the statutory cap on the compensatory award.

These individual financial remedies are unlikely to satisfy the requirement of real and effective protection under Article 11. First, the financial remedies do not include a punitive element, and this may be necessary to ensure that they are sufficiently dissuasive to deter wrongdoing. Secondly, there is no collective remedy for the trade union itself. In *Wilson*, the ECtHR recognised that the trade union has its own Article 11 rights that need to be protected. Collective remedies might include financial compensation to the union, or bargaining orders to compel the employer to negotiate with the union. Thirdly, the primary remedy for trade union dismissals should be reinstatement or re-engagement rather than compensation. Individual compensation is no substitute for the visible restoration of the union's presence in the workplace.

3. Blacklisting and Human Rights

In the introduction to this chapter, we referred to the practice of blacklisting, which consists in the inclusion of workers who are trade union members and who exercise trade union rights in a secret list that employers consult in order to dismiss them and refuse employment opportunities to them. Blacklisting raises pressing questions under Article 11 of the ECHR but also under Article 8 (the right to private life), alone or together with Article 14 (prohibition of discrimination).[39] More precisely, being included in a list of trade union members compiled by employers to be used in hiring or retention decisions clearly interferes with Article 11. Article 11(2) of the ECHR permits limitations to the right to form and join trade unions, but any limitation must have a legitimate aim. Blacklisting has no legitimate aim, as its purpose is to discriminate against workers who exercise a Convention right. Because of the discriminatory element, the inability to obtain a job and dismissals on the basis of the blacklists also violate Article 14 together with Article 11. There is extensive evidence that blacklisting has ruined people's lives.[40] This can also be seen as a violation of the right to work, with all the severe implications that this has for someone's life.[41] The right to work is not guaranteed explicitly in the ECHR, but it has been protected in case law on other provisions.[42] Blacklisting also raises questions on the protection of the right to private life under Article 8, a provision that is interpreted broadly by the Court, because of the exclusion of individuals from work opportunities with its grave implications for their private and family life.[43]

---

[39] Article 14 is not a free-standing provision. It can only be violated when invoked together with some other Convention right. See further chapter 4.

[40] See K Ewing, *Ruined Lives – Blacklisting in the Construction Industry* (Liverpool, Institute of Employment Rights, 2013).

[41] On the value and legal protection of the right to work, see V Mantouvalou (ed), *The Right to Work: Legal and Philosophical Perspectives* (Oxford, Hart, 2015).

[42] See chapter 8. See also V Mantouvalou, 'The Protection of the Right to Work Through the European Convention on Human Rights' (2014) 16 *Cambridge Yearbook of European Legal Studies* 313; R O'Connell, 'The Right to Work in the ECHR' (2012) *European Human Rights Law Review* 176.

[43] See chapters 13 and 14. For further discussion of blacklisting, see V Mantouvalou, 'Labour Rights, Human Rights and Criminal Wrongs' in A Bogg et al (eds), *Criminality at Work* (Oxford, OUP, 2020).

When the blacklisting scandal came to light in 2009, a fine of £5,000 was imposed on a person who held an important role in the Consulting Association for the reason that he processed personal information without having registered as a data controller with the Information Commissioner on the basis of the Data Protection Act 1998. None of the companies that were members of the Consulting Association were prosecuted. Some blacklisted workers applied to employment tribunals, and in 2010 the Employment Relations Act 1999 (Blacklists) Regulations 2010 came into force, which made blacklisting a civil wrong. The Regulations include provisions that define blacklisting, make it unlawful for organisations to refuse employment, dismiss or cause detriment to individuals who are included in a blacklist, and make it unlawful for agencies to refuse service to blacklisted workers. The Regulations make blacklisting unlawful, but not a criminal offence.

Despite the human rights implications, the ECtHR declared inadmissible two cases on blacklisting,[44] though it did accept that there had been an interference with Convention rights.[45] Mr Smith and Mr Brough were blacklisted and suffered significantly because of their inclusion in the lists. Mr Brough claimed that blacklisting violated Article 11 of the ECHR, but the Court dismissed his claim for non-exhaustion of domestic remedies, which in this case consisted in not having raised an ECHR argument in employment tribunal proceedings. Mr Smith was an agency worker, who worked in the construction industry. He claimed that the collection of his personal data through blacklisting was in breach of Article 8, that English law did not protect him as an agency worker who was blacklisted because of his union activities, and did not provide him a remedy for that, and that he was not protected from discrimination as a union member and agency worker under Article 14. The Court accepted that there had been an interference with Article 8, and explained that national authorities have a margin of appreciation in securing compliance with the provision.[46] In this regard, it found that the authorities had made the retention of personal data a criminal offence under the Data Protection Act 1998, and that they also allowed for a civil remedy, through which the applicant was awarded compensation. The Court ruled that the application was incompatible with the Convention *ratione personae*,[47] because the state had met its positive obligations under the Convention by criminalising the unlawful retention of personal data, and by creating a civil remedy, which the applicant pursued and through which he obtained compensation. In reaching the decision, the Court took into account the fact that 'it was the actions of private companies rather than the national authorities'.[48] It is important to note that this occurred before the revelations that there was state involvement in blacklisting.[49] The Court also examined the admissibility of the case on the basis of Article 35(3)(c),[50] and ruled that the applicant had not suffered 'significant disadvantage', because domestic courts recognised the injustice that he suffered, and he was awarded compensation. The Court then turned to the

---

[44] *Brough v UK*, App No 52962/11, Admissibility Decision of 30 August 2016; *Smith v UK*, App No 54357/15, Admissibility Decision of 28 March 2017. For discussion of the *Brough* decision, see K Ewing and J Hendy, 'Article 11(3) of the European Convention on Human Rights' (2017) *European Human Rights Law Review* 356 at 373 ff.
[45] *Smith*, above n 44, [36].
[46] paras 36–37.
[47] ECHR, Article 35(3).
[48] *Smith*, above n 44, [40].
[49] www.theguardian.com/uk-news/2018/mar/23/officers-likely-to-have-passed-personal-files-to-blacklisters-says-met.
[50] Paragraph 3 of Article 35 says that a case will be declared inadmissible if '(b) the applicant has not suffered a significant disadvantage, unless respect for human rights as defined in the Convention and the Protocols thereto requires an examination of the application on the merits and provided that no case may be rejected on this ground which has not been duly considered by a domestic tribunal'. On this admissibility criterion, see D Shelton, 'Significantly Disadvantaged? Shrinking Access to the European Court of Human Rights' (2016) 16 *Human Rights Law Review* 303; N Vogiatzis, 'The Admissibility Criterion Under Article 35(3)(b) ECHR: A "Significant Disadvantage" to Human Rights Protection?' (2016) 65 *International and Comparative Law Quarterly* 185.

question whether respect for human rights required the examination of the complaint, which it rejected. This was because domestic courts had recognised the injustice of blacklisting, and parliamentary and other national bodies had scrutinised and condemned the practice. These decisions have been criticised, while it has been proposed that in order to deter blacklisting effectively, it should be punished as a criminal offence.

The ECtHR has ruled that Article 11 requires 'real and effective protection against anti-union discrimination',[51] but the legal framework on blacklisting does not meet this standard. In parliamentary debates on blacklisting in 2017, it was argued that there is a strong case to criminalise it, and provide for severe sanctions, including high fines and possible imprisonment for the worst cases,[52] and bans on companies that have engaged in blacklisting from the award of public contracts.[53] Representatives of trade unions giving evidence to the Scottish Affairs Committee of the House of Commons said that blacklisting would not cease unless legal sanctions against the practice were strengthened: 'It is happening, and it will continue in the UK until blacklisting is made a criminal offence punishable by imprisonment and unlimited fines. Until that legislation is brought in by whichever Government decides to bring it in, it will continue.'[54] Given that there is evidence that blacklisting still happens, criminalisation can serve to condemn employers who engage in the harmful conduct, and to reduce the instances of it.

4. The Closed Shop

'Negative' Freedom of Association under UK Law

The positive right to join a trade union is protected under international and European human rights law. What about the negative right *not* to join a trade union? This question arises within the context of the 'closed shop' and other forms of 'union security' arrangement. These terms describe a situation where a worker is required to be a trade union member as a condition of their employment. In the UK in the post-war decades, these practices were relatively widespread and estimated to directly affect one in six British workers.[55]

In fact, 'union security' covers a wide range of industrial relations practices.[56] Pre-entry closed shops are where the worker is required to be a union member as a pre-condition of employment. They provided unions with significant control over the labour supply, which enabled them to maintain strong bargaining power by limiting the pool of workers. Post-entry closed shops were more common. These required the worker to join a trade union once they were in employment. In North America, 'agency shops' permit workers to pay the union a fee to support its collective bargaining services in lieu of trade union membership. This could be rationalised on the basis that since the union is providing a valuable service to the worker by negotiating improved terms and conditions on their behalf, it is right that they should pay an agency fee to the union for that service.

---

[51] *Danilenkov*, above n 14, [124].
[52] House of Commons, Hansard, 5 September 2017, Vol 628, col 68WH.
[53] ibid, Chuka Umunna MP, col 69WH.
[54] House of Commons, Scottish Affairs Committee, 'Blacklisting in Employment: Addressing the Crimes of the Past; Moving Towards Best Practice', Sixth Report of Session 2013–2014, para 51. See also A Just, 'A Manifesto Against Blacklisting' in D Smith, *Blacklisting: The Need for a Public Inquiry* (Liverpool, Institute of Employment Rights, 2017) 39.
[55] Lord Wedderburn, *The Worker and the Law*, 3rd edn (1986) 371.
[56] The classic account is still WEJ McCarthy, *The Closed Shop in Britain* (Blackwell, 1964).

It is unusual for any of these union security arrangements to be enforced directly by governments through legal duties. Indeed, the ILO regards state-enforced arrangements as a violation of freedom of association.[57] They are generally enforced by employers and trade unions themselves. Employers may either refuse to employ (in pre-entry closed shops) or dismiss/penalise non-members (in post-entry closed shops). Trade unions can threaten strike action to pressurise employers to enforce closed shops through refusals of employment, dismissals, or other economic penalties. In this way, enforcement is usually through 'social' rather than direct legal sanctions.

From a human rights perspective, closed shops have always been controversial. Critics of closed shops sometimes invoke freedom of association as a fundamental civil liberty. The right to join a trade union must also encompass a right not to join. They have been described as the 'positive' and 'negative' counterparts of freedom of association, flipsides of the same freedom, and required as a matter of logic. The argument from legal logic has sometimes been dismissed as 'shallow legalism'.[58]

A better human rights argument might be the importance of personal autonomy and choice, and the role of human rights in supporting individual freedom. Forcing a worker to join a trade union against their wishes is an infringement of their personal freedom. It also exposes the worker to arbitrary power by trade unions. If they are expelled from the union, for example, they would not only lose their membership; they might also lose their job. This also engages the right to work. A human rights approach at least requires this interference to be justified under a proportionality standard.

Defenders of closed shops usually pointed to broader functional arguments based on the positive social consequences of union security.[59] They prevented workers from free-riding on the sacrifices of other workers, stopping them from taking the benefits of collective bargaining without shouldering some of the burdens such as striking. This also supports the bargaining strength of the union, which is a collective benefit for everyone in the bargaining unit. Finally, closed shops limited the scope for inter-union conflict, and this cohesion could also be a benefit for the employer in avoiding wasteful disputes. The overall utility of the arrangement justified the costs to individual freedom, which in many cases were relatively modest anyway.

The position under UK law is now simply stated. All forms of closed shop and union security arrangement are legally unenforceable by both employers *and* trade unions. This unenforceability is because of legislation. Across the 1980s, the closed shop was subjected to increasing statutory restriction by the Conservative Government. The last vestiges of the pre-entry closed shop were finally made unenforceable in 1990. These statutory developments probably had less to do with a human rights agenda and more to do with the dominant ideology favouring deregulated labour markets and limits on trade union power.[60] This political hostility was puzzling in some respects. Closed shop agreements were contracts, and neoliberal ideology supported freedom of contract. Ultimately, however, union security was another obstacle to the unimpeded labour market. It tended to increase the bargaining strength of trade unions, and therefore it needed to be removed. Interestingly, no subsequent Government has proposed to reverse this strict legal position on enforcing the closed shop.

Under s 137 of TULRCA 1992, it is unlawful to refuse employment because of trade union membership. While this provision covers membership and non-membership symmetrically, the

---

[57] ILO (1994), *General Survey on Freedom of Association and Collective Bargaining*, [102]–[103].
[58] Wedderburn, above n 55, 363.
[59] McCarthy, above n 56.
[60] For historical context, see PL Davies and MR Freedland, *Labour Legislation and Public Policy* (OUP, 1993) ch 9.

real target of s 137 was preventing enforcement of the pre-entry closed shop. For post-entry closed shops, all forms of employer pressure are now prohibited in TULRCA 1992. In relation to inducements and detriments, under s 145A and s 146 the relevant statutory provisions each include references to inducing (s 145A(1)(d)) or compelling (s 146(1)(c)) the worker 'to be or become a member of any trade union or of a particular trade union or of one of a number of particular trade unions'. Most importantly, it is an automatically unfair dismissal where the reason or principal reason for it is that the employee (s 152(1)(c)) 'was not a member of any trade union, or of a particular trade union, or one of a number of particular trade unions, or had refused, or proposed to refuse, to become or remain a member'. These statutory restrictions in ss 146 and 152 also prevent the enforcement of US-style 'agency fee' arrangements in lieu of union membership, in s 146(3) and s 152(3).

There are special remedies for trade union dismissals, which include a minimum basic award;[61] the possibility of joining the trade union as a party to the proceedings where it has exercised industrial pressure on the employer to induce the dismissal;[62] and scope for interim relief which requires the employer to reinstate or re-engage the employee until the dismissal claim has been determined by the tribunal.[63]

In relation to unions, there is also a comprehensive prohibition of industrial action and other forms of industrial pressure to enforce closed shop practices. It is unlawful to refuse to deal with suppliers because the work is not done by union members (s 145), and any contractual term to that effect is void (s 144). This prevents trade unions from placing pressure on employers to maintain lists of union-approved suppliers, which would operate like a form of 'secondary' boycott of non-union suppliers. Finally, the trade dispute immunity, which protects trade unions from tort liability for organising industrial action, is removed where the action is undertaken to enforce a closed shop (s 222).

We will now consider whether this strict approach prohibiting enforcement is compatible with international and European human rights law.

The Closed Shop and Human Rights

The fundamental ILO Conventions on freedom of association and collective bargaining, C87 and C98, do not address the closed shop directly. Article 1(2)(a) of C98 refers to protection against acts that 'make the employment of a worker subject to the condition that he shall *not* join a union or shall *relinquish* trade union membership'. This appears to protect the positive freedom of association while leaving some space for pre-entry closed shops. Article 1(2)(b) refers more broadly to prejudicial acts 'by reason of union membership'. The ILO Committee of Experts has adopted a permissive approach to closed shops. Provided that these arrangements are not compelled by legislation, and are based in collective agreements, they are neither mandated nor proscribed by the right to organise.

In Europe, the closed shop is now regarded as a violation of the right to organise across different human rights instruments. Under the ESC, the European Committee of Social Rights (ECSR) regards compulsory union membership as incompatible with Article 5 and the right to organise.[64] While Jacobs has suggested there might be some limited scope for 'agency fee' arrangements

---

[61] TULRCA 1992, s 156. This award is currently £7,836.
[62] TULRCA 1992, s 160.
[63] TULRCA 1992, s 161.
[64] See, eg, *Confederation of Swedish Enterprise v Sweden* (Collective Complaint no 12/2002).

under Article 5,[65] the ECSR's hostility to closed shops is now an entrenched feature of Article 5. Interestingly, point 11 of the Community Charter of the Fundamental Social Rights of Workers, adopted as a political declaration in 1989 by 11 Member States, also provided for the freedom to join or not to join trade unions.

The position under Article 11 of the ECHR has been more dynamic. Broadly speaking, the early case law was cautiously discouraging of closed shops given their detrimental effects on 'negative' freedom of association. In more recent case law, this caution has disappeared and the positions under the ESC and the ECHR are now substantially aligned against closed shops.

In *Young, James, and Webster v UK*, three applicants had been dismissed from employment at British Rail because they refused to join one of the three unions specified in the closed shop agreement.[66] The ECtHR emphasised that it was not assessing the general legitimacy of closed shops under Article 11. It was focused on the concrete situation of the applicants. They had been dismissed pursuant to a closed shop agreement that had been concluded after they had been employed at British Rail. Their refusal was based in conscientious objections to trade union policies and activities and, in Mr Young's case, the union's political affiliation. The closed shop agreement restricted the applicants' choices about which unions they could join. The ECtHR also emphasised that dismissal was 'a most serious form of compulsion'.[67] For these reasons, the treatment of the applicants under the closed shop agreement had interfered with their Article 11 freedom of association rights. The ECtHR did not regard this interference as necessary in a democratic society. Even if there had been no compulsion to join a union applied to existing non-union employees, as in this case, railway unions would not have been prevented from striving for the protection of their members' occupational interests.[68]

At this stage, the ECtHR was cautious about the closed shop. While freedom of association required 'some measure of freedom of choice as to its exercise',[69] the Court did not say that negative freedom of association was on an equal footing with positive freedom of association. For example, if there had been an exception for existing employees, or if there had been a broad permitted choice of trade unions in the closed shop agreement, this might have made a difference. There was also a strong dissenting opinion by the Danish, Icelandic and Swedish judges, who considered that Article 11 should be neutral on the closed shop. This alignment probably reflected the importance of specific industrial relations traditions to the legitimacy of the closed shop, rather than abstract arguments about individual freedom of choice.

Some years later, in *Sorensen and Rasmussen v Denmark*, pre-entry closed shops in Denmark were treated as a violation of freedom of association.[70] The applicants objected to union membership on conscientious political grounds. According to the Court, the compulsion to join the union as a condition of access to employment 'struck at the very substance of the freedom of association guaranteed by Article 11 of the Convention'.[71] In support of its conclusions, it used an integrated approach and referred to the ESC and the Community Charter of Fundamental Social Rights of Workers.[72] Since there was little support across Europe for closed shops, they were unlikely to be indispensable for the trade union's ability to represent the occupational

---

[65] A Jacobs, 'Article 5: The Right to Organise' in N Bruun, K Lorcher, I Schomann and S Clauwaert (eds), *The European Social Charter and the Employment* Relation (Hart, 2017) 220, 243.
[66] *Young, James, and Webster v UK* [1981] ECHR 4.
[67] ibid [55].
[68] ibid [64].
[69] ibid [52].
[70] *Sorensen and Rasmussen v Denmark* (2008) 46 EHRR 29.
[71] ibid [64].
[72] ibid [72]–[73].

interests of members effectively.[73] In listing the 'essential elements' of freedom of association under Article 11, the ECtHR now includes 'the prohibition of closed-shop agreements' in that list.[74] The scope for permissible closed shop agreements under Article 11(2) has now all but disappeared.

From a human rights perspective, the individual worker's negative freedom to disassociate is now strongly protected under European instruments. Historically, these developments caused some scepticism among labour lawyers about the role of human rights in undermining collective solidarity.[75] Before concluding this discussion, we should note that not everyone agrees that human rights require the prohibition of the closed shop. First, there may still be scope for the 'agency shop' where a worker is required to pay a fee to the union to reimburse it for its collective bargaining services. This is far less intrusive on the individual's freedom because it does not require membership and the fee subsidises the 'industrial' rather than political activities of the union. It also addresses the free-rider problem effectively. Secondly, it would be better to distinguish between conscientious objection and freedom of choice in protecting the right not to join a trade union. Where a worker has a conscientious objection to union membership, for political or religious reasons, compulsion is far more serious than if the worker is simply a free-rider who would prefer to choose not to pay for collective benefits.[76] Freedom of conscience is likely to be much more important in systems like France where trade unions are divided along ideological or confessional lines, and where a Catholic worker may otherwise be compelled to join a communist trade union.

Finally, we should remember that negative freedom of association claims can relate to different associative rights and activities other than membership. For example, in *Gustafsson v Sweden*, the negative claim related to an employer's freedom to opt out of a collective agreement rather than compulsory membership of an association.[77] In such cases, the negative freedom could have deregulatory effects on a public scheme with the objective of protecting workers' conditions of employment. The necessity test for justifying restriction of the freedom to opt out of collective agreements ought to be satisfied more easily here than in a closed shop case.

5. Trade Union Autonomy and Human Rights

Many of the human rights themes under the 'closed shop' discussion are also relevant to the trade union's freedom of association. In closed shops, the focus is on the individual's freedom not to join the trade union. In relation to trade unions and their members, the focus is on the group's freedom to determine its relationship with its own members. This includes the permitted scope for refusals to allow an individual to join the union ('exclusion'), or the discipline or expulsion of the member because of a disciplinary offence or some other breach of membership eligibility rules.

From a human rights perspective, there are two general issues that underpin the law in this area. The first concerns the scope of the trade union's negative freedom of association. Just as individuals can refuse to associate with a trade union, to what extent can unions refuse to associate with an individual? In a formal sense, the freedom to disassociate might seem to be symmetrical in both cases, so that the same considerations should apply. In substantive terms,

---

[73] ibid [75].
[74] See eg *Association of Civil Servants and Union for Collective Bargaining and others v Germany* [2022] ECHR 543, [57].
[75] Lord Wedderburn, 'Freedom of Association or Right to Organise? The Common Law and International Sources' in Lord Wedderburn, *Employment Rights in Britain and Europe* (London, Lawrence & Wishart, 1991), originally published in (1987) *Industrial Relations Journal* 244.
[76] See S White, 'Trade Unionism in a Liberal State' in A Gutmann, *Freedom of Association* (Princeton UP, 1998) ch 12.
[77] *Gustafsson v Sweden* [1996] ECHR 20.

there may be differences in the social and economic consequences of giving equal protection to negative freedom of association for trade unions. Organised groups like trade unions can wield much more power than individuals. Where a group with social power excludes an individual from membership, there are risks that it could abuse its dominant position. Individuals might be excluded from material benefits for bad reasons such as sex or race. Even without this discriminatory context, social ostracism in the workplace can be unpleasant for excluded workers. In closed shop situations, the arbitrary exclusion of workers from trade union membership can lead to loss of employment and infringement of the right to work. By contrast, the consequences of an individual worker disassociating from the union are likely to be marginal to the union's ability to pursue its activities. This asymmetry in social and economic consequences might justify a different approach to individual and collective 'negative' freedom of association.

The second issue concerns the protection of individual autonomy and choice for trade union members. As we have seen, individual autonomy has been recognised by the ECtHR as an important value underlying Article 11. Does the protection of individual autonomy include giving workers a free choice between competing trade unions, creating a kind of marketplace for union representation? This would justify imposing some legal limits on the ability of trade unions to coordinate their organisational activities. Considerations of individual autonomy might also justify limits on the union's ability to discipline or expel members for refusing to participate in a strike. If we prioritise individual autonomy over collective solidarity, participation in strike action should be the individual's sovereign choice. Interestingly, the strongest counterargument to this would be based in freedom of contract. Where an individual chooses to join a trade union, and they enter into a contract of membership, they have freely assumed the legal obligations of membership.

The leading ECtHR judgment on the trade union's freedom of association is *ASLEF v UK*.[78] The ECtHR considered the scope of the trade union's freedom to determine its own membership criteria under UK law by reference to Article 11. The case arose out of the union's attempts to expel Mr Lee from the trade union because of his association with a far right political party, the British National Party (BNP). This was based in the union's view that Mr Lee's political association was antithetical to its anti-fascist values as an organisation. These values were inscribed in the constitutional objects of ASLEF which included a commitment to socialist principles and anti-racism. The union's ability to determine its membership criteria was extensively regulated and restricted by statute. In particular, TULRCA 1992 prohibited exclusion or expulsion of a trade union member where this related to membership of a political party. While there was some uncertainty during the domestic litigation about whether the expulsion related to his conduct or BNP membership, ASLEF considered itself bound to retain Mr Lee in its membership. This compelled association was in contravention of its own internal rules and objects.

The Court found that UK law violated Article 11. As with *Wilson*, the Court in *ASLEF* based its reasoning on the 'integrated approach'. The Court referred to ILO materials.[79] Trade union autonomy is a fundamental principle under ILO C87 Article 2, which provides that 'Workers and employers, without distinction whatsoever, shall have the right to establish and, subject only to the rules of the organisation concerned, to join organisations of their own choosing without previous authorisation.' This is subject to Article 8 which requires organisations to respect the general law of the land in exercising their rights under C87. The Court also referred to the ESC, and the ECSR's criticisms of the statutory rules under consideration in the *ASLEF* case itself.[80] These were held to infringe Article 5 ESC.

---

[78] *ASLEF v UK* [2007] ECHR 184.
[79] ibid [25].
[80] ibid [22]–[24].

The Court drew an explicit parallel with the individual's negative freedom:

> As an employee or worker should be free to join, or not join a trade union without being sanctioned or subject to disincentives (*e.g. Young, James and Webster v. the United Kingdom*, judgment of 13 August 1981, Series A no. 44, *mutatis mutandis*, *Wilson & the National Union of Journalists and Others*, cited above), so should the trade union be equally free to choose its members. Article 11 cannot be interpreted as imposing an obligation on associations or organisations to admit whosoever wishes to join. Where associations are formed by people, who, espousing particular values or ideals, intend to pursue common goals, it would run counter to the very effectiveness of the freedom at stake if they had no control over their membership.[81]

The limits to this freedom were determined by the protection of individuals from the abuse of dominant position by the union:

> the State must nonetheless protect the individual against any abuse of a dominant position by trade unions (see *Young, James and Webster* judgment, cited above, § 63). Such abuse might occur, for example, where exclusion or expulsion from a trade union was not in accordance with union rules or where the rules were wholly unreasonable or arbitrary or where the consequences of exclusion or expulsion resulted in exceptional hardship (see *Cheall*, cited above, *Johanssen v. Norway*, no. 13537/88, Comm. Dec. 7.5.90).[82]

The three circumstances of 'abuse of dominant position' were not engaged on the facts in *ASLEF*. The expulsion was in accordance with the rules of the organisation. The exclusion of members of racist/far right political parties could not be described as 'wholly unreasonable or arbitrary'. Finally, the consequences of exclusion/expulsion would not result in 'exceptional hardship' because there was no closed shop and Mr Lee would continue to enjoy the benefits of collective bargaining. The *ASLEF* judgment led to important changes to the statutory framework.

We will consider two areas where the rights of unions and union members have come into conflict: exclusion from membership; and discipline/expulsion from the trade union. In both areas, applying the *ASLEF* principles, statutory regulation has tipped the balance too far in favour of individual autonomy. It gives insufficient weight to the trade union's human rights.

Trade Union Exclusion: Common Law and Statute

At common law, the fundamental starting-point is freedom of contract. *Faramus v Film Artistes' Association* concerned an exclusion within the context of a closed shop.[83] The applicant had not disclosed his criminal convictions which were of a minor nature and some of which had been acquired during the Nazi occupation of Jersey. The eligibility rules of the union prohibited membership for those who had been convicted of a criminal offence. When his youthful indiscretions came to light, he was excluded from the union. The House of Lords enforced the rule, there being no common law basis to disapply it.

This 'freedom of contract' approach provided strong protection for the trade union's autonomy to determine its own eligibility rules. It did not provide protection for an individual who had been subjected to 'exceptional hardship' in the application of this rule to his individual circumstances. While some courts tried to limit the harsh exclusionary effects of these rules using common law public policy, such as the 'right to work', this did not provide an effective legal basis for protecting individuals from abuse of dominant position.[84] From an Article 11 perspective,

---

[81] ibid [39].
[82] ibid [43].
[83] [1964] AC 925.
[84] *Nagle v Feilden* [1966] 2 QB 633.

the common law was weighted too far in favour of trade union autonomy. This was particularly problematic during the closed shop period, when the loss of membership could lead to the loss of employment.

The main source of legal protection is now s 174 of TULRCA 1992 which is very prescriptive in specifying four *permissible* grounds of exclusion/expulsion. These are where there is: (i) an 'enforceable membership requirement' which determines eligibility by reference to matters such as occupation, trade, profession or qualifications (s 174(3)); (ii) geographical restrictions on the scope of membership limited to particular parts of Great Britain (s 174(2)(b)); (iii) where a union is restricted to an employer or associated employers, employment with that employer; (iv) exclusion or expulsion is 'entirely attributable to conduct of his' (s 174 (2)(d)).

The 'conduct' ground looks to be very broad. It is, however, hedged with significant restrictions. It does not include 'excluded conduct' as defined in s 174(4). This includes being or ceasing to be a member of another trade union, being or ceasing to be employed by a particular employer, or conduct which would count as 'unjustifiable discipline' under s 65 of TULRCA 1992. Critically, this category of 'unjustifiable discipline' includes refusing to participate in strike action. The practical effect of these exclusions from 'conduct' is to protect the individual's freedom to choose which union to join: they cannot be excluded or expelled for joining a different trade union to one which customarily organises in their workplace.[85] This also inhibits the scope for unions to coordinate their organisational efforts through rules enforced by 'social' sanctions such as ordering the expulsion of 'poached' members.

Following *ASLEF*, there are now very complicated rules regulating the exclusion or expulsion of individuals because of party political membership. This is restricted to situations where membership is contrary to a rule or objective that it is 'reasonably practicable' to ascertain (s 174(4C)); the union is acting in accordance with its own rules (s 174(4G)(a)); the exclusion or expulsion is procedurally fair (s 174(4H); the individual must not suffer loss of livelihood or exceptional hardship (s 174(4G)(c)). These statutory restrictions are far more onerous than the ones envisaged by the ECtHR in *ASLEF* itself.

Overall, the statutory position under s 174 strikes the balance very strongly in favour of individual choice. It does not give sufficient weight to trade union autonomy. While there is no doubt that trade unions should be bound by general laws such as the Equality Act 2010,[86] it is less clear why unions should not be able to exclude strike-breakers or those who might be more appropriately represented by a different trade union. Given that the closed shop is no longer enforceable, the arguments in favour of trade union autonomy are even stronger.

Trade Union Discipline: Common Law and Statute

At common law, the courts were innovative in using public policy to uphold the principles of natural justice in trade union cases.[87] The judicial development of principles of natural justice in the contract of membership went far beyond what was happening in the employment contract. In *Esterman v NALGO*, the court even issued an injunction to restrain an internal disciplinary process where a union member had a conscientious objection to impending strike action.[88] This era of judicial creativity reflected concerns about the closed shop and the abuse of dominant

---

[85] B Simpson, 'Individualism versus Collectivism: an Evaluation of section 14 of the Trade Union and Employment Rights Act 1993' (1993) 22 *ILJ* 181.
[86] Trade unions fall within its scope under Equality Act 2010, s 57.
[87] *Edwards v SOGAT* [1971] Ch 354.
[88] [1974] ICR 625.

position by strong trade unions. In this social context, the courts were less concerned with trade union autonomy and the union's freedom of association rights.

These old common law cases have now been eclipsed by statutory regulation. Under s 64(1) of TULRCA 1992, trade union members now have a right not to be unjustifiably disciplined by the union. Some of these provisions protect union members where they have raised concerns about union governance, such as the disposal of union property. They are akin to statutory provisions protecting whistleblowers from victimisation by employers.

More controversially, it also includes the failure to participate in a strike or other industrial action (s 65(2)(a)). This must be viewed in the wider context of UK strike law, which imposes strict requirements of democratic support in a ballot as precondition of a lawful strike. This means that an individual member can either not vote at all or vote against the strike. They can then still refuse to strike even if the statutory support thresholds for lawful strike action are satisfied. It is difficult to see how this is compatible with *ASLEF*. Union rules requiring members to obey a lawful strike instruction cannot be described as 'wholly unreasonable or arbitrary'. Effective strikes depend upon solidarity and the enforcement of internal union discipline. And in the absence of a closed shop, expulsion from the union does not result in 'exceptional hardship' to the member. This is a situation where 'freedom of contract', enforcing the member's assumed duties under the contract of membership, would accord with Article 11.

6. Conclusion

Over the last two decades, the legal protection of freedom of association as a fundamental human right has been transformed under Article 11. A textbook chapter on human rights and employment law written in the late 1990s may well have struck a sombre note on the scope for human rights to protect 'collective' rights and values. It may well have been very critical of the 'individualism' of human rights. Such an analysis would not be persuasive today.[89] Furthermore, human rights litigation has also led to significant changes to legislation, as in the Employment Relations Act 2004. Human rights matter in Parliament as much as in the courts.

Human rights law now strikes a better balance between individual and collective freedoms. While there are still gaps in protection for the right to organise and blacklisting, there have been significant improvements in legal protection as a result of human rights. The protection against discrimination and victimisation, rooted in ideals of legal equality, has led to strong judicial protection and beneficial statutory reforms. The most urgent candidate for further reform is criminalisation of blacklisting practices and the provision of more effective remedies for trade unionists in situations of victimisation.

In relation to closed shops and the trade union's freedom to determine its own membership rules, the current state of human rights law and domestic legislation is still in need of improvement. The individual worker's negative freedom to disassociate from the union is treated as paramount under both Article 11 and TULRCA 1992. By contrast, the trade union's own negative freedom to disassociate is subject to extensive limitations. This means that human rights law can obstruct solidarity at work, undermining the union's ability to protect its members' interests where the economic power of employer and union are still very unequal.

---

[89] These ideas of 'collectivism' and 'individualism' are themselves very complex and can be used in the literature in contradictory ways: see A Bogg, '"Individualism" and "Collectivism" in Collective Labour Law' (2017) 46 *ILJ* 72.

6
Human Rights and Worker Voice

1.	Industrial Democracy, Worker Voice, and Human rights	4.	The EU Social Model: From Consultation to Collective Bargaining?
2.	Sources of Legal Protection: ILO and EU	5.	Conclusion
3.	Trade Union Recognition and Collective Bargaining		

1. Industrial Democracy, Worker Voice, and Human Rights

Imagine a government that assigns almost everyone a superior whom they must obey. Although superiors give most inferiors a routine to follow, there is no rule of law. Orders may be arbitrary and can change at any time, without prior notice or opportunity to appeal. Superiors are unaccountable to those they order around. They are neither elected nor removable by their inferiors. Inferiors have no right to complain in court about how they are being treated, except in a few narrowly defined cases. They also have no right to be consulted about the orders they are given.[1]

The political philosopher Elizabeth Anderson could be describing life in an autocratic dictatorship such as North Korea. In fact, she is describing the lives of workers in a liberal democracy, the United States, but as it plays out in many US workplaces today. Her argument points to the gulf between, on the one hand, democratic citizenship in politics and society, and, on the other hand, democratic citizenship at work.

The US system of labour law represents an extreme case of this problem of workplace autocracy. This is because of very low levels of unionisation and limited general protections from unfair dismissal (so-called 'employment at will' because the employer can terminate the employment contract at very short notice without any need to justify termination). Yet Anderson's arguments are relevant to workers in the UK too. Although there are more legal restrictions on managerial prerogative than in the US, employers still enjoy significant authority to direct the running of the workplace. Workers are subject to a contractual duty to obey the lawful and reasonable instructions of the employer.[2] They are also subject to rules imposed unilaterally, either through the contract or through employer policies and handbooks, that affect important aspects of workers' lives. This includes pay, work schedules, timing of holidays, and even

---

[1] E Anderson, *Private Government: How Employers Rule Our Lives (and Why We Don't Talk about It)* (Princeton UP, 2017) 37.
[2] *Laws v London Chronicle (Indicator Newspapers) Ltd* [1959] 1 WLR 698.

economic decisions leading to the closure or sale of the business. These decisions may be more important in the daily lives of workers than many of those taken by the elected government.

Without an effective voice at work, managerial power may be arbitrary and unaccountable to those over whom the power is exercised, the workers. These critical insights are not new in labour law. These concerns were often grouped together under the general term 'industrial democracy'.[3] Still, it is interesting that they are now back on the agenda of politics again. It may reflect deeper concerns about the disempowerment of workers in an era of declining unionisation.

This democratic agenda for labour law was once described by Keith Ewing as 'to untangle the contradiction identified by Hugh Collins, namely that while the principles of self-determination and democracy govern the relations between the individual and the state, "these cherished values … appear to be eclipsed as soon as we enter the workplace", where "we find a system of autocratic power exercised by the management over the work-force."'[4] These analogies between the state and the firm have sometimes led scholars to draw upon the language of constitutional values to reflect upon how firms and labour markets should be governed.[5] Theories of industrial democracy have used analogies with general democratic theory, for example by comparing collective bargaining with the activities of pressure groups vying for influence in the wider democratic process.[6] Historically, this focused on collective bargaining between employers and trade unions. Collective bargaining meant that workers could influence terms and conditions of employment through their union representatives by negotiating collective agreements. There are limits to how far these analogies between states and firms can go.[7] In a political democracy, political representatives are subject to periodic elections and in this way they are directly accountable to the electorate. In firms, by contrast, managers are not subject to periodic elections by their workers and they cannot be removed by popular vote! Given the ownership of firms, managers are accountable to their shareholders, not their workers. That said, it is also far easier for workers to resign and 'exit' their employers than it is for people to repudiate their national citizenship: this option of 'exit' provides an important check on employer power.

Different theories of labour law converge on the fundamental value of democracy at work. Three leading theories are dignity, freedom as non-domination, and capabilities. From a dignity perspective, Allan Flanders famously argued that the strongest justification for collective bargaining was a dignitarian one: it 'defines their rights, and consequently their status and security … Equally they are interested in participating as directly as possible in the making and administration of these rules in order to have a voice in shaping their own destiny and the decisions on which it most depends.' By giving workers some role in shaping their destiny at work, this respects their agency and their self-determination. From a freedom as non-domination perspective, the subjection of workers to unaccountable managerial power exposes them to the risk of arbitrary treatment.[8] Even if workers are lucky enough to be treated well, this vulnerability to arbitrary treatment undermines their freedom. By giving workers voice to contest managerial power, this

---

[3] For a classic account from the 'industrial relations' literature of the 1960s, see HA Clegg, *A New Approach to Industrial Democracy* (Blackwell, 1960).

[4] KD Ewing, 'Democratic Socialism and Labour Law' (1995) 24 *Industrial Law Journal* 103, 112.

[5] R Dukes, *The Labour Constitution* (OUP, 2017).

[6] See RA Hyman, 'Pluralism, Procedural Consensus and Collective Bargaining' (1978) 16 *British Journal of Industrial Relations* 16.

[7] Although some democratic theorists have proposed that there should be much greater democratisation of firms: see RA Dahl, *A Preface to Economic Democracy* (University of California Press, 1986).

[8] P Pettit, *Republicanism: A Theory of Freedom and Government* (OUP, 1997).

provides a check against arbitrary treatment and it can ensure that managerial power is more accountable.[9] Finally, 'capabilities' is concerned with the real opportunities for workers to pursue lives that they have reason to value. This capabilities approach has been particularly influential in theories of labour law.[10] Martha Nussbaum identifies 'control over one's political and material environment' as a central capability.[11] 'Control' over one's material environment encompasses democracy at work.

The importance of democracy at work has led some scholars to argue that there is a human right to voice at work, rooted in the fundamental value of democracy in free societies.[12] What would a human right to voice at work include? There are many different theories of democracy, which may reflect different underlying values and concerns. This complexity is also reflected in the idea of a human right to voice at work. It is not reducible to a single idea. It is probably better to think of this human right as encompassing a range of different approaches to democracy at work. A comparative perspective shows that different countries adopt different legal models. These models of the human right to voice at work vary across four dimensions.

The first is between 'single channel' representation through trade unions or 'dual channel' representation based on universal coverage. Historically, UK labour law was based on the 'single channel' model.[13] Independent trade unions provided an effective voice for organised workers, usually through collective bargaining over terms and conditions of employment. The 'dual channel' model reflected many European systems which provided for standing institutional arrangements for elected workplace representatives. This includes the German system of enterprise-based works councils, although in practice many elected works council representatives are also trade unionists.[14] Nor are works councils 'universal' in practice, but they are relatively easy to establish because they are facilitated by the legal framework

The second is the nature of the process for voice, and the degree of effective influence over managerial prerogative. The provision of information can reduce unfair surprise in managerial decisions, supporting dignitarian interests. It does not provide any influence over decision-making. The next tier is the process of 'weak' consultation which envisages 'an exchange of views and establishment of a dialogue'.[15] 'Stronger' forms of consultation might be 'with a view to reaching an agreement'. At the apex, collective bargaining resulting in a collective agreement enables the joint authorship of conditions of employment. Some legal systems may even provide for codetermination rights which give worker representatives an effective veto over certain managerial decisions.

The third relates to the subjects of worker voice. Most workers are keen to influence the core elements of the wage-work bargain such as pay rates, working time, and holidays. Specific events that affect workers' interests very significantly, such as a transfer of undertakings or collective redundancies, might also trigger a process for worker voice. Even if the decision cannot be reversed, consultation and negotiation might lead to mitigation of its effects. The inclusion

---

[9] A Bogg and C Estlund, 'Freedom of Association and the Right to Contest: Getting Back to Basics' in A Bogg and T Novitz (eds), *Voices at Work: Continuity and Change in the Common Law World* (OUP, 2014).

[10] B Langille, 'The Capability Approach to Labour Law – Why are We Here?' in B Langille (ed), *The Capability Approach to Labour Law* (OUP, 2019).

[11] M Nussbaum, *Creating Capabilities: The Human Development Approach* (Harvard UP, 2011) 167.

[12] V Mantouvalou, 'Democratic Theory and Voices at Work' in A Bogg and T Novitz (eds), *Voices at Work: Continuity and Change in the Common Law World* (OUP, 2014) 221.

[13] P Davies and C Kilpatrick, 'UK Worker Representation After Single Channel' (2004) 33 *Industrial Law Journal* 121.

[14] J Rogers and W Streeck, 'The Study of Works Councils: Concepts and Problems' in J Rogers and W Streeck (eds), *Works Councils: Consultation, Representation and Cooperation in Industrial Relations* (University of Chicago Press, 1995) 11–16; W Streeck, 'Works Councils in Western Europe: From Consultation to Participation', ibid, 313–14.

[15] Information and Consultation of Employees Regulations 2004 (SI 2004/3426), reg 2.

of issues around the strategic direction of the enterprise are more contested. These are often regarded as central to the managerial prerogative, and the laws on worker voice less likely to encroach on it. As new challenges arise, such as AI and algorithmic management, it is important that voice institutions keep pace with these developments.

Finally, the law on worker voice is generally focused on process rather than outcomes. This no doubt reflects the importance of the underlying democratic principles. Under UK law, for example, the legal default in the workplace is generally non-union.[16] Recognition for collective bargaining must usually be positively sought by workers and trade unions. Where there is collective bargaining, the fundamental value of 'autonomy' of the parties means that governmental agencies are reluctant to force the parties to agree to specific terms. Nor is it mandatory for firms to implement general consultation procedures in national or transnational undertakings. Instead, the legal framework provides for a 'trigger' to initiate a process for negotiating a consultation procedure. Employees may never pull the trigger, and even if they do, they still have significant latitude to agree their own tailored arrangements.

Interestingly, corporate governance is another important vehicle for worker voice. For example, the reform of corporate law to include workers in board-level representation could provide a powerful way of enhancing voice. Such corporate governance measures have not generally been treated as human rights entitlements. This may be because they involve broader structural reform of the 'constitution' of firm governance, a matter of company law rather than human rights law.[17] While we do not focus on company law measures in this chapter, their overall importance to worker participation should not be overlooked. It is also an important reminder that we can pursue important employment law goals effectively other than through human rights techniques.

2. Sources of Legal Protection: ILO and EU

There is no 'human right to voice at work' protected in any international human rights instrument. Instead, specific mechanisms of worker voice, such as collective bargaining or consultation, are protected as human rights. In this section, we shall focus on the International Labour Organization (ILO) and the European Union (EU). Historically, the ILO has focused strongly on collective bargaining, whereas the EU was more focused on information/consultation. Recently, however, the EU has provided important support to collective bargaining in Directive 2022/2041 on adequate minimum wages in the European Union. We will consider the position on collective bargaining under Article 11 of the European Convention on Human Rights (ECHR) in more detail when we examine UK law on recognition and collective bargaining.

The fundamental right of collective bargaining is central to the ILO. This is reflected in its constitutional recognition in both the Declaration of Philadelphia[18] and the ILO Declaration on Fundamental Principles and Rights at Work 1998. Convention 98, the Right to Organise and Collective Bargaining Convention (1949), is a fundamental convention. The key provision

---

[16] For an interesting argument about switching this default, so that workers must opt out rather than opt in to unionisation, see M Harcourt, G Gall, RV Kumar, R Croucher, 'A Union Default: A Policy to Raise Union Membership, Promote the Freedom to Associate, Protect the Freedom not to Associate and Progress Union Representation' (2019) 48 *Industrial Law Journal* 66.
[17] PL Davies and Lord Wedderburn, 'The Land of Industrial Democracy' (1977) 6 *Industrial Law Journal* 197, for a historical perspective on company law reform and industrial democracy.
[18] III(e).

in C98 is set out in Article 4, which may be one of the most important articles in international labour law:

> Measures appropriate to national conditions shall be taken, where necessary, to encourage and promote the full development and utilisation of machinery for voluntary negotiation between employers or employers' organisations and workers' organisations, with a view to the regulation of terms and conditions of employment by means of collective agreements.

In terms of legal form, this does not appear to be formulated as a *right* either of trade unions or workers. Nor does it envisage a correlative legal *duty* on employers to negotiate with a union. Instead, it specifies a positive obligation on the state 'to encourage and promote' machinery for voluntary collective bargaining. Even then, the positive obligation is conditioned by the fact that auxiliary support should be 'appropriate to national conditions' and only 'where necessary'. Further specification of the scope and content of the state's positive obligation is set out in Article 5 of Convention 154, Collective Bargaining Convention (1981).

The open-textured nature of these fundamental norms is a necessary response to the diversity of collective bargaining models around the world. Collective bargaining may be focused at the level of the enterprise, sector, or national level dialogue. It is sometimes correlative to a directly enforced legal duty to bargain, especially in enterprise-based systems such as the US and Canada. In sectoral bargaining, by contrast, there may be no direct legal duty to bargain but strong indirect support of collective agreements through administrative machinery guaranteeing or extending their normative effects. The remedies for failures to bargain may be financial or based in injunctive relief. International standards need to be formulated at a high level of generality to accommodate these reasonable national variations in collective bargaining models.

This approach is also reflected in the work of the ILO Committee on Freedom of Association (CFA). Its work has developed general principles that set broad parameters for a 'right' to collective bargaining without being too prescriptive. In particular, the CFA has emphasised the fundamental importance of the 'voluntary character' of effective collective bargaining, which limits the extent to which direct compulsion can be used to promote it.[19] It has also tried to steer a course between national models that oblige the social partners to negotiate and those that do not: both are permissible.[20] The CFA also treads carefully where national models allocate preferential bargaining rights to 'representative' trade unions.

In enterprise-level collective bargaining, for example, the CFA recognises the legitimacy of exclusive bargaining rights for the most representative union in the bargaining unit.[21] However, this must be subject to safeguards such as independent verification of representative status, and regular opportunities for other unions to assess the support levels of competing unions. Minority unions must be permitted to represent their members and speak on their behalf, even where they do not have formal bargaining rights.[22] The CFA Digest, which runs to hundreds of pages, is not devoid of principles, however. The collated decisions provide determinate guidance to member states and a critical yardstick to evaluate diverse national models of collective bargaining. Similar general principles can be seen in the decisions of the European Committee of Social Rights in respect of Article 6 of the European Social Charter (ESC), which requires that member states ensure 'effective exercise of the *right* to bargain collectively'.[23]

---

[19] ILO, *Freedom of Association: Digest of Decisions and Principles of the Freedom of Association Committee of the Governing Body of the ILO*, 6th edn (2018) 1313.
[20] ibid 1317–18.
[21] ibid 1350–51.
[22] ibid 1387.
[23] Council of Europe, *Digest of the Case Law of the European Committee of Social Rights* (2022).

The right to consultation is not entirely absent from the ILO and the ESC. Article 6 ESC includes the promotion of joint consultation as an aspect of the right to bargain collectively. ILO Consultation (National and Industrial Levels) Recommendation 113 (1960) also recommends the promotion of effective consultation and cooperation. Yet consultation is subsidiary and an adjunct to the ILO's overriding emphasis on collective bargaining. For example, Recommendation 113 provides that 'Such consultation and co-operation should not derogate from freedom of association or from the rights of employers' and workers' organisations, including their right of collective bargaining.'

By contrast, the EU's approach to voice at work is focused more strongly on information and consultation of employees. Some labour lawyers were very critical of this emphasis on consultation over collective bargaining at the European level. For example, Lord Wedderburn considered that EU-level consultation would only be effective where it was supported by strong collective bargaining with autonomous trade unions.[24] Otherwise, 'Without the constraints of autonomous collective bargaining, management prerogative can turn consultation into a highway for "personalised contracts".'[25] The recent directive on adequate minimum wages in the EU does indicate a shift towards EU-level regulatory support for collective bargaining. European law on consultation was also controversial in requiring dual channel representation so that employees without a trade union were not denied their information and consultation rights. This challenged the historical approach in UK industrial relations, which was 'single channel' trade union representation based on collective bargaining.[26] This 'dual channel' information and consultation still represents the dominant EU approach to worker voice. Promoting broader representational coverage of workers could fit better with the democratic justification for consultation. However, it is also important to consider the independence and expertise of these non-union channels of representation.

Article 27 of the EU Charter of Fundamental Rights provides that 'Workers or their representatives must, at the appropriate levels, be guaranteed information and consultation in good time in the cases and under the conditions provided for by Union law and national laws and practices'. As the Explanatory Note on Article 27 makes clear, this right to information and consultation is also reflected in Article 21 of the revised European Social Charter 1996 and points 17 and 18 of the Community Charter on the Fundamental Social Rights of Workers 1989. In *AMS*, the Court of Justice took the view that Article 27 depended upon further legislative action for its specification and implementation and so could not be relied upon directly by individual parties in litigation.[27] However, the Court also considered that this right was 'fundamental' in nature.[28]

There has been extensive legislative activity on information and consultation at the EU level. These instruments give concrete legal specification to the human right to information and consultation. The first wave of activity occurred in the 1970s. This was focused on information and consultation within the context of economic restructuring and change. For example, the duty to consult on collective redundancies originated in Directive 75/129/EEC.[29]

---

[24] Lord Wedderburn, 'Consultation or Collective Bargaining in Europe: Success or Ideology?' (1997) 26 *Industrial Law Journal* 1.
[25] ibid 32.
[26] PL Davies, 'A Challenge to Single Channel' (1994) 23 *ILJ* 272.
[27] Case C-176/12 *Association de mediation sociale v Union locale des syndicats* [2014] IRLR 310.
[28] ibid [42].
[29] See now Council Directive 98/59/EC of 20 July 1998 on the approximation of the laws of the Member States relating to collective redundancies [1998] OJ 225/16.

Information and consultation duties are also triggered where there is a transfer of undertakings.[30] The second wave of activity was focused on providing for more general structures of information and consultation, allowing workers and their representatives to anticipate and shape economic changes rather than reacting to them. This might also give workers a more effective opportunity to influence those business strategies, rather than just mitigating their effects.

The first major intervention was action on European Works Councils which was first agreed in 1994.[31] Given its focus on transnational Community-scale entities operating across different Member States, this area was well-suited to legislative action at the European level. Otherwise there would be a serious regulatory deficit that could not be addressed within Member States. It was revised in 2009 to ensure better coordination between transnational and national consultation processes,[32] and further revisions are anticipated. In 2002, the EU legislated for general information and consultation in national level firms.[33] We have already noted the significant variations across different European countries in respect of worker voice, trade unions, and structures of collective bargaining and consultation. This legislative intervention needed to be sensitive to these variations so as not to disrupt or undermine existing national protections for worker participation. It was focused heavily on a process for negotiating consultation procedures rather than imposing prescriptive templates. A more prescriptive approach could be a serious problem where there were already works councils, for example. We will consider the EU framework on information and consultation in more detail later in the chapter.

In the next section, we consider the law on trade union recognition and collective bargaining in more detail. It will begin with the right to collective bargaining under Article 11 of the ECHR. The case law on Article 11 has been through a dynamic and exciting period in recent times. This followed a long period where the Court adopted a cautious approach to trade union rights. We will then examine the detailed statutory law in the UK on recognition and collective bargaining from the perspective of Article 11. While the case law under Article 11 has sometimes been viewed as giving rise to radical possibilities for improving UK law, the actual impact of Article 11 has been quite modest. This may reveal something about the potential (and limitations) of human rights law to generate radical legal changes.

3. Trade Union Recognition and Collective Bargaining

The ECHR and Article 11

Until the early 2000s, the ECtHR adopted a cautious approach to the development of positive trade union rights under Article 11. Article 11 protects the 'right to form and join trade unions for the protection of his interests'. This was always regarded by the ECtHR as requiring states to

---

[30] Council Directive 2001/23/EC of 12 March 2001 on the approximation of the laws of Member States relating to the safeguarding of employees' rights in the event of transfers of undertakings, businesses or parts of undertakings or businesses [2001] OJ L82/16, Article 7.

[31] Council Directive 94/45/EC of 22 September 1994 on the establishment of a European Works Council or a procedure in Community-scale undertakings and Community-scale groups of undertakings for the purposes of informing and consulting employees [1994] OJ L254/64.

[32] Council Directive 2009/38/EC of 6 May 2009 on the establishment of a European Works Council or a procedure in Community-scale undertakings and Community-scale groups of undertakings for the purposes of informing and consulting employees (recast).

[33] Council Directive 2002/14/EC of 11 March 2002 establishing a general framework for informing and consulting employees in the European Community [2002] OJ L80/29.

take *some* positive legal measures in their national laws so that trade unions could protect their members' occupational interests through collective action. While this might include collective bargaining, there were other ways in which states might implement the right that the trade union should be heard.[34] This reflected the generally wide margin of appreciation for states given the sensitive issues of social and economic policy in the regulation of industrial relations systems. While some academics were critical of what they regarded as an 'anti-collectivist' agenda,[35] it is also important to acknowledge national sensitivities around trade union laws. They display a great variety across Europe and reflect the diverse histories of trade union movements and social change. The Court's cautious approach during this period may have been pragmatic as much as it was ideological.

An important shift occurred in *Wilson v UK*.[36] Under UK law at the time, employers were free to offer financial inducements to workers to persuade them to opt out of union representation. The withholding of offers did not constitute 'action short of dismissal' because of their trade union membership. The ECtHR concluded that the state had failed in its positive obligations to secure the Article 11 rights of both the workers and the trade union itself from interference by the employer:

> it is of the essence of the right to join a trade union for the protection of their interests that employees should be free to instruct or permit the union to make representation to their employer or to take action in support of their interests on their behalf. If workers are prevented from so doing, their freedom to belong to a trade union, for the protection of their interests, becomes illusory. It is the role of the State to ensure that trade union members are not prevented or restrained from using their union to represent them in attempts to regulate their relations with their employers.[37]

The ECtHR did not go on to consider whether the interference could be justified under Article 11(2). This perhaps reflects the gravity of individual trade union victimisation and discrimination, which strikes at the very core of freedom of association. It is difficult to imagine how individual union victimisation could be justified under any circumstances. It should also be recalled that the strict protective approach in *Wilson* involved a private sector employer. The judgment was also notable for its use of the 'integrated approach', developing its interpretation of Article 11 using relevant ILO and ESC provisions.

It was perhaps easier for a court to take this step in *Wilson* because individual discrimination wrongs are very serious violations of human rights. At this stage, the Court was not prepared to recognise a fundamental right to bargain collectively. Nor was it necessary for it to do so in this case. The Court was also reluctant to trespass on the state's 'collective' arrangements for recognition and collective bargaining, which (unlike individual victimisation) continued to fall within the state's wide margin of appreciation:

> Compulsory collective bargaining would impose on employers an obligation to conduct negotiations with trade unions. The Court has not yet been prepared to hold that the freedom of a trade union to make its voice heard extends to imposing on an employer an obligation to recognise a trade union. The union and its members must however be free, in one way or another, to seek to persuade the employer to listen to what it has to say on behalf of its members.[38]

---

[34] *Swedish Engine Drivers' Union v Sweden* (1979-80) 1 EHRR 617.
[35] Lord Wedderburn, 'Freedom of Association or Right to Organise? The Common Law and International Sources' in Lord Wedderburn, *Employment Rights in Britain and Europe* (Lawrence & Wishart, 1991), originally published in (1987) 18 *Industrial Relations Journal* 244.
[36] (2002) 35 EHRR 20.
[37] ibid [46].
[38] ibid [44].

The ECtHR appeared to take a momentous step in *Demir and Baykara v Turkey*.[39] This arose out of the non-recognition of the trade union's legal personality and the resulting annulment of a collective agreement in the public sector. The claims in *Demir* were based on the right to form a trade union (which depended upon the legal recognition of corporate personality) and the right to collective bargaining (which concerned the annulment of the collective agreement). According to the Grand Chamber, the 'integrated approach' supported the explicit recognition of the fundamental right to bargain collectively under Article 11. There were ambitious predictions about the impact of *Demir* on Article 11 and in national laws.[40] The subsequent reception of *Demir* into the Article 11 case law was rather more constrained than many had hoped. In particular, the facts in *Demir* involved a direct state interference with the trade union's legal personality and its collective agreement. As such, it was not a pure state 'positive duty' case. These extreme facts of direct state interference may have muted the subsequent legal impact of *Demir*.

This restrictive reading of *Demir* was adopted in *UNITE the Union v UK*.[41] Given their specific vulnerabilities, a special protective regime applied to the collective bargaining position of agricultural workers in the UK. These Agricultural Wages Boards (AWB) provided a state-supported institutional mechanism for setting wages and other conditions of employment. Following a public consultation exercise, the Government abolished AWBs. While agricultural workers were not prevented from using the general recognition legislation, this was practically unavailable because it was limited to employers who employed 21 or more workers. This excluded the vast proportion of agricultural workers who were employed in smaller undertakings. The Court rejected the application as manifestly ill-founded. Unlike *Demir*, there were no direct restrictions on the ability of unions to bargain collectively.[42] Even though voluntary collective bargaining was practically non-existent in the agricultural sector, there was no positive obligation on the state to introduce specific machinery for agricultural workers. The court also emphasised the wide margin of appreciation under Article 11. Given the extreme circumstances in *UNITE*, it is difficult to see what scope remains for a positive obligation to support collective bargaining under the ECHR.[43]

Finally, the ECtHR recognises the special position of 'representative' trade unions in national bargaining systems. In *Association of Civil Servants and Union for Collective Bargaining and Others v Germany*, the Court considered legal rules regulating conflicts between collective agreements in the German labour relations system.[44] The relevant legislation prioritised collective agreements negotiated by the most representative unions. This made it difficult for minority unions to negotiate and apply their own collective agreements. The ECtHR concluded that there was no violation. The Court reiterated that under Article 11 'States remained free to organise their collective bargaining system so as, if appropriate, to grant special status to representative trade unions'.[45] It was also important in this case that these particular rules were designed to strengthen the system of collective bargaining, not undermine it.[46] Accordingly, the state had a wide margin of appreciation in organising its collective bargaining system and determining legal criteria of representativeness.

---

[39] (2009) 48 EHRR 54.
[40] KD Ewing and J Hendy, 'The Dramatic Implications of Demir and Baykara' (2010) 39 *Industrial Law Journal* 2.
[41] App No 65397/13, 3 May 2016.
[42] ibid [65].
[43] For criticism, see K Arabadijeva, 'Another Disappointment in Strasbourg: Unite the Union v United Kingdom' (2017) 46 *ILJ* 289.
[44] *Association of Civil Servants and Union for Collective Bargaining and Others v Germany* [2022] ECHR 543.
[45] ibid [60].
[46] ibid [69].

Overall, then, the ECtHR has adopted a cautious approach to the right to collective bargaining under Article 11. The initial flurry of excitement about *Demir* is now long forgotten. The Court applies a wide margin of appreciation to member states in their collective bargaining systems, such as the level of bargaining, designating trade unions as representative, the enforcement of any legal duties to bargain, and so forth. Nor is there a legal requirement of compulsory recognition under Article 11. This margin is greatly reduced where individual trade unionists have been victimised (*Wilson*) or where the state itself has intervened directly to restrict or undermine collective bargaining (*Demir*). The state's positive obligation to promote collective bargaining is not yet well-developed, and there would seem to be little scope for it after *UNITE*. The basic minimum under Article 11 is that the union must be free to organise strike action to seek recognition in a purely voluntary system, and workers must be protected from victimisation.

Schedule A1 of TULCRA 1992 and Article 11 ECHR

What does the right to bargain collectively look like in UK law and practice? It is framed around the concept of 'recognition'. There are two forms of recognition, voluntary and statutory. UK law gives priority to voluntary over statutory recognition, and this is reflected in the legal machinery. Voluntary recognition depends upon employer consent. Where the employer recognises the union for the purposes of collective bargaining, this is described as voluntary recognition. It describes a situation where the employer recognises the union for the purposes of negotiation with a view to striking a bargain.[47] The union may induce an employer to recognise it for negotiation through rational persuasion or threats of strike action. The employer may prefer to avoid the time and expense of defending a statutory claim under the statutory procedure. It may also accord voluntary recognition for more cynical reasons, for example selecting a 'sweetheart' union that it considers more cooperative or compliant with a managerial agenda.

Where an employer is not prepared to agree to voluntary recognition, an independent trade union can make an application for statutory recognition under the procedure set out in Schedule A1 of TULRCA 1992.[48] The Schedule sets out detailed and prescriptive legal steps for the relevant adjudicative body, the Central Arbitration Committee (CAC), to consider the union's recognition application. The policy of Schedule A1 is to favour voluntary recognition over statutory recognition, and the law nudges the parties towards voluntary arrangements. This fits with the historical context of 'collective laissez-faire' and voluntarism.[49] It also reflects a practical judgement that long-term bargaining relationships are more likely to be enduring where the parties are committed to its success rather than subject to legal compulsion.

The Schedule A1 procedure is based upon a model of majority worker support. This majoritarian approach is the specific legal model of representativeness codified in the statute. The principal function of the CAC is to assess the level of worker support, and its discretion is relatively constrained. Although this fundamental majoritarian principle is simply stated, the legal procedure itself is complex. Before considering whether this legislative approach is within the UK's margin of appreciation, we will first set out the main legal steps for a Schedule A1 claim. It is highly detailed so as to limit the scope for CAC discretion and so minimise its exposure to judicial

---

[47] *NUGSAT v Albury Brothers Ltd* [1979] ICR 84, CA.
[48] On the recognition procedure in its political context, see A Bogg, *The Democratic Aspects of Trade Union Recognition* (Hart, 2009).
[49] R Dukes, 'Otto Kahn-Freund and Collective Laissez-Faire: An Edifice without a Keystone?' (2009) 72 *Modern Law Review* 220.

review proceedings. In this respect, it has been successful and so avoided some of the problems of earlier statutory recognition procedures enacted in the 1970s.[50]

The application under Schedule A1 must be made by an independent trade union on behalf of a group of workers and addressed to an employer that employs at least 21 workers.[51] If there is no voluntary agreement between the parties, the CAC must then assess at this preliminary stage whether the union's application can proceed under the legislation. The application may only be accepted if there is no existing union recognition in place, reflecting the legislative priority of voluntary recognition.[52] The legislator was keen to avoid the use of Schedule A1 in situations of inter-union conflict, where unions are fighting over the same group of workers. Additionally, the CAC must assess the likely credibility of the application: at least 10% of the workers in the union's proposed bargaining unit must be members of the union, and the CAC must consider it likely that a majority of workers in the bargaining unit will support the union's recognition claim.[53] This filter ensures that legal and administrative resources are being directed at meritorious cases.

If the application is accepted, the CAC must consider whether the union's proposed bargaining unit is 'appropriate' by reference to statutory criteria, the most important of which is that the unit is 'compatible with effective management'.[54] Once the bargaining unit is settled, the CAC must then assess the level of worker support in the bargaining unit. There are two ways in which this can be demonstrated. The first is through majority union membership, although such cases tend to be rarer because workers are more likely to join unions once they are being represented and can experience its benefits.[55] The second is through a ballot of the bargaining unit, where a majority (and 40 per cent of those entitled to vote) must vote in favour of union recognition.[56] Where the union achieves the support threshold, the parties will at this stage usually agree a voluntary bargaining procedure. However, the CAC may specify a 'method' of bargaining which covers pay, hours, and holidays.[57] There is no explicit legal 'good faith' duty to bargain with a view to reaching an agreement in this 'method'.

The Schedule A1 procedure has had a long statutory life compared with previous and short-lived historical experiments with statutory recognition in the 1970s. Its direct impact on collective labour relations has not been very extensive, and the annual number of Schedule A1 applications is usually in the tens rather than the hundreds. Scholars have criticised a range of flaws in its legal design: its deference to existing recognition arrangements gives employers too much power to pre-empt statutory applications by more representative trade unions; it does not tackle employer hostility to unionisation effectively enough; the process is too cumbersome and unwieldy to be effective; and it is based upon neutrality rather than positive state support for collective bargaining.[58]

From the perspective of our book, the critical question is whether these design flaws amount to a violation of Article 11. The regulatory challenge is that there are a great variety of collective

---

[50] B Simpson, 'Judicial Control of the CAC' (2007) 36 *Industrial Law Journal* 287.
[51] TULRCA 1992, Sch A1, para 10.
[52] ibid para 35.
[53] ibid paras 36(1)(a) and 36(1)(b).
[54] ibid para 18.
[55] Even where there is majority membership, the CAC may order a ballot in certain specified situations, for example where this would be in the interests of good industrial relations: ibid paras 22(3) and (4).
[56] ibid para 29.
[57] Trade Union Recognition (Method of Collective Bargaining) Order 2000 (SI 2000/1300).
[58] R Dukes, 'The Statutory Recognition Procedure 1999: no Bias in Favour of Recognition?' (2008) 37 *ILJ* 236.

bargaining models across Europe, and the standards in Article 11 must be capable of accommodating this divergence. Courts are also reluctant to encroach on democratic institutions where there has been a considered attempt to legislate on collective bargaining. The issues are often viewed as highly political, so that the courts must be careful to observe proper constitutional limits. The effect of this has been effectively to insulate Schedule A1 from legal challenge using Article 11 in the English courts. This dominant judicial approach is reflected in a trio of cases culminating in the recent Supreme Court judgment in *Deliveroo*.

The first case in the trio is *R (Boots Management Services Ltd.) v Central Arbitration Committee*.[59] This involved a voluntary recognition with a non-independent association, the Boots Pharmacists Association (BPA), the effect of which was to block a statutory application by an independent union, the Pharmacists' Defence Association (PDAU). The barrier to the PDAU's application was not absolute. Since the BPA was non-independent, an individual worker could trigger a process leading to a de-recognition ballot. If the BPA was de-recognised, the PDAU would then be clear to make a statutory application. According to Underhill LJ, since the barrier was not absolute, the legislative measure was within the state's wide margin of appreciation under Article 11. The fact that a legislative choice might be viewed as sub-optimal did not mean it was a human rights violation. However, the Court of Appeal did raise the issue of whether the complete removal of the statutory procedure or a very serious inadequacy with it might constitute an Article 11 violation. This was a very high threshold. Any legislative specification of an abstract right inevitably involves a limitation on who enjoys the right, the circumstances in which it can be claimed, and against whom that right can be asserted. The state enjoys a wide margin of appreciation to make those choices through its democratic institutions.

The second case also concerned 'representativeness'. In *R (Independent Workers Union of Great Britain) v Central Arbitration Committee*, the IWGB was blocked from using Schedule A1 because of an existing voluntary agreement with an independent trade union.[60] This was different to *Boots* because there was no possibility of seeking de-recognition under the legislation. This meant that the IWGB was prevented from using Schedule A1 for as long as the voluntary recognition arrangement continued. The Court of Appeal again concluded that the legislator's choice of legal rules on access to Schedule A1 was within the state's margin of appreciation. There are winners and losers whenever Parliament decides on a statutory scheme. That is an unavoidable consequence of legislating. In this case, the workers concerned also had the benefit of existing recognition with a well-established and reputable independent trade union. Both Bean LJ and Underhill LJ questioned whether the removal of the Schedule A1 might constitute a violation of Article 11. In other words, this left open the possibility that there might be a positive obligation to provide some legal support for recognition, even if the detail of the scheme was ultimately a matter for Parliament.

Finally, the recent Supreme Court judgment in *Deliveroo* now effectively closes off that small opening for Article 11.[61] Strictly speaking, these observations on the positive obligation were *obiter* because the case turned upon whether riders were in an 'employment relationship' under Article 11. Having concluded that they were not in an 'employment relationship', and hence did not enjoy trade union rights under the ECHR, the issue of positive obligation was not necessary to deciding the case. According to the Supreme Court, the ECtHR's case law under Article 11 did not support

---

[59] [2017] EWCA Civ 66, [2017] IRLR 355. For a human rights analysis, see A Bogg and R Dukes, 'Article 11 ECHR and the Right to Collective Bargaining' (2017) 46 *Industrial Law Journal* 543.
[60] [2021] EWCA Civ 260, [2021] ICR 729.
[61] *IWGB v CAC and another* [2023] UKSC 43.

the view that there was a positive obligation to maintain a legal procedure like Schedule A1.[62] Does this mean that a state need do nothing by way of positive legal support for collective bargaining? For example, in a purely voluntary system based on the common law, gig workers would be unprotected from basic forms of individual victimisation for trade union activities; and the organiser of strike action could potentially be sued in tort. They would then be unable to engage in activities to persuade the employer to listen to the trade union. This would constitute a violation of Article 11. In fact, this is effectively the situation now left by the judgment in *Deliveroo* for the riders, because the most basic protections in TULRCA 1992 (such as protection from detriment) depend on worker status. The Supreme Court held that that the Riders were not in an 'employment relationship', and this meant that they were unprotected from trade union detriments under the 1992 Act. *Deliveroo* is unlikely to be the last word on Article 11 rights in the gig economy.

Collective Bargaining and Individual Offers

Following *Wilson v UK*, a new statutory provision was enacted in the Employment Relations Act 2004 to regulate 'offers' within the context of recognition and collective bargaining. This is now set out in s 145B of TULRCA 1992. This provision is wider than the facts in *Wilson* itself, where the offers were tied to the relinquishment of union representation. Under s 145B, a worker who is a member of an independent trade union that is recognised or seeking recognition has a right not to have an offer made to him in certain 'collective bargaining' contexts. Those offers must, if accepted by other workers to whom offers had been made, lead to the 'prohibited result'. This result is that the workers' term (or terms) of employment would not (or would no longer) be determined by collective agreement. It does not matter if the bypassing of collective bargaining is temporary (in a current bargaining round) or amounts to a permanent exclusion of collective bargaining. Nor is it necessary for the offers to have been accepted in fact. The enquiry requires the tribunal to imagine the position if the offers were accepted, as a hypothetical matter.

If this counterfactual condition on 'prohibited result' is satisfied, the liability enquiry then shifts to the employer's 'sole or main purpose'. The assessment of the employer's 'sole or main purpose' is guided by s 145D which provides (amongst other things) that it is relevant 'that the offers were made only to particular workers, and were made with the sole or main purpose of rewarding those particular workers for their high level of performance or of retaining them because of their special value to the employer'. Where unlawful offers are made, there is a penal financial award currently set at £5,128 for each offer.

At the time of its enactment, the provision was subjected to various criticisms from an Article 11 perspective.[63] It did not give the union an independent right to enforce the provision, but depended upon individual workers enforcing the right. The remedy was individual rather than collective, and so would fail to compensate the union for its own losses such as the loss of representative standing in the workplace. The 'sole or main purpose' test also set a difficult evidential threshold, although this was deliberately designed to allow employers and workers some freedom to negotiate individualised 'performance related pay'.

The leading Supreme Court judgment is now *Kostal UK Ltd v Dunkley and others*.[64] The employer issued direct offers to workers during a collective bargaining round and before the bargaining procedure had been exhausted. The Supreme Court agreed that these offers violated

---

[62] ibid [134].
[63] A Bogg, 'Employment Relations Act 2004: Another False Dawn for Collectivism?' (2005) 34 *ILJ* 72–75.
[64] [2021] UKSC 47.

s 145B. The judgments differed as to the correct basis for this. The majority judgment was given by Lord Leggatt. He focused on the 'prohibited result' requirement. This depended upon a causation test to ascertain whether the offers, if accepted, would lead to the prohibited result.[65] If the offers had been made *during* a collective bargaining process, the matter might otherwise have been dealt with through the collective negotiation because it was still ongoing. By contrast, if the offers were made once the bargaining process was exhausted, there could be no liability because there was no scope for the matter to be negotiated collectively anyway. The offers would be causally irrelevant. The employer's 'sole or main purpose' is less important than this objective causation enquiry, although it does provide a defence to an employer who honestly believed that the bargaining was exhausted. In practice, a well-advised employer can now easily avoid s 145B liability by ensuring that its offers are timed to wait until the exhaustion of the collective bargaining process.

By contrast, Lady Arden and Lord Burrows focused on the mental element for liability.[66] On their approach, whenever individual offers were made to a group of workers, they would always have the 'prohibited result' because such terms were being determined by individual agreement, not collective agreement. In practice, liability would depend upon whether an employer could identify a reasonable business case for making those offers. Where there was a credible explanation related to the needs of the business, the employer's 'sole or main purpose' was unlikely to be present. This would depend upon a common-sense judgement by the tribunal. While the minority approach lacks the legal certainty of the majority, it also means that tribunals can scrutinise sharp bargaining conduct of employers who may go through the motions of bargaining in bad faith to reach an impasse and then maker individual offers. In strict legal terms, this may appear a little messier than the majority judgment. However, this vagueness gives tribunals scope to enforce the statute effectively, especially in bad faith bargaining situations where employers run down the clock to exhaustion of the bargaining process.

Interestingly, despite their differences, both majority and minority approaches are likely to fall within the margin of appreciation under Article 11. This particular statutory provision originated in an individual victimisation case, *Wilson*, where there is a much reduced margin. By contrast, *Kostal* and s 145B is more focused on a 'collective' issue, which is the use of legal measures to support good faith collective bargaining. In this collective context, the margin of appreciation is generally wider.

4. The EU Social Model: From Consultation to Collective Bargaining?

A glance at the EU Charter of Fundamental Rights suggests strong protection for the right to worker voice in EU law. Article 27 protects the right to information and consultation, and Article 28 protects the right to negotiate and conclude collective agreements. This is further reinforced by the replication of Article 11 ECHR in (confusingly) Article 12 of the Charter, which must, of course, be interpreted in accordance with the ECtHR's case law.[67] However, this straightforwardly protective picture masks a much more complex history.

Many Member States have strong traditions of worker voice, with constitutional protections for key rights such as freedom of association and the right to strike. But these traditions are

---

[65] ibid [65].
[66] ibid [129].
[67] EUCFR, Article 52(3).

very diverse, ranging from the use of collective bargaining to set terms and conditions across the labour market as a whole, in Scandinavian countries such as Sweden, to dual channel models with collective bargaining and works councils, in Germany, to the single channel, 'collective laissez-faire' approach found in the UK. This wide range of different practices has meant that Member States have, at times, sought to guard their autonomy with some vigour. This helps to explain the exclusion of freedom of association and the right to strike from the EU's legislative competence in Article 153(5) TFEU. However, Article 153 does provide competence over 'information and consultation of workers' and 'representation and collective defence of the interests of employers and workers, including co-determination'. And there is a strong cross-border interest in worker voice. For example, if a firm with multiple sites in different EU countries is considering a closure on economic grounds, its choice may, in part, be influenced by workers' ability to protest that closure as protected by national law. Similarly, worker voice mechanisms may be a factor in where firms decide to locate or incorporate.

Where the EU has responded to these pressures and intervened to create opportunities for worker voice, it has faced two significant challenges. One is common to any attempt to legislate on worker voice: it is not possible to compel parties to negotiate with each other or to reach agreement. It is only possible to provide a procedural framework within which this can take place. The other challenge, specific to the EU, is the diversity of national traditions just described. This means that when the EU does set out frameworks, it generally needs to keep them vague, in order to accommodate differences between Member States and to secure political support. This raises the question whether the EU's interventions in the sphere of worker voice are sufficient to effect meaningful change at the national level.

Here, we examine EU law's protection of worker voice in three historical phases: the 1970s directives dealing with major workplace changes, such as redundancies, broader efforts to encourage worker voice through more general consultation mechanisms in the 2000s, and the more recent focus on collective bargaining, despite the limits on competence, through the Directive on Adequate Minimum Wages in particular.[68] But first, it is important to mention the constitutional place of worker voice in the EU, through the social dialogue procedure.

Social Dialogue

Under Article 154 TFEU, the Commission is obliged to consult representatives of management and labour, known as the social partners, before making proposals about labour law issues, and on the details of any proposal it makes. The social partners are BUSINESSEUROPE (representing private firms), SMEunited (small businesses) and SGI Europe (public employers) on the employer side, and the ETUC on the worker side. Under Article 155 TFEU, the social partners may decide, during the consultations under Article 154, to reach an agreement themselves on a particular matter. This may operate either as a social partner agreement to be implemented at national level by employers and trade unions, or it may be enacted as a directive by the Council.

The social dialogue has produced three major directives: on parental leave, part-time work and fixed-term work.[69] There have also been several autonomous agreements, on matters such

---

[68] Directive 2022/2041/EU on adequate minimum wages in the European Union.
[69] Directive 1996/34/EC concerning the framework agreement on parental leave; Directive 2010/18/EU on the revised framework agreement on parental leave (repealed by Directive 2019/1158/EU on work–life balance with effect from 2 August 2022); Directive 97/81/EC concerning the framework agreement on part-time working; Directive 1999/70/EC concerning the framework agreement on fixed-term work.

as stress and harassment at work.[70] But the procedure has not lived up to its early promise. After the three directives, the social partners could not reach agreement on a revision to the Working Time Directive, and no further directives have emerged since the 2000s. There have been several different attempts to explain the failure of the social dialogue, but probably the most plausible is the lack of incentive on employers to agree to new binding initiatives. In 'ordinary' collective bargaining, unions back up their demands with threats of industrial action. There is no equivalent in the social dialogue. Instead, the parties bargain in the 'shadow' of the activities of the Commission and the other EU institutions.[71] If there was a clear indication that, if negotiations failed, a directive would be enacted through the usual legislative process, the employer side might have a reason to engage in the social dialogue in order to help shape the outcome. But this has not always been guaranteed, making it difficult for the worker side to get leverage. And if a directive was on the cards, there would be no incentive for the worker side to make concessions during social dialogue. There is no particular reason to suppose that a planned 'relaunch' of the social dialogue under the European Pillar of Social Rights will be able to overcome these difficulties.[72] Another Commission proposal is to develop a means of tracking Member States' implementation of the social partners' autonomous agreements, which are largely invisible at present.[73] It remains to be seen what impact this will have.

The social dialogue promises to give a 'constitutional' role to worker voice at the heart of the EU legislative process, but it has not lived up to that promise, largely because of its structural inadequacies. Perhaps paradoxically, the seemingly less powerful mechanism for consulting the social partners before enacting legislation may be a more effective way to include worker (and employer) voice.

Business Reorganisations

The 1970s saw a period of economic crisis in the EU, with rising unemployment.[74] Three directives were enacted to address some of the consequences: the Collective Redundancies Directive (CRD),[75] the Acquired Rights Directive (ARD)[76] and the Employer Insolvency Directive.[77] These sought to protect workers when their employer proposed large-scale redundancies, when the firm for which they worked changed hands, or when their employer became insolvent. The directives include both substantive and procedural protections. Both the CRD and the ARD protect workers' rights to be consulted about the changes taking place. We will take the CRD as an example.

The CRD provides for consultation in Article 2, as follows:

1. Where an employer is contemplating collective redundancies, he shall begin consultations with the workers' representatives in good time with a view to reaching an agreement.

---

[70] Framework Agreement on Stress at Work (2004); Framework Agreement on Harassment and Violence at Work (2007).
[71] For analysis, see JME Sørensen, M Würtzenfeld and MP Hansen, 'Explaining the deadlock of the European social dialogue: negotiating in the shadow of hierarchy' (2022) 42 *Journal of Public Policy* 323.
[72] European Pillar of Social Rights, Principle 8.
[73] Commission, 'Strengthening social dialogue in the European Union: harnessing its full potential for managing fair transitions' COM (2023) 40 final.
[74] For detail, see Jeff Kenner, *EU Employment Law: From Rome to Amsterdam and Beyond* (Hart, 2003) ch 2.
[75] Directive 98/59/EC on the approximation of EU countries' laws regarding collective redundancies.
[76] Directive 77/187/EEC on the approximation of the laws of the Member States relating to the safeguarding of employees' rights in the event of transfers of undertakings (as amended by Directive 98/50/EC and consolidated in Directive 2001/23/EC).
[77] Originally Directive 80/987/EEC. The current text is Directive 2008/94/EC on the protection of employees in the event of the insolvency of their employer.

2. These consultations shall, at least, cover ways and means of avoiding collective redundancies or reducing the number of workers affected, and of mitigating the consequences by recourse to accompanying social measures aimed, inter alia, at aid for redeploying or retraining workers made redundant.

Consultation may be defined in different ways, giving a greater or lesser role in the ultimate decision to the people being consulted. The CRD adopts a relatively strong definition, using the phrase 'with a view to reaching an agreement'.[78] This does not mean that the parties are obliged to agree, but it clearly requires a sincere effort in that direction. This gives a more powerful role to worker voice, closer to what we find in collective bargaining.

The Directive is specific about a number of factors which contribute to an effective consultation process. First, it requires the consultation to take place 'in good time' when the employer is 'contemplating' collective redundancies.[79] This reflects the fact that it is difficult to influence the outcome when the employer has already made its decision and consults late in the day. Of course, the provision can be difficult to enforce in practice, but its good intentions are clear.[80] Second, Article 2(2) sets out in some detail what the consultation process is to cover. When a large number of workers is being made redundant, it is tempting to focus on preventing that from happening, but the detail provided in the Directive encourages the parties to pay attention to other significant possibilities, such as reducing the numbers or providing support to the workers who are losing their jobs. Third, Article 2(3) sets out in some detail the information to be provided to the representatives. This is important because no meaningful discussion can take place unless the representatives have a clear idea of what is being proposed and why.

Two important elements of the protection on offer are left to the Member States to determine, in accordance with the EU's usual practice. These are the identification of the representatives and the remedies for a failure to consult. However, in both cases, the Member States' discretion is not unlimited. The UK initially implemented the CRD by providing that employers should consult trade union representatives, in accordance with the UK's 'single channel' tradition.[81] However, this meant that workers in non-unionised workplaces had no effective right to be consulted. The CJEU ruled that this amounted to a failure to implement the Directive properly, so the UK had to create a mechanism for the election of representatives in non-unionised workplaces.[82] The remedies provided by the Member State in the event of non-compliance with the duty to consult must meet the usual tests of equivalence and effectiveness.[83] In the UK, non-compliance with s 188 of TULRCA 1992 attracts a so-called 'protective award' of up to 90 days' pay for each affected employee.[84] The courts have struggled to implement this provision, ultimately concluding that it is, in effect, a penalty applied to the employer which should reflect the seriousness of the breach, so the highest possible award should be made in respect of a total failure to consult.[85] A prohibition on implementing the redundancies until the consultation has been carried out would be a much more effective remedy.[86]

---

[78] CRD, Article 2(1).
[79] CRD, Article 2(1).
[80] See eg Case C-44/08 *AEK ry v Fujitsu Siemens Computers Oy* [2010] ICR 444.
[81] Case C-383/92 *Commission v UK* [1994] ECR I-2479. For discussion, see P Davies, 'A Challenge to Single Channel' (1994) 23 *ILJ* 272; P Davies and C Kilpatrick, 'UK Worker Representation After Single Channel' (2004) 33 *ILJ* 121.
[82] Case C-496/22 *EI v SC Brink's Cash Solutions SRL* ECLI EU:C:2023:741.
[83] Case C-12/08 *Mono Car Styling SA v Odemis* EU:C:2009:466, [2009] ECR I-6653.
[84] TULRCA 1992, s 189.
[85] eg *E Ivor Hughes Educational Foundation v Morris* [2015] IRLR 696.
[86] See ACL Davies, *Valuing Employment Rights: A Study of Remedies in Employment Law* (Hart, 2024) ch 6.

The fact that the CRD implements the right to worker voice has had some impact on its interpretation and application. The claimants in the *Vining* case were 'parks police officers' employed by a local council.[87] They were not consulted when collective redundancies were proposed because the duty to consult (TULRCA 1992, s 188, implementing the CRD) did not apply to people in 'police service'.[88] The Court of Appeal held that, although consultation was not the same as collective bargaining, it was protected by Article 11 ECHR. The Government had provided no explanation for the exclusion of the parks police officers, so there was no possibility of justification under Article 11(2). Using s 3 of the Human Rights Act 1998, s 188 of TULRCA 1992 could be interpreted so as to include them.

Although EU law typically sets minimum standards for labour rights on which Member States are permitted to improve, there are limits to this principle. In the case of the CRD, this became apparent in *AGET Iraklis*.[89] In that case, a firm sought to challenge a rule of Greek law that required the permission of a government minister before collective redundancies could take place. The firm argued that the rule interfered with its freedom of establishment under Article 49 TFEU, and with its freedom to run a business, protected by Article 16 of the EU Charter of Fundamental Rights. The CJEU accepted that Member States could provide additional protection beyond that set out in the Directive, and that helping to safeguard jobs was a legitimate objective. However, it found that the Greek legislation did amount to a disproportionate interference with the employer's interests, because the criteria attaching to the grant of permission were too vague, and because the CRD sought to provide safeguards in collective redundancy situations rather than to stop redundancies going ahead altogether.

General Duties to Consult

The 1970s directives imposed duties to consult on specific occasions when workers were affected by changes to the business. Subsequent directives sought to promote the idea of worker voice as a more general requirement for firms. This is likely to be a more effective way of integrating worker voice into firms' decision-making than requirements to consult only in times of crisis. We examine two directives here: on European or Transnational Works Councils, and Information and Consultation.[90]

The original Directive on European Works Councils was passed in 1994,[91] with a revision enacted in 2009.[92] The provisions apply to firms with at least 1,000 workers, with at least 150 in each of two or more Member States.[93] It is not compulsory to set up a European Works Council (EWC): negotiations may be initiated by management on its own initiative or on the request of 100 employees or their representatives in at least two Member States.[94] This requires a degree of coordination among the workforce even to get the negotiations off the ground. As we noted at the outset, parties cannot be forced into an agreement, so the Directive seeks to facilitate this by providing a process with some default rules which can be applied if

---

[87] *Wandsworth LBC v Vining* [2017] EWCA Civ 1092, [2018] ICR 499.
[88] TULRCA 1992, s 280.
[89] Case C-201/15 *AGET Iraklis* EU:C:2016:972, [2017] 2 CMLR 32. For discussion, see Stefano Giubboni, 'Freedom to Conduct a Business and EU Labour Law' (2018) 14 *European Constitutional Law Review* 172.
[90] For reasons of space, we are unable to consider worker involvement provisions in European company law here.
[91] Directive 94/45/EC on European Works Councils.
[92] Directive 2009/38/EC on European Works Councils (Recast).
[93] EWC Directive, Article 2.
[94] ibid Article 5(1).

agreement cannot be reached. If a valid request is received, management must set up a Special Negotiating Body (SNB).[95] The role of the SNB is to negotiate arrangements for an EWC, such as its composition and the frequency of its meetings.[96] The default rules apply if management refuses to set up the SNB or if agreement cannot be reached after three years.[97] These default rules are quite limited in content, which makes it difficult for SNBs to negotiate for more elaborate arrangements. For example, they limit EWCs to one meeting per year, plus the possibility of emergency meetings in relation to collective redundancies or plant closures,[98] and the information to be provided relates mainly to the firm's financial situation rather than to its broader policies:

> The information of the European Works Council shall relate in particular to the structure, economic and financial situation, probable development and production and sales of the Community-scale undertaking or group of undertakings. The information and consultation of the European Works Council shall relate in particular to the situation and probable trend of employment, investments, and substantial changes concerning organisation, introduction of new working methods or production processes, transfers of production, mergers, cut-backs or closures of undertakings, establishments or important parts thereof, and collective redundancies.[99]

The ETUC has suggested that EWCs should be encouraged to look at broader issues such as the impact of climate change and the transition towards a greener economy, the firm's plans in relation to algorithmic management and artificial intelligence (some, but not all, of which might be captured by 'new working methods') and labour rights in supply chains.[100]

One potential area of concern about EWCs from the perspective of worker voice is that the Directives use a relatively weak definition of consultation: the 'establishment of dialogue and exchange of views'.[101] There is no reference to attempting to reach an agreement, an approach we encountered above in the CRD. Although the role of the EWC is for the parties to determine, it seems unlikely that management would be willing to go beyond what the Directive envisages, and the Directive clearly leaves the ultimate decision-making power in the hands of the employer.

Another issue is the limitation of the EWC to the consideration of 'transnational' issues, a provision introduced in 2009.[102] The intention behind this was to help the EWC to mesh more effectively with national information and consultation arrangements, by carving out a distinctive role for information and consultation at EU level. 'Transnational' is defined in the Directive as concerning the EU-wide firm as a whole, or undertakings in two or more Member States.[103] This has the potential to generate disputes about whether a particular issue is 'transnational' or not, and is relatively easily bypassed. For example, a firm seeking to close an undertaking in one Member State could argue that this was not a transnational matter, even though this may involve an implicit choice not to close a different undertaking, and may have implications for workers in other parts of the group.

---

[95] ibid Article 5.
[96] ibid Article 6.
[97] ibid Article 7.
[98] ibid Annex 1, paras 2 and 3.
[99] ibid para 1(a).
[100] ETUC response to the second-phase consultation of Social Partners under Article 154 TFEU on a possible revision of the European Works Council Directive (2009/38/EC) (October 2023).
[101] EWC Directive, Article 2(1)(g).
[102] ibid Article 1(3).
[103] ibid Article 1(4).

At the time of writing, there are ongoing discussions about a further revision to the Directive. The Commission has published a proposal[104] following calls from the European Parliament to strengthen the Directive,[105] and a failed attempt to pursue a revision through the social dialogue procedure. The proposal includes a default rule of two meetings per year instead of one, and clarifications to the definition of a 'transnational' issue. Although it also includes changes to the definition of consultation, it would still leave the ultimate decision firmly in the hands of management.[106]

While the EWC Directive seeks to create opportunities for worker voice at the EU level, another initiative, the Information and Consultation (I&C) Directive, seeks partially to harmonise information and consultation arrangements in national firms.[107] This was less easy to justify as an EU measure, because the cross-border implications are less obvious. However, Member States with elaborate information and consultation mechanisms feared that they might be at a disadvantage relative to Member States with fewer or no such obligations, and there was also a concern that the EWC Directive could not function effectively without equivalent national arrangements. The I&C Directive was eventually agreed in 2002. It applies to larger national firms: Member States may choose to apply it to 'undertakings employing at least 50 employees' or 'establishments employing at least 20 employees'.[108] It leaves substantial discretion to the Member States to decide how I&C mechanisms should be set up and what form they should take.

The Directive is more specific about the subject-matter for information and consultation, setting out three different levels of employee involvement. First, information must be provided on 'the recent and probable development of the undertaking's or the establishment's activities and economic situation'.[109] Second, information and consultation must take place on 'the situation, structure and probable development of employment within the undertaking or establishment and on any anticipatory measures envisaged, in particular where there is a threat to employment'.[110] Third, consultation 'with a view to reaching agreement' must take place 'on decisions likely to lead to substantial changes in work organisation or in contractual relations'.[111] This latter provision ensures that the Directive is consistent with other EU measures, such as the CRD.

There is a dearth of reliable information about the impact of the Directive in the Member States.[112] The Directive is necessarily vague, in order to enable Member States to adapt it to their traditions of worker voice. However, a potential disadvantage of this approach is that the Directive may not be rigorous enough to support the creation of effective information and consultation mechanisms in Member States where no such tradition exists. For example, the UK

---

[104] Commission, *Proposal for a Directive of the European Parliament and of the Council amending Directive 2009/38/EC as regards the establishment and functioning of European Works Councils and the effective enforcement of transnational information and consultation rights* COM(2024)14 final.

[105] European Parliament resolution of 2 February 2023 with recommendations to the Commission on Revision of European Works Councils Directive (2019/2183(INL)).

[106] For criticisms, see ETUC press release, Improvements to European Works Councils under new draft directive (24 January 2024).

[107] Directive 2002/14/EC establishing a general framework for informing and consulting employees in the European Community.

[108] ibid Article 3.

[109] ibid Article 4(2)(a).

[110] ibid Article 4(2)(b).

[111] ibid Article 4(2)(c).

[112] Commission Staff Working Document, 'Fitness check' on EU law in the area of Information and Consultation of Workers SWD(2013) 293 final.

implemented the Directive in 2004.[113] Given that this was a time of declining trade union membership, this could have provided an opportunity to give workers an alternative route to securing some voice at work, or to give trade unions a different way of engaging with workers and employers in non-unionised workplaces.[114] Instead, the UK's implementation was formulaic and had little effect in practice.

A final point to note is that the CJEU has not given particularly strong effect to the right to worker voice underpinning the I&C Directive. In the *AMS* case, the Court was asked to consider the effect of French legislation which excluded workers with a particular type of contract from counting towards the firm size threshold for the application of the information and consultation provisions.[115] This amounted to a failure to implement the Directive correctly. However, the issue arose in a horizontal dispute between workers and their employer, in which the Directive could not be invoked, because of the general rule that directives do not have horizontal direct effect. The claimant tried to argue in favour of a general principle of worker voice, relying on Article 27 of the EU Charter of Fundamental Rights, in order to get the national rule disapplied.[116] But the Court refused to accept this approach, noting that the right set out in Article 27 required further specification in EU and national law, and could not be regarded as capable of being invoked by individuals.

Collective Bargaining

Although, as we noted above, the EU does not have competence to legislate on core collective matters, this does not mean that EU law is wholly irrelevant to the sphere of collective bargaining. One common phenomenon in EU law – which is particularly significant in relation to the right to strike – is where a fundamental right in the collective sphere comes into conflict with some other element of EU law.[117] We will examine an example of this in this section. Much more significantly, the recent Directive on Adequate Minimum Wages[118] deals directly with collective bargaining, pushing at the boundaries of the EU's competence in order to pursue a commitment to wage adequacy set out in the European Pillar of Social Rights.[119] If successful, this Directive may transform the EU into a significant supporter of worker voice in wage-setting.

One area in which there has been a potential for conflict between EU law and collective bargaining is in relation to precarious workers. As chapter 3 explained, a significant challenge in modern labour law is in classifying workers who work on a casual basis, whether through online platforms or more traditional means. National legal systems often treat these individuals as self-employed rather than as employees, even though they only supply their labour. This poses problems at the boundary between labour law and competition law. An agreement between workers and an employer is, of course, a collective agreement and exempt from competition law,[120] whereas an agreement among self-employed workers to set prices for a work

---

[113] Information and Consultation of Employees Regulations 2004 (SI 2004/3426).
[114] See Davies and Kilpatrick, above n 81.
[115] Case C-176/12 *Association de mediation sociale v Union locale des syndicats CGT* EU:C:2014:2, [2014] 2 CMLR 41.
[116] By analogy with Case C-555/07 *Kücükdeveci v Swedex GmbH & Co KG* [2010] ECR I-365.
[117] Another example in the collective bargaining context is Case C-426/11 *Alemo-Herron v Parkwood Leisure Ltd* EU:C:2013:521, [2014] 1 CMLR 21, on which see Jeremias Prassl, 'Freedom of contract as a general principle of EU law? Transfers of undertakings and the protection of employer rights in EU labour law' (2013) 42 *Industrial Law Journal* 434.
[118] Above n 68.
[119] European Pillar of Social Rights, Principle 6.
[120] Case C-67/96 *Albany International BV* EU:C:1999:430, [1999] ECR I-5751.

provider may be in breach of competition law. This issue has been addressed by the CJEU in the *FNV Kunsten* case.[121] In that case, a group of self-employed orchestral musicians who worked as substitutes sought to agree a fair rate for their work with the employer. The CJEU held that if they were 'false self-employed', in the sense that they (in reality) worked under the direction of the employer and took no commercial risk, their agreement would be an exempt collective agreement. The Commission followed this up in 2022 with guidance on the application of competition law to self-employed persons in order to remove this obstacle to collective bargaining on the part of precarious workers.[122] The proposed Directive on Platform Work, agreed but not yet published at the time of writing, also makes various provisions relating to consultation and representation of platform workers, though it remains to be seen how many of these will feature in the final text.[123] The original draft included a right for platform workers' representatives to receive information from platforms about their workers, a right to information and consultation on changes to algorithmic management systems, and the provision of a channel for communication among platform workers (which could be a significant support to organising).

A much more significant move by the EU in relation to collective bargaining is the new Directive on Adequate Minimum Wages.[124] This Directive, which must be transposed by November 2024, is based on the competence to address working conditions under Article 153(1)(b) TFEU. It stretches the EU's competence because of the express exclusion of pay under Article 153(5), though the Commission has argued that it is within competence because it does not seek to set levels of pay in itself. The Directive adopts a two-pronged strategy to address minimum wages. First, it requires states with statutory minimum wages to ensure that they are set at an adequate level. The provisions here include an obligation to consult the social partners when setting the minimum wage rate.[125] Second, it requires all states to promote collective bargaining on wage-setting. This second objective will be our focus here.

Article 4(1) is worth quoting in full:

With the aim of increasing the collective bargaining coverage and of facilitating the exercise of the right to collective bargaining on wage-setting, Member States, with the involvement of the social partners, in accordance with national law and practice, shall:

(a) promote the building and strengthening of the capacity of the social partners to engage in collective bargaining on wage-setting, in particular at sector or cross-industry level;

(b) encourage constructive, meaningful and informed negotiations on wages between the social partners, on an equal footing, where both parties have access to appropriate information in order to carry out their functions in respect of collective bargaining on wage-setting;

(c) take measures, as appropriate, to protect the exercise of the right to collective bargaining on wage-setting and to protect workers and trade union representatives from acts that discriminate against them in respect of their employment on the grounds that they participate or wish to participate in collective bargaining on wage-setting;

---

[121] Case C-413/13 *FNV Kunsten Informatie en Media v Netherlands* EU:C:2014:2411, [2015] 4 CMLR 1.
[122] Commission Communication, Guidelines on the application of Union competition law to collective agreements regarding the working conditions of solo self-employed persons (2022/C 374/02).
[123] Commission, Proposal for a Directive of the European Parliament and of the Council on improving working conditions in platform work COM(2021) 762 final.
[124] Directive (EU) 2022/2041. For discussion, see L Ratti, 'The Sword and the Shield: The Directive on Adequate Minimum Wages in the EU' (2023) 52 *ILJ* 477; L Ratti, E Brameshuber and V Pietrogiovanni (eds), *The EU Directive on Adequate Minimum Wages: Context, Commentary and Trajectories* (Hart, 2024); and chapter 10 below.
[125] ibid Article 7.

(d) for the purpose of promoting collective bargaining on wage-setting, take measures, as appropriate, to protect trade unions and employers' organisations participating or wishing to participate in collective bargaining against any acts of interference by each other or each other's agents or members in their establishment, functioning or administration.

This sets out a complex mix of obligations for the Member States. Some, such as (c) and (d), focus on the core protection of freedom of association in the relevant jurisdiction, for example, through legislation prohibiting anti-union discrimination and protecting the autonomy of trade unions and employers' associations. Paragraph (b) could, in part at least, be addressed through duties to provide information to support collective bargaining, but may require other measures to 'encourage' collective bargaining. Paragraph (a) focuses on capacity-building and could potentially include a wide range of measures concerned with resources, training and expertise for trade union representatives.

The provisions of Article 4(1) are further reinforced by the arguably more striking provisions in Article 4(2). These require any Member State with collective bargaining coverage of below 80% to 'provide for a framework of enabling conditions for collective bargaining', either by law or by agreement with the social partners, and to 'establish an action plan to promote collective bargaining'. The framework of enabling conditions could take a variety of forms, but a procedure for recognising trade unions for the purposes of collective bargaining could form a part of that framework. For countries with low levels of trade union membership, a significant drive to increase those levels might have to be the starting-point.

Collective bargaining coverage is hugely varied across the EU, from 97% in Italy to 6% in Estonia.[126] Interestingly, though, much of the opposition to the Directive came from Nordic states with relatively high levels of collective bargaining coverage, which were opposed to any move to make statutory minimum wages compulsory and to any interference with their approach to collective bargaining.[127] At the time of writing, Denmark has announced that it will bring an action for annulment of the Directive before the CJEU.[128] It seems unlikely that this will succeed, given that the CJEU is not particularly keen on finding directives to be invalid. The Court has already accepted that many measures in EU law, such as equality law, have indirect consequences for pay, and that this is legitimate despite the exclusion in Article 153(5).[129]

Improving collective bargaining coverage in any particular state requires creative endeavour by the national authorities and by trade unions themselves, with sensitivity to national conditions and traditions. All EU Member States have ratified the core ILO Conventions on freedom of association and collective bargaining, discussed above, so there are interesting questions about what the Directive will add. This is particularly so given that the Commission is not an expert advisor on, or enforcer of, collective bargaining-related duties. The Directive is a striking new departure for the EU, but its practical impact remains to be seen.

---

[126] www.eurofound.europa.eu/en/european-industrial-relations-dictionary/collective-bargaining-coverage#:~:text=Eurofound's%20analysis%20of%20collective%20agreements,%25)%20and%20Sweden%20(89%25).

[127] K Ahlberg, 'Denmark takes minimum wage directive to the EU Court' (19 January 2023), available at: www.nordiclabourjournal.org/nyheter/news-2023/article.2023-01-16.8551998747. The author notes that not all Scandinavian countries opposed the Directive, with Finland being a strong supporter.

[128] Case C-19/23 *Denmark v Parliament and Council.*

[129] See eg Case C-501/12 *Specht* EU: C:2014:2005, para 33.

5. Conclusion

Democracy is an enduring value in employment law. The debates around voice at work are as relevant today as they were in the factories of the 19th century, even though the modern context leads to different priorities. Pay-setting is always likely to be a core issue of industrial democracy, and here collective bargaining has a distinctive role to play. However, worker representatives are now as likely to be interested in the coding of management algorithms or sexual harassment at work as the timing of rest breaks. Historically, the dominant democratic method in British labour law was based upon collective bargaining between trade unions and employers. Today, the democratic terrain is more complex and contested in British workplaces. Collective bargaining remains an important method for many workers, especially in the public sector. The most important legacy of European law has been the spread of consultation mechanisms in a range of business decisions. For a growing number of private sector workers, the most pressing challenge of all will be to ensure that they have any effective voice at work at all.

It is therefore unsurprising that democracy at work should also be central to the human rights agenda. Generally speaking, the influence of the EU has been most significant in relation to information and consultation, although there is now a greater willingness to promote collective bargaining. By contrast, collective bargaining continues to be central to the ILO's mission. The ECtHR now recognises collective bargaining as a fundamental right under Article 11, reflecting an expanding and dynamic jurisprudence on trade union rights. These ECHR developments tend to suggest that conflicts between worker solidarity and 'individualistic' human rights are overstated, because human rights (especially freedom of association) can provide an important support for collective activities in the workplace.

We should also be careful in overstating the radical impact of human rights law on workplace governance. Even in workplaces with collective bargaining and consultation, managers are still very much in charge and they are still mostly answerable to their shareholders. The sheer variety of different models of worker voice across different countries means that international and European standards try to respect those differences. This also means that states are left with a wide freedom to determine their own institutional arrangements for collective bargaining and consultation. Comparative law reveals that there is no single correct template for democracy at work. This is surely an important reason why 'margin of appreciation' is so important in Article 11 cases. In the British national context, courts are also sensitive to the politically controversial nature of industrial relations. Where Parliament has legislated in a particular way, as with Schedule A1 on collective bargaining, the courts have been conscious of their own limitations in terms of expertise and democratic legitimacy. The effective realisation of the human right to voice at work depends ultimately on the mobilisation of workers' social power. This may in fact be the oldest truth in labour law.

7

The Right to Strike

1.	The Moral and Political Foundations of a Human Right to Strike	4.	The Right to Strike at the Collective Level
2.	The Right to Strike as a Human Right: Sources of Legal Protection	5.	The Right to Strike in EU Law: Free Movement vs The Right to Strike
3.	The Right to Strike at the Individual Level	6.	The Right to Strike in UK Labour Law: Right or Immunity?

1. The Moral and Political Foundations of a Human Right to Strike

According to a group of leading scholars, 'the common elements of the right [to strike] certainly include (1) the withdrawal of labour by workers (2) which is coordinated and (usually) simultaneous.'[1] This provides an excellent starting point, though it is probably still incomplete. Otherwise, it would cover a group of workers who decided jointly to absent themselves from work to go on a recreational fishing trip.[2] To this basic definition, we might add (3) a coordinated withdrawal of labour with the specific purpose of expressing a grievance and exerting economic pressure to defend and promote workers' occupational interests.[3] This will often be directed at employers in a dispute over terms and conditions of employment. The right to strike is also an element in a flourishing democratic and civic culture.[4] The repression of strikes can be the mark of an authoritarian regime.[5]

Striking involves the deliberate causing of economic harm. In this respect, the human right to strike is unusual. This is because its effective exercise depends upon the intentional infliction of disruption and harm on a third party, such as an employer, consumer, or government. Without this purposive dimension, the right to strike would be useless because striking workers would have no means of effectively defending their interests. For this reason, the legal

---

[1] J Vogt, J Bellace, L Compa, KD Ewing, Lord Hendy, K Lorcher and T Novitz, *The Right to Strike in International Law* (Hart, 2020) vii.

[2] For the fishing trip example, originally posed by Chief Justice MacKeigan of Nova Scotia, we are indebted to B Langille, 'What is a Strike?' (2009–10) 15 *Canadian Labour and Employment Law Journal* 355, 358.

[3] On this expressive dimension of striking, see A Bogg and C Estlund, 'The Right to Strike and Contestatory Citizenship' in H Collins, G Lester and V Mantouvalou (eds), *Philosophical Foundations of Labour Law* (OUP, 2018) 229, 238.

[4] On democracy, citizenship, and work, see R Dukes and W Streeck, *Democracy at Work: Contract, Status and Post-Industrial Justice* (Polity, 2023).

[5] A Bogg, 'Beyond Neo-liberalism: The Trade Union Act 2016 and the Authoritarian State' (2016) 45 *Industrial Law Journal* 299.

implementation of a human right to strike has always been coupled with a very careful consideration of limitations on its exercise. Striking usually involves a clash of rights and interests. In fact, it is intrinsic to striking that there should be such a clash.

Most countries protect the right to strike either in a constitution or labour legislation.[6] As we shall see, it is also widely recognised as a fundamental human right in international instruments. There are a range of general moral and political arguments for protecting the right to strike as a human right. The choice of supporting argument will have implications for the legal detail of the human right. These will include the identity of the right-holder (is it the trade union's right? the worker's individual human right? or both together?); the purposes for which strike action is legally protected (political strikes? collective bargaining strikes?); whether any procedural conditions such as ballots or notice requirements are justifiable; and the scope of limitations on the right's exercise.

The most basic argument for a right to strike is a liberty argument, based in what Gourevitch has described as 'classical liberal theory'.[7] Individuals are at liberty to bargain and dispose of their labour in the market. Since they enjoy freedom of contract as individuals, freedom of association ensures that they can bargain collectively. This includes the freedom to withhold labour. This 'classical liberal theory' argument was historically important in the 19th century in challenging special legal restrictions on trade union activity in the laws of conspiracy and master and servant.[8] It is less clear that it is so relevant today. It seems to support only a 'liberty' to withdraw labour rather than a positive 'right'. This 'liberty' would not be sufficient to justify duties on the employer to not dismiss or penalise the striking worker, for example.

A more promising modern foundation for the right to strike is the 'social democratic' justification.[9] On this approach, the right to strike is instrumental in addressing inequality of bargaining power in the individual employment contract. Without collective bargaining through trade unions, supported by a right to strike, individual workers are exposed to serious risks of contractual exploitation. This social democratic approach is the most familiar to employment lawyers given its similarities with the general 'inequality of bargaining power' justification for employment law. Unlike the 'classical liberal theory' foundation, the social democratic justification would support positive duties on employers to avoid discriminating against strikers. It might also justify positive obligations on the state to provide a system of employment law that facilitates collective bargaining and strike action.

Finally, Gourevitch has defended a 'radical view' of the right to strike as a right to resist economic oppression.[10] The most disadvantaged workers in liberal capitalist economies experience poverty, precarious housing and finances, and structural oppression. Their ability to organise effective strike action is undermined by the ease with which powerful employers can hire replacement labour or repress trade union activity. This structural oppression cannot be addressed by either the classical liberal or social democratic versions of the right to strike. This is because they do not protect more effective forms of worker resistance such as sit-ins, mass picketing, or property damage and trespass. The reconciliation of the right to strike with other basic liberties recognised by the legal system, such as the employer's property rights, leaves structural oppression intact. This 'radical view', which has much in common with theories of civil disobedience,

---

[6] For a comprehensive comparative overview, see B Waas (ed), *The Right to Strike: A Comparative View* (Kluwer, 2014) ch 1.
[7] A Gourevitch, 'The Right to Strike: A Radical View' (2018) 112 *American Political Science Review* 905, 911.
[8] For discussion, see PS Atiyah, *The Rise and Fall of Freedom of Contract* (OUP, 1979) 528–33.
[9] Gourevitch, above n 7, 911–13.
[10] Gourevitch, above n 7, 913–15.

is not strongly reflected in human rights *law*. This is because of the Rule of Law, and the courts' concern to protect the rights of others to ensure the overall coherence and integrity of the legal system.

The moral and political foundations of the right to strike are also relevant to the scrutiny of restrictions on the right to strike. The right to strike is a qualified right in international human rights law. Careful scrutiny of whether restrictions are justified is especially important here, simply because it is intrinsic to an effective strike that the interests of others will be affected. On the 'classical liberal theory' approach, for example, the right to strike may be easily extinguished by the rights of others. On the 'radical view', by contrast, the rights of non-strikers and employers to be free from union coercion may be given insufficient protection by the law. The 'social democratic' justification looks for an intermediate accommodation of competing rights, and it provides the closest fit with the right to strike in international human rights law. For example, the International Labour Organization's (ILO's) Committee on Freedom of Association has held that:

> The conditions that have to be fulfilled under the law in order to render a strike lawful should be reasonable and in any event not such as to place a substantial limitation on the means of action open to trade union organizations.[11]

The formula under Article 11(2) of the European Convention on Human Rights (ECHR) provides a more detailed proportionality method for evaluating restrictions. These restrictions must be 'prescribed by law' and 'necessary in a democratic society' in the interests of 'national security or public safety', 'prevention of disorder or crime', 'protection of health or morals', and the 'protection of the rights and freedom of others'. For example, striking may be restricted in 'essential services' where there is endangerment of the life, personal safety, or health of the public; or circumstances of 'acute national emergency'.[12] Under the last heading, the courts usually consider the general economic harms which may be imposed on others, such as employers, consumers, other workers, and the wider economic and political system.[13] We need to examine any legal restrictions justified by general economic harms very strictly, given the nature of striking as an economically harmful activity.

2. The Right to Strike as a Human Right: Sources of Legal Protection

The academic literature on the moral and political foundations of a right to strike suggest that the right could be derived from a range of well-established human rights. For example, some writers have argued that the right to strike is closely connected to the fundamental freedom from forced labour.[14] This human right is unlikely to provide a complete basis for the right to strike in situations where employees are free to resign from their contracts. Usually, striking is undertaken as a temporary withdrawal of labour, and strikers want their jobs back at the end of the dispute. Given that strikes are expressive activities, often linked to protest and freedom of assembly, the right to

---

[11] B Gernigon, A Odero and H Guido, *ILO Principles Concerning the Right to Strike* (International Labour Office: Geneva, 2000) 25.
[12] ibid 22–24.
[13] For an excellent analysis of such arguments, see T Novitz, *International and European Protection of the Right to Strike* (OUP, 2003) ch 4.
[14] R Ben Israel, *International Labour Standards: The Case of Freedom to Strike* (Kluwer, 1988) 24–25.

strike might also be derived from freedom of expression.[15] The degree of protection afforded to 'striking as expression' may depend upon whether it is characterised as political or commercial speech. Political expression attracts stronger protection under Article 10 ECHR, but industrial disputes may be treated as commercial speech. There is also the difficulty that there are other less damaging ways of expressing a grievance that do not involve striking, such as leafletting.

In practice, the derivation of a human right to strike in human rights law has been focused on freedom of association. The specific content of this protection varies across different regimes of human rights law, but broadly speaking they fall within what Gourevitch has described as a 'social democratic' foundation. The right to strike is justified principally by its instrumental role in equalising the bargaining strength of workers and employers.

The starting point for the right to strike in international law is the ILO. The fundamental instrument from which the right to strike has been derived in international labour law is the core Freedom of Association and Protection of the Right to Organise Convention No 87 (1948). This does not protect the right to strike expressly. Instead, the right to strike has been derived through interpretation by the ILO committees. Article 3 provides that:

1. Workers' and employers' organisations shall have the right to draw up their constitutions and rules, to elect their representatives in full freedom, to organise their administration and activities and to formulate their programmes.
2. The public authorities shall refrain from any interference which would restrict this right or impede the lawful exercise thereof.

On its ordinary meaning, this 'full freedom' to organise 'activities' must encompass trade union activities such as the right to strike.[16] This is supported by a purposive interpretation of freedom of association based on Article 10, which provides that 'In this Convention the term *organisation* means any organisation of workers or of employers for furthering and defending the interests of workers or of employers.' As the 'social democratic' justification makes clear, trade unions cannot 'further and defend' workers' social and economic interests without the ability to organise strike action. In addition, the other core freedom of association Convention, the Right to Organise and Collective Bargaining Convention No 98 (1949) protects individual strikers from acts of victimisation. Article 1 provides that 'Workers shall enjoy adequate protection against acts of anti-union discrimination in respect of their employment', and this prohibits reprisals against individual strikers.[17] The collective freedoms of C87 and the individual freedoms of C98 provide complementary support for the right to strike in the ILO.

The legal principles regulating and conditioning the right to strike have been developed through the ILO committees over a long period of time. These committees have not been constrained by a comprehensive definition of the right to strike codified in the text of a dedicated instrument. Also, their deliberations lack the formality of court-based judgments. This flexibility has led to a dynamic body of principles covering the full range of legal issues with strikes, such as ballots, notice requirements, political strikes, sympathy and secondary action, essential services and minimum service levels, and individual reprisals. Overall, the ILO's legal conception of the right to strike is broad, and it is recognised as 'one of the essential means by which

---

[15] See, for example, S Kupferberg, 'Political Strikes, Labor Law and Democratic Rights' (1985) 71 *Virginia Law Review* 685; Bogg and Estlund, above n 3.
[16] Vogt and others, above n 1, ch 5.
[17] Gernigon and others, above n 11, ch 6.

workers and their organizations may promote and defend their economic and social interests'.[18] According to Novitz, this is not restricted to the negotiation of collective agreements or the conduct of collective bargaining, but is a wider '"socio-economic" right ... connected to workers' civil liberties and entitlement to democratic participation'.[19]

However, the lack of a clear textual basis for the right to strike has also meant that the ILO's work depends upon a tripartite political consensus on the legitimacy of the committee system. This has been disrupted from time to time, as with the Employers' Group's objections to the legal authority of the ILO Committee of Experts in 2012.[20] Although there was a 'ceasefire' in this dispute, allowing the ILO's supervisory institutions to continue their work, the disagreement has rumbled on. Article 37 of the ILO Constitution makes the International Court of Justice (ICJ) the ultimate arbiter of interpretive disputes about Conventions, and in 2023, the ILO's Governing Body took the extraordinary decision to refer the question of whether C87 protects the right to strike to the ICJ.

Within the Council of Europe, the right to strike is protected under both the European Social Charter (ESC) and the ECHR.

Despite the broad European consensus on its fundamental status as a right, there are wide variations in its implementation across different legal systems. In Italy and France, for example, it is regarded as an individual right of workers albeit exercised collectively. This has implications for the implementation of the right, for example by making it more difficult to justify certain limitations on 'wildcat' or unofficial strike action not organised by a trade union. In Germany, by contrast, the right to strike is usually interpreted as an organic right derived from the capacity of representative trade unions to conduct collective bargaining.[21] The institutions of the Council of Europe must tread a delicate line, sensitive to this reasonable variation while safeguarding the fundamental elements of the right.

The ESC protects the right to strike expressly in Article 6. This article is concerned with 'ensuring the effective exercise of the right to bargain collectively'. The 'effective exercise' of the right to bargain collectively requires states to 'recognise the right of workers and employers to collective action in cases of conflicts of interest, including the right to strike'. While the text of this protection appears narrow, linking the right to strike to the right to bargain collectively, in practice the European Committee of Social Rights has interpreted the right broadly and generously.[22] Limitations and conditions on the exercise of the right to strike must also be construed strictly, so that workers and trade unions are enabled to protect workers' social and economic interests.[23]

Unlike the ESC, there is no textual protection of the right to strike in Article 11 of the ECHR. Instead, it protects the 'right to form and join trade unions for the protection of his interests'. This purposive requirement that freedom of association be 'for the protection of his interests' has provided a strong basis for judicial recognition of the right to strike. Following recognition of the right to strike in *Enerji Yapi-Yol Sen v Turkey*,[24] there is now a very extensive body of case law on the right to strike under Article 11. This has been supported by

---

[18] Committee on Freedom of Association Digest of Decisions (1996) para 475, cited in Novitz, above n 13, 290.
[19] Novitz, above n 13, 290.
[20] C La Hovary, 'Showdown at the ILO? A Historical Perspective on the Employers' Group's 2012 Challenge to the Right to Strike' (2013) 42 *Industrial Law Journal* 338.
[21] Waas, above n 6, 237.
[22] Vogt and others, above n 1, 101–06.
[23] ibid 103.
[24] [2009] ECHR 2251.

the 'integrated' approach to interpretation, with the ECtHR sometimes using 'external' legal sources such as the ILO and ESC to support its own legal reasoning.[25]

The variety of legal forms of the right to strike in European countries means that the margin of appreciation concept has been particularly important under Article 11. This is demonstrated by *RMT v United Kingdom*.[26] This case involved a challenge to the ban on secondary strike action in UK law. 'Secondary' strike action can be distinguished from 'primary' strike action. A 'primary' dispute is between workers and their own employer about their terms and conditions. 'Secondary' strike action is parasitic on a primary dispute. It involves other groups of workers taking action in support of the workers in the primary dispute. Most European countries permit some form of secondary strike action where there is a nexus with the primary dispute, for example where there is a community of interest between the groups of workers or the employers are connected in some way. The UK is unusual in opting for a complete ban. In a controversial judgment, the ECtHR treated secondary action as 'an accessory rather than a core aspect of trade-union freedom'.[27] This supported a wide margin of appreciation for the state in justifying restrictions under Article 11(2):

> In previous trade-union cases, the Court has stated that regard must be had to the fair balance to be struck between the competing interests of the individual and of the community as a whole. Since achieving a proper balance between the interests of labour and management involves sensitive social and political issues, the Contracting States must be afforded a margin of appreciation as to how trade-union freedom and protection of the occupational interests of union members may be secured.[28]

In the 'collective' aspects of the right to strike, *RMT* demonstrates that the ECtHR is particularly sensitive to the democratic pedigree of legislation in achieving the balance between competing interests. After *RMT*, the Court will generally be reluctant to interfere with a legislative determination of 'collective' conditions for the right to strike. Many of the leading cases involving the right to strike have concerned very intrusive restrictions with claims brought mainly against Turkey or Russia. *RMT* was viewed by the Court as a less extreme case. The judgment has been criticised for its undue deference to restrictive legislation, and its failure to adopt the 'integrated approach'.[29]

This does not mean that Article 11 is irrelevant as a source of legal protection. First, even in 'collective' cases like *RMT*, the margin of appreciation does have limits. In *Ognevenko*, for example, a train driver was dismissed for participating in a strike organised by the union which violated a legal prohibition of strikes in rail transportation. The claimant succeeded in his Article 11 claim. The complete legislative ban on strike action for railway workers was outside the state's margin of appreciation. Railway transportation was not an 'essential service' in international law, and even if it could be so characterised, there was no evidence that the government had considered less intrusive measures such as a minimum service level.[30] The finding of a violation was no doubt also supported by the fact that an individual striker had been dismissed as a result of the 'collective' unlawfulness, with dismissal the 'most severe penalty' with a serious chilling effect on trade union activities.[31]

---

[25] See, for example, *Ognevenko v Russia* [2019] IRLR 195, [70].
[26] [2014] IRLR 467.
[27] *RMT v UK*, ibid, [77].
[28] ibid [86].
[29] A Bogg and KD Ewing, 'The Implications of the RMT Case' (2014) 43 *Industrial Law Journal* 221.
[30] Above n 25, [77].
[31] ibid [83].

This is linked to a second point. Where individual strikers have been subjected to detriments with the intention of deterring them from or penalising them for participating in lawful strikes, the margin of appreciation is extremely narrow. This is so even where the detriment is light, such as disciplinary warnings;[32] or suits for civil damages even where these are paid by the union.[33] The state is also under a positive obligation to provide 'real and effective protection' against trade union victimisation, which includes access to effective civil remedies against adverse treatment.[34] Given that strike action falls within the general scope of 'trade union activity' under Article 11,[35] this 'real and effective protection' would include detriment and dismissal of individual strikers. Indeed, it is extremely difficult to think of situations where the victimisation of strikers engaged peacefully in lawful strike action could be justified.

Finally, the ECtHR has said that it considers the 'totality of measures' enacted by the state in protecting the 'substance' of the freedom under Article 11.[36] Specific legal restrictions, if considered singly, can appear reasonable and modest. Take, for example, the requirement of a 50 per cent turnout threshold for valid strike ballots. This threshold ensures that the ballot enjoys a greater measure of democratic legitimacy than majority support on a low turnout. However, the cumulative interaction of multiple restrictions such as the complexity of the balloting rules, notice requirements, the potential for imposed minimum service levels, and the procedural availability of interim injunctions, can effectively stifle the right to strike. The 'totality' approach is valuable in enabling the ECtHR to be sensitive to these cumulative effects. In practice, this 'totality' approach seems to have been limited by other factors, such as the Court's focus on the specific facts of the dispute giving rise to the application. In *RMT*, for example, there was little evidence of a broader consideration of the 'totality' of legal restrictions in UK law.

3. The Right to Strike at the Individual Level

We will now consider the legal position of the individual striker under UK law and whether these legal protections satisfy the requirements of the right to strike in international and European human rights law. The basic starting-point is the common law position of the individual striker. We will then consider the statutory protections available to workers where they are dismissed or subjected to detriment for participating in a strike. The common law still operates very harshly against individual strikers, because the common law does not yet recognise a right to strike. The legal protections are provided by statute.

Strikes and the Common Law

Let us first consider a complete withdrawal of labour by the individual striker. At common law, the strike will usually be a repudiatory breach of contract by the individual striker, because if an

---

[32] *Karacay v Turkey*, App No 6615/03, 27 March 2007.
[33] *Dilek v Turkey*, App No 74611/01 and others, 17 July 2007.
[34] *Danilenkov v Russia* [2009] ECHR 1243.
[35] *RMT v UK*, above n 26, [77].
[36] *Association of Civil Servants and Union for Collective Bargaining and Others v Germany* [2022] ECHR 543, [56].

employee declines to do any work in accordance with their contract, this subverts the entire basis of the wage-work bargain.[37]

As a matter of general contract law, three main consequences flow from this for the legal position of the individual striker. First, an employee who is on full strike for a day is not entitled to any payment in respect of that day. The calculation of what counts as a day's pay depends upon the contract. While quantifying pay for a daily deduction can be surprisingly complex, given the sheer variety of contractual payment techniques, there is no human rights objection to the general principle of 'no work, no wages'. This means that proportionate deductions from wages are permitted under both ILO and ESC principles on the right to strike.[38]

Secondly, because a strike is a repudiation of one of the essential conditions of the contract, the employer is entitled at common law to summarily dismiss the striker without notice.[39] It is irrelevant that the strike is lawful and organised by a trade union. The employer's power to terminate the contract is analysed as a purely contractual matter. International standards on the right to strike certainly require that the individual striker is protected from dismissal, and is provided with real and effective remedies and enforcement procedures. Under the ILO framework, individual protections from dismissal are based in Article 1 of C98, Right to Organise and Collective Bargaining Convention, 1949.[40] The ECtHR has also emphasised the need for real and effective protection from anti-union discrimination.[41]

Finally, because the striker is in breach of contract, the employer can sue the individual striker for damages for loss caused by the breach. In industrial relations terms, it is unusual for individual strikers to be sued for damages in contract. The trade union will usually have deeper pockets, and in any event suing individual strikers is likely to be viewed as vindictive and inflammatory. As Keith Ewing has argued, the reasoning in the very few reported cases on the measure of damages is 'very difficult to follow' and even 'perverse'.[42] Even if an employer has no intention of suing individual strikers, the *threat* to sue under conditions of legal uncertainty is likely to have a chilling effect on strikers. It is clear that the exposure of strikers to a risk of civil liability is a violation of the right to strike under Article 11 ECHR.[43] From a human rights perspective, where an individual is participating in lawful and official strike action, it may be that the contract should be treated as suspended rather than breached.[44] This would ensure that they cannot be sued for contractual damages. For a short period, this suspension theory proved attractive to Lord Denning in *Morgan v Fry*.[45] However, it did not find broader favour in the courts. Scholars such as Lord Wedderburn were also cautious because its application depended upon controversial policy choices which were best resolved by Parliament rather than the courts. The suspension of the contract would not necessarily prevent an employer from imposing penalties on the striker (though it would at least prevent an action for damages for breach of contract). Fuller protection would require statutory protections from detriment.

---

[37] *Simmons v Hoover Ltd* [1977] ICR 61, 76.
[38] Gernigon and others, above n 11, 48. See eg the ECSR Conclusions XIII-1 France – Article 6(4) and Conclusions 2010 France – Article 6(4), in each case holding that a rule deducting 1/30th of salary for strikes of less than a day was not in conformity with Article 6(4).
[39] *Simmons*, above n 37.
[40] Gernigon and others, above n 11, 37.
[41] *Danilenkov*, above n 34.
[42] KD Ewing, *The Right to Strike* (OUP, 1991) 19.
[43] *Dilek*, above n 33.
[44] For a discussion of Lord Wedderburn's wrestling with this idea of contractual suspension through his early career, see A Bogg, 'The Hero's Journey: Lord Wedderburn and the "Political Constitution" of Labour Law' (2015) 44 *Industrial Law Journal* 299, 337–46.
[45] [1968] 2 QB 710, 728.

What about the common law position of strikers engaged in action short of a full strike? This could involve a wide range of actions with the purpose of interfering with the employer's business operations. It includes the 'go slow' or 'work to rule', both of which involve performing to the strict letter of the contract but with the object of disrupting the enterprise. It may also include the refusal to perform certain duties, such as the refusal to mark examinations, or a refusal to undertake certain extra activities such as voluntary overtime. In most cases, these forms of action will involve a breach of contract. Even if they do not breach an express term, they will usually breach an implied term, such as the duty of cooperation[46] or the duty of obedience.[47]

The courts have consistently taken the view that the employer is entitled to refuse partial performance.[48] Where there has been a refusal of partial performance, the logic of *Miles* is that the employee is entitled to no payment until the employee is willing to perform the contract. The consequences of this orthodox contractual approach can be harsh. In *Wiluzynski v Tower Hamlets*, for example, employees refused to answer councillors' queries over a five-week period, which amounted to about three hours' work in total. The employees were informed that if they attended work, it would be on a voluntary basis. In these circumstances, the employer was entitled to withhold pay for the entire period. There are limits to this. While the employer need not prevent the employee from working, the legal test of refusal should focus on substance not form. Where the employer is issuing instructions to the employer, for example, this could constitute evidence that partial performance has been accepted.

If partial performance has been accepted, the proper basis for assessing the level of payment remains obscure. Some cases have endorsed an 'equitable set off' approach, so that the employer deducts an amount from the payment corresponding to the losses caused by the breach of contract.[49] Other judgments have denied that there is any contractual right to pay during a strike at all, and that the employee must recover payment for the services provided to the employer on a restitutionary basis.[50] The problem with these private law approaches is that they leave the employee vulnerable to disproportionate deductions of pay. There are also real problems of 'access to justice'. It is simply unrealistic to imagine that most employees would be able to pursue an expensive restitutionary claim against their employers when they are already losing pay in the strike.

From a human rights perspective, the answers to these difficult questions on partial strike action are not always clear cut. Many legal systems that protect a right to strike do not protect all forms of strike action. Sometimes, action short of a strike is treated as an 'abuse' of the right to strike and outside the scope of legal protection. It is also difficult to see how a doctrine of contractual suspension would work if some work is being performed under the contract. The employer's refusal of partial performance does not seem to raise human rights concerns. Where partial performance has been accepted, however, the ability of the employer to implement punitive and disproportionate deductions does engage issues under Article 11. It is effectively a form of individual sanction imposed on the striker with the intention of penalising or deterring them from participating in lawful strike action. As we have seen, the margin of appreciation is very narrow for cases involving individual penalties against strikers under Article 11.

---

[46] See *Secretary of State for Employment v ASLEF (No 2)* [1972] 2 QB 455, which involved consideration of the contractual implications of a 'work to rule'.
[47] *Sim v Rotherham Metropolitan Borough Council* [1987] Ch 216.
[48] *Miles v Wakefield Metropolitan District Council* [1987] IRLR 193, especially Lord Bridge and Lord Brightman.
[49] *Sim*, above n 47.
[50] *Miles*, above n 48, per Lord Brightman.

Strikes and Statutory Protections: Unfair Dismissal

The dismissal of strikers represents one of the most serious infringements of the right to strike. According to the ILO, dismissal of strikers is a very serious abuse of freedom of association, and a prohibited form of discrimination against those participating in legitimate trade union activities.[51] The ECtHR also regards dismissal as a very serious form of penalty that strikes at the core of Article 11.[52] The approach to dismissal protection under UK law depends upon the categorisation of the industrial action. The statute adopts three categories, which are linked to three different levels of protection. These are set out in the Trade Union and Labour Relations (Consolidation) Act 1992 (TULRCA 1992), ss 237, 238A and 238.

The most limited form of statutory protection is where the industrial action is 'unofficial'. 'Unofficial' is defined in TULRCA 1992, s 237(2). Interestingly, the definition does not include situations where there are no union members engaged in a strike. Instead, the definition is engaged only where there are some union members taking part in industrial action and that action has not been 'authorised or endorsed' by a relevant trade union official. There is a broad definition of 'authorised or endorsed' that is set out in TULRCA 1992, s 20. Where the industrial action is 'unofficial', the tribunal has no jurisdiction to consider an unfair dismissal claim unless it can be shown that an automatically unfair reason for dismissal applies (for example, pregnancy or acting as a worker representative). In effect, then, dismissal for participating in an unofficial strike is automatically fair.

The law's policy to deter 'unofficial' industrial action is understandable because there is a public interest in encouraging dispute resolution through negotiation with trade unions. It is also not clear that this treatment of unofficial strikers violates Article 11 because the ECtHR indicated in *Baris v Turkey* that legal protections can be restricted to lawful and official strike action organised by a trade union.[53]

The most extensive form of statutory protection is where the industrial action is 'protected'. As unfair dismissal protection, it is restricted to 'employees' and does not extend to 'limb (b)' workers. Where the striking employee is dismissed for participating in 'protected' industrial action, this is automatically unfair under TULRCA 1992, s 238A. The definition of 'protected' is set out in s 238A(1). It is action that the employee is induced to commit 'by an action which by virtue of section 219 is not actionable in tort'. This means that the organiser of the strike action must have satisfied the requirements for a lawful strike, which we discuss in detail below. The *individual* employee's protections depend upon the lawfulness of the strike at the *collective* level. Controversially, there is also a time limit on the protection under s 238A. The protection runs for the first 12 weeks of the dispute: s 238A(3). Where an employee is dismissed (even after the end of the dispute or once they have stopped striking) for participating in 'protected' action within this 12-week period, the dismissal is automatically unfair. The 12-week period may be extended where a tribunal finds that 'the employer had not taken such procedural steps as would have been reasonable for the purposes of resolving the dispute to which the protected industrial action relates': s 238A(5).

The introduction in 1999 of 'protected industrial action' was a significant advance on the existing protections for individual strikers. Nevertheless, it is less clear that s 238A goes far enough in protecting the right to strike. First, it only protects 'employees', whereas trade union

---

[51] Gernigon and others, above n 11, 37.
[52] *Ognevenko*, above n 25.
[53] *Baris v Turkey*, App No 66828/16, 27 January 2020.

rights under Article 11 extend to a wider category of those in an 'employment relationship'.[54] Secondly, the ILO has criticised the 12-week limit on the basis that there is never any justification for dismissing strikers, whatever the time frame.[55] Thirdly, while the remedy of reinstatement or re-engagement is available where there has been a breach of s 238A, the ILO makes clear that reinstatement should be the standard remedy in cases of anti-union victimisation. The protections in the legal system, which includes its procedure and remedies, must be real and effective.[56] While the restriction of s 238A to collectively lawful strike action has been criticised, we have already seen that under *Baris v Turkey* this may well be legitimate under Article 11.[57]

The third residual category under s 238 applies where ss 237 and 238A are not otherwise applicable. For example, s 238 would apply where a strike extended beyond the protected period under s 238A, or a union lost its s 219 immunity because of procedural irregularities in the conduct of the strike. It is also the case that strike action involving union members must be 'authorised or endorsed' by the union, otherwise the s 237 exclusion of tribunal jurisdiction for 'unofficial' action will apply. Section 238 does not apply where every striking employee is dismissed. Where dismissals are implemented selectively in a s 238 situation, the tribunal will have jurisdiction to consider unfair dismissal claims. This still means that it is possible for the employer to dismiss fairly, particularly where it has done so through fair procedures.

The 'selective dismissal' category is a messy compromise that gives some limited protection to individual employees. Given that the conditions of 'collective' lawful strike action are so complicated, so that it is relatively easy to drop out of s 238A while the union is making a good faith effort to comply with the law, the limited protections for individual strikers under s 238 may be criticised from an Article 11 perspective. This is because both the union and the individual striker may end up with reduced protection while making every reasonable effort to comply with the law.

Strikes and Statutory Protections: 'Detriment' Short of Dismissal

The protections under ss 237–238A only apply to employees who have been dismissed. There are many ways in which employers can penalise individual strikers other than through dismissal, such as demotion, suspension, fines, disciplinary warnings, and disproportionate pay deductions. In *Secretary of State for Business and Trade v Mercer*, the Supreme Court considered if a worker proposing to strike was protected from 'detriment' under TULRCA 1992, s 146.[58] This was because it concerned her participation in the 'activities of an independent trade union'. The Supreme Court concluded that strike action was excluded from s 146, principally because it was not 'at an appropriate time'. This meant that there was no statutory protection for the claimant, Ms Mercer, who (on the agreed facts) had been suspended for activities connected to a lawful and official strike.

It followed that her only available domestic redress was under the Human Rights Act 1998 (HRA 1998). This required the Supreme Court to consider whether her Convention rights under Article 11 had been infringed as a result of the exclusion of industrial action from s 146. If there was an Article 11 infringement, could it be remedied by a s 3 interpretation or a s 4 declaration of incompatibility?

---

[54] *Sindicatul 'Pastoral Cel Bun' v Romania* [2014] IRLR 49.
[55] ILO Committee on Freedom of Association, *Compilation of Decisions* (6th edn, 2018) para 815.
[56] See *Danilenkov*, above n 34.
[57] App No 66828/16, 27 January 2020.
[58] *Secretary of State for Business and Trade v Mercer* [2024] UKSC 12.

Giving a unanimous judgment for the Supreme Court, Lady Simler considered that the absence of *any* legal protection from detriment for individuals engaged in a lawful strike was not compatible with Article 11. She did not agree that any individual sanction, however light, was liable to have a dissuasive effect such as to infringe Article 11. In this respect, she considered that the ECtHR case law allowed a wider margin of appreciation to states in 'horizontal' cases involving private sector employers. By contrast, even minimal sanctions were likely to infringe Article 11 where they were imposed by the state as a public employer.[59] Lady Simler also regarded the 'core' and 'essential' distinctions on the right to strike in the *RMT* judgment as interchangeable.[60] Since the right to strike was neither 'core' nor 'essential', it followed that there was a wider margin of appreciation in respect of regulation of the right to strike under Article 11.[61] Despite the breadth of the margin of appreciation, however, the complete absence of *any* statutory protection from detriment meant that the state had not struck a fair balance in relation to individual strikers exposed to victimisation in private sector strikes.[62] As such 'section 146 of TULRCA both encourages and legitimises unfair and unreasonable conduct by employers'.[63]

The Supreme Court's reasoning on Article 11 is of fundamental significance in recognising that the right to strike is protected as a matter of UK law. Some aspects of its approach are open to criticism, and two aspects will be considered briefly here. The first is the distinction between private sector and public sector employment. In *Danilenkov*, for example, the ECtHR observed that it did not matter whether the state was the direct employer or if it was responsible for securing the effective enjoyment of Article 11 rights of workers employed in the private sector.[64] *Danilenkov* followed the approach in *Wilson v UK*, where the ECtHR found that a legal framework permitting the use of financial offers by private sector employers to induce trade union members to opt out of collective bargaining was a violation of Article 11.[65] In *Wilson*, the ECtHR did not even consider the issue of justification under Article 11(2).

The second aspect is the distinction between 'core' and 'essential'. While the reasoning of the ECtHR is sometimes a little opaque, these two terms are not interchangeable in *RMT*. The right to strike is not yet designated as an 'essential' trade union freedom, though it is an integral prop to other 'essential' rights such as the right to make representations and the right to bargain collectively. In *RMT*, the distinction between 'core' and 'accessory' is being used in a different sense, to emphasise gradations of importance *within* a specific right ('essential' or otherwise). In *RMT*, the Court was drawing a distinction between primary strike action, which was 'core' and deserving of stronger protection, and 'secondary' strike action which was 'accessory' and therefore amenable to a wider margin of appreciation. The situation in *Mercer* involved a primary strike, and hence it was at the 'core' of the right to strike.

The misstep of the Supreme Court is in its failure to recognise that the targeted victimisation of individual workers engaged in lawful and protected trade union activity attracts the strongest protection under Article 11. This dimension of constitutional equality engages the fundamental constitutional responsibility of the court in human rights cases.[66]

---

[59] ibid [75].
[60] *RMT v UK*, above n 24.
[61] *Mercer*, above n 58, [69].
[62] ibid [90].
[63] ibid [89].
[64] *Danilenkov v Russia*, above n 34.
[65] *Wilson and Palmer, National Union of Journalists and others v UK* (2002) 35 EHRR 523.
[66] MP Foran, *Equality Before the Law: Equal Dignity, Wrongful Discrimination, and the Rule of Law* (Hart, 2023).

The Supreme Court did not consider that a s 3 interpretation was possible because it involved controversial policy choices between incommensurable options. This would lead the Supreme Court to stray beyond an interpretive role into the activity of legislating, which would have been constitutionally improper. This reticence has a long and respectable history, and was reflected in Lord Wedderburn's earlier reservations about judges developing a doctrine of contractual suspension and thereby usurping the democratic role of the legislature. Having determined the s 3 issue, the Supreme Court then considered a s 4 declaration. While the existence of incommensurable policy choices counted against a s 3 interpretation, this counted in favour of a s 4 declaration. It was constitutionally appropriate for these matters to be considered by the Executive and Parliament. Since there were no countervailing reasons against issuing a s 4 declaration, the Supreme Court declared s 146 of TULRCA 1992 incompatible with Article 11.

Any domestic protection for private sector workers now awaits legislative action. Interestingly, workers employed directly by the state appear to be protected very strongly under Article 11, as recognised by Lady Simler where she refers to the stringent protections against even 'minimal sanctions'.[67] Such workers may be able to pursue action against a 'public authority' directly under s 6 of the HRA 1998. While the Supreme Court did not agree that all detriments for private sector workers infringed Article 11, it indicated that suing strikers for damages for breach of contract or suspension without pay was likely to be encompassed by Article 11.[68] The protection might not extend to situations where 'the manner of the breach is harmful or disruptive', which seems to envisage some kind of 'malice' or 'abuse of rights' constraint.[69] The Supreme Court also indicated that deductions from pay are not sanctions and nor should they be considered 'detriments'.[70] While this principle is undoubtedly correct in full strikes, there are difficult boundary issues where strikers are engaged in action short of full strike and are exposed to disproportionate deductions with the purpose of deterring or penalising the worker. Clearly, *Mercer* is far from the last word on these thorny issues.

4. The Right to Strike at the Collective Level

We will now consider the treatment of the right to strike at the collective level in the UK: in other words, the rules governing trade unions and those who organise strikes. These will be examined under four main headings. First, we assess the purposes for which a legitimate strike can be organised. These draw a strong link between the right to strike and collective bargaining, and are more limited than some of the purposes permitted by the international instruments discussed in section 2. We then examine the procedural conditions on organising a lawful strike, which include the requirement to hold a ballot and to serve the employer with various notices. While procedural conditions can be legitimate, it is important that they do not inhibit the effective exercise of the right to strike. Third, we examine new legislation requiring minimum levels of service to be maintained in certain public services during industrial action. While the international instruments permit restrictions on the right to strike in 'essential services', UK law goes well beyond what might reasonably be permitted on that score. Fourth, we examine the remedies an employer may obtain in the event of an unlawful strike. One of the most important factors here

---

[67] Mercer, above n 58, [76].
[68] ibid [87].
[69] ibid [83].
[70] ibid [61].

is the ease with which an employer may be able to take the momentum out of the union's action by obtaining an interim injunction to stop the strike going ahead.

Legitimate Purposes: Trade Disputes, Political Strikes, Secondary Action

We noted above that individuals taking part in strike action are in breach of their contracts of employment. Those who organise strikes are also engaged in unlawful acts at common law, but under the law of tort. Most straightforwardly, persuading someone to go on strike usually amounts to the economic tort of 'inducing breach of contract'. But there are more elaborate torts too: interfering with the claimant's business by unlawful means, or intimidation. The legal mechanism for enabling strikes to be organised is to grant unions and strike organisers 'immunity' from liability in tort if certain conditions are met. We return in the conclusion to the question whether an immunity can be sufficient to provide effective protection to the right to strike. Here, we examine the conditions for securing the immunity in greater detail.

The key provision is s 219 of TULRCA 1992 which provides protection for certain listed torts where they are committed by someone acting 'in contemplation or furtherance of a trade dispute'. One immediate problem with s 219 is that the strategy of listing the protected torts is vulnerable to developments at common law. This problem was acute in the 1970s when there was open hostility towards trade unions from some of the judges.[71] Although the common law continues to evolve and create uncertainty around the margins, as it did in the *OBG* case, it seems less likely nowadays that judges would invent new torts to restrict industrial action.[72]

The test for 'contemplation or furtherance' is subjective: what matters is that the trade union or strike organiser believed that the action would support the dispute, not whether it was effective in practice.[73] A 'trade dispute' is defined in s 244(1). The dispute must be between 'workers and their employer' and it must relate 'wholly or mainly' to one or more of a list of matters, including terms and conditions of employment, hiring, discipline, dismissal, work allocation, trade union membership, facilities for union officials, and arrangements for recognition and collective bargaining.

It is evident from this list that, to be lawful in the UK, strike action must be closely related to collective bargaining: either to the mechanics of bargaining, or to the topics typically addressed during the process of collective bargaining. Political strikes – which are, to some extent at least, permitted under the ILO approach, discussed above – are not covered. This can cause particular difficulties for unions in the public sector, especially when combined with the requirement that the strike should relate 'wholly or mainly' to one or more of the listed matters. For example, as the *Mercury* case demonstrates, where a union wishes to strike in protest at a proposal to privatise a public service, it must take care to explain the purpose of the strike in terms of threatened job losses or pay cuts, rather than as a protest against the general policy of privatisation.[74]

Specific provision is made in ss 224 and 225 for the immunity to be lost in various situations amounting to secondary action. For example, under s 224, there is no immunity for inducing breach of contract where the employer party to the contract is not a party to the dispute. As we saw above, an attempt to argue in the *RMT* case that this restriction was in breach of Article 11 ECHR was unsuccessful.[75]

---

[71] eg *Rookes v Barnard* [1964] AC 1129.
[72] *OBG Ltd v Allan* [2007] UKHL 21, [2008] 1 AC 1.
[73] *Express Newspapers Ltd v McShane* [1980] AC 672, HL; *Duport Steels Ltd v Sirs* [1980] 1 WLR 142, HL.
[74] *Mercury Communications Ltd v Scott-Garner* [1984] Ch 37.
[75] Above n 24.

Procedural Conditions: Ballots and Notice Requirements

Although the immunity is potentially available to anyone who organises a strike, most strikes are, in practice, organised on behalf of a trade union. Where this is the case, the union must comply with rules requiring a ballot before the strike can take place, and must give a series of notices to the employer regarding the ballot and the proposed action. The immunity will be lost if any of these requirements is not observed.

TULRCA 1992, s 20(2) sets out when a union will be held responsible for a strike. A noteworthy feature of this provision is that it does not limit the union's responsibility to the people who are empowered under the union's own rules to call a strike. This creates a risk of a situation in which a strike is called by a person not authorised by the union but nevertheless covered by s 20, without the proper procedures having been followed. In this situation, the union has the option of repudiating the strike by following the process set out in s 21. While this protects the union from liability in tort, it renders the strike 'unofficial'. This has severe consequences for the striking workers, because they lose their protection against dismissal, as detailed in section 3. This puts the union in an impossible situation.

The union must secure the support of its members in a ballot before the strike can go ahead. This interference in a trade union's autonomy to arrange its own internal affairs is often said to be justified because of the impact of the strike on the employer and the wider community, though of course in practice it would be a foolish trade union leader who called a strike without being sure of a decent level of support. In general terms, the ILO accepts that a balloting requirement may be legitimate, as long as it does not render the right to strike ineffective or excessively difficult to exercise.[76] This might be the case where, for example, a very high level of support is required in order for the strike to be approved.

The requirement to hold a ballot is set out in s 226. The trade union must appoint a scrutineer to oversee the ballot and the ballot must be postal, at no cost to the members.[77] The latter is particularly problematic for unions because of the expense involved and the difficulty of getting members to return their ballot papers (as opposed to voting online, for example). The voting paper itself must be in a form prescribed by the statute, including a warning that going on strike involves a breach of the contract of employment, though there is some wording explaining the unfair dismissal protection outlined above.[78]

One area of particular risk for trade unions is balloting the wrong people. The requirement, in s 227(1), is legally straightforward but practically challenging:

> Entitlement to vote in the ballot must be accorded equally to all the members of the trade union who it is reasonable at the time of the ballot for the union to believe will be induced by the union to take part or, as the case may be, to continue to take part in the industrial action in question, and to no others.

Under s 232A, the immunity is lost if a member is induced to take part in the action when they were not given an opportunity to vote in accordance with s 227. It is easy to imagine how a union, faced with organising a large ballot, might miss some members out or send ballot papers to the wrong people. Section 232B allows for mistakes to be disregarded where they are 'accidental and on a scale which is unlikely to affect the result of the ballot'. In the *Serco* case, the Court of Appeal

---

[76] ILO Committee on Freedom of Association, *Compilation of Decisions* (6th edn, 2018), paras 805–10.
[77] TULRCA 1992, ss 226B, 230.
[78] TULRCA 1992, s 229.

held that this should be construed to protect the union against inadvertent errors even if they could have been avoided, for example, by more accurate record-keeping.[79]

Under s 226(2)(a)(iia), there must be a turnout of at least 50 per cent in the ballot. In most cases, a majority of those voting is then sufficient. However, in 'important public services' (as designated by the Secretary of State in the health, education, fire, transport, nuclear and border security sectors), there is a further requirement that at least 40 per cent of those entitled to vote in the ballot voted in favour of the strike.[80] When introducing these thresholds, the government argued that they were necessary to ensure that strikes had strong support, given the disruption they caused. However, a strike is unlikely to be successful – or disruptive – unless it has strong support, and a system of postal balloting may not be the best way of ascertaining union members' views. Electronic balloting could provide a more effective way of maximising participation and so promoting democratic legitimacy. If the ballot result is in favour of industrial action, the union's mandate generally lasts for six months from the date of the ballot.[81] This means that the union must reballot its members if the dispute has not been resolved before the end of that period.

English law also requires the union to give the employer a series of notices: notice that the ballot is to take place,[82] notice of the ballot result,[83] and notice of the strike itself.[84] Although a strike with no notice at all would maximise the disruption to the employer (which, as we noted above, is the objective of the strike), the ILO accepts the legitimacy of a requirement to give some notice that the strike is to take place, provided that it does not render the right ineffective.[85] The requirement to give ballot notices has been explained by governments as a way of enabling the employer to check that the ballot has been properly conducted, but is less obviously justified in international law. But the real issue with the notices is the complex requirements for giving a proper notice and the risk that the union might make a mistake which renders the strike unlawful, even if it is doing its best to comply.

An example will help to illustrate the point. Under s 226A, the union must give the employer notice of the date of the ballot and a copy of the ballot paper. The notice must tell the employer the total number of employees, giving job categories and workplaces, together with 'an explanation of how [the] figures were arrived at'.[86] One of the cases which eventually reached the ECtHR, in *RMT v UK*, *EDF Energy Powerlink Ltd*, illustrates the challenge involved.[87] In that case, the union had identified the relevant employees as 52 'engineers and technicians' at a site employing 155 people. The employer argued that it used a more precise system of job classification and could not therefore identify the employees involved. An injunction was granted on the basis that, although the union did not systematically record the information, it could have made more effort to discover it given the small number of people involved. This aspect of the complaint was dismissed by the ECtHR in *RMT* as inadmissible, because the union had subsequently managed to organise a lawful strike.[88] The additional administrative burden placed on

---

[79] London & Birmingham Railway Ltd v Associated Society of Locomotive Engineers and Firemen; Serco Ltd v National Union of Rail, Maritime & Transport Workers [2011] EWCA Civ 226, [2011] ICR 848.
[80] TULRCA 1992, s 226(2C).
[81] TULRCA 1992, s 234.
[82] TULRCA 1992, s 226A.
[83] TULRCA 1992, s 231A.
[84] TULRCA 1992, s 234A.
[85] ILO Committee on Freedom of Association, *Compilation of Decisions* (6th edn, 2018) para 799.
[86] TULRCA 1992, s 226A(2)(c). The union is not obliged to name the individuals involved: s 226A(2G).
[87] *EDF Energy Powerlink Ltd v National Union of Rail, Maritime and Transport Workers* [2009] EWHC 2852 (QB), [2010] IRLR 114.
[88] Above n 24.

the union – which makes the right to strike harder to exercise – was not considered. The Court of Appeal has also given detailed consideration to the compatibility of the notice provisions with Article 11 in the *Metrobus* case, holding that none represented a disproportionate restriction on the right to strike, despite the obligation under Article 11 to consider the cumulative effect of the 'totality' of restrictions.[89]

Minimum Service Levels and 'Essential Services'

There are some sectors in which the disruptive effect of industrial action may be particularly severe, threatening the life, safety or health of the community. It has long been accepted that strikes can be banned in 'essential services', such as the police, for this reason.[90] Governments typically make arrangements to ensure that an independent body determines pay and conditions in sectors subject to a strike ban. In other services, such as the NHS, strikes have been permitted, but unions have usually agreed with employers that some workers should continue to work so that there is cover in the event of an emergency.[91] The Strikes (Minimum Service Levels) Act 2023, amending TULRCA 1992, is a highly controversial new statute which seeks to restrict industrial action in certain public services by imposing a requirement to continue to provide a minimum level of service during a strike.

Under the new s 234B, the Secretary of State is empowered to make regulations providing for minimum service levels in (broadly) the sectors identified above as requiring a higher ballot threshold for a strike: health, education,[92] fire and rescue, transport, border security and nuclear. These are a mix of sectors regarded by the ILO as 'essential services' in which strikes can be restricted (health, fire and rescue, nuclear) and sectors regarded by the ILO as services of 'public importance' in which minimum service levels can be required (education, transport, border security).[93]

Once regulations have been made, an employer may issue a trade union with a 'work notice' under s 234C, once the union has given notice of a strike under s 234A. Although there is no obligation on the employer to issue a notice, it seems likely that public sector employers in particular will be pressured by the government, or aggrieved service users, into doing so. The notice must identify who is required to work during the strike to provide the minimum service, and what work they are required to do. The employer may not target union members (or non-members) or union activists in deciding who to name in the work notice.[94] The employer must consult the union before issuing the notice, and 'have regard to' the union's views.[95] There are serious consequences if an employee subject to a work notice fails to comply with it. They might be disciplined or dismissed by the employer, and would not benefit from the unfair dismissal protection under s 238A.

Under s 234E, the union loses its immunity if it 'fails to take reasonable steps' to ensure that the members (but not non-members) named in the work notice comply with it. These

---

[89] *Metrobus Ltd v Unite the Union* [2009] EWCA Civ 829, [2010] ICR 173.
[90] eg ILO Committee on Freedom of Association, *Compilation of Decisions* (6th edn, 2018) para 840.
[91] There is a criminal offence of wilfully breaching a contract in a way that will endanger life or cause serious bodily injury under TULRCA 1992, s 240.
[92] The 2016 Act only addresses schools under this heading, but this provision also covers further and higher education.
[93] See I Katsaroumpas, 'Crossing the Rubicon: The Strikes (Minimum Service Levels) Act 2023 as an Authoritarian Crucible' (2023) 52 *Industrial Law Journal* 513, 534–35.
[94] s 234C(6).
[95] s 234C(8).

are specified in a Code of Practice issued under s 203.[96] The union must identify its members named in the work notice and send them a communication encouraging them to comply with the work notice, and instruct the picket supervisor to use 'reasonable endeavours' to stop picketers discouraging workers subject to a work notice from crossing the picket line to go to work. As with the provisions on strike ballots and notices, there are risks that a union may be found not to have taken sufficient steps despite making an effort to do so. For example, the Code says:

> A failure by the union to identify a small number of their members, and therefore missing these members from subsequent steps, may not constitute a failure in carrying out the overall obligation to take reasonable steps, as long as the union made a reasonable attempt to identify such members. This would be for a Court to determine based on the facts of each case.[97]

As Katsaroumpas points out, the element of uncertainty inherent in the idea of 'reasonable steps' may have a chilling effect on the exercise of the right to strike.[98]

If the union fails to comply with the Code, the immunity is lost and the union would be potentially liable in damages to the employer. The extent of any losses will vary according to the circumstances. The statute does at least confine damages to the additional losses incurred by the employer as a result of the non-compliance, not the losses caused by the strike as a whole.[99] Damages are also subject to statutory maximum limits set out in further detail below. However, probably the most serious consequence of non-compliance is for the striking workers themselves. If the union loses the immunity, the strike is no longer covered by s 238A which, as explained above, makes it automatically unfair to dismiss striking employees engaged in 'protected' action.

A number of commentators have noted that the Act is constitutionally problematic: it sets out a framework for the operation of minimum service levels, but leaves the details to be laid down in regulations which are largely a matter for ministers.[100] Thus, it was not fully apparent when the legislation itself went through Parliament how it would be used. The true picture is beginning to emerge at the time of writing. In schools, the government has consulted (but not decided) on various options, including a proposal to require pupils aged between 4 and 11 to be able to attend school during a strike (which would mean no possibility of strike action in primary schools), and a proposal for secondary pupils to attend where they are in an exam year or vulnerable, or where their parents are essential workers.[101] In relation to the border force, the requirement is for border security services to be provided as normal, raising a serious question as to whether any meaningful strike action will be able to take place in this setting at all.[102]

In all these instances, the so-called minimum service has been set at a very high level. While it may be argued that this reflects the importance of the services involved, it severely undermines any capacity for unions in these sectors to take meaningful and impactful strike action which is,

---

[96] Department for Business and Trade, *Minimum Service Levels: updated Code of Practice on Reasonable Steps* (November 2023).
[97] ibid para 21.
[98] Above n 93.
[99] s 234E(2).
[100] eg KD Ewing and J Hendy, *Strikes (Minimum Service Levels) Act 2023* (IER, November 2023); Katsaroumpas, above n 93.
[101] Department for Education, *Minimum Service Levels in Education* (November 2023).
[102] The Strikes (Minimum Service Levels: Border Security) Regulations 2023 (SI 2023/1353); Home Office, *Border Security: Minimum Service Levels during Strike Action* (November 2023). See Joint Committee on Human Rights, letter to the Secretary of State (24 November 2023).

after all, intended to be disruptive. It seems likely that there will be a variety of challenges to the provisions before domestic courts and international institutions.

The prospects for a successful Article 11 ECHR challenge may have reduced following the recent Grand Chamber judgment in *Humpert and Others v Germany*.[103] The case involved a challenge to the longstanding prohibition of strikes by civil servants in Germany. This arrangement is deeply embedded in the constitutional traditions and values of Germany, and this no doubt affected the Court's approach to it. The Court concluded that the prohibition was not a violation because civil servants were provided with other compensatory guarantees to ensure that their occupational interests could be protected by the trade union. Under the Minimum Service Levels framework, the strike is restricted rather than prohibited so that unions can still undertake *some* strike action. This factor was important in *RMT* as well. It is also possible for unions to organise industrial action short of a full strike and avoid the legislation entirely. In these circumstances, and following *Humpert*, the 2023 legislation may be within the state's margin of appreciation under Article 11.

Remedies: Damages and Injunctions

If the union or strike organiser does not comply with the various requirements discussed above, the immunity will not be applicable and the strike – if it goes ahead – will involve the commission of various torts. The usual remedy is therefore an award of damages. However, in practice, most employers would prefer to stop the strike going ahead. This can be done by obtaining an injunction.

Under s 22 of TULRCA 1992, there is a statutory limit on the damages which may be awarded against a union which varies according to the union's number of members:

Less than 5,000	£40,000
5,000 or more but less than 25,000	£200,000
25,000 or more but less than 100,000	£500,000
100,000 or more	£1,000,000

These limits were last increased in 2022. The purpose of the damages award is to compensate the employer for any losses caused by the strike, not to punish the union, so the amount of damages will correspond to the employer's legally-recognised losses. The maximum limits give unions some certainty about the 'worst-case scenario' they may face if the action is not immune.

An injunction may be obtained to restrain a union or strike organiser from going ahead with an unlawful strike. In practice, most cases involve an interim injunction. This may be awarded pending a hearing to determine whether or not the strike is unlawful. The employer must show a *prima facie* case of unlawfulness and that the 'balance of convenience' favours the granting of the injunction.[104] These thresholds are relatively low: the complexity of the rules around industrial action, particularly balloting and notice requirements, make it easy to show that something may have gone wrong, and the employer can usually make a strong argument on the balance of

---

[103] *Humpert and Others v Germany* [2023] ECHR 1008.
[104] *American Cyanamid Co v Ethicon Ltd* [1975] AC 396.

convenience because of the disruptive impact of the strike. Under s 221, the court must be satisfied that all reasonable steps have been taken to get the union before the court when an injunction is sought (interim injunctions can generally be obtained without the defendant being present) and must have regard to the likelihood that the union would establish the immunity at trial, but these measures do not appear to have done much to redress the balance. Once an interim injunction has been granted, the trade union will typically reconsider its strategy rather than pursuing the matter to a final hearing. Breach of an injunction amounts to contempt of court and attracts serious penalties which are not subject to the limits in s 22.

5. The Right to Strike in EU Law: Free Movement vs The Right to Strike

The right to strike is recognised in EU law, but it sits in some tension with the fundamental principles of the EU internal market.[105] Although this is less of a concern in the UK after the UK's exit from the EU, it remains an issue for trade unions within the Member States.[106]

The two leading cases on the right to strike in EU law are *Viking* and *Laval*. In *Viking*, a trade union organised a blockade of a shipping firm when it proposed to re-flag a ship from Finland to Estonia.[107] Re-flagging is an exercise of freedom of establishment in EU law: the freedom of a business to move from one Member State to another. It usually happens where the regulatory regime in the new flag state is less strict – and therefore cheaper to comply with – than in the old flag state, though in *Viking* itself, the employer denied that it intended to cut the terms and conditions of the affected workers. Until the *Viking* case, freedom of establishment had been applied largely against the Member States, to challenge restrictions they might place on where a company could be established. But the Court of Justice held that it could also apply 'horizontally' to a trade union. The Court recognised that the trade union in *Viking* was exercising the right to strike, an important move given that the case pre-dates the EU Charter, in which the right to strike is expressly protected. However, it held that the task for the national court was to examine whether the trade union's exercise of the right to strike was a proportionate restriction on the employer's freedom of establishment.

In *Laval*, the employer had won a contract to build a school in Sweden, and sought to bring a 'posted' workforce from Latvia to carry out the work.[108] This is an exercise of freedom to provide services under EU internal market law. A Swedish trade union organised a blockade of the building site because the employer refused to agree to the applicable Swedish collective agreement for its workers. Again, it was held that the trade union's exercise of the right to strike had to be tested for its proportionality against the employer's exercise of its freedom to provide services. An added complication was that there is a Directive which allows Member States to regulate some aspects of the terms and conditions of 'posted' workers, but Sweden was found not to have implemented the Directive properly.[109]

---

[105] A different approach has been taken in competition law: eg Case C-413/13 *FNV Kunsten Informatie en Media v Netherlands* EU:C:2014:2411, [2015] 4 CMLR 1.
[106] N Countouris and KD Ewing, *Brexit and Workers' Rights* (Institute of Employment Rights, 2019).
[107] Case C-438/05 *International Transport Workers' Federation v Viking Line ABP* EU:C:2007:772, [2007] ECR I-10779.
[108] Case C-341/05 *Laval un Partneri Ltd v Svenska Byggnadsarbetareforbundet* EU:C:2007:809, [2007] ECR I-11767.
[109] Directive 96/71/EC concerning the posting of workers in the framework of the provision of services (amended 2018).

These decisions gave rise to a large critical literature.[110] For labour lawyers, it was a significant problem that the decisions appeared to prioritise the employer's internal market freedoms over the right to strike. While it is perfectly legitimate to restrict the right to strike, as we noted above, the usual enquiry in a human rights forum would be whether proposed restrictions on the right were proportionate, not whether the exercise of the right itself was a proportionate restriction on something else. However, within the logic of EU law, which treats the internal market rules as fundamental, it was perhaps difficult for the Court of Justice to reason in this other way, particularly given that both strikes were exceptionally effective and therefore disruptive in effect. The ILO[111] and the European Committee on Social Rights[112] have been critical of the Court's decision. Perhaps most significantly, so has the ECtHR. In the *Holship* case, the Court found no violation where the Norwegian Supreme Court had found a boycott to be incompatible with EEA law after careful balancing of the competing considerations.[113] But, in an unusual move, it went on to say this:

> From the perspective of Article 11 of the Convention, EEA freedom of establishment is not a counterbalancing fundamental right to freedom of association but rather one element, albeit an important one, to be taken into consideration in the assessment of proportionality under Article 11, paragraph 2.[114]

This is a clear indication that the ECtHR regards the fundamental freedoms in EU law as having a lesser status than Convention rights, taking the opposite position to the Court of Justice.

In domestic law, it is often possible to reverse an unwanted judicial decision by legislation, but this was more challenging in the EU context. The right to strike is specifically excluded from the EU's legislative competence in the field of labour law, presumably because Member States wanted to protect their autonomy in this area and did not anticipate the Court's dramatic intervention.[115] The EU instead proposed what became known as the Monti II Regulation, using an internal market Treaty basis, which would have required the Court to balance the right to strike against the economic freedoms.[116] This proposal was rejected by national parliaments using the 'yellow card' procedure. But the EU has reformed the Posted Workers Directive to allow 'host' states to impose a wider range of provisions on posted workers and to strengthen its enforcement.[117]

There is some evidence that the Court has also moderated its approach. For example, in *Commission v Germany*, the Court addressed a situation in which German local authorities had placed contracts for pension provision without putting them out to tender in accordance with

---

[110] eg ACL Davies, 'One Step Forward, Two Steps Back? The Viking and Laval Cases in the ECJ' (2008) 37 *ILJ* 126; MR Freedland and J Adams-Prassl (eds), *Viking, Laval and Beyond* (Hart, 2014); P Syrpis and T Novitz, 'Economic and Social Rights in Conflict: Political and Judicial Approaches to their Reconciliation' (2008) 33 *EL Rev* 411.
[111] eg CEACR Observation, adopted 2009, published 99th ILC session (2010), in relation to the BALPA dispute in the UK.
[112] *Swedish Trade Union Confederation (LO) v Sweden* (ECSR 85/2012) (2015) 60 EHRR SE7.
[113] *Norwegian Confederation of Trade Unions (LO) v Norway* (2021) 73 EHRR 16. It may be worth noting that the Court assumed that the *Bosphorus* presumption (that EU law is compatible with the Convention) did not apply to EEA law for the purposes of deciding this case.
[114] ibid [118].
[115] Article 153(5) TFEU.
[116] Proposal for a Council Regulation on the exercise of the right to take collective action within the context of the freedom of establishment and the freedom to provide services, COM (2012) 130.
[117] Directive 2018/957. The Court rejected a challenge to the revision in *Hungary v European Parliament: Re The Posted Workers Directive* [2021] 2 CMLR 9.

EU public procurement law.[118] The local authorities had placed the contracts with national providers named in a collective agreement with their workers. The Court held that this was unlawful, but made potentially significant comments about the need to 'reconcile' the social objectives of the collective agreement and the requirements of EU law. As Barnard suggests,[119] this could provide a way for the Court to return to some of the approaches found in the case law prior to *Viking* and *Laval*, in which the Court appeared to be more willing to balance fundamental rights and economic freedoms.[120]

6. The Right to Strike in UK Labour Law: Right or Immunity?

Does UK labour law recognise a 'right' to strike or a mere 'immunity', and does it matter anyway? Historically, there was a lively debate about whether the form of legal protection mattered. The leading proponents for recognising a right to strike were Elias and Ewing. In particular, they argued that 'Judges might be less jealous of a right than an immunity and might consequently respond more positively to a new hierarchy of norms which places the right to strike above other competing common law claims.'[121] This reflects a view of rights that they are special legal claims attracting stricter legal protection. By contrast, Lord Wedderburn was dismissive of what he regarded as a 'semantic' argument about words. The debate about rights versus immunities was 'no more useful today as a contribution to the politics of labour law than a dispute about the number of shop stewards able to dance on the head of a pin'.[122] What mattered more was the substance of the legal protections, and whether they were enforced by a sympathetic judiciary in specialist labour courts with the expertise to understand industrial relations.

Some of the legal problems that triggered the debate are no longer so pressing, such as the 'discovery' of new economic torts by the courts to police the strike activities of unions. It is also unclear to what extent this debate really matters under human rights law. Under the ESC, for example, the parties undertake to 'recognise' the right to strike under Article 6(4). This could be viewed as requiring states to give the 'right' formal legal recognition rather than through a limited immunity. By contrast, the ECtHR has tended to give greater emphasis to the 'substance' of legal protections in the member state.[123] Also, the recognition of the right to strike by the ECtHR now brings it into play indirectly in the UK legal system, by virtue of the HRA 1998 and its provisions 'bringing rights home'.

Where rights have real value (both substantive and rhetorical) is in the treatment of individual strikers. The prohibition of penalties against and victimisation of individual strikers is a fundamental feature of the human right to strike. This has provided a critical language for political campaigning and strategic litigation. It also supports a 'suspension' approach to the contract of employment, rather than treating striking as a repudiatory breach, especially where there is a

---

[118] Case C-271/08 *Commission v Germany* EU:C:2010:426.
[119] C Barnard, 'A Proportionate Response to Proportionality in the Field of Collective Action' (2012) 37 *European Law Rev* 117.
[120] eg Case C-112/00 *Eugen Schmidberger Internationale Transporte Planzuge v Austria* EU:C:2003:333, [2003] ECR I-5659.
[121] P Elias and K Ewing, 'Economic Torts and Labour Law: Old Principles and New Liabilities' (1982) 41 *Cambridge Law Journal* 321, 358.
[122] Lord Wedderburn, *Employment Rights in Britain and Europe* (Lawrence & Wishart, 1991) 95.
[123] *Association of Civil Servants and Union for Collective Bargaining and Others*, above n 36, [56].

complete withdrawal of labour. However, human rights arguments may have less impact on the 'collective' aspects of industrial action. The margin of appreciation ensures respect for democratic choices in selecting conditions for the lawful exercise of the right to strike, such as ballots and notice requirements or substantive restrictions on strike purposes. A comparative perspective shows that there are many different ways of implementing it while still being faithful to the ideal of rights.[124] Sometimes this may have led courts to excessive deference to legislative choices. However, the ECtHR has also indicated that it will consider the 'totality' of measures, which may include examining the cumulative effects of strike laws. This totality approach has yet to be applied vigorously by the ECtHR, and it would provide a powerful tool for ensuring a broader contextual evaluation of signatory states' legal rules on strike action.

---

[124] A Bogg, 'The Right to Strike, Minimum Service Levels, and European Values', available at https://papers.ssrn.com/sol3/papers.cfm?abstract_id=4410323.

8
The Right to Work

1.	The Right to Work in International Human Rights Law	5.	Prison Labour
2.	Can Certain Jobs be Prohibited?	6.	Welfare-to-Work
3.	Regulatory Exclusions from Jobs and Work Sectors	7.	Conclusion
4.	Employers' Controls Over Access to Work		

In July 2008, a Burmese national arrived in the Republic of Ireland seeking asylum. Pending the outcome of his claim for refugee status, which eventually took eight years, he was required to live in state accommodation, received an allowance of 19 euros a week, but by statute, he was forbidden to seek or enter into employment. In 2013, he was offered employment in the facility that housed him, but the minister refused permission to work. The applicant sought a declaration on the incompatibility of the law prohibiting his employment with the Charter of Fundamental Rights of the European Union (CFREU), the European Convention on Human Rights (ECHR), and the Irish constitution. Although not expressly mentioned in the Irish constitution, the Supreme Court of Ireland held a right to work had been established as an implied or an 'unenumerated' right. This right is a 'freedom to seek work which however implies a negative obligation not to prevent the person from seeking or obtaining employment, at least without substantial justification'.[1] On the question whether a right to work was limited to Irish citizens, the Court concluded that the right goes to the essence of human personality, so that to deny it to anyone would be to fail to recognise their essential equality as human persons.[2] The Court cited with broad approval a General Comment of the UN Committee on Economic, Social and Cultural Rights:[3]

> The right to work is essential for realizing other human rights and forms an inseparable and inherent part of human dignity. Every individual has the right to be able to work, allowing him/her to live in dignity. The right to work contributes at the same time to the survival of the individual and to that of his/her family, and insofar as work is freely chosen or accepted, to his/her development and recognition within the community.[4]

---

[1] *NVH v Minister for Justice and Equality* [2017] IESC 35 (30 May 2017) [12]. Cf D McCormack-George, 'The Right to Work in Irish Law' (2019) 42 *Dublin University Law Journal* 119.
[2] *NVH v Minister for Justice and Equality*, ibid [13].
[3] ibid [16].
[4] General Comment No 18 on the Right to Work, adopted on 24 November 2005, at para 1.

The Court concluded that, although some restrictions on the right to work were justifiable, where there is no temporal limit on the asylum process, the complete exclusion from employment was unconstitutional.[5] The case provides a clear vindication of a human right to work.

Most people in contemporary societies work. However, many may find the idea of a *right* to work puzzling. Some may not want to work. They may instead prefer to pursue their hobbies or other activities that they find valuable in life. Could there be a hidden agenda? A duty to work disguised as a right?[6] Even if we think that work is an important good, does it make sense to talk about a right to work?[7] Questions such as these will be explored in this chapter.

To reach the conclusion that the right to work is a universal human right, the Supreme Court of Ireland recognised many features of the value of work. Work is important because of the income it generates. Without this income, most would not be able to meet other basic needs or pursue their interests. Yet work is not only about income. It is also a space with actual opportunities of living, through self-development and the development of valuable relations with others. The Supreme Court of Ireland noted, for instance, how the applicant's inability to work had caused him to feel depressed, frustrated, and to lack self-belief.[8] It has been argued that the central goods of work consist in excellence, social contribution, community, and social recognition.[9] Unless they work, people may be unable to access these goods in the modern world. The justification for having a right to work, not merely a necessity or a duty to work, relies on these sorts of reasons that may justify other human rights too.

Elements of the human right to work, in turn, have been grounded not only in values such as dignity and autonomy that are typically viewed as foundations of other rights, but also on the value of self-realisation.[10] Through work people meet physical and intellectual challenges, get a sense of achievement, and create meaning for their lives, which they would not be able to fulfil were they deprived of the right to work. All this suggests that the right to work may be grounded on traditional justifications of human rights, but also that it has its own special justification.

For these reasons we must accept that the right to work is morally important. Yet what is the meaning of the right to work in human rights law? It may seem too imprecise at first. What duties does it impose? Does the right to work mean that everyone should have a job? Does it require that people have the job of their dreams? Can we ever be forced to work in a job that is not the work of our choice? Can the right to work be used as a right against strike action by those who do not

---

[5] *NVH v Minister for Justice*, above n 1, [21]. On the right to work of asylum seekers, see further P Herzfeld Olsson and T Novitz, 'Access to Work for Those Seeking Asylum: Concerns Arising from British and Swedish Legal Strategies' (2024) *Industrial Law Journal*.

[6] See the discussion in A Paz-Fuchs, 'The Right to Work and the Duty to Work' in V Mantouvalou (ed), *The Right to Work – Legal and Philosophical Perspectives* (Oxford, Hart Publishing, 2015) 177. A duty to work enforced through anti-parasite laws was common in the laws and constitutions of former states in the USSR and other Communist countries, but it is also found in some socialist inspired constitutions such as the French Constitution of 1958, which incorporates the Preamble to the Constitution of 1946, stating that 'everyone has a duty to work, and a right to employment': see S Robin-Olivier, 'The French Approach to the Right to Work: The Potential of a Constitutional Right in Ordinary Courts' in Mantouvalou, *The Right to Work*, 195.

[7] See the discussion in A Bogg, 'Only Fools and Horses: Some Sceptical Reflections on the Right to Work' in Mantouvalou, *The Right to Work*, 149; and JW Nickel, 'Giving Up on the Human Right to Work' in Mantouvalou, ibid, 137.

[8] *NVH v Minister for Justice*, above n 1, [20].

[9] A Gheaus and L Herzog, 'The Goods of Work (Other than Money!)' (2016) 47 *Journal of Social Philosophy* 70. See also DL Blustein, 'The Role of Work in Psychological Health and Well-Being' (2008) 63 *American Psychologist* 228; K Arnold et al, 'Transformational Leadership and Psychological Well-Being: The Mediating Role of Meaningful Work' (2007) 12 *Journal of Occupational Health Psychology* 193.

[10] H Collins, 'Is There a Human Right to Work?' in Mantouvalou, *The Right to Work* (n 6) 17. Self-realisation may require not only obtaining a job of one's choice, but also the opportunity to perform work in that job and to retain one's skills and expertise rather than being kept idle: *William Hill Organisation Ltd v Tucker* [1999] ICR 291, CA.

participate in a strike? To answer these questions, we turn to the legal protection of the right to work in international human rights law.

1. The Right to Work in International Human Rights Law

A good starting point when thinking about the right to work in human rights law is the Universal Declaration of Human Rights (UDHR). Article 23(1) states:

> Everyone has the right to work, to free choice of employment, to just and favourable conditions of work and to protection against unemployment.

It is ambiguous whether this provision represents four separate rights, or one right, the right to work, which is composed of three elements. We prefer the interpretation that the provision contains four complementary rights. In the first phrase, the right to work includes the right not to be excluded from the possibility of working and the correlative freedom not to work. The right to free choice of employment in the second phrase includes the elimination of unnecessary barriers to access particular types of jobs. It also implies a right to be free from being compelled to work at a particular kind of job. In the third phrase, the right to work applies to jobs with just and favourable conditions, not exploitative jobs. Finally, the right also imposes positive duties on the state and perhaps others to protect people from unemployment and to safeguard decent working conditions. To refer to a classic typology of duties imposed by human rights, the right to work gives rise to duties to 'respect, protect and fulfil'.[11] The fact that the right to work and the right to fair working conditions were included in the UDHR indicates that the drafters viewed unemployment as an evil, and that working in unjust conditions is a wrong that the state has to address. The right to fair and just working conditions is discussed more fully in chapter 11.

When the international community separated civil and political from economic and social rights, the rights to work and to fair working conditions were only explicitly protected in social rights documents, including the European Social Charter (ESC) and the International Covenant on Economic, Social and Cultural Rights (ICESCR), which were not justiciable through individual petition.[12] Those rights are not expressly mentioned in the ECHR. As a consequence, the right to work is relatively underexplored in case law of courts and other bodies that hear individual petitions. However, the meaning of the right has been elucidated in the deliberations of the committees tasked with monitoring compliance with social and economic rights.

ICESCR

The right to work is protected in the ICESCR, Article 6, which states in its first paragraph: 'The States Parties to the present Covenant recognize the right to work, which includes the right of everyone to the opportunity to gain his living by work which he freely chooses or accepts, and will take appropriate steps to safeguard this right.' Article 7 of the Covenant protects the right to fair and just conditions of work, and Article 8 protects trade union rights.

---

[11] See H Shue, *Basic Rights: Subsistence, Affluence and U.S. Foreign Policy*, 2nd edn (Princeton, Princeton University Press, 1996).

[12] There is a more recent Collective Complaints Protocol under the ESC, and an individual communications Protocol under the ICESCR: see above chapter 2.

Like other socio-economic rights in the ICESCR, the right to work is not interpreted as imposing on state authorities an immediate obligation to provide a job to everyone. However, it does contain some immediate obligations: for example, the right to work contains a right not to be forced to work, and states have a duty to prohibit discrimination in access to and retention of employment. In addition, the right also imposes certain duties of progressive realisation. These immediate state duties also arguably include the right to be protected from unjustifiable dismissal.[13]

The Committee on Economic, Social and Cultural Rights (CESCR) provides authoritative interpretations of the Covenant through its General Comments.[14] According to General Comment No 3 of the CESCR, '[t]he concept of progressive realization constitutes a recognition of the fact that full realization of all economic, social and cultural rights will generally not be able to be achieved in a short period of time.'[15] The second paragraph of Article 6 ICESCR provides that the steps that the authorities ought to take for the full realisation of the right include technical and vocational programmes, and policies that will lead to full employment.

The CESCR has issued General Comment No 18 on the Right to Work, which commences with the statement quoted by the Supreme Court of Ireland mentioned in our introduction.[16] Like other human rights, the right to work here is linked to human dignity, because the General Comment recognises that without work and the income that it generates, most people would not be able to satisfy their basic needs. From the wording of the General Comment, it is a right that every human being has simply by virtue of being human.

The right to work has not been interpreted as a right of everyone to have a job or to have the job of their choice. The state is not presented as employer of last resort. According to General Comment 18, the right to work may be violated when the authorities do not take all necessary steps to ensure its realisation. The state must refrain from pursuing policies that lead to massive unemployment, and also pursue policies that create opportunities for employment.[17] This latter aspect of the right to work imposes a duty on the authorities to promote employability, in other words. On this basis, state authorities have positive duties to promote education and training of individuals in a way that will make them capable of accessing jobs. Moreover, economic policies of the state must lead to the creation of jobs, so that everyone has the opportunity to work.

In General Comment 18, the Committee explained that the right to work should be read holistically: Articles 6–8 are interdependent, and the right to work should be viewed as a right to decent work.[18] States must take steps to protect the rights of workers to enjoy just and favourable conditions of work, to form trade unions and freely to choose and accept work. This brings to mind the agenda of the International Labour Organization (ILO) that insists that its guiding mission should be decent work for all.[19] This Comment does not address the problem that there may arise a tension between the right to work and the right to decent work in the sense that governments often find it easier to manage the economy in ways to produce jobs than to ensure

---

[13] See chapter 18.
[14] C O'Cinneide, 'The Right to Work in International Human Rights Law' in Mantouvalou, *The Right to Work* (n 6) 99, 102–11. See, generally, M Langford and J King, 'Committee on Economic, Social and Cultural Rights' in M Langford (ed), *Social Rights Jurisprudence* (Cambridge, CUP, 2008) 477.
[15] CESCR, General Comment No 3, para 9.
[16] General Comment No 18, 2005, para 1, above n 4.
[17] General Comment No 18, para 26.
[18] General Comment No 18, paras 7–8.
[19] https://www.ilo.org/global/topics/decent-work/lang--en/index.htm.

that all jobs are secure and fairly paid.[20] Furthermore, the globalised economy constantly puts pressure on governments to preserve jobs by cutting costs to employers, including the costs of compliance with employment rights.[21]

ESC

At regional level, in Europe, the right to work is protected in Article 1 of the ESC:

With a view to ensuring the effective exercise of the right to work, the Contracting Parties undertake:

(1) to accept as one of their primary aims and responsibilities the achievement and maintenance of as high and stable a level of employment as possible, with a view to the attainment of full employment;
(2) to protect effectively the right of the worker to earn his living in an occupation freely entered upon;
(3) to establish or maintain free employment services for all workers;
(4) to provide or promote appropriate vocational guidance, training and rehabilitation.

Article 2 of the ESC protects the right to just working conditions, Article 3 provides for health and safety at work, and Article 4 protects the right to fair remuneration.[22] The European Committee of Social Rights (ECSR) has deemed the right to work to be of 'fundamental importance' since the effective exercise of several essential rights contained in the ESC – rights to just conditions of work, to safe and healthy working conditions, to fair remuneration and to organise and bargain collectively – is 'inconceivable unless the right to work is guaranteed first'.[23] This suggests that there is a relationship of indivisibility and interdependence between these rights, with the right to work being a pre-condition for the enjoyment of other rights.

There is no question that the meaning of the promotion of full employment needs to be examined further. In relation to the relevant state duties, the ECSR examines a range of indicators in order to assess whether states comply with their relevant obligations, including states' public commitments to promote full employment and expenditure on employment measures.[24] Even though the ECSR grants wide discretion to member states in this area, it has found that there is non-conformity with Article 1(1) when there was no clear public commitment to full employment or when there was high youth and long-term unemployment and low participation in active labour market programmes.[25] In other words, the ECSR understands the objective of full

---

[20] For example the EU Employment Strategy to create more and better jobs is described as 'little more than a pipe dream', for the policy of 'flexicurity' seems to lead to job creation of precarious work: M Freedland and N Kountouris, 'The Right to (Decent) Work in a European Comparative Perspective' in Mantouvalou, *The Right to Work* (n 6) 123, 129; cf D Ashiagbor, *The European Employment Strategy: Labour Market Regulation and New Governance* (Oxford, OUP, 2005). See also the pressures for flexibility emanating from the Organisation for Economic Cooperation and Development, the World Bank and the International Monetary Fund: K Rittich, 'The Right to Work and Labour Market Flexibility: Labour Market Governance Norms in the International Order' in Mantouvalou, *The Right to Work* (n 6) 316.

[21] G Mundlak, 'Working Out the Right to Work in a Global Labour market' in Mantouvalou, *The Right to Work* (n 6) 291.

[22] On the interpretation of the right to work by the European Committee of Social Rights (ECSR), see O'Cinneide, n 14; S Deakin, 'Article 1: The Right to Work' in N Bruun, K Lorcher, I Schomann and S Clauwaert (eds), *The European Social Charter and the Employment Relation* (Oxford, Hart Publishing, 2017) 147. For further analysis of the right to work under the ESC and the EU Charter of Fundamental Rights, see also D Ashiagbor, 'The Right to Work' in G de Burca and B de Witte (eds), *Social Rights in Europe* (Oxford, OUP, 2005) 241.

[23] Council of Europe, European Committee of Social Rights, *Conclusion I* (First supervision cycle, 1969–70, Denmark, Germany, Italy, Ireland, Sweden, Norway, United Kingdom) 13.

[24] O'Cinneide, above n 14, 114–15.

[25] Conclusions XVI-I, Netherlands (Netherlands, Antilles and Aruba); Conclusions 2004-1, Bulgaria.

employment in Article 1(1) as requiring states to adopt a coherent employment policy which aspires to full employment.

The ECSR has identified three different types of protection of the right to work contained in Article 1(2) that states should apply.[26]

(1) The prohibition of all forms of discrimination in employment. As discussed in chapter 4, human rights law requires everyone to be treated as an equal. A recognition of the right to work encourages equal treatment and equal opportunity, but also different treatment to adjust for disadvantages. For example, the law of disability discrimination usually requires an employer to make reasonable adjustments in order to enable persons with a disability to obtain work of their choice.[27] The requirement to make reasonable adjustments for disability as an aspect of the right to work is also recognised in other international Conventions.[28]

(2) The prohibition of forced or compulsory labour on the basis that this is incompatible with the value of 'an occupation freely entered into'. Some forms of forced labour amount to slavery and similar kinds of oppression that are also contrary to Article 4 ECHR discussed in chapter 9. Here the focus is on economic and legal coercion applied to force a person into or to continue in an unwanted occupation.

(3) The prohibition of any practice that might interfere with workers' right to earn their living in an occupation freely entered upon.

EU Charter of Fundamental Rights

The EU Charter of Fundamental Rights contains social rights alongside civil and political rights. The right to work in this context is protected in Article 15, under the heading 'Freedoms'. Article 15(1) says that '[e]veryone has the right to engage in work and to pursue a freely chosen or accepted occupation'. It is significant that, as the Explanations to the Charter note, Article 15 is rooted in the freedom, recognised in Article 1(2) ESC, to choose one's economic activities, rather than in the other ESC subsections which locate the right to work in the idea of access to, and availability of, work. So, the most prominent dimension of the ESC's understanding of the right to work – namely, the right to have work made available, implying a duty on the state to provide work – is missing from the EU's version of this right.[29]

This brief survey of the protection of the right to work in international human rights law illustrates both how this right is regarded as fundamental to any scheme of human rights and

---

[26] ECSR, 'Conclusions II, Statement of Interpretation on Article 1(2)', 4.
[27] Equality Act 2010, s 20; *Archibald v Fife Council* [2004] UKHL 32, [2004] ICR 954.
[28] United Nations, *Convention on the Rights of Persons with Disabilities* (12 December 2006) Article 27; E Albin, 'Universalising the Right to Work of Persons with Disabilities' in Mantouvalou, *The Right to Work* (n 6) 61; ILO, C159 – Vocational Rehabilitation and Employment (Disabled Persons) Convention, 1983 (No 159); A O'Reilly, The Right to Decent Work of Persons with Disabilities (Geneva, ILO, 2007); *Guevara Díaz v Costa Rica*, judgment of 22 June 2022, Series C, No 453 (Inter-American Court of Human Rights), noted by A Trebilcock, 'Inter-American Court of Human Rights Takes on Disability Discrimination in Relation to the Right to Work' (2023) 9 *International Labor Rights Case Law* 48; SR Galicia, 'The Right to Be Free of Discrimination on the Basis of Disability with Regard to Employment' (2023) 9 *International Labor Rights Case Law* 213.
[29] H Collins, 'Progress Towards the Right to Work in the United Kingdom' in Mantouvalou, *The Right to Work* (n 6) 227, 229–30. On the right to work in the EU Charter, see further E Frantziou and V Mantouvalou, 'Article 15 – Freedom to Choose an Occupation and Right to Engage in Work' in S Peers, T Hervey, J Kenner and A Ward (eds), *The EU Charter of Fundamental Rights – A Commentary*, 2nd edn (Oxford, Hart, 2021) 449.

how it has many ramifications in relation to work ranging from entry into jobs, the working conditions enjoyed in jobs, and termination of employment. For this reason, the right to work will be discussed in many other chapters in this book. In this chapter we focus on topics where what is at stake is arguably the core meaning of the right to work – the right of the worker to earn their living in an occupation freely entered upon. That right was denied explicitly in the Irish case discussed at the commencement of this chapter. More often interference with that right involves indirect practices and regulations.

2. Can Certain Jobs be Prohibited?

If people have a right to work in the job of their choice, can state authorities ever ban a particular type of job even if people want to do it? Are some types of work so contrary to human rights, public morality, public policy, or public order that they should be completely banned by law? If people want to perform such jobs, it will inevitably be questioned whether this is an informed rational choice or one that it produced either by coercion or misinformation. If the latter, there must be a question whether this work is really a job of their choice that ought to be protected.

In *Wackenheim v France*,[30] the UN Human Rights Committee (HRC), monitoring compliance with the International Covenant on Civil and Political Rights (ICCPR), considered a case that raised this issue. Mr Wackenheim was a person with dwarfism, who in 1991 appeared in 'dwarf tossing' events in France. Wearing protective equipment, he allowed himself to be thrown short distances onto an air bed by customers of the venue staging the events. This was his job, the way in which he made a living. However, later that year the French authorities said that dwarf tossing should be banned because *inter alia* it violated Article 3 of the European Convention on Human Rights (the prohibition of inhuman and degrading treatment). Mr Wackenheim submitted a communication to the HRC claiming that the ban from working had a negative impact on his life and constituted a violation of his dignity, invoking provisions such as the prohibition of discrimination, the right to liberty and security of the person, and the right to privacy.

Mr Wackenheim believed that the ban, which meant that he could not engage in the work of his choice, was incompatible with his dignity, while the authorities took the view that the work that he wanted to do was incompatible with his dignity. The HRC only examined whether the ban violated the prohibition of discrimination in the merits of the communication, and ruled that it did not violate Article 26 of the ICCPR, because the different treatment of people with dwarfism in this instance was justified by the protection of their dignity. Many other questions could be asked in relation to the problems set by this specific case, such as what other work opportunities Mr Wackenheim had and what social welfare support was available to him. Yet the case illustrates well the different values that support the right to work and the controversies that can arise in relation to certain occupations.

A particularly controversial area where related considerations arise and are regularly debated involves sex work.[31] Sex work is prohibited to varying extents in many legal orders. In some countries like Russia and much of the United States, sex work is 'fully criminalised', meaning it is

---

[30] *Wackenheim v France*, Communication No 854/1999: France. 26/07/2002 CCPR/C/75/D/854/1999.
[31] See J Flanigan and L Watson, *Debating Sex Work* (Oxford, OUP, 2019). See further the discussion in M Madden Dempsey, 'Sex, Work, and Criminalisation' in Bogg et al (eds), *Criminality at Work* (Oxford, OUP, 2020) 173; K Cruz, 'The Work of Sex Work: Prostitution, Unfreedom, and Criminality at Work' in Bogg, ibid 192. We are grateful to Danielle Worden for comments on this issue.

a criminal offence to sell or pay for sex. Sex work is 'partially criminalised' in others: in the UK, for instance, it is not a criminal offence to exchange sex for money, but other related activities, such as advertising in certain areas and running a brothel, are a criminal offence. In Aotearoa/New Zealand, on the other hand, sex work is decriminalised because, for the most part, sex work is treated no differently to other labour industries. Others have the 'sex-buyer model' under which the sale of sex is decriminalised but purchasing sex and other related offences remain illegal.

The main argument in favour of decriminalisation is that sex work should be lawful like other work because this is the best way of protecting the right to work and the safety of workers. In New Zealand, for instance, the first two stated purposes of the legislative decriminalisation of sex work are to 'safeguard the human rights of sex workers and protect them from exploitation' and 'promote their welfare and occupational health and safety'.[32] The criminalisation of sex work, on the other hand, jeopardises all this and appears to be mainly influenced by moralistic judgments on the nature of this work. Examples like these suggest that even work that some regard as unacceptable and incompatible with human dignity is work that is regarded as valuable and important by others.

A further example of banning conduct that could be classified as work involves the criminalisation of begging.[33] People who beg ask passers-by for money in public spaces. Those who beg are often rough sleepers, which means that they sleep in the open air or in spaces that are not designed for habitation (such as car parks).[34] Empirical research in the UK has shown that many people who beg are homeless before starting to beg, and further examined how homelessness occurs in the first place.[35]

Even though those who beg are often viewed as passive recipients of support, there is not always a sharp division between begging and work. A line of literature explores begging as work,[36] while categories of people who may be prosecuted as beggars may be street vendors or sex workers. ILO research defined begging as 'a range of activities whereby an individual asks a stranger for money on the basis of being poor or needing charitable donations for health or religious reasons. Beggars may also sell small items, such as dusters or flowers, in return for money that may have little to do with the value of the item for sale.'[37] The ILO definition suggests that the boundary between begging and work is not always clear. Conduct, such as the activity of street vendors, may be classified as begging but can also be viewed as work.[38] Other street life categories that may bear similarities to begging include charity collections, busking, and 'Big Issue' vending.[39]

---

[32] Prostitution Reform Act, s 3(a)–(b).

[33] We find this, for instance, in the UK Vagrancy Act 1824, s 3.

[34] See S Fitzpatrick and C Kennedy, 'The Links between Begging and Rough Sleeping: A Question of Legitimacy' (2001) 16 *Housing Studies* 549; Public Health England (PHE), 'Evidence Review: Adults with complex needs (with a particular focus on street begging and street sleeping)' (PHE Publications, 2018) 28–29.

[35] See S Fitzpatrick, G Bramley and S Johnsen, 'Pathways into Multiple Exclusion Homelessness in Seven UK Cities' (2012) 50 *Urban Studies* 148.

[36] AK Kassah, 'Begging as work: a study of people with mobility difficulties in Accra, Ghana' (2008) 23 *Disability and Society* 163; SE Lankenau, 'Stronger than Dirt – Public Humiliation and Status Enhancement among Panhandlers' (1999) 28 *Journal of Contemporary Ethnography* 288; J Lenhard, 'The Hopeful Labour of Begging – Homeless People's Struggles for a Better Life in Paris' (2021) 39 *Society and Space* 792.

[37] ILO, 'A Rapid Assessment of Bonded Labour in Domestic Work and Begging in Pakistan' (2004) 22.

[38] On challenges faced by street vendors, see ILO, 'The Regulatory Framework and the Informal Economy' (no date): www.ilo.org/wcmsp5/groups/public/@ed_emp/@emp_policy/documents/publication/wcms_210451.pdf.

[39] The Big Issue is a magazine sold by homeless people in the UK. On all these categories, see J Hermer, *Begging, Law and Power in Public Spaces* (Oxford, Hart, 2019) ch 3.

The criminalisation of begging has concerned human rights institutions during the last few years both at supranational and at national level.[40] Significantly, the criminalisation of begging was examined under the ECHR in the judgment *Lacatus v Switzerland*.[41] Even though the Court did not examine begging as work in this case, it ruled that begging falls within the scope of the right to private life, and that its blanket ban is incompatible with the provision. The African Court on Human and Peoples' Rights also found that the criminalisation of begging violates a number of provisions of the African Charter of Human and Peoples' Rights. In its Advisory Opinion, it explained that by criminalising vagrancy, these laws punish the most underprivileged and marginalised people in society, and violate the prohibition of discrimination and the right to equality before the law,[42] the right to dignity,[43] the right to liberty,[44] the right to a fair trial,[45] freedom of movement,[46] and the protection of the family.[47]

It is important not to normalise begging as a way to make a living for people who are destitute. State duties towards individuals who beg are far broader than the decriminalisation of begging. However, decriminalisation of begging is a first step towards protecting the rights of those faced with poverty and disadvantage, and people who may engage in work, such as street vendors and sex workers, who may be faced with criminal prosecution under laws banning begging.[48]

3. Regulatory Exclusions from Jobs and Work Sectors

A further related issue involves the question whether the authorities can ban groups of individuals from engaging in specified categories of jobs. Such bans are likely to interfere with the right of workers to take an occupation of their choice. In the UK, it is not much more than a century ago when women were banned by law from most professions and from standing for political office. It was only in the second half of the 20th century that married women were permitted to continue working in many kinds of jobs. Formal and informal racial and religious barriers to particular occupations were commonplace in many countries. A combination of the right to equal treatment and the right to work has slowly dismantled all those unjustified interferences with the right to work. Yet many other barriers remain, and these require careful legal scrutiny under human rights law.

A good illustration of this is the case *Sidabras and Dziautas v Lithuania*.[49] The applicants were former employees of the Soviet Security Service ('KGB'). The first applicant was employed by the KGB from 1975 to 1986. After 1990 he started working as a tax inspector at the Inland Revenue. The second applicant worked as a KGB officer from 1985 to 1991.

---

[40] See, for instance, UN Human Rights Council, *Report of the UN Special Rapporteur on Extreme Poverty and Human Rights*, Magdalena Sepúlveda Carmona, UN Doc A/66/265 (2011), paras 30–33.
[41] *Lacatus v Switzerland*, App No 14065/15, Judgment of 19 January 2021 (in French only). For critical analysis, see S Ganty, 'The Double-Edged ECtHR *Lăcătuş* Judgment on Criminalisation of Begging: *Da Mihi Elimo Sinam Propter Amorem Dei*' (2022) 3 *European Convention on Human Rights Law Review* 393.
[42] Articles 2 and 3 of the African Charter of Human and Peoples' Rights.
[43] Article 5.
[44] Article 6.
[45] Article 7.
[46] Article 12.
[47] Article 18.
[48] On begging and human rights, see further V Mantouvalou, 'Structural Injustice and Human Rights: The Case of Begging' in V Mantouvalou and J Wolff (eds), *Structural Injustice and the Law*, forthcoming (London, UCL Press, 2024).
[49] *Sidabras and Dziautas v Lithuania*, App Nos 55480/00 and 59330/00, Judgment of 27 July 2004.

After 1991 he was employed as a prosecutor at the Office of the Prosecutor General, investigating organised crime and corruption. In 1998 Lithuania enacted the Law on the Evaluation of the USSR State Security Committee and the Present Activities of Permanent Employees of the Organisation. The Act characterised the USSR State Security Committee (part of which was the KGB) as a criminal organisation that had committed a number of serious crimes, such as war crimes and genocide. Permanent employees of the KGB, as a result, were barred from taking up a wide range of jobs in the public and private sector for 10 years after the entry into force of the law. Both Mr Sidabras and Mr Dziautas were found to fall within the scope of the Lithuanian Act, were dismissed from their jobs and were unable to find a job in the posts prescribed by it. Having exhausted domestic remedies, they brought a complaint to the European Court of Human Rights (ECtHR). Considering the question whether the right to private life was engaged, the Court said that the ban 'affected their ability to develop relationships with the outside world to a very significant degree and has created serious difficulties for them in terms of earning their living, with obvious repercussions on the enjoyment of their private lives'.[50] The extensive implications of the restriction engaged the right to private life, and led to a violation of Article 14 ECHR (prohibition of discrimination) together with Article 8 ECHR (the right to private life).

A notable feature of the *Sidabras* case is that, in examining whether the right to private life of the applicants was engaged, the Court took note of materials of the ECSR on the right to work under Article 1(2) of the ESC, and of the ILO in relation to ILO Convention 111 on Discrimination (Employment and Occupation) of 1958. In assessing the scope of Article 8 ECHR, the Court said that:

> having regard in particular to the notions currently prevailing in democratic States, the Court considers that a far-reaching ban on taking up private sector employment does affect 'private life'. It attaches particular weight in this respect to the text of Article 1 § 2 of the European Social Charter and the interpretation given by the European Committee of Social Rights ... and to the texts adopted by the ILO ... It further reiterates that there is no watertight division separating the sphere of social and economic rights from the field covered by the Convention ...[51]

This use by the ECtHR of Article 8 to protect the right to work has been repeated.[52] In *Campagnano v Italy*,[53] national law banned those registered as bankrupt from carrying on various occupations such as director of a company, a trustee, an auditor, an arbitrator, lawyer, notary or management consultant for five years after the declaration of bankruptcy. The Court held that the law was a disproportionate interference with Article 8. Similarly, in *Mateescu v Romania*,[54] a general practitioner and university lecturer in medicine was denied entry into the legal profession even though he had passed all the examinations and completed the necessary training because the domestic law was interpreted to mean that being a doctor was a profession that was incompatible with being a lawyer. Relying on Article 8, the ECtHR held that the Romanian courts' interpretation of the domestic legislation was not foreseeable and therefore the ban on doctors also being lawyers was not in accordance with the law and therefore not justified.

---

[50] ibid [48].
[51] *Sidabras*, para 47.
[52] R O'Connell, 'The Right to Work in the ECHR' (2012) 2 *European Human Rights Law Review* 176.
[53] *Campagnano v Italy*, App No 77955/01, (2009) 48 EHRR 43, [2006] ECHR 241.
[54] *Mateescu v Romania*, App No 1944/10, [2014] ECHR 37.

Similar issues involving restrictions on access to particular kinds of work were examined by the UK Supreme Court (UKSC) in the case *R (Wright) v Secretary of State for Health*.[55] The case involved care workers who were placed on a list of people who, because of allegations of misconduct, the truth of which had not yet been determined, would be viewed as unsuitable to work with vulnerable adults. Any care worker included in that list was deprived of employment as a care worker and prevented from getting any other such employment in the sector of care work. Under the legislative framework at the time, care workers included in that list had no opportunity for a judicial hearing before being placed on the list, but only an opportunity for an administrative process after being included in that list. The UKSC examined whether this was compatible with the right to a fair trial under Article 6 of the ECHR and the right to private life under Article 8 of the ECHR. In this context, the Court examined in essence care workers' right to work. It ruled that the procedure of banning care workers on an interim basis from working with vulnerable adults, without giving them adequate opportunity to respond to the allegations, was incompatible with the right to a fair trial. Referring to the *Sidabras* case, it also maintained that the scheme may engage Article 8 on the right to private life because of its extensive implications for workers' private life, including their stigmatisation.

These cases are significant. They show that the right to work can be indirectly protected by courts in the context of the right to private life, the prohibition of discrimination, or the right to a fair trial. They emphasise the importance of work for people, not only because of the income that work generates but also because of its contribution to social interaction and private life more generally. They also exemplify that there is no sharp division between civil and social rights, and that a violation of a social right such as the right to work may give rise to a violation of the right to private life.[56]

The law of the European Union can also be used as a ground for challenging regulatory restrictions on access to work in the Member States. The free movement of workers is guaranteed by Article 45 TFEU. This right applies to all citizens of the EU who are seeking work. The right is protected against direct discrimination on grounds of nationality and also against indirect discrimination such as language requirements that have the effect of putting all nationals of other Member States at a particular disadvantage. In order to overcome the barrier to the right to free movement of workers that can be presented by justifiable rules requiring formal professional qualifications, the EU provides a general scheme for the mutual recognition of professional qualifications between Member States. Following the exit from the EU of the UK, none of these protections for the right to work apply to workers from the EU who migrate to the UK. Nevertheless, direct or indirect discrimination on grounds of nationality in order to obtain access to jobs may still be impugned under Article 8 of the ECHR. For instance, in *Bigaeva v Greece*,[57] a Russian national had by reason of a mistake been admitted into the Greek legal profession and permitted to take the professional examinations and to enter a training contract. The subsequent steps taken by Greek authorities to exclude her from the legal profession on the ground of her nationality were held to be contrary to Article 8 of the ECHR in conjunction with Article 14.

---

[55] *R (Wright) v Secretary of State for Health* [2009] UKHL 3, [2009] AC 739.
[56] See further V Mantouvalou, 'Work and Private Life: Sidabras and Dziautas v Lithuania' (2005) 30 *European Law Review* 573.
[57] *Bigaeva v Greece* [2011] ECHR 2164.

4. Employers' Controls Over Access to Work

Many restrictions on access to employment imposed in the past by employers and associations of employers are now unlawful under laws against discrimination such as the Equality Act 2010 in the UK.[58] Although these prohibitions against discrimination on grounds of race, sex, age and other protected characteristics are usually regarded as part of the right to equal treatment, in their origin as political movements these restrictions on employment opportunities were often attacked as interferences with the right to work.[59]

Restrictions on access to employment or particular trades and professions imposed by associations of employers such as guilds and private regulatory authorities may be regarded as unlawful, either as unlawful restraints on trade and so contrary to competition laws,[60] or as irrational decisions by private bodies that perform regulatory functions.[61] The restrictions are only likely to be valid if they identify necessary educational qualifications and experience in order to perform the particular job to an adequate standard.

Trade unions often try to negotiate with employers a closed shop under which employers agree not to hire any non-union members. Closed shop agreements enable the union to discipline its members and, by creating greater solidarity, strengthen their hand in bargaining with employers. But the law now recognises a right not to be a member of a trade union under Article 11 ECHR, with the effect that closed shops are unlawful.[62] This protects the right to work of those who do not want to be a member of a recognised trade union.[63]

5. Prison Labour

We mentioned earlier that Article 6 of the ICESCR on the right to work contains 'the right of everyone to the opportunity to gain his living by work which he freely chooses or accepts'. In its General Comment on the right to work, the CESCR explained that

> [s]tates parties are under the obligation to *respect* the right to work by, inter alia, prohibiting forced or compulsory labour and refraining from denying or limiting equal access to decent work for all persons, especially disadvantaged and marginalized individuals and groups, including prisoners or detainees, members of minorities and migrant workers.[64]

Article 1(2) of the ESC also protects the right to work 'in an occupation freely entered upon'. On the basis of this provision, the ECSR has examined prison labour to assess whether it is compatible with the right to work. Does having work opportunities in prison promote the right to work? Or does it constitute a violation of the right to choose an occupation freely?

It is important to appreciate that work in prison is typically not part of prisoners' punishment: the European Prison Rules explicitly say that '[p]rison work shall be approached as a positive

---

[58] See chapter 4.
[59] J Shim, *Equality or the Right to Work? Explaining and Justifying Employment Discrimination Law* (PhD London School of Economics, 2008) ch 6.
[60] *The Case of the Tailors of Habits &c. of Ipswich* (1614) Michaelmas Term, 12 James 1, Coke's Reports, Vol 11, 53a (KB). Cf H Collins, 'Progress Towards the Right to Work in the United Kingdom', above n 29, 227, 247–48.
[61] *Nagle v Feilden* [1966] 2 QB 633, CA.
[62] TULRCA 1992, s 137(1). See further chapter 5 on closed shops and on blacklisting.
[63] In the USA, anti-union laws are frequently described as 'right to work' laws.
[64] General Comment 18, para 23.

element of the prison regime and shall never be used as a punishment'.[65] Even though work in prison is not part of punishment and legally required, it is often compulsory in practice.[66] Prisoners are not free to decide whether they will work, for if they refuse to work, they may be sanctioned with reduced visits from friends and family, reduced television or gym time, less or no income and even solitary confinement. In this way, those in prison are in effect compelled to work by the prison authorities. It is generally accepted that work in prison is beneficial for many reasons – for instance to deal with boredom, gain income to support dependants, and gain new skills. However, compulsion to work of those who are deprived of their physical freedom and are in a position of vulnerability for this reason should be examined closely for it may be incompatible with respecting the right to work and the prohibition of forced labour. How should we approach the compulsion to work of prisoners?

In addition to the compulsion to work, working conditions of the incarcerated are not equal to working conditions of those who do the same work outside prison, even if they are employed by private entities. In many legal orders, working prisoners are excluded from rights such as the right to a minimum wage, working time and the right to form and join trade unions. Not only do they not have a right to choose whether they will work, in other words, but they are also employed with very little or no pay or protection of other labour rights, in conditions that can be described as exploitative. Even though it is typically said that prisoners do not forfeit all their rights while their physical freedom is limited in prison,[67] the compulsion to work under threat of sanctions raises questions under human rights law. That they have no freedom to move freely or to have a normal social or family life can be viewed as a necessary implication of imprisonment. Working without workers' rights is not. It increases the vulnerability of this group to exploitation,[68] which is incompatible with a broadly conceived right to work.

An important issue to highlight, though, is that international human rights and constitutional rights documents that prohibit forced and compulsory labour explicitly exclude prison labour from the prohibition. Article 4 of the ECHR states: 'For the purpose of this Article the term "forced or compulsory labour" shall not include [...] any work required to be done in the ordinary course of detention imposed according to the provisions of Article 5 of this Convention or during release from such detention.'[69] The ILO draws a distinction between private and public prisons in the Forced Labour Convention No 29, and imposes specific requirements regarding the regulation of private use of prisoners' labour.[70] Article 2(1) of the Convention says that 'forced or compulsory labour shall mean all work or service which is exacted from any person under the menace of any penalty and for which the said person has not offered himself voluntarily'. Article 2(2) contains exceptions, with the relevant one for present purposes being the following:

> (c) any work or service exacted from any person as a consequence of a conviction in a court of law, provided that the said work or service is carried out under the supervision and control of a public authority and that the said person is not hired to or placed at the disposal of private individuals, companies or associations.

---

[65] Article 26(1).
[66] For discussion see R Lippke, 'Prison Labour: Its Control, Facilitation, and Terms' (1998) 17 *Law and Philosophy* 533.
[67] ibid 543.
[68] V Mantouvalou, *Structural Injustice and Workers' Rights* (Oxford, OUP, 2023) ch 4.
[69] ILO Forced Labour Convention, 1930 (No 29), Article 4, para 3(a).
[70] See C Fenwick, 'Private Use of Prisoners' Labor: Paradoxes of International Human Rights Law' (2005) 27 *Human Rights Quarterly* 249, 273; F Milman-Sivan, 'Prisoners for Hire: Towards a Normative Justification of the ILO's Prohibition of Private Forced Prisoner Labor' (2013) 36 *Fordham International Law Journal* 1619.

These exclusions of working prisoners may have been deemed acceptable in the past,[71] but they are not acceptable anymore. The ILO examined in 2007 whether prison labour for private employers complies with Convention No 29, and developed principles in the area.[72] In order for prison work for private employers to comply with the Forced Labour Convention, what is needed is the formal written consent of the prisoner and working conditions similar to a free labour relationship (in relation to wage levels, social security and occupational safety and health). These would indicate that labour is voluntary.[73]

The ECSR also considered prison labour in the context of Article 1, para 2 of the ESC, which protects the right to work in an occupation freely entered upon. It reached similar findings to the ILO, namely that working conditions in prison have to be regulated strictly, and that when employed by private employers, prisoners have to be employed with their consent and in conditions as similar as possible to working conditions outside prison.[74] The Committee further said that the prohibition of discrimination concerns their pay, working hours and other working conditions, as well as social security rights.[75]

The Grand Chamber of the ECtHR examined prison labour in *Stummer v Austria*,[76] which involved affiliation of working prisoners with an old age pension system. Here the applicant was not entitled to an old age pension despite having worked for lengthy periods of time in the prison kitchen and bakery, because he had not accumulated the required minimum of contributions in order to have this entitlement. Even though the majority of the Court recognised that prisoners should enjoy all rights except their physical liberty while incarcerated, they did not find that the applicant's rights were violated.

However, there were powerful dissenting opinions in *Stummer* on the human rights of working prisoners. Judge Tulkens particularly highlighted in her dissent on Article 4:

> [C]an it really still be maintained in 2011, in the light of current standards in the field of social security, that prison work without affiliation to the old-age pension system constitutes work that a person in detention may *normally* be required to do? I do not think so. This, in my view, is the fundamental point. Nowadays, work without adequate social cover can no longer be regarded as normal work. It follows that the exception provided for in Article 4 § 3 (a) of the Convention is not applicable in the present case. *Even a prisoner cannot be forced to do work that is abnormal.*

Compulsion to work and exclusion from labour and social security rights while working raises pressing questions in relation to its compatibility with the prohibition of forced and compulsory labour, which is an aspect of the right to work, while the blanket exclusion of prison labour from the prohibition of forced labour is outdated, according to Judge Tulkens.

6. Welfare-to-Work

It was noted above that under international conventions on the right to work, states have positive duties to promote full employment, have employment strategies and promote employability.

---

[71] See, for instance, *Van Droogenbroeck v Belgium*, [1982] ECHR 3.
[72] ILO Report of the Committee of Experts for the Application of Conventions and Recommendations, 'Eradication of Forced Labour', International Labour Office, 2007.
[73] ibid paras 59–60 and 114 ff.
[74] Conclusions XVI-1, Germany.
[75] Conclusions 2012, General Introduction, Statement of Interpretation of Article 1 para 2.
[76] *Stummer v Austria* (2012) 54 EHRR 11.

On this basis, through welfare-to-work schemes, welfare benefits for working age people are most of the time conditional upon them making an effort to obtain work. These schemes are a part of 'activation policies' that encourage active engagement with the labour market. They make welfare benefits conditional upon looking for and accepting work, failing which people lose access to welfare support and may be unable to meet their basic needs.

It could be said that the purpose of welfare conditionality schemes is to promote the right to work. However, these schemes raise two issues of interference with the right to work, which we examine in turn: (1) Does conditionality in effect amount to coercion to work or forced labour? (2) Does conditionality unjustifiably interfere with the right to freely choose an occupation?

Prohibition of Forced and Compulsory Labour

While conditionality of welfare benefits is not a new development in social policy,[77] in recent years the schemes have become particularly punitive in many countries.[78] In the UK, the sanctions can be very harsh for failure to attend a meeting or attend a job interview, even for reasons outside one's control. Welfare claimants can lose access to all social support for long periods of time, ranging from months to years. As the German Constitutional Court has held with respect to its own national scheme, without a guarantee of an existential minimum of welfare support, the penalties may be disproportionate and violate human dignity.[79] Does this compulsion to take a job amount to an interference with Article 4 ECHR or other international human rights instruments?

Article 4 of the ECHR prohibits forced and compulsory labour.[80] But it exempts in its third paragraph 'any work or service which forms part of civic obligations'. In the relevant case law on welfare-to-work, the ECtHR has not ruled that there has been a violation of the Convention thus far. In *Schuitemaker v the Netherlands*,[81] the applicant, a philosopher by profession, was asked to take 'generally accepted' work (rather than work that was 'deemed suitable' for her). If she did not comply with the condition, her benefits would be reduced. She claimed that this was contrary to Article 4. In rejecting her claim, the Court said that:

> it must in general be accepted that where a State has introduced a system of social security, it is fully entitled to lay down conditions which have to be met for a person to be eligible for benefits pursuant to that system. In particular a condition to the effect that a person must make demonstrable efforts in order to obtain and take up generally accepted employment cannot be considered unreasonable in this respect. This is the more so given that Dutch legislation provides that recipients of benefits pursuant to the Work and Social Assistance Act are not required to seek and take up employment which is not generally socially accepted or in respect of which they have conscientious objections.

The question arises whether the UK Universal Credit system satisfies this test in that it both imposes very severe sanctions and forces people sometimes into precarious and badly paid work that may not count as 'generally accepted employment'.

---

[77] A Paz-Fuchs, *Welfare to Work* (Oxford, OUP, 2008) ch 2.
[78] On the UK scheme which is especially punitive, see M Adler, *Cruel, Inhuman or Degrading Treatment? Benefit Sanctions in the UK* (London, Palgrave Macmillan, 2018) ch 2.
[79] BVerfG 1 BvL 7/16 (05.11.2019).
[80] For a detailed overview of the case law, see E Dermine, 'Activation Policies for the Unemployed and the International Human Rights Case Law on the Prohibition of Forced Labour' in E Dermine and D Dumont (eds), *Activation Policies for the Unemployed, the Right to Work and the Duty to Work* (Brussels, Peter Lang, 2014) 103.
[81] *Schuitemaker v the Netherlands*, App No 15906/08, admissibility decision of 4 May 2010. See also *Talmon v the Netherlands* [1997] ECHR 207.

The HRC also examined related complaints under Article 8 of the ICCPR that contains a prohibition of slavery, servitude, forced and compulsory labour, which is similar to Article 4 of the ECHR.[82] It considered the exemption of normal civic obligations from the prohibition of forced labour and said:

> to so qualify as a normal civil obligation, the labour in question must, at a minimum, not be an exceptional measure; it must not possess a punitive purpose or effect; and it must be provided for by law in order to serve a legitimate purpose under the Covenant. In the light of these considerations, the Committee is of the view that the material before it, including the absence of a degrading or dehumanizing aspect of the specific labour performed, does not show that the labour in question comes within the scope of the proscriptions set out in article 8.

The HRC accepted that people may have a duty to work as part of their normal civic obligations. When looking at particularly precarious jobs, though, such as zero-hour contracts for a private employer, can we say that these constitute a normal civic obligation?

The UK Supreme Court considered welfare-to-work and human rights in a 2013 judicial review case, *Reilly*.[83] One of the questions for the Court was whether a law that made benefits conditional on Ms Reilly working in a shop (Poundland), in a position that would not advance her employment prospects and chosen career in museums, was contrary to Article 4 ECHR. The Supreme Court ruled that the provision of a conditional benefit of that kind comes nowhere close to the type of exploitative conduct at which Article 4 is aimed.[84] It recognised that Article 4 has exploitation at its heart,[85] but said that to find a violation, work has to be not just compulsory and involuntary, but the duty and its performance must be 'unjust', 'oppressive', 'an avoidable hardship', 'needlessly distressing' or 'somewhat harassing'.[86] The threshold set by the UK Supreme Court, the HRC and the ECtHR is high,[87] but there are examples of welfare conditionality claimants nowadays where such conditions might be met.[88]

Right to Work

A specific aspect of welfare conditionality schemes that may be incompatible with the right to work involves working conditions. Studies have shown that schemes of strict conditionality can be seen as 'a driver of in-work poverty' and 'force unemployed persons to accept jobs regardless of the pay levels'.[89] Looking at the welfare conditionality arrangements in the UK, it can be argued that they can turn the unemployed poor into working and exploited poor because people are

---

[82] *Faure v Australia*, Comm 1036/2001, UN Doc A/61/40, Vol II, at 97 (HRC, 2005).

[83] *R (on the application of Reilly and Anor) v Secretary of State for Work and Pensions* [2013] UKSC 68. There have already been successful instances of judicial review on the basis that the regulations that involve the calculation of Universal Credit (Universal Credit Regulations 2013 (SI 2013/976)) were wrongly interpreted. See *R (on the application of Johnson and Others) v Secretary of State for Work and Pensions* [2019] EWHC 23 (Admin).

[84] ibid [83].

[85] ibid [81].

[86] ibid [89]. These terms were borrowed from *Van der Mussele v Belgium* [1983] ECHR 13, [37].

[87] See also E Dermine, 'Limitation of Welfare to Work: The Prohibition of Forced Labour and the Right to Freely Chosen Work' in A Eleveld, T Kampen and J Arts (eds), *Welfare to Work in Contemporary European Welfare States* (Bristol, Policy Press, 2020) 67.

[88] V Mantouvalou, 'Welfare to Work, Structural Injustice and Human Rights' (2020) 83 *Modern Law Review* 929. However, establishing a violation of the prohibition of forced labour may be challenging. See A Almutawa and B Almajed, 'The Prohibition of Forced or Compulsory Labour and Conditional Welfare under the United Kingdom's Universal Credit Scheme' (2023) 43 *Legal Studies* 734.

[89] D Seikel and D Spannagel, 'Activation and In-Work Poverty' in H Lohmann and I Marx (eds), *Handbook on In-Work Poverty* (Cheltenham, Edward Elgar, 2018) 245 at 257.

compelled to accept precarious work, such as zero-hour contracts, for otherwise they may face destitution.[90]

The severity of the issues that arise from the UK system were highlighted by the UN Special Rapporteur on Extreme Poverty and Human Rights, Philip Alston, following a visit to the UK in 2018 that focused on the problems of Universal Credit and in-work poverty.[91] The role of the Special Rapporteur is to examine and report on the rights of those living in extreme poverty. Alston emphasised that in the UK there are 14 million people in poverty, that 60% of those who are in poverty are in families where someone works, and 2.8 million people in poverty are in families where all adults work full time.[92] He noted that the denial of benefits has pushed certain categories of claimants into unsuitable work,[93] and explained that people want to work, and take work that is badly paid and precarious in order to meet their basic needs.[94] Having spoken with Universal Credit claimants, he said that not only did they have to 'fill out pointless job applications for positions that did not match their qualifications', but also that they had to 'take inappropriate temporary work just to avoid debilitating sanctions'.[95] Are these schemes compatible with human rights law?

Aspects of welfare-to-work schemes may violate elements of the right to work in international human rights law.[96] In the ICESCR, as mentioned earlier, the right 'includes the right of everyone to the opportunity to gain his living by work which he freely chooses or accepts', and requires that the authorities 'take appropriate steps to safeguard this right'.[97] On the basis of Article 6 and General Comment 18, the right to work guarantees a right to decent work.[98] It can be argued that certain precarious types of work, such as zero-hours work, can be exploitative or abusive. Forcing people into this kind of work under the threat of serious sanctions and destitution can therefore be viewed as a violation of the right to work.

Welfare-to-work schemes with harsh sanctions, which require people to accept work that is not suitable, may also raise questions under the right to work in Article 1(2) of the ESC that protects the right to work in an occupation freely chosen. The standards set in the context of the Charter are often used by the ECtHR to illuminate the interpretation of rights protected in the ECHR.[99] The ECSR has found in this context that contracting parties may violate the provision when they have schemes with excessive conditionality. As was said earlier, there are different types of activation policies and different kinds of welfare conditionality schemes, some of which are stricter than others.[100] According to the ECSR, welfare-to-work may be

---

[90] Mantouvalou, above n 88. The ILO Global Survey on the Eradication of Forced Labour has also explained that the requirement to work could be contrary to forced labour if work is used as a penalty and there are no safeguards that will guarantee that it is compatible with the 1930 Forced Labour Convention (No 29) and the 1952 Social Security Convention (No 102), particularly with respect to its suitability: International Labour Conference, Global Survey on the Eradication of Forced Labour, 2007, para 205.

[91] Report of the UN Special Rapporteur on Extreme Poverty and Human Rights, Visit to the UK and Northern Ireland, A/HRC/41/39/Add.1, 23 April 2019.

[92] ibid [28].

[93] Alston makes this point in relation to people with disabilities, for instance, in [4] of his Report.

[94] ibid [8].

[95] ibid [57].

[96] For a detailed overview of the principles, see E Dermine, 'Activation Policies for the Unemployed and the International Human Rights Case Law on the Right to Freely Chosen Work' in E Dermine and D Dumont (eds), *Activation Policies for the Unemployed, the Right to Work and the Duty to Work* (Brussels, Peter Lang, 2014) 139.

[97] Article 6 ICESCR.

[98] General Comment No 18, para 7.

[99] See above, discussion on *Sidabras*.

[100] For an overview, see the volume above, n 96.

incompatible with Article 1(2), when work is inconsistent with human dignity or more generally when it is exploitative.[101]

The Committee has explained that activation policies violate the right to freely chosen work if they require claimants to accept work that is not suitable.[102] Do precarious work arrangements, such as zero-hours contracts, constitute suitable employment? The answer to this question may be negative because the concept of suitable employment is defined by reference to a decent wage.[103]

To conclude this section, work is an important good. Schemes that encourage individuals to work are potentially valuable and can promote the right to work, as we have seen in experiments where people were guaranteed work.[104] Welfare conditionality schemes with harsh sanctions, on the other hand, can violate the right to work.

7. Conclusion

As we have noted, the right to work has many important dimensions and plays a pivotal role in the protection of human rights at work. References to the right appear in many other chapters. Indeed, it can be argued that the right to work provides the foundation for all labour laws.[105] In this chapter we have focused on the point that work is an important good for individual wellbeing and personal development. Policies that promote full employment are a key component of the state's positive duties under the right to work. Restrictions on the right to work either for particular groups or for particular jobs must be subject to scrutiny and be justified as proportionate. Compulsion to work in exploitative conditions under the threat of severe sanctions and the fear of poverty and destitution may be viewed as incompatible with the right.

---

[101] See ECSR Conclusions 2012, Statement of Interpretation, Article 1(2). See further the discussion by S Deakin, 'Article 1 – The Right to Work' in N Bruun, K Lorcher, I Schoemann and S Clauwaert (eds), *The European Social Charter and the Employment Relation* (Oxford, Hart, 2017) 147 at 159.

[102] Criteria on the meaning of 'suitable employment' are found in a Guide drafted in 2010 by the Committee of Experts on Social Security, in charge of the promotion of the European Social Security Code.

[103] On this see E Dermine, above n 96 at 166 ff.

[104] See M Kasy and L Lehner, 'Employing the Unemployed of Marienthal: Evaluation of a Guaranteed Job Programme' (2023) CESifo Working Paper No 10394, available at https://ssrn.com/abstract=4431385; see also E Mork, L Ottosson and U Vikman, 'To Work or Not to Work? Effects of Temporary Public Employment on Future Employment and Benefits', IZA DP No 15071.

[105] For discussion of this idea in Japan, see K Arita, 'The Development of Right to Work Theories of Labour Law in Japan: A Comparative Perspective' in Mantouvalou, *The Right to Work* (n 6) 209.

9

Migration, Slavery, Servitude, Forced Labour and Human Trafficking

1.	Labour Migration	4.	Undocumented Workers
2.	Agricultural Work and Seasonal Visas	5.	Slavery, Servitude, Forced and Compulsory Labour
3.	Domestic Labour and the UK Overseas Domestic Worker Visa	6.	UK Modern Slavery Act 2015
		7.	Conclusion

Ella migrated to work in Qatar, under a *kafala* visa, and came to the UK accompanying her employers under a UK Overseas Domestic Worker visa.[1] Both are very restrictive visa schemes that effectively tie workers to an employer. This means that they cannot change employer for otherwise they become undocumented. While in the UK, Ella worked day and night as a domestic worker, cared for one of her employers who had serious health issues and the family's youngest child, and slept in the storage room. She was paid about £200 per month. The employers did not give her food and she was very hungry, so she left them after a few days in London. By leaving them she became undocumented because of her visa conditions. She had four young children back home, and she needed to continue working to support them, which is why she could not return to her country of origin, the Philippines. After leaving her employers in the UK, she started looking for other work as a domestic worker. She found some part-time jobs, but they were always underpaid, and often employers offered hourly pay that was below the national minimum wage: 'Sometimes if you have an interview and you tell [the prospective employers] that you don't have papers, they take advantage of you and they give you a small salary,' she said. When the employers were away on holidays, they did not pay her. She also had some health issues but did not go to the doctor because she was undocumented. Ella is one of thousands of migrant domestic workers who arrive in the UK every year, accompanying an employer under a UK Overseas Domestic Worker (ODW) visa. About 20,000 ODW visas are issued each year, according to statistics provided by the Home Office.

Is it fair for workers to be employed in such conditions? What is the role of restrictive visa schemes in making these workers particularly vulnerable to exploitation? How about the status of being an undocumented worker? Is the treatment of these groups of workers compatible with

---

[1] Ella's story (not her real name) is based on interviews of migrant domestic workers conducted by Virginia Mantouvalou. See further, V Mantouvalou, '"Am I Free Now?" Overseas Domestic Workers in Slavery' (2015) 42 *Journal of Law and Society* 329.

the prohibition of slavery, servitude, forced and compulsory labour? In this chapter we address these questions. The chapter, first, discusses two particularly restrictive visa schemes for migrant workers that have been linked to labour exploitation, including some of its more severe forms, and then considers the status of being an undocumented worker. After that, it turns to the prohibition of slavery, servitude, forced and compulsory labour under the European Convention on Human Rights (ECHR) and relevant International Labour Organization (ILO) instruments to assess the compatibility of the treatment of these workers with the relevant instruments. We look at case law that has ruled that migrant workers are sometimes victims of the worst forms of labour exploitation. The final part of the chapter turns to the UK Modern Slavery Act 2015 (MSA 2015). The MSA 2015 was adopted to address some of these problems by primarily criminalising employers' conduct. We raise doubts as to whether it is an effective tool to address this major social problem.

1. Labour Migration

Migration is part of life for many people in the modern world, who may move from one country to another for personal, economic or other reasons. Labour migration has become a central concern for labour and human rights law scholars in recent years.[2] The ability to migrate and work is valuable not only for the person who migrates, but also for the host country and for the worker's home country. This is why it is sometimes described as a 'triple win': it is said that the schemes that regulate labour migration are beneficial for the country of nationality of the worker because they send remittances to support family, the country of destination because the workers cover labour shortages, and the workers themselves who earn income that they need. However, as Ella's story suggests, migrant workers may face significant challenges and be severely exploited at work. Migrant workers are often more vulnerable than other groups of workers, because they may face language barriers, lack networks of support and may work in precarious sectors, such as domestic work, construction or agriculture. What is particularly troubling, though, is that immigration rules may set conditions that increase workers' vulnerability and 'fashion precarious work'.[3]

Many countries have labour migration schemes for so called 'highly skilled' workers. Under these schemes, people with a certain level of skills and education can move to another country to work with relative ease, either having a job offer or without a job offer.[4] In the context of the European Union, there is free movement of all workers since its inception.[5] This is a fundamental right of workers who are citizens of EU Member States, also protected in the EU Charter of Fundamental Rights.[6] A lot of people move freely from one EU country to another to work, but for workers from outside the EU there are restrictions.

---

[2] See, for instance, C Costello and M Freedland (eds), *Migrants at Work – Immigration and Vulnerability in Labour Law* (Oxford, OUP, 2014); B Ryan and R Zahn (eds), *Migrant Labour and the Reshaping of Employment Law* (Oxford, Hart, 2023); J Howe and R Owens (eds), *Temporary Labour Migration in the Global Era* (Oxford, Hart, 2016).

[3] B Anderson, 'Migration, Immigration Controls, and the Fashioning of Precarious Work' (2010) 24 *Work, Employment and Society* 300. See further V Mantouvalou, *Structural Injustice and Workers' Rights* (Oxford, OUP, 2023) ch 3.

[4] This is the case with the UK High Potential Individual visa.

[5] Article 45 TFEU.

[6] See Article 15 on the freedom to choose an occupation and the right to engage in work that provides as follows: '2. Every citizen of the Union has the freedom to seek employment, to work, to exercise the right of establishment and to provide services in any Member State. 3. Nationals of third countries who are authorised to work in the territories of

There are some immigration routes for workers typically viewed as low-skilled. However, these generally impose limitations in terms of the length of time that the migrant worker can stay in a country. They may also bind the worker to a particular employer, and restrict the right to be accompanied by family members or to form relations with locals.[7] The resulting problem is that these schemes create special relations of dependency of the worker on the employer, in addition to the standard inequality of power that characterises a typical employment relation. A further concern is that workers may be exploited or abused, but will be reluctant to question their treatment or leave their employer because they fear deportation.[8] The UK Seasonal Worker visa and the Overseas Domestic Worker visa, to which we now turn, exemplify the problems created by restrictive temporary labour migration schemes in particularly precarious sectors.

2. Agricultural Work and Seasonal Visas

Agricultural work is a low paid sector with a high concentration of workers under temporary labour migration schemes. The ILO has described workers in agriculture as the 'poorest of the rural poor'.[9] Work in this sector is challenging for several reasons.[10] It is typically seasonal work with the implication being that workers do not have a guaranteed income throughout the year.[11] This makes it an unattractive option for many people. Moreover, these workers may be reluctant to claim a pay rise or enforce their legal rights because the employer may not want to rehire them for the season that follows. In addition, agricultural work is dangerous. According to estimates of the ILO, over 170,000 agricultural workers are killed each year at work around the world.[12] According to the Health and Safety Executive, the UK regulator on matters of health and safety at work, agriculture has the highest rate of fatal injury of workers if compared to all key sectors.[13] Many are injured in industrial accidents with the machinery used, or poisoned by pesticides. As agricultural workers are often temporary workers, they are more likely to be involved in accidents because they are often new to the work that they do.

Working in rural areas means that workers are isolated: they cannot easily access legal advice or be accessed by trade unions. The accommodation of agricultural workers can also constitute

---

the Member States are entitled to working conditions equivalent to those of citizens of the Union.' On this, see further E Frantziou and V Mantouvalou, 'Freedom to Choose an Occupation and Right to Engage in Work' in S Peers, T Hervey, J Kenner and A Ward (eds), *The EU Charter of Fundamental Rights – A Commentary*, 2nd edn (Oxford, Hart, 2021) 449.

[7] See, for instance, D Rajkumar, L Berkowitz, LF Vosko, V Preston and R Latham, 'At the Temporary–Permanent Divide: How Canada Produces Temporariness and Makes Citizens Through its Security, Work, and Settlement Policies' (2012) 16 *Citizenship Studies* 483.

[8] On challenges faced by undocumented workers in agriculture, see, for instance, the judgment of the European Court of Human Rights in *Chowdury v Greece*, App No 21884/15, Judgment of 30 March 2017. See also R Kukreja, 'Visible Yet Invisible: The Disciplinary Mechanism of Self-Surveillance Among Undocumented South Asian Male Migrants in Rural Greece' (2021) 47 *Journal of Ethnic and Migration Studies* 3660.

[9] ILO, Agricultural Wage Workers: The Poorest of the Rural Poor, Press Release, 23 September 1996.

[10] As highlighted in ACL Davies, 'Migrant Workers in Agriculture' in Costello and Freedland (eds), *Migrants at Work*, above n 2, 79 at 80–81.

[11] On this point and further discussion of the key features of agricultural work, see, for instance, P Hurst in collaboration with P Termine and M Karl, 'Agricultural Workers and their Contribution to Sustainable Agriculture and Rural Development', International Labour Organization, Food and Agriculture Organization, International Union of Food, Agricultural, Hotel, Restaurant, Catering, Tobacco and Allied Workers' Associations, 2007, p 23.

[12] ILO, 'Agriculture: A Hazardous Work', available at www.ilo.org/safework/areasofwork/hazardous-work/WCMS_110188/lang--en/index.htm.

[13] See Health and Safety Executive, 'Fatal Injuries in Agriculture, Forestry and Fishing in Great Britain 2021/22', available at www.hse.gov.uk/agriculture/resources/fatal.htm.

a challenge. It is often provided by the employer, as farms may be in remote locations and it is convenient to live close to work, but may be of substandard quality.[14] However, the fact that accommodation may be provided by the employer also means that if a worker leaves their job, they will lose this accommodation. For migrant workers, the implication of this may be that they become homeless. Finally, agricultural workers are often employed through agencies, a reality which creates further challenges because it is not always clear who is the employer: the agency or the farm business.[15]

Workers in agriculture are often recruited under temporary labour migration programmes, namely schemes whereby migrant workers arrive in a country to work, often without a route to permanent residence or citizenship. Legal rules that restrict these workers' rights exacerbate their vulnerability, as the UK Seasonal Worker visa shows.

The UK Seasonal Worker Visa

While the UK was a member of the EU, with free movement rules in place, there were relatively limited needs for workers from outside the EU.[16] The end of free movement, which followed Brexit, led to a new scheme that can serve to illustrate how restrictions on visa conditions create particularly serious problems for workers' rights.[17] From 2019, following the decision to leave the EU, the UK reintroduced a Pilot Seasonal Worker visa, which it expanded later on.[18] The pilot involved 2,500 workers initially and has gradually been increasing to 55,000 workers in 2023. The scheme was renamed the Seasonal Worker visa. The visa would be used for recruitment in horticulture, but was expanded to cover other fields, such as poultry.[19]

The programme is a sponsored visa which is run by certain approved intermediaries, and not by the farms directly. These have to be endorsed by the Department for Environment, Food and Rural Affairs, and licensed by the Gangmasters and Labour Abuse Authority.[20] The visa contains a number of conditions, which restrict workers' freedom. For instance, its duration is up to six months for every 12-month period, the workers cannot get a permanent job, be accompanied by family members or have recourse to public funds, which include a range of social benefits that are available to people on a low income.[21] The temporary nature of the visa and the fact that workers cannot be accompanied by family members means that it will often be those who

---

[14] See, for instance, The Voice Investigation on 'Strawberry Slavery', available at www.voice-online.co.uk/news/2021/10/10/strawberry-slavery/.

[15] The discussion of the challenges of the sector draws on Davies (n 10). On agency work, see ACL Davies, 'The Implementation of the Directive on Temporary Agency Work in the UK: A Missed Opportunity' (2010) 1 *European Labour Law Journal* 303. See also J Fudge and K Strauss (eds), *Temporary Work, Agencies and Unfree Labour – Insecurity in the New World of Work* (Abingdon, Routledge, 2016).

[16] The UK had a seasonal worker visa between 1945 and 2013 when it was discontinued. On the history of the scheme, see ACL Davies, 'Problems Continue in the Horticulture Sector: The Seasonal Workers Pilot Review 2019' (2022) 51 *Industrial Law Journal* 494.

[17] For an overview, see M Gower, S Coe and I Stewart, 'Recruitment Support for Agricultural Workers', Commons Library Debate Pack, 24 May 2022, CDP 2022/0094.

[18] See the Immigration Rules Appendix Temporary Work – Seasonal Worker, 2016, available at www.gov.uk/guidance/immigration-rules/immigration-rules-appendix-t5-temporary-worker-seasonal-worker.

[19] See Department for Environment, Food and Rural Affairs, Government Food Strategy, June 2022, p 10.

[20] See Guidance, Workers and Temporary Workers: Guidance for Sponsors: Sponsor a Seasonal Worker, SE 2.5, available at www.gov.uk/government/publications/workers-and-temporary-workers-guidance-for-sponsors-sponsor-a-seasonal-worker/workers-and-temporary-workers-guidance-for-sponsors-sponsor-a-seasonal-worker-accessible-version.

[21] SE 1.7, Appendix SAW 7.2.

are younger and probably less experienced who use this migration route.[22] There is no English language requirement for the workers.

Crucially, the fact that intermediaries are involved creates special dependency of the workers, not on the end user alone but also on the intermediaries themselves. The intermediaries are required by the scheme to make sure that workers are normally permitted to move to another employer. The official Guidance provides:

> You must not *normally* refuse requests from participating workers to change employers. Participating workers can change employers if they wish and must *normally* be allowed to do so, unless there are significant reasons not to permit this (for example, their visa will imminently expire and the duration of the necessary training requirements would make such a move impractical).[23]

There is no free and unconditional right to change employer. Workers have to request to change employer, and intermediaries must not *normally* turn down the request.

A Review by the Home Office and the Department for Agriculture, Food and Rural Affairs on the first year of its operation (2019–20)[24] did not identify instances of extreme labour exploitation but uncovered other concerning issues, such as a lack of personal protective equipment for workers, poor living conditions and allegations of unfair treatment by the employers, including racism and other forms of discrimination.

However, civil society organisations, academic scholars and journalists have uncovered serious instances of abuse. Research has shown that workers' recruitment, working conditions, and living conditions exhibit elements of compulsion and duress, and that workers cannot leave their employer.[25] The fact that workers are not free to change employer, but are only permitted to change *normally*, has been presented as a factor that creates vulnerability, particularly because some workers incur debts in order to travel to the UK which means that they cannot easily leave the job and return to their home country.[26] Workers stay with employers even if they are ill-treated, as they have debts to pay back, and they need to work until they are able to do so. An investigation by the *Bureau of Investigative Journalism* and *The Guardian* found that some workers who come to the UK under the Seasonal Worker visa may pay extortionate recruitment fees to recruitment agents, and blamed this on the underfunding of labour enforcement agencies and the quick expansion of the Seasonal Worker visa scheme.[27] Many workers interviewed said that they were unable to change employer and that the intermediaries create fear in order to control workers,[28] with workers reportedly saying that 'all that is missing is a whip'.[29]

---

[22] See Written Evidence submitted by Focus on Labour Exploitation to the EFRA Committee Inquiry into Labour Shortages in the Food and Farming Industry, January 2022, para 12, available at www.labourexploitation.org/publications/flex-written-submission-efra-committee-inquiry-labour-shortages-food-and-farming.
[23] See 'Workers and Temporary Workers: guidance for sponsors', SE 3.8, April 2023 (emphasis added).
[24] Home Office and DEFRA, *Seasonal Workers Pilot Review 2019* (December 2021), www.gov.uk/government/publications/seasonal-workers-pilot-review/seasonal-workers-pilot-review-2019.
[25] I Thiemann et al, 'UK Agriculture and Care Visas: Worker Exploitation and Obstacles to Redress', Modern Slavery and Human Rights Policy & Evidence Centre, 11 March 2024; Focus on Labour Exploitation and Fife Migrants Forum, 'Assessment of the Risks of Human Trafficking for Forced Labour on the UK Seasonal Workers Pilot', 2021 (hereafter FLEX Report). See also Work Rights Centre, 'Weed Out Exploitation', 2 March 2022; and Davies, above n 2, 496 ff.
[26] FLEX Report, 58; Thiemann et al, above n 25, 25–26.
[27] E Mellino, R Pangeni and P Pattisson, 'Migrant Fruit Pickers Charged Thousands in Illegal Fees to Work in UK Farms', The Bureau of Investigative Journalism, 27 May 2022.
[28] Work Rights Centre (n 25) 4.
[29] E Mellino and M Chapman, '"All that Is Missing is a Whip": Home Office Ignored Migrant Worker Abuses on Farms', The Bureau of Investigative Journalism, 22 October 2023.

3. Domestic Labour and the UK Overseas Domestic Worker Visa

Another example of a very restrictive visa scheme is the UK Overseas Domestic Worker (ODW) visa, mentioned in the introduction to this chapter. Domestic workers are workers undertaking various household tasks, such as cleaning, cooking, and caring for children or the elderly. They are sometimes employed part-time, working for a few hours a day for different employers, and sometimes full-time, working for one employer. Some domestic workers live in the employers' household. These live-in domestic workers are mostly migrants who migrate to work as domestic workers and send income back to their families.[30] This group of workers face challenges that other migrant workers may also face, such as language barriers, lack of friends and family in the destination country, and a lack of knowledge of existing networks of support and of their legal rights. Building new networks is almost impossible because they work in private households. An important particularity of the sector is that domestic workers have extremely few opportunities to develop social relations at work: they are isolated, they do not have a circle of co-workers with whom they would regularly interact; they interact mostly with their employer. This also creates challenges for attempts to unionise. It is hard for trade unions to reach out to workers who are employed in private households. The great majority of domestic workers are women.[31]

Domestic workers are excluded from protective rules or treated differently to other workers in fields such as working time regulation,[32] regulation of night work,[33] and occupational health and safety protection.[34] The ILO has adopted a special Convention on Domestic Workers, recognising the particularities of the sector and the challenges faced by this group of workers.[35] However, immigration rules further exacerbate this situation.[36] Temporary migration schemes for this kind of work that does not depend on seasonal factors create the sense that workers work for a family rather than being part of the labour market.[37]

The UK has a particularly restrictive scheme for domestic workers. The ODW visa effectively ties domestic workers to the employer with whom they arrived in the country.[38] The recent history of the scheme shows how it was developed and maintained despite evidence of abuse and exploitation, and persistent calls for reform. In 1998, immigration rules allowed domestic

---

[30] Some data is available in the 2010 ILO Report, 'Promoting Decent Work for Domestic Workers', para 20. For analysis, see B Anderson, *Doing the Dirty Work? The Global Politics of Domestic Labour* (London, Zed Books, 2000).

[31] ILO Report (n 30) para. 21. For analysis, see B Ehrenreich and AR Hochschild (eds), *Global Woman* (New York, Granta Books, 2003); H Lutz, *The New Maids: Transnational Women and the Care Economy* (London, Zed Books, 2011) 18.

[32] ILO Report (n 30) 48–50.

[33] ibid.

[34] ibid 61 ff. On examples of legal exclusions of domestic workers from protective laws, see more generally V Mantouvalou, 'Human Rights for Precarious Workers: The Legislative Precariousness of Domestic Labor' (2012) 34 *Comparative Labor Law and Policy Journal* 133; See also N Sedacca, 'Domestic Workers, the "Family Worker" Exemption from Minimum Wage, and Gendered Devaluation of Women's Work' (2022) 51 *Industrial Law Journal* 771. On the role of the law in the regulation of domestic work, see A Blackett, *Everyday Transgressions – Domestic Workers' Challenge to International Labor Law* (Ithaca NY, Cornell University Press, 2019).

[35] ILO Domestic Workers Convention 189 (2011). On this, see E Albin and V Mantouvalou, 'The ILO Convention on Domestic Workers: From the Shadows to the Light' (2012) 41 *Industrial Law Journal* 67; A Blackett, 'The Decent Work for Domestic Workers Convention and Recommendation 2011' (2012) 106 *American Journal of International Law* 778.

[36] On domestic work and migration, see M Galliotti, 'Making Domestic Work a Reality for Migrant Domestic Workers', ILO Domestic Work Policy Brief No 9, 2015.

[37] ILO Report (n 30) 10.

[38] Between 2012 and 2016 they never had a right to change employer, while after 2016 they have a right to change employer only in very limited circumstances.

workers to change employers but not work sector. This was the outcome of a successful campaign by domestic workers, trade unions, and other civil society organisations that supported them.[39] A domestic worker who had been employed by an employer for at least one year abroad could accompany a foreign national who entered the country for a period of six or 12 months, which was renewable. After five years, the worker could apply for settlement. Even though the domestic worker had entered the country with a specific employer, the worker was not tied to that employer. The Draft International Labour Organization Multilateral Framework on Labour Migration of 2005[40] and the UN Special Rapporteur on the Human Rights of Migrants cited the 1998 ODW visa as best practice.[41] In the UK, it was viewed as a safeguard against trafficking in human beings.[42]

However, in 2012 the UK Government introduced a visa regime that did not permit domestic workers to change employer. This occurred against the backdrop of an outcry by domestic workers' organisations that emphasised that the rules would trap these workers in serious exploitation and abuse. The point was that the workers would either be fearful to leave exploitative employment relations because they would not want to become undocumented or that, if they left, their undocumented status would trap them in badly paid and exploitative work. Under the 2012 scheme, domestic workers' residency status was lawful only for as long as the employer with whom they entered employed them, to a maximum of six months.

The story of Ella in our introduction exemplifies the problem, but there are many other stories: over the years there is increasing evidence that this visa is problematic and that migrant domestic workers suffer serious exploitation and abuse.[43] With some limited changes introduced in 2016, domestic workers have an unconditional right to change employer but this is restricted to the six months of the duration of the visa.[44] In practice, this change is generally viewed as ineffective because new employers are very unlikely to hire a domestic worker for a period of less than six months (which may be remaining on their visa).[45] In addition, domestic workers who are recognised as victims of human trafficking can change employer and stay in the UK for up to two years,[46] but this change is not satisfactory either, given the fear of deportation that makes

---

[39] For further details, see Anderson, *Doing the Dirty Work?*, above n 30, ch 6. See also E Albin and V Mantouvalou, 'Active Industrial Citizenship of Domestic Workers: Lessons Learned from Unionizing Attempts in Israel and the United Kingdom' (2015) 17 *Theoretical Inquiries in Law* 321.

[40] See Draft ILO Multilateral Framework on Labour Migration, available at www.ilo.org/public/english/standards/relm/gb/docs/gb295/pdf/tmmflm-1.pdf, para 82.

[41] See the Report of the Special Rapporteur on the Human Rights of Migrants, Addendum: Mission to the United Kingdom of Great Britain and Northern Ireland, available at www.refworld.org/cgi-bin/texis/vtx/rwmain?docid=4c0623e92, paras 60–61.

[42] Home Affairs Committee, 'The Trade in Human Beings: Human Trafficking in the UK', Sixth Report of Session 2008-2009, Vol I, 9 June 2011.

[43] See the briefings of the NGO Kalayaan at www.kalayaan.org.uk/. Further reports and discussions of this include M Simons, '"They Treated Me Like an Animal": How Filipino Domestic Workers Become Trapped', *The Guardian*, 26 October 2023; R Wright, 'Slavery Behind Closed Doors', *Financial Times*, Weekend Magazine, 22/23 February 2020; Human Rights Watch, 'Hidden Away', March 2014; J Ewins, 'Independent Review of the Overseas Domestic Worker Visa', 16 December 2015; Mantouvalou, above n 1.

[44] The right to change employers is not in the Immigration Rules but is explained on the government's website 'Overseas Domestic Worker visa', Home Office, 'Immigration Rules. Appendix Overseas Domestic Worker – Updated 5 October 2023', available at www.gov.uk/guidance/immigration-rules/immigration-rules-appendix-overseas-domestic-worker.

[45] See the statement by Baroness Hamwee, in the discussion of the Nationality and Borders Bill, HL Deb 10 February 2022, vol 818, col 1911. See also the joint statement of Kalayaan, Immigration Law Practitioners' Association, Liberty, the Voice of Domestic Workers, Joint Council for the Welfare of Immigrants and Kanlungan, 1 March 2022, available at https://ilpa.org.uk/wp-content/uploads/2022/02/ILPA-JCWI-Kalayaan-and-Others-Briefing-Overseas-Domestic-Workers-Amendment-Report.pdf.

[46] Home Office, 'Immigration Rules. Appendix Domestic Worker who is a Victim of Modern Slavery – Updated 31 January 2024', available at www.gov.uk/guidance/immigration-rules/immigration-rules-appendix-domestic-worker-who-is-a-victim-of-modern-slavery.

workers reluctant to contact the authorities, the challenges in being recognised as a victim of trafficking, and the fact that some will not have a right to work during lengthy periods.[47]

What emerges thus far is that migrant workers in precarious sectors, such as agriculture and domestic work, are employed under visas that make them particularly prone to exploitation. If they escape exploitative employers, they often become undocumented, even more vulnerable, and trapped in cycles of exploitation, with legal rules again having a significant role to play as we see below.

4. Undocumented Workers

Workers become undocumented because they have escaped exploitative employers under a scheme such as the above, because they entered a country without a work visa, or because they otherwise broke their visa conditions. Undocumented workers are usually employed in precarious sectors and sectors with low union density, such as domestic labour, sex work, agriculture, construction and manufacturing.[48] Employers may prefer to employ undocumented workers rather than documented migrants or local workers exactly because they fear deportation. However, their legal status creates vulnerability and workers who are exploitable and regularly exploited.[49]

The doctrine of illegality in English private law exemplifies and exacerbates the vulnerability of undocumented workers. According to this doctrine, illegal acts cannot form the basis for enforcing any rights that arise out of that illegal context. When applied in the employment context, this means that someone who has no right to work, but is nonetheless employed, may not be able to claim rights linked to their contract of employment because the employment is illegal. This doctrine may be suitable for some private law relationships. Is it suitable in the context of employment, and particularly when we are looking at labour rights of migrant workers, such as their right to unpaid wages or their right not to be harassed or discriminated against because of their race or sex?

The UK Supreme Court (UKSC) examined the question in the case of *Hounga v Allen*.[50] Ms Hounga was a Nigerian national who came to the UK to work as a domestic worker for the Allen family. She would look after the children and would be treated as a member of the family, being provided with accommodation and boarding. Before arriving in the UK, she had been promised that she would attend school, would be paid £50 a month, and would also have her travel to the UK paid. In order to come to the country, she made false statements to obtain a passport and a six-month visa, which she overstayed. In the UK she looked after the three children of the family and cleaned the house. During the 18 months that she was employed, she suffered serious physical abuse. She claimed that the employer slapped her, regularly hit her, pulled her ears and hair. The employer would put her arm around her neck, so that she could not breathe, would throw her on the floor and kick her stomach and head. She also claimed that the employer

---

[47] On the right to work of domestic workers in the process of being recognised as victims of trafficking, see the 2019 Kalayaan Report by N Sedacca and A Sharp, 'Dignity, Not Destitution – The Impact of Differential Rights of Work for Migrant Domestic Workers Referred to the National Referral Mechanism'. For a criticism of the 2016 changes, see Kalayaan, 'Overseas Domestic Workers Left in the Dark by the Immigration Act 2016', 28 June 2016.
[48] B Anderson, *Us and Them? The Dangerous Politics of Immigration Control* (Oxford, OUP, 2013) 79 ff.
[49] On illegality and vulnerability, see NP De Genova, 'Migrant "Illegality" and Deportability in Everyday Life' (2002) 31 *Annual Review of Anthropology* 419.
[50] *Hounga v Allen and Another* [2014] UKSC 47, [43]–[44].

would bang her head on the wall and call her an 'animal'. Once she was threatened with a knife, and was told that she would be killed. At some point, Ms Hounga was physically pushed out of the house. Eventually someone found her in a distressed state and took her to the social services.

Was Ms Hounga entitled to compensation for unfair dismissal, breach of contract, unpaid wages and holiday pay? UK tribunals and courts found that as these claims were contractual, Ms Hounga was not entitled to them. However, when it came to her discriminatory dismissal, her claim was not to be barred by the illegal contract because it was a tort law claim. The UKSC explained that the doctrine of illegality is founded on a public policy consideration, which is to preserve the integrity of the legal system that was not even clearly relevant in this instance. Yet there are other public policy considerations, as the UKSC highlighted, and more specifically the public policy to combat human trafficking that was clearly applicable in this case. As there was strong evidence that the Allen family were guilty of human trafficking, they could not rely on the defence of illegality.

A different angle on the question of the rights of undocumented workers emerged in the case of *Okedina v Chikale*,[51] where the Court of Appeal examined whether contractual claims of a migrant domestic worker employed under an illegal contract could be barred by the doctrine of illegality. Crucially, in this case, the worker was unaware that she did not have the right to work. The employer, who had exploited her and withheld her passport, had falsely reassured her that her visa was being renewed. When she was dismissed and evicted from the employer's home, she brought several contractual claims, including holiday pay and minimum wage. The Court of Appeal found that the fact that Ms Okedina had been misled was crucial, and her contractual claims succeeded despite the illegality of the contract. The criminality was her employer's, not her own. These cases illustrate not only the serious ill-treatment of migrant workers under restrictive visa schemes, but also the unsuitability of some general private law doctrines for the employment relationship.

It is also important to underline here that, in some legal orders, being undocumented has further legal implications for workers. For instance, in some countries, undocumented workers do not have a right to join a trade union.[52] Illegality bars the judicial protection of labour rights, as the EU Fundamental Rights Agency highlighted in a survey of EU Member States,[53] and has as an effect the unjust enrichment of the employer.[54] Perhaps the worst instantiation of the role of the law for undocumented workers is when working without a work visa or other right to work documentation becomes a criminal offence. The UK Immigration Act 2016 not only criminalises 'illegal working' but also allows for workers' salaries to be seized by the authorities under the Proceeds of Crime Act 2002, a policy adopted in the context of the creation of a 'hostile environment' for undocumented migrants.[55] In this way, undocumented workers' labour is a criminal offence, for which not only are they not compensated but for which they are punished further through the confiscation of their wages. Undocumented migrant workers affected by hostile immigration

---

[51] *Okedina v Chikale* [2019] EWCA Civ 1393. For analysis, see A Bogg, '*Okedina v Chikale* and Contract Illegality: New Dawn or False Dawn?' (2020) 49 *Industrial Law Journal* 258.

[52] See Fundamental Rights Agency Report, 'Fundamental Rights of Migrants in an Irregular Situation in the European Union', 2011, p 55, which refers to Cyprus, Latvia and Lithuania.

[53] ibid. See also N Countouris, 'The Legal Determinants of Precariousness in Personal Work Relations' (2012) 34 *Comparative Labor Law and Policy Journal* 21 at 27–28.

[54] On this, see E Dewhurst, 'The Right of Irregular Immigrants to Back Pay' in Costello and Freedland (eds), *Migrants at Work* (n 2).

[55] For analysis of the effects of 'hostile environment' policies on workers' rights, see N Sedacca, 'Migrant Work, Gender and the Hostile Environment: A Human Rights Analysis' (2024) 53 *Industrial Law Journal* 63. For an overview of 'hostile environment' policies, see M Griffiths and C Yeo, 'The UK's Hostile Environment: Deputising Immigration Control' (2021) 41 *Critical Social Policy* 521.

policies may face many human rights violations, including violations of the right to work, the right to private life and the prohibition of slavery, servitude, forced and compulsory labour, as Sedacca explained.[56] In the section that follows we turn to slavery, servitude, forced and compulsory labour to assess how the prohibition applies to migrant workers.

5. Slavery, Servitude, Forced and Compulsory Labour

Some characterise the treatment of migrant workers in the above situations as 'modern slavery', which is a term used to describe the worst instances of labour exploitation.[57] Does it violate the prohibition of slavery, servitude, forced and compulsory labour that we find in human rights law? Forced and compulsory labour is prohibited under the ILO Declaration of Fundamental Principles and Rights at Work (1998), the ILO Forced Labour Convention 29 (1930), the ILO Abolition of Forced Labour Convention 105 (1957) and the ILO Forced Labour Protocol (2014). It is also prohibited under several international and regional human rights documents. The ECtHR has developed extensive case law on Article 4 of the ECHR, which contains a prohibition of slavery, servitude, forced and compulsory labour. In this context the ECtHR has examined the treatment of migrant workers, looking at both undocumented workers and workers under very restrictive visa schemes.[58] In the relevant case law, the Court also generally takes note of human trafficking documents of the United Nations,[59] the EU[60] and the Council of Europe,[61] which it uses in the interpretation of Article 4 of the ECHR.

The case of *Siliadin v France*[62] was the first time in the history of the ECHR that the ECtHR found a violation of Article 4. The applicant was a Togolese national who was brought to France to work and be educated, but was instead kept at home as a domestic worker. She had to clean the house and the employer's office and to look after three children; she slept on the floor in their room; she rarely had a day off; she was almost never paid. At some point Ms Siliadin escaped and brought a case to the French courts. In her application to Strasbourg, the complaint was that French law did not criminalise her treatment. The Court examined the scope of Article 4 in detail, explaining that Ms Siliadin's situation was not 'slavery', because the employer did not exercise a right of legal ownership over the worker. Slavery and legal ownership go hand in hand, according to this judgment. Yet it classified it as 'servitude', which is still in the scope of Article 4. On servitude, it said that 'what is prohibited is a "particularly serious form of denial of freedom" … It includes, "in addition to the obligation to perform certain services for others … the obligation for the 'serf' to live on another person's property and the impossibility of altering his condition".'[63] Being a minor at the time, Ms Siliadin had to work almost 15 hours a day, seven days per week. She had not chosen to work for her employers, she had no resources, was isolated, had no money

---

[56] Sedacca, ibid.
[57] We discuss the term further below, in the context of the UK Modern Slavery Act 2015.
[58] See M Jovanovic, *State Responsibility for 'Modern Slavery' in Human Rights Law: A Right Not to Be Trafficked?* (Oxford, OUP, 2023). See also V Stoyanova, *Human Trafficking and Slavery Reconsidered* (Cambridge, CUP, 2017).
[59] Protocol to Prevent, Suppress and Punish Trafficking in Persons, especially Women and Children ('the Palermo Protocol'), supplementing the United Nations Convention against Transnational Organised Crime.
[60] Article 5(3) of the EU Charter of Fundamental Rights and Directive 2011/36/EU of the European Parliament and of the Council of 5 April 2011 on preventing and combating trafficking in human beings and protecting its victims.
[61] Council of Europe Convention on Action against Trafficking in Human Beings.
[62] *Siliadin v France* [2005] ECHR 545.
[63] ibid [123].

to move elsewhere, and 'was entirely at [the employer's] mercy, since her papers had been confiscated and she had been promised that her immigration status would be regularised, which never occurred'.[64] This treatment was classified as servitude. Importantly, *Siliadin* also established that Article 4 is relevant to private relations, and imposes a duty on the authorities to criminalise non-state conduct that falls short of Article 4 standards.[65] Given that most instances of forced labour occur in the private economy,[66] the decision of the Court to extend human rights principles in the private sphere is crucial.

Domestic labour has been examined in more recent case law too. In *CN v UK*,[67] for instance, the Court explained specifically that 'domestic servitude … involves a complex set of dynamics, involving both overt and more subtle forms of coercion, to force compliance', which requires 'an understanding of the many subtle ways an individual can fall under the control of another'.[68]

The appalling treatment of undocumented workers in agriculture was examined in *Chowdury v Greece*.[69] These workers had been promised 22 euros for seven hours of work and three euros for each hour of overtime, but ended up working for 12 hours a day, with armed guards supervising them, and were told that they would only be paid if they continued working for their employer. When they claimed unpaid wages, they were shot by armed guards. The situation of systematic exploitation in the region of Manolada, Greece, was widely known. It had been covered in the national press and by the Ombudsman who had reported extensively on the issue. In this case the Court clarified that immigration law itself should be scrutinised and that 'it must respond to concerns regarding the incitement or aiding and abetting of human trafficking or tolerance towards it'.[70]

Examining the question of whether these workers had freely agreed to work, or whether they had been coerced, the Court said that when an employer takes advantage of workers' vulnerability, they do not offer their labour voluntarily even if they initially consented, explaining that this question involves the assessment of a range of facts.[71] In examining whether labour is 'forced', the Court did not only assess physical coercion and violence. It said that any penalty imposed 'can also take subtler forms, of a psychological nature, such as threats to denounce victims to the police or immigration authorities when their employment status is illegal'.[72] In *Chowdury*, the ECtHR questioned whether the workers had consented to their working conditions, and placed special attention on the fact that when they agreed to do the work, they were in a situation of vulnerability as irregular migrants without resources and at risk of being arrested, detained and deported. They were aware that if they stopped working, they would never receive their unpaid wages that were overdue, the amount of which was constantly increasing.[73] On this basis, the Court classified their treatment as forced labour and found that

---

[64] ibid [126].
[65] See H Cullen, '*Siliadin v France*: Positive Obligations under Article 4 of the European Convention on Human Rights' (2006) 6 *Human Rights Law Review* 585; V Mantouvalou, 'Servitude and Forced Labour in the 21st Century: The Human Rights of Domestic Workers' (2006) 35 *ILJ* 395.
[66] See ILO, 'The Cost of Coercion', International Labour Conference, 98th Session 2009, Report I(B).
[67] *CN v UK*, App No 4239/08, Judgment of 13 November 2012.
[68] ibid [80].
[69] *Chowdury v Greece* [2017] ECHR 300.
[70] ibid [87].
[71] ibid [96]. For further analysis of consent in this context, see M Niezna, 'Consent to Labour Exploitation' (2024) 53 *Industrial Law Journal* 3, available at https://doi.org/10.1093/indlaw/dwad036.
[72] See also *Zoletic v Azerbaijan* [2021] ECHR 789, [151].
[73] *Chowdury*, above n 69, [95].

the Greek authorities violated Article 4 because they did not implement sufficient operational measures to prevent human trafficking and protect the workers, and did not investigate effectively the complaints or punish those responsible.

The above cases involve undocumented workers, and they develop a number of positive obligations for the authorities to criminalise the workers' treatment and enforce the law. In addition to those, the Court has also recognised that a very restrictive visa scheme can also violate Article 4 of the Convention. *Rantsev v Cyprus and Russia*[74] was the first ever Strasbourg case on trafficking for sexual exploitation. This involved a woman from Russia who arrived in Cyprus under an 'artiste visa'. An 'artiste' was defined in the legislation as 'any alien who wishes to enter Cyprus in order to work in a cabaret, musical-dancing place or other night entertainment place and has attained the age of 18 years'.[75] There was significant evidence that this visa scheme was connected to sex trafficking.[76] Under the scheme, Ms Rantseva received a temporary work and residence permit. Having worked at a cabaret for three days, she escaped, only to be captured soon after and be taken to the police. Since her immigration status was not irregular, the police returned her to her employer. Later that night she was found dead on the street below the flat where she was staying. The case was taken to the ECtHR by the victim's father.

The Court examined whether human trafficking for sexual exploitation is covered by Article 4 and explained that:

> trafficking in human beings, by its very nature and aim of exploitation, is based on the exercise of powers attaching to the right of ownership. It treats human beings as commodities to be bought and sold and put to forced labour, often for little or no payment, usually in the sex industry but also elsewhere .... It implies close surveillance of the activities of victims, whose movements are often circumscribed .... It involves the use of violence and threats against victims, who live and work under poor conditions ....[77]

Without distinguishing between the four concepts of Article 4, the Court was prepared to rule that trafficking falls within its ambit because it is incompatible with human dignity and other underlying values of the Convention. In relation to the immigration rules, of particular concern was the fact that cabaret managers made an application for an entry permit for the artiste in a way that rendered the worker dependent on the employer or agent and in this way vulnerable to human trafficking.[78] The conditions of the scheme gave cabaret owners and managers a significant power to control cabaret dancers by encouraging them to track down artistes who were missing or otherwise take personal responsibility for them. In light of this, the Court ruled that Cyprus violated the Convention.[79]

These cases underline the point that serious labour exploitation falls within the scope of Article 4 of the ECHR, as well as being incompatible with ILO, EU and other Council of Europe documents, that migrant workers are prone to such treatment and that state authorities have to take positive steps to address this situation. However, the main legal obligations that the ECtHR has examined and developed over the years are obligations to criminalise employers' conduct, investigate and enforce criminal laws. A criminal law response has traditionally been associated

---

[74] *Rantsev v Cyprus and Russia* [2010] ECHR 22.
[75] ibid [113].
[76] ibid [80] ff.
[77] ibid [281].
[78] ibid [89], [91], [94], [100].
[79] The Court also ruled that Russia violated the ECHR with respect to its procedural obligations under Article 4. Other case law that has followed has paid further attention to obligations of member states to investigate effectively cases of human trafficking. See the Grand Chamber case *SM v Croatia* (2021) 72 EHRR 1, App No 60561/14, Judgment of 25 June 2020.

with the law on human trafficking.[80] Is criminalisation sufficient when tackling labour exploitation, including exploitation of the most serious form? We will address this question by focusing on the UK Modern Slavery Act 2015.

6. UK Modern Slavery Act 2015

The UK Modern Slavery Act 2015 (MSA 2015) was presented as path-breaking in criminalising 'modern slavery'.[81] The MSA 2015 codified and consolidated existing legislation[82] and increased penalties for the most serious offenders. Soon after the MSA 2015 was enacted, Theresa May, as Prime Minister, wrote:

> These crimes must be stopped and the victims of modern slavery must go free. This is the great human rights issue of our time, and as Prime Minister I am determined that we will make it a national and international mission to rid our world of this barbaric evil.[83]

The stated purpose of the MSA 2015 consisted of facilitating the work of prosecutors and the police with regard to modern slavery,[84] and increasing the rates of prosecutions, which were viewed as low.[85] According to the Act it is a criminal offence to keep someone in slavery or servitude or to require them to perform forced or compulsory labour,[86] or to engage in the trafficking of a person with intent to exploit.[87] In both cases, any purported 'consent' on the part of the victim must be disregarded.[88] Courts are expressly directed to interpret the s 1 offence in line with Article 4 ECHR so, at a definitional level, domestic legislation should keep pace with the ECHR.[89]

Even though the focus on severe labour exploitation and its criminalisation may have been welcomed, the Act can also be criticised.[90] If there is a serious commitment to tackle severe labour exploitation, is it sufficient to criminalise employers or traffickers? Shouldn't the authorities be considering and addressing the underlying reasons why workers become vulnerable to such exploitation, such as the visa schemes discussed above? The fact that the Overseas Domestic Worker visa remained in place during the passing of the MSA 2015, despite concerted efforts by civil society to liberalise its terms, brings these questions into sharp focus.

---

[80] For criticism, see H Shamir, 'A Labor Paradigm for Human Trafficking' (2012) 60 *UCLA Law Review* 76; I Thiemann, 'Beyond Victimhood *and* Beyond Employment? Exploring Avenues for Labour Law to Empower Women Trafficked into the Sex Industry' (2019) 48 *ILJ* 199; C Costello, 'Migrants and Forced Labour: A Labour Law Response' in A Bogg, C Costello, A Davies and J Prassl (eds), *The Autonomy of Labour Law* (Oxford, Hart Publishing, 2015).

[81] See Home Office, 'Historic Law to End Modern Slavery Passed' (26 March 2015) at www.gov.uk/government/news/historic-law-to-end-modern-slavery-passed.

[82] Sexual Offences Act 2003, ss 57–59; Asylum and Immigration (Treatment of Claimants) Act 2004, s 4, as amended by ss 109 and 110 of the Protection of Freedoms Act 2012, and s 71 of the Coroners and Justice Act 2009.

[83] T May, 'My Government will lead the way in Defeating Modern Slavery', *The Telegraph*, 31 July 2016, available at www.telegraph.co.uk/news/2016/07/30/we-will-lead-the-way-in-defeating-modern-slavery/.

[84] Hansard, HC 8 July 2014, vol 584, col 171.

[85] For instance, in 2013 there were only 68 convictions: Hansard, HC 8 July 2014, Vol 584, col 175.

[86] MSA 2015, s 1.

[87] MSA 2015, s 2.

[88] MSA 2015, ss 1(5) and 2(2).

[89] MSA 2015, s 1(2).

[90] For more detail on many of the points made in this section, see V Mantouvalou, 'The UK Modern Slavery Act 2015 Three Years On' (2018) 81 *Modern Law Review* 1017. For further analysis of the concept of 'modern slavery', see A Paz-Fuchs, 'Badges of Modern Slavery' (2016) 79 *Modern Law Review* 757.

Moreover, the enactment of criminal offences does not exhaust the state's duties under Article 4.[91] As we know from the case law discussed earlier, the state is also obliged to have effective arrangements in place to investigate possible instances of modern slavery and to prosecute offenders, to support victims of modern slavery, and to ensure that victims receive compensation.[92] There are weaknesses in all three areas. For example, although the overall level of police investigations and prosecutions has risen since the pandemic, this is from a low starting-point and is unlikely to reflect the true scale of the problem.[93] In addition, support for victims is provided through the National Referral Mechanism, the main administrative mechanism dealing with modern slavery allegations and identifying victims.[94] Where there are reasonable grounds to believe that a person is a victim, they are given a minimum 45-day recovery period during which they receive government support. This allows time for the competent authority to make a final decision on their status. Once the final decision is made, individuals who are found to be victims receive a further period of 'move on' support tailored to their circumstances. One issue here is that the support on offer is still relatively short-term and may be insufficient to provide meaningful help to victims who have experienced serious trauma.[95] Moreover, delays in decision-making on matters such as housing or benefits may leave victims destitute, in potential breach of Article 3 ECHR that prohibits inhuman and degrading treatment.[96]

Victims who are migrants and do not have a right to be in the UK may be given discretionary leave to remain, for example, where this is necessary to assist their recovery or where police enquiries into their situation are ongoing.[97] However, in practice, this only happens in a tiny proportion of cases.[98] Many victims are deterred from approaching the authorities to report offences because they are afraid that they will be deported. This can lead to a cycle in which the deported person is re-trafficked to the UK and subjected to further exploitation. Furthermore, the MSA 2015 does not create a right for victims to obtain a civil remedy. Section 8 provides for a reparation order, but this only applies where the perpetrator has been convicted and has been made the subject of a confiscation order. Although the Government has argued that victims would be able to bring other kinds of claims, ordinary tort or employment law may not provide full redress for all the wrongs they are likely to have suffered. This may be a particular difficulty where the worker has committed a criminal offence connected with their migration status, and the doctrine of illegality operates as a bar to their legal claim against the employer.

There are further criticisms of the MSA 2015, which cannot be developed fully here.[99] There is no question that severe labour exploitation is a grave moral wrong. However, the MSA 2015 has not been successful in meeting the key aim of increasing prosecutions, and has not provided adequate protection and remedies to victims. In any case, criminal law alone cannot be sufficient in addressing labour exploitation, not least because it focuses on individual conduct rather than the underlying structural reasons that make migrant and other workers vulnerable to this conduct.

---

[91] Though it is one of the duties: *Siliadin*, above n 62.
[92] *Rantsev*, above n 74.
[93] Independent Anti-Slavery Commissioner (IASC), *Annual Report 2021–2022* (April 2022), 24–32.
[94] Modern Slavery Act 2015, Pt 5; Nationality and Borders Act 2022, Pt 5.
[95] British Red Cross, *Hope for the Future: Support for Survivors of Trafficking after the National Referral Mechanism* (July 2019). For further issues affecting migrant domestic workers in the National Referral Mechanism, see N Sedacca and A Sharp, 'Dignity Not Destitution: The Impact of Differential Rights to Work for Migrant Domestic Workers', UK Labour Law Blog, 12 April 2019.
[96] *R (Limbuela) v Secretary of State for the Home Department* [2005] UKHL 66, [2006] 1 AC 396.
[97] Nationality and Borders Act 2022, s 65.
[98] IASC, 19.
[99] See further Mantouvalou, above n 90.

7. Conclusion

Temporary labour migration schemes are typically described as a triple win, as we said earlier. However, the history and current evidence on the operation and effects of the programmes show that they actually create 'perfect immigrants'[100] to the particular benefit of employers and the state, rather than the workers themselves. Migrant workers under restrictive visa schemes and undocumented migrants are faced with some of the most severe forms of labour exploitation, and the authorities have obligations to address this under human rights law. Human and labour rights monitoring bodies have at times classified workers' treatment as slavery, servitude, forced and compulsory labour. It is important to appreciate, though, that criminalising employers' conduct for this treatment is not sufficient. Migrant workers should enjoy protection of labour rights equal to all other workers.[101] Immigration rules and other rules that increase their vulnerability to exploitation should change if state authorities are to comply with their human rights obligations.

---

[100] See C Hahamovitch, 'Creating Perfect Immigrants: Guestworkers of the World in Historical Perspective' (2003) 44 *Labor History* 69.
[101] See Inter-American Court of Human Rights, Advisory Opinion OC-18/03, 2003, Legal Status and Rights of Undocumented Migrants, available at www1.umn.edu/humanrts/iachr/series_A_OC-18.html.

10

The Right to Fair Pay

1. Three Interpretations of the Right to Fair Pay
2. Collective Bargaining
3. A Living Wage
4. Fairness within Organisations
5. Conclusion

1. Three Interpretations of the Right to Fair Pay

In the 19th century, trade unionists frequently invoked the rallying cry 'A Fair Day's Wages for a Fair Day's Work'. That slogan sounds reasonable and is widely accepted. Yet views differ about what should be regarded as fair pay (and a fair day's work). Influenced by the ideology of freedom of contract, the common law of contract endorsed the view that the terms of a contract were fair if both parties had freely consented to it and each had provided consideration – work in return for pay. Most people realised, however, that the market rate for pay could at times slip below what workers needed to survive, leaving them in abject poverty. That might happen when there were high levels of unemployment or when a powerful employer could impose wage cuts or avoid inflation-matching increases. Employers often have that strong bargaining power because many workers need to maintain their income in order to survive, whereas employers can hold out and live off their capital until the market price of labour is to their liking. Employers may also use their stronger bargaining power to renege on the deal in various ways such as delays in payment, unreasonable deductions from pay, and attempts to replace payment in a valid currency with various forms of credit such as credit at the employer's shop. All these devices to subvert the market rate of pay need to be prohibited by the law.[1]

At the opposite extreme to the common law of contract, Marxists such as Friedrich Engels argued that, far from being the embodiment of fairness, every contract of employment was an instance of exploitation, in which capital kept the fruits of the work of labour in the form of profits rather than allocating those rewards to the workers themselves.[2] In Engels' view, fairness would only be achieved if workers kept all of the profits for themselves, which could only realistically happen if they seized control of the means of production.[3]

---

[1] ILO Protection of Wages Convention, 1949 (No 95). In UK law the main protections against unauthorised deductions of wages are in the Employment Rights Act 1996, Pt II, ss 13–27.
[2] F Engels, 'A Fair Day's Wages for a Fair Day's Work', The Labour Standard No 1, May 7, 1881.
[3] 'Labour is, besides the earth, the only source of wealth; capital itself is nothing but the stored-up produce of labour. So that the wages of Labour are paid out of labour, and the working man is paid out of his own produce. According to what we may call common fairness, the wages of the labourer ought to consist in the produce of his labour.' ibid.

During the 20th century, whilst preserving the general framework of the capitalist labour market, though with some experiments in public ownership of the means of production, three rather different views of the meaning of the right to fair pay emerged in international declarations of labour rights and standards.

(1) *Collective bargaining.* A fair wage is produced by the market, provided that there is equality of bargaining power between capital and labour. Equality of bargaining power would be achieved by trade unions bargaining collectively on behalf of workers with their employers. Through collective bargaining, workers would receive a fair share of the profits of the business. The law would also need to prevent unfair competition in the labour market such as products made by unpaid forced labour.

(2) *A living wage.* A fair wage would be the market rate provided that it reached a minimum standard. That standard required a living wage through which a worker and their dependants could achieve a decent standard of living appropriate for the society in which they lived. There must be sufficient income not only to afford subsistence and shelter but also the ability to live a life of dignity. That living wage could be achieved by minimum wages and/or welfare benefits. A safety net of a minimum level of income would be applied to those unable to work either as a result of recession and wide scale unemployment or because the workers had become infirm or disabled.

(3) *Relative wages within organisations.* A third interpretation of fair wages required fair differentials between the wages of different groups of workers within productive organisations. For instance, this view rejected discrimination in rates of pay on grounds of sex or race. More generally, fair pay should reflect a person's contribution to the success of a productive organisation. Differences in rates of pay could only be justified if they were deserved.

To a considerable extent, these three interpretations of the right to fair pay are compatible. They were combined, for instance, in the Declaration of Philadelphia in 1944 at the formation of the International Labour Organization.[4] Article III(e) requires member states to respect the right to collective bargaining,[5] and Article III(d) requires 'policies in regard to wages and earnings, hours and other conditions of work calculated to ensure a just share of the fruits of progress to all, and a minimum living wage to all employed and in need of such protection'. Similarly, the Universal Declaration of Human Rights 1948 (UDHR), Article 23[6] and the European Social Charter 1961 (ESC)[7] both support the right of workers to join a trade union for the protection of their interests

---

[4] Declaration concerning the aims and purposes of the International Labour Organisation, The General Conference of the International Labour Organization, Twenty-sixth Session in Philadelphia, 10 May 1944.

[5] ibid, III(e) 'the effective recognition of the right of collective bargaining, the cooperation of management and labour in the continuous improvement of productive efficiency, and the collaboration of workers and employers in the preparation and application of social and economic measures'.

[6] Universal Declaration of Human Rights 1948, Article 23, '1. Everyone has the right to work, to free choice of employment, to just and favourable conditions of work and to protection against unemployment. 2. Everyone, without any discrimination, has the right to equal pay for equal work. 3. Everyone who works has the right to just and favourable remuneration ensuring for himself and his family an existence worthy of human dignity, and supplemented, if necessary, by other means of social protection. 4. Everyone has the right to form and to join trade unions for the protection of his interests.'

[7] European Social Charter 1961, Article 4 – The right to a fair remuneration, 'With a view to ensuring the effective exercise of the right to a fair remuneration, the Contracting Parties undertake: 1 to recognise the right of workers to a remuneration such as will give them and their families a decent standard of living; 2 to recognise the right of workers to an increased rate of remuneration for overtime work, subject to exceptions in particular cases; 3 to recognise the right of men and women workers to equal pay for work of equal value; 4 to recognise the right of all workers to a reasonable

and insist that workers should receive a wage that is sufficient for a life of dignity, which can be understood as a decent standard of living for themselves and their dependants. They also require non-discrimination in pay: equal pay for equal work.

The three interpretations of the right can usually be combined and applied cumulatively by a legal system, though sometimes there may be friction. Complexities might arise, for instance, if a collective agreement produces levels of wages for different groups in an organisation that some regard as unfair differentials that do not satisfy the principle of equal pay for equal work. Similarly, trade unions are sometimes concerned that the introduction of a mandatory minimum wage by law might discourage workers from joining trade unions for the purpose of collective bargaining. When exploring the legal implications of those three interpretations of the right to fair pay, we must also consider the proper scope of exclusions from the right.

2. Collective Bargaining

As discussed in chapters 5, 6, and 7 above, Article 11(1) of the European Convention on Human Rights protects the right of everyone to form and join trade unions for the protection of their interests. This right has been interpreted by the ECtHR to include not only the right to join a trade union, but also to have a trade union represent a person for the purpose of collective bargaining, and, subject to many restrictions, for a trade union to organise industrial action in support of collective bargaining.[8] We need not go into further details here. The question is rather whether the right to fair pay is essentially the same as the right to collective bargaining.

To interpret the right to fair pay as being comprised primarily of a right for collective bargaining to set pay has the attraction to many that it does not question the market system for determining pay. Collective bargaining does not replace the market, but is supposed to correct the market by equalising the bargaining power of the parties when setting rates of pay. It does not question whether market rates of pay, whether set through individual or collective bargaining, are unfair and should be replaced by government interventions. The state avoids having to impose wage rates or replace the labour market for wages. Instead, the right to fair pay is supported by the policy that Otto Kahn-Freund called 'collective laissez-faire'.[9]

Some legal controls of the functioning of the labour market are nevertheless required. The labour market must be protected from unfair competition. For example, the government must prevent the undercutting of market rates for pay by the use of cheap labour such as prisoners, trafficked workers, and undocumented workers. This protectionism may also include the exclusion of competition from cheaper foreign imports in order to protect the domestic labour market from undercutting.[10] At the same time, the law plays an important auxiliary role in the facilitation of the functioning of collective bargaining. The law needs to protect against anti-union discrimination and to supply a mechanism by which representative unions can compel

---

period of notice for termination of employment; 5 to permit deductions from wages only under conditions and to the extent prescribed by national laws or regulations or fixed by collective agreements or arbitration awards. The exercise of these rights shall be achieved by freely concluded collective agreements, by statutory wage fixing machinery, or by other means appropriate to national conditions.' Article 5 concerns the right to organise a trade union, and Article 6 requires the state to support collective bargaining between trade unions and employers.

[8] *Demir and Baykara v Turkey* [2008] ECHR 1345.
[9] O Kahn-Freund, 'Labour Law' in O Kahn-Freund, *Selected Writings* (London, Stevens, 1978) 1, 8.
[10] Foreign Prison-Made Goods Act 1897. The US law is broader because it includes forced labour as well as prison labour: 19 US Codes § 1307 (Section 307 Tariff Act 1930).

employers to come to the bargaining table and bargain in good faith about wages without the need for damaging industrial action.

For much of the 20th century, most workers in industrial economies benefitted from effective collective bargaining. Their wages were enhanced and wage differentials were compressed as a result of collective bargaining. Unions also bargained for benefits in addition to pay such as reduced hours of working, paid holidays, occupational pensions, health insurance, and other fringe benefits. In the middle of the 20th century, the combination of taxation and union wage effect was to make the United Kingdom a more equal society in terms of the distribution of wealth than it ever had been and is now.

As an interpretation of the right to fair pay, however, collective laissez-faire has several obvious flaws. In the first place, why should we think that collective labour has equal bargaining power to that of employers? It can be argued that unions are either too weak or too strong, depending on your point of view, so that the collective agreements that are concluded are unfair to one party or the other. Even if there is equality of bargaining power, a second reason for doubting that collective bargaining adequately defends the right to fair pay is to ask why should we regard the outcome of the collective agreement as necessarily fair? Those who are paid the lowest wages under the collective agreement may argue that the result is unfair, either because it does not provide them with a living wage or because it indirectly discriminates against protected groups such as women and minorities. Moreover, the reliance on collective bargaining for wage determination is likely to favour economic sectors where it is relatively straightforward to organise trade unions and maintain solidarity, as is often the case in factories, mines and transport. Where organisation is harder, as in the case of homeworkers, farm workers, platform workers, and where jobs are typically precarious, collective bargaining, even if it exists, is unlikely to secure significant benefits for members of the union.

Continuing reliance on the right to collective bargaining as the principal embodiment of the right to fair pay must also be questioned in the light of the decline of trade union power in the United Kingdom. The union wage premium is an estimation based on government household surveys of the average beneficial effect on wages for trade union members in comparison with workers whose pay is individually negotiated. Estimates of the size of the union wage premium vary, but it seems to have fallen from about 25 per cent in the 1990s to about 3–4 per cent in the 2020s.[11] During the same period, the percentage of the UK workforce who were union members declined from about 32 per cent to 22 per cent. Factors other than union density are also likely to have reduced the union wage effect, such as austerity measures in the public sector, and in the private sector increased global competition and concerns that higher wages will induce employers to relocate to a different country.[12] Assuming it is correct that the current union wage premium is only a few percentage points, it must be questioned whether collective bargaining continues to provide a mechanism for equalising bargaining power in order to secure a fair wage.

Such criticisms force the conclusion that the right to fair pay must also include the two other dimensions mentioned above: a minimum wage and protection against unfair differentials in pay.

---

[11] A Bryson, 'Union wage effects: what are the economic implications of union wage bargaining for workers, firms, and society?', IZA World of Labor session at the Society of Labor Economists (SOLE) Conference (Virginia, US, 2014); Statista, 'Trade union wage premium in the United Kingdom from 1995 to 2022' (May 2023) www.statista.com/statistics/287278/uk-trade-union-wage-premium/#statisticContainer..

[12] E Barth, A Bryson and H Dale-Olsen, 'Union Density Effects on Productivity and Wages' (2020) 130 *The Economic Journal*, Issue 631, 1898.

3. A Living Wage

A right to a living wage or an adequate wage appears in most declarations of human rights that include social and economic rights.[13] The requirement for workers to be paid a living wage is often regarded as a way of conferring dignity on workers.[14] A minimum wage is also supported on the grounds that it fosters self-respect and contributes to some extent to make society more equal.[15]

Dignity and Decency

Article 23(3) of the Universal Declaration of Human Rights of 1948 (UDHR) states:

> Everyone who works has the right to just and favourable remuneration ensuring for himself and his family an existence worthy of human dignity, and supplemented, if necessary, by other means of social protection.

The text is ambiguous whether the right concerns pay itself, as opposed to household income from both pay and other forms of social support such as Universal Credit and the National Health Service in the UK. Given that in Article 23(3) the right to just and favourable remuneration can be achieved, where necessary, by welfare measures, a human right to be paid fairly by one's employer appears to be qualified by the alternative of a resort to state support or 'social protection'. That interpretation of the right is arguably unsatisfactory, because welfare payments may not achieve 'an existence worthy of human dignity' in the same way as a fair wage. While a living wage achieves self-esteem for workers who can support their households through their own efforts, welfare dependency often incurs calculated humiliation and the anxiety caused by a rigid and incomprehensible bureaucratic social security machine.[16] For this reason, perhaps only a fair wage can achieve the objective of Article 23(3): 'an existence worthy of human dignity'.

This ambiguity has been resolved in subsequent conventions on human rights.[17] Article 4 of the European Social Charter 1961 (ESC) is concerned with pay, not household income:[18]

> All workers have the right to a fair remuneration sufficient for a decent standard of living for themselves and their families.

Similarly, Article 7 of the International Covenant on Economic, Social and Cultural Rights (ICESCR) supports a right to fair wages without qualification.[19]

---

[13] A notable exception is the International Covenant on Economic, Social and Cultural Rights, Adopted and opened for signature, ratification and accession by General Assembly resolution 2200A (XXI) of 16 December 1966 (ICESCR), though the requirement of fair pay in Article 7 presumably rules out extremely low wages.

[14] G Davidov, 'A Purposive Approach to the National Minimum Wage Act' (2009) 72 *Modern Law Review* 581.

[15] B Rogers, 'Justice at Work: Minimum Wage Laws and Social Equality' (2014) 92 *Texas Law Review* 1543.

[16] J Wolff, 'Fairness, Respect, and the Egalitarian Ethos' (1998) 27 *Philosophy and Public Affairs* 97.

[17] However, there is no right to fair remuneration in the European Union Charter of Fundamental Rights, due in part to hostility by Member States to such a broad principle, but also because the issue of fair wages is generally outside of the competence of the European Union: J Hunt, 'Fair and Just Working Conditions' in T Harvey and J Kenner (eds), *Economic and Social Rights under the EU Charter of Fundamental Rights: A Legal Perspective* (London, Bloomsbury, 2006) 45, 54.

[18] The European Social Charter 1961, and the Revised European Social Charter 1996 are expressed in identical terms.

[19] ICESCR (n 13).

But what does the right to fair pay require if it supports a life of dignity and decency? Article 25 of the UDHR provides helpful guidance:

> Everyone has the right to a standard of living adequate for the health and well-being of himself and of his family, including food, clothing, housing and medical care and necessary social services, and the right to security in the event of unemployment, sickness, disability, widowhood, old age or other lack of livelihood in circumstances beyond his control.

In other articles, the UDHR upholds a right to free education and a right to participate in the culture of a community.

Article 43 of the Indian Constitution obliges the state to ensure that all workers, industrial or otherwise, are provided with a living wage and assured of a decent standard of living. A decent standard of living has been interpreted to mean not only subsistence, such as food and shelter, but also necessary medical expenses, some education, and necessary transport costs.[20] The courts of India also insist that the living wage must be regularly uprated to match the increase in the cost of living.[21]

Calculating the Minimum Standard

How can one calculate the exact wages that may be required to satisfy the right to fair pay? In its Convention that encourages the development of a minimum wage, following its tradition of supporting bipartisan processes, the ILO focuses on the importance of wide consultation about setting the minimum wage including consultation with unions and employers. The Convention only lists the factors that should be taken into account when setting the minimum wage without indicating what outcome is preferred:

> The elements to be taken into consideration in determining the level of minimum wages shall, so far as possible and appropriate in relation to national practice and conditions, include–
>
> (a) the needs of workers and their families, taking into account the general level of wages in the country, the cost of living, social security benefits, and the relative living standards of other social groups;
> (b) economic factors, including the requirements of economic development, levels of productivity and the desirability of attaining and maintaining a high level of employment.[22]

The European Committee of Social Rights (ECSR), which interprets the ESC, maintains that to achieve a decent standard of living, the minimum net remuneration should not normally fall below 60% of the net average wage in the country. Using this formula, the task is to find the average weekly wage of all workers after tax and social security is deducted, calculate 60% of that average weekly wage, and compare that result to the statutory minimum wage or, where appropriate, the minimum wage set by a national or sectoral level collective agreement. If the national minimum wage is less, it is probably insufficient to meet the criterion of a 'decent

---

[20] *Chandra Bhavan Boarding And Lodging ... vs The State Of Mysore And Anr*, 29 September 1969, 1970 AIR 2042, 1970 SCR (2) 600, Supreme Court of India. The authors are grateful to Emily Strachan for research into case law related to the right to fair pay in international and national courts.
[21] *Abdul Ahad Ganai And Ors vs Ut Of J&K & Ors*, 26 December, 2022, High Ct of Jammu & Kashmir and Ladakh at Srinagar. https://indiankanoon.org/doc/72347136/.
[22] Minimum Wage Fixing Convention, 1970 (No 131), Article 3.

standard of living'. In order to resist that conclusion, states can produce evidence to demonstrate compliance with the standard by showing how the costs of healthcare, transport, tax credits, and education are covered by other welfare measures, so that the national minimum wage, when combined with those welfare benefits, achieves the goal of a decent standard of living.[23] France was able to defend its minimum wage that fell slightly below the 60% threshold on those grounds,[24] but the United Kingdom's defence of its national minimum wage has so far been unsuccessful.[25] Similarly the Greek Government could not avoid a finding of violation of Article 4.1 ESC by failing to provide statistics on net wages. The Committee used publicly available statistics on gross wages to estimate that the minimum wage largely set by collective agreements, which had been lowered as a result of the financial crisis in 2009, was plainly unfair.[26] The ECSR did not appear to regard the budgetary crisis of the Greek Government as relevant to the issue of compliance with the Charter.

A Directive of the European Union on adequate minimum wages provides a more precise suggestion about the formulation of a minimum wage standard.[27] Owing to the limited competence of the EU in the field of wages,[28] the Directive does not require a particular minimum wage level or a statutory mechanism for setting one, but it does require the Member States to have procedures in place, whether through collective bargaining or statutory wage-fixing bodies involving social partners, that should ensure that all workers receive an adequate wage that provides a decent standard of living. Although no precise formula for setting minimum wages is required by the Directive, para 28 of the Preamble indicates both the use of median and average national wages:

> The assessment might be based on reference values commonly used at international level such as the ratio of the gross minimum wage to 60 % of the gross median wage and the ratio of the gross minimum wage to 50 % of the gross average wage, which are currently not met by all Member States, or the ratio of the net minimum wage to 50 % or 60 % of the net average wage. The assessment might also be based on reference values associated to indicators used at national level, such as the comparison of the net minimum wage with the poverty threshold and the purchasing power of minimum wages.

In recent years, the UK Government has introduced first a National Minimum Wage and then what is called a 'National Living Wage' for those aged 23 or more.[29] The revised stated purpose of the National Living Wage is to attain two-thirds of the median hourly earnings of workers aged 21 or above by 2024.[30] If this goal is achieved, the statutory minimum wage law in the UK may comply with the standard set by the ECSR, especially if working tax credits are taken into account, though the comparison is difficult because the UK law is based on median wages, not average wages, it excludes youth workers and apprentices, and calculations are performed on gross wages rather than net. Median hourly earnings are preferred to average wages as the basis for the calculation because the average wage can provide a distorted picture if there are a few who

---

[23] Z Adams and S Deakin, 'Article 4: The Right to a Fair Remuneration' in N Braun, K Lorcher, I Schomann and S Clauwaert (eds), *The European Social Charter and the Employment Relation* (Oxford, Hart Publishing, 2017) 198, 205–11.
[24] ECSR Conclusions XVIII-I (2007) France.
[25] ECSR Conclusions XVI-2 (2003) United Kingdom; Conclusions XXII-3 – United Kingdom – Article 4.1 (2023).
[26] Assessment of follow-up: Greek General Confederation of Labour (GSEE) v Greece, Complaint No 111/2014, decision on the merits of 23 March 2017, Resolution CM/ResChS(2017)9; Complaint No 111/2014.
[27] Directive (EU) 2022/2041 of the European Parliament and of the Council of 19 October 2022 on adequate minimum wages in the European Union.
[28] Article 153(5) TFEU.
[29] National Minimum Wage Act 1998; National Minimum Wage Regulations 2015 (SI 2015/621).
[30] National Minimum Wage: Low Pay Commission Report 2022 (January 2023).

earn very high incomes. The UK National Living Wage of 66 per cent of the median wage may well conform to the EU suggested standard of 60% of the gross median wage, even though the UK calculations of the median wage exclude workers aged under 21.

Pensions

Does the right to fair pay apply when a worker is no longer able to work through infirmity and old age? Pensions in old age, disability benefits, and sick pay may be regarded purely as part of the state's social security system, which is funded from taxation. Yet it is possible to regard pensions as a kind of deferred pay to which a worker has contributed through savings from regular income. Most occupational pension schemes also include a contribution from the employer, which is a cost in addition to wages. Similarly, sick pay may be included in the contract of employment as a benefit or be part of medical insurance provided by the employer. Do such arrangements fall within the scope of the right to fair pay? International human rights law does not provide much guidance, though Article 45(b) of the Charter of the Organisation of American States includes both direct and deferred pay within its scope:

> Work is a right and a social duty, it gives dignity to the one who performs it, and it should be performed under conditions, including a system of fair wages, that ensure life, health, and a decent standard of living for the worker and his family, both during his working years and in his old age, or when any circumstance deprives him of the possibility of working …

Exclusions from the Living Wage

Most jurisdictions recognise five main exclusions from the right to a living wage. These are well-established, though they often provoke controversy:

(1) *Family members.* Where members of the family contribute to a family business, such as a shop or market stall, but they all live together as a family unit that informally shares the income to pay for food and shelter and other necessities, the exact wages of each family member will not be assessed by the legal requirements of any statutory minimum wage.[31] Controversially, this family member exception was extended in the UK to domestic workers who, though not members of the family, are treated as such in many respects because they live in and share meals (which they have usually cooked as well). This exemption was open to abuse, because employers could qualify for the exemption by not paying wages at all or providing merely pocket money. This exclusion of domestic workers treated like members of the family was abolished in 2024.

(2) *Independent contractors.* Individuals who are self-employed and not classified as workers are also excluded from minimum wage laws and sectoral collective agreements. Their income depends on how many clients they can attract and the fees they can charge for their services. Many of the poorest people in the world including in the UK are self-employed and have no claim for a living wage. To take advantage of this exclusion, some employers try to manipulate their contracts for work by presenting employees as self-employed. Countering

---

[31] National Minimum Wage Regulations 2015, reg 57(3). Natalie Sedacca, 'Domestic Workers, the "Family Worker" Exemption from Minimum Wage, and Gendered Devaluation of Women's Work' (2022) 51(4) *Industrial Law Journal* 771.

that practice, the courts often penetrate to the reality of these examples of the bogus self-employed by examining what happens in practice.[32] It is also possible for legislation to extend the minimum wage and similar employment rights to independent contractors if they are economically dependent on a single employer and are to some extent in a relation of subordination. In the UK, the statutory category of 'worker' applies to these kinds of self-employed workers who deserve the statutory right to a minimum wage.[33] As the *Uber v Aslam* case illustrated, platform workers typically fit into this category of independent contractors who are nevertheless entitled to certain statutory protections such as a minimum wage.[34]

(3) *Education and training.* Where the predominant purpose of a contractual arrangement is to provide professional experience and to improve the practical skills of young persons, it will also fall outside legal requirements for a living wage even if the person is expected to work as part of that arrangement. This exclusion applies to trainee schemes and apprenticeships. In the UK, apprentices are entitled to a lower rate of pay for the national minimum wage. Article 7.5 of the ESC permits the payment of lower wages to apprentices on the ground that the on-the-job training they receive is a valuable benefit. The European Social Committee has warned that apprenticeships should not be used to underpay young workers and that the pay should increase as they acquire stills, starting at at least one-third of the national minimum wage and reaching two-thirds by the end of the apprenticeship.[35] The risk posed by this exclusion from a statutory minimum wage is that employers may try to disguise what in practice is a job as some kind of training opportunity. This abuse is particularly notorious in the case of unpaid 'internships' in sectors such as journalism, fashion, and the House of Commons. It is possible to challenge bogus internships by demonstrating that work is being performed for the benefit of the employer without a significant educational element. Cases that are properly exempt from the minimum wage include students having work experience as part of their university course, work-shadowing by school age children, and apprentices.

(4) *Youth workers.* In the first few years after leaving school, young people typically receive a reduced wage even if they are performing the same job as older colleagues. Unequal treatment may be justified in some cases by a young person's lack of experience, but the lower rate applies even if experience is unnecessary. It seems likely that employers have strong bargaining power when hiring young people fresh out of school because teenagers cannot demonstrate their capabilities and will often be anxious to find a job as soon as possible. Article 7.5 of the ESC states that national laws must provide for the right of young workers to a fair wage. In its assessment of Montenegro, the European Social Committee concluded that a young worker's wage may be less than the adult starting wage, but any difference must be reasonable and the gap must close quickly. For 15–16-year-olds, a wage of 30 per cent lower than the adult starting wage is acceptable. For 17–18-year-olds, the difference may not exceed 20 per cent. Since a young worker's wage corresponded to only 37.8 per cent of the average wage, it was too low to secure a decent standard of living.[36] In the UK in 2024 the national living wage for adults aged 23 and above is £11.44, whereas 18–20 year olds are only entitled to £8.60, the difference being greater than 20 per cent.[37]

---

[32] *Autoclenz Ltd v Belcher* [2011] UKSC 41, [2011] ICR 1157.
[33] National Minimum Wage Act 1998, s 54; Employment Rights Act 1996, s 230(3).
[34] *Uber BV v Aslam* [2021] UKSC 5, [2021] ICR 657; *Pimlico Plumbers Ltd v Smith* [2018] UKSC 29, [2018] ICR 1511.
[35] Conclusions 2019 – Montenegro – Article 7-5 2019/def/MNE/7/5/EN.
[36] ibid.
[37] National Minimum Wage (Amendment) (No 2) Regulations 2024 (SI 2024/432).

(5) *Prisoners and detainees.* Many prisoners and other kinds of detainees such as asylum seekers are expected to work. This requirement is usually justified as part of a programme of rehabilitation, so that on release prisoners are more likely to be able to obtain gainful employment. Much of the work performed in prisons is necessary for the functioning of the prison, such as cooking, cleaning, laundry work, and maintenance. This is cheap labour because in most countries, prison labour is either not paid at all, or paid only a token amount. In the UK, s 45 of the National Minimum Wage Act 1998 excludes prison work from the statutory minimum wage. The European Court of Human Rights has decided that work in prisons is not the same as employment, so that normal workers' rights such as the right to join a trade union can be excluded because this is a decision within the margin of appreciation of each member state of the Council of Europe.[38] Similarly, the courts in the UK appear to share the view that prisoners do not have contracts for the performance of work since the activity is mandated and regulated by prison rules.[39] In those rules, the Prison Service Order 4460 Annex B lays down a minimum wage for prisoners working inside prisons of £4 for a full week's work, though in practice research of the Howard League for Penal Reform found in 2011 that the average pay of prisoners was a bit less than £10 per week.[40] Similarly, detainees in UK immigration centres are treated as if they were prisoners, though they are encouraged to help with the domestic side of the centre in return for pay with a cap much lower than the national minimum wage.[41]

4. Fairness within Organisations

The right to fair pay has also been interpreted to require fair pay relative to other workers. Ever since the UDHR of 1948, declarations of the right to fair pay have included a principle against discrimination. Article 23(2) of the Declaration states: 'Everyone, without any discrimination, has the right to equal pay for equal work.' Article 4 of the ESC also prohibits discrimination between men and women. Article 7 of the ICESCR apparently supports an unlimited right to fair wages: 'Fair wages and equal remuneration for work of equal value without distinction of any kind …'[42] That Article supports a right to 'fair wages' that goes beyond equal pay for equal work, which would possibly include a right to challenge unfair differentials in pay.

This third interpretation of the right to fair pay concerns comparisons of wages between groups of workers. Comparison can be made horizontally and vertically.[43] A horizontal comparison is a claim that another group of workers is paid more even though their work is of no greater value or that the differential in pay is excessive. A vertical comparison compares the wages of low paid groups with those of high earners in order to claim that the pay of high earners is

---

[38] *Yakut Republican Trade Union Federation v Russia* [2021] ECHR 1033.
[39] *Cox v Ministry of Justice* [2016] UKSC 10, [2016] AC 660, UKSC; *R v Secretary of State for the Home Department ex parte Davis* (25 April 1994, unreported); *Pimm v (1) Sodexo Justice Services Limited (2) Secretary of State for Justice (Intervener)*, Case No 3312375/2019.
[40] V Mantouvalou, 'Pay for Work in Prison', UK Labour Law Blog, 12 December 2022.
[41] K Bales and L Mayblin, 'Unfree Labour in Immigration Detention: Exploitation and Coercion of a Captive Immigrant Workforce' (2018) 47 *Economy and Society* 191; Z Adams, *Labour and the Wage* (Oxford University Press, 2020) 220–22.
[42] Article 7 ICESCR (n 13).
[43] Human Rights Council, Twenty-ninth session, Report of the Special Rapporteur on extreme poverty and human rights, Philip Alston, A/HRC/29/31, para 7.

excessive and therefore unfair. Vertical comparisons are often linked to criticisms of increasing inequality in western societies between the extremely rich and the majority of the workforce. Gross inequalities are believed to pose risks to social cohesion, political participation, housing, and long-term sustainable development.[44] But even if there were no growth in social inequality, it would still be possible to interpret the right to fair pay as a tool for challenging the excessive pay of 'fat cats' such as chief executive officers of large corporations.

Before we examine legal claims based on such horizontal and vertical comparisons, it is necessary to reflect on the meaning of fairness in this context. What is striking about this third interpretation of the right to fair pay is the rejection of the normal assumption about fair prices that an undistorted market provides the correct price. To make comparisons between groups of workers, two other criteria appear to dominate in moral and legal reasoning. These are the principles of desert and recognition.

Desert

Within employer organisations, desert is the most frequently cited moral principle for the distribution of rewards such as pay and promotion. It is generally believed that employees should be paid according to the value of their contribution to the productive organisation. Those who work hard and achieve much in their jobs for the benefit of the goals of the organisation should be rewarded for that contribution. It follows as well that those who contribute little should not expect high levels of pay.

Desert is a very different principle of justice than the one applicable to ordinary market transactions. In other bilateral exchanges such as sales of goods, justice will normally be satisfied by some kind of equivalence in the exchange or merely the opportunity to bargain for the best price. In general, the market price will be regarded presumptively as what is fair. Within an organisation, however, fairness is not based on market price, though of course the rates of pay are likely to be influenced by the market price for labour because of the need to recruit and retain staff. In the 'internal labour market' or pay scales of productive organisations, what typically matters more than external market rates are relativities between different jobs including both horizontal and vertical pay equity. In large organisations, wages are normally set primarily by reference to the grade of the job according to the rules of the organisation, though increasingly with an additional discretionary bonus element to recognise especially valuable contributions by individuals.

The reason why desert is the appropriate moral principle for fair pay is that productive organisations are voluntary organisations that pursue a particular goal such as assembling a popular make of car, creating software systems, or providing a world-class education to students. As in any kind of team production, members of the organisation should be rewarded according to their contribution to the purpose of the organisation. If the principle of desert is ignored or flouted, members of the team will either cease to pull their weight or quit altogether.[45] Desert is therefore an existential principle for productive organisations.

The great difficulty presented by desert as a moral standard is that an individual's contribution is always hard to measure. As in a sports team, a successful goal-scorer or a manager may be highly lauded and rewarded, but every member of the team's contribution is in fact essential to their success, as is usually revealed when a player is sent off. Where work involves the creation of

---

[44] United Nations, Social and Economic Affairs, *Sustainable Development Goals 2030*, Goal 10.
[45] JB Wade, CA O'Reilly, III and TG Pollock, 'Overpaid CEOs and Underpaid Managers: Fairness and Executive Compensation' (2006) 17(5) *Organization Science* 527.

separate items, such as sewing t-shirts together, pressing widgets, or stuffing cuddly toys, merely counting the number of pieces completed may provide a rough measure of desert. As soon as work involves making decisions, coordinating work with others, exercising discretion, planning the performance of tasks, and generally using intellectual abilities and discretion, desert based on contribution cannot be measured with objectivity and precision. Furthermore, some argue that desert should also include the extent that a job contributes to benefits to society as a whole, such as the contribution of nurses to health care or teachers to education. Placing a value on the value of a job in terms of social welfare is bound to be controversial. For instance, it might be said that professional sports players provide little public benefit from hitting or kicking a ball about, whereas others might argue that supporters derive more satisfaction from the performance of their team than any other aspects of their lives. Although desert by reference to contribution and social benefit is therefore usually indeterminate in its guidance about levels of pay, if an organisation needs every job to be performed effectively, every employee's contribution is indispensable and valuable and needs to be rewarded at a level that is perceived to match the level of desert.

Recognition

Due recognition requires treatment by other members of the employer organisation not only with respect and courtesy, but also in ways that enable everyone to have a positive understanding of themselves or self-respect. It reinforces the human motivation to achieve satisfaction from doing a job well.[46] Fair wages are a clear signal that a worker is respected by others for their contribution to the organisation through the performance of their job. Due recognition requires the organisation to show that all members are valued and respected as persons for their indispensable contribution to the productivity of the organisation.

Due recognition through fair wages for the lowest paid is especially important, because they are likely to be disproportionately drawn from disadvantaged groups such as racial minority groups, women, and migrants, for whom recognition is often especially difficult. Again, this moral principle of recognition rejects the market rate of pay as a standard of fairness. The market rate for disadvantaged groups may be significantly below the market rate for white male workers even though there is no significant difference in their skills and competence to perform the job. The recognition principle insists that everyone should receive a wage that confers respect on this member of the organisation. Often a 'living wage' will satisfy the requirement of recognition, but not if other groups of workers receive a higher wage for performing a similar job.

Horizontal Comparisons

For horizontal comparisons, we consider whether two workers or groups of workers who perform similar jobs are receiving the same wages. Alternatively, it is possible to attempt an objective evaluation of their contribution to the goals of the organisation and assess whether their contributions are of equal value. In law, horizontal comparisons are most frequently used for the purpose of claims for equal pay for women. These claims often highlight the pattern of inequality between work that is predominantly being performed by women such as caring and cleaning and other kinds of jobs that are mostly performed by men. Although some of that difference between men's and women's wages may be explicable by reference to objective criteria such as skills and

---

[46] JA Stiglitz, *The Price of Inequality* (London, Penguin, 2013) 139.

qualifications, there is certainly a component of prejudice and stereotypes that contribute to the setting of the pay of women at lower rates. A famous example arose when the women sewing machinists at the Ford Car Plant in Dagenham went on strike because they were rated unskilled and were therefore low paid, whereas the male workers on the conveyor belt were awarded the status of skilled workers with higher pay. This strike became a powerful symbol that eventually forced a change of policy inside the trade unions, and then the UK Government was compelled to enact the Equal Pay Act 1971.

The current UK law on equal pay for women is contained in the Equality Act 2010, which itself is largely based on the law of the European Union. Under the law of the European Union, not only must the pay of women be the same as men if they are doing the same job, but also they should be paid equally if their work is of equal value to that of a male colleague.[47] In *Enderby v Frenchay Health Authority*,[48] a female speech therapist was permitted to claim that her work, which was predominantly performed by women, was of equal value to that of two very different kinds of jobs, clinical psychologists and pharmacists, which were predominantly performed by men. The very idea that jobs can be of equal value invokes a criterion of contribution and desert. The value of the job cannot be determined by reference to its prevailing market rate, for it is of course usually that market rate that is being challenged by the claimant. The appeal to some other way of valuing the job in equal value claims clearly looks at the putative contribution of a woman and her male comparator to the outcomes of the productive organisation. The granting of the claim to women also illustrates the principle of due recognition for all members of the organisation.

Under the law of equal pay for women, an employer may justify a difference in pay even though it violates the principle of equal pay for equal work if the employer can establish that there is a material factor that explains the difference in pay which is not in itself a factor tainted by sex. Attempts by employers to reintroduce references to market rates of pay in support of the material factor defence are unlikely to be successful, because the market rates are likely to be tainted by prejudicial stereotypes such as the view that women's work such as cleaning and caring is less important. In *Enderby v Frenchay*, the employer claimed that assuming the jobs were of equal value, paying the pharmacists more was justifiable on the ground that there was a shortage of candidates for the job. The European Court of Justice (ECJ) accepted that this could be a justification for a pay difference provided that the difference in pay was proportionate to the legitimate aim of recruitment. In *Enderby v Frenchay*, the employer also sought to justify the difference in pay on the ground that the rates were set by different collective bargaining processes. The ECJ rejected this justification, for collective agreements that have set different rates for jobs of equal or comparable value may have been influenced by negative stereotypes about the value of women's work. This case illustrates the tension between the conception of the right to fair pay as one requiring collective bargaining and the different conception that the right to fair pay requires fair differentials in the workplace. When these two conceptions clash, as they did in *Enderby v Frenchay*, the ECJ favours the latter view, no doubt in part because the right to equal pay (but not the right to collective bargaining) is embedded in the Treaties governing the EU.

---

[47] Treaty on the Functioning of the European Union (Consolidated) 01/03/2020, Article 157(1): 'Each Member State shall ensure that the principle of equal pay for male and female workers for equal work or work of equal value is applied.' Directive 2006/54/EC (Sex Equality) ([2006] OJ L204/23).

[48] Case C-127/92 *Enderby v Frenchay Health Authority* [1993] ECR I-5535, [1994] ICR 112, ECJ.

Women who suffer disadvantages in their pay and terms and conditions have to use the law of equal pay, but other disadvantaged groups may suffer from indirect discrimination in pay, in particular migrants, racial minority groups (and the two together), and older workers. They can bring claims for indirect discrimination on the ground that they are members of a protected group that suffers disproportionate disadvantage in their pay or other terms and conditions. Again, any discrepancy in pay can be justified by the employer if it is a proportionate means of pursuing a legitimate aim.

The horizontal comparisons used in this third interpretation of the right to fair pay tend to be confined to a single business organisation or at most industrial sector where sectoral collective bargaining exists. The reasons for confining the comparison to a single employer is that one employer cannot control what other employers pay their workers, and different employers may be more profitable and therefore able to reward their staff differentially. For this reason, a claim for equal pay can normally only be made within the same organisation. There must be a single employing entity that determines the pay of the woman and her comparator.[49] Where, however, a collective agreement purports to set the rates of pay for several organisations or as wide as a whole industrial sector, horizontal comparisons are possible to raise all workers covered by the collective agreement to the levels of pay it sets. There are some limited exceptions to the 'single source' principle. For example, after 12 weeks of employment by a client, temporary agency workers, who are employed by their agency, are entitled to compare their wages with directly employed staff of the client and demand equal wages. There is also special provision in the Equality Act 2010 that holds the main employer liable for the terms and conditions of workers employed by a contractor.[50] The exceptional provision in the Equality Act 2010 was used to hold the core employer liable for indirect race discrimination for condoning the practice of the subcontractor paying its workers, who were all black migrant workers, only the national minimum wage when the directly employed staff (who were mostly white) were paid the much higher London living wage.[51] Outside the scope of this unusual provision, it is normally not possible to hold one employer responsible for the practices and conduct of another: if an outsourced contractor pays very low wages or refuses to recognise a trade union for the purposes of collective bargaining, it is of no concern to the core business.

Horizontal comparisons have sometimes included historical comparisons for the same group of workers. The current wages paid to a group are arguably unfair if they are the result of a unilaterally imposed pay cut, or the failure of the wages to keep their real value or purchasing power due to rising inflation. For example, in Lithuania, the right to fair pay is a constitutional right, and it has been interpreted to prohibit imposed pay cuts during the expected duration of employees' contracts except perhaps in cases of emergency when the cut must be proportionate.[52] Similarly, the right to fair pay under the Kenyan Constitution has been interpreted to prohibit unilateral pay cuts without discussion, warnings, or giving reasons.[53] The same right was also violated where a person was required to 'act up' to a more senior role in the organisation, without receiving the pay for the job for six years.[54]

---

[49] Case C-320/00 *Lawrence v Regent Office Care Ltd* [2002] ECR I-7325.
[50] Equality Act 2010, s 41.
[51] *Boohene & Ors v The Royal Parks Ltd* (ET Cases 2202211/2020, 2204440/2020 & 2205570/2020), reversed on appeal on the ground of insufficiency of evidence to support the conclusion: *The Royal Parks Ltd v Boohene & Ors* [2023] EAT 69 (5 May 2023).
[52] Ruling on wages of officers of the system of the internal service [2009] LTCC 29; Case No 14/07-17/08-25/08-39/08 (11 December 2009).
[53] *Fredrick Ouma v Spectre International Ltd* [2013] eKLR, http://www.kenyalaw.org/caselaw/cases/view/88118.
[54] *Oyatsi v Judicial Service Commission* (Petition E111 of 2021) [2022] KEELRC 3 (KLR) (10 March 2022), http://kenyalaw.org/caselaw/cases/view/230130.

Vertical comparisons

Within organisations there is usually a hierarchy of pay. In many organisations, these differences are formalised in systems of pay scales and banding of jobs that allocate a particular rate of pay to a job according to its position in the hierarchy. The pay grading system is designed to recruit, retain, and to incentivise workers to work hard at their jobs in the hope of promotion. For the most part, this grading system is likely to correspond to perceptions of desert and recognition. If a salary scale does not correspond to those criteria, the right to fair pay could be regarded as providing the basis for a challenge to unfair differentials.

Unfortunately, the remuneration committees of the boards of directors of large companies that set the pay of the top executives do not pay much attention to those values and fairness. Instead, they tend to look at market rates of pay for top executives in a global labour market and to insist on highly geared performance-related pay systems in order to align the interests of the executives with the shareholders. A typical remuneration package therefore includes a high fixed salary with the possibility of a substantial bonus that may treble remuneration if the value of the shares increases.[55]

Does the right to fair pay demand that a limit should be set on excessive differentials of pay within organisations, especially with respect to the salaries of chief executive officers? Such proposals are no doubt fuelled by concerns about rising inequalities in our society, though it is unclear whether such measures would help much as the evidence suggests that the greatest disparities of wealth derive from ownership of capital and the way it is taxed. Furthermore, it is unlikely that any agreement could be reached about what the maximum ratio of wages between top and bottom in organisations should be or where to set the maximum amount.

There is considerable divergence between organisations in their views about what are fair differentials between different pay grades. Prime Minister David Cameron suggested that pay ratios between top and bottom in the Civil Service should not exceed 20:1. That proposal was defeated, as was a referendum in Switzerland that sought to limit the pay ratio in all businesses to 12:1.[56] Some faith organisations and churches insist on narrower wage dispersal, as in the case of the Quakers who adopt a maximum differential of 4:1.[57] There are a number of voluntary codes of practice that propose maximum wage ratios. For instance, 'Wagemark' is an international wage standard used to certify that the ratio between a business, non-profit organisation, or a government agency's highest and lowest paid earners (defined as the average pay of the bottom decile) is no more than 8:1. In a survey of employees' attitudes to pay ratios, a quarter thought ratios were irrelevant, but among those who though they did matter, around a third thought that a CEO's pay should be less than five times an average employee's salary, and around a fifth believed it should be between five and 10 times above. Those in the not-for-profit and public sectors were more likely to say that the pay ratio should be less than five times.[58] In practice, however, in the large FTSE 100 companies, remuneration committees are happy to endorse ratios well in excess of 100:1, and the divergence is even greater in the USA. Their sole concern appears to be market rates, not fair pay within the organisation. Given this variation in the ratios that are deemed acceptable, it is hard to avoid the conclusion that any fixed upper

---

[55] MT Moore, 'Corporate Governance, Pay Equity, and the Limitations of Agency Theory' (2015) 68 *Current Legal Problems* 431.

[56] A Atkinson, *Equality: What can be Done?* (Cambridge, MA, Harvard University Press, 2015) 151.

[57] Similarly, *Traidcraft* (a Christian trading organisation) limits pay disparity to 6:1. Impact and Performance Report for Traidcraft 2013–14, 42.

[58] CIPD, Pulse Survey, 'The view from below: What employees really think about their CEO's pay packet' (December 2015) 4: The-view-from-below_2015-what-employees-think-CEO-pay-packet__tcm18-8916.pdf (cipd.co.uk).

limit would meet strong resistance from powerful organisations. A weaker, though workable, alternative may be to require organisations to develop transparent pay ratios that they are not permitted to exceed.[59] Breach of those rules might give rise to a claim for compensation from the lowest paid or perhaps some kind of additional taxation. For example, the City of Portland in the USA has introduced increased local business taxation by 10 per cent for resident large companies that exceed a ratio of CEO to median worker above 100:1, and the surtax is 25 per cent if the ratio exceeds 250:1.[60]

One attempt to control the pay of top earners was a measure against bankers' bonuses. Following the financial crash of 2008, it was believed that employees of investment banks had too much incentive to engage in risky trades because they stood to gain multi-million bonuses if their bets with their clients' money paid off. As part of an EU-led reform of the banking sector, the Capital Requirements Directive,[61] which was intended to restore stability to the financial sector, included a rule that capped bankers' bonus at 100 per cent of their fixed annual salaries or 200 per cent with shareholder approval.[62] The limited evidence has not established whether this measure has contributed to a reduction of risky transactions.[63] There may be many other causes of diminished risk-taking such as increased capital requirements for banks. Nor does the measure appear to have significantly reduced the high salaries of bankers, but merely led to an increase in the fixed salary element and a decrease in the bonus element, the latter dropping from 53 per cent to about 40 per cent of total remuneration package. Following persistent opposition by Conservative-led governments and commercial banks, the UK financial regulator consulted on detailed proposals to remove limits on bonuses in order to restore the performance-related incentives to banking employees and to enable banks to reduce labour costs during a downturn.[64] No concern is expressed by government or the regulator about the high level of wages in some banks however they may be composed. On the contrary, high wages are regarded as ensuring that the financial sector is competitive for attracting the best talent internationally. The law in the UK has now been changed to remove the cap on bankers' bonuses.[65] The fate of the regulation of bankers' bonuses demonstrates the strength of the opposition to controls over top salaries.

Nevertheless, concerns about the adverse effects of growing inequality in society provide the backdrop for ambitious proposals for a maximum wage or a right against extreme wage inequality.[66] Such a right may be grounded in the opaque phrase in the Declaration of Philadelphia that wages and other conditions of work should be set 'to ensure a just share of the fruits of progress for all'.[67] A maximum wage could be enforced through high levels of taxation above

---

[59] H Collins, 'Fat Cats, Production Networks, and the Right to Fair Pay' (2022) *Modern Law Review* 1.

[60] City of Portland (Charter, Code and Policies) ARB-LIC-5 Pay Ratio Surtax: www.portland.gov/policies/licensing-and-income-taxes/fees/lic-502-pay-ratio-surtax.

[61] Capital Requirements Directive (2013/36/EU) – CRD IV; and Capital Requirements Directive (2019/878/EU) – CRD V.

[62] Rule 15.9(3) of the Remuneration Part of the Prudential Regulation Authority Rulebook.

[63] Stefano Colonnello, Michael Koetter, and Konstantin Wagner, 'Compensation Regulation in Banking: Executive Director Behavior and Bank Performance after the EU Bonus Cap' (2023) 76 *Journal of Accounting and Economics* 101576.

[64] Prudential Regulation Authority of the Bank of England, CP15/22 – Remuneration: Ratio between fixed and variable components of total remuneration ('bonus cap') (19/12/2022).

[65] Bank of England, PS9/23 – Remuneration: Ratio between fixed and variable components of total remuneration ('bonus cap'), PRA policy statement 9/23, FCA policy statement 23/15.

[66] I Katsaroumpas 'A Right Against Extreme Wage Inequality: A Social Justice Modernisation of International Labour Law?' (2021) 32(2) *King's Law Journal* 260; M Ramsay, 'A Modest Proposal: The Case for a Maximum Wage' (2005) 11(4) *Contemporary Politics* 201.

[67] KD Ewing and Lord Hendy KC, '"A Just Share of the Fruits of Progress": What does it mean?' in B Langille and A Trebilcock (eds), *Social Justice and the World of Work: Essays in Honour of Francis Maupain* (Oxford, Hart Publishing, 2023) 65.

a certain level of income and by conditions attached to public procurement. On the difficult question of how the maximum might be specified, the answer might be a parliamentary vote, perhaps informed by a Commission of experts and consultation with social partners.[68]

5. Conclusion

Although a right to fair pay is present in both international declarations of human rights and in some national constitutions, there is no consensus on what the right requires and how it should be achieved. Where most of a nation's labour force benefits from effective collective bargaining, the question of fair pay is answered by support for collective bargaining and the extension of those standards to the whole workforce. In the 21st century, however, we have become aware that in advanced economies the impact of collective bargaining has rapidly declined in most countries, and in developing economies trade union representation is patchy and does not protect whole sectors of the informal economy. These developments have advanced the case for legislation that guarantees a living wage, one that enables a person to live a life of dignity. At the same time, an awareness of the growing disparities of wealth in most countries, which is partly due to huge differences in pay between the CEOs of companies and the lowest paid decile in those companies, has led to an increased insistence on fairness in wage setting, so that those at the top are not paid excessively, but at the same time the lowest wages signal that the employees' contributions are valued and that their independent interests and dignity are recognised. However the right to fair pay is understood, effective legislation is always difficult, because it challenges greed, the power of the wealthy, and may disrupt market mechanisms with adverse consequences such as unemployment and the export of jobs abroad.

---

[68] Katsaroumpas, above n 66, 281–82.

11

The Right to Reasonable Limitation of Working Hours

1. Introduction
2. Sources and Themes
3. Weekly Working Time
4. Paid Annual Leave
5. Rights to Leave for Family Reasons
6. Rights Relating to the Organisation of Working Time
7. Conclusion

1. Introduction

This chapter considers rights relating to working time. These rights have long been a concern of the labour movement, reflected in the fact that the very first International Labour Organization (ILO) Convention, in 1919, dealt with the length of the working week.[1] Economic and social rights instruments typically recognise the right to a maximum limit on the working day and working week, and the right to paid holidays. We discuss the formulation and implementation of these rights, and the challenges posed to working hours by issues such as 'on call' time and the constant intrusion of work into home life through technology. Another important group of rights relating to working time are rights to leave from work for family reasons. Early initiatives here tended to focus on maternity leave, though the focus has now shifted to more neutral parental leave rights with a view to promoting both equality at work and equal parenting. Finally, we consider a more modern group of rights intended to give workers greater control over the amount and distribution of their working hours, for example, through the right to request flexible working or the right to request predictable working arrangements. But before turning to these various groups of rights, we identify the main sources of rights relating to working time, and the major themes that will run throughout the chapter.

2. Sources and Themes

In this section, we consider some of the possible bases for a right to reasonable limitation of working hours. Understanding why it is that workers need a particular right helps us to interpret and apply that right more appropriately. We consider three possible bases here: dignity, health and safety, and equality. It is worth noting at the outset that rights relating to working time

---

[1] ILO Convention No 1, Hours of Work (Industry) Convention, 1919.

feature in instruments concerned with economic and social rights rather than civil and political rights, though very long hours working with no breaks is often a characteristic of forced labour, which is prohibited by these instruments.[2]

Article 24 of the Universal Declaration of Human Rights (UDHR) sets out the right in the following terms:

> Everyone has the right to rest and leisure, including reasonable limitation of working hours and periodic holidays with pay.

This suggests that 'rest and leisure' is a right in itself. Article 7(d) of the International Covenant on Economic, Social and Cultural Rights (ICESCR) is in similar terms. One way of thinking about this is that a working person's dignity is infringed if they are expected to work very long hours with no rest and no time away from the workplace. Work cannot take up the whole of a person's life: time is needed to sleep, to relax, to be with family and friends, and to engage in other valuable activities such as volunteering, exercising or pursuing other personal interests. Of course, what constitutes a 'reasonable' limitation is somewhat arbitrary and often culturally determined. The European Social Charter (ESC) offers a bit more detail on these points, as do the various ILO instruments. It is noteworthy that the original ESC prescribed a minimum of two weeks' paid annual leave, whereas the 1996 revision now provides for four weeks' paid annual leave as a minimum.[3]

The health and safety justification for the regulation of working time is a feature of EU law, and has a quirky history.[4] In the 1980s and 1990s, the EU institutions and many Member States wanted to enact new directives on labour law matters, but were constrained by the UK's opposition and use of its veto to block such initiatives. One of the Treaty provisions which only required qualified majority voting – and thus could not be blocked by the UK's veto – dealt with health and safety.[5] The Working Time Directive was therefore agreed using the health and safety basis.[6] The UK brought proceedings in the CJEU alleging that the Directive was outside the EU's powers.[7] This was rejected by the Court. It adopted a broad definition of health and safety, focusing on the worker's wellbeing, rather than the narrow 'prevention of accidents and avoidance of disease' definition which was proposed by the UK Government.[8] On this view, the Working Time Directive was well within the EU's competences. Despite the unusual history, the connection between health and safety and rights to reasonable limitations on working time is relatively clear-cut. A worker who is tired is more prone to making mistakes, which may injure the worker, colleagues or customers. This argument is particularly important in safety-critical industries such as transport. A worker who is tired over the long term is more prone to ill-health, both mental and physical. These are strong arguments for limiting working hours.

The equality justification for limiting working hours is less obvious, but potentially quite important for some of the reasons given in chapter 4. As we explained there, the majority of unpaid work in the home (cooking, cleaning, looking after children and so on) remains the responsibility of women, even though many women now spend a significant amount of time engaged in paid work outside the home. Limits on working time can make it easier for parents of any gender and in any kind of family structure to achieve a better balance between their work

---

[2] See chapter 9.
[3] ESC (1961), Article 2(3); ESC (1996), Article 2(3).
[4] J Kenner, *EU Employment Law from Rome to Amsterdam and Beyond* (Hart, 2003) ch 3.
[5] Article 118a EEC.
[6] Directive 93/104/EC, now Directive 2003/88/EC.
[7] Case C-84/94 *United Kingdom v Council (Working Time Directive)* [1996] ECR I-5755.
[8] ibid [15].

and their home life. As we shall see, the law often provides a mix of rights to time off for family purposes (such as maternity, paternity and parental leave) and rights to work flexibly.[9] Both of these approaches can help women to manage their competing responsibilities and can provide more opportunities for men to play a fuller part in family life.

One significant challenge in relation to the regulation of working time is to determine whether that regulation protects workers' interests or workers' choices.[10] Rights can do either of these things. If a right protects workers' interests, we would generally expect to find that it was binding and could not be waived. For example, it is often argued that (a small part of) the right to maternity leave should be compulsory, in order to protect the health of the woman who has recently given birth and to give her time to recuperate.[11] However, rights which protect workers' choices are more flexible. For example, while many instruments propose a right to paid annual leave, it is often not compulsory to take the leave, and many working people do not use their full entitlement in any given year. This is so even though the right cannot formally be waived by workers under EU law. There are lots of possible reasons for the failure to take leave: an ambition to get ahead at work, for example, or (more negatively) pressure from the employer not to use the full entitlement. This highlights one of the problems with protecting workers' choices. On the one hand, this empowers workers to exercise their rights as they see fit and to gain greater control over their lives. On the other hand, we cannot always be sure that a worker's choice is freely exercised without interference by the employer, particularly given the inequality of bargaining power which generally obtains in the working relationship.

One particularly important factor to consider when thinking about working time, and workers' choices in relation to working time, is the connection between working time and pay. For many working people who are paid per hour or per day, this connection is direct and immediate: their earnings are determined by how many hours they work. From this perspective, limits on working time need to be considered in conjunction with other requirements, such as the minimum wage, in order to ensure that workers who work a standard working week as permitted by the law can live on their earnings.[12] This is also one of the reasons why many human rights instruments emphasise that the right to annual leave is a right to *paid* leave.[13] A right to unpaid leave is of limited value, particularly to low-paid workers who may not be in a position to save any money in order to support themselves whilst taking leave. However, this has not stopped the creation of rights to unpaid (or low paid) leave in some contexts, notably parental leave.[14] We discuss the implications of this in greater detail below. Another important link between working time and pay is the possibility of earning extra money by working beyond usual hours. In many workplaces, it is common for 'overtime' to be paid at a higher rate. This may give workers a strong incentive to work longer hours – for example, to waive their right not to work more than a certain number of hours in the week – in order to increase their earnings. On the other hand, mandatory overtime rates may deter employers from relying on long hours working, and encourage them to seek more creative solutions to the organisation of work.

---

[9] See eg ESC (1996), Articles 8 and 27.
[10] For discussion, see the analysis of derogations in A Bogg and M Ford, 'Article 31' in S Peers et al (eds), *The EU Charter of Fundamental Rights: a Commentary*, 2nd edn (Hart, 2021).
[11] See S Fredman, 'Reversing Roles: Bringing Men into the Frame' (2014) 10 *International Journal of Law in Context* 442, 450–51, for competing views on this point.
[12] Subject also to social security provisions. Directive 2022/2041/EU on adequate minimum wages in the EU has the potential to fill a significant gap in the EU's legal framework on these issues.
[13] eg the ESC, above n 3.
[14] eg in the UK, the Maternity and Parental Leave etc Regulations 1999 (SI 1999/3312), regs 13–16.

A final theme which will run throughout the chapter is the different experiences of working time for individuals with different types of employment relationship.[15] Traditional rights relating to working time, such as the maximum limit on the working week or the right to a rest break during the day, were developed to address the needs of a 'typical' employee working a regular working week in an office or factory. The main problem faced by these employees was a long hours culture and a lack of rest and leisure time. In the modern economy, work has become much less regular for many people, with a significant proportion of workers now working on a casual 'as required' basis. Some, but by no means all, of this casual work takes place in the gig economy. As chapter 3 demonstrated, one problem faced by casual workers is the difficulty of establishing that they have 'worker' status in law in order to access statutory employment protections including, in many jurisdictions, rights to reasonable limitations on their working hours.[16] However, even if these individuals do fall within the law's protection, as is increasingly the case, their working time needs are complex. One problem is that casual workers may spend significant amounts of time either waiting for or looking for work. Although the UK Supreme Court's decision in the *Uber* case upheld a finding that the drivers were working whenever they were logged on, in the relevant area, waiting for work, this may not be the case for all platforms or jurisdictions, and is not necessarily true of other types of casual work.[17] This 'available' time is not genuine rest or leisure time, but may not be counted by the law as work time either.[18] Another problem is that casual work is usually presented as 'flexible', with ample opportunities for casual workers to fit their jobs around their other interests and commitments.[19] However, this flexibility is often misleading because of the role played by customer demand in the allocation of work. A food delivery rider who wants to make money needs to be available for work at busy times, such as evenings, when customers are ordering food. Their earnings may be significantly affected if they take a rest break at a busy time. It is therefore important to consider whether rights relating to working time which were formulated for a particular type of working pattern remain helpful and relevant for this important group of workers.

3. Weekly Working Time

In this section, we consider the right to 'reasonable limitation of working hours', which typically includes a maximum limit on the working week and rights to rest breaks both during the working day and between shifts. We also consider the blurred boundary between working time and non-work time generated by modern technology, which has led to calls for the protection of workers' right to 'disconnect'.

Human rights instruments, such as the ICESCR and the ESC, tend to be vague about the working week, calling for 'reasonable daily and weekly working hours' without specifying exact limits.[20] The ILO instruments set the limit at 48 hours per week, with a working day of eight hours.[21]

---

[15] For discussion, see ILO, *Working Time and Work-Life Balance Around the World* (January 2023).
[16] eg in the UK, the Working Time Regulations 1998 (SI 1998/1833) apply to 'workers', reg 2.
[17] *Uber BV v Aslam* [2021] UKSC 5, [2021] ICR 657, [121]–[138].
[18] ACL Davies, 'Getting More than you Bargained for? Rethinking the Meaning of "Work" in Employment Law' (2017) 46 *ILJ* 477. In the context, see Agnieszka Piasna, 'Algorithms of Time: How Algorithmic Management Changes the Temporalities of Work and Prospects for Working Time Reduction' [2023] *Cambridge Journal of Economics* (forthcoming).
[19] For a classic critique, see Sandra Fredman, 'Women at Work: The Broken Promise of Flexicurity' (2004) 33 *ILJ* 299.
[20] ICESCR, Article 7(d); ESC, Article 2(1) (both versions).
[21] ILO Convention No 1, Hours of Work (Industry) Convention, 1919; Convention No 30, Hours of Work (Commerce and Offices) Convention, 1930.

The EU Working Time Directive also uses 48 hours as the limit on weekly working time, averaged over 17 weeks, but does not specify the appropriate length of the working day.[22] It provides instead for a right to an 11-hour rest break in every 24-hour period, which could allow for much longer shifts, subject to the overall limit on the working week.[23]

One of the most contentious features of the EU Directive is the so-called 'opt-out'. This provision allows Member States to legislate for individuals to opt out of the 48-hour limit on the working week.[24] If the purpose of the Directive is to protect workers' health and safety, it seems odd that an opt-out is permitted. However, the opt-out could be regarded as a means of protecting workers' autonomy and choice, as discussed above, by allowing them to choose to work longer hours – perhaps at certain points during their lives – in order to boost their earnings. A particular problem with the opt-out, given the inequality of bargaining power between employers and most individual workers, is ensuring that the worker is making a genuine choice to opt out. Research in the UK – where many workers are opted out – suggests that employers often insist on the opt-out when the worker is offered a job, creating the impression that signing is a condition of getting the job.[25] Various reforms have been suggested to address this, such as requiring the opt-out to be signed separately.[26] Even if the opt-out were to be abolished, it is worth noting that workers who do not have formal start and finish times ('unmeasured' work) are excluded anyway,[27] and that the 48-hour limit is an average over 17 weeks (extendable to 52 weeks by collective negotiation) which could still permit some very long working weeks.[28] It might also create greater incentives for employers to design their written contracts to exclude worker status.

An interesting feature of the ESC, in both versions, is the ambition for 'the working week to be progressively reduced to the extent that the increase of productivity and other relevant factors permit'.[29] The ILO's Forty-Hour Week Convention, of 1935, is in a similar vein, requiring signatory states to declare their 'approval' of a 40-hour week with no reduction in living standards.[30] For many in the labour movement, the 48-hour week was just intended to be a starting-point for further reductions in the working week, perhaps as new technologies helped to drive productivity improvements. While the long-run data indicates that working hours have fallen sharply, particularly in nations of the Global North, over the past 150 years, those falls have tailed off and calls for further reductions in the working week have become less mainstream.[31] Some have argued for shorter working weeks as a way of tackling unemployment. This is often given as a reason for the legislation introducing a 35-hour week in France, though from that perspective, the initiative has not been successful.[32] Unsurprisingly, given that there is a cost associated with

---

[22] Directive 2003/88/EC, Article 6.
[23] ibid Article 3.
[24] ibid Article 22.
[25] C Barnard et al, 'Opting Out of the 48-Hour Week: Employer Necessity or Individual Choice? An Empirical Study of the Operation of Article 18(1)(b) of the Working Time Directive in the UK' (2003) 32 *Industrial Law Journal* 223.
[26] A change proposed by the Commission in one of its many (unsuccessful) attempts to reform the Directive: Commission, *Proposal for a Directive amending Directive 2003/88/EC concerning certain aspects of the organisation of working time* (COM (2004) 607 final), 5–6.
[27] Above n 22, Article 17.
[28] ibid Articles 16 and 19.
[29] Article 2(1).
[30] ILO Convention No 47, Forty-Hour Week Convention, 1935, Article 1 (ratified by a mere 15 countries).
[31] C Giattino et al, 'Working Hours' (2020), available at https://ourworldindata.org/.
[32] For detail and discussion, see C Dufour, 'Reduction of Working Time in France: a Lone Knight' in Maarten Keune and Béla Galgóczi (eds), *Collective Bargaining on Working Time: Recent European Experiences* (ETUI, 2006); S Laulom, 'A New Agenda for Reforms in France: New Complexities and Flexibilities of Labour Law' (2016) 39 *Dublin University Law Journal* 93; S Lehndorff, 'It's a Long Way from Norms to Normality' (2014) 67 *International Labour Review* 838.

each person a firm employs, employers have not been willing to hire additional workers even when hours are limited. In the UK, some employers have recently taken part in an experiment to test a four-day week, in which workers were encouraged to do their usual work in four days rather than five, for the same wage.[33] Many firms reported positive outcomes, with workers feeling happier because of the extra day off, and being more productive during the remaining time. However, it is not clear whether this approach would work in all types of firm and economic sector.

A particular challenge for 'progressive reduction' approaches is the link between work and pay. The human rights instruments discussed above call for living standards to be maintained as hours are reduced, but for many workers and employers, there is a close relationship between hours worked and pay: if a worker wants to do fewer hours, they will receive less pay. It is very difficult to break out of this mentality. Moreover, many workers consider themselves 'underemployed': they earn less money than they would like and are willing to work more hours than they can get.[34] Progressive reduction schemes have no direct appeal for this group, nor are they designed to benefit them indirectly by creating demand for more workers, since the assumption is that existing workers will continue to carry out the same work, but in a shorter time.

A second element of the right to a 'reasonable limitation' of working hours is the right to rest breaks. One aspect of this right is the right to take breaks during the working day. The EU Directive provides for a rest break if the working day is longer than six hours.[35] The duration and other details of the break may be specified in national legislation or collective agreements. In the UK, the minimum statutory break has been set at a rather meagre 20 minutes, and it need not be paid.[36] Although the rest break right may seem trivial, it is an important recognition that workers are humans, not robots, and have basic physical needs to attend to during the working day. The EAT has held that the employer need not force a worker to take a rest break, but it is the employer's responsibility to organise the working day so that there is an opportunity to take a break.[37] One area ripe for challenge is where workers are set tough targets (for example, packers in a warehouse required to pack a set number of items per hour) which mean that, in practice, they cannot realistically take the breaks to which they are entitled for fear of missing their targets and incurring a disciplinary penalty.

Another right in the international instruments is a right to a 'weekly rest period'. In the ESC, the duration is unspecified, but there is an expectation that it should, 'as far as possible, coincide with the day recognised by tradition or custom in the country or region concerned as a day of rest'.[38] The ILO standard is for 24 hours in every seven days.[39] The Working Time Directive makes the same provision, which is added on to the 11 hours' rest in every 24 hours in Article 3.[40] The UK implementation allows the 24-hour period to be varied by the employer to 48 hours in every 14 days.[41] Interestingly, when the UK challenged the health and safety basis of the Directive, the

---

[33] Autonomy Research, *The Results Are In: the UK's Four-Day Week Pilot* (February 2023), available at www.4dayweek.co.uk/.
[34] For statistical analysis, see S Dey-Chowdhury et al, *Alternative Measures of Underutilisation in the UK Labour Market* (September 2022), available at www.ons.gov.uk. The underemployment rate in the UK is very low at the time of writing.
[35] Directive 2003/88/EC, Article 4.
[36] Working Time Regulations 1998 (SI 1998/1833), reg 12. There is no right to payment in reg 12.
[37] *Grange v Abellio London Ltd* [2017] ICR 287.
[38] ESC, Article 2(5) (both versions).
[39] ILO Convention No 14, Weekly Rest (Industry) Convention, 1921; Convention No 106, Weekly Rest (Commerce and Offices) Convention, 1957.
[40] Above n 22, Art 5.
[41] Above n 36, reg 11.

only provision the CJEU struck down was one designating Sunday as the preferred day of rest.[42] This was held not to be justified as a health and safety measure because, from that perspective, it did not matter when the rest was taken. However, the broader right to rest and leisure can justify the protection of a particular day, as noted above, because there is some value in a majority of people having the same day as a rest day, in order to facilitate valuable community activities outside work.[43]

The discussion so far has assumed a relatively clear distinction between working time and rest time. Indeed, the CJEU has held that there is a binary distinction between the two: time is either work or rest.[44] However, the position in practice is often much more complex than that. One problem is 'on call' time. There are many jobs (security guards, carers, medical professionals, emergency workers and so on) where there is a requirement to spend a period of time 'on call', ready to respond to an emergency. Depending on the circumstances, this time may be spent at home (which might need to be within a certain distance of the workplace) or at the workplace itself, and there may be variations in the extent to which the worker is permitted to engage in other activities during the 'on call' time. For example, a doctor might be required to stay in the hospital but provided with sleeping accommodation. These situations challenge the work/non-work binary, because employers will typically argue that a person who is asleep cannot be working, whereas workers will point out that they are not at liberty to do whatever they want during on call time. The CJEU has taken a relatively strict approach to on call time, focusing largely on the worker's location. A worker who is required to be at the workplace will generally be seen as working, even if they are permitted to sleep.[45] If the worker is at home, the time may be work or rest depending on the extent of the constraints they face.[46]

This version of 'on call' time is, at least, a formal part of the working person's employment arrangements. Precarious workers experience an even more pernicious version of this type of time. These workers typically have to make themselves available for work, for example, by logging in to an app and scrolling through potential jobs, but with no guarantee of receiving any work or pay.[47] Employers benefit from having a pool of workers available, but this type of time is not normally paid: inherent in the 'gig' economy is the idea that working people are paid for the tasks they undertake, not for the time they spend working. The UK Supreme Court's decision in the *Uber* case makes some inroads into this problem, by upholding the tribunal's decision that the drivers were 'working' for working time (and minimum wage) purposes when they were logged in to the app and waiting in their vehicles in the relevant area, as well as when they were driving to collect a customer or taking them to their destination.[48] However, given the diversity of precarious jobs, it cannot be assumed that all future cases will be decided in the same way. This is an area in which the right to 'reasonable limitations' on working hours is not being implemented effectively.

---

[42] Case C-84/94 *United Kingdom v Council (Working Time Directive)* [1996] ECR I-5755.
[43] See A Bogg, 'Of Holidays, Work and Humanisation: A Missed Opportunity?' (2009) 34 *European Law Review* 738. Of course, the choice of Sunday has historic religious connotations which may be problematic in making it easier for some groups to have time for religious observance without interfering with the working week, an issue we explore further in chapter 17.
[44] Case C-303/98 *SIMAP v Conselleria de Sanidad y Consumo de la Generalidad Valenciana* EU:C:2000:528, [2000] ECR I-7963, [47].
[45] eg *SIMAP*, above n 44; Case C-151/02 *Landeshauptstadt Kiel v Jaeger* EU:C:2003:437, [2003] ECR I-8389.
[46] See Case C-518/15 *Ville de Nivelles v Matzak* ECLI:EU:C:2018:82, and cases discussed in Leszek Mitrus, 'Defining Working Time Versus Rest Time: An Analysis of the Recent CJEU Case Law on Stand-By Time' (2023) 14 *European Labour Law Journal* 35.
[47] See the literature at n 18, above.
[48] Above n 17.

Another modern problem blurring the lines between work and rest is the use of technology. Even if a worker 'clocks off' and leaves the workplace to go home after doing the relevant number of hours of work permitted by law, they may carry on performing work tasks on their phone or laptop once they have got home.[49] Workers who work from home some or all of the time may find the precise distinction between work and non-work time even harder to identify.[50] While some workers may welcome the flexibility of being able to spend time at home whilst keeping an eye on urgent work matters, others experience stress and burnout through the requirement to be 'always on' and at the employer's disposal even when supposedly resting.[51]

This set of issues has led to increasing interest in the academic literature, some states and the EU in a 'right to disconnect'.[52] This is the idea that the employer would be forbidden from contacting the worker (or perhaps requiring a response) outside formal working hours, perhaps with exceptions for genuine emergencies. The thinking is that this would help to reinstate the formal boundary between work and rest. Again, however, there is a problematic dynamic around interests and choices. As noted above, some workers may prefer to deal with some work issues remotely, and once the employer receives responses from these workers, others may feel pressured to work too, in order to appear committed or to win a promotion. But a complete ban on working remotely outside formal working hours would be difficult to police and might seem intrusive, and might have the counterproductive consequence of forcing workers to spend more time at the office.

Another option, rather than developing a specific 'right to disconnect', may be to ensure that existing limits on working time clearly include this type of work and are effectively monitored and enforced.[53] One possible solution offered by Katsabian is to harness the very technology used to facilitate working from home in order to record working time and make transparent exactly when and for how long a person is working.[54] EU law is already moving in this direction: although the Working Time Directive does not contain any express obligation on Member States to require employers to monitor their workers' working hours, the Court of Justice has held that this is implicit in order to fulfil the Directive's worker-protective purpose.[55] However, there is significant potential for monitoring to contribute to a high-stress atmosphere for workers and to raise privacy concerns where it intrudes into a worker's home.[56] This is an area ripe for regulation.

---

[49] T Katsabian, 'It's the End of Working Time as We Know It: New Challenges to the Concept of Working Time in the Digital Reality' (2020) 65 *McGill Law Journal* 379.

[50] Eurofound, *Right to Disconnect: Exploring Company Practices* (EU, 2021), esp 4–7.

[51] See S Turkle, 'Always-On/Always-On-You: The Tethered Self' in James E Katz and Manuel Castells, *Handbook of Mobile Communication Studies* (Cambridge, MA: MIT Press, 2008).

[52] In the EU, countries including Belgium, France, Greece, Italy, Slovakia and Spain all have versions of this right: Eurofound, *Right to Disconnect*, above n 50, ch 1. See also L Lerouge and F Trujillo Pons, 'Contribution to the Study on the "Right to Disconnect" from Work: Are France and Spain Examples for other Countries and EU law?' (2022) 13 *European Labour Law Journal* 450. The latest position in the EU is set out in A Saliba, 'The Right to Disconnect' (January 2024), available at www.europarl.europa.eu/legislative-train/theme-a-europe-fit-for-the-digital-age/file-al-legislative-proposal-to-the-commission-on-the-right-to-disconnect.

[53] The position varies across EU countries. See Eurofound, above n 50, 12.

[54] Above n 49.

[55] Case C-55/18 *Federación de Servicios de Comisiones Obreras v Deutsche Bank SAE* ECLI:EU:C:2019:402. For the UK position, see Pt 3 of the Employment Rights (Amendment, Revocation and Transitional Provision) Regulations 2023 (SI 2023/1426).

[56] Eurofound, *Employee Monitoring and Surveillance: the Challenges of Digitalisation* (EU, 2020), esp ch 3.

4. Paid Annual Leave

The right to paid annual leave, like the right to reasonable limits on the working week, is also a longstanding concern of the labour movement, and is widely recognised in international human rights instruments. The ICESCR provides in Article 7 for paid public holidays and for a right to paid annual leave, but without specifying a particular duration. The original ESC offered a right to two weeks' paid annual leave, which was increased to four weeks in the 1996 revision.[57] The EU Working Time Directive requires Member States to provide a minimum of four weeks' paid annual leave.[58]

The CJEU has taken a particularly strong stance that the right to paid annual leave is a fundamental social right of working people. It is worth exploring this idea before examining the Court's more detailed rulings, because it has been hugely influential over the Court's approach. The Court's framing of the right first emerged in the *BECTU* case and has been repeated on many subsequent occasions.[59] It reflects the unqualified nature of the right found in the Directive and, of course, its international recognition. Nowadays, the right features in Article 31(2) of the EU Charter of Fundamental Rights (EUCFR), which reinforces its fundamental status.[60] This recognition of the right's importance has generated some significant interpretive principles for the Court, notably a strict insistence that Member States implement the Directive correctly and do not add limitations which are not authorised (as was the case in *BECTU* itself), and the principle that workers should usually be able to take 'actual rest', which we explore in more detail below.[61]

The fundamental status of the right has been further reinforced in some of the Court's more recent decisions relating to horizontal effect. The *Bauer* case concerned a German rule which provided that the payment in lieu of annual leave did not accrue to the worker's estate when the worker's employment terminated upon death.[62] The Court held that the Directive did not establish the right to paid annual leave, which was instead derived from the ESC, ILO instruments and statements of rights at EU level, such as the Community Charter of the Fundamental Social Rights of Workers. Thus, although the claimant could not rely on the Directive against another private party, the employer, because directives do not have horizontal direct effect, it was possible to rely on the right itself, as set out in Article 31(2) EUCFR. This meant that the national court was expected to give effect to the right, for example, by interpreting or disapplying incompatible national rules.

An important feature of the right in the EU context (and in the UK) is that it is a protected choice. There is no compulsion on workers to take their paid annual leave, though the CJEU has recently taken some steps towards ensuring that workers are given a genuine opportunity to exercise their right. In the *Kreuziger* and *Shimizu* cases, workers challenged the compatibility with EU law of German legislation which provided that the worker would forfeit payment in lieu of annual leave on the termination of the employment relationship where the worker had

---

[57] ESC, Article 2(3) (both versions).
[58] Directive 2003/88/EC, Article 7.
[59] Case C-173/99 *R (BECTU) v Secretary of State for Trade and Industry* EU:C:2001:356, [2001] ECR I-4881, [43].
[60] See A Bogg and M Ford, 'Article 31' in S Peers et al (eds) *The EU Charter of Fundamental Rights: A Commentary*, 2nd edn (Hart, 2021).
[61] *BECTU*, above n 59, [43]–[44].
[62] Case C-569/16 *Stadt Wuppertal v Bauer* EU:C:2018:871, [2019] 1 CMLR 36.

not attempted to use their leave before the termination date.[63] The CJEU held that this rule was incompatible with EU law unless the employer could show that it had given the worker an opportunity to exercise the right. This would include encouraging the worker to take leave, providing information about leave entitlements, and making clear the consequences of failing to take leave by the relevant date. Only if it could be shown that the worker had made a deliberate and informed choice not to exercise the right to take leave would it be permissible to forfeit the payment in lieu. The obligation on the employer to facilitate the taking of leave is further reinforced by the decision in *King*, in which it was held that the employer would be liable for a payment in lieu with no limitation, in a case where the worker had been refused paid leave over many years on the basis of an argument by the employer (found by the court to be incorrect) that the individual was self-employed and therefore ineligible.[64]

In addition to this pressure on the employer, there are also a number of features of EU law which seek to nudge workers in the direction of taking leave. One is that it is not possible for the employer to provide a payment in lieu of leave unless the employment relationship is at an end.[65] While this is a highly paternalistic provision, because many workers would prefer to trade their leave for extra money, it does remove a strong disincentive to taking leave. Another is that the CJEU has insisted that leave must be paid at a worker's usual rate.[66] This includes extra payments not labelled as salary provided that they are paid regularly. This helps to ensure that workers do not lose out financially by taking leave, despite the efforts of many employers to stretch the boundaries of this principle, reflected in the large volume of litigation on the point. Relatedly, the CJEU also ruled against the practice of 'rolled-up' holiday pay, in which the worker is paid a higher hourly rate to include some holiday pay, but then not paid when they take time off work.[67] This practice is popular with some workers because of the increase in their hourly rate, but the Court held that it deterred people from taking holiday because they would not be paid when they did so, and it was not reasonable to expect people to save the extra money. The UK Government has reintroduced the possibility of rolled-up holiday pay for workers with irregular hours post-Brexit.[68] It has continued to be used in casual work environments in particular despite the CJEU's ruling. Finally, the CJEU has also been supportive of the idea that a worker who is prevented from taking holiday, for example, because of ill-health, should be able to take the leave at a later date, even if this involves adjusting national rules on the 'carrying over' of leave from one year to the next.[69]

A final point to note about annual leave is that, although its purpose is to give the worker an opportunity to rest (in EU law at least, to protect the worker's health and safety), there is not usually any obligation on the worker to use the time for that purpose.[70] Indeed, the linguistic shift from 'holiday' to 'annual leave' reflects the fact that workers typically use leave for a variety of purposes, including child care and what might be termed 'life admin' as well as for rest and leisure. In some countries, notably Germany, the worker is prohibited from taking paid employment elsewhere during a period of leave. The health and safety justification suggests that the

---

[63] Case C-619/16 *Kreuziger v Land Berlin* EU:C:2018:872, [2019] 1 CMLR 34; Case C-684/16 *Max-Planck-Gesellschaft zur Förderung der Wissenschaften eV v Shimizu* EU:C:2018:874, [2019] 1 CMLR 35.
[64] Case C-214/16 *King v Sash Window Workshop Ltd* EU:C:2017:914, [2018] ICR 693.
[65] Directive 2003/88/EC, Article 7(2).
[66] eg Case C-155/10 *Williams v British Airways Plc* EU:C:2011:588, [2012] ICR 847.
[67] Case C-131/04 *Robinson-Steele v RD Retail Services Ltd* EU:C:2006:177, [2006] ECR I-2531, on which see AL Bogg, 'The Right to Paid Annual Leave in the Court of Justice: The Eclipse of Functionalism' (2006) 31 *European Law Review* 892.
[68] Employment Rights (Amendment, Revocation and Transitional Provision) Regulations 2023 (SI 2023/1426).
[69] eg Case C-520/06 *Stringer v Revenue and Customs Commissioners* EU:C:2009:18, [2009] ECR I-179.
[70] See A Stöhr, 'The purpose of annual leave and its relevance for legislation and interpreting the law' (2024) *International Journal of Comparative Labour Law and Industrial Relations* (forthcoming).

worker's interest in resting should probably be protected by a ban of this kind, whereas if the aim is to protect the worker's choice, that seems likely to include a choice to use the time for any purpose (subject, perhaps, to contractual restrictions on working for a competitor). It is also worth noting that a better work/life balance generally – through shorter working weeks and greater flexibility – might give workers more scope to use their annual leave for genuine rest rather than to juggle other responsibilities.

5. Rights to Leave for Family Reasons

Older human rights instruments focus primarily on maternity leave, and approach the topic from the perspective of a perceived need to 'protect' working mothers. As we noted in chapter 4, while maternity leave serves important purposes, it may also reinforce a perception that women are primarily responsible for childcare. More modern human rights instruments and national laws now incorporate rights to paternity or parental leave, with a view to promoting equal parenting. We examine each type of leave in turn, before offering some broader reflections on these rights.

Article 8 of the original ESC is a good starting-point for the analysis of maternity leave. It provided:

> With a view to ensuring the effective exercise of the right of employed women to protection, the Contracting Parties undertake:
>
> 1. to provide either by paid leave, by adequate social security benefits or by benefits from public funds for women to take leave before and after childbirth up to a total of at least twelve weeks;
> 2. to consider it as unlawful for an employer to give a woman notice of dismissal during her absence on maternity leave or to give her notice of dismissal at such a time that the notice would expire during such absence;
> 3. to provide that mothers who are nursing their infants shall be entitled to sufficient time off for this purpose …[71]

The revised ESC makes two significant changes: the length of leave is increased to 14 weeks, and the right to protection against dismissal applies from when the woman notifies her employer of the pregnancy until the end of her maternity leave.[72] This captures three important points relating to the specific situation of the pregnant woman: the need for paid time off work around the time of childbirth, protection against dismissal and time off for breastfeeding.

EU law largely reflects the ESC. The Pregnant Workers Directive provides for 14 weeks of paid leave, of which at least two must be compulsory, and for protection against dismissal, though it only addresses health and safety issues in relation to breastfeeding.[73] However, practice in EU countries varies enormously.[74] At one extreme, Bulgaria provides over a year of maternity leave, whereas Germany provides 14 weeks. Levels of payment vary, with many Member States providing for full pay throughout, but others providing reduced or variable pay. The UK provides for up to 52 weeks' leave, but 39 weeks' pay, at 90% of average weekly earnings for the first six weeks, and whichever is lower of 90% of average weekly earnings or a fixed sum (currently £172.48 per week) for the remaining 33 weeks. The final 13 weeks of leave are unpaid. Another

---

[71] See also Article 10(2) ICESCR, in a similar vein but with less detail.
[72] ESC (1996), Article 8.
[73] Directive 92/85, esp Articles 8 and 10.
[74] European Parliament, *Maternity and Paternity Leave in the EU* (March 2022), available at www.europarl.europa.eu/RegData/etudes/ATAG/2019/635586/EPRS_ATA(2019)635586_EN.pdf.

variable is compulsion: compulsory leave is two weeks in the UK, but 20 weeks (the full amount of leave available) in Italy. Finally, Sweden appears to offer no maternity leave at all, but this is because it provides a single system of gender-neutral parental leave, with 240 days of paid parental leave available to each parent. Under the shared parental leave scheme in the UK, two parents with responsibility for a child can choose to share the 50 weeks of non-compulsory leave and 37 weeks of pay on the rates set out above.

There are three points to note about these arrangements. First, compulsory maternity leave is controversial. As we noted at the outset, rights relating to working time may protect interests or choices, and compulsory maternity leave is a clear example of the former. Some writers argue that women should be able to decide how much leave to take, though Fredman notes that a short period of compulsory leave may be helpful to protect women against pressure to return to work before they are ready to do so, even if it may also force others into unwanted time away from work.[75] Second, pay is particularly important in ensuring that women can take the leave offered to them, and that it does not become the preserve of the wealthy. Ideally, the state should cover the cost of this leave, so that it does not fall on the employer. This recognises the social importance of having a family, and helps to reduce the risk that employers might discriminate against women who they believe will take time off for maternity leave. Third, it is clear that many EU countries have not caught up with the important equality considerations at play in this area. At one time, it was seen as an important ambition of the women's movement to increase the availability of maternity leave. However, this risks entrenching the stereotype that women are primarily responsible for childcare, even though this can just as easily be shared by both parents. Models such as that in Sweden, which provide leave for both parents, are much more likely to encourage equal parenting.

One measure adopted by some states to encourage fathers to take a greater role in childcare is paternity leave. In EU law, paternity leave was introduced in the Work-Life Balance Directive, with implementation from 2022.[76] This is a right for the 'second' parent to take at least 10 working days of leave around the time of the birth of the child. This must be paid, as a minimum, at the same level as sick pay. Research conducted in 2022 but prior to the implementation date revealed that four Member States provided no paternity leave at all, and another five provided fewer than 10 days.[77] The majority provided either two or four weeks of leave, with a couple of outliers providing longer periods. While paid paternity leave is clearly a good thing, it seems unlikely that these relatively limited rights will do much to promote a culture of equal parenting. This is particularly the case if the leave is optional (which is the case in most Member States) and not paid in full (which varies across the Member States).[78]

Perhaps a more promising option is parental leave. This forms a part of a much more comprehensive right governing the reconciliation of work and family life in Article 27 of the revised ESC, which is worth quoting in full:

With a view to ensuring the exercise of the right to equality of opportunity and treatment for men and women workers with family responsibilities and between such workers and other workers, the Parties undertake:

1. to take appropriate measures:
    a. to enable workers with family responsibilities to enter and remain in employment, as well as to re-enter employment after an absence due to those responsibilities, including measures in the field of vocational guidance and training;

---

[75] Above n 11.
[76] Directive 2019/1158, Article 4.
[77] European Parliament, above n 74.
[78] ibid.

b. to take account of their needs in terms of conditions of employment and social security;
   c. to develop or promote services, public or private, in particular child daycare services and other childcare arrangements;
2. to provide a possibility for either parent to obtain, during a period after maternity leave, parental leave to take care of a child, the duration and conditions of which should be determined by national legislation, collective agreements or practice;
3. to ensure that family responsibilities shall not, as such, constitute a valid reason for termination of employment.

While this is vague as to the details, it states clearly that parental leave should be available to either parent, and situates it clearly within an equality framework, both between men and women and between workers who are parents and workers who are not. In EU law, there is a requirement under the Work-Life Balance Directive to provide a minimum of four months of parental leave, at least two months of which should not be transferable between parents.[79] Member States must also make provision for payment for the two non-transferable months.[80] The leave may be taken flexibly rather than in blocks, though the details are left to the Member States to determine.[81] In the UK, in addition to the right to shared parental leave, discussed above, there is a right to 18 weeks' unpaid parental leave, which can generally only be taken in one-week blocks.[82] The importance of parental leave is that it is open to both parents in a couple and, particularly when some of the leave is non-transferable, there is an incentive on each parent to take some leave, otherwise the right will be lost. This is a useful way of shaping people's preferences without compelling them to act in particular ways. However, where the right is unpaid, it may be difficult for some parents to take advantage of it. This may also have discriminatory consequences where one parent (often the father) earns more than the other (often the mother), because the lower-earning parent may come under pressure to be the one who takes time off.

There are three broader points to note about these various forms of leave. First, taking the UK as an example, these various forms of leave are provided to working people who are classified as 'employees' rather than 'workers', often with a period of qualifying employment to be completed before they become entitled.[83] This partly reflects the way in which these rights have developed over time, but may also indicate a view that it does not make sense for people with precarious working arrangements – who work intermittently anyway – to have formal leave from work. However, the practical effect of this is that a person with a precarious working arrangement who needs to take a break from the labour market for maternity or childcare reasons will have no guarantee of being able to return to their former role when they are ready to do so, because their right to return is not protected in law and the employer will usually have found other casual workers to fill the gap. This situation is hard to defend from an equality perspective. Second, and relatedly, where leave is unpaid or not paid at the worker's full wage, it is much less likely to be used. A right to take unpaid leave does not protect a worker's choice very effectively if the worker simply cannot afford to choose the leave. As noted above, the cost of providing leave need not fall on the employer. Third, while leave is an important right to help parents balance work and family life, for example, by allowing them to take time off during school holidays, it can only ever be for limited periods of time. Enabling parents to work more sensible or flexible hours in

---

[79] Directive 2019/1158, Article 5.
[80] ibid Article 8.
[81] ibid Article 5(6).
[82] Employment Rights Act 1996, s 76; Maternity and Parental Leave etc Regulations 1999 (SI 1999/3312), regs 13–16A.
[83] eg Maternity and Parental Leave etc Regulations 1999 (SI 1999/3312), reg 13(1).

general terms may be more helpful. Limiting the working week arguably benefits all workers, but it benefits parents in particular. Another option is to provide rights relating to flexible working, to which we will now turn.

6. Rights Relating to the Organisation of Working Time

In this section, we consider a group of rights which can be summarised as 'rights relating to the organisation of working time'. This may seem like an odd idea. Surely it is for the employer, as the person paying for the work, to decide when it takes place? Indeed, the power to decide when work takes place has often been seen as a key indicator of the presence of an employment relationship between the parties.[84] One way to get greater worker input into the organisation of working time is through collective bargaining: as we have seen, trade unions have often concerned themselves with long hours working or overtime payments. The Working Time Directive also recognises the general importance of organisation of working time in Article 13 on 'Pattern of work': 'Member states shall take the measures necessary to ensure that an employer who intends to organise work according to a certain pattern takes account of the general principle of adapting work to the worker.'[85] To date, this 'humanisation of work' principle has had limited regulatory effects. But the law nowadays offers some legal options for individual workers to request adjustments to their working hours.

One route to achieving control over working hours is through a duty placed on the employer to accommodate the employee for a particular reason. A key example of this is disability discrimination law, where it is recognised that equal treatment will often be insufficient to ensure the individual's full participation in the labour market.[86] The employer might be required to offer different or more flexible working hours in order to enable the worker to manage their workload in the context of their medical condition. As we shall see in chapter 17, attempts by employees to get their working hours changed to fit around their religious observance (where there is typically no duty to accommodate) have been less successful. The ECtHR's early decisions indicated that it was the employee's responsibility to find a job which did not interfere with their religious observance.[87] However, there are signs that, in future, a proportionality approach would be used, so the employer would be required to demonstrate that a duty on the employee to work at a particular time was a proportionate means of achieving a legitimate aim within the business.[88] This would depend on the facts of the case.

Another option is a more general right to request flexible working. This right applies in EU law to parents of children under the age of eight, and to carers,[89] and in the UK, to all employees.[90] The use of the term 'request' is significant. The right does not reverse the basic assumption that it is for the employer to decide the employee's working arrangements. But it does provide an

---

[84] eg *Ready Mixed Concrete (South East) Ltd v Minister of Pensions and National Insurance* [1968] 2 QB 497, 515.
[85] For discussion of this principle, see Bogg and Ford, above n 10.
[86] Equality Act 2010, s 20, and see chapter 4.
[87] See eg *X v UK*, Commission Decision, 12 March 1981; *Stedman v United Kingdom* (1997) 23 EHRR CD 168.
[88] *Eweida v United Kingdom* (2013) 57 EHRR 8, [83].
[89] Directive 2019/1158/EU on work-life balance for parents and carers, Article 9. Member States may, of course, make the right more widely available.
[90] Employment Rights Act 1996, ss 80F–80I. This was originally subject to a 26-week qualifying period, but this was repealed in April 2024 when the Employment Relations (Flexible Working) Act 2023, s 1, and the Flexible Working (Amendment) Regulations 2023 (SI 2023/1328) entered into force.

opportunity to ask the employer to consider other options. These do not necessarily relate to working hours – the right can be used to vary the place of work, for example – but the right is often used to request reduced or flexible hours. A cynic might respond that a right to 'request' is useless: it is always possible to ask an employer for a change in one's terms and conditions, but there is no guarantee of success. However, this type of legal right places a process around the employer's discretion – requiring the employer to consider the request within a specific timeframe, for example – and limits the reasons the employer can give for refusing the request.[91] While a determined employer may still be able to resist, others may be prompted to consider flexibility where this had not previously been offered. The Covid-19 pandemic has also contributed to this change because the period of enforced working from home highlighted, for some people at least, the benefits of greater flexibility. TUC evidence in the UK suggests that the majority of rights to request flexible working are agreed by employers.[92]

One noticeable difference between the EU and UK approaches is that the former is confined to parents and carers, whereas the UK, having initially gone down the same route, now makes the right more widely available. A significant benefit of the more general approach is that it avoids intrusive enquiries by employers about a person's family responsibilities, and reduces the risk that employers might avoid employing parents because they might want to exercise the right. However, a more general right groups together people with strong reasons for requiring flexibility with people who simply prefer a different pattern of working. This may mean that the right is not taken so seriously.

A final point to note is that the right to request flexible working tends to be a right for the privileged: in the UK case, 'employees' rather than 'workers', typically in stable jobs with fixed working hours.[93] A person working on a casual basis will usually be a 'worker', so legally ineligible for the right, and would in any event find it difficult to claim flexibility when they do not have a stable working relationship to start with. This highlights a key division in the labour market that is obscured by undifferentiated use of the term 'flexibility': between stable work that is adapted to the employee through the right to request flexible working, and employer-friendly flexibility that leaves precarious workers at the employer's beck and call, with less opportunity to fit their work around their other commitments.[94] A right to have a say in the organisation of working time would need to apply to both groups of working people in order to be truly effective.

In the EU, the Directive on Transparent and Predictable Working Conditions makes some tentative steps towards addressing the needs of precarious workers for more reliable working hours.[95] First, it requires that workers whose work schedule is unpredictable may only be required to work within 'predetermined reference hours and days' and if they are given reasonable notice.[96] They should not be penalised for turning down a shift where either (or both) of these conditions is (are) not met. Second, once a shift has been assigned to a worker, Member States must provide for the worker to be compensated if it is cancelled 'after a specified reasonable deadline'.[97] From a working time perspective, the first of these is particularly important, since it gives workers a clear indication of when they cannot be called in to work at all, and gives them the opportunity to turn down last-minute shifts without suffering adverse

---

[91] Employment Rights Act 1996, s 80G, and see *Commotion Ltd v Rutty* [2006] ICR 290.
[92] TUC, *The Future of Flexible Work* (June 2021), available at https://www.tuc.org.uk/research-analysis/reports/future-flexible-work?page=6.
[93] Employment Rights Act 1996, s 80F.
[94] See Fredman, above n 19.
[95] Directive 2019/1152/EU on transparent and predictable working conditions in the European Union.
[96] ibid Article 10.
[97] ibid Article 10(3).

consequences. However, two problems remain: workers may not feel able to turn down shifts, even if they have a legal right to do so, because of the financial consequences, and employers may have subtle ways of penalising them which may be difficult to challenge in court. For example, it would be hard to prove that the worker had been offered slightly fewer shifts for a few weeks as a punishment.

Another option, found in both the Directive[98] and the Workers (Predictable Terms and Conditions) Act 2023 in the UK, is to give precarious workers the right to request a more stable contract. The Act uses the same mechanism as the right to request flexible working for traditional employees: the employer must consider the request according to the process set out in the statute and can only reject it on the listed grounds. However, although circumstances may vary widely, there is a significant difference between the two rights. Where an employee has a stable job but wishes to perform it in a different way, the employer may incur some inconvenience but is unlikely to incur significant additional costs. But where the worker has a precarious job and is seeking more work or more stable work, two of the legitimate reasons given in the Act for rejecting the request are likely to come into play: 'the burden of additional costs' and 'insufficiency of work during the periods the worker proposes to work'.[99] It seems likely that a higher proportion of these requests will be turned down by employers.

7. Conclusion

As this chapter has demonstrated, the right to reasonable limitation of working hours continues to capture a central concern of working people: that working lives should be organised in such a way as to enable them to earn a decent living, whilst having sufficient time available for other activities unrelated to work. Although this ambition has manifested itself in different ways over the years – from early campaigns to limit the working week, to more modern concerns with the right to disconnect – the underlying problem is fundamentally the same. In entering into an employment relationship, the working person inevitably cedes some control over their time to the employer, but the employer's control should not be without boundaries. It is these boundaries that the right seeks to police.

---

[98] ibid Article 12.
[99] Workers (Predictable Terms and Conditions) Act 2023, s 80IC(1)(c).

12
Business, Supply Chains and Human Rights

1. Background
2. Self-Regulation by MNCs
3. Home State Initiatives
4. International Initiatives
5. Conclusion

Much of our discussion in this book has been concerned with the regulation of employment relationships, and the human rights dimensions of those relationships, within a particular state. In this chapter, we turn to a complex set of problems surrounding the regulation of employment relationships across national borders, in the corporate structures and supply chains[1] of multinational companies (MNCs). The central question to be addressed is: should a large MNC be responsible for ensuring that its subsidiaries and suppliers respect workers' fundamental human rights, even if this is not required by the authorities in the 'host' states in which they are operating? And if the answer to that question is yes, which regulatory technique or combination of techniques should be used to impose that responsibility since, *ex hypothesi*, regulation by the host state is lacking?

The chapter begins by unpacking the assumptions underpinning these questions, before examining three main regulatory options: self-regulation by MNCs themselves, regulation by so-called 'home' states in which MNCs are headquartered, or international initiatives addressing all parties to the problem. This is a big topic which has generated a huge number of different types of initiative, so we will not be able to cover them all in detail, but we will attempt to explore three main questions. First, what is the coverage of any particular initiative, both in terms of the workers it seeks to protect and the labour rights it covers? Second, how, if at all, are standards monitored and enforced? And third, to what extent, if at all, does the mechanism enable the voices of affected workers to be heard?

1. Background

Over the course of the 20th century, as it became easier to transport goods around the world and to communicate quickly and cheaply with people in other countries, firms began to close their manufacturing bases in the Global North – with relatively high production costs – and purchase components or goods from firms in the Global South at lower cost.[2] In some cases,

---

[1] Note that despite the linear implications of the word 'chain', this metaphor usually describes a complex, multidimensional network of different firms involved in the process of turning raw materials into goods for sale.

[2] For a historical overview, see MJ Trebilcock, R Howse and A Eliason, *The Regulation of International Trade*, 4th edn (Routledge, 2013) ch 1.

this has also extended to services, with many firms outsourcing their call centres or 'back office' functions to low-cost locations. The cost-benefit analysis of the changes brought about by this process of globalisation is, inevitably, complex. Workers in the Global North, particularly in manufacturing, have lost their jobs, but consumers have benefited from lower prices. Workers in the Global South have gained access to new sources of work and income, but wider economic benefits may not always have materialised because MNCs' profits are typically realised elsewhere.

We can only touch briefly here on the factors driving the process of globalisation. For many states in the Global South, a key source of comparative advantage over states in the Global North is a plentiful supply of workers who are willing to work for lower wages.[3] This is regarded as a legitimate form of competition in a capitalist market system. But it ceases to be legitimate where those lower wages are below a decent minimum for the country concerned, or where low labour costs are achieved by disregarding other rights such as health and safety standards. So how does this come about?[4] One factor is pressure from MNCs on suppliers or prospective suppliers to keep costs down in order to retain or win lucrative contracts.[5] There is a constant threat of losing business to competitors who are willing to supply the same goods at an even lower price. Another, linked, factor is pressure from MNCs on states. A state might be tempted to put a stop to the downward spiral by promoting collective bargaining or setting a minimum wage, but the threat that national firms might lose out to firms in other states with less regulation applies here too. This is sometimes framed in terms of a 'race to the bottom' in labour standards, as states compete to attract investment by lowering the level of regulation.[6] While the idea of a 'race to the bottom' may be exaggerated, there is certainly some pressure on states not to regulate. There may also be challenges in setting up an effective regime of labour inspection and enforcement when a state with limited resources has many other calls on its budget. This can result in a situation in which labour exploitation in supply chains is commonplace, but MNCs can defend themselves by claiming that they are in full compliance with local laws and standards.[7]

The perception that host states cannot or will not regulate MNCs has led to the development of three main groups of alternative regulatory strategies. In practice, the groups are not analytically watertight, but it helps to separate them for the purposes of exposition and critical analysis. One group consists of self-regulatory initiatives by MNCs themselves. MNCs with a strong brand identity, such as major retailers, may be the subject of adverse media attention and consumer boycotts if poor labour standards are detected in their supply chains. This has prompted many MNCs to draw up their own 'code of conduct' for subsidiaries and suppliers, or to sign up to a code drawn up by a non-governmental organisation (NGO). Another group of initiatives involves action by the home states of MNCs, typically wealthier states of the Global North. These states may place obligations on MNCs headquartered in their jurisdiction to *report* on any steps they are taking or, more strongly, to *take steps* to eliminate human rights abuses from their supply chains. Another option may be to sue the parent company in the home state (which is likely to

---

[3] See Trebilcock et al, above n 2, for a useful explanation of comparative advantage.

[4] For an argument that globalisation is inherently incompatible with human rights, see eg Paul O'Connell, 'On Reconciling Irreconcilables: Neo-liberal Globalisation and Human Rights' (2007) 7 *Human Rights Law Review* 483.

[5] See M Anner, 'CSR Participation Committees, Wildcat Strikes and the Sourcing Squeeze in Global Supply Chains' (2018) 56 *International Journal of Employment Relations* 75; ILO, *Decent Work in Global Supply Chains* (2016) ch 2. But see also M Starmanns, *Purchasing Practices and Low Wages in Global Supply Chains: Empirical Cases from the Garment Industry* (ILO, 2017) for challenges facing purchasers in improving wage levels.

[6] For discussion, see BA Hepple, *Labour Laws and Global Trade* (Hart, 2005) ch 1.

[7] Some of the challenges for MNCs in operating in states with inadequate regulation are explored in A Griffith, L Smit and R McCorquodale, 'Responsible Business Conduct and State Laws: Addressing Human Rights Conflicts' (2020) 20 *Human Rights Law Review* 641.

have more resources) for compensation for losses suffered as a result of human rights abuses in the supply chain. A third group of initiatives arise at the international level. Early schemes, such as the International Labour Organization (ILO) and Organisation for Economic Co-operation and Development (OECD) codes, focused principally on the activities of MNCs themselves.[8] More recent efforts have sought to strike a balance between the responsibilities of MNCs and states, though agreement on a legally binding treaty on the subject remains elusive.

This chapter explores three key questions in relation to these various measures. One relates to their scope: which labour rights do they include? A common problem is focusing on a very narrow range of labour rights, such as slavery and forced labour, rather than trying to tackle exploitation in broader terms. Another set of questions looks at how MNCs' behaviour is monitored and what enforcement actions are taken when breaches are uncovered. A particular worry is that firms may commit to certain standards without putting in place effective checks on compliance, so that the whole process is little more than 'window-dressing'. Alternatively, firms may react to instances of non-compliance by taking extreme measures, such as dropping a supplier. While this removes the breach of labour rights from the MNC's supply chain, it does little to help the affected workers, who are left with no job at all. A third issue is whether any of these initiatives does enough to ascertain and act on the preferences of the affected working people.[9] While it may arguably be necessary as a temporary measure to use international or extraterritorial strategies to tackle human rights abuses in supply chains, it is clearly not desirable over the longer term that host states or workers should remain disempowered. Engaging with workers themselves could help to identify ways of supporting them both to bargain with their employer and to campaign for reform more widely within their state.

2. Self-Regulation by MNCs

A corporation wishing to enforce ethical standards through its supply chain can either develop its own code of practice,[10] or adopt one developed by a non-governmental organisation (NGO).[11] There is also a UN-led initiative, the UN Global Compact, which firms can join.[12] Although this is obviously international, given the involvement of the UN, it has more in common with corporate and other codes, and will therefore be considered here.

In terms of content, a number of these initiatives draw on the ILO Declaration of Fundamental Principles and Rights at Work ('ILO Declaration') which was proclaimed in 1998 during something of an identity crisis for the ILO.[13] There was a perception that, while the ILO was good at developing detailed labour standards through Conventions, it was less good at promoting and enforcing labour rights on the world stage.[14] The ILO responded by identifying

---

[8] ILO, Tripartite Declaration of Principles concerning Multinational Enterprises and Social Policy (1977, as amended); OECD, Guidelines for Multinational Enterprises (1976, as amended).

[9] For critique, see eg PC Zumbansen, 'Law as Critical Cartography: Global Value Chains, Borders, and the Spatialization of Vulnerability', McGill SGI Research Papers in Business, Finance, Law and Society, Research Paper No 2023-04.

[10] For an overview, see L Compa and T Hinchliffe-Darricarrere, 'Enforcing International Labor Rights through Corporate Codes of Conduct' (1995) 33 *Columbia Journal of Transnational Law* 663.

[11] There is growing interest in shareholder activism to encourage corporations to comply with environmental, social and governance standards (ESG). We do not have space to explore this option here.

[12] https://unglobalcompact.org/.

[13] ILO Declaration of Fundamental Principles and Rights at Work (1998, amended 2022).

[14] For discussion, see P Alston, '"Core Labour Standards" and the Transformation of the International Labour Rights Regime' (2004) 15 *European Journal of International Law* 457; BA Langille, 'Core Labour Rights: The True Story' (2005) 16 *European Journal of International Law* 409.

freedom of association, equality, freedom from forced labour and freedom from child labour as 'core' labour rights. In 2022, health and safety was added to the list.[15] The ILO itself used the Declaration to encourage states to ratify the Conventions associated with these rights, and directed a lot of its technical support activity to encouraging greater compliance with them. However, an important side-effect of the Declaration is that it has become a focal point for corporate codes of conduct. For example, the UN Global Compact includes the four original principles from the Declaration.

There are some obvious advantages and disadvantages to corporate initiatives focused around the Declaration. On the one hand, the Declaration does capture some very fundamental labour rights. The inclusion of freedom of association is particularly important. Firms might be tempted to ignore this right because it poses challenges to their authority to determine terms and conditions of employment, but if it is respected, it has the potential to empower workers to improve their terms and conditions of employment in ways not mentioned by the Declaration itself.[16] On the other hand, the Declaration is extremely narrow. The Ethical Trading Initiative (ETI), a code which is popular with many UK-based retailers, adds a number of other requirements, including the payment of a living wage, the provision of regular employment, and the avoidance of excessive working hours.[17] While the promotion of freedom of association and collective bargaining may enable workers to secure some of these benefits for themselves, it may be preferable to insist on observance of the basic conditions of decent work via a code in the first instance.

A common criticism of corporate and other codes is that it is relatively easy for a firm to sign up, but less clear that there is any meaningful impact from doing so. One question is whether firms make an effort to monitor compliance.[18] In theory at least, the very presence of a code should provide an economic incentive to engage in some monitoring: if a firm has committed itself publicly to particular standards, adverse publicity and reputational damage will ensue if trade unions, NGOs or journalists uncover evidence of breaches, or if there is a scandal such as a serious health and safety incident.[19] Many firms engaged in audit or management consultancy offer a monitoring service. Some codes have sought to supplement this with some kind of reporting mechanism. For example, the UN Global Compact encourages firms to fill in a 'Communication on Progress' questionnaire.[20] The contents are telling. Statistical data is collected on a few issues, such as the gender pay gap and the accident rate within the firm. In other areas, the focus is on the firm's policies on labour rights issues (with some attention to their content), and whether it has engaged with stakeholders or taken action to prevent or mitigate risks associated with particular labour rights. The questionnaire asks about the content of a firm's policy on freedom of association and about details of any collective agreements, but there is no requirement to have a policy on collective bargaining and no requirement to submit information about

---

[15] ILO Press Release 10 June 2022, International Labour Conference adds safety and health to Fundamental Principles and Rights at Work.
[16] See Hepple, above n 6.
[17] www.ethicaltrade.org/.
[18] For a critical account of audit efforts, see S Kuruvilla and N Li, 'The Reliability of Supplier Data and the Unique Role of Audit Consultants' in S Kuruvilla (ed), *Private Regulation of Labor Standards in Global Supply Chains* (Cornell University Press, 2021).
[19] Many MNCs were prompted to act by the Rana Plaza disaster, in which over 1,000 workers were killed and thousands more injured when a garment factory (in which clothes were made for many well-known brands) in Bangladesh collapsed. See A Trebilcock, 'The Rana Plaza Disaster Seven Years On: Transnational Experiments and Perhaps a New Treaty?' (2020) 159 *International Labour Review* 545.
[20] https://unglobalcompact.org/participation/report/cop.

collective bargaining coverage. Even where this kind of initiative collects useful information, there is a lot of work to be done in analysing the results. The assumption seems to be that trade unions, NGOs and journalists will make use of the material, but they may lack the resources to do so.

Another issue is how the corporation reacts if it discovers a breach of its code. From a business perspective, the simplest and most obvious thing to do is to terminate the contract of the offending supplier.[21] However, as the example of child labour illustrates, this can be highly problematic: termination would leave the affected children and their families worse off financially, and is unlikely to result in better outcomes, such as the children going to school. The ETI frames the obligation relating to child labour carefully (emphasis added):

> There shall be no *new* recruitment of child labour.[22]
>
> Companies shall develop or participate in and contribute to policies and programmes which provide for the *transition* of any child found to be performing child labour to enable her or him to attend and remain in quality education until no longer a child; 'child' and 'child labour' being defined in the appendices.[23]

There is also a complex issue surrounding the allocation of responsibility for breaches of workers' rights in supply chains. The adoption of a code tends to create the impression that multinationals are themselves supportive of workers' rights, but are let down by bad actors in distant corners of the supply chain. However, to take so-called 'fast fashion' as an example, a firm which requires a supplier to produce a new line of clothing with a very quick turnaround to respond to a trend may be contributing to the problem.[24] For example, the only way for the supplier to fulfil the order in time may be to require its workers to work dangerously long hours. While regulatory failures in the host state may mean that there is no working time legislation or, more likely, no effective enforcement of working time legislation, MNCs themselves are usually responsible for the commercial pressure which leads to long hours working. Of course, the presence of a corporate code may provide suppliers with some leverage – if the MNC wants safe working practices, it may have to pay more or wait longer for the goods – but suppliers are always vulnerable to being undercut by competitors. In short, it is not clear how effective corporate codes are likely to be in tackling the deeper structural problems which lead to labour rights violations in supply chains.

Finally, it seems likely that corporate initiatives have varying degrees of success in relation to worker voice.[25] Although the UN Global Compact and the ETI code, among others, address freedom of association, codes drafted by firms themselves are less likely to prioritise or even include this right. This reduces the chances of workers being able to influence their own terms and conditions of employment. While firms often engage with NGOs, it is important to examine whether the claim of any particular NGO to speak on behalf of a group of workers is borne out by the facts.

---

[21] See S Dadush, 'Contracting for Human Rights: Looking to Version 2.0 of the ABA Model Contract Clauses' (2018–19) 68 *American University Law Review* 1519.
[22] ETI Base Code, above n 17, para 4.1.
[23] ibid para 4.2.
[24] ILO, above n 5, ch 2.
[25] For discussion of some of the challenges, see M Fischer-Daly and C Raymond, 'Freedom of Association and Collective Bargaining in Global Supply Chains' in S Kuruvilla (ed), *Private Regulation of Labor Standards in Global Supply Chains: Problems, Progress, and Prospects* (Cornell University Press, 2023); S Zajak, 'Channels for Workers' Voice in the Transnational Governance of Labour Rights?' (2017) 8 *Global Policy* 530.

3. Home State Initiatives

We turn now to strategies which might be employed in the home states of MNCs, where the parent company in the group or the owner of the brand at the top of the supply chain has its headquarters. There is a certain logic to home state action. If host states are unable or unwilling to regulate, home states seem to be the obvious alternative. They can tackle the problem from the top down, focusing on the people in charge and the firms with the deepest pockets (which is particularly important from the perspective of liability to pay compensation). But there are concerns and criticisms too. One problem is that home states' motives may be questioned: are they genuinely concerned about the rights of workers around the world, or are they attempting to protect the interests of their own labour markets (by reducing competition from elsewhere) or even to engage in some kind of neo-colonial attempt to export their own norms to other countries?[26] Another, more prosaic problem is that these initiatives may simply be ineffective. In particular, the focus on the firm at the top of the supply chain raises the problem that it may simply deny responsibility for legally separate firms at the bottom, or claim that it did all it could reasonably have been expected to do to ensure that they did not infringe workers' rights. We will consider two main examples here: legislation requiring firms to report on their efforts to protect workers' rights in their supply chains or to adopt particular approaches to monitor supply chains, such as human rights due diligence (HRDD), and claims against MNCs in contract or tort.

Disclosure and Due Diligence Legislation

A number of states have legislated to require multinational corporations headquartered in their jurisdiction to report on the measures they are taking to combat abuses of labour rights in their supply chains.[27] Some of the earlier measures were relatively light-touch, simply requiring firms to report, but more recent initiatives have become more prescriptive about the measures a firm should be taking. As we shall see, reporting obligations rely on the assumption that firms will want to maintain a positive reputation in order to discourage them from failing to report, reporting untruthfully or reporting that their efforts are minimal or non-existent. They are a form of 'naming and shaming'. However, the effectiveness of this type of regulatory strategy depends on whether a firm's public reputation is important to its business, and on whether NGOs, journalists or others read and publicise the contents of the disclosures.

Section 54 of the Modern Slavery Act 2015 in the UK is an example of a disclosure obligation at the light-touch end of the spectrum.[28] Firms with a turnover of more than £36 million are obliged to make a statement of the steps they are taking, if any, to combat modern slavery in their own business and in their supply chain. In theory at least, the Secretary of State may seek an injunction to require a firm to produce a statement if it fails to do so, but at the time of writing, this power has never been used.[29] One particular problem with the UK legislation is that the identification of firms in terms of annual turnover means that only the firms themselves

---

[26] For a powerful response to this claim, see D Palombo, 'Transnational Business and Human Rights Litigation: An Imperialist Project?' (2022) 22 *Human Rights Law Review* 1.
[27] There is growing interest in legislating to regulate corporate ESG disclosures to shareholders, but this is not discussed here for reasons of space.
[28] For discussion, see V Mantouvalou, 'The UK Modern Slavery Act 2015 Three Years On' (2018) 81 *MLR* 1017.
[29] Modern Slavery Act 2015, s 54(11).

can determine whether they reach the threshold, making it difficult for the Secretary of State (as the enforcement authority) or any other interested party to draw up a definitive list of the firms which should be producing statements. Another problem is that there is no obligation on a firm to state that it is taking any steps: if it has chosen not to address modern slavery at all (and is prepared to take the reputational consequences), it may make a statement to that effect.[30] Finally, and most obviously, the Act is concerned only with 'modern slavery': slavery, forced labour and trafficking. It does not address other serious violations such as hazardous working conditions or a ban on unionising. After a critical independent review of the Act, the Government accepted that there were problems and proposed some modest reforms, but little action has been forthcoming and it is not clear that they remain part of the Government's policy agenda.[31]

Other states in Europe have adopted more rigorous legislation. In Norway, legislation enacted in 2021 and entering into force in 2022 requires larger firms either headquartered in Norway or liable to pay tax there to carry out due diligence in accordance with the OECD Guidelines for Multinational Enterprises (discussed below).[32] The due diligence must relate to 'fundamental human rights and decent working conditions'.[33] This is broad in scope, since it is not confined to a narrow set of labour rights (such as those in the ILO Declaration) and could include wages and working hours, among other things. Due diligence requires the MNC to 'identify and assess actual and potential adverse impacts' which the firm has caused or to which it has contributed, or which are 'directly linked' to it via the supply chain.[34] Again, this seems to be a relatively broad definition of the firm's responsibility, though it will no doubt be open to interpretation in practice. The Act expressly includes an obligation to provide remedies as well as to mitigate adverse effects.[35] However, its impact may be undermined by the statement that the requirement to conduct due diligence should be proportionate to the firm's likely effect on human rights.[36] This may enable some firms to classify themselves as 'low risk' and escape some of the more searching obligations by that means. The legislation also requires firms to publish an annual account of their activities and to respond to requests for information.[37] This may be helpful in enabling journalists, NGOs, trade unions and others to identify and publicise problems as a means of encouraging firms to comply, although, as noted above, this depends on these actors having sufficient resources to do so.

At the time of writing, the EU is in the process of agreeing the Corporate Sustainability Due Diligence Directive (CSDDD).[38] This Directive will require each Member State to ensure that large firms with their registered office in that Member State 'conduct human rights and environmental due diligence' as laid down in the Directive.[39] It also applies to larger firms established in third countries.[40] The Annex to the proposed Directive lists a wide range of sources for human

---

[30] Modern Slavery Act 2015, s 54(4)(b).
[31] Home Office, *Independent Review of the Modern Slavery Act: Final Report* (May 2019); *Government Response to the Independent Review of the Modern Slavery Act* (July 2019).
[32] M Krajewski, K Tonstad and F Wohltmann, 'Mandatory Human Rights Due Diligence in Germany and Norway: Stepping, or Striding, in the Same Direction?' (2021) 6 *Business and Human Rights Journal* 550. An English language version of the Act is available at: https://lovdata.no/dokument/NLE/lov/2021-06-18-99/%C2%A72#%C2%A72.
[33] Transparency Act (Norway), s 4.
[34] ibid.
[35] ibid.
[36] ibid.
[37] ibid, ss 5–7.
[38] The final text has not yet emerged from the legislative process, so the discussion here is based on the Commission's original proposal: Commission, Proposal for a Directive on Corporate Sustainability Due Diligence and amending Directive (EU) 2019/1937 (COM(2022) 71 final). The text as enacted may be different.
[39] ibid Article 4. The scope of the draft Directive is set out in Article 2.
[40] ibid Article 2.

rights, going beyond the core ILO Conventions and including rights in the Universal Declaration of Human Rights (UDHR), International Covenant on Civil and Political Rights (ICCPR) and International Covenant on Economic, Social and Cultural Rights (ICESCR). The precise due diligence requirements laid down by the Directive include having a due diligence policy, identifying actual and potential adverse impacts, preventing or mitigating those impacts and ending adverse impacts.[41] Firms are to provide a complaints procedure for affected individuals, trade unions and NGOs, and to publish details of their due diligence activities in their annual report (unless already subject to other corporate reporting obligations).[42] Importantly, though, the Directive goes beyond reporting: Member States are required to put in place a supervisory authority with the power to impose sanctions linked to the firm's turnover if national obligations derived from the Directive are not met.[43] It is worth noting that this would represent a significant shift from older schemes requiring firms to report on activities largely of their own choosing, towards a much stricter approach in which firms are expected to have a particular set of policies and practices in place.

Civil Liability for Human Rights Abuses

Another possible route for dealing with human rights abuses in supply chains is through litigation. In some respects, the most obvious targets are the firms at the bottom of the supply chain which could be sued, for example, in employment or personal injury law, in the 'host' country. However, there have been a number of attempts to litigate against the firm at the top of the supply chain in its home jurisdiction, which will often be the US or the UK. This may happen either because the law or the legal system is deficient in the host country, so that it is difficult to establish liability, or, more often, because the firm at the bottom of the supply chain has limited resources.[44] The firm at the top of the supply chain typically has much deeper pockets. Most claims have been made in contract or tort,[45] but there are usually several legal obstacles to overcome, as well as the obvious practical hurdles of international litigation, even with the support of NGOs.

For some years, it seemed as if tort claims in the US would be the most promising avenue to pursue.[46] Many major transnational corporations are domiciled in the US. The Alien Tort Claims Act appeared to allow a claim to be brought in a US court in respect of a violation of *ius cogens* norms committed anywhere in the world against a US-domiciled defendant.[47] While not all labour violations reach the level of *ius cogens*, some of the most serious ones, such as the use of forced labour, would probably do so. However, in the *Kiobel* decision, the court applied a presumption against the extraterritorial application of US law.[48] This meant that the facts of any case had to 'touch and concern' the US in order to fall within the courts' jurisdiction. The exact parameters of this phrase are unclear, and it is open to interpretation by other courts, but it makes it much more difficult to use the Alien Tort Claims Act in a supply chain situation.

---

[41] ibid Articles 4–8.
[42] ibid Articles 9 and 10–11.
[43] ibid Articles 17–20.
[44] See GL Skinner with R Chambers and S McGrath, *Transnational Corporations and Human Rights* (Cambridge University Press, 2020) ch 3.
[45] A false or misleading advertising claim is another possibility, but this is more readily available to consumers rather than workers: A Reddy, 'Nike Settles With Activist In False-Advertising Case', Washington Post (13 September 2003).
[46] R Chambers and G Berger-Walliser, 'The Future of International Corporate Human Rights Litigation: A Transatlantic Comparison' (2021) 58 *American Business Law Journal* 579.
[47] Alien Tort Statute (US) 1789, 28 USC § 1350 (2012).
[48] *Kiobel v Royal Dutch Petroleum Co* 569 US 108, 109–10 (2013).

In the UK, there are two possible routes to establishing liability: vicarious liability or direct liability on the part of the parent company.[49] Vicarious liability is almost impossible to use in the supply chain context, because it requires a relationship 'akin to employment' between the defendant (the company at the top of the supply chain) and the tortfeasor (the company lower down in the supply chain which has harmed the claimant worker).[50] Although vicarious liability has been broadened in recent years, it does not apply where the tortfeasor is an independent contractor as against the defendant, which is typically the case in the scenario we are considering. However, there is a possibility of establishing a form of direct liability on the part of the parent company by applying the ordinary rules on duty of care, following the approach in *Vedanta*.[51] Thus, a parent company might be liable if it issued group-wide policies which were followed by a subsidiary and were the source of the harm, where it controlled the operations of the subsidiary in ways which made it responsible for harm, or where it held itself out as controlling the subsidiary but then failed to do so. For example, in *Chandler*, it was established that a parent company was liable in negligence to the employees of a subsidiary whose health had been damaged by the subsidiary's failure to take proper safety precautions when producing asbestos.[52] The parent company's liability was established because it had set up the manufacturing process and handed it over to the subsidiary.

A promising feature of *Vedanta* is that it allows for various possibilities for parent company liability even in the case of separate legal entities with limited control. For example, it might be argued that by publishing a corporate code of conduct, a parent firm had held itself out as controlling the activities of subsidiaries, so that it could be liable if workers were harmed as a result of non-compliance. However, a number of problems remain.[53] First, the tort route is unlikely to capture the full range of labour violations. It is much more promising for health and safety breaches causing physical injury to workers than it is for dismissal of trade union activists, where it is hard to see how a plausible tort claim might be formulated. Second, much will turn on the precise wording of any corporate policies and their implementation by the parent company. Third, even if it can be established in principle that the parent company owes a duty of care to the workers, there are many more elements to be satisfied before it can be shown that the firm has breached that duty and is liable. For example, in the 'omission' scenario outlined above, the parent company could argue that it took all reasonable steps to ensure that subsidiaries complied, and was therefore not in breach of any duty of care towards affected workers. Fourth, it is possible that, under rules of private international law, even if a case is heard in the English courts, liability is determined under the law of the country in which the breach took place. If this is less generous or well-developed, claimants may be at a further disadvantage.

Another possibility is to use the law of contract as the basis for a claim, given that terms relating to the treatment of workers may be included in a contract between a firm and its suppliers.[54] However, there are two obvious problems here. First, the term supply 'chain' masks the complexity of the huge networks many firms use. Appropriately drafted contract clauses may not be included in all the contracts between all the different suppliers, regardless of the preferences of the firm at the top of the network, leaving some workers without protection. Second, in

---

[49] For a detailed analysis, see D Cabrelli, 'Liability for the Violation of Human Rights and Labour Standards in Global Supply Chains: A Common Law Perspective' (2019) 10 *Journal of European Tort Law* 108.
[50] See eg *Barclays Bank Plc v Various Claimants* [2020] UKSC 13, [2020] AC 973.
[51] *Vedanta Resources Plc v Lungowe* [2019] UKSC 20, [2020] AC 1045. See also *Okpabi v Royal Dutch Shell Plc* [2021] UKSC 3, [2021] 1 WLR 1294.
[52] *Chandler v Cape Plc* [2012] EWCA Civ 525, [2012] 1 WLR 3111.
[53] Cabrelli, above n 49.
[54] See S Dadush, above n 21.

English law at least, the doctrine of privity is an obvious obstacle to workers being able to rely on terms in a contract between the lead firm and their employer. Of course, one of the exceptions to privity under s 1 of the Contracts (Rights of Third Parties) Act 1999 is where the clause in question was intended to benefit the third party. This could be applicable to clauses requiring workers to be treated in particular ways. However, the position is not straightforward. The parties can expressly exclude third party liability and, in any event, the courts may conclude that the relevant clause was not intended to be enforceable by the third party under s 1(2).

These various limitations have led to growing calls for states to legislate for civil liability. This is the approach adopted in France under the new 'duty of vigilance' legislation.[55] This requires large firms headquartered in France[56] to prepare a 'vigilance plan' in accordance with the UN Guiding Principles on Business and Human Rights (to be discussed in detail in the next section) for their subsidiaries and sub-contractors with which they have an established commercial relationship. The 'vigilance plan' should identify risks to human rights (among other factors) and prevent severe impacts on those rights. What distinguishes the French legislation from reporting obligations is that the firm is also under a duty to implement the plan effectively.[57] However, it is unclear what exactly this entails and there is no official guidance on what firms should do. The enforcement mechanism, which can be initiated by trade unions or NGOs, consists of a two-stage process in which the firm is first given a notice to comply, followed by the possibility of an injunction and a periodic penalty payment if it still fails to do so.[58] This applies whether or not any damage has occurred. Most interestingly, where there is evidence of damage, there is the possibility of bringing a claim against the parent company for failure to comply with the duty of vigilance, for example, by preparing an inadequate plan or failing to take sufficient steps to implement it. However, the claimant will have to show that the parent company's failure was the cause of the harm they suffered, making it potentially quite difficult for workers to establish liability when they work for a supplier at the 'end' of the supply chain.[59]

A potentially significant new development at EU level is the inclusion of a civil liability provision in Article 22(1) of the proposed CSDDD, if it were to be enacted as originally drafted by the Commission:

Member States shall ensure that companies are liable for damages if:

(a) they failed to comply with the obligations laid down in Articles 7 and 8 and;
(b) as a result of this failure an adverse impact that should have been identified, prevented, mitigated, brought to an end or its extent minimised through the appropriate measures laid down in Articles 7 and 8 occurred and led to damage.[60]

Much will depend on how the Member States implement this provision within their own legal systems.[61] But there are a couple of limits on the face of Article 22 itself. First, it is necessary to show that harm was caused by the firm's failure to take 'appropriate' due diligence measures.

---

[55] See S Cossart, J Chaplier and T Beau de Lomenie, 'The French Law on Duty of Care: A Historic Step Towards Making Globalization Work for All' (2017) 2 *Business and Human Rights Journal* 317; E Avourey and S Brabant, 'The French Law on the Duty of Vigilance: Theoretical and Practical Challenges Since its Adoption' (2021) 6 *Business and Human Rights Journal* 141.

[56] As with the position in UK law, there is considerable uncertainty as to which firms are subject to the duty, discussed in Avourey and Brabant, above n 55.

[57] Above n 55.

[58] ibid.

[59] ibid.

[60] For analysis and comparison with the UK approach, see P Davies, 'Corporate Liability for Wrongdoing within (Foreign) Subsidiaries: Mechanisms from Corporate Law, Tort and Regulation' (NUS Law Working Paper 2023/007).

[61] It is perhaps worth noting that this is why the EU initiative is best regarded as a home state strategy rather than an international one.

This may open up a defence that the firm did take 'appropriate' measures (even if they failed) or that the harm could not have been prevented. Second, Article 22 limits a firm's liability for the actions of other firms with which it has an 'indirect' business relationship, provided that it has taken the actions set out in Articles 7 and 8. Nevertheless, the provision is a significant step forward. It requires states to legislate for civil liability even in extraterritorial situations, thereby removing one of the major obstacles blocking tort claims.[62] The CSDDD also places an obligation on the Commission to publish model contract clauses to assist firms in fulfilling the requirements under Articles 7 and 8 to contract with their direct business partners for compliance with the firm's code of conduct.[63] This could prove significant in overcoming the limitations of firms' own contracting practices as identified above.

Summary

Fears that home state initiatives would pose a major threat to the sovereignty or economic advantage of host states have (so far at least) been unfounded, given their limited impact. Reporting or due diligence obligations are relatively light-touch, and do little more than put into statutory form what many firms claim to be doing already through their own codes. Their impact is likely to be varied, depending in particular on how sensitive a firm is about its reputation with consumers. Litigation has more potential – it more clearly involves workers and their representatives, and it could have an impact on a firm's finances – but this potential has not yet been realised and there may be too many obstacles in the way. One feature common to all these types of initiative is that they require active trade unions or NGOs to support litigation or to make use of the information generated by reporting or due diligence exercises. In other words, they seem almost to 'contract out' a lot of monitoring and enforcement activity to groups which are not well-resourced and may not be best placed to bear that burden.

But the tide is clearly turning, first through national initiatives and now through the proposed EU CSDDD. This has a number of strengths from a worker-protective perspective when compared with some of the earlier measures. First, it includes detailed substantive due diligence obligations across a wide range of human rights norms, not just an obligation to report on whatever the firm chooses to do. Second, it requires the creation of national supervisory authorities with the power to impose sanctions for non-compliance, instead of relying on softer, reputational impacts. And third, it bridges the gap between initiatives focused on corporate behaviour and initiatives driven by victims, by requiring Member States to legislate for civil liability. Of course, it remains to be seen on what terms the Directive has been agreed, and what impact it will have in practice.

4. International Initiatives

A final group of initiatives to consider are those at international level. Given the dynamics of globalisation, discussed above, it seems obvious that one way to tackle them would be for states

---

[62] Above n 38, Article 22(5).

[63] ibid Article 12. An academic working group has already drafted some model clauses which are available online: see M Scheltema, 'European Model Clauses (third draft)', available at www.eur.nl/en/esl/media/2023-10-european-model-clauses-supply-chains0. The American Bar Association has published something similar: see DV Snyder, SA Maslow and S Dadush, 'Balancing Buyer and Supplier Responsibilities: Model Contract Clauses to Protect Workers in International Supply Chains, Version 2.0', and see S Dadush, 'Contracting for Human Rights: Looking to Version 2.0 of the ABA Model Contract Clauses' (2019) 68 *American University Law Review* 1519.

to work together to reassert their authority over MNCs. However, those same dynamics also make it difficult to achieve consensus, given that states are competing against each other for inward investment. States in the Global South often suspect that human rights initiatives driven by states in the Global North are in fact motivated by protectionism (seeking to limit the competition their own markets face) rather than genuine concern for the welfare of workers and others. We examine three international efforts: the OECD guidelines, the UN Guiding Principles, and the proposed binding treaty on business and human rights.

OECD MNE Guidelines

International initiatives to deal with the challenges posed by MNCs are by no means a new phenomenon. There are two major initiatives dating back to the 1970s, one set up by the ILO and the other by the OECD. Both take the form of guidelines addressed primarily to MNCs themselves. The OECD guidelines were revised in 2023.[64] They refer to the rights in the ILO Declaration, including health and safety, but go further in some respects. For example, there are duties to provide information to worker representatives and facilities to enable them to carry out their functions.[65] Thus, there is more detail on what it means to recognise freedom of association and collective bargaining than is found in some other instruments. Another important feature of the guidelines is a duty to notify and consult in the event of collective redundancies, which is rarely found elsewhere but may be a significant issue in the context of the global competition for investment outlined at the start of the chapter.[66] The OECD guidelines are enforced via a network of national contact points (NCPs) in 51 states, which have a role in promoting the guidelines and providing what is referred to as a non-judicial grievance mechanism for complaints about non-compliance.[67] For example, it would be possible for an interested party, such as a trade union or NGO, to complain to the UK NCP about the activities of a firm headquartered in the UK, even if the breach of the guidelines took place elsewhere. The NCPs typically encourage firms to change their policies and practices and may be able to secure remedies, though they proceed by persuasion and have no formal powers. Their impact is therefore variable in practice.[68]

UN Guiding Principles

The UN Guiding Principles on Business and Human Rights were proposed by UN Special Representative John Ruggie (and are therefore often referred to as the 'Ruggie principles') and endorsed by the UN Human Rights Council in 2011.[69] The Principles have three core elements: the state's duty to *protect* human rights, firms' responsibility to *respect* human rights, and the need to provide access to *remedies* for victims of violations.[70]

---

[64] www.oecd.org/corporate/mne/.
[65] OECD Guidelines for Multinational Enterprises on Responsible Business Conduct, p 28, para 2.
[66] ibid, p 29, para 6.
[67] https://mneguidelines.oecd.org/ncps/.
[68] For critical analysis, see K Bhatt and G Erdem Türkelli, 'OECD National Contact Points as Sites of Effective Remedy: New Expressions of the Role and Rule of Law within Market Globalization?' (2021) 6 *Business and Human Rights Journal* 423.
[69] UN Guiding Principles on Business and Human Rights (2011).
[70] For an overview, see L Catá Backer, 'On the Evolution of the United Nations' "Protect-Respect-Remedy" Project: The State, the Corporation and Human Rights in a Global Governance Context' (2011) 9 *Santa Clara J Int'l L* 37.

The significance of this framework is two-fold. First, it emphasises that both firms and the state must take responsibility in the sphere of human rights, but in different ways.[71] The state has a wide-ranging responsibility under international human rights instruments to fulfil both negative and positive obligations in relation to human rights. The responsibility of business is narrower: firms 'should avoid infringing on the human rights of others and should address adverse human rights impacts with which they are involved'.[72] This is an attempt to carve out an area of responsibility for firms, whilst retaining respect for state sovereignty and refraining from making firms responsible for all the problems of the states in which they operate. Previous initiatives directed at MNCs, such as the ILO and OECD guidelines, struggled to capture this distinction. Second, the framework places considerable emphasis on the state's responsibility to provide effective redress mechanisms, and on firms' responsibility to provide redress, for victims.[73] Earlier initiatives (such as the UN Global Compact, discussed above) tended to be more 'promotional' in nature and to ignore the possibility that violations might still occur.

The Principles require firms to respect 'at a minimum' the rights contained in the International Bill of Human Rights and the ILO Declaration.[74] This is somewhat confusing, since the small selection of rights in the ILO Declaration is, of course, already contained in the International Bill of Human Rights, but presumably it would have been politically difficult not to mention the ILO. One potential area of difficulty lies in determining what exactly a firm needs to do in order to 'respect' a particular right – such as freedom of association – in any given context. For example, it is tolerably clear that a firm would breach the requirement if it dismissed workers on grounds of their trade union membership or activities, but it is unclear to what extent it might also require positive steps, such as recognition of a trade union for the purposes of collective bargaining.[75] It is difficult to obtain guidance on these issues from other sources, such as the ILO, because ILO Conventions are addressed to states.

There are two major criticisms of the Principles. One is that they focus primarily on the responsibility of host states and firms, and do not elaborate particularly strongly on any responsibility of *home* states to regulate MNCs extraterritorially.[76] The commentary to Principle 2 indicates that home states may choose to regulate MNCs' activities but are not under any obligation to do so. This position looks increasingly outdated now that many states are starting to consider due diligence or even civil liability legislation, as discussed above. The other relates to the relationship between firms' obligation to undertake due diligence[77] and their duty to respect human rights.[78] If a firm has done its due diligence but is nevertheless found to have failed to respect workers' rights, does it have a defence? Bonnitcha and McCorquodale argue that the Principles are ambiguous on the point, with the potential to leave some MNCs with the impression that their main responsibility is to do due diligence, rather than to avoid infringing workers' rights.[79] This would weaken the content of the Principles very considerably. However, the Principles themselves

---

[71] The framework is derived from H Shue, *Basic Rights: Subsistence, Affluence, and U.S. Foreign Policy*, 2nd edn (Princeton University Press, 1996).
[72] Above n 69, Principle 11.
[73] ibid, Principles 22 and 25.
[74] ibid, Principle 12.
[75] cf the OECD guidelines, discussed above.
[76] See D Davitti, 'Refining the Protect, Respect and Remedy Framework for Business and Human Rights and its Guiding Principles' (2016) 16 *Human Rights Law Review* 55.
[77] Above n 69, Principle 17.
[78] ibid, Principle 11.
[79] J Bonnitcha and R McCorquodale, 'The Concept of "Due Diligence" in the UN Guiding Principles on Business and Human Rights' (2017) 28 *European Journal of International Law* 899.

make clear that due diligence is not a defence,[80] and state instead that firms should address any adverse impacts they discover through due diligence, including by providing affected workers with a remedy.[81] Ruggie himself appears to have regarded due diligence as a process for discovering impacts, rather than as the standard of firms' behaviour.[82] Nevertheless, the various criticisms of the Principles, coupled with their status as non-binding guidance, have led to ongoing calls for a stronger international regime.

Draft Binding Instrument

In 2014, the UN Human Rights Council adopted a resolution setting up a process to negotiate a legally binding international instrument on business and human rights.[83] At the time of writing, these negotiations are ongoing and the instrument has been through a number of drafts.[84]

The proposed instrument would be binding on signatory states, reflecting the fact that states – not corporations[85] – are the subjects of international law. It does not distinguish between home and host states, or between MNCs and companies in the supply chain. Instead, it places quite basic obligations on all states to regulate all firms in the following terms:

State Parties shall adopt appropriate legislative, regulatory, and other measures to:

(a) prevent the involvement of business enterprises in human rights abuse;
(b) ensure respect by business enterprises for internationally recognized human rights and fundamental freedoms;
(c) ensure the practice of human rights due diligence by business enterprises; and,
(d) promote the active and meaningful participation of individuals and groups … in the development and implementation of laws, policies and other measures to prevent the involvement of business enterprises in human rights abuse.[86]

Under Article 8, states must provide a system of legal liability applicable to firms operating within their territory, including for their transnational activities, which provides remedies to victims. Thus, although there are some references to extraterritorial regulation by home states and to HRDD by businesses, the emphasis – as it is in the Principles, discussed above – is on reasserting the regulatory authority of host states. There has been some criticism of the instrument for this breadth of focus. Some states in the Global South would like to see a clearer focus on the potential harm caused by MNCs, with provisions specific to them, perhaps enforced by an international tribunal.[87] However, there are a number of problems with this idea, not least the obvious issue that the direct cause of harm to workers is usually a subsidiary or supplier located within the host state.

---

[80] Above n 69, Principle 17 and commentary.
[81] ibid, Principle 22.
[82] JG Ruggie and JF Sherman, 'The Concept of "Due Diligence" in the UN Guiding Principles on Business and Human Rights: A Reply to Jonathan Bonnitcha and Robert McCorquodale' (2017) 28 *EJIL* 921.
[83] Full details are available here: www.ohchr.org/en/hr-bodies/hrc/wg-trans-corp/igwg-on-tnc.
[84] References in this section are to the July 2023 draft.
[85] There have been calls for an instrument that would bind MNCs, but there are a number of obstacles to this: L McConnell, 'Assessing the Feasibility of a Business and Human Rights Treaty' (2017) 66 *International and Comparative Law Quarterly* 143.
[86] Updated Draft Legally Binding Instrument to Regulate, in International Human Rights Law, the Activities of Transnational Corporations and Other Business Enterprises (July 2023), Article 6.2.
[87] R Morgantini, 'A Binding Treaty to Tackle Corporate Impunity or an Empty Instrument?', available at www.business-humanrights.org/en/blog/a-binding-treaty-to-tackle-corporate-impunity-or-an-empty-instrument/.

The most obvious flaw in the draft binding instrument links back to our starting-point: globalisation itself. Of course, it would be best if all states regulated firms operating in their territories, but it is precisely because of pressure from MNCs and competition with other states that they do not. The draft binding instrument would help to combat these problems if it was very widely ratified, but the same factors that make states reluctant to regulate firms in the first place also seem likely to make them reluctant to ratify the proposed treaty. It remains to be seen how the negotiations will develop, and whether the EU's greater involvement in this area (through the CSDDD) will help to unblock international action on the topic.

5. Conclusion

A striking feature of this chapter is the sheer number of schemes designed to get MNCs to take action on labour rights (and other similar issues) in their supply chains. The landscape is crowded. Although there are many overlaps, such as references to the international norms in domestic due diligence legislation, the proliferation of regulatory strategies may be a problem in itself, creating confusion for everyone involved. But are any of the strategies producing results? It is certainly getting increasingly difficult for MNCs to ignore the pressure to act on workers' rights or to claim ignorance of the issues.[88] But the rights involved are typically quite narrowly framed, and as compliance improves, there will be a need to develop more ambitious targets, going beyond the ILO Declaration. It is not clear how this will be achieved. There is also a considerable gap between firms' stated commitments and effective monitoring and enforcement of those commitments, particularly when it comes to remedies for workers who have been harmed by a breach. While cross-border litigation may seem to be an obvious avenue for redress, there are many practical and legal obstacles in the way of getting MNCs to pay compensation. It remains to be seen whether new initiatives in Europe will be able to overcome some or all of these obstacles. Finally, there is still a strong sense that human rights are being 'done to' workers in supply chains rather than 'done with' them. Workers' voices rarely seem influential in this space. Some would argue that this does not matter when universally applicable fundamental rights are at issue, but this argument is less persuasive from a labour law perspective.

---

[88] See P Muchlinski, 'The impact of the UN Guiding Principles on Business Attitudes to Observing Human Rights' (2021) 6 *Business and Human Rights Journal* 212.

13

The Right to Private Life at Work

1.	Private Life at Work	4.	Data Protection
2.	Workplace Monitoring and Surveillance	5.	Testing
3.	Blurred Boundaries	6.	Conclusion

'It's not prison. It's work.'[1] Courtenay Brown described in these words the working conditions and constant surveillance, working about 10 hours a day in a section of Amazon Fresh on groceries to be directed to delivery trucks. There were cameras everywhere, she explained, and she was being measured by a system calculating the number of items that were being loaded on the trucks by her team. Workers held scanners to track inventory, which Amazon used to put pressure on them to be more productive. 'They basically can see everything you do, and it's all to their benefit,' the worker said. 'They don't value you as a human being. It's demeaning,' Brown explained.

Even though Amazon is perhaps one of the more extreme examples, excessive surveillance and monitoring in the workplace is not unique to Amazon, and technological advances have increased employers' power on this front.[2] Tools that track productivity, also known as Bossware, are used increasingly by employers who find that they make it simpler for them to measure and monitor workers' performance in ways that could not have been imagined in the past.[3] Employers may believe that algorithmic management techniques improve efficiency and productivity, but they give workers the sense that their subordination to management is intensified, that they are not trusted, that they are treated unfairly, and that their autonomy and privacy are not respected.[4] Furthermore, the automated decision-making systems that control their working lives will frequently appear arbitrary, unaccountable, and beyond the reach of the influence of workers and their representatives.[5] Technological developments may affect

---

[1] J Greene, 'Amazon's Employee Surveillance Fuels Unionization Efforts: "It's not Prison, it's Work"', *Washington Post*, 2 December 2021. See, further, 'Amazon Workers Face "Increased Risk of Mental Illness"', 25 November 2013, available at www.bbc.com/news/business-25034598; J Bloodworth, *Hired – Six Months Undercover in Low-Wage Britain* (Atlantic Books, 2018). See also Michael Sainato, 'Accidents at Amazon: Workers Left to Suffer After Warehouse Injuries', *The Guardian*, 30 July 2018.

[2] See, generally, K Levy, *Data Driven – Truckers, Technology, and the New Workplace Surveillance* (Princeton University Press, 2023); A Bernhardt, L Kresge and R Suleiman, 'Data and Algorithms at Work – The Case for Worker Technology Rights', UC Berkley Labor Center, November 2021.

[3] Z Corbyn, '"Bossware is coming for almost every worker": the software you might not realize is watching you', *The Guardian*, 27 April 2022; L Cater and M Heikkila, 'Your Boss is Watching: How AI-Powered Surveillance Rules the Workplace', *Politico*, 27 May 2021.

[4] E Segal, 'How Productivity and Surveillance Technology Can Create a Crisis for Businesses', *Forbes*, 18 August 2022; J Stanley, 'The Nightmarish Loss of Workplace Privacy', ACLU, 26 August 2022.

[5] P Collins and J Atkinson, 'Worker Voice and Algorithmic Management in Post-Brexit Britain' (2023) 29 *Transfer: European Review of Labour and Research* 37; V Doellgast and I Wagner, 'Collective regulation and the future of work in the digital economy: Insights from comparative employment relations' (2022) 64 *Journal of Industrial Relations* 438.

everyone, but workers under precarious work arrangements, including those employed in the gig economy, may be monitored and managed more closely than people in standard employment relations.[6]

Does the right to private life (or privacy) in human rights law protect workers from workplace monitoring and surveillance? How about when people work from home? These are the questions that this chapter addresses. A significant theme that emerges is that the boundaries between life and work are increasingly blurred for most workers, particularly with new technologies that enable remote working and monitoring. These blurred boundaries will be explored both in this and the chapter that follows, which considers protection of the right to private life for activities outside the workplace and working time, including the use of social media.

1. Private Life at Work

Article 8 of the European Convention on Human Rights (ECHR) protects the right to private and family life.[7] It states:

1. Everyone has the right to respect for his private and family life, his home and his correspondence.
2. There shall be no interference by a public authority with the exercise of this right except such as is in accordance with the law and is necessary in a democratic society in the interests of national security, public safety or the economic well-being of the country, for the prevention of disorder or crime, for the protection of health or morals, or for the protection of the rights and freedoms of others.

The ECHR provision sets out a qualified right (rather than an absolute one) and provides for possible limitations: any interference with the right must pursue a legitimate aim, be 'in accordance with the law', which means that it must have 'some basis in domestic law',[8] and 'necessary in a democratic society'. This latter part of the test means that any restriction 'corresponds to a pressing social need and, in particular, that it is proportionate to the legitimate aim pursued'.[9] In light of this, a first question is whether the right to private life is applicable at all to life at work.[10]

Many people assume that private life involves activities at home, whereas when we are in the workplace, we are in public space and hence outside the scope of the right to private life. Could anything that we do in the workplace and during working time fall in the scope of the right to private life? How about when people work from home? The ECtHR has generally interpreted the

---

[6] See, for instance, A Rosenblat and L Stark, 'Algorithmic Labor and Information Asymmetries: A Case Study of Uber's Drivers' (2016) 10 *International Journal of Communication* 1166. See also more generally, J Prassl, *Humans as a Service – The Promise and Perils of Work in the Gig Economy* (OUP, 2018); J Adams-Prassl, H Abraha, A Kelly-Lyth, M 'Six' Silberman and S Rakshita, 'Regulating Algorithmic Management' (2023) *European Labour Law Journal*.

[7] The right to private and family life is also protected in Article 7 of the EU Charter of Fundamental Rights, while Article 8 of the Charter protects personal data. The right to privacy is also guaranteed in Article 12 of the Universal Declaration of Human Rights and Article 17 of the International Covenant on Civil and Political Rights.

[8] *Leander v Sweden* (1978) 9 EHRR 433, [50].

[9] *Pretty v UK* [2002] ECHR 427, [70].

[10] On the right to privacy at work, see generally M Otto, *The Right to Privacy in Employment: A Comparative Analysis* (Oxford, Bloomsbury Publishing, 2016) 82; F Hendrickx and A Van Bever, 'Article 8 ECHR: Judicial Patterns of Employment Privacy Protection' in F Dorssemont, K Lorcher and I Schomann (eds), *The European Convention on Human Rights and the Employment Relation* (Oxford, Hart, 2013).

right to private life broadly, to include activities far beyond what people do in a private household, and to cover conduct taking place in public space,[11] access to work and protection from unjustified dismissal.[12] Several aspects of individual autonomy fall within the scope of the right to private life, in other words, and not only intimate aspects of personal life at home.

Niemietz v Germany[13] set out a general principle on work and private life. It involved the question whether the police could search a lawyer's office for the purposes of a criminal investigation. In considering whether the office can form part of someone's private life, the Court said in a much-cited passage that:

> it would be too restrictive to limit the notion to an 'inner circle' in which the individual may live his own personal life as he chooses and to exclude therefrom entirely the outside world not encompassed within that circle. Respect for private life must also comprise to a certain degree the right to establish and develop relationships with other human beings.[14]

It went on to note that 'there appears … to be no reason in principle why this understanding of the notion of "private life" should be taken to exclude activities of a professional or business nature' and stated that 'it is, after all, in the course of their working lives that the majority of people have a significant, if not the greatest, opportunity of developing relationships with the outside world'.[15] *Niemietz* was significant because it emphasised that someone's workplace is not outside the scope of the right to private life. But what are the further implications for private life at work? Can the employer ever monitor workers and what are the limitations?

2. Workplace Monitoring and Surveillance

The early cases of the Court on workplace monitoring and surveillance involved phone tapping. In *Halford v United Kingdom*,[16] the ECtHR had to consider whether monitoring of the telephone conversations of Ms Halford, a senior police officer who had brought a sex discrimination complaint against her employer, violated her right to private life. The Government claimed that she did not have a reasonable expectation of privacy for phone calls from her phone provided by her employer. However, the Court responded that she had not been warned that her calls would be monitored so the right to private life was applicable to her communications, as she had also been specifically told that one of her work phones was designated for her private use. Even if a worker is not specifically told that they can use their phone, email and other such forms of communication for personal purposes, they still have a 'reasonable expectation of privacy' when using them at work.[17]

The principle of the reasonable expectation of privacy plays a fundamental role in determining whether Article 8 of the ECHR is applicable in the employment relation. It might imply that if the employer informs a worker that they will be monitored, the worker has no reasonable expectation of privacy. However, this interpretation would make the reasonable expectation of privacy

---

[11] *Von Hannover v Germany* (2005) 40 EHRR 1.
[12] *Sidabras and Dziautas v Lithuania* [2015] ECHR 674, see further chapter 8; *Denisov v Ukraine* [2018] ECHR 1061, see further chapter 18.
[13] *Niemietz v Germany* [1992] ECHR 80.
[14] ibid [29].
[15] ibid.
[16] *Halford v UK* [1997] ECHR 32.
[17] *Copland v UK* [2007] ECHR 253.

unsuitable for the employment context.[18] It would suggest that the employer has unlimited power to monitor every aspect of workers' life, insofar as it has first notified them. This brings to the forefront the following problem: employers can (and often do) include terms in the employment contracts or rulebooks, setting out extensive monitoring practices and other restrictions of rights. As employees are generally offered their contract of employment on a take it or leave it basis, and have no bargaining power to negotiate different terms,[19] these terms may waive all expectations of privacy.[20] The contract can be used as a vehicle of domination of the employer over the worker.[21] The analysis of privacy on the basis of consent and expectations needs further refinement. A concern with placing the expectations of privacy in the centre of the analysis in the employment context is that if an expectation of privacy is viewed as a *descriptive* term, it may lead to 'the possibility of a downward spiral', and that the state, the employer or other powerful actors can create conditions where there is no expectation of privacy.[22] This concern is grounded on the feature of submission in the employment relation. The employer may simply say to workers that they should have no expectation of privacy. This raises the following pressing question: Are contractual terms and other policies determined by the employer that waive the right to private life at work compatible with the ECHR? What is the weight to be given to the employees' consent to these terms?

The reasonable expectation of privacy and its limitations were discussed in the landmark case *Barbulescu v Romania*.[23] Mr Barbulescu was employed by a private company as an engineer in charge of sales. He was asked by his employer to set up a Yahoo messenger account to respond to customers' enquiries. At some point he was informed that his account was monitored for a few days and that it emerged that he used it for personal communications, which he refuted in writing. However, a transcript of his communications showed that he had used the account to communicate with family members about personal matters involving health and sex life. He was dismissed for using the account in a manner that breached the employer's internal regulations, which prohibited using the employer's resources for personal matters. In assessing the complaint, the Court stated that states are required to not only have an adequate legislative framework in place to ensure the protection of workplace privacy, but also to ensure that domestic courts provide an appropriate balance when considering the conflicting interests of the employers and employees.[24]

The ECtHR developed criteria, which should guide national courts that assess the compatibility of monitoring with the Convention. It said:

[T]he domestic authorities should treat the following factors as relevant:

(i) whether the employee has been notified of the possibility that the employer might take measures to monitor correspondence and other communications, and of the implementation of such measures. While in practice employees may be notified in various ways depending on the particular

---

[18] The test has also been criticised in the context of media law. See E Barendt, '"A Reasonable Expectation of Privacy": A Coherent or Redundant Concept?' in AT Kenyon (ed), *Comparative Defamation and Privacy Law* (Cambridge, CUP, 2016) 96.

[19] See H Collins, 'Is the Contract of Employment Illiberal?' in H Collins, G Lester and V Mantouvalou (eds), *Philosophical Foundations of Labour Law* (OUP, 2019) 48.

[20] M Niezna and G Davidov, 'Consent in Contracts of Employment' (2023) 86 *Modern Law Review* 1134; H Collins and V Mantouvalou, 'Human Rights and the Contract of Employment' in Freedland (ed), *The Contract of Employment* (Oxford, OUP, 2015) 158; G Morris, 'Fundamental Rights: Exclusion by Agreement?' (2001) 30 *ILJ* 49.

[21] See V Mantouvalou, 'Advancing Human Rights, Capabilities and Non-Domination at Work' in G Davidov, B Langille and G Lester (eds), *Oxford Handbook on the Law of Work* (Oxford, OUP, 2024).

[22] J Atkinson, 'Workplace Monitoring and the Right to Private Life at Work' (2018) 81 *MLR* 688 at 696.

[23] *Barbulescu v Romania*, [2017] ECHR 742. See Atkinson, ibid.

[24] *Barbulescu*, ibid [121].

factual circumstances of each case, the Court considers that for the measures to be deemed compatible with the requirements of Article 8 of the Convention, the notification should normally be clear about the nature of the monitoring and be given in advance;

(ii) the extent of the monitoring by the employer and the degree of intrusion into the employee's privacy. In this regard, a distinction should be made between monitoring of the flow of communications and of their content. Whether all communications or only part of them have been monitored should also be taken into account, as should the question whether the monitoring was limited in time and the number of people who had access to the results .... The same applies to the spatial limits to the monitoring;

(iii) whether the employer has provided legitimate reasons to justify monitoring the communications and accessing their actual content .... Since monitoring of the content of communications is by nature a distinctly more invasive method, it requires weightier justification;

(iv) whether it would have been possible to establish a monitoring system based on less intrusive methods and measures than directly accessing the content of the employee's communications. In this connection, there should be an assessment in the light of the particular circumstances of each case of whether the aim pursued by the employer could have been achieved without directly accessing the full contents of the employee's communications;

(v) the consequences of the monitoring for the employee subjected to it ...; and the use made by the employer of the results of the monitoring operation, in particular whether the results were used to achieve the declared aim of the measure ...;

(vi) whether the employee had been provided with adequate safeguards, especially when the employer's monitoring operations were of an intrusive nature. Such safeguards should in particular ensure that the employer cannot access the actual content of the communications concerned unless the employee has been notified in advance of that eventuality.[25]

It reiterated that 'in order to be fruitful, labour relations must be based on mutual trust',[26] and further stated that when communications are monitored, the authorities should ensure that workers have access to a remedy before a judicial body that will determine the lawfulness of monitoring in light of the above criteria.[27] The Grand Chamber ruled that Mr Barbulescu's dismissal for using his work Yahoo Messenger for private communications constituted a violation of his right to private life under the ECHR, and in a striking passage it emphasised that workers' 'private social life' at work 'cannot be reduced to zero'.[28]

The *Barbulescu* case shows that what constitutes reasonable expectation of privacy at work does not depend only on notification by the employer but that there is, instead, a normative threshold and that several criteria should guide courts assessing compliance with the right to private life. This can only be viewed as a welcome development. Notification by the employer that a worker is being monitored cannot be sufficient to remove any claim to privacy protection of the worker. If there were no normative threshold and the reasonable expectation of privacy only depended on the employer's whim, this could lead to domination over the worker by the employer, who would be able to intrude into any aspect of the worker's private life having simply given a warning.

Other case law considered academics' right to privacy in university lecture theatres. The non-covert surveillance during their teaching, with the recordings kept for one month to be consulted by the faculty dean, was found to fall within the scope of Article 8. The Court explained that

---

[25] ibid [121].
[26] ibid.
[27] ibid [122].
[28] ibid [80].

'university amphitheatres are the workplaces of teachers. It is where they not only teach students, but also interact with them, thus developing mutual relations and constructing their social identity.'[29] It held that the monitoring in this case violated the right to private life.

However, the Court has not always been as clear on whether prior notification of the nature and extent of monitoring is essential for compliance with Article 8, as became evident in case law that involves a conflict between the workers' right to privacy, on the one hand, and the employer's right to property.[30] In *Lopez Ribalda v Spain* the employer, a supermarket, had suspicions of theft, and installed cameras without notifying its employees (cashiers and sales assistants) about all cameras installed.[31] The applicants were dismissed because the cameras for which they had not been notified showed that they had been stealing from the supermarket. The Grand Chamber of the Court explained that in this case there was a conflict between the workers' right to private life and the employer's right to property and the smooth operation of the business. It highlighted that in certain areas in the workplace, such as toilets or cloakrooms, there is a heightened expectation of privacy and stronger protection of the right to private life. Private offices are also covered by a high expectation of privacy. However, areas where the public have access should be differentiated. The Court took into account a number of other considerations, such as the fact that the employer had a reasonable suspicion of theft, and concluded that even though the employees had not been notified in advance about all cameras involved, the balancing exercise employed by domestic courts was satisfactory and compatible with the Convention.

The idea that there is no need to notify workers in advance if the employer has a suspicion of theft or other misconduct may be viewed as a concerning development. Warning about concrete measures of monitoring seems to be a basic guarantee. The idea that a suspicion of theft is sufficient can lead to troubling outcomes and may be abused by employers. For instance, would the employer have this right to monitor without a warning in a case of suspected 'time theft'?[32] There is a risk that the employer can use suspicions as an excuse to engage in extensive covert monitoring. It is worth noting that in *Lopez Ribalda*, Judges De Gaetano, Yudkivska and Grozev disagreed with the majority of the Court. They stressed the threats to workers' privacy because of new technologies, explained that the Court should have applied the *Barbulescu* criteria, including that of prior notification of the workers about the extent of their surveillance, and emphasised that the employer should have informed the police of its suspicions instead of taking the matter into its own hands.

What we have seen this far is that in addressing workers' privacy in case law that increasingly considers intrusions through technological tools, the Court has developed criteria to guide domestic authorities regarding the applicability and scope of Article 8, which take into account the particularities of the employment context. However, the test developed in *Barbulescu* does not address all problems of private life at work.

3. Blurred Boundaries

Technology creates increasingly blurred boundaries between personal and professional life. This can be observed in many aspects of the work/life balance, including the use of apps and cloud storage for professional and personal purposes and working from home practices.

---

[29] *Antovic and Mirkovic v Montenegro* [2017] ECHR 1068, [44].
[30] See *Kopke v Germany* [2010] ECHR 1725. *Lopez Ribalda v Spain* [2019] ECHR 752.
[31] *Lopez Ribalda*, ibid.
[32] On time theft, see the Canadian case *Besse v Reach CPA Inc*, 2023 BCCRT 27.

Personal Devices Used for Work, Cloud Storage and Other Such Practices[33]

A new practice that brings these blurred boundaries to the forefront is the use of personal devices for work purposes, including access to work email or other apps that the employer requires workers to use, the use of cloud storage for work and personal purposes and the use of apps that may be accessible from work and private devices.

In the past, people had documents that were work-related in filing cabinets in their offices, while personal documents, photos and other items were at home. There was a clear separation between personal and professional life. This is no longer the case. For instance, employers encourage 'Bring Your Own Device' (BYOD) practices, and scholars have over the years explored its potential but also raised concerns involving IT security, workers' privacy, working time, and other reasons.[34] Workers use cloud storage and other systems to back up both personal and professional materials, which are accessible by the employer. Even where individuals have not actively saved files onto these systems, it is often the default location for backups of devices or apps, which may store data such as messages in places that the user was not expecting. To give another example of how blurred the boundaries between personal and professional life are, workers may use messaging services, such as WhatsApp, which for ease and convenience they may install both on their personal and professional devices. Moreover, they may use these services for both personal and professional reasons. To make things even more complicated, some employers incentivise or even require their workers to connect their devices.[35]

Aspects of the problems that arise from the increasingly blurred boundaries between personal and professional life were illustrated in a High Court case, *FKJ v RVT and Others*.[36] The claimant was a solicitor working for a law firm. RVT was her supervisor. The claimant was dismissed for falsifying a timesheet and brought a claim to the employment tribunal primarily arguing that she had been subjected to sex discrimination by her supervisor, including inappropriate comments and sexual touching. She lost in the employment tribunal but much of the evidence used was based on her WhatsApp messages, which showed that the conduct was consensual. There were 18,000 messages (about 900 pages), including private and intimate messages to her partner, friends and others, including information on her health and sex life. Her claim in the High Court was that her WhatsApp messages had been hacked by RVT who scanned her phone WhatsApp QR code that is needed to authorise connecting WhatsApp to another device (her work computer in this case). RVT said that some of the messages were found in her work computer when he reviewed it, and other messages were sent to him by an anonymous source. There is no need to go into further detail on the specific case. What it illustrates is that someone's communications through means that may seem private and may involve some of the most intimate aspects of the person's private life, can become relevant in workplace disputes, and the employer may be able to access them.

---

[33] See generally, V Mantouvalou and M Veale, 'Blurred Boundaries: Rescuing Workers' Privacy in the Process of Searching Data and Devices', forthcoming.

[34] See eg L Blair, 'Contextualizing Bring Your Own Device Policies' (2018) 44 *Journal of Corporation Law* 151; Y Wang, J Wei and K Vangury, 'Bring Your Own Device Security Issues and Challenges', IEEE 11th Consumer Communications and Networking Conference (CCNC) (2014); J Ibarra Jimenez and H Jahankhani, 'Bring Your Own Device: GDPR Compliant or Headache? The Human Aspect in Security and Privacy', *Cyber Security Practitioner's Guide* (World Scientific, 2019); D Kahvedžić, 'Digital Forensics and the DSAR Effect' (2021) 22 ERA Forum 59; DR Stewart, 'Killer Apps: Vanishing Messages, Encrypted Communications, and Challenges to Freedom of Information Laws When Public Officials Go Dark' (2019) 10(1) *Case Western Reserve Journal of Law, Technology and the Internet*.

[35] Z Schiffer, 'Apple Cares About Privacy unless you Work at Apple', www.theverge.com/22648265/apple-employee-privacy-icloud-id.

[36] *FKJ v RVT and Others* [2023] EWHC 3 (KB).

In the *FKJ* case, the employer used the messages in tribunal proceedings as a defence in a discrimination claim, and the messages were obtained without prior knowledge or cooperation of the employee. In *Garamukanwa v UK*,[37] the applicant's WhatsApp messages, email communications and photos found in his mobile device had been used in disciplinary proceedings that led to his dismissal, and he complained that this constituted a violation of his right to private life. Some of these materials were passed to the employer, an NHS Trust, by the police that held it in the context of a harassment complaint by a colleague of his. Others were voluntarily shared by him. The ECtHR declared the application inadmissible, explaining that the applicant had no reasonable expectation of privacy for all these materials and communications: during the disciplinary proceedings he did not complain about their use, while he also provided further intimate materials to the disciplinary panel. Yet this case also exemplifies how work and private materials, some of which can be of the most intimate nature, can become relevant in employment disputes, revealed to the employer and relevant to disciplinary proceedings.

More generally, sometimes there may be legal basis for a court or tribunal to order someone to share messages that the person may have viewed as private, as evidence in legal proceedings.[38] This makes the issue more difficult to navigate: the employers will often have a legitimate reason to request access to devices or storage on the basis of rights of third parties. Many legal regimes provide for access to a variety of types of information which may be held on workers' devices. For instance, in the context of legal proceedings in a tribunal, an employer may be under a legal duty to share WhatsApp messages between employees in the context of a subject access request[39] in a claim of unfair dismissal or discrimination. Does the right to private life offer protection to workers in this case, when personal and professional devices and apps blur the boundaries?

The ECtHR examined a related question in *Libert v France*, a case that involved a work device that contained personal material.[40] The applicant who was in charge of general surveillance at the national railway company found out that, during a period that he had been suspended from work, his work computer had been seized and searched, and a large number of pornographic images and films were found in the hard disk. The search occurred despite the fact that he had stored these materials in a file named 'fun' in a folder in the D:\ drive, which he had labelled 'personal data'. As a result of this finding, he was dismissed. He claimed that the fact that the hard drive was searched *without him being present* violated his right to private life. The first question for the Strasbourg Court was whether the search was in accordance with law. The French Court de Cassation had ruled in a separate case that for a search of files that are labelled as 'personal' to take place, the employee had to be present unless there is a serious risk or other exceptional circumstances.[41] For this reason, the ECtHR accepted then that there was a legal basis for the search. On the question whether the employer had a legitimate aim, the Court accepted that this was the case given that it had a right to ensure that work equipment is used in line with its contracts and other regulations. When it came to the test of proportionality for the restriction of Libert's right, the Court referred to its margin of appreciation, considered the rulings of the national courts which had taken into account the right considerations (such as the fact that the nature of his job would have required him to be a role model in that respect and the fact that the pornographic materials took up a lot of space on the D:\ drive), and found that there had been no violation of the right to private life.

---

[37] *Garamukanwa v UK* [2019] ECHR 445.
[38] See Mantouvalou and Veale, above n 33.
[39] Data Protection Act 2018, s 45(1).
[40] *Libert v France* [2018] ECHR 185.
[41] ibid [44].

As *Libert* involved pornographic materials, the case was more difficult than had it involved other private materials, such as personal, private, family and intimate photos of his. The nature of the materials affected the Court's decision to recognise a margin of appreciation to the French authorities.[42] It is generally questionable whether employees should be role models in their private lives, an issue to which we return in the chapter that follows. What is more interesting to note is that even though *Libert* was about a work computer, and not a personal device, it can help identify safeguards that should apply in relation to practices that blur the personal/professional boundaries. The right to private life in this context has to be understood as giving power to the worker to control the process of a search both *ex ante* in order to limit the frequency of the problem and *ex post*, namely during a search of someone's private device or storage where there is no clear separation of work and private materials.[43]

The blurring of the lines in the context of workplace monitoring was examined further in case law involving GPS equipment installed in a company vehicle, which collected data on issues such as distances travelled and places visited.[44] Employees were permitted to use the vehicle for personal purposes but they would have to reimburse the employer for the relevant expenses. The collection of the data was very extensive as employees were not permitted to deactivate the system, which collected this information both in relation to their work and private travel. In this case, the data was used as the basis for the applicant's dismissal because it was found that he had recorded travel for private purposes as work travel and because the GPS showed that he was not working his contracted hours. The dismissal impacted his private life in two ways: both through the collection of data involving his private life and because of the effects of a dismissal on someone's private life.[45] The Court examined the balancing exercise performed by domestic courts, which had ruled that only geolocation data that involved the distances travelled could be used by the employer in this case, and this had a legitimate aim, which was the monitoring of company expenditure. The GPS data could not be used to monitor the worker's performance or working hours. In relation to the distances travelled, the data could legitimately be used as evidence of gross misconduct justifying dismissal, according to the ECtHR. In the circumstances, and given the careful balancing exercise employed by national courts, the Court concluded that there was no violation of Article 8 of the ECHR.

As we see in this case law, the ECtHR is increasingly conscious of the challenges set to workers' privacy because of technology. The Court applies its criteria and pays careful attention to the reasoning of national courts. Yet additional challenges emerge when it comes to remote working practices and broader 'working from home' practices. When someone's job is not in an office or other public space, but in the privacy of a household, monitoring and surveillance raise distinct challenges. What implications does this have for office workers working from home? How about domestic workers who work from someone else's home?

Office Workers Working from Home

'How many days a week are you expected to go to the office?' This is a very common question asked nowadays, which would have been unimaginable for most people before the Covid-19 pandemic in 2020. At the beginning of the pandemic, a lot of people started working from home. For

---

[42] It is common for courts to do this in cases that may raise sex-related issues. See also *Pay v UK*, [2008] ECHR 1007, discussed further in chapter 14.
[43] See Mantouvalou and Veale, above n 33.
[44] *Florindo de Almeida Vasconcelos Gramaxo v Portugal* [2022] ECHR 1073.
[45] ibid [96]. See further chapter 18.

many workers and employers this was a major and positive development. It was helpful for both employers and workers as they could continue operating and retain their jobs at a time when people were urged or required to 'stay at home'.[46]

When people are in the office, the employer has a sense of control: workers can be seen sitting in front of their computers, typing, reading and having meetings. When working from home, employers are deprived of the ability to see and physically access workers. This made some employers suspicious. Were people really working from home? Or were they looking after children, home-schooling or engaging in leisure activities? This tested the limits of trust that is supposed to be a founding block of the employment relationship.

Against this background, it was increasingly reported that technological tools known as 'Bossware' were used to monitor productivity.[47] These include tools monitoring keystrokes, website visits, tracking movements of workers, and even cameras. After the pandemic, hybrid working became the norm for many people. Office workers combine a few days in the office and a few days working from home, and it is reported that 'Bossware is everywhere, and it's getting more nightmarish'.[48]

Do workers have a right to privacy when working from home? Is the protection of their privacy heightened exactly because they work away from the office and in their personal setting, where they have a stronger expectation of privacy? On the one hand, it could be said that we simply need to apply the criteria developed in *Barbulescu*, and require the employer to inform the workers about the nature and extent of monitoring, without reducing privacy to zero. That would mean that employers are free to monitor extensively people in their own households, insofar as they inform them while recognising that there may be a limited space that cannot be monitored. Yet such an approach could justify intrusive monitoring and surveillance in one's household and could pose serious risks to privacy, such as inadvertently watching and exposing some of the most intimate aspects of people's private lives.[49] A different approach supports the position that when working from home, workers have a stronger expectation of privacy than when working in the office. This can be grounded on case law of the ECtHR about the right to private life at home.[50] On this view, one's private home should be protected especially strongly from external, including employers', interference. The ECtHR has ruled that monitoring when someone is 'in the sanctity of her home' is a particularly serious affront to dignity and a grave breach of the right to private life.[51] The fact that life at home involves some of the most intimate aspects of one's self and identity should be reflected in the interpretation of the right to private life when working from home, affording workers stronger protection and imposing limits on employers' powers.

---

[46] See, for instance, the UK campaign here: www.gov.uk/government/news/new-tv-advert-urges-public-to-stay-at-home-to-protect-the-nhs-and-save-lives#:~:text='Stay%20at%20home%2C%20save%20lives,on%20Friday%208%20January%202021.

[47] See A Jack, 'Growth of Staff Monitoring Software Stokes Debates Over Rights and Morals', *Financial Times*, 22 September 2021; V Romei, 'Surveillance Risks "Spinning Out of Control", Warns UK Workers' Union', *Financial Times*, 28 February 2022.

[48] M Carnegie, 'The Creepy Rise of Bossware', *Wired*, 23 July 2023.

[49] There were many examples of accidental exposure of intimate moments during the pandemic. See, for example, A Kassam, 'Man Offers to Resign After Showering During Live Video Meeting', *The Guardian*, 3 July 2020.

[50] For the two different approaches, see P Collins, 'The Right to Privacy, Surveillance by Software, and the "Home Workplace"', UK Labour Law Blog, 3 September 2020, and E Frantziou, 'The Right to Privacy when Working from Home ("WFH"): Why Employee Monitoring Infringes Article 8', UK Labour Law Blog, 5 October 2020. See also J Hariharan and H Noorda, 'Employee Monitoring as a Form of Imprisonment', UK Labour Law Blog, 19 May 2021.

[51] *Khadija Ismayilova v Azerbaijan* [2019] ECHR 11.

Domestic Workers Working from (Other People's) Home

While most people started working from home after the start of the Covid-19 pandemic, domestic workers have always worked from (other people's) home. For live-in domestic workers particularly, the employers' home is both their workplace and their home. This reality gives rise to a number of challenges, including significant restrictions of the right to privacy of the worker, as well as conflicts between workers' rights to privacy and fair working conditions, on the one hand, and employers' rights to privacy.

Live-in domestic workers have a room in the employer's home. This may mean that they are always on call, and that the employer may always be able to interfere with their private life. Sometimes migrant domestic workers may not even have their own room in the employers' home, as we saw in the judgment of the ECtHR, *Siliadin v France*,[52] where the applicant was sleeping on the floor in the children's bedroom. In this kind of case, workers have extremely limited privacy (if any at all) but this issue is often accompanied by other types of exploitation and ill-treatment. In the ECtHR, the ill-treatment and exploitation of domestic workers has generally been examined under Article 4 of the ECHR that prohibits slavery, servitude, forced and compulsory labour,[53] and not as a violation of the right to private life.

When considering domestic workers' right to private life, what is significant is that the workplace of a domestic worker is also the employer's household. Should labour inspectors have a power to enter private households to inspect the working conditions of domestic workers? There is a conflict of rights between the employers' right to privacy and the workers' right to fair and just working conditions. How should this be resolved? In some legal orders, the law excludes private households from labour inspections, giving precedence to the employers' privacy over workers' rights.[54] The UK even used this as a reason to refrain from ratifying the ILO Convention on Domestic Workers that protects a number of labour and other human rights of this group of workers. The Government representative in the ILO proceedings said: 'we do not consider it appropriate, or practical, to extend criminal health and safety legislation, including inspections, to cover private households employing domestic workers. It would be difficult, for instance, to hold elderly individuals, who employ carers, to the same standards as large companies.'[55]

Migrant domestic workers who accompany their employer under a visa that ties them to the employer or a visa that obligates them to live in the employer's home are known to live and work in poor conditions, with no private space and with very limited opportunities to have a private life or contact with the outside world.[56] The exclusion of their workplace from labour inspections should not be accepted without qualification. This is supported by the fact that the European Committee of Social Rights (ECSR) and the Group of Experts on Action against Trafficking in Human Beings (GRETA) have insisted on the importance of labour inspections in private households in order to examine the working conditions of domestic workers, notwithstanding that such inspections can interfere with the employers' private life.[57] It is important to note here that

---

[52] *Siliadin v France* [2005] ECHR 545.
[53] This issue is discussed in chapter 9.
[54] See, for instance, s 51 of the UK Health and Safety at Work Act 1974, entitled 'Exclusion of application to domestic employment', which states that '[n]othing in this Part shall apply in relation to a person by reason only that he employs another, or is himself employed, as a domestic servant in a private household'.
[55] Statement by Ms Warwick, International Labour Conference Record of Proceedings 15 June 2011, 25(rev), p 22.
[56] See, for instance, *Siliadin v France*, above n 52; *CN v UK* [2010] ECHR 380; V Mantouvalou, '"Am I Free Now?" Overseas Domestic Workers in Slavery' (2015) 42 *Journal of Law and Society* 329; N Sedacca, 'Migrant Domestic Workers and the Right to Private and Family Life' (2019) 37 *Netherlands Quarterly of Human Rights*.
[57] GRETA, Second Report on Spain, 2018, para 90; ECSR, 2020 Conclusions on Albania. The living conditions of domestic workers when in a situation of servitude have also been presented as giving rise to a violation of the right

some legal orders permit inspections in private households while protecting employers' privacy through measures such as the prior authorisation of the inspection by a judicial body or the consent of the employer.[58]

Further difficult questions affecting people who work in private households arise in relation to babysitters, carers or nannies who look after young children, elderly people, or others in need of care at home. People who employ domestic workers may feel anxious about leaving their dependants, particularly young babies, with someone whom they know little. Installing a camera (known as a 'nanny cam') may give them a sense of safety and peace of mind. However, for the worker (babysitter, carer or nanny), knowing that they are constantly monitored may induce anxiety, while covert surveillance for which the worker has not been informed may violate the right to privacy.[59] The criteria developed in *Barbulescu* and other case law, including clear advance notification of the nature and extent of monitoring, should apply here, if someone seeks to monitor workers in intimate settings. Even though anxiety about leaving babies, young children, elderly people and others with a carer may be human nature, it is important to appreciate that electronic monitoring may undermine the relationship of trust and violate the worker's right to private life.

4. Data Protection

A further specific problem that emerges with new technological tools is that not only can employers monitor workers closely, but they can also collect and store extensive data, including personal and sensitive data. Legislation on the right to privacy that also applies in the workplace is to be found in data protection laws,[60] such as the EU General Data Protection Regulation of 2016.[61] In the UK there is the Data Protection Act 2018 (DPA 2018),[62] sitting alongside the UK General Data Protection Regulation, which, as assimilated EU law, contains the majority of substantive provisions relating to data protection at work. The DPA 2018 incorporates some key principles: lawfulness, fairness, transparency, purpose limitation, data minimisation, accuracy. These principles constitute a good starting point for employers' use of personal data but are not specifically tailored for the employment relationship which is typically characterised by inequality of bargaining power between the worker and the employer. However, there is Guidance by the Information Commissioner, which focuses specifically on privacy at work, and aims to create more certainty on monitoring and data at work, protect workers' rights and support employers.[63] Aspects of the guidance involve the collection of 'special category data', which involve racial or ethnic origin, political opinions, religious or philosophical beliefs, trade union

---

to housing. See J Hohmann, 'Conceptualising Domestic Servitude as a Violation of the Human Right to Housing and Reframing Australian Policy Responses' (2022) 31 *Griffith Law Review* 98.

[58] See ILO Report IV(1), 'Decent Work for Domestic Workers', International Labour Conference, 99th session, 2010, para 249.

[59] For a broader discussion of privacy in intimate settings and technology, see K Levy and B Schneier, 'Privacy Threats in Intimate Relationships' (2020) 6 *Journal of Cybersecurity* 1. See also L Stark and K Levy, 'The Surveillant Consumer' (2018) 40 *Media, Culture & Society* 1.

[60] See F Hendrickx, 'Protection of Workers' Personal Data: General Principles', ILO, May 2022.

[61] Regulation (EU) 2016/679 of the European Parliament and of the Council of 27 April 2016 on the protection of natural persons with regard to the processing of personal data and on the free movement of such data, and repealing Directive 95/46/EC (General Data Protection Regulation) *OJ* L 119, 4.5.2016, 1–88.

[62] This replaced the Data Protection Act 1998.

[63] Available at https://ico.org.uk/about-the-ico/media-centre/news-and-blogs/2023/10/ico-publishes-guidance-to-ensure-lawful-monitoring-in-the-workplace/.

membership, genetic data, biometric data, health or disability, sex life, or sexual orientation. The guidance also specifically discusses criminal offence data to which data protection law also gives special protection.[64]

In the context of access to work, one crucial question is whether data on prior convictions, police cautions, and reprimands (for children) are collected and disclosed in accordance with data protection law and Article 8 ECHR. In a case that involved retention and disclosure of a police caution issued to the applicant, which led to the withdrawal of a job offer and harmed her employment prospects, the ECtHR ruled that 'the indiscriminate and open-ended collection of criminal record data' by the authorities is unlikely to be compatible with the ECHR, unless there are 'clear and detailed statutory regulations clarifying the safeguards applicable and setting out the rules governing, *inter alia*, the circumstances in which data can be collected, the duration of their storage, the use to which they can be put and the circumstances in which they may be destroyed'.[65] In this case, the Court found that the UK did not comply with its obligations under Article 8. Since then, the UK rules governing retention and disclosure have been tightened considerably, though the use of criminal record checks has been considerably expanded. Usually, there will be a check by an employer with the Disclosure and Barring Service for criminal convictions, excluding those that have been 'spent' by the effluxion of time.[66] For a wide range of jobs involving criminal justice and health professions, the employer must check for all convictions and adult cautions even if spent.[67] An employer must carry out an even more comprehensive check for jobs involving contact with children and the provision of health and social care services, which includes any information whatsoever that the police have on their database, including youth cautions (which involve no judicial determination of criminal behaviour)[68] and mere allegations of wrongdoing.[69] The UK Supreme Court has held that these detailed regulations comply with Article 8 because the law is precise and accessible, the disclosure serves a legitimate aim such as the protection of children and the public, and the interference with privacy is proportionate.[70] The Court acknowledged that sometimes the disclosed information is irrelevant or hardly pertinent, but argued that employers must use their judgement in determining whether to use this information. The danger is, of course, that employers carrying out these mandatory enhanced checks will simply reject candidates for jobs if there is the slightest hint on the police record of something untoward, even if the police have concluded that there was no misconduct. 'In these days of keen competition and defensive decision-making will the candidate with the clean record not be placed ahead of the other, however apparently irrelevant his offence and even if otherwise evenly matched?'[71]

The EU is proposing more intense regulation of data protection in the context of platform workers who are subject to automated monitoring and decision-making systems used by digital labour platforms. In Chapter III of the proposed Directive on Platform Work,[72] EU legislation

---

[64] Article 10 of the UK GDPR.
[65] *MM v United Kingdom*, [2012] ECHR 1906, [199].
[66] Rehabilitation of Offenders Act 1974.
[67] Rehabilitation of Offenders Act 1974 (Exceptions) Order 1975 (SI 1975/1023), as amended on many occasions, including changes in view of a declaration of incompatibility with Article 8 in *R (T) v Chief Constable of Greater Manchester Police (Liberty intervening); R (B) v Secretary of State for the Home Department (Liberty intervening)* [2014] UKSC 35, [2015] AC 49.
[68] Crime and Disorder Act 1998, s 66ZA.
[69] Police Act 1997, ss 113A and 113B; upheld as compatible with Article 8 in *R v National Police Chief's Council* [2020] EWCA Civ 1348, [2021] ICR 425.
[70] *R (on the application of P and others) v Secretary of State for Justice and others* [2019] UKSC 3, [2020] AC 185.
[71] *R (T) v Chief Constable of Greater Manchester Police*, above n 67, [45] per Lord Wilson.
[72] Proposal for a Directive of the European Parliament and of the Council on improving working conditions in platform work 2021/0414(COD) 10107/23 Brussels, 7 June 2023 (Council position).

will ban the processing of certain kinds of data altogether. This ban applies to the emotional and psychological state of the person, or the collection of data while the person is not working. The proposal also requires greater information about these automated systems to be provided to the workers, and human monitoring of these decision-making systems including the power to override such decisions. There will also be a duty placed on labour platforms to inform and consult workers or their representatives on the introduction and changes in the use of automated monitoring or decision-making systems. These measures are clearly guided by concerns for privacy as well as the intensification of subordination in employment. Although the proposed Directive will not apply to workers in the UK, it provides a persuasive illustration of what further measures are required to protect the privacy of workers in the emerging world of algorithmic management.

5. Testing

Some employers use blood or urine tests of employees for detecting drugs and alcohol. Compulsory tests are interferences with the right to privacy under Article 8 ECHR,[73] and information obtained is likely to be confidential personal information linked to a person's health regulated by the data protection legislation.[74] Accordingly, involuntary testing must be justified as a necessary and proportionate measure to achieve a legitimate aim under Article 8(2) ECHR, and the test results processed in accordance with the principles of data protection laws. The Information Commissioner's Employment Practices Guidance suggests that, in the absence of a compelling health and safety reason for testing, normally an employer should use less intrusive means of monitoring the workforce. It also suggests that testing following an incident is less intrusive of privacy than random testing of the workforce in general.

Random testing for alcohol in jobs where the safety of others is at stake is normally regarded as justifiable under Article 8(2) ECHR. Examples of such jobs include pilots of planes, train drivers, bus drivers, and construction workers. The extent to which such safety concerns justify testing was considered in *Madsen v Denmark*.[75] The applicant worked on a ship, not as a sailor involved in the running of the ship, but rather as a member of the crew looking after passengers. He objected to having to take a random test for alcohol (though he in fact tested negative). Because he was involved in passenger safety to some extent, at least in case of an emergency, the ECtHR held that occasional random alcohol tests, about once a year, were a proportionate and necessary measure to protect the right to life of the passengers. On that view, train and flight crews would also have to submit to random tests. But where no safety concerns exist, testing for alcohol is likely to be an unjustifiable interference with the right to privacy. In the UK, an employee might resign and claim compensation for constructive unfair dismissal.

Random testing for drugs is much harder to justify. Unlike testing for alcohol, the methods for testing for residues of drugs in the blood cannot inform the employer whether work performance was adversely affected in fact. Furthermore, it seems that in the UK drugs are seldom used in the workplace, so that the regulator of health and safety at work (the Health and Safety Executive) has been unable to find a link between drugs and workplace accidents, thereby removing one of the main justifications for random testing.

These principles are applicable to other kinds of testing. Genetic testing for investigations of an employee's likely future health is so far unreliable, expensive and of dubious predictive value.

---

[73] *X v Austria*, [1979] ECHR 6; *Peters v Netherlands*, App No 21132/93 (1994) 77A DR 75.
[74] General Data Protection Regulation 2016, Article 9(2). Data Protection Act 2018, s 10.
[75] *Madsen v Denmark* [2002] ECHR 855.

In the UK, because such testing is unlikely to be proportionate or satisfy the requirements for fair processing of sensitive personal data, the Information Commissioner has determined that such information should not be collected.[76] In the United States, federal regulation controls the use of genetic information.[77]

Some employers also use various kinds of personality testing for job applicants. Data driven web systems assess video interviews automatically according to algorithms chosen to some extent by the client, thereby reducing selection to an automated process. Such tests may involve questions that probe deeply into an employee's private life on the premise that difficult personal circumstances or unusual lifestyles may interfere with performance on the job. This invasion of privacy is, of course, consensual in the sense that an applicant has the choice to refuse the test and forgo the job. Do job applicants have any legal remedy if they refuse to take a personality test and are consequently not considered for a position? Although some use of tests may help to overcome unconscious bias, it may be possible to claim indirect discrimination on the ground of race or sex if it can be shown that the personality test in practice has a disproportionate adverse effect on the recruitment of a member of a protected group. For instance, if the questions ask about criminal records or arrests of family members, a black applicant is likely to be disadvantaged because of the higher rates of arrest in that community. But provided employers comply with the data protection principles with respect to the results of the tests, there is no obvious route for challenging the use of such tests on the grounds that they amount to an unjustified interference with privacy.

6. Conclusion

Our opening example on monitoring and surveillance by Amazon may represent one of the more extreme instances of intrusions of privacy. However, it is not unique and there are worrying patterns affecting all workers. Employers' interference with workers' private life is gradually increasing and technology facilitates this. Workers in precarious sectors may be monitored even more closely, and have even more limited power to resist by objecting to monitoring or changing jobs. Employers may present monitoring as justified for reasons of efficiency and other business interests. However, both the reasons and the proportionality of the measures must be scrutinised closely. The right to privacy in the workplace encompasses many aspects of individual dignity and autonomy, and organisations and human and labour rights monitoring bodies have shown awareness of the value of privacy for workers' dignity and autonomy, and the importance of placing control on collection and use of personal data. Working from home presents workers with distinct threats to their private life, given that activities at home generally involve some of the most personal and intimate aspects of one's life, while those working from other people's homes are faced with the problem that their workplace is not accessible to the authorities because of the employers' right to privacy. Workers' private life should not be reduced to zero, though, as the ECtHR said in *Barbulescu*. Quite to the contrary: their dignity and autonomy should be protected from employers' domination both when they are at work, and when they are away from work, as the chapter that follows explains.

---

[76] Information Commissioner's Office, 'Employment practices and data protection: information about workers' health' (August 2023).

[77] Under Title II of the Genetic Information Nondiscrimination Act of 2008, it is illegal to discriminate against employees or applicants because of genetic information. It prohibits the use of genetic information in making employment decisions, restricts employers and other entities from requesting, requiring or purchasing genetic information, and strictly limits the disclosure of genetic information. PT Kim, 'Regulating the Use of Genetic Information: Perspectives from the US Experience' (2010) 31 *Comparative Labour Law and Policy Journal* 693.

14

Private Life Away from Work

1.	Dismissal and the Right to Private Life	5.	Criminal Convictions
2.	Spatial Isolation and Private Life	6.	Employers' Reputation
3.	Relevant Factors and Criteria	7.	Reconceptualising Privacy: A Sharp Line for Life Away from Work
4.	Sexual Intimacy: None of the Employer's Business	8.	Conclusion

Driving back home on a winter Saturday night, Mr X stopped at a transport café between two towns to use the lavatory. In the toilet he met a man with whom he had consensual sex. A police officer entered the toilet and arrested them both. Mr X, 'very shocked and frightened', was driven to the police station and put in a cell. He was interviewed and was reassured that further action would not be taken unless he reoffended within five years. Having been cautioned for gross indecency, his name was placed on the Sex Offenders Register. His offence was to have engaged in homosexual activity in public with a consenting adult under s 13 of the Sexual Offences Act 1956, as amended by the Sexual Offences Act 1967. Mr X was employed by a charity organising activities for young offenders. His employer, who had access to the Register, was informed of the offence. Mr X was dismissed.

Mr Pay performed shows in hedonist and fetish clubs in his leisure time and was also a director of a company selling products connected with bondage and sadomasochism on the internet; photographs of him and semi-naked women and men were available online. Mr Pay was employed as a probation officer. At some point he disclosed to his employer that he belonged to a number of organisations, and the employer was later informed about his activities in detail. Although his off-duty conduct had no impact on his performance at work, the employer held the view that it was incompatible with his professional duties as a probation officer. Mr Pay was dismissed.

Should it ever be lawful for people to lose their job due to the way that they act in their leisure time, away from work, for reasons connected with their intimate relationships? Or is this conduct part of their private life? Can the right to private life extend to activities in public space? And can life away from work ever constitute a legitimate reason for disciplinary action? This chapter addresses these and other related questions, focusing particularly on personal and intimate relationships that people develop outside the workplace and working time.[1]

---

[1] Parts of this chapter draw on V Mantouvalou, 'Human Rights and Unfair Dismissal: Private Acts in Public Spaces' (2008) 71 *Modern Law Review* 912. Dismissal for conduct away from work involving social media activity is discussed in chapter 16.

1. Dismissal and the Right to Private Life

Both Mr X and Mr Pay challenged their dismissals in employment tribunals and courts. UK law provides protection of employees against dismissal. The fairness enquiry is set out in the Employment Rights Act 1996 (ERA 1996). Section 94(1) provides that '(a)n employee has the right not to be unfairly dismissed by his employer'. The employer needs to present a reason for dismissal that has to involve conduct, capability or qualifications, redundancy or 'some other substantial reason'.[2] Section 98(4) deals with fairness, and states that it 'depends on whether in the circumstances … the employer acted reasonably or unreasonably in treating it as a sufficient reason for dismissing the employee' which should also be 'determined in accordance with equity and the substantial merits of the case'. However, from early on, tribunals and courts accepted that employers had a very broad 'range of reasonable responses'.[3] They recognised to employers a significant degree of discretion, ruling that even if a dismissal is harsh, it can be fair.[4]

Being particularly sensitive to business interests in the promotion of economic efficiency, they exhibited at the same time a striking reluctance to afford similar attention to the interests of the employees in job security, which obtained a subordinate status in judicial reasoning in cases challenging the legality of disciplinary powers. Due to this unwillingness to scrutinise managerial prerogative, all but the most perverse cases of termination of employment were deemed to be lawful.[5]

Against this background, it is evident that the prospects of success for a claim challenging the legality of dismissal for activities that could be classified as private were slim. In 1975, for instance, in *Spiller v Wallis Ltd*,[6] the employer, a supermarket, dismissed Mrs Spiller for having adulterous relationships contrary to the company policy. Her dismissal was held to be fair. In *Saunders v Scottish National Camps Association*,[7] the applicant's dismissal on the grounds of his homosexuality was equally deemed unproblematic. In *Mathewson v RB Wilson Dental Laboratories*,[8] where the applicant was caught by the police with a small amount of cannabis when he was having a lunch break, and was therefore one hour late for work, the court found his resulting dismissal 'harsh but fair'. Off-duty conduct formed the basis for a lawful reason for termination of employment, as it was unequivocally found not to be wholly unreasonable, while considerations regarding the implications for the employees' private lives were probably irrelevant when determining legality.

However, Mr X and Mr Pay argued that they were unfairly dismissed under s 98 of the Employment Rights Act 1996, examined and interpreted in line with the right to private life under the Human Rights Act 1998 (HRA 1998) that incorporated European Convention (ECHR) rights into domestic law.[9] According to s 3 of the HRA 1998, courts have a duty to interpret national legislation, including employment legislation, in a manner compatible with the HRA 1998. In addition, s 6(1) states that '[i]t is unlawful for a public authority to act in a way which is incompatible with one or more of the Convention rights'. The term 'public authorities' also includes courts and tribunals, which have to take into account Convention rights in the development of common law.

---

[2] ERA 1996, s 98(1) and 98(2).
[3] See *Iceland Frozen Foods Ltd v Jones* [1983] ICR 17.
[4] See H Collins, *Justice in Dismissal* (OUP, 1992) ch 1.
[5] For analysis and critique, see generally, Collins, above n 4.
[6] *Spiller v FJ Wallis Ltd* [1975] IRLR 362, IT.
[7] *Saunders v Scottish National Camps Association Ltd* [1980] IRLR 174, EAT; [1981] IRLR 277, Court of Session.
[8] *Mathewson v RB Wilson Dental Laboratories* [1988] IRLR 512, EAT.
[9] See Human Rights Act 1998, ss 3 and 6 on the interpretive duties of courts and the duties of public authorities.

The relevant Convention right is Article 8 of the ECHR that protects the right to private and family life.[10] It states:

1. Everyone has the right to respect for his private and family life, his home and his correspondence.
2. There shall be no interference by a public authority with the exercise of this right except such as is in accordance with the law and is necessary in a democratic society in the interests of national security, public safety or the economic well-being of the country, for the prevention of disorder or crime, for the protection of health or morals, or for the protection of the rights and freedoms of others.

The right to private life has a broad scope and does not only cover activities in one's home in ECHR case law. The ECtHR has stated that Article 8 'encompasses, inter alia, the right to personal autonomy and personal development'.[11] It has further found that it protects 'the right to establish and develop relationships with other human beings and the outside world',[12] and protects 'an individual's physical and social identity'.[13] The provision

> secure[s] to the individual a sphere within which he can freely pursue the development and fulfilment of his personality ... and concerns rights of central importance to the individual's identity, self-determination, physical and moral integrity, maintenance of relationships with others and a settled and secure place in the community.[14]

Article 8 also extends to the workplace, as we saw in chapter 13, where it protects aspects of the employee's private life from employer intrusion through monitoring and surveillance.[15] Does the right to private life protect workers for their activities away from the workplace and working time?

UK tribunals and courts accepted from early on that the law of unfair dismissal should be interpreted in line with the HRA 1998. However, in *X v Y*, Mummery LJ said:

> The applicant's conduct did not take place in his private life nor was it within the scope of application of the right to respect for it. It happened in a place to which the public had, and were permitted to have, access; it was a criminal offence, which is normally a matter of legitimate concern to the public; a criminal offence is not a purely private matter; and it led to a caution for the offence, which was relevant to his employment and should have been disclosed by him to his employer as a matter of legitimate concern to it. The applicant wished to keep the matter private. That does not make it part of his private life or deprive it of its public aspect.[16]

A similar argument was advanced when looking at the dismissal of Mr Pay, notwithstanding that he had not acted illegally. Both the Employment Tribunal and the Employment Appeal Tribunal held that his private life was not in question. Mr Pay's activities 'had been publicised on the website of Roissy of which he was a director and ... he was present in bars and clubs, to which the public was admitted, promoting the interests of Roissy in [bondage, domination and sado-masochism]'.[17]

This approach to the right to private life that protects a right to act in seclusion and leaves outside its scope conduct that takes place in public space has also been followed in decisions on

---

[10] The right to private and family life is also protected in Article 7 of the EU Charter of Fundamental Rights, while Article 8 of the Charter protects personal data. The right to privacy is also guaranteed in Article 12 of the Universal Declaration of Human Rights and Article 17 of the International Covenant on Civil and Political Rights.
[11] *A, B and C v Ireland* [2010] ECHR 2032, [212].
[12] *Pretty v the United Kingdom* [2002] ECHR 427, [61].
[13] *Mikulic v Croatia* [2002] ECHR 27, [53].
[14] See, eg, *A-MV v Finland*, [2017] ECHR 273, [76].
[15] *Niemietz v Germany* [1992] ECHR 80; *Barbulescu v Romania* [2017] ECHR 742.
[16] *X v Y* [2004] EWCA Civ 662, [2004] ICR 1634, [2004] IRLR 624, [52].
[17] *Pay v Lancashire Probation Service* [2004] ICR 187, EAT, [36].

dismissal because of workers' activity on social media.[18] In *Crisp v Apple Retail*,[19] for instance, the Employment Tribunal found that Mr Crisp's Facebook comments that were critical of his employer's products did not engage his right to private life. His Facebook profile was not private for the reason that his friends could access it, and forward his comments to others. He could not have an expectation of privacy on the internet, on the view of the tribunal, and as an employee of Apple, a company that specialises in technology, he should have known that. As he had no expectation of privacy for comments he posted on Facebook, his right to private life was not engaged,[20] and his dismissal by the tech giant was ruled to be harsh but fair.

Evidence of the same thinking on the right to private life can be found in more recent decisions. In the Employment Tribunal case of *Lawrence v Secretary of State for Justice*,[21] Mrs Lawrence was dismissed from her post as a Delivery Manager in the public sector for posting sexually graphic images and videos of herself on the internet. She brought a claim of unfair dismissal and invoked, inter alia, her right to private life under Article 8 of the ECHR. The tribunal dismissed this argument, saying that '[t]he activity was a public activity. Inhibiting a public activity by dismissal from employment is not a matter to which article 8 extends.'[22]

We see that UK courts and tribunals examining intimate, sex-related or other personal activities and views outside the workplace and working time focus on a spatial criterion as a central factor determining whether a dismissal implicates the right to private life. This means that the activity is not protected under Article 8 if it takes place in public space or in space to which the public has access. The right to private life is not engaged at all in these instances, so tribunals and courts do not reach the second stage in the process of reasoning which examines whether the restriction is proportionate to the aim pursued. Is it correct to say that conduct away from the workplace and working time is never covered by the right to private life in the employment context, if it takes place in public space?

2. Spatial Isolation and Private Life

The understanding of the right to private life that protects only activities in a private or secluded location is not compatible with the interpretation of the provision by the ECtHR, which has found that the right to private life applies in public space. When Mr Peck, for instance, challenged the decision of UK authorities to provide to newspapers and TV programmes CCTV footage of him attempting to commit suicide – recognisable images of which were then publicly transmitted – the Court rejected the view that these images remained outside the scope of Article 8, simply because they were captured in public. Placing its attention on the question whether the applicant could have foreseen that they would have been used in this way,[23] it found a breach of the right to private life. In a further landmark case, Caroline Von Hannover, the Princess of Monaco, alleged that publication in the tabloid press of photographs of her, taken while she was in public – in restaurants, on holidays with family and friends, shopping at the market – constituted a violation of her private life.[24] The ECtHR decisively rejected the dominant view in

---

[18] See further chapter 16.
[19] *Crisp v Apple Retail (UK) Ltd*, ET/1500258/11, 5 August 2011.
[20] ibid [45].
[21] *Lawrence v Secretary of State for Justice*, ET/3401016/2016, 23 March 2017 (Employment Tribunal).
[22] ibid [42].
[23] *Peck v UK* [2003] ECHR 44, [62].
[24] *Von Hannover v Germany* [2004] ECHR 294.

German jurisprudence that privacy is to be equated to seclusion: 'the criterion of spatial isolation, although apposite in theory, is in reality too vague and difficult for the person concerned to determine in advance'. Germany violated the right to private life.[25]

Moreover, this narrow interpretation of the right to private life can be criticised for being particularly ill-suited in the employment context. As we said, case law on work and private life reads the right to private life broadly, covering several activities that do not take place in private space, and protecting several aspects of individual autonomy. In *Niemietz v Germany*, considering whether the office can form part of someone's private life, the Court said that

> it would be too restrictive to limit the notion to an 'inner circle' in which the individual may live his own personal life as he chooses and to exclude therefrom entirely the outside world not encompassed within that circle. Respect for private life must also comprise to a certain degree the right to establish and develop relationships with other human beings.[26]

In *Sidabras*,[27] the Court read the right to work into the right to private life. Even more to the point, the Court has accepted that dismissal for activities outside the workplace and working time can lead to a violation of the right to private life even if these activities do not necessarily take place in private space. In *Ozpinar v Turkey*,[28] the applicant was a judge and was dismissed following complaints about her close personal relationships, the clothes and make-up she used, and the fact that she did not live with her mother, among other issues. The ECtHR accepted that the applicant's dismissal was for reasons that were covered by her right to private life in relation to these complaints that were not relevant to her performance at work, and accepted that there was an interference with Article 8,[29] which was not justified.[30] For life away from work to be used as a reason for dismissal, in other words, what matters is whether the activities in question have a connection to the performance of someone's duties at work.

This case law suggests that the applicable criteria on the scope of the right to privacy are not based on the place where the conduct occurred. The employer may wish to control many aspects of workers' lives, but the right to private life can place limitations to this power, particularly when it comes to off-duty conduct. ECtHR case law supports the position that workers have a right to live their life autonomously away from work, without employers dictating how they will do this in line with their preferences. Employees are not role models that should lead their private lives according to the moral standards that some groups espouse and may associate with the performance of their duties, as *Ozpinar* showed.

3. Relevant Factors and Criteria

Academic scholarship describes the right to private life as 'contextually dependent'.[31] This means that it should be interpreted in line with the particular context where it is considered.[32]

---

[25] ibid [75]. For a similar position adopted by the House of Lords on the publication of the applicant's photo, captured when she was in public, see *Campbell v MGN Ltd* [2004] UKHL 22.
[26] *Niemietz*, above n 15, [29].
[27] *Sidabras and Dziautas v Lithuania* [2004] ECHR 395.
[28] *Ozpinar v Turkey* [2010] ECHR 2268.
[29] ibid [43]–[48].
[30] The Court concluded that Article 8 was violated.
[31] FD Schoeman, 'Privacy and Intimate Information' in FD Schoeman (ed), *Philosophical Dimensions of Privacy – An Anthology* (Cambridge, CUP, 1984) 403 at 404.
[32] See further Mantouvalou, above n 1. On dismissal for conduct away from work, see also A Sanders, 'The Law of Unfair Dismissal and Behaviour Outside Work' (2014) 45 *Legal Studies* 328; M Finkin, 'Life Away from Work' (2006) 66

The inequality of power between the employer and the worker, the importance of a work/life balance and other such employment-related principles should determine the interpretation of employees' right to private life in the employment context.[33]

Once we accept that the right to private life is not determined by the space where an act takes place, we can accept that in principle it may cover activities that take place in public space, outside the workplace and working time. The next step would be to employ a test of proportionality in line with the second paragraph of Article 8 of the ECHR. The test of proportionality typically means that as soon as an interference with a Convention right has been established, the employer's action must have been necessary and appropriate to achieve a legitimate aim. The ECtHR asks whether the employer's reason for disciplinary action was in pursuit of an aim, such as the efficiency of the business, protection of health and safety, or the avoidance of adverse publicity and possible damage to reputation among customers of the business or public service. In what follows, we examine some central considerations to be taken into account in this context on the basis of case law of the ECtHR.

The cases of *Obst* and *Schuth*[34] involved dismissal by organisations that promote a particular ideology or ethic, also known as ideological organisations, and illustrate the Court's main considerations when applying the test of proportionality in dismissal for reasons involving people's private life. The employers, religious organisations, dismissed the applicants because they both had extramarital affairs. Generally speaking, one would think that whether someone has an extramarital affair is not the employer's business.[35] However, when considering employees of organisations committed to a particular ethic, things may be different. Mr Obst was employed as director for Europe of public relations by the Mormon Church, and Mr Schuth was employed as an organist and choirmaster by the Catholic Church. The Court applied a test of proportionality in both cases and reached different outcomes on each application. It emphasised that

> [w]hilst it is true that, under the Convention, an employer whose ethos is based on religion or on a philosophical belief may impose specific duties of loyalty on its employees, a decision to dismiss based on a breach of such duty cannot be subjected, on the basis of the employer's right of autonomy, only to a limited judicial scrutiny exercised by the relevant domestic employment tribunal without having regard to the nature of the post in question and without properly balancing the interests involved in accordance with the principle of proportionality.[36]

The post that someone has in the organisation is a consideration to be taken into account when assessing the fairness of dismissal, and the dismissal of Mr Obst was ruled to be compatible with the Convention. He had been raised as a member of the Mormon Church, and was aware that his conduct would be contrary to its beliefs, which he represented, as he was responsible for its public relations. According to the Court, by signing his contract with the Mormon Church, he knew that he agreed to marital fidelity that was a central issue for this Church.

The same could not be said about Mr Schuth, in the view of the Court. His job as an organist and choirmaster was not so closely connected to the Catholic Church's mission, and during his years of employment he never argued against the Church's beliefs. His contract did not imply that he agreed to marital fidelity, and his affair had not been publicised in a way that could harm the

---

Louisiana Law Review 945; S Sugarman, 'Lifestyle Discrimination in Employment' (2003) 24 *Berkeley Journal of Employment and Labor Law* 377.

[33] See further Mantouvalou, ibid.
[34] *Obst v Germany*, App No 425/03; *Schuth v Germany*, App No 1620/03, judgments of 23 September 2010.
[35] Some employers seek to limit relationships between co-workers and develop rules to that end, which become all the more intrusive. On this, see J Crispin, 'We might soon be forbidden from falling in love at work. Do we want that?', *The Guardian*, 5 November 2019; and E Jacobs, 'Is Friendship Employers' Business', *Financial Times*, 15 November 2023.
[36] *Schuth*, above n 34, [69].

Church's image. At the same time, the fact that Mr Schuth would have great difficulty in obtaining a job with another employer because of the nature of his work was an additional weighty consideration, particularly when the employer has a 'predominant position in a given sector or activity'.[37] The dismissal of Mr Schuth was ruled to be in breach of Article 8 of the Convention.

The above cases show that in ideological organisations where the employee may have certain duties to comply with a particular ethic, a test of proportionality is crucial when it comes to activities in the employee's private life. Factors that the Court considered in applying the test of proportionality include the question whether the employer's sanction involves the deprivation of a job, livelihood, and possibly a career. These factors are sensitive to the employment context and the importance of work (as the main means by which most people make a living) and private life, which is where many people develop their most intimate interpersonal relations. Perhaps more problematic is the fact that the Court also paid attention to whether the applicants had agreed to marital fidelity in their employment contracts in *Schuth* and *Obst*. There is a concern that since most contractual terms are devised and imposed by an employer, apparent consent to those terms given by an employee may be illusory and effectively coerced.[38] Even ideological organisations cannot, through the employment contract, freely impose on employees duties that dominate their entire life, as the Court observed in *Schuth*.[39]

The criteria for the assessment of dismissal because of private life were more recently revisited in *Fernandez Martinez v Spain*,[40] which divided the Grand Chamber. The case had to examine the decision not to renew the contract of the applicant, a Catholic priest, who had been a Catholic religion and ethics teacher at a secondary state school since 1991. The applicant was ordained as a priest in 1961, and in 1984 he requested that he be exempted from the obligation of celibacy. He did not receive an answer, got married and had five children. In 1996, he was named in a newspaper as a priest who was married and belonged to an organisation that supports optional celibacy for priests. Following the publication, the Diocese of Carthagena informed the Ministry of Education that he was no longer suitable as a teacher of Catholic religion. For this reason, the Ministry did not renew his contract as a school teacher. The ECtHR examined his claim under Article 8 of the Convention. A narrow majority of 9 to 8 ruled that there was no breach of the ECHR. The majority balanced the applicant's private life against the autonomy of the religious organisation. The fact that the state (and not the religious organisation itself) employed the applicant did not affect the ruling of the Court. The decision of the majority was that the interference with the applicant's private life was not disproportionate in light of the interests of the religious organisation to autonomy.

In an insightful dissenting opinion, though, Judges Spielmann, Sajo, Karakas, Lemmens, Jaderblom, Vehabovic, Dedov and Saiz-Arnaiz criticised the decision of the majority. They said that '[w]hile it is true that, under the Convention, an employer whose ethos is based on religion or on a philosophical belief may impose specific duties of loyalty on its employees, a decision to dismiss based on a breach of such duty, must be subjected to a form of judicial scrutiny that involves a proper balancing of the right of the religious community to respect for its autonomy against the individual's human rights, in accordance with the principle of proportionality'.[41]

---

[37] *Schuth*, above n 34, [73].
[38] See H Collins and V Mantouvalou, 'The Contract of Employment and Human Rights' in M Freedland (ed), *The Contract of Employment* (Oxford, OUP, 2016). See also G Morris, 'Fundamental Rights: Exclusion by Agreement?' (2001) 30 ILJ 49. See *Eweida and Others v UK* [2013] ECHR 37. See further M Niezna and G Davidov, 'Consent in Contracts of Employment' (2023) 86 *Modern Law Review* 1134.
[39] *Schuth*, above n 34, [70].
[40] *Fernandez Martinez v Spain* [2014] ECHR 615.
[41] ibid, dissent, [22].

The dissenting Judges explained that it was the publicity given to the applicant's marital status that led to his dismissal, and emphasised that a crucial factor in the balancing exercise was that the applicant's teaching ability had not been affected by his private conduct; his private life, in other words, had had no impact on his workplace performance. The dissenting Judges were also particularly attentive to the particularities of the employment relation and the value of work for the individual, and explained that dismissal should be a last resort, criticising the fact that the authorities had failed to consider offering the applicant an alternative post that would not involve teaching religion and ethics.

In this line of cases, we see that in assessing whether a dismissal is compatible with the right to private life, a number of factors are pertinent, including the nature of the employer's organisation, the nature of the job, the question whether the person can find a new job and the question whether the conduct in question has an effect on someone's workplace performance.

4. Sexual Intimacy: None of the Employer's Business

The above ECtHR case law on ideological organisations suggests that private relationships that people develop outside work are in principle covered by the right to private life and can lead to its violation. When it comes to employers that do not promote a particular ethic, friendships or other intimate relationships away from work should be viewed as even less relevant to the retention of someone's work. This argument finds support in the jurisprudence of the ECtHR, which has recognised the importance of sex life for private life. In the landmark case of *Dudgeon v UK*,[42] which involved legislation banning homosexual activities between consenting adults, the Court stated that sexuality constitutes a 'most intimate aspect of private life',[43] and ruled that although public authorities generally enjoy a certain margin of appreciation in implementing the rights of the Convention, they can only interfere with such rights if they have particularly serious reasons.

More generally, concerns voiced by employers that the sex life of their employees might adversely affect business reputation should be tested with great caution because of the importance of privacy and sexual intimacy for dignity and autonomy, in order to eliminate the possibility of indirect imposition of moralistic preferences of either the employer or the wider public on employees. Societal prejudice on sex-related matters and sexuality has historically been widespread, and has frequently led to injustice has been exemplified in cases such as *Smith and Grady v UK*,[44] where the applicants were discharged from the armed forces because of their sexual orientation. In examining their complaint, the ECtHR stressed that the applicants' discharge stemmed primarily from a 'predisposed bias on the part of the heterosexual majority against a homosexual minority'[45] rather than evidence that they could not perform their job. It concluded that the UK violated the ECHR.

The case of Mr Pay, the probation officer who was dismissed because of his conduct away from work, that we discussed earlier in this chapter, went up to the ECtHR.[46] The Strasbourg Court

---

[42] *Dudgeon v UK* [1981] ECHR 5.
[43] ibid [52].
[44] *Smith and Grady v United Kingdom* [1999] ECHR 72. See also *Lustig-Prean and Beckett v United Kingdom* [1999] ECHR 71.
[45] *Smith and Grady*, ibid [97].
[46] *Pay v UK* [2009] IRLR 139 (ECtHR). Noted in V Mantouvalou and H Collins, 'Private Life and Dismissal: Pay v UK' (2009) 38 *ILJ* 244.

declared the application inadmissible for being manifestly ill-founded, having made an assessment of the merits of the complaint. In relation to the question whether the right to private life was applicable to the activities of Mr Pay, the ECtHR placed emphasis on the points that the applicant's performances were in a nightclub likely to be frequented only by a self-selecting group of like-minded people, that the photographs of his act that were published on the internet were anonymised and that the applicant claimed that the public performance aspect of his act was a fundamental part of his sexual expression. In other words, although the public could go to the nightclub, just as they could go to the toilet of the café where Mr X was caught engaged in sexual activity in *X v Y*, that did not necessarily make it a public place, outside the zone of respect for private life. A picture on the internet, similarly, might not involve a forfeiture of the right to privacy. For these reasons, the ECtHR concluded: 'In these circumstances, the Court is prepared to proceed on the assumption, without finally deciding, that Article 8 is applicable.' The decision in *Pay v UK* casts further doubt on the approach of tribunals and courts with respect to the scope of the right to privacy.

However, even though the ECtHR was prepared to accept in *Pay* that the right to private life was applicable to the activities of the applicant, it conceded that the restriction of Article 8(1) had been in accordance with the law and in pursuit of a legitimate aim of the employer, namely the protection of the reputation of the probation service. It then applied a test of proportionality in order to establish whether dismissal was a justified measure to pursue this aim. In doing so, it stated that national authorities have a 'margin of appreciation', which is a well-established doctrine that the Court uses when it wishes to allow national authorities a degree of discretion in the regulation of sensitive social and political matters.

The ECtHR recognised that the dismissal was a severe measure because of its effects on Mr Pay's reputation and on his chances of exercising the profession for which he had been trained and acquired skills. In these circumstances, the Court suggested that it might have been more proportionate for the employer to take less severe measures, short of dismissal, particularly as Mr Pay's activities had not yet become public knowledge. That option, however, had been foreclosed by Mr Pay himself, as a result of his failure to curb those aspects of his activities such as the pictures on the internet that were most likely to enter the public domain. In the end, therefore, the ECtHR concluded that the interference with Mr Pay's right was proportionate.

Although his dismissal was triggered by activities related to his sexual activities, which the Court has in the past described as a 'most intimate aspect of private life',[47] which places limitations on the scope of the margin of appreciation, in *Pay* it permitted national authorities to take a restrictive approach to matters involving the applicant's sexual practices. The fact that Mr Pay worked with sex offenders, which seems to have influenced the English courts in their approach to the case, should not have provided necessarily a justification for the interference with his right to privacy. Even if his off-duty conduct could be viewed as related to the nature of his job, his employers could have taken a proportionate measure of redeploying him to other tasks of the probation service.

It should be added here that a dismissal also has effects on the reputation of the worker who loses their job because of their private activities. This was analysed carefully by the Grand Chamber of the ECtHR in the case of *Denisov v Ukraine*,[48] where the Court provided extensive explanation of the relevance of the right to private life in dismissal. It said that, on the one hand, dismissal may be because of an employee's private life activities; and on the other, it may have grave effects on an employee's private life, including their reputation. A dismissal because

---

[47] *Dudgeon*, above n 42, [52].
[48] *Denisov v Ukraine* [2018] ECHR 1061. Discussed further in chapter 18.

of someone's intimate activities may have especially grave consequences on their reputation, which have to be carefully considered when assessing whether it is compatible with the right to private life.

A specific concern that emerges from cases such as *Pay v UK* is that employers and others may have prejudicial attitudes on sex-related matters. This can be illustrated by the case of *IB v Greece*,[49] which involved dismissal because of an employee's HIV status. Mr IB was dismissed from his job in a jewellery shop when colleagues of his found out that he was HIV-positive. They refused to work with him, demanding his dismissal. The employee challenged the dismissal as unlawful. However, the Greek Court of Cassation upheld the dismissal on the ground that it was not motivated by hostility towards his HIV status on the part of the employer, but by the need to ensure the peaceful running of the business. The ECtHR ruled that his dismissal in response to workforce pressure violated Article 14 (the prohibition of discrimination) in conjunction with Article 8 of the Convention. The ECtHR resisted the argument that business interests justified the dismissal. It emphasised that 'HIV-positive persons have to face up to a whole host of problems, not only medical, but also professional, social, personal and psychological, and above all sometimes to deeply rooted prejudices even among the most highly educated people',[50] and explained that prejudice cannot be used as a pretext for dismissal.[51] There is no question that there is significant stigma and prejudice affecting people who are HIV-positive, a social problem also recognised by the International Labour Organization.[52] Prejudice may affect other dismissals involving sexual activities or sexual orientation, which can be scrutinised under the Convention.

The principle that people's prejudice cannot justify a dismissal suggests that the ECtHR should have found in favour of Mr Pay. He did not engage in criminal activity. His sexual activities were seen as unconventional but there was no evidence that they had any impact on his ability to do his job.

Dismissal because of someone's personal relations may impair all relations of sexual intimacy for a variety of reasons. Societal beliefs about morality change and people are often prejudiced on sex-related matters. An employer may dismiss the employee because it has a view about morality that conflicts with the employee's, it disapproves of the employee's sex life, or it deems the employee's choices unconventional or immoral and hence incompatible with business interests. Yet discipline or dismissal for such reasons risks leading to an indirect imposition of the employer's personal morality upon the employee. It can damage individual choice and the liberty to have relationships which may be highly valued as essential for a person's well-being.

5. Criminal Convictions

Criminal convictions may set a tough task for courts and tribunals when determining fairness in dismissal. In the case of *X v Y*, which we discussed earlier in this chapter, Mummery LJ suggested that criminal activities are not private and that they are outside the scope of Article 8. However, given that the interpretation of the right to private life by UK courts in employment law cases has been questioned on the basis of Strasbourg case law, the statement of Mummery LJ

---

[49] *IB v Greece*, App No 552/10, Judgment of 3 October 2013.
[50] ibid [80].
[51] ibid [87].
[52] ILO Recommendation No 200 concerning HIV and AIDS and the World of Work, 2010. See also the judgment of the Constitutional Court of South Africa, *Hoffmann v South African Airways* (CCT 17/00) of 28 September 2000.

should be scrutinised more closely. People who commit a criminal offence are faced with the consequences of their actions in the criminal justice system, which also has the principle of double jeopardy that means that someone should not be put on trial twice for the same crime. Is it always fair for someone to lose their job following any criminal conviction?

Criteria that we presented earlier in this chapter become relevant here too: the nature of someone's job and the nature of the employer's business are relevant to the question whether they can lose their job because of a criminal conviction. Moreover, the nature of the conviction itself should be examined. A conviction for a criminal offence that is related to the nature of someone's job may render dismissal lawful, carrying significant weight in the test of proportionality – an issue that can be illustrated by a variety of examples: conviction for theft of a cashier employed by a supermarket, or conviction for possession of child pornography of a person employed by a nursery. Criminal offences such as these may have a devastating effect on the relation of trust and confidence between the employer and the employee, on the performance of contractual duties, on the employer's reputation or on the rights of others.

However, a criminal conviction may sometimes be irrelevant to the retention of or access to employment. This position probably underlies the statement of a Canadian adjudicator, who examined the legality of the dismissal of someone who was employed as a psychologist at a centre that treated inmates with mental health problems, because of his conviction for criminal harassment of his former girlfriend. The adjudicator found that the dismissal was unlawful, suggesting that '[a]n employer is generally not considered to be the custodian of an employee's moral character'.[53] Similarly, in *CJD v the Royal Bank of Scotland*,[54] it was ruled that a dismissal of an employee who assaulted his partner at home, who was also a work colleague, was unlawful. The Court of Session accepted that conduct outside the workplace can constitute a reason for dismissal if it 'reflects in some way upon the employer-employee relationship'.[55] In this case the dismissal was ruled to be unfair.

A similar approach in relation to criminal activities is supported by the decision of the ECtHR in *Thlimmenos v Greece*.[56] Mr Thlimmenos was a Jehovah's Witness, a religious group committed to pacifism, who was convicted under Greek legislation for refusing to wear a military uniform for the purposes of his mandatory military service. Because of his conviction, he could not be appointed to the position of a chartered accountant, although he had been successful in the examinations. The ECtHR held that the facts of the case fell within the ambit of freedom of religion and constituted a violation of Article 14 in conjunction with Article 9, famously stating that prohibition of discrimination 'is also violated when States without an objective and reasonable justification fail to treat differently persons whose situations are significantly different'. It concluded that the crime committed by Mr Thlimmenos, unlike other crimes that could have obstructed the performance of his job as an accountant, should not have been used to justify his exclusion from the profession.

To conclude this section, while the commission of a criminal offence is a public matter for the purposes of the criminal justice system, a criminal conviction should not always be viewed as falling outside the scope of the right to private life in the employment context. A criminal conviction may frequently be immaterial to the nature of someone's employment and may have no link

---

[53] Cited in a decision of 16 June 2008 of the Federal Court in *Attorney General of Canada v Frederick James Tobin* 2008 FC 740 at [42], which overturned the decision of the adjudicator, holding that there was a link between the criminal offence and the nature of his employment.
[54] *CJD v Royal Bank of Scotland* [2013] CSIH 86.
[55] ibid [43].
[56] *Thlimmenos v Greece* [2000] ECHR 162.

to the performance of their work and other aspects of workplace relations. To this, it should be added that conduct is sometimes wrongly criminalised, as the case of *Thlimmenos* reminds us. Moreover, it is important to bear in mind that if current or prospective employers had the power to exclude someone convicted of any criminal offence, offenders would never be able to find a job and would, therefore, be condemned to permanent unemployment and stigmatisation, without a route to social reintegration.

6. Employers' Reputation

It was earlier said that an aspect of business interests that is often invoked by employers when dismissing people for intimate conduct involves the reputation of the business, with the reputational risk often being remote. Protection of reputation may constitute a legitimate aim to be pursued. Employees have a duty of loyalty towards their employer, and deliberate infliction of reputational damage may breach that. However, given the value of intimate relationships for individual autonomy, which is a central value that underlies privacy, an attack on business reputation has to be particularly serious for limitations on private life to be justified. Respect for autonomy does not permit the imposition of the employer's moral views and preferences on employees,[57] unless a workplace has the promotion of a particular moral outlook as its central aim, as we said earlier. The issue of the employer's reputation should be approached with particular care, because it may constitute a pretext,[58] it may disguise an employer's moralistic views about how employees should lead their lives, or it may lead to the imposition of majority views (through pressure from the tabloid press, for instance) on individuals, minorities or other groups.

7. Reconceptualising Privacy: A Sharp Line for Life Away from Work

Reconceptualising the right to private life in cases of dismissal for off-duty conduct requires a sharp distinction between life at work and life outside work.[59] This provides a more appropriate criterion in a fresh approach to the interpretation of the condition of fairness in dismissal because of an employee's leisure activities. This is because life outside work is valuable. It is our time to act autonomously, to develop meaningful relationships with others and to engage in conduct that we find gratifying, without fear that it may impact on the retention of our job with all its devastating implications. The intrusion of the employer in decisions on how we spend our leisure time can have a damaging effect on our autonomy: it can threaten our work/life balance, it can harm our relations of love, friendship and trust, as well as all intimate relations that most of us value. Termination of employment because of our off-duty conduct can lead to a relationship of domination.

Support for this argument can also be found in the UK Supreme Court, as Sanders emphasised.[60] In a discussion of the scope of Article 8 of the ECHR in a different context,

---

[57] *Smith and Grady*, above n 44.
[58] See, for instance, *Mason v Huddersfield Giants Ltd*, 2014 WL 3925309, 15 July 2014.
[59] See also Mantouvalou, above n 1.
[60] Sanders, above n 32, 334.

the House of Lords underlined the importance of leisure time for 'identity and personal development'.[61] It was explained that 'some will be fortunate enough to find this kind of fulfilment in their job, but others will pursue it in their leisure hours'.[62]

On the basis of the argument developed in this chapter, it would be a positive starting point if courts stated clearly that life away from work should in principle be protected from employers' intrusion, irrespective of whether it is in public or private space. There should be a presumption of privacy. Drawing a clear, bright line that separates workplace conduct or performance, and off-duty conduct, can protect employees from employers' oppression, and can also help employers who are concerned about their reputation.

8. Conclusion

Tribunals and courts in the UK place excessive attention on the location where the worker's off-duty conduct took place in their assessment whether a dismissal violates the right to private life. However, Strasbourg case law suggests that this approach is erroneous. When examining the right in the employment context, it is not the space where the activities took place that should be viewed as determinative but the protection of workers against employers' power, who may seek to impose their views on how they should live their life away from work. The test of fairness in dismissal should not recognise wide discretion to the employer. It should, instead, be a test of proportionality, which both assesses whether the employer has a legitimate aim and whether disciplinary action or dismissal is strictly required in pursuing this aim. The power of employers to dismiss workers because of their private life can pose threats to people's autonomy and amount to domination.[63] Protecting the autonomy of workers against employer interference when they are away from the workplace and working time is crucial,[64] for otherwise the employer will become a moral arbiter of workers' private life. This position may be advocated in some management literature[65] but is incompatible with workers' right to private life.

---

[61] *R (Countryside Alliance) v A-G* [2007] UKHL 52, [139].
[62] ibid [97].
[63] Mantouvalou, above n 1.
[64] See R Lippke, 'Work, Privacy, and Autonomy' (1989) 3 *Public Affairs Quarterly* 41.
[65] M Kaptein, 'Prescribing Outside-Work Behavior: Moral Approaches, Principles and Guidelines' (2019) 31 *Employee Responsibilities and Rights Journal* 165.

15

Freedom of Expression Connected to the Performance of Work

1.	Tension between Freedom and Contractual Terms	4.	Whistle-blowing
2.	Valuable Speech and Abuse	5.	Academic Freedom
3.	Trade Union Activities	6.	Conclusion

The European Convention on Human Rights (ECHR), Article 10 (freedom of expression) states:

1. Everyone has the right to freedom of expression. This right shall include freedom to hold opinions and to receive and impart information and ideas without interference by public authority and regardless of frontiers. ...
2. The exercise of these freedoms, since it carries with it duties and responsibilities, may be subject to such formalities, conditions, restrictions or penalties as are prescribed by law and are necessary in a democratic society, in the interests of national security, territorial integrity or public safety, for the prevention of disorder or crime, for the protection of health or morals, for the protection of the reputation or rights of others, for preventing the disclosure of information received in confidence, or for maintaining the authority and impartiality of the judiciary.

The European Court of Human Rights (ECtHR) frequently repeats that freedom of expression protected by Article 10 of the Convention 'constitutes one of the essential foundations of a democratic society and one of the basic conditions for its progress and for each individual's self-fulfilment'.[1] Furthermore, Article 10 applies 'not only to "information" or "ideas" that are favourably received or regarded as inoffensive or as a matter of indifference, but also to those that offend, shock or disturb'.[2] These statements emphasise that the right to freedom of expression is not confined to political speech and expression of opinions in the media and public forums. Freedom of expression is valuable both for social progress, as in the case of scientific research and literature, and more generally for everyone's personal development. To pursue fulfilling lives and self-realisation, we need to have access to the world of ideas and opinions and be able to debate with others on every possible topic. We need to have access to ideas and opinions that we find shocking and offensive, because only by sifting those ideas in the hard light of day and critical enquiry are we likely to get to the truth of the matter or a morally acceptable position. The enormous value of freedom of expression to individual autonomy and truth is the reason why it is the first casualty of dictatorships and wars.

---

[1] *Lingens v Austria* (1986) 8 EHRR 407, [41].
[2] ibid.

But do these vaulting aspirations about the right to freedom of expression in a liberal society have any relevance to employment and the workplace? We examine this question in this chapter and the next. In this chapter, the focus is on speech that is closely connected to the performance of work. In the following chapter, the focus shifts to speech and communications by employees that occur outside working time and the performance of the job.

1. Tension between Freedom and Contractual Terms

The argument that the right to freedom of expression has no application to the workplace relies on views about the purpose of employment relations and their standard legal structure. If the purpose of employment is regarded as merely an exchange of work for a productive organisation in return for wages, it is unclear why the value of freedom of expression to democratic debate, scientific progress, the arts, and personal development is at stake. If employment is primarily a contractual exchange, much like a sale of goods, its main value lies in its enhancement of wealth and welfare, not the development of democratic, scientific, and cultural discourse.

This view is reinforced by the express or implied terms of a contract of employment. Usually, they curtail opportunities for discussion and debate. An employee's duties to be loyal to the employer, to provide faithful service, and to obey lawful instructions assume an employment relation in which the worker follows instructions rather than debates what should be done, and respects the confidences of the employer's business in order to promote the interests of the employer. Employees who openly criticise their managers or cast doubt on their employer's views about how to conduct a business are vulnerable to justified dismissal on the grounds of disobedience and disloyalty.

Furthermore, dissension and debate are likely to disrupt the efficiency of a productive organisation. The expression of offensive or disturbing views may provoke disharmony among colleagues in the workplace, which is likely to diminish levels of cooperation, communication, and to distract from the necessity of getting on with the job. Disruptive speech is also likely to be a breach of the implied term of cooperation or good faith in the contract of employment.

For all these reasons, it may be doubted whether the right to freedom of expression has any application to employment and the workplace. Employees are free to have their own opinions and ideas, but the law appears to say they should keep them to themselves until they leave work, and even then, as we shall discover in the next chapter, the employer may try to suppress freedom of expression away from the workplace on such grounds as loyalty and confidentiality. This severe restriction of freedom of speech in employment might be supported as an interpretation of the opening phrase of Article 10(2) ECHR, which speaks of justified limitations based on the 'duties and responsibilities' of individuals. It is arguable that the express and implied terms of the contract of employment are relevant 'duties and responsibilities' which are valid restrictions on the freedom prescribed by law. Yet heavy restrictions of free speech at work on the basis of the contract of employment may not be compatible with values reflected in human rights law.[3]

In opposition to this heavy restriction on freedom of expression in the workplace, Sabine Tsuruda argues that the law should require employers to treat employees as 'equal moral agents'

---

[3] See H Collins, 'Is the Contract of Employment Illiberal?' in H Collins, G Lester and V Mantouvalou (eds), *Philosophical Foundations of Labour Law* (Oxford, OUP, 2018) 188.

or in other words as persons with dignity who seek an autonomous life.[4] Although restrictions on disruptive and disloyal speech may be justified for reasons of maintaining cooperation and efficiency in the workplace, employees should be granted space to make criticisms of their manager, to push back against unfair instructions, and to resist having to endorse either expressly or implicitly the moral perspective of their employer. In short, to deny some freedom of expression to employees is to reduce them to instruments of the employer's will rather than independent persons of equal moral worth. Human rights law may lend support to this argument by helping scrutinise contractual terms that limit the enjoyment of human rights at work.[5]

This tension between the value of freedom of expression and the demands of a productive organisation is present in all the issues considered in this chapter. Even though human rights law can support workers' freedom of expression against employers, as we see in this and the next chapter, this fundamental conflict is rarely visible in cases that come before the UK courts. It is unusual for the right to freedom of expression even to be mentioned. Instead, the question posed is whether the employee was in breach of an important term of the contract such as the terms requiring confidentiality, loyalty, or trust and confidence. Courts focus on the question of whether the term has been broken and the gravity of the breach. They rarely consider the further question of whether disciplinary action for breach of contract is a proportionate interference with the right to freedom of expression.[6]

For example, a schoolteacher was dismissed for publishing a work of fiction entitled 'Stop! Don't Read This!' that she had written with the cooperation and support of some especially disruptive final year students. The book drew on the slang and everyday experiences of these teenage boys, including their criminal behaviour, breaches of school rules, and sexual fantasies. Although the headteacher had praised the teacher's inspirational work with the boys and had awarded her promotion, her summary dismissal shortly thereafter was justified mainly on the ground that the text broke a requirement of confidentiality. The book had been published on the internet by its printers without the knowledge of the teacher. Because the names of the boys and some of the teachers at the school could be identified, the headteacher and governors decided that there had been a breach of confidence and the teacher was summarily dismissed.[7] Although the boys concerned and their parents were delighted with the book and joined a petition from all the pupils to have the teacher reinstated, the governors remained intransigent. When her case came before the General Teaching Council to decide whether she should be struck off the list of qualified teachers for misconduct, it decided that she had no case to answer. Nevertheless, an employment tribunal (ET) upheld the fairness of her dismissal; no mention of the right to freedom of expression was made in the case.[8]

Similarly, a nurse was held by the Employment Appeal Tribunal (EAT) to have been fairly dismissed for making a joke.[9] At the end of her shift, she passed through A&E, where nurses were having difficulty in restraining and medicating a strong man having a fit. She assisted by sitting on the patient's feet as he lay in the prone position wearing a surgical gown. But the patient

---

[4] S Tsuruda, 'Working as Equal Moral Agents' (2020) 26 *Legal Theory* 305.
[5] G Morris, 'Fundamental Rights: Exclusion by Agreement?' (2001) 30 *Industrial Law Journal* 49; H Collins and V Mantouvalou, 'Human Rights and the Contract of Employment' in M Freedland (gen ed), *The Contract of Employment* (Oxford, Oxford University Press, 2016) 188, 200–02; G Davidov and M Niezna, 'Consent in Contracts of Employment' (2023) 86 *Modern Law Review* 1134, 1157 ff.
[6] P Wragg, 'Free Speech Rights at Work: Resolving the Difference between Practice and Liberal Principle' (2015) 44 *Industrial Law Journal* 1.
[7] T McVeigh, 'Leonora Rustamova: I Taught my Pupils to Enjoy Books – and Got Fired' *The Observer*, 27 March 2011.
[8] *Rustamova v Governing Body of Calder High School*, UKEAT/0284/11/ZT Nov 2013.
[9] *Bowater v NW London Hospitals NHS Trust* [2011] EWCA Civ 63, [2011] IRLR 331.

twisted over and raised his legs, so that she ended up astride his naked genitals. Embarrassed, she commented, 'It's been a few months since I have been in this position with a man underneath me.' Neither the patient nor any member of the public heard the remark. Six weeks later and following a hearing, senior nursing staff dismissed her summarily for gross misconduct consisting of unprofessional behaviour. The ET held that she had been unfairly dismissed, but the EAT allowed an appeal on the ground that the ET's decision was perverse and that a reasonable employer could have dismissed the nurse for such a lewd remark. The Court of Appeal restored the decision of the ET, observing that the ET was entitled to conclude on the facts that no reasonable employer would dismiss the nurse for what was intended as an embarrassed humorous remark solely directed to herself and colleagues. No mention was made of the right to freedom of expression. It seems that embarrassed humour and spontaneous remarks can only survive an employer's controls over speech at work if the employer cannot point to even a minimal risk of harm to its reputation and professional standards.

In a few cases, though the right to freedom of expression may not be expressly relied upon by the court, the value of freedom of expression may be present in the interstices of the legal reasoning. In *Smith v Trafford Housing Trust*,[10] an employee was demoted for breach of the employer's contractual code of conduct by posting on his personal Facebook page his view that gay marriage in church was 'an equality too far'. The code of conduct forbade speech and postings that might cause offence to colleagues or bring the employer into disrepute. A member of staff had complained that the employee's 'homophobic' remark had caused her concern and distress. Recognising the relevance of the rights to freedom of expression and freedom of religion, Briggs J held that the broadly worded code of conduct had to be interpreted so that it did not apply to personal comments posted at weekends to friends. The demotion and pay cut had therefore been a breach of contract by the employer. The legal reasoning avoids the conflict between the code of conduct and the right to freedom of expression by interpreting the code narrowly so that its interference with freedom of expression was in effect proportionate.

Perhaps the most extensive ground on which employers justify restrictions on freedom of expression by employees at work relies on the assumed preferences and feelings of customers of the business. Employers impose restrictions because employees' words or other ways of expressing themselves might offend or simply put off potential customers. These restrictions might include the approved language in which staff should engage with customers, such as calling them 'sir' or 'madam', but may also extend to dress and appearance codes. One case involved lapel badges that a woman wore at work. These badges used lesbian logos and rallying cries such as 'Lesbians Ignite'. On refusing to remove the badges, she was dismissed. The EAT upheld the fairness of the dismissal, because the employer was entitled to take measures to avoid any risk that any customers might be offended and there was no need for the employer to demonstrate that any such problem had arisen.[11] Similarly, employers' restrictions on employees having visible tattoos are routinely justified by the risk of possible offence or discomfort to customers.[12] In such cases, there is no mention that the interference with freedom of expression of employees and the restrictions on their personal autonomy in order to achieve conformity with conventional standards should have been restricted to a proportionate measure.[13]

These examples demonstrate that the right to freedom of expression is often regarded by tribunals and employers as irrelevant or of marginal importance in cases where dismissal is a

---

[10] *Smith v Trafford Housing Trust* [2012] EWHC 3221 (Ch), [2013] IRLR 86.
[11] *Boychuck v H J Symons Holdings Ltd* [1977] IRLR 395, EAT.
[12] V Nath, S Bach and G Lockwood, 'Dress Codes and Appearance at Work: Body Supplements, Body Modification and Aesthetic Labour', ACAS Research Paper 07/16 (2016).
[13] KE Klare, 'Power/Dressing: Regulation of Employee Appearance' (1992) 26 *New England Law Review* 1395.

response to the words or messages expressed by an employee. Instead, the express and implied contractual obligations of the employee predominate in the typical legal analysis of domestic courts. Once it is established that the employee has disobeyed the code of conduct in breach of the duty of obedience, there is no further assessment of the proportionality of the interference with the right by the dismissal. Similarly, once the implied term of confidentiality has been broken, there is no further examination of the appropriateness and necessity for dismissal. It is assumed in these cases that the employer's interest in upholding the terms of the contract overrides any interest of the employee (or society as a whole) in preventing interferences with the right to freedom of expression.

That priority awarded to contractual terms over protection of human rights applies to most examples of decisions by tribunals and courts in the United Kingdom. If we turn to decisions of the ECtHR, however, the legal analysis is more nuanced. In particular, the Court requires a test of proportionality to be deployed in order to determine whether the interference with the right to freedom of expression was justified.[14] In *Fuentes Bobo v Spain*,[15] an employee, together with others, was involved in a wide-ranging dispute with his employer, a public broadcasting service. During an interview on the radio about his dispute, he was impolite and used vulgar language when criticising the company and the way it was being managed. The employer dismissed him on the ground that his remarks injured the reputation of the company and some of its staff. The applicant argued that by upholding the fairness of his dismissal, the Spanish courts had violated his right to freedom of expression. The Grand Chamber of the ECtHR agreed on the basis that there was 'no reasonable relation of proportionality' between the penalty of dismissal and the legitimate aim of protecting the reputation of the employer and its staff. The Court insisted that in their assessment of proportionality, the courts should have taken into account the fact that the remarks were spontaneous and that some of the harsh comments had been introduced or provoked by the radio interviewers. This decision demonstrates how the Convention requires an assessment of the proportionality of an employer's disciplinary sanction. Even though the Court grants national courts a margin of appreciation, namely a degree of discretion, it concluded in this case that the finding of a fair dismissal was not the product of a reasonable assessment of proportionality.

Rather exceptionally for the UK context, this use of Article 10(2) and a test of proportionality was applied in *Hill v Great Tey Primary School*.[16] A dinner assistant at the school interrupted four boys whipping a girl's legs with a skipping rope in the playground. She took the girl to the nurse and the boys to the Headmistress, reporting to her what had happened. The head teacher reported to the girl's parents that she had been treated for an accident and that she had been hurt by some other children. Later that day, the dinner assistant happened to meet the child's mother, and believing that she had not heard what had happened in full, described the whole incident to her. The parents then approached the police. The head teacher suspended the dinner assistant, who then contacted the local press. The governors subsequently dismissed the assistant for breach of confidence. An ET subsequently held that the dismissal had been unfair because of procedural irregularities, but it reduced the claimant's compensation to close to

---

[14] See *Vogt v Germany* (1996) ECHR 34, discussed further in chapter 16. See also P Collins, *Putting Human Rights to Work* (Oxford, Oxford University Press, 2022) 133; H Collins, 'The Protection of Civil Liberties in the Workplace' (2006) 69 *MLR* 619; L Vickers, *Freedom of Speech and Employment* (Oxford, OUP, 2002) 40; V Mantouvalou, '"I Lost my Job Over a Facebook Post: Was that Fair?" Discipline and Dismissal for Social Media Activity' (2019) 35 *International Journal of Comparative Labour Law and Industrial Relations* 101.

[15] *Fuentes Bobo v Spain* (2001) 31 EHRR 50 (Grand Chamber).

[16] [2013] ICR 691, EAT. For another example where a test of proportionality was applied in a case of unfair dismissal, see *Webb v London Underground Ltd*, 3306438/2021, 2 February 2023, discussed further in chapter 16.

zero for contributory fault because the dismissal would have been fair but for the procedural irregularity. On appeal, the EAT found an error of law because the tribunal had not properly applied Article 10(2). The correct approach was to consider whether a breach of confidentiality falls within the exceptions in Article 10(2) – yes, 'preventing the disclosure of information received in confidence' – whether this restriction was provided by law – yes, the implied term of confidentiality in contracts of employment – and whether the sanction of dismissal was proportionate, being both appropriate and necessary in the circumstances. The case was remitted to a tribunal to consider these questions. The approach used in the *Great Tey Primary School* case is both correct in principle and sets out a clear method for considering the legitimacy of restrictions imposed by employers on employees' freedom of expression.

2. Valuable Speech and Abuse

Assuming that there is some scope for freedom of expression at work, despite the duties and responsibilities of employees under their contracts of employment, the question arises whether all kinds of speech are protected no matter what their form or content.[17] For instance, is protection only afforded to speech that is regarded as valuable or important? It might be possible to distinguish, for example, between remarks made in the public interest and those merely voicing a personal grievance of an employee against a manager or a co-worker. Similarly, a line might be drawn between civil and respectful speech, on the one hand, and words and images that are deliberately offensive and abusive of identifiable individuals on the other. If such distinctions can be drawn, protection for freedom of expression at work might not be available for harping complaints or abusive remarks.

Such distinctions have often been rejected in contexts apart from work: '[A] freedom which is restricted to what judges think to be responsible or in the public interest is no freedom. Freedom means the right to publish things which government and judges, however well motivated, think should not be published. It means the right to say things which "right thinking people" regard as dangerous or irresponsible. This freedom is subject only to clearly defined exceptions laid down by common law or statute.'[18]

There is some support for limitations on freedom of expression in Article 10(2) of the ECHR. Certainly, where the speech concerned amounts to an unjustifiable attack on the reputation of others, it is very unlikely to be protected by the Convention. One might also argue that if restrictions on freedom of expression can be justified in the name of 'prevention of disorder or crime, for the protection of health or morals', it should be possible to argue that communications that serve those goals in the public interest, such as the prevention of crime or injuries to the workforce, should receive strong protection under the Convention. We consider the special protection of whistle-blowers who speak out in the public interest below. Yet it does not follow that speech that is not in the public interest should not be included within the right to freedom of expression.

In France, this question of inherent limits on the right to freedom of expression based on the content of the speech has been debated for the purpose of an interpretation of its labour law code, the Code du Travail, Article L 2281-1, which states: 'Employees enjoy a right to freedom of expression, both as individuals and collectively in accordance with the terms and conditions

---

[17] See, generally, Wragg, above n 6. See also Vickers, above n 14, ch 2.
[18] Hoffmann LJ, *R v Central Independent Television plc* [1994] Fam 192, 203.

of their work.'[19] The right can be exercised during working time, but for meetings of workers during working hours the timing and place of the meeting should normally be agreed with the employer. There is protection against dismissal in response to an exercise of freedom of expression. Is this right limited to speech concerning matters of public interest or general importance? No: it can include letters of complaint or messages designed to question the validity of a manager's criticism of an employee. Employees have a right to personal and collective expression on the content, conditions of exercise, and the organisation of their work. Opinions expressed in this context such as complaints about overwork cannot be sanctioned.[20] Yet the French courts have limited freedom of expression if the words are regarded as mostly abuse. Dismissal may be justified where the language degenerates into the making of defamatory, abusive, or excessive remarks. Temperate criticisms of managerial decisions and their competence in their jobs will not count as abuse.

Should the approach of the French courts be followed in respect of the exclusion of abuse from the right to freedom of expression? It is suggested that such an exclusion would be a mistake. Freedom of expression must be extensively protected, even if judges find the ideas distasteful and shocking. Abusive language is in principle covered by Article 10(1). Nevertheless, abusive remarks may be unjustified under Article 10(2) in many contexts. *Sanders v Kingston*[21] concerned a dismissal, in accordance with special statutory rules, of the elected Conservative leader of Peterborough town council for what the court regarded as expressions of personal anger and abuse conveyed to the media. If the remarks had amounted to political expression, the test of proportionality would have protected the councillor, as local democracy must be safeguarded against government interference. In this case, however, the abuse was not concerned with the business of the council. In an ordinary work context, abusive language is likely to be disruptive to the productive organisation and show disrespect to colleagues. It may also amount to harassment contrary to the Equality Act 2010. In such cases of serious disruption and harassment, disciplinary action is likely to be regarded as a proportionate response. But it is questionable whether abusive language should always be excluded, for it is arguable that it should sometimes be protected, especially in the context of trade union activities and industrial conflict.

3. Trade Union Activities

Freedom of speech as part of the activities of members of trade unions deserves special treatment for three main reasons. First, freedom of expression overlaps in this context with the right under Article 11 of the ECHR of freedom of association, which includes the right to join a trade union for the representation of workers' interests. As explained in other chapters, that right normally includes the right to bargain collectively and to take industrial action subject to any justifiable limitations applied by law. The realisation of the right in Article 11 necessarily includes the freedom of expression of members and officials of trade unions to support membership, recruitment and organisation of workers, and the need for collective solidarity. The vital importance of freedom of expression to trade union activities is recognised in the

---

[19] 'Les salariés bénéficient d'un droit à l'expression directe et collective sur le contenu, les conditions d'exercice et l'organisation de leur travail.'
[20] *K v Installux*, ECLI:EN:CCASS:2022:SO00945, Cour de Cassation, Chambre Sociale, 21 Septembre 2022.
[21] *Sanders v Kingston* [2005] EWHC 1145 (Admin).

Declaration of Philadelphia 1944, which, in Article 1(b), stated that 'freedom of expression and of association are essential to sustained progress'.

Secondly, we should recognise that as one of the main purposes of trade unions is to present and protect the interests of their members, these interests such as better pay and conditions are likely to conflict with those of their employers and more broadly with rich and powerful groups in society. Trade union officials therefore must challenge and criticise the conduct of employers and often governments whenever there is a dispute about wages, conditions of work, or other kinds of treatment of the workforce. In situations of industrial conflict, tempers may run high, aspersions may be cast on motives and strategies, and allegations of intransigence and belligerence may be commonplace. In this inherently conflictual environment, the language used may degenerate into abuse and offensive remarks. Yet trade union officials need to encourage their members and adopt forthright positions if they are to have any chance of success against the usually stronger bargaining power of employers. In so far as freedom of expression is being used to represent the interests of the members of the trade union, intemperate speech needs to be tolerated because trade union officials may not be able to serve their members' interests adequately if they need to be careful about everything they say.

Thirdly, the speech of trade union officials and their members is special because of its contribution to democracy in the whole of society. Trade unions provide one mechanism of civil society through which ordinary working people can find a voice. Meetings in the workplace enable workers to discuss the issues that concern them with others who find themselves in similar situations in a way that is often hard to arrange outside the workplace. Trade unions can also express views about local and national political issues in the media. They may also provide financial and organisational support for political parties. To a considerable extent their contribution to politics provides a vital countervailing force to the power of owners of capital who own the media and thereby greatly influence the agenda of politics and the outcomes of elections. By linking the freedom of expression of trade unions and their members to freedom of association, the ECHR appreciates the important contribution made by such working-class organisations to democratic government.

The question arises whether these three considerations in favour of freedom of speech by trade union representatives provide a complete protection against adverse action by employers. This issue was raised before the Grand Chamber of the ECtHR in *Palomo Sanchez v Spain*.[22] The workers were deliverymen for a bakery. They had brought legal proceedings against the employer in pursuit of their claim for salaried-worker status, which attracted social security benefits, rather than being self-employed. When the employer rejected the claim, the applicants formed a trade union to represent their interests. Two deliverymen who belonged to a different workers' organisation had testified against the union in the legal proceedings concerning the claim for salaried-worker status. The union activists responded by publishing in their newsletter a report of their eventual success in the case together with a satirical cartoon of the employer's director of human resources, seated behind a table, under which was drawn an individual on his hands and knees with his back to the viewer, and pictures of the workers who had testified against the union looking at the scene, awaiting their turn to 'satisfy' the director. Inside the bulletin, two articles, worded in crude and vulgar terms, criticised the fact that those two individuals had testified in favour of the company. Following the applicants' dismissal for misconduct for harming the dignity and reputation of other employees and their resulting unsuccessful legal claims for unfair dismissal, the union was disbanded. The applicants argued before the ECtHR that their freedom of expression had been unjustifiably constrained. But a majority of the ECtHR disagreed,

---

[22] *Palomo Sanchez and Others v Spain* [2011] ECHR 1319, [2011] IRLR 934 (Grand Chamber).

explaining that, although a trade union and its activists must be able to express themselves freely, Article 10 also carries with it duties and responsibilities. The attacks on the individuals in the bulletin were offensive, intemperate, gratuitous and in no way necessary for the legitimate defence of the applicants' interests. The Court quoted the responsible body of the ILO, the Committee on Freedom of Association in its digest of decisions published in 2006, which stated:

> 154. The full exercise of trade union rights calls for a free flow of information, opinions and ideas, and to this end workers, employers and their organizations should enjoy freedom of opinion and expression at their meetings, in their publications and in the course of other trade union activities. Nevertheless, in expressing their opinions, trade union organizations should respect the limits of propriety and refrain from the use of insulting language.

In the view of the majority of the Court, in denying the claims for unfair dismissal, the Spanish courts had correctly balanced the right to freedom of expression against the protection of the rights of others.

As this case demonstrates, though Article 10 is likely to protect serious and substantiated criticisms of co-workers and senior management uttered by union officials, it may not protect offensive remarks and unsubstantiated allegations that damage others' reputations. The majority of the ECtHR was not prepared to create an exemption from the normal principles applied under Article 10 for speech connected to union representation of the interests of the workforce. However, a dissenting minority argued that because the intemperate remarks had been made in the course of attempts to achieve recognition of the union, in the light of Article 11 and its protection of the formation of trade unions for the protection of workers' interests, the balance should be struck in favour of protecting the freedom of speech of the union organisers.[23] Furthermore, the minority drew an analogy between trade union speech and the vital importance of unrestricted freedom of speech in the press and media for the protection of democratic government. They said that trade unions play the role of a 'watchdog' in a similar way to the press in a democracy.[24] Even though there is a need to protect the reputation of others, the dissent argued that the cartoon did not overstep the boundaries of the Convention, which protects even speech that 'shocks, offends and disturbs'.[25] While the cartoon was vulgar and tasteless, it did not involve the depicted persons' private lives but was critical of their work-related activities. Their dismissal could have a chilling effect on conduct of trade union freedom,[26] and is particularly harsh in a context of high unemployment, on the view of the dissenting judges. Apart from defamation, restrictions on freedom of the press are unlikely to be justifiable. Freedom of expression by trade union officials in connection with their role should, according to the minority view, receive a similar level of protection. The minority quoted with approval the statement: 'since trade unions play an important role, in that they express and defend ideas of public interest in professional and employment-related matters, their freedom to put forward opinions warrants a high degree of protection'.[27] Subsequent decisions of the ECtHR have addressed the question of protection of freedom of speech of trade union representatives almost entirely within the framework of Article 11, which may strengthen the protection of trade union speech by enhancing its weight in the balancing process under the test of proportionality.[28]

Under UK law, the freedom of expression of members of trade unions is protected primarily by statute. The Trade Union and Labour Relations (Consolidation) Act 1992 (TULRCA 1992),

---

[23] Joint dissenting opinion of Judges Tulkens, David Thor Bjorgvinsson, Jociene, Popovic and Vucinic.
[24] Dissent, para 7.
[25] Dissent, para 10.
[26] Dissent, para 17.
[27] J-P Margeunaud and J Mouly, 'La Liberté d'Expression Syndicale, Parent Pauvre de la Démocratie', *Rec Dalloz*, 2010, p 1456.
[28] *Straume v Latvia* [2022] ECHR 409.

s 146 protects a worker against detriment imposed for the sole or main purpose of 'preventing or deterring him from taking part in the activities of an independent trade union at an appropriate time', or punishing the worker for so doing. TULRCA 1992, s 152 renders a dismissal for the same purpose automatically unfair. The phrase 'activities of an independent trade union' has been interpreted broadly by the courts, so that it includes attending and participating in meetings and freedom of expression more generally. It applies to speech directed towards internal debate and criticism of the union, as in the case where a woman was reprimanded by her employer for criticising her union's weak stance on equal pay for women.[29] The courts understand trade union activities to mean collective activities such as meetings, so protection does not cover an individual employee organising a petition about a health and safety issue.[30]

Does the statutory protection in the UK provide equivalent or better safeguards for freedom of expression for trade union members than the ECHR? The courts make a distinction between detriment or dismissal for trade union activities and disciplinary measures taken for separate instances of misconduct. For example, if a trade union representative is given information by the employer in strict confidence, sharing that information with members in breach of confidence is a separate act of misconduct that removes the statutory protection.[31] In contrast, if a union representative indicates to the employer that he has been leaked information that apparently reveals a breach of a redundancy procedure agreement by the employer, that statement or allegation is part of trade union activities. For an employer to find misconduct when the representative was defending the interests of their members would undermine the important protection for trade union representatives provided by Parliament.[32] The Court of Appeal has approved the statement that activities that are unprotected must be 'wholly unreasonable, extraneous or malicious acts done in support of trade union activities'.[33] But this limitation certainly does not apply to critical remarks about the attitude of employers made in the context of a union membership meeting.

During a presentation to new pub managers at a meeting where the employer had permitted the shop steward to recruit new members, he said: 'You will get threatened and if you get hurt it will be the union who will fight for you, not the company. At the end of the day the company is concerned with profits and this comes before everything else.' The Court of Appeal unanimously restored the finding of unfair dismissal by the ET, with Pill LJ observing that in the speech there was 'nothing beyond the rhetoric and hyperbole which might be expected at a recruiting meeting for a trade union or, for that matter, some other organisation or cause. Neither dishonesty nor bad faith are suggested.'[34] The result of these cases appears to be that freedom of expression is protected unless the speech amounts to either dishonest falsehoods or serious misconduct that is severable from the trade union activity. The courts in the UK have not yet considered in reported cases vulgar, sarcastic, and deliberately offensive speech of the kind that the ECtHR found had arguably crossed the line in *Palomo Sanchez*.[35]

In this field of trade union activities, it is important to consider finally the issue of victimisation of trade union representatives. Disciplinary action against trade union representatives

---

[29] *British Airways Engine Overhaul Ltd v Francis* [1981] ICR 278, EAT.
[30] *Chant v Aqua Boats Ltd* [1978] ICR 643, EAT.
[31] *Azam v Ofqual*, [2015] 3 WLUK 560, 19 March 2015, EAT.
[32] *Morris v Metrolink Ratp Dev Ltd* [2018] EWCA Civ 1358, [2019] ICR 90.
[33] *Lyon v St James Press Ltd* [1976] ICR 413, EAT per Phillips J, approved in *Bass Taverns Ltd v Burgess* [1995] IRLR 596, CA, and *Morris v Metrolink* (n 32).
[34] *Bass Taverns Ltd v Burgess* [1995] IRLR 596, 598.
[35] On free speech and trade union rights, see further A Bogg and V Mantouvalou, 'Free Speech and Strike Action', UK Labour Law Blog, 20 March 2020.

is likely to have a chilling effect on all their activities. Who will want to stand up and forcefully represent the interests of their members if they will lose their job? Even if representatives receive substantial compensation for unfair dismissal, they may still be deterred from taking on the role as a trade union representative, because their job may be personally too valuable both materially and psychologically. The ECtHR has recognised that dismissal is the harshest sanction in this context and creates the risk that it will intimidate and suppress all trade union activity. The Court has therefore said that any disciplinary action should be proportionate, with the strong hint that it will rarely be so if it deters trade union membership and activities. This question of proportionality was another ground for disagreement in *Palomo Sanchez*. The majority thought that the dismissal for abusive remarks was proportionate, but the minority argued that the interference with Article 10 read with Article 11 by a dismissal with no possibility of reinstatement did not meet a 'compelling social need' and could not be regarded as 'necessary in a democratic society' and that it appeared to be manifestly disproportionate to the aims pursued.

Unusually, under UK law, to address the problem of victimisation, a dismissed employee may apply to an ET for 'interim relief' against dismissal.[36] If the ET thinks it likely that the dismissal will be found to be unfair, it can ask the employer to reinstate the employee. If that request is refused, the ET may make an order that the contract of employment continues notwithstanding the dismissal until the determination or settlement of the complaint. Such an order in effect requires the employer to continue to pay wages and other benefits, but does not require the employer to permit the union representative to return to work. Ultimately, a tribunal cannot force the employer to reinstate an employee even if the dismissal is for trade union activities. For this reason, strong unions resort to industrial action to protect their members.[37] It seems that the remedies under UK law do not meet the international standards set by the ECHR and ILO Convention 135 concerning Protection and Facilities to be Afforded to Workers' Representatives in the Undertaking, Article 1: 'Workers' representatives in the undertaking shall enjoy effective protection against any act prejudicial to them, including dismissal, based on their status or activities as a workers' representative or on union membership or participation in union activities, in so far as they act in conformity with existing laws or collective agreements or other jointly agreed arrangements.' There must be a doubt whether 'effective protection' against dismissal is provided by slightly more generous compensation for unfair dismissal than is usually ordered. Employers are unlikely to be deterred from dismissing employees who challenge their authority and judgment.

4. Whistle-blowing

Employees blow the whistle when they report misconduct and unlawful activity committed by their employers to a third party such as the police or the media. According to the Council of Europe, 'the term whistle-blower must be broadly defined so as to cover any individual or legal entity that reveals or reports, in good faith, a crime or lesser offence, a breach of the law or a threat or harm to the public interest of which they have become aware either directly or indirectly'.[38] Whistle-blowing is viewed as an important guarantee in a healthy democracy.[39] However,

---

[36] TULRCA 1992, s 161.
[37] H Collins, KD Ewing and A McColgan, *Labour Law*, 2nd edn (Cambridge, Cambridge University Press, 2019) 505.
[38] Council of Europe Parliamentary Assembly Resolution 2300: Improving the Protection of Whistle-blowers All Over Europe (1 October 2019) para 5.
[39] ibid para 1.

whistle-blowers almost certainly breach the implied obligations of confidentiality and discretion in contracts of employment. Under the ordinary law of employment, therefore, employers can fairly dismiss such whistle-blowers. The common law did not develop an exception where the whistle-blower was acting in the public interest by reporting crime, corruption, or actions that put public safety at risk. Nor was such an exception included in the statutory law of unfair dismissal, though it was envisaged in the ILO Convention on Termination of Employment.[40] The Council of Europe and the European Union have also recommended that Member States adopt a framework protecting whistle-blowers.[41]

The Public Interest Disclosure Act 1998 was pathbreaking legislation in the UK. For the first time, it conferred protection for whistle-blowers against unfair dismissal and other detrimental disciplinary action. If the reason for the disciplinary action is that the worker has made a 'qualifying disclosure' to an 'appropriate person', the action is unlawful. The legislation was originally conceived as a consumer protection measure: employees would be encouraged to report that products were unsafe and might cause personal injuries. But the legislation could also be supported as a technique for reducing bribery, money laundering, and corruption in the conduct of private companies and government bodies.[42]

The Foundation in Human Rights

A decade later, the Grand Chamber of the ECtHR decided in *Guja v Moldova* that disciplinary action in response to whistle-blowing might amount to an unjustified interference with the right to freedom of expression.[43] A press officer in the Prosecutor General's office of Moldova was dismissed for leaking two letters to the press. The letters implied that there was improper ministerial interference in criminal proceedings being taken against four police officers. The ECtHR stressed that employees, especially civil servants who have access to sensitive information, normally owe a duty of loyalty, reserve and discretion to their employers. Nevertheless, if there was a strong public interest, disclosure of confidential information should be protected under Article 10, subject to a requirement of proportionality. In the first instance, the employee should disclose concerns about wrongdoing to a superior or other competent authority. Where that course of action was impracticable, the information could, as a last resort, if no other route was possible, be disclosed to the public and the media. Before doing so, the ECtHR emphasised that the employee must verify as far as possible that the information was accurate and reliable. The value of freedom of expression in this context is regarded by the ECtHR as not so much about the freedom of the speaker as the right of the public to access accurate information related to the public interest.[44] Under the test of proportionality, a court

---

[40] ILO Convention, Convention 158 on Termination of Employment (1982) Article 5: 'The following, *inter alia*, shall not constitute valid reasons for termination: (c) the filing of a complaint or the participation in proceedings against an employer involving alleged violation of laws or regulations or recourse to competent administrative authorities;' See also Revised European Social Charter 1996, Article 24 and Appendix.

[41] See Council of Europe Parliamentary Assembly, above n 38, and Directive (EU) 2019/1937 of the European Parliament and of the Council of 23 October 2019 on the protection of persons who report breaches of Union law (2019) OJ L305/17.

[42] The Council of Europe had agreed a Criminal Law Convention on Corruption of 4 November 1999, which urged member states to create a comprehensive criminal code against bribery and corruption and which provided in Article 22 for the necessity of protection of whistleblowers ('collaborators of justice').

[43] *Guja v Moldova* [2008] ECHR 144 (Grand Chamber). As is not unusual in whistle-blowing cases, as soon as Guja was reinstated following this decision, he was dismissed again on a pretext, and so he proceeded to a second victory in the ECtHR a decade later: *Guja v Moldova (No 2)* [2018] ECHR 206.

[44] For critical analysis of the case law, see D Kagiaros, 'Reassessing the Framework for the Protection of Civil Servant Whistleblowers in the European Court of Human Rights' (2021) 39 *Netherlands Quarterly of Human Rights* 220.

should also consider the motive of the reporting employee and whether the harm suffered as a result of the disclosure outweighed the public interest in knowing the truth. In this case, the dismissal was unjustified because there was a strong public interest in uncovering political interference with the Rule of Law and the criminal justice system.

Protection of the public interest was then extended to the private sector and matters that were not so clearly of significant public importance. In *Heinisch v Germany*,[45] a nurse in a care home for the elderly complained on several occasions about shortages of staff that placed the patients at risk as well as putting intolerable pressure on staff. After a year or so and two inspections by a regulator that tended to confirm her complaints, having given the employer notice, she went to the criminal prosecutor to ask them to launch criminal proceedings against her employer. She was dismissed and her dismissal was upheld as lawful in the German courts. Her application to the ECtHR was successful. The Court held that in applying the test of proportionality, the national courts had failed to balance correctly the important public interest in receiving information about the level of care for the elderly in such institutions against the employer's interest in its business reputation. In addition, the ECtHR also noted how the severe sanction of dismissal seemed disproportionate, because it could have a chilling effect on all freedom of speech in the public interest by workers.

One important consequence of the application of human rights law is that protection for whistle-blowers extends beyond the normal personal scope for employment law.[46] In principle, anyone who suffers economic sanctions from another for justifiably reporting their unlawful or corrupt conduct should have their freedom of expression protected. For this reason, the legislation in the UK extends beyond employees to include a special category of 'workers', a word that has a wider meaning than the normal statutory definition. The effect of the Employment Rights Act 1996 (ERA 1996), s 43K(1) is to include workers within triangular relationships such as agency workers and to regard both agency and customer as responsible. It also includes subcontractors who are not required to perform the work personally themselves but who can delegate or employ others.[47] The UK Supreme Court in *Gilham v Ministry of Justice* in effect extended the meaning of 'worker' also to include an office holder such as a district judge on the ground that to exclude office holders was unjustifiable discrimination in the enjoyment of Convention rights contrary to Article 14 ECHR read in conjunction with Article 10.[48]

The human rights basis for the protection of whistle-blowers is also reflected in the way the legislation provides similar protection to that afforded to other social rights. There is no qualifying period of continuous employment for protection from dismissal or detriment, which means that

---

[45] *Heinisch v Germany* [2011] ECHR 1175, [2011] IRLR 922 (ECtHR).
[46] See chapter 3; see also P Collins, above n 14, 120; J Atkinson, 'Employment Status and Human Rights: An Emerging Approach' (2023) 86 *Modern Law Review* 1166. See also the EU Directive 2019/1937 of 23 October 2019 on the protection of persons who report breaches of Union law, Article 4.
[47] ERA 1996, s 43K(1) 'For the purposes of this Part "worker" includes an individual who is not a worker as defined by section 230(3) but who—

(a) works or worked for a person in circumstances in which—
 (i) he is or was introduced or supplied to do that work by a third person, and
 (ii) the terms on which he is or was engaged to do the work are or were in practice substantially determined not by him but by the person for whom he works or worked, by the third person or by both of them,
(b) contracts or contracted with a person, for the purposes of that person's business, for the execution of work to be done in a place not under the control or management of that person and would fall within section 230(3)(b) if for "personally" in that provision there were substituted "(whether personally or otherwise)".

[48] *Gilham v Ministry of Justice* [2019] UKSC 44, [2019] ICR 1655.

whistle-blowers are protected from dismissal from day one of their employment. Dismissal for making a protected disclosure is automatically unfair. The tribunals can award unlimited compensation for detriment and dismissals. Moreover, unlike any other claim for unfair dismissal, compensation can include compensation for injury to feelings, which is a type of aggravated damages for the affront to dignity of a person who is acting in the public interest.

The Public Interest

Under the UK legislation, the subject matter of a protected disclosure is broadly described in the ERA 1992, s 43B to include for instance any failure to comply with a legal obligation.

(1) In this Part a 'qualifying disclosure' means any disclosure of information which, in the reasonable belief of the worker making the disclosure, is made in the public interest and tends to show one or more of the following—
  (a) that a criminal offence has been committed, is being committed or is likely to be committed,
  (b) that a person has failed, is failing or is likely to fail to comply with any legal obligation to which he is subject,
  (c) that a miscarriage of justice has occurred, is occurring or is likely to occur,
  (d) that the health or safety of any individual has been, is being or is likely to be endangered,
  (e) that the environment has been, is being or is likely to be damaged, or
  (f) that information tending to show any matter falling within any one of the preceding paragraphs has been, is being or is likely to be deliberately concealed.

Perhaps surprisingly, this list does not apparently include such matters as gross waste or mismanagement of funds and serious misuse or abuse of authority.[49] It is usually important for an employee to be able to point to unlawfulness or the risk of unlawfulness, not merely to something of which the employee disapproves.[50]

The crucial limitation on protected disclosures is that in the reasonable belief of the employee, they must serve the 'public interest'. The statute does not contain any definition of the public interest, so the concept must be elucidated by the courts. They have attempted to draw a distinction between, on the one hand, personal or individual grievances such as a complaint about a deduction from pay, and, on the other hand, breaches of the law, questionable accounting practices, or breaches of contract terms that have broader implications that deserve exposure in the public interest.[51] For instance, if an unlawful deduction from pay by the employer also pushes the worker below the statutory minimum wage, this might turn the private grievance into a matter of public interest, because it is an important public policy that everyone should receive at least the minimum wage.

The Protection of Confidentiality and Loyalty

Although the protection of whistle-blowers is guaranteed by the underlying protection of Article 10 ECHR, the ECtHR has stressed that even for disclosures in the public interest, employees must still respect their obligations of confidentiality and loyalty to their employer as far as possible. The main impact of the duty of confidentiality is strong pressure on employees

---

[49] Based on USA Whistleblower Protection Act 1989 – which protects federal employees who expose government violations of law, gross waste of funds, or specific danger to public health or safety. The reform is proposed in Protect, *Draft Whistleblowing Bill* (updated May 2022).
[50] *Eiger Securities LLP v Korshunova* [2017] ICR 561, EAT.
[51] *Chesterton Global Ltd v Nurmohamed* [2017] EWCA Civ 979, [2018] ICR 731.

to direct their disclosure in the first instance to the management of their own organisation. In accordance with this approach, the broad design of the UK legislation is to permit disclosure in only two ways. The first route is to disclose the information to the employer (ERA 1996, s 43C) or the relevant prescribed regulator of a particular field (ERA 1996, s 43F).[52] In the case of disclosure to the prescribed regulator, not only must the employee work out which is the correct regulatory authority for the particular concern being voiced,[53] but the employee must also believe the disclosure to be substantially true rather than merely having a suspicion based on reasonable grounds.

Disclosure to others apart from the employer or the regulator is constrained by detailed rules that keep pressure on the employee to preserve confidentiality.

43G Disclosure in other cases

(1) A qualifying disclosure is made in accordance with this section if—
  (a) ...
  (b) the worker reasonably believes that the information disclosed, and any allegation contained in it, are substantially true,
  (c) he does not make the disclosure for purposes of personal gain,
  (d) any of the conditions in subsection (2) is met, and
  (e) in all the circumstances of the case, it is reasonable for him to make the disclosure.

(2) The conditions referred to in subsection (1)(d) are—
  (a) that, at the time he makes the disclosure, the worker reasonably believes that he will be subjected to a detriment by his employer if he makes a disclosure to his employer or in accordance with section 43F,
  (b) that, in a case where no person is prescribed for the purposes of section 43F in relation to the relevant failure, the worker reasonably believes that it is likely that evidence relating to the relevant failure will be concealed or destroyed if he makes a disclosure to his employer, or
  (c) that the worker has previously made a disclosure of substantially the same information—
    (i) to his employer, or
    (ii) in accordance with section 43F.

The requirement of reasonableness permeates this control over when disclosures can be made to third parties. The statute indicates that a tribunal should take into account such matters as the seriousness of the offence, the person to whom the disclosure is made, the employee's duty of confidentiality, and the action, if any, that the employer has already taken.[54] The strict conditions in s 43G that are designed to preserve confidentially can only be modified where the unlawfulness that is being reported is 'exceptionally serious'.[55] But even in such circumstances, the requirement of reasonableness and the need to respect confidentiality persists, so that it is unlikely that a whistle-blower who goes immediately to the press or posts on social media will be protected. The same and possibly stricter protections for confidentiality are applied by the ECtHR: 'It is important to establish that, in making the disclosure, the individual acted in good faith and in the belief that the information was true, that it was in the public interest to disclose it and that no other, more discreet means of remedying the wrongdoing was available to him or her.'[56]

---

[52] Public Interest Disclosure (Prescribed Persons) Order 2014 (SI 2014/2418) as amended.
[53] Disclosure to the wrong regulator removes protection: *ALM Medical Services Ltd v Bladon* [2002] ICR 1444, CA.
[54] ERA 1996, s 43G(3).
[55] ERA 1996, s 43H.
[56] *Heinisch v Germany*, above n 45, [69].

The main impact of the obligation of loyalty is that the disclosure to persons other than the employer or regulator should not be made for purposes of personal gain. The meaning of personal gain in this context presumably refers primarily to payments made by the news media to an employee for giving them a tip-off. The acceptance of a payment seems to tarnish the motives of the whistle-blower, though it is unclear why that should matter if indeed the revelations are in the public interest. Furthermore, the ability to accept a payment may encourage valuable whistle-blowing, for otherwise employees may calculate that speaking out is not worth the harm to their income caused by the loss of their job. In the USA, to encourage the disclosure of corruption in government contracts, whistle-blowers are rewarded by a sharing of the savings to the taxpayer.[57]

The obligation of loyalty may also explain the frequent reference to a requirement of 'good faith' in judging whether a disclosure should be protected. This requirement tries to distinguish between disclosures that are made as part of a grudge against the employer as opposed to disclosures by an employee standing up for the public interest. Yet such a distinction concerning the motives of employees for making the disclosure is often impossible to draw, because employees who are ignored or silenced may develop a grudge against their managers even though their underlying concern is with the public interest.[58] Under the UK legislation, a tribunal may use a finding of bad faith to reduce the amount of compensation payable, but not to prevent the disclosure from being a protected one.[59] This provision about compensation apparently means that a disclosure which was made in the reasonable belief that it was in the public interest might nevertheless be found to be made in bad faith, which seems unlikely.

Finally, it is worth noting that many employers try to ensure confidentiality and loyalty by inserting express terms into the contract of employment that forbid disclosures to outsiders with the sanction of summary dismissal. To protect the right to freedom of expression of whistle-blowers, the UK statute renders terms of contracts that prevent protected disclosures void.[60] But disclosures of material that is not judged to be of public interest or material that does not reveal wrongdoing, but merely questionable judgement, can be effectively suppressed by injunctions to enforce non-disclosure agreements. It is questionable whether non-disclosure agreements should validly apply to allegations of sexual harassment which may point to unlawful conduct under the Equality Act 2010 or a criminal sexual assault.

5. Academic Freedom

Do special rules for freedom of expression apply in the context of universities and institutions of scientific research? In this context, there is an important principle of protecting the arts and sciences from interference by powerful interest groups and governments. That principle was stated in the Charter of the Fundamental Rights of the EU, Article 13: 'The arts and scientific research shall be free of constraint. Academic freedom shall be respected.' There is no express mention of such a right in the ECHR, but the ECtHR acknowledges that it deserves strong

---

[57] False Claims Act, 31 USC ss 3729, 3730(h) – permits the Government to recover triple damages from contractors defrauding the federal government, and gives individual whistleblowers 15–25% of the government's recovery.
[58] J Gobert and M Punch, 'Whistleblowers, the Public Interest, and the Public Interest Disclosure Act 1998' (2000) 63 *Modern Law Review* 25.
[59] ERA 1996, ss 49(6A) and 123(6A).
[60] ERA 1996, s 43J.

protection under Article 10 ECHR.[61] The right to academic freedom appears to have two complementary elements.

First, there is an obligation to protect freedom of speech within institutions engaged in the arts and scientific research. As Frankfurter J once stated:

> It is the business of a university to provide that atmosphere which is must conducive to speculation, experiment and creation. It is an atmosphere in which there prevail 'four essential freedoms' of a university – to determine for itself on academic grounds who may teach, what may be taught, how it shall be taught, and who may be admitted to study.[62]

The obligation applies to governments, courts, and churches, which must respect the autonomy of universities, but it also applies to the universities themselves: universities should permit and encourage freedom of expression in all aspects of artistic and scientific endeavour. There is a risk that attempts to 'no-platform' speakers whose views are found by some to be morally offensive will seriously diminish the value of universities and other institutions as sites of seeking truth through dialogue.[63] Diversity in the faculty and student body has also been regarded as vital to promote universities as a marketplace of ideas.[64]

Secondly, academic freedom means that there is an individual right of researchers and scholars to be permitted to talk and write about their ideas and research. This right must be a strong one so that the freedom to express new ideas can overcome the problem that it may cause shock and offence to some listeners. Yet the individual right may not be sufficiently strong as to protect the choice of professors to teach subjects that no students want to learn about or to use pedagogical techniques that put excessive stress on the students.[65]

In the UK, the individual right of academics to freedom of expression is secured in the first instance by the statutes of the university. Under the Education Reform Act 1988, s 202(2)(a), University Commissioners have to approve those statutes, and they must have regard to the need to ensure that 'academic staff have freedom within the law to question and test received wisdom, and to put forward new ideas and controversial or unpopular opinions, without placing themselves in jeopardy of losing their jobs or privileges they may have at their institutions'. This phrase is understood to include the freedom to criticise the decisions and policies of the administration of the university itself.[66] If a member of the academic staff is dismissed for publications or speech, a claim for breach of contract resulting from breach of the university statutes should be available.

Alternatively, a dismissed employee of the university may bring a claim for unfair dismissal under the Employment Rights Act 1996, arguing that the fairness of the dismissal should be assessed in a way that is compatible with rights under the ECHR. Under Article 10 ECHR, the ECtHR has strongly protected academic freedom to the extent of protecting opinions that offend

---

[61] J Murray, 'The Thinkery and the Academy: Examining the Legal Parameters and Interactions of Academic Freedom and Freedom of Expression Under English Law' (2023) 76 *Current Legal Problems* 345. For theoretical analysis of the relationship between free speech and academic freedom, see B Simpson, 'The Relationship Between Academic Freedom and Free Speech' (2020) 30 *Ethics* 287.

[62] *Sweezy v New Hampshire* 354 US 234 (1957) 263, quoting the Conference of Representatives of the University of Cape Town, the University of Witwatersrand and the Open Universities of South Africa (1957) 10–12.

[63] V Tadros, 'The Rights and Wrongs of No-Platforming' (2022) 85 *Modern Law Review* 968; G Letsas, 'There Is No Free Speech Right to a University Platform', *Times Higher Education*, 31 March 2022.

[64] Powell J in *Regents for the University of California v Bakke* 438 US 265 (1978). That justification for affirmative action for racial minorities was subsequently rejected: *Students for Fair Admissions v Harvard*, 600 US 181 (2023).

[65] E Barendt, *Academic Freedom and the Law* (Oxford, Hart Publishing, 2010) 2.

[66] Barendt, ibid 98.

and even defame individuals. In *Mustafa Erdogan v Turkey*,[67] a professor of constitutional law published an article that criticised a decision of the Turkish constitutional court as erroneous in law, and he argued that the judges were biased and incompetent. Three of the judges of the constitutional court won a claim for damages for defamation in the domestic courts. The ECtHR held that the publication was on a matter of public interest (the exclusion of a political party from parliament) and offered opinions based on facts, so that this interference with freedom of expression could not be justified as necessary in a democratic society. Within the academic's area of expertise, this freedom applies not only to scientific publications and the classroom but also to statements in the press and social media. Academic writing and speech that will not be protected under Article 10 includes mere insults, offensive views not based on fact, such as 'holocaust deniers', and speech that is calculated to attack the human rights of others, such as incitements to racial hatred. There will be difficult borderline cases. For instance, in a classroom discussion of the proper relation between law and morality, a professor might express the view that the law should uphold conventional moral values for the sake of social cohesion, giving as an example the prohibition of abortion. Many students might find such views offensive, because they deny rights to autonomy and privacy for women. The expression of such views by the professor may be protected under Article 10, though their mode of expression might justify proportionate restrictions.

Finally, a member of academic staff who feels that there is interference with academic freedom by the university may make a complaint to a regulator, the Office for Students, about the failure of the governing body of a university to take all reasonably practicable steps to protect academic freedom.[68] This route differs in some respects from the strong protections under Article 10. The scope of academic freedom is not limited to the academic's area of expertise, but it is limited by existing laws such as the law of defamation.[69] Universities can defeat the complaint by demonstrating that they took all practicable steps to protect the academic's freedom of expression. If the complaint is upheld by the regulator, the academic can bring a civil claim for compensation for pecuniary or non-pecuniary loss.[70]

6. Conclusion

Our examination of the law protecting employees' freedom of expression in connection with the performance of work has revealed that although freedom of speech is always constrained by express and implied contractual obligations, courts and tribunals should assess whether restrictions on freedom of speech are proportionate. This assessment of proportionality takes into account many factors including the exceptional importance of the protection of speech that serves the public interest, speech that represents the interests of workers to their employer, and the vital importance of freedom of speech in scientific research and scholarly enquiry.

Yet speech observes no physical barriers. Words and the ideas they express permeate all barriers created to censor, suppress, and revise them. On the internet, the more foolish, offensive, and inaccurate the ideas and language used, the faster they spread around the world. Speech therefore seeps from words used in connection with the performance of work to the outside world, but

---

[67] *Mustafa Erdogan v Turkey* [2014] ECHR 530.
[68] Higher Education (Freedom of Speech) Act 2023; J Murray, 'The Higher Education (Freedom of Speech) Act 2023: An Employment Focused Overview' (2023) 52 *Industrial Law Journal* 791.
[69] Higher Education Research Act 2017, Pt A1, as amended by Higher Education (Freedom of Speech) Act 2023, s 1.
[70] Higher Education Research Act 2017, Pt A7, as amended by Higher Education (Freedom of Speech) Act 2023, s 4.

also passes in the other direction, from personal life outside work back to haunt the employee in the workplace. The division between this chapter about speech in connection with work and the next that concerns speech outside work is therefore certainly not watertight. The division does highlight, however, the potential for considerations of respect for private life to be at the forefront of the legal analysis of speech outside work, though as we shall see, that potential is largely unrealised.

16

Freedom of Expression Outside Work

1.	Private Life and Social Media	5.	Political Speech
2.	Freedom of Belief	6.	Offensive Speech and Hate Speech
3.	Unfair Dismissal and Freedom of Expression	7.	Conclusion
4.	Legitimate Interests of Employers		

Ms Gibbins was employed by the British Council as Head of Global Estates, overseeing the management of the Council's property. One day when she was logged onto Facebook, she saw on her newsfeed a photograph of Prince George, who was 2 years old at the time, which had been posted on the page of the band Dub Pistols, accompanied by the comment, 'I know he's only 2 years old, but Prince George already looks like a Fucking Dickhead.' The image appeared on her feed because some of her friends had commented on it. She added the following comment: 'White privilege. That cheeky grin is the (already locked-in) innate knowledge that he is Royal, rich, advantaged and will never know *any* difficulties or hardships in life. Let's find photos of 3yo Syrian refugee children and see if they look alike, eh?' She further explained that she disagrees with systems that privilege some people over others, that she is a socialist, atheist and Republican, and that in her view a royal family has no place in a modern democracy.

Ms Gibbins had the highest Facebook privacy settings, but her employer could nevertheless be identified. Despite her privacy settings, someone came across the post and sent it to the tabloid press. The story was misreported on the front page of *The Sun*, which said that Prince George was 'hit by vile rant from British Council boss paid thousands by taxpayers to promote UK'. The front page attributed the offensive comment about Prince George to Ms Gibbins. The misquotation was circulated widely online and in the press (the *Metro* newspaper, and the *Daily Mail*), and great pressure was put on the British Council, including by members of the far right group Britain First. Following hasty disciplinary proceedings, Ms Gibbins was dismissed for gross misconduct and specifically because she had brought the British Council into disrepute. The Employment Tribunal found her dismissal lawful, having rejected her claims of discrimination because of philosophical belief, wrongful dismissal, and unfair dismissal.[1]

In liberal political theory, it is usually the state that is viewed as a threat to free speech, with a key concern being that of paternalism. The idea is that the state should not choose which views are valuable for people to hold and express, and which are not. Yet the power of the employer to decide what speech is compatible with its economic interests, or what kind of expression is

---

[1] *Gibbins v British Council*, 2200088/2017, 3 November 2017, ET.

agreeable to it on moral grounds, has not been scrutinised with similar intensity.[2] The realisation that there are types of speech that are protected against state interference, but not against employer interference, is particularly problematic. Spontaneous remarks that may be disagreeable, distasteful or possibly offensive to some on social media may still have value for individual autonomy – not only for the protection of the autonomy of those who express them, but also for the autonomy of those who are exposed to these views, as by being exposed to them they can freely decide whether to endorse or reject them.

The *Gibbins* case is typical of contemporary disputes regarding the exercise of the right to freedom of expression by employees outside working hours and not directly connected to the performance of their jobs. Many people lose their job because of views that they express on social media, and many claims have been brought before courts and tribunals.[3] Is it fair for individuals to be dismissed because of views that they express outside the workplace and working time, on social media or elsewhere away from work? The first issue raised by such cases is whether the speech outside work has any connection to the employer and the employment relation. Many people think that how they express themselves in their leisure time is none of the employer's business, a matter that falls squarely within their private life. The second issue that needs to be considered is whether the law against discrimination on the ground of philosophical belief in the Equality Act 2010 can protect employees against dismissal and other disciplinary action imposed by the employer in response to the views expressed outside work. Thirdly, if the conduct falls outside the protection of beliefs, can an employee bring a legal claim against dismissal or other disciplinary action on the basis of a claim for unfair dismissal or breach of contract. Finally, for all of these legal claims, the outcome may turn on how the courts balance the interest of the employee in the enjoyment of their Convention rights, particularly Articles 9 (freedom of belief) and 10 (freedom of expression), against the legitimate interests of the employer such as the protection of its reputation. This balancing exercise, which is often conducted through a test of proportionality, must also take into account the nature of the speech itself. For instance, the expression of political views may receive stronger protection than offensive remarks, and some speech such as the expression of hatred against a group may merit no protection at all.

1. Private Life and Social Media

In the past, people would express views away from work, in discussions with their friends, colleagues, and others, but those not present, such as the employer or the broader public, would not easily be able to discover these views. Unless individuals chose to publicise their opinions, they were normally not shared widely. People's political views or their approach to other controversial issues were unlikely to become known to the employer. A significant shift occurred with the use of social media. Everyone can now voice their opinions with great ease and speed in the public domain, in a way that is permanent and can often be accessed by colleagues, customers, the general public, and the employer. Moreover, through their profile on social media platforms, individuals can often be linked to their workplace and their employing organisation. This occurs,

---

[2] See E Anderson, *Private Government – How Employers Rule Our Lives (and Why We Don't Talk about It)* (Princeton, Princeton University Press, 2017).

[3] For an overview of the issues in several different jurisdictions, see the special issue (2017–2018) 39 *Comparative Labor Law and Policy Journal* on 'Employer Access and Use of Employee Social Media' and (2019) 35 *International Journal of Comparative Labour Law and Policy*.

for instance, when workers name their employer explicitly on their profile or when they have connections that help identify it. Unlike conversations with a closed group in the pub, a café or by the office watercooler, comments on social media can reach a very broad audience and leave a permanent record.

With the use of social media, many aspects of our personality and life that would have been kept private or expressed to a small group become part of the public space. Some people may realise this and may have consented to sharing information with a large number of others by having their social media profile open to the public; others may not realise immediately, or even at all, that some information that they share is accessible to the broader public. Some social media platforms give users limited control over who can access their posts. They often revise their (often unnecessarily complicated) privacy settings, so posts which users considered to be private, shared with a small number of followers or friends, become part of the public space, accessible by anyone. In addition, posts, sometimes spontaneous or expressed in a heated moment, may be shared by others and reach a great number of users, far greater than the audience that people originally intended to reach. A comment for a few dozen followers can be potentially viewed by thousands of people.

With the growing use of social media, domestic courts and tribunals, and the ECtHR have been faced with a number of new questions involving disciplinary action and freedom of expression away from work, as the *Gibbins* case illustrates. Several further stories exemplify the problem. A cheerleader was dismissed for posting a photo of herself in lingerie on her Instagram page.[4] A woman employed by a US government contractor lost her job because she was photographed extending her middle finger at the motorcade of President Trump when she was away from work, and she posted the photo on her Facebook and Twitter page.[5] An employee of a care home was dismissed for posting on Facebook a video and a photo of a music night, which she regularly organised for the residents, where one of them with Down's syndrome was visible, and was tagged.[6] Gary Lineker, a hugely popular sports commentator, was suspended by the BBC because of his comments on social media that the Illegal Migration Bill that targets an extremely vulnerable group of people is immeasurably cruel.[7] The examples are endless. Can views expressed on social media constitute a legitimate reason for dismissal?

Such dismissals and disciplinary action may implicate aspects of the right to private life, which we examined in chapter 14. Many users of social media seem to think that their use of the platforms outside working hours and not involving discussion of issues closely related to their work is a private matter. But UK courts and tribunals have rejected that view on the ground that the posts can easily be disseminated and viewed by large numbers of people. The expression of an opinion that was intended to be shared with a small group of friends can rapidly go viral if others find it controversial, and the algorithms of social media tend to highlight such statements to other users. Statements on social media are therefore regarded by the courts and tribunals as a public activity that does not trigger the consideration of Article 8 of the European Convention on Human Rights (ECHR) at all.[8]

---

[4] See M Brady, 'NFL Cheerleader Says She Was Fired Over Instagram Photo', BBC, 29 March 2018, www.bbc.com/news/world-us-canada-43576681.
[5] M Haag, 'Woman Who Was Fired for Giving Trump the Middle Finger Sues Former Employer', *NY Times*, 5 April 2018, www.nytimes.com/2018/04/05/us/juli-briskman-middle-finger-trump.html.
[6] 'I Lost my Job Over a Facebook Post – Was that Fair?', BBC, 6 November 2017, www.bbc.com/news/stories-41851771.
[7] See the discussion in G Letsas and V Mantouvalou, 'Censoring Gary Lineker', UK Labour Law Blog, 13 March 2023.
[8] See *Crisp v Apple Retail (UK) Ltd*, ET/1500258/11, 5 August 2011. For further analysis of the meaning of privacy in the context of social media, see V Mantouvalou, '"I Lost my Job Over a Facebook Post: Was that Fair?" Discipline and Dismissal for Social Media Activity' (2019) 35 *International Journal of Comparative Labour Law and Industrial Relations* 101. See also H Nissenbaum, 'Respecting Context to Protect Privacy' (2015) *Science and Engineering Ethics* 1.

Because the right to privacy does not usually apply to the use of social media on the view of UK tribunals and courts, our focus in this chapter concerned with speech outside of work is primarily on freedom of belief under Article 9 and freedom of expression under Article 10 ECHR. The ECtHR has recognised the importance of social media for freedom of expression in a case involving political speech, and protected workers from dismissal for political speech on social media. In *Cengiz and Others v Turkey*,[9] the applicants were law lecturers and professors in different institutions in Turkey, experts in human rights law and free speech. They complained to the ECtHR because Turkey blocked access to YouTube, a platform where people can post and view video files. The applicants, active YouTube users, complained that their freedom of expression was violated, because blocking the site restricted their right to share and access information and ideas. They argued that this was particularly important for their job as academics, as they used the platform to upload and access professional video files. The Court said that:

> User-generated expressive activity on the Internet provides an unprecedented platform for the exercise of freedom of expression .... In this connection, the Court observes that YouTube is a video-hosting website on which users can upload, view and share videos and is undoubtedly an important means of exercising the freedom to receive and impart information and ideas. In particular, as the applicants rightly noted, political content ignored by the traditional media is often shared via YouTube, thus fostering the emergence of citizen journalism. From that perspective the Court accepts that YouTube is a unique platform on account of its characteristics, its accessibility and above all its potential impact, and that no alternatives were available to the applicants.[10]

2. Freedom of Belief

Article 9 ECHR protects freedom of religion and freedom of philosophical belief.[11] It guarantees the right to manifest such a belief, but this is qualified by a test of proportionality in order to protect the rights of others. As in cases such as *Gibbins*, employers may object to the manifestation of a particular belief on the ground that it interferes with their rights, such as their good reputation.

In domestic law, the normal way to protect the right to freedom of belief is through a claim for direct discrimination under the Equality Act 2010. A philosophical belief is a protected characteristic.[12] Direct discrimination arises where, because of a protected characteristic, one person treats another less favourably than that person treats or would treat others.[13] Less favourable treatment might include dismissal, other forms of disciplinary action, and a refusal to hire someone on the ground of their protected belief.

In anti-discrimination law, an employer is not usually able to justify direct discrimination. In the case of discrimination on the ground of belief, however, the courts and tribunals assess whether or not there has been discrimination on the ground of philosophical belief by applying Article 9 ECHR, which protects the manifestation of religious and other beliefs, including its test of proportionality in Article 9(2). If there is no justified manifestation of a protected belief in accordance with Article 9, the claim for direct discrimination will fail. Claims by employees on the ground of direct discrimination for a protected philosophical belief therefore raise three major questions.

---

[9] *Cengiz and Others v Turkey* [2015] ECHR 1052.
[10] ibid [52].
[11] Freedom of religion is considered in chapter 17 below.
[12] Equality Act 2010, s 10.
[13] Equality Act 2010, s 13.

The Scope of Protected Belief

The first question is whether the asserted belief is a (philosophical) belief of the kind protected by Article 9. To answer that question, a convenient summary of the case law on Article 9 was provided in *Grainger Plc v Nicholson*,[14] where the belief was about the moral imperatives arising from climate change. The criteria for assessing whether the belief qualified for protection are:

(i) The belief must be genuinely held.

(ii) It must be a belief and not … an opinion or viewpoint based on the present state of information available.

(iii) It must be a belief as to a weighty and substantial aspect of human life and behaviour.

(iv) It must attain a certain level of cogency, seriousness, cohesion and importance.

(v) It must be worthy of respect in a democratic society, be not incompatible with human dignity and not conflict with the fundamental rights of others.[15]

Criterion (ii) derives from *McClintock v Department of Constitutional Affairs*,[16] where a distinction was drawn between a belief of such fundamental importance that it was analogous to a religious belief under Article 9, and provisional belief based on the current state of the evidence, which was unprotected. The odd result of this distinction is that a bigoted belief based on no evidence at all might be protected whereas a more thoughtful, rational belief would be unprotected.[17] Criterion (iii) attempts to draw a distinction between mere lifestyle choices and those choices about how to live one's life that are based on profound philosophical beliefs about being human and the meaning of life. Being a vegetarian, for instance, might fall either side of the line depending on the reason for that choice of diet. It has often been observed that tribunals should not require too much under criterion (iv): some internal inconsistency in the belief can be ignored and so too a lack of cohesion between different elements of a belief.[18] An ET has doubted, however, whether a holocaust denier whose beliefs rejected all contrary evidence could satisfy this requirement (and other requirements).[19]

The final criterion under the *Grainger* test for philosophical belief proves to be the most troublesome. Many controversial beliefs cause anger precisely because they appear to deny fundamental rights to others and thus fail to treat others with equal respect and dignity. A common example, considered in chapter 17, are Christian beliefs that oppose same-sex marriage. Here we focus on 'gender critical beliefs' in which exponents reject gender fluidity, insist that gender at birth is immutable, and maintain that trans people cannot ever become members of their chosen sex. Does the holding of such a belief without more amount to a conflict with the rights of others, in this case those who are transgender? Or is it necessary to satisfy criterion (v) that the holder of the belief actually takes steps that in some way interfere with the rights of others? That issue divided the ET and the EAT in *Forstater v CGD Europe*.[20] In this case, the claimant had lost her job resulting from expression of views on social media. Being concerned that proposed changes to the law would make legal recognition of self-identified gender easier, she posted her belief that gender identity was fixed at birth, was either male or female, and could

---

[14] *Grainger Plc v Nicholson* [2009] UKEAT 0219_09_0311, [2010] ICR 360, EAT, drawing heavily on *Campbell and Cosans v United Kingdom* (1982) 4 EHRR 293 (concerning corporal punishment in schools).

[15] *Grainger*, ibid [24]; cf K Patten, 'Protected Beliefs Under the Equality Act: Grainger Questioned' (2024) *Industrial Law Journal* (Jan 3, advanced access).

[16] [2008] IRLR 29, EAT.

[17] G Pitt, 'Keeping the Faith: Trends and Tensions in Religion and Belief Discrimination' (2011) 40 *ILJ* 384, 389.

[18] *R (on the application of Williamson) v Secretary of State for Education and Employment* [2005] UKHL 14, [2005] 2 AC 246, HL.

[19] *Ellis v Parmagan Ltd* (unreported, 2 February 2014), ET.

[20] *Forstater v CGD Europe*, ET 2200909/2019, 18 December 2019; UKEAT/0105/20/JOJ, [2022] ICR 1, EAT).

not be changed. The ET held that the claimant's belief was incompatible with human dignity and the fundamental rights of others in view of the fact that even if a trans person had a Gender Recognition Certificate,[21] the claimant would still not accept that person as having changed gender even though in law they had.[22] The EAT reversed that decision, insisting that a belief was protected under Article 9 ECHR unless it amounted to the complete denial of rights to another person, such as the treatment of Jews in Nazi Germany. It was unlikely that a widely held belief that had not been made unlawful by legislation could be disqualified from protection. Accordingly, the gender critical belief itself, though offensive to some people, was protected under the law of direct discrimination.[23]

Conduct Connected to the Belief

The second question for claims of direct discrimination on the ground of belief is whether conduct that provided the reason for the imposition of a detriment on the claimant by the employer was a manifestation of that philosophical belief. In *Higgs v Farmor's School*,[24] the claimant was employed in a secondary school as a pastoral administrator and work experience manager through which she had contact with parents and pupils. One parent complained about her social media posts in which the claimant had forcibly expressed strong concerns about relationships education in primary schools. These posts grew from her beliefs including lack of belief in gender fluidity and same-sex marriage. The school suspended her and then, after a disciplinary investigation and hearing, dismissed her for gross misconduct. The claimant brought a claim for direct discrimination and harassment on the ground of a protected belief. In this case, in rejecting her claim, the ET had failed properly to engage with the question whether there was a sufficiently close or direct nexus between her protected beliefs and the content of her posts, which was an error of law.[25] The EAT held that her Facebook posts were clearly closely connected to her beliefs. The case was then remitted for the tribunal to consider the third question.

Proportionality

The third question involves the test of proportionality. Here the issue concerns the manner of expression and the degree to which it interfered with the rights of others. Employers may have to tolerate views that they find objectionable or inconvenient. But if those views are expressed intemperately, in ways that are calculated to offend others and are likely to harm the reputation of the employer, restrictions on freedom of speech about protected beliefs may be proportionate. If the restrictions are proportionate, the fundamental belief is not protected against such restrictions on its manifestation. Accordingly, a claim for direct discrimination on the ground of freedom of belief will not succeed because the interference with its manifestation was proportionate. Although there is no general defence of justification to direct discrimination, a belief is only protected against unjustified restrictions on manifestations of that belief.

---

[21] Gender Recognition Act 2004.
[22] *Forstater* (ET) (n 20) [84].
[23] *Forstater* (EAT) (n 20) [111].
[24] *Higgs v Farmor's School* [2023] EAT 89, [2023] ICR 1072.
[25] This test was approved in *Page v NHS Trust Development Authority* [2021] EWCA Civ 255, [2021] ICR 941, [68].

The test of proportionality requires the employer to point to a legitimate aim,[26] such as the protection of its business interests, and show that the detriment such as dismissal was imposed in accordance with the law. The final part of the test of proportionality follows the guidance of Lord Reed in *Bank Mellat v HM Treasury (No 2)*:[27]

(1) whether the objective of the measure is sufficiently important to justify the limitation of a protected right;

(2) whether the measure is rationally connected to the objective;

(3) whether a less intrusive measure could have been used without unacceptably compromising the achievement of the objective; and

(4) whether, balancing the severity of the measure's effects on the rights of the persons to whom it applies against the importance of the objective, to the extent that the measure will contribute to its achievement, the former outweighs the latter.[28]

In making this assessment of proportionality in the context of the manifestation of freedom of belief, it is important to remember that if the form of manifestation falls also within the ambit of Article 10 ECHR on freedom of expression, the assessment of proportionality must also bear in mind considerations of the vital importance of freedom of speech in a democratic society, especially if the speech concerns matters of public interest and political debate.

Drawing on those general principles, Eady J in *Higgs v Farmor's School* suggested that the following considerations should be taken into account in the context of employment and the manifestation of belief:

> regard should be had to: (i) the content of the manifestation; (ii) the tone used; (iii) the extent of the manifestation; (iv) the worker's understanding of the likely audience; (v) the extent and nature of the intrusion on the rights of others, and any consequential impact on the employer's ability to run its business; (vi) whether the worker has made clear that the views expressed are personal, or whether they might be seen as representing the views of the employer, and whether that might present a reputational risk; (vii) whether there is a potential power imbalance given the nature of the worker's position or role and that of those whose rights are intruded upon; (viii) the nature of the employer's business, in particular where there is a potential impact on vulnerable service users or clients; (ix) whether the limitation imposed is the least intrusive measure open to the employer.[29]

Applying these considerations, it is possible that although the employee's belief is a protected belief under the Equality Act 2010, the particular way in which it is manifested may fall outside the protection. For example, although a gender critical belief is a protected belief, if the holder of such a belief manifests it in a way that causes offence to others, a restriction imposed by an employer may be proportionate and legitimate. For instance, in *Mackereth v Department for Work and Pensions*,[30] a doctor holding gender critical beliefs based on Christianity was held to have a protected belief under s 10 of the Equality Act 2010, but because he manifested it by refusing to address applicants for disability payments by their chosen gender pronouns, disciplinary action would be justified because it was a necessary and proportionate means of achieving the legitimate aims of ensuring that applicants were treated with respect and in accordance with their rights. Similarly, a particular manifestation of a belief might amount to unlawful harassment by the holder of the belief against a fellow worker. The definition of harassment under s 26(1) of

---

[26] On legitimate aims in this context see below, section 4 of this chapter.
[27] *Bank Mellat v HM Treasury (No 2)* [2013] UKSC 39, [2014] AC 700.
[28] ibid [74].
[29] *Higgs*, above n 24, [94].
[30] *Mackereth v Department for Work and Pensions* [2022] EAT 99, [2022] ICR 1609.

the Equality Act 2010 is unwanted conduct related to a relevant protected characteristic that has the purpose or effect of violating the victim's dignity, or creating an intimidating, hostile, degrading, humiliating or offensive environment for the victim. It is possible that posts on social media away from work might be understood as creating a hostile atmosphere for a trans person or a gay or lesbian person at work. If the employer failed to act to prevent the creation of the hostile environment, it would be vicariously liable for the unlawful harassment.[31] The prevention of harassment by appropriate means should normally amount to a proportionate interference with the right to the protection of fundamental beliefs and freedom of expression as its legitimate aim is the protection of the rights of others.

3. Unfair Dismissal and Freedom of Expression

In cases where employees express views away from work that result in dismissal by the employer, they may also challenge the dismissal (or disciplinary action) as a breach of contract,[32] or more probably under the law of unfair dismissal, which has been previously discussed in outline in chapter 2. As we noted there, the test of fairness for claims for unfair dismissal in the Employment Rights Act 1996 (ERA 1996), s 98(4) asks 'whether in the circumstances … the employer acted reasonably or unreasonably in treating it as a sufficient reason for dismissing the employee' which should also be 'determined in accordance with equity and the substantial merits of the case'. However, tribunals and courts accept that employers have a very broad 'range of reasonable responses' to the misconduct of an employee.[33] They grant to employers a significant degree of discretion, ruling that even if a dismissal is harsh, it can be fair.[34] Following the enactment of s 3 of the Human Rights Act 1998, it was accepted that s 98(4) of the ERA 1996 has to be interpreted in line with Convention rights.[35] In addition, s 6(1) states that '[i]t is unlawful for a public authority to act in a way which is incompatible with one or more of the Convention rights'. The term 'public authorities' also includes courts and tribunals, which must take into account Convention rights in the development of common law.

The Convention rights that might be regarded as relevant to an assessment of the fairness of dismissal for manifestation of a belief outside of the workplace and working time are the right to private life and freedom of expression. We analysed the right to private life in Article 8 in relation to activities away from the workplace and working time earlier in this chapter and in chapter 14, and it is important to reiterate here the central challenge: social media posts are very rarely private in practice, in the sense that they can be accessed by several people who can share them further with the broader public. For this reason, UK tribunals and courts may not accept that this is part of workers' private life. As we have explained, this interpretation of the right to private life is problematic and potentially incompatible with the interpretation of the right under the ECHR, as the scope of privacy is not determined by the space where the relevant conduct took place.[36]

---

[31] Equality Act 2010, s 109; *Tower Boot Co Ltd v Jones* [1997] ICR 254, CA.
[32] *Smith v Trafford Housing Trust* [2012] EWHC 3221 (Ch), [2013] IRLR 86; see chapter 15.
[33] See *Iceland Frozen Foods Ltd v Jones* [1983] ICR 17.
[34] See H Collins, *Justice in Dismissal* (Oxford, OUP, 1992) ch 1.
[35] *X v Y* [2004] EWCA Civ 662, [2004] ICR 1634, [2004] IRLR 624.
[36] See the discussion in chapter 14. See also Mantouvalou, above n 8. For further challenges to privacy in the age of social media, see T Katsabian, 'Employees' Privacy in the Internet Age' (2019) *Berkeley Journal of Employment and Labor Law* 203.

Turning to freedom of expression, the right is protected under Article 10(1) of the ECHR that reads as follows, insofar as relevant: 'Everyone has the right to freedom of expression. This right shall include freedom to hold opinions and to receive and impart information and ideas without interference by public authority and regardless of frontiers.' The ECtHR has recognised that freedom of expression 'constitutes one of the essential foundations of a democratic society and one of the basic conditions for its progress and for each individual's self-fulfilment'.[37] Theoretical literature grounds it on a plurality of foundations, such as the discovery of the truth,[38] personal development,[39] democracy,[40] or autonomy.[41] Robust protection of free speech can promote all these values. It is generally accepted that different types of speech justify different degrees of protection,[42] with the example of political speech as a kind of speech that warrants particularly high protection because of the special value of pluralism in a democracy. However, it is striking to think that a lot of what we are free to say in a state that values free speech without interference by the authorities may be hindered by the economic power of the employer, who may dismiss workers because of views expressed that it finds objectionable, offensive or simply unconventional.[43] Is this fair?

As we know from previous chapters, having a right to something does not mean that we enjoy absolute protection against interference with our right.[44] Rights can come into conflict with other rights or other important values. Article 10(2) ECHR recognises that rights can be restricted if there is a legitimate aim, such as the protection of the reputation or the rights of others, and in a manner that is proportionate to the aim pursued.[45] The question in connection with unfair dismissal is whether the test of fairness or reasonableness in the statute is amended or made more stringent because the employer's reason for a dismissal involves an interference with Article 10. For instance, in a case such as *Gibbins* discussed in the introduction to this chapter, in connection with a claim for unfair dismissal, should a tribunal apply the normal test of whether or not the dismissal fell within the range of reasonable responses to the employee's conduct, or should the tribunal apply the arguably more stringent test of proportionality contained in Article 10(2) ECHR?

In the previous chapter concerning freedom of speech at work, we noted that tribunals rarely considered the question of the application of Article 10, and if they did in a case of dismissal, it seemed to be assumed that because the employee's actions constituted a breach of contract, such as a breach of confidence, the dismissal was within the range of reasonable responses and was therefore fair. Exceptionally, in *Hill v Great Tey Primary School*, even though there was arguably a breach of confidence by the employee, the EAT nevertheless insisted that the ET should have considered also the question of proportionality. That requirement is reinforced

---

[37] See, for instance, *Lingens v Austria* (1986) 8 EHRR 407, [41].
[38] JS Mill, *On Liberty* (Amherst, Prometheus Books, 1986).
[39] E Barendt, *Freedom of Speech* (Oxford, OUP, 2007).
[40] C Sunstein, *Democracy and the Problem of Free Speech* (New York, Free Press, 1995).
[41] Mill, above n 38; TM Scanlon, 'A Theory of Freedom of Expression' (1972) 1 *Philosophy and Public Affairs* 204.
[42] TM Scanlon, *The Difficulty of Tolerance – Essays in Political Philosophy* (Cambridge, CUP, 2009) 84.
[43] See the analysis in H Collins, 'Is the Contract of Employment Illiberal?' in H Collins, G Lester and V Mantouvalou (eds), *Philosophical Foundations of Labour Law* (Oxford, OUP, 2018) 48.
[44] With exceptions, such as the prohibition of torture, inhuman and degrading treatment, and slavery, servitude, forced and compulsory labour.
[45] Article 10(2) provides: 'The exercise of these freedoms, since it carries with it duties and responsibilities, may be subject to such formalities, conditions, restrictions or penalties as are prescribed by law and are necessary in a democratic society, in the interests of national security, territorial integrity or public safety, for the prevention of disorder or crime, for the protection of health or morals, for the protection of the reputation or rights of others, for preventing the disclosure of information received in confidence, or for maintaining the authority and impartiality of the judiciary.'

by frequent statements of the ECtHR that as dismissal is the most serious form of disciplinary action, with very significant effects on workers' interests, reputation and private life,[46] the test of proportionality can provide more suitable protection of employees, taking into account not just business interests but a broader range of considerations.

In connection with other Convention rights, however, the English Court of Appeal has applied the range of reasonable responses test of the law of unfair dismissal, and claimed that all the considerations relevant to a test of proportionality under the Convention can be considered within the test of reasonableness.[47] While that claim may be true, the issue is rather whether other, potentially irrelevant considerations under an enquiry into the protection of human rights may be included in the reasonableness assessment,[48] and whether under the test of reasonableness the tribunal focuses adequately on the importance of upholding Convention rights as opposed to the business interests of employers.[49]

Despite the lax nature of the test of the range of reasonable responses, it is possible that some dismissed employees can bring a successful claim. For instance, in *London Borough of Hammersmith and Fulham v Keable*,[50] a journalist recorded a conversation between participants in rival demonstrations in which one person was very critical of the Zionist movement in the past. Without permission, selected statements were then used by the journalist for the purpose of running a story on the internet that this person was antisemitic. Eventually this person's name was linked to his employer in the media, which led to suspension and then dismissal. Although the dismissal was held to be unfair because of procedural reasons, the ET also held that the dismissal was outside the range of reasonable responses of the employer. To reach that conclusion, which was upheld on appeal, the ET considered the following factors:

a. The Claimant made comments outside the workplace in his private capacity with no discernible link to his employment at all;

b. The Claimant did not himself publish the comments;

c. The comments were not found by the [employer] to be discriminatory, anti-Semitic, or racist;

d. The comments were not alleged to be unlawful or criminal or libellous;

e. The comments were not alleged to have been expressed in an abusive threatening, personally insulting, or obscene manner;

f. The Claimant was acknowledged … to have a right to attend demonstrations in his own time and express his own opinions.[51]

This decision demonstrates that although the range of reasonableness test in the law of unfair dismissal confers a wide discretion on employers, there are limits on when disciplinary action responding to speech outside of work can be regarded as fair.

Whether the test of proportionality or the test of reasonableness applies to a claim, a core element of the enquiry is to balance the interests of the employer against those of the employee in freedom of expression. To complete this chapter, we next consider which interests of the

---

[46] *Denisov v Ukraine*, App No 76639/11, [2018] ECHR 1061; see also *Szima v Hungary* [2013] IRLR 59, [2012] ECHR 1788, that involved demotion rather than dismissal.

[47] *Copsey v WBB Devon Clays Ltd* [2005] EWCA Civ 932, [2005] ICR 1789; *Turner v East Midland Trains Ltd* [2012] EWCA Civ 1470, [2013] ICR 525.

[48] See the discussion of *Copsey*, ibid.

[49] See H Collins, 'The Protection of Civil Liberties in the Workplace' (2006) 69 *Modern Law Review* 619; Mantouvalou, above n 8; P Wragg, 'Free Speech Rights at Work: Resolving the Differences Between Practice and Liberal Principle' (2015) 44 *ILJ* 1.

[50] [2021] UKEAT 2019-733, [2022] IRLR 4.

[51] *Hammersmith v Keable*, ibid [42].

employer are likely to be regarded as legitimate interests in these balancing tests. Finally, we need to consider the significance of different kinds of speech to the balancing exercise. Here we contrast the special importance attached to political speech in contrast to the exclusion of hate speech from protection.

4. Legitimate Interests of Employers

Business Interests

What constitutes a legitimate aim when limiting human rights in the employment context is not uncontroversial. At a general level, it can be said that the promotion of business interests such as profits and efficiency is a legitimate aim for the employer who takes disciplinary action. 'Business interests' is a vague concept, though, that needs to be further refined. The ECtHR has suggested that a potential, remote risk to business interests is not sufficient: the employer needs to demonstrate how the worker's conduct affected its interests. The analysis of business interests should primarily centre on the employee's workplace performance. Employees who spend much of their working time on social media, and hence cannot perform their job satisfactorily, may legitimately be disciplined for their activity. Disciplinary action is also justified when employees use social media to harass or bully other workers. But where the freedom of expression occurs away from work and does not interfere with the performance of the job, the protection of business interests does not appear to be a legitimate justification for disciplinary action.

Employer's Reputation

An aspect of business interests that is often invoked in dismissals for social media use is the protection of the reputation of the employer. For example, the main reason for the dismissal in *Gibbins* was an attempt by the employer to address what it regarded as damage to its reputation as a representative of Britain and the monarchy abroad. Protection of reputation may constitute a legitimate aim to be pursued. Employees have a duty of loyalty towards their employer, and deliberate infliction of reputational damage may breach that term of the contract. In ECtHR case law on freedom of expression, the protection of reputation of an individual (not an employer) is analysed as an aspect of Article 8, and is viewed as a legitimate reason to set limits to free speech. However, given the conflict with the right to free speech, the Court has ruled that a careful balancing exercise must be performed. 'In order for Article 8 to come into play ... an attack on a person's reputation must attain a certain level of seriousness and in a manner causing prejudice to personal enjoyment of the right to respect for private life.'[52] With the employer being an economic entity, and not generally a private person, the Convention provision at stake is the right to private property, which is protected in Article 1 of Protocol 1.

There are several considerations to keep in mind when resolving the conflict between freedom of expression of the worker, on the one hand, and business reputation of the employer on the other. These explain also why there is a need for very close scrutiny of alleged reputational damage. First, a significant danger with accepting too quickly that actual or potential damage to reputation justifies dismissal is that this may open the door for societal prejudice and majoritarian preferences to dictate which views and preferences are acceptable. In the case of *Gibbins*,

---

[52] *Axel Springer v Germany* [2012] ECHR 227, (2012) 55 EHRR 6, 32 BHRC 493, [2012] EMLR 15, [83].

for instance, it was particularly troubling to see that the tabloid press played a major role in pressurising the employer to dismiss her. This is even more troubling given that they misreported the incident causing serious damage. In any case, the role of human rights law is exactly to protect individuals and minorities from the imposition of majoritarian views and preferences. Unpopular political views may have an effect on business reputation, but courts and tribunals should pay close attention to alleged reputational damage as a reason for dismissal, because it may introduce majoritarian preferences that can oppress workers with unpopular views.

The nature of the employer's business and the nature of a person's job should be carefully considered in assessing whether disciplinary action or dismissal is proportionate to the aim of preventing damage to the employer's reputation. Respect for autonomy that underlies aspects of human rights law does not permit the imposition of the employer's political views and other preferences on employees, unless a particular workplace has the promotion of a particular political or other ethical outlook as its central aim. If the employer holds itself out as having a particular ethic or set of values, such as a church, restrictions on freedom of expression by employees may be justified as protections of the employer's reputation, whereas the same statements would not provide a legitimate justification for interference with freedom of expression if carried out by ordinary employers. The nature of the job is also important to consider in this context.[53] Returning to the case of *Gibbins*, if it is accepted that the British Council was committed to certain values such as upholding the British monarchy, it does not follow that her republican remarks should justify dismissal. It is important to recall that her job was not public-facing, so it is difficult to see why she should accept limitations on her freedom of political expression since her remarks would not normally be associated with the employer.

It is also important to appreciate that sometimes employers use the effects of social media posts on their reputation as a pretext to discipline or dismiss, without this being the real reason for the termination. This can be seen in the case of *Mason*.[54] Mr Mason, a rugby player, was contracted by Huddersfield Giants to play for four years. During a traditional, long, drinking session with his co-players, Mr Mason left his phone briefly, which another player used to take a photo of his anus. Later, Mr Mason's girlfriend tweeted the image through his phone and account, tagging another player. Mr Mason's followers (over 4,000 of them) could access the photo. Mr Mason deleted the tweet two days later, but his employer decided to terminate his contract for gross misconduct. His contract provided that he should preserve the club's name and reputation, and that he should not engage in any conduct that could bring the club into disrepute. His employer explained that players are role models, and they should use social media responsibly. The High Court that heard the case found his dismissal wrongful. Judge Saffman explained, inter alia, that it was not immediately obvious that the photo on social media was of someone's anus, as it was said that it looked more like a photograph of a 'hairy peach'. He also suggested that there was a certain degree of hypocrisy in dismissing Mr Mason for his social media post which was viewed as incompatible with family values, given that the particular club (as many other rugby clubs) had a tradition of the so-called Naked Monday, where players had to undertake a naked run in public. How could a post of a naked body part be viewed as problematic by the employer, who at the same time permitted naked runs of players in public spaces? The case suggested that the real reason for termination was Mr Mason's performance, which had not been as his employer expected. *Mason* is not the only case where social media activity is a mere pretext for dismissal, while the real reason involves workplace relations.

---

[53] See further *Obst* and *Schuth* discussed in chapter 14.
[54] *Mason v Huddersfield Giants Ltd* [2013] EWHC 2869 (QB).

Finally, it is worth noting that the manner of the expression may accentuate or reduce the risk of possible damage to the reputation of the employer. Where language is crude and offensive, the risk of damage to reputation may be greater than when controversial views are articulated in a moderate, reasoned way. As Briggs J said in *Smith v Trafford Housing Trust*:[55] 'I cannot envisage how his moderate expression of his particular views about gay marriage in church, on his personal Facebook wall at a weekend out of working hours, could sensibly lead any reasonable reader to think the worst of the Trust for having employed him as a manager.'[56]

5. Political Speech

The ECtHR has protected workers from discipline or dismissal for views expressed outside the workplace and working time in case law involving political speech under Article 10 and participation in political parties as an aspect of freedom of association under Article 11. Indeed, one of the oldest employment-related cases of the ECtHR was about political expression. In *Vogt v Germany*,[57] the applicant was employed as a secondary school teacher and was dismissed from her job for breaching her duty of political loyalty as she was an active member of the Communist party that aimed to overthrow the political structure of the state and the constitutional system.

The Court found that there had been a breach of her freedom of expression and thought. It said that the right to obtain a job in the public sector does not fall within the scope of Article 10, but stated that '[t]his does not mean, however, that a person who has been appointed as a civil servant cannot complain on being dismissed if that dismissal violates one of his or her rights under the Convention'.[58] It went on to explain that

> [f]reedom of expression constitutes one of the essential foundations of a democratic society and one of the basic conditions for its progress and each individual's self-fulfilment. Subject to paragraph 2 of Article 10 (art. 10-2), it is applicable not only to 'information' or 'ideas' that are favourably received or regarded as inoffensive or as a matter of indifference, but also to those that offend, shock or disturb; such are the demands of that pluralism, tolerance and broadmindedness without which there is no 'democratic society'.[59]

The Court accepted that civil servants may have special duties of loyalty but found that the dismissal of Ms Vogt was disproportionate to the aim pursued. The Court paid attention to the reputational damage inflicted on Ms Vogt through her dismissal, the fact that loss of her job would probably mean loss of livelihood as all teaching posts were in the public sector, while also noting that her political views and activities away from work had had no impact on her workplace performance.[60] The Court also accepted that teachers are 'figures of authority to their pupils',[61] and for this reason they have certain duties to act as such in their life away from work. Yet it found no evidence that Ms Vogt openly expressed anti-constitutional sentiments outside work, while the political party in which she was involved was lawful. Her dismissal was therefore found to violate the ECHR.

---

[55] *Smith v Trafford Housing Trust* [2012] EWHC 3221 (Ch).
[56] ibid [63].
[57] *Vogt v Germany* [1996] ECHR 34.
[58] ibid [43].
[59] ibid [52].
[60] ibid [60].
[61] ibid.

Dismissal because of political affiliation was also at stake in the case *Redfearn v United Kingdom*.[62] Mr Redfearn, a white British man, was employed by Serco, a private bus company that provided transport services to local authorities. He transported children and adults with physical and mental disabilities in the city of Bradford, an area containing a majority Asian population. He was employed for less than one year. When it became known to Serco that he was an active member of the British National Party (BNP), an extreme right-wing political party, which is notorious not only for its anti-immigration and anti-European Union positions, but also, ironically, for its policy of withdrawal from the ECHR, he was transferred to a mail delivery post. When he was elected as a local BNP councillor, following representations by the local trade union, he was summarily dismissed. The reason given for his dismissal was that his continued employment would create potential health and safety risks for it could cause anxiety among Asian customers and perhaps even provoke violence. It might also harm the reputation of Serco with possible negative implications for its business with the local council of Bradford.

The right to claim unfair dismissal under the ERA 1996 is subject to a qualifying period of employment that was raised from one year to two years in April 2012.[63] Exceptions to this qualifying period apply to instances where employees claim other statutory rights. Claims under the anti-discrimination laws in the Equality Act 2010 are also exempt from any qualifying period. However, Mr Redfearn lacked the qualifying period of employment and did not fall within any of the exceptions to that requirement. He could therefore not bring a claim for unfair dismissal. Moreover, he could not bring a discrimination claim because the law does not prohibit discrimination on the grounds of political beliefs.

The ECtHR examined *Redfearn* under Article 11 (freedom of association) interpreted in light of Article 10. All members of the Court accepted that in general a qualifying period for claims of unfair dismissal could be justified as an aspect of economic policy. UK governments have often asserted that a qualifying period helps to reduce levels of unemployment in the economy by removing a deterrent against employers hiring new staff.[64] But the majority noted that there were many exceptions to the qualifying period for unfair dismissal, and that anti-discrimination laws apply from day one of employment. In view of these exceptions, a majority of the Court held that the UK Government could not successfully justify the absence of an exception in this case to protect employees against unfair dismissal or discrimination on the ground of membership of a political party or political opinion. The Court said that there should be legislation which protects individuals from dismissal that implicates Article 11, instead of leaving individuals in a regulatory gap.[65] In assessing the situation, the Court placed attention, inter alia, on the fact that Mr Redfearn was 'a first class employee' and that at the time he was dismissed he was 56 years old, which would make it difficult for him to find another job.[66]

In this case law, we see that the ECtHR espouses strong protection of political association and political expression: it defends the right to freedom of association and expression for members of political parties against interference by an employer, even if those political parties hold objectionable views, such as those of the BNP, and oppose fundamental principles of the Convention or the constitutional orders of the Member States. The Court endorses strongly the post-war commitment to multi-party democracy and acts forcefully against any challenge posed

---

[62] *Redfearn v United Kingdom* (2013) 57 EHRR 2.
[63] s 108(1) as amended by the Unfair Dismissal and Statement of Reasons for Dismissal (Variation of Qualifying Period) Order 2012 (SI 2012/989). On the qualifying period, see further chapter 3.
[64] *R v Secretary of State for Employment, ex parte Seymour Smith* [2012] UKHL 12, [2000] ICR 244.
[65] Following *Redfearn*, the Government removed the continuity requirement where the dismissal relates to an employee's political opinions or affiliation: ERA 1996, s 108(4).
[66] Above n 62, [45]–[46].

to this fundamental ingredient of liberal democracies, particularly one emanating from private employers.[67]

Can people lawfully be dismissed for expressing political views on social media? In *Melike v Turkey*,[68] the applicant, an employee at the Ministry of National Education, was dismissed because she 'liked' on Facebook various articles that had been posted by others. They criticised the authorities for oppressive practices and religious figures for sexist comments, encouraged protest against these practices, denounced abuse of pupils in institutions run by the authorities and other such issues. The Court examined the case under the right to freedom of expression. It found that the matters at stake were unquestionably matters of public interest, and explained that when it comes to issues of political speech or issues of general public interest, there is particularly limited scope for restrictions.

To return to the case of *Gibbins*, given the special weight typically attached to political expression, and the role of social media for free speech, it is clear that her remarks on Facebook on white privilege and royalty qualify for protection under the right to free speech. However, the Tribunal focused on the fact that she associated herself with an offensive post in relation to her discrimination claim, and did not enter into a discussion of freedom of expression in her claim of unfair dismissal. It applied the test of reasonable responses, which is found in s 98 of the ERA 1996. It said:

> no member of the tribunal was able to say that no reasonable employer could dismiss the claimant for these reasons and after this process. A robust leadership may have sought to face down the press by disciplining the claimant short of dismissal, but it cannot be said the decision was one that no reasonable employer could have made. Clearly the claimant deserves some sympathy for her slip of judgment, but that does not mean the decision was unfair.[69]

This test is clearly unsuitable for a dismissal that interferes with the right to freedom of expression generally, and political expression particularly.

6. Offensive Speech and Hate Speech

Finally, in the protection of freedom of expression, the content of the expression itself is relevant to the question of how far it can be protected under the test of proportionality. As we have noted already, the mere fact that speech and other modes of expression are found offensive does not mean that they are unprotected under Article 10. Nevertheless, in making an assessment of the proportionality of an employer's restrictions on freedom of expression, the content of the speech, its intended impact, and the offence caused to others will be relevant to the determination of the lawfulness of the restrictions. What needs to be remembered, however, is that even unthinking, ranting, offensive speech is an expression of personal autonomy.[70] The mere fact that some people may be offended, and that therefore the employer prefers not to risk its reputation in possibly being associated with the remarks, is not necessarily a sufficient justification for disciplinary action including dismissal.[71] The tribunals may not always sufficiently appreciate that offensive

---

[67] Although the Court refrains from passing judgment on the policies of the BNP, the authors do not share the same hesitation in condemning every aspect of the BNP's racist programme.
[68] *Melike v Turkey* [2021] ECHR 511.
[69] *Gibbins*, above n 1, [141].
[70] See the discussion of autonomy in TM Scanlon, *The Difficulty of Tolerance* (Cambridge, CUP, 2003) 15 ff.
[71] J Rowbottom, 'To Rant, Vent and Converse: Protecting Low Level Digital Speech' (2012) 71 *Cambridge Law Journal* 355; and Wragg, above n 49.

speech may sometimes have to be tolerated by employers and that it is not the employer's role to decide what speech is acceptable.

For example, Mr Laws was employed by a retailer with 300 stores in the UK.[72] He was responsible for assessing risk and preventing loss in about 100 of the stores. The employer had several official Twitter accounts for the stores, and Mr Laws also opened a personal one to follow them. He did not identify his employer on his account, but he was followed back by 65 of the stores when he was linked to the employer in someone else's tweet, which he retweeted. At some point, it was found out that Mr Laws had posted offensive tweets on various groups, such as dentists, caravan drivers, a hospital Accident and Emergency Department, Newcastle supporters, and disabled people, from his Twitter account that was accessible by the public. He was dismissed. The EAT examined the question whether the Twitter account had acquired a sufficiently work-related context, and whether the settings were public or private. Having been satisfied that the context was sufficiently work-related, and that many could access Mr Laws' tweets, it found the dismissal fair. The *Laws* case shows how personal messages can become attributed to the employer simply by virtue of one's job. It also demonstrates how unthinking, spontaneous, offensive remarks on social media, perhaps intended as a joke, can disseminate quickly and raise questions about the ethical standards of an employee, which in turn might be attributed to the employer. The tribunals seem to diminish the protection for freedom of expression outside work to vanishing point in such cases even though the test of proportionality should require the employer to demonstrate the necessity and appropriateness of the sanction of dismissal.

Nevertheless, there will be instances where freedom of expression is deliberately being used not only to cause offence but to stir up hatred of groups of people and to undermine respect for human rights.[73] In such instances, the test of proportionality is likely to provide scant protection against interferences with the right to freedom of expression. This can be exemplified by the case of *Webb v London Underground*.[74] Ms Webb worked for 35 years for London Underground, her latest position being a train manager. She was dismissed because of comments she posted on Facebook that were offensive and racist in relation to the killing of George Floyd, an African American man murdered by a white police officer in the US. The murder was followed by protests across the US and elsewhere in the world, with a key slogan being that 'Black Lives Matter'. Ms Webb commented that Floyd was 'scum', suggested that he was responsible for several crimes, and was critical of the fact that there had been no responses similar to those following his murder after the murder of a white man in the UK, Lee Rigby. Colleagues of hers saw the messages, which were very widely shared, and found them racist and offensive.

The tribunal examined whether her dismissal violated the right to freedom of expression among other issues.[75] It accepted that dismissal was justified for the protection of the employer's reputation and the rights of others, explaining that many had found her comments deeply offensive, racially divisive, and inflammatory. The tribunal also paid attention to the fact that the employer was a high-profile public body, and that its response would be scrutinised very closely in the public domain on such a political matter that had gained global interest and publicity. Her dismissal was found to be a proportionate measure (though it was ruled to be unfair on procedural grounds for the reason that the employer had refused to engage with the Article 10 defence).

---

[72] *Game Retail Ltd v Laws*, UKEAT/0188/14/DA, 3 November 2014, 2014 WL 6862769.
[73] For an argument that there should be a clear distinction between offensive speech and hate speech, see N Hatzis, *Offensive Speech, Religion, and the Limits of the Law* (Oxford, OUP, 2021), ch 1.
[74] *Webb v London Underground Ltd*, 3306438/2021, 2 February 2023, ET.
[75] The ET found that Article 8 was not engaged in this context. See [95]–[97].

This tribunal decision appears to be in line with the case law of the ECtHR on justified restrictions to free speech. The Court has noted that

> tolerance and respect for the equal dignity of all human beings constitute the foundations of a democratic, pluralistic society. That being so, as a matter of principle it may be considered necessary in certain democratic societies to sanction or even prevent all forms of expression which spread, incite, promote or justify hatred based on intolerance … , provided that any 'formalities', 'restrictions' or 'penalties' imposed are proportionate to the legitimate aim pursued.[76]

Against this background, speech that incites racial hatred has been found to be legitimately restricted in the case of a well-known footballer who was fined for his comments,[77] and in the case of a journalist and pundit who was convicted for speech that was viewed as inciting hatred and discrimination towards the French Muslim community.[78] To reach this conclusion, the Court either considers the speech in question to be legitimately restricted under Article 10(2) ECHR or to be excluded under Article 17 as a prohibited abuse of a right.[79] The ECtHR is clear that speech that calls for direct use of violence and strong negative labelling of individuals and groups is covered by Article 17.[80] Yet what constitutes hate speech is not always sufficiently clear, and this line of case law of the Court has been criticised for being unprincipled and for not upholding liberal values.[81]

7. Conclusion

Free speech is an important right in modern liberal societies, as the ECtHR has repeatedly recognised. Having a right to freedom of expression outside the workplace and working time is crucial for individual autonomy and democracy. Social media have brought new challenges for workers, employers and courts dealing with complaints of disciplinary action and dismissal. There is nowadays greater potential for reputational damage than in the past because of the spontaneous nature of the posts, and the reach and impact that they can have. Yet free speech is important, and people value using social media to express views on all kinds of issues. The employer should not have the power to police these views, adopt restrictive social media policies and discipline employees for comments that may be controversial or disagreeable to it.

For reasons such as these, a bright line could be usefully drawn by courts when assessing cases of social media activity and other speech away from the workplace.[82] When it comes to the effect of this on business interests, it would be a positive starting point if courts stated clearly that employees' social media posts that have no link to workplace performance or the nature of the

---

[76] *Erbakan v Turkey*, App No 59405/00, Judgment of 6 July 2006, [56].
[77] See *Simunic v Croatia*, App No 20373/17, Admissibility Decision of 22 January 2019.
[78] *Zemmour v France* [2022] ECHR 1130.
[79] Article 17 provides as follows: 'Nothing in this Convention may be interpreted as implying for any State, group or person any right to engage in any activity or perform any act aimed at the destruction of any of the rights and freedoms set forth herein or at their limitation to a greater extent than is provided for in the Convention.'
[80] See, for instance, *Hizb Ut-Tahrir and others v Germany* [2012] ECHR 1045, [74], where the Court focused on Articles 11 and 17.
[81] For criticism of the approach of the Court, see G Letsas, 'Free Speech, Balancing, and the Margin of Appreciation' in Charles Girard and Pierre Auriel (eds), *Cambridge Handbook on Freedom of Expression and Democracy – European Perspectives* (Cambridge, CUP, 2025, forthcoming). See also A Buyse, 'Dangerous Expressions: The ECHR, Violence, and Free Speech' (2014) 63 *International and Comparative Law Quarterly* 491. Cf J Waldron, *The Harm in Hate Speech* (Cambridge MA, Harvard University Press, 2013).
[82] See also Mantouvalou, above n 8.

job should never be understood to represent the employer's views. There should be a presumption of privacy or protected speech. Drawing a clear, bright line that separates workplace conduct or performance, and off-duty social media activity, can protect employees from employers' oppression, and can also help employers who are concerned about the effect of social media on their reputation. This position was adopted in the case of Adrian Smith, where the Court ruled that

> [t]he right of individuals to freedom of expression and freedom of belief, taken together, means that they are in general entitled to promote their religious or political beliefs, providing they do so lawfully. Of course, an employer may legitimately restrict or prohibit such activities at work, or in a work related context, but it would be prima facie surprising to find that an employer had, by the incorporation of a code of conduct into the employee's contract, extended that prohibition to his personal or social life.[83]

While it may be acceptable for the state to outlaw some types of speech, such as hate speech or speech that incites violence, and for the employer to limit some types of speech in the workplace for the purpose of harmonious relations, giving the employer the power to determine the value of speech on social media or elsewhere outside work carries significant dangers. Free speech should be defended rigorously in the workplace, for otherwise employers can exercise tyrannical power over employees who hold views that they find disagreeable or distasteful.

---

[83] *Smith*, above n 55, [66].

17

Freedom to Manifest a Religion

1. Religious and Other Beliefs
2. Framing of Claims
3. Working Hours
4. Dress Codes
5. 'Conscientious Objection' to Providing a Particular Service
6. Expressing Religious Views
7. Religious Organisations as Employers
8. Conclusion

Article 9 of the European Convention on Human Rights (ECHR) makes specific provision for religious and other beliefs:

1. Everyone has the right to freedom of thought, conscience and religion; this right includes freedom to change his religion or belief and freedom, either alone or in community with others and in public or private, to manifest his religion or belief, in worship, teaching practice and observance.
2. Freedom to manifest one's religion or beliefs shall be subject only to such limitations as are prescribed by law and are necessary in a democratic society in the interests of public safety, for the protection of public order, health or morals, or for the protection of the rights and freedoms of others

As we shall see, while 'religious beliefs' is often a useful shorthand, legal protections of this kind typically extend to non-religious beliefs (agnosticism, atheism, humanism and so on) and other belief systems not related to religion. In the employment context, the focus is on the extent to which a working person should be allowed or enabled to 'manifest' their religion or belief in the workplace. This is a qualified right which can be restricted on various grounds including, importantly, the protection of the rights and freedoms of others.

In English law and EU law, the starting-point for analysis of employees' claims based on religion is usually equality law, interpreted in the light of Article 9 and other human rights obligations. Religious and other beliefs are a 'protected characteristic' for these purposes, so the question becomes whether the employer has discriminated, directly or indirectly, against a person because of their beliefs. In most cases, the discrimination will be indirect, so attention will shift to justification: whether the employer's rule or policy is a proportionate means of achieving a legitimate aim. For example, an employer might adopt a dress code which applies to the whole workforce equally, but has an adverse impact on an employee whose religious beliefs require them to wear a particular type of clothing. The court would consider the employer's reasons for adopting the dress code – which might include factors such as presenting a neutral image to customers, or observing health and safety requirements – in deciding the case. The precise interaction between Article 9 and equality law can sometimes present difficulties, which we examine in greater detail below.

It is probably worth noting at the outset that the protection of religion in particular is not without its critics, even though the protection is even-handed as between believers and non-believers.[1] This is because many adherents to the major world religions hold views which conflict with other strands of equality law, such as gender or sexual orientation.[2] Few religious groups recognise equal marriage for gay couples, for example. In practice, the law manages these conflicts by paying careful attention to the context in which they arise, and by balancing the claims of believers against the need to protect the rights and freedoms of others. On the one hand, religious organisations benefit from some exceptions to equality law to allow them to discriminate in accordance with their beliefs, for example, when appointing people to leadership positions within the organisation. On the other hand, a state official who refuses on grounds of their personal religious beliefs to perform civil wedding ceremonies for gay couples may legitimately be dismissed by their employer in pursuit of its policy of providing equal access to public services for everyone.[3]

This chapter begins by examining the meaning of 'religious beliefs' and identifying the other types of belief that attract the law's protection.[4] It then turns to the four main areas in which a working person's desire to manifest their beliefs may be an issue at work: working hours, dress codes, conscientious objection, and the expression of religious views. It concludes by examining the position of religious organisations as employers, and the extent to which they can require the people they employ to abide by their religious teachings.

1. Religious and Other Beliefs

The freedom simply to hold a particular religious or other belief as 'a matter of individual thought and conscience' is 'absolute and unqualified' under Article 9.[5] Most conflicts, whether at work or in other contexts, arise where a person wishes to 'manifest' their belief in some way. For these purposes, there is greater scrutiny of whether the person's belief falls within the category of beliefs protected by the law.

The breadth of Article 9 is captured in the ECtHR's judgment in *SAS v France*:

> [Article 9] is, in its religious dimension, one of the most vital elements that go to make up the identity of believers and their conception of life, but it is also a precious asset for atheists, agnostics, sceptics and the unconcerned ... That freedom entails, inter alia, freedom to hold or not to hold religious beliefs and to practise or not to practise a religion.[6]

This makes clear that freedom of religion includes freedom not to have any religious beliefs at all. The Court has recognised most major world religions, but typically avoids trying to develop a definition or to apply it to a particular group,[7] in the interests of being neutral as

---

[1] See F Raday, 'Culture, Religion, and Gender' (2003) 1 *ICON* 663; and for a discussion with a UK focus, A McColgan, 'Class wars? Religion and (In)Equality in the Workplace' (2009) 38 *ILJ* 1.
[2] M Bell, 'Bridging a Divide: a Faith-Based Perspective on Anti-Discrimination Law' (2020) 9 *OJLR* 56; C McCrudden, *Litigating Religions: An Essay on Human Rights, Courts, and Beliefs* (OUP, 2018).
[3] See the *Ladele* case, decided together with *Eweida v United Kingdom* (2013) 57 EHRR 8, noted by R McCrea, 'Religion in the Workplace: *Eweida and Others* v *United Kingdom*' (2014) 77 MLR 277.
[4] For a more detailed account of many of the issues discussed here, see L Vickers, *Religious Freedom, Religious Discrimination and the Workplace*, 2nd edn (Oxford, Hart, 2016).
[5] ibid [80].
[6] *SAS v France* (2015) 60 EHRR 11, [124].
[7] *Chappell v UK* (1988) 10 EHRR CD 510.

between different religions and sects.[8] The only situation in which an organisation might be deemed not to be a religion is where it is not genuine, such as an organisation set up to parody religion.[9]

Article 9 also protects a range of other beliefs that are not religious, provided that they occupy a significant position in the lives of their believers. Guidance in *Campbell and Cosans v UK* indicates that the following requirements must be met:

— beliefs must 'attain a certain level of cogency, seriousness, cohesion and importance'[10] and must be more than a matter of opinion;[11]
— they must 'relate to a weighty and substantial aspect of human life and behaviour';[12]
— they must be 'worthy of respect in a "democratic society" and … not incompatible with human dignity', and must not conflict with the fundamental rights of others.[13]

The case itself concerned the applicants' strongly held belief that corporal punishment of children in schools was morally wrong, which was accepted as a 'philosophical conviction' for the purposes of the Protocol 1, Article 2 right to education. A range of different beliefs, such as pacifism[14] and veganism,[15] have been recognised as qualifying for protection under Article 9.

English law treats 'religion or belief' as a protected characteristic by virtue of s 4 of the Equality Act 2010. Under s 10(1), 'religion means any religion and a reference to religion includes a reference to a lack of religion', and under s 10(2), 'belief means any religious or philosophical belief and a reference to belief includes a reference to a lack of belief'. In the leading case of *Grainger*, the EAT followed the *Campbell and Cosans* guidance in determining what kinds of beliefs qualify for protection as 'philosophical beliefs'.[16] It upheld the tribunal's decision to recognise the claimant's belief in the imminent climate emergency as a philosophical belief. It further indicated that it was no bar to a belief being protected that it did not govern all aspects of the claimant's life, that it was a political philosophy, or that it was based on science. The distinction between a belief and an opinion has potentially important consequences in English law. Under the Convention, this simply acts as a dividing line between Article 9 and Article 10, whereas in English law, expressions of opinion fall outside the scope of discrimination law and attract more patchy protection, as discussed in chapter 16.

The limitation that a belief must not conflict with the rights of others allows courts and tribunals to reject certain beliefs, such as fascist and racist beliefs, as unworthy of protection.[17] However, in *Forstater*, the EAT controversially took the view that this should be construed in the light of Article 17 ECHR, so that a belief would only fall outside the scope of Article 9 if it 'involves a very grave violation of the rights of others, tantamount to the destruction of those rights'.[18] On this basis, it held that the claimant's belief that a person's biological sex at birth

---

[8] *Metropolitan Church of Bessarabia v Moldova* (2002) 35 EHRR 13, [116].
[9] *De Wilde v Netherlands* (2023) 76 EHRR SE4.
[10] *Campbell and Cosans v UK* (1982) 4 EHRR 293, [36].
[11] ibid.
[12] ibid.
[13] ibid.
[14] *Arrowsmith v UK* (1981) 3 EHRR 218.
[15] *CW v UK* (1993) 16 EHRR CD44.
[16] *Grainger plc v Nicholson* [2010] ICR 360.
[17] eg *Cave v The Open University*, 5 May 2023, ET, holding that a belief in 'English nationalism' was unworthy of protection.
[18] *Forstater v CGD Europe* [2022] ICR 1.

was immutable did qualify for protection. Critics have argued that this is an overly narrow way of construing the relevant criterion, in that a belief may be incompatible with the dignity and rights of others without necessarily reaching the Article 17 'destruction' threshold.[19]

The approach of EU law to the types of beliefs qualifying for protection may be somewhat narrower than those taken by the ECtHR and the English courts. The Equal Treatment Directive (ETD) refers, in Article 1, to 'religion or belief'.[20] In *WABE*, the Court held that these two terms should be treated as 'two facets of the same single ground of discrimination'.[21] In the *LF* case, the Court interpreted 'religion or belief' as meaning 'religious belief and philosophical or spiritual belief', but not political beliefs, which are mentioned separately in Article 21 of the EU Charter of Fundamental Rights (EUCFR).[22] As a result, the ETD was held not to cover 'political or trade union belief; nor does it cover artistic, sporting, aesthetic or other beliefs or preferences'.[23] Of course, it remains open to the Member States to offer more broadly-framed protection, to include political beliefs, but it is not permissible for implementing legislation to split 'religion or belief' into two separate protected characteristics. The EAT in *Grainger* drew a distinction between a political philosophy, which qualified for protection, and a political belief, which did not, so it may be that the Court of Justice is reaching for a similar distinction in *LF*.[24] Further clarification may be required.

2. Framing of Claims

As noted above, conflicts in the workplace typically arise not because of the beliefs a person holds, but because of the way in which they wish to 'manifest' those beliefs. Before we discuss some examples, it may be helpful to say something about how the different legal regimes under consideration 'frame' a dispute between a worker and their employer.

The ECtHR, as a supranational court, is concerned to flesh out the positive duties Article 9 places on the state to secure people's ability to manifest their beliefs at work or in any other context.[25] It is thus not directly concerned with the immediate dispute between the worker and their employer. The state benefits from a margin of appreciation. This means that the Court will sometimes focus less on the outcome and more on whether the affected worker had sufficient opportunity to challenge the employer's actions in the domestic courts.[26] As well as the usual proportionality test, the Court also uses the definition of 'manifestation' as a device to limit Article 9 claims. Article 9 lists four forms of manifestation – 'worship, teaching, practice and observance' – but nothing appears to turn on the precise categorisation of any particular belief-motivated act. What is important is that the act is 'intimately linked to the religion or belief'.[27] This is clear from *Eweida*, in which the Court stated that not 'every act which is in some way

---

[19] S Cowan and S Morris, 'Should "Gender Critical" Views about Trans People be Protected as Philosophical Beliefs in the Workplace? Lessons for the Future from *Forstater, Mackereth and Higgs*' (2022) 51 *ILJ* 1.
[20] Directive 2000/78.
[21] Case C-804/18 *IX v WABE ev* EU:C:2021:594, [2022] ICR 190, [47].
[22] Case C-344/20 *LF v SCRL* EU:C:2022:774, [2023] ICR 133, [27]–[28]. For discussion, see E Howard, '*LF v SCRL* and the CJEU's Failure to Engage with the Reality of Muslim Women in the Labour Market', *Industrial Law Journal*, forthcoming.
[23] *LF*, ibid [28].
[24] ibid.
[25] *Eweida*, above n 3, [84].
[26] *Schüth v Germany* (2011) 52 EHRR 32.
[27] *Eweida*, above n 3, [82].

inspired, motivated or influenced by [the belief] constitutes a "manifestation" of the belief'.[28] Instead, 'the existence of a sufficiently close and direct nexus between the act and the underlying belief must be determined on the facts of each case'.[29]

In equality law, attention is squarely on the employer, and the claim must be framed either as direct discrimination – the use of religion or belief as a decision-making criterion by the employer – or as indirect discrimination – an apparently neutral provision, criterion or practice applied by the employer which has an adverse impact on the claimant. The CJEU has confirmed that the ETD protects against adverse impacts on the way in which the claimant wishes to manifest their belief, even though this terminology is not expressly used in the Directive.[30] The indirect discrimination approach can cause problems where the claimant's mode of manifesting their religious belief is particular to them.[31] For example, *Eweida* itself concerned a Christian who wanted to wear a cross, but this is not generally regarded as a requirement of Christianity, nor is it a common practice among believers.[32] On a strict application of the Equality Act 2010, s 19(2)(b), persons who share the claimant's belief are not put at a disadvantage by an employer's jewellery ban because they do not see themselves as obliged to wear a cross. The ECHR offers much clearer protection to purely individual choices. Under Article 9, the applicant does not have to establish that the particular way in which they wish to manifest their belief is a 'duty mandated by' their religion or belief or a preference shared by other believers.[33] This issue could be resolved by reading s 19(2)(b) compatibly with Article 9 under s 3 of the Human Rights Act 1998 (HRA 1998), though this does involve a significant departure from the original intention of s 19 to combat group disadvantage. However, the domestic courts have so far been reluctant to take this step.[34]

To address gaps in the law of indirect discrimination, a public sector employee may be able to rely directly on Article 9 by making a claim in the ordinary courts under the HRA 1998, s 7. Furthermore, all employees may be able to claim unfair dismissal if their employment has been terminated for a manifestation of religion. An employment tribunal will be required to assess the reasonableness of the dismissal in a way that is compatible with the right to manifest a religion or a belief. Although the 'range of reasonable responses' test of fairness in the law of unfair dismissal appears rather less demanding on employers than the requirements for justification under Article 9 and discrimination law (to be considered next), so far the English courts have perhaps surprisingly insisted that the two standards produce the same result.[35] Accordingly, dismissals that interfere with an employee's right to manifest a religion will be held to be fair if reasonable employers would have dismissed in the circumstances.

Turning to the framework for justification for interferences with manifestations of religion, direct discrimination is, of course, not normally open to justification by the employer outside the specific context of 'genuine occupational requirements', to which we will return below. However, this creates the potential for conflict with Article 9, where the potential for justification is ever-present. For example, under Article 9, it is always possible to justify an interference

---

[28] ibid.
[29] ibid.
[30] Case C-157/15 *Achbita v G4S Secure Solutions NV* EU:C:2017:203, [2017] 3 CMLR 21, [28].
[31] See J Adenitire, 'Protecting Solitary Beliefs against Discrimination' (2021) 50 *ILJ* 196.
[32] *Eweida*, above n 3.
[33] ibid [82].
[34] *Gray v Mulberry Co (Design) Ltd* [2019] EWCA Civ 1720, [2020] ICR 715, though cf *Mba v Merton LBC* [2013] EWCA Civ 1562, [2014] ICR 357.
[35] *Copsey v WWB Devon Clays Ltd* [2005] EWCA Civ 932, [2005] ICR 1789; *Turner v East Midland Trains Ltd* [2012] EWCA Civ 1470, [2013] ICR 525.

with religious expression whether that interference applies to all religions (and thus falls within the equality law category of indirect discrimination) or targets a particular religion or belief (and thus counts as direct discrimination in equality law terms). The domestic courts are still grappling with this problem. In *Higgs*, the EAT drew a distinction between 'objectionable' and legitimate manifestations of belief.[36] This introduces a justification test into direct discrimination by asking first whether the manifestation was objectionable (by assessing whether it was legitimate for the employer to interfere with it under Article 9) and then holding that objectionable manifestations fall outside the scope of protection of religion or belief under domestic equality law. While this deals with the issue, it adds another layer of complexity to the law.[37]

Whatever form a case takes, it is clear that the proportionality test plays a fundamental role. While the ECtHR recognises the importance of the freedom to manifest – 'bearing witness in words and deeds is bound up with the existence of religious convictions'[38] – the right to do so is heavily qualified because of its potential to impact the rights and freedoms of others:[39]

> Article 9 does not always guarantee the right to behave in the public sphere in a manner which is dictated by one's religion or beliefs.[40]

Employers' justificatory arguments may take a variety of different forms, but one argument which is often made before both the ECtHR and the CJEU is that the employer wishes to pursue a policy of 'neutrality'. For example, the employer's dress code may prohibit the wearing of any religious symbols in order to present a neutral image to customers. This may form part of a broader argument that religious or other beliefs should be a private matter, kept separate from working life. An individual should be free to worship or practise their religion outside working hours, but should not attempt to do or say anything faith-based at work. Employers' neutrality policies appear to have been inspired in many cases by state traditions of secularity. The French approach of laïcité is a well-known example.[41] Religious symbols are prohibited in public spaces such as schools and municipal buildings, in order to create a neutral environment in which the state does not appear to support any particular belief system.

Neutrality policies are controversial for a number of reasons. The label itself is somewhat misleading: a firm could also be neutral as between different religions by allowing all employees to wear items manifesting their beliefs.[42] It may also be questioned whether the justifications for having a secular state apply equally to private employers,[43] though in the EU context, employers may be able to invoke Article 16 EUCFR to reinforce their desire to adopt a particular attitude towards religion and belief.[44] Finally, it is worth noting that many religious people would argue that any attempt to apply a strict public/private divide misunderstands the all-encompassing nature of religious belief.

It is worth noting one significant critique of the current legal framework. Some commentators have argued that the concept of 'reasonable accommodation', which already applies in disability

---

[36] *Higgs v Farmor's School* [2023] EAT 89, [2023] ICR 1072.
[37] For discussion, see M Foran, 'Discrimination and Manifestation of Belief: *Higgs v Farmor's School* [2023] EAT 89', *Industrial Law Journal*, forthcoming.
[38] *Eweida*, above n 3, [80].
[39] ibid [126].
[40] *SAS v France*, above n 6, [125].
[41] See M Hunter-Henin, 'Why the French don't like the Burqa: Laïcité, National Identity and Religious Freedom' (2012) 61 *ICLQ* 613; E Daly, The Ambiguous Reach of Constitutional Secularism in Republican France: Revisiting the Idea of Laïcité and Political Liberalism as Alternatives' (2012) 32 *OJLS* 583.
[42] C Barnard, 'Headscarves, Tolerance and EU Law: *Achbita, Bougnaoui* and *WABE*' in J Adams-Prassl, A Bogg and ACL Davies (eds), *Landmark Cases in Labour Law* (Hart, 2022).
[43] See Hunter-Henin, above n 41.
[44] *Achbita*, above n 30, [38].

discrimination law, should be extended to religion or belief.[45] This would require employers to make positive adjustments to the workplace – hours of work or dress codes, for example – to accommodate their workers' religious beliefs. Since these adjustments would have to be 'reasonable', there would be limits, for example, where the proposed adjustment conflicted with the rights and freedoms of others. One perceived advantage of this approach is that it is more targeted: as noted above, individual believers often have quite specific concerns and preferences, not related to those of a wider group of believers, which could more easily be addressed through an accommodation approach.

We now turn to consider the four main areas of conflict between workers and their employers relating to religion or belief: working hours and the treatment of days or dates of religious significance, dress codes, conscientious objection to the performance of particular work tasks, and the expression of religious or other beliefs either at or outside the workplace.

3. Working Hours

A number of religions designate particular days of the week or dates during the year as sacred, but this may be a source of conflict where the employer requires the worker to be at work on the days or dates in question.

Historically, the European Commission on Human Rights was not sympathetic to workers' claims in this context. In a series of decisions concerning workers who did not want to work at specific times despite a contractual obligation to do so, the Commission characterised the problem as the workers' refusal to work their contracted hours, and held that they had the option of resigning if their contracted hours were incompatible with their religious beliefs.[46] However, the Court has moved away from resignation as a solution in other cases involving workers' rights, and in *Eweida* gave a strong indication that this approach would not be taken in future:

> Given the importance in a democratic society of freedom of religion, the Court considers that, where an individual complains of a restriction on freedom of religion in the workplace, rather than holding that the possibility of changing job would negate any interference with the right, the better approach would be to weigh that possibility in the overall balance when considering whether or not the restriction was proportionate.[47]

In practice, it seems likely that any future decision on Article 9 rights in relation to working hours would consider the circumstances in which the requirement to work had arisen and what efforts had been made by the employer to accommodate the employee's religious beliefs. In the domestic case of *Copsey*, the employer had moved to a system of seven-day working in order to meet increased demand for its products.[48] This caused a difficulty for an employee who refused, on religious grounds, to work on a Sunday, and was dismissed. The Court of Appeal disagreed on the applicability of Article 9, given the confusing Commission decisions discussed above, but noted that the employer had not acted unreasonably (in the unfair dismissal sense) because it had offered the employee the option of taking a generous redundancy package or applying for other

---

[45] eg J Bowers, 'Accommodating Difference: How is Religious Freedom Protected When It Clashes with Other Rights; Is Reasonable Accommodation the Key to Levelling the Field?' (2021) 10 *OJLR* 275; E Griffiths, 'The "Reasonable Accommodation" of Religion: Is this a Better Way of Advancing Equality in Cases of Religious Discrimination?' (2016) 16 *International Journal of Discrimination and the Law* 161.
[46] See eg *X v UK*, Commission Decision,12 March 1981; *Stedman v United Kingdom* (1997) 23 EHRR CD 168.
[47] *Eweida*, above n 3, [83].
[48] *Copsey v WWB Devon Clays Ltd* [2005] EWCA Civ 932, [2005] ICR 1789.

roles which did not involve Sunday working. Similarly, in *Mba*, the Court of Appeal upheld the tribunal's finding that an employer running a residential care home for children had no alternative but to require the claimant to work on Sundays, contrary to her religious beliefs.[49]

One argument which has not been fully tested in court, at least in the systems under consideration, is a discrimination argument based on the differential treatment of majority and minority groups within a particular society.[50] For example, despite increasing secularisation, Sunday remains a traditional day off for many working people in the UK. This means that it is much easier for Christians (historically, at least, a majority group) to reconcile work and religious observance than it is for members of minority groups. The courts often take into account contextual information in other kinds of indirect discrimination claim. For example, women's greater share of responsibility for child-care has been taken into account when assessing requirements to work full-time or to work particular shift patterns.[51] This would not mean that the employer could not justify the choice of a traditional working week, but it might force the employer to give more active consideration to the reasons underpinning the choice, rather than just relying on convention or habit.

We noted above that some commentators have argued that employers should be placed under a positive duty to accommodate their workers' religious beliefs.[52] Working hours are one of the areas in which this approach might make a significant difference. Under a duty to accommodate, the employer might be obliged to come up with different shift systems for different members of staff to accommodate their religious beliefs about appropriate days for work, always assuming that it was reasonable to do so.[53] For example, if the business was open seven days a week, it might be possible to give workers different days off according to their religious preferences. Under a proportionality analysis, by contrast, the focus is on the employer's justification for the shift system it has adopted, despite its discriminatory effect, so there is less scope for the active consideration of alternatives.

4. Dress Codes

Another area of potential conflict relates to employers' dress codes and their impact on workers who wish to wear a symbol or item of clothing reflecting their religion or belief. We examine whether these cases should be treated as examples of direct or indirect discrimination, before considering the application of the proportionality test.

Although dress codes are usually formulated in general terms, for example, by prescribing a uniform in detail or by barring religious or political symbols, it is possible for a rule purporting to be neutral to be targeted at a particular group on the facts.[54] Under the CJEU's approach in *CHEZ*, this can be treated as direct discrimination.[55] This argument was accepted in *WABE*, in which the Court acknowledged that a policy banning 'conspicuous, large-sized' religious symbols

---

[49] *Mba*, above n 34.
[50] An argument based on Article 9 in conjunction with Article 14 was dismissed with little discussion in *Ahmad v United Kingdom* (1982) 4 EHRR 126.
[51] eg *London Underground Ltd v Edwards (No 2)* [1999] ICR 494.
[52] Above n 45.
[53] Of course, another option would be to make a request for flexible working under s 80F of the Employment Rights Act 1996, though the employer arguably has greater scope to turn down such requests on business grounds.
[54] Barnard, above n 42, 334–36.
[55] Case C-83/14 *CHEZ* EU:C:2015:480, [2016] 1 CMLR 14.

could constitute direct discrimination where it was 'inextricably linked to one or more specific religions or beliefs'.[56] This was for the national court to determine on the facts.

In most cases, policies requiring all workers to dress neutrally or to refrain from wearing any visible symbols (not just conspicuous ones) will be treated as a form of indirect discrimination, so attention shifts to the employer's ability to justify its requirements as a proportionate means of achieving a legitimate aim.[57] Sometimes, the employer may be able to point to a specific justification relating to the nature of the work. In *Chaplin*, one of the cases heard with *Eweida* in the ECtHR, the employer successfully argued that it was proportionate to restrict the wearing of jewellery by a nurse because it might cause a health and safety hazard when handling patients, with the effect that the claimant could not wear a cross in accordance with her religious beliefs.[58] The employer had also offered a number of alternative solutions.

Another justification offered by employers in some cases has been that customers prefer not to see employees wearing visible religious or other symbols. In EU law, this argument was rejected by the Court in *Bougnaoui* (in the context of an argument about 'genuine occupational requirements').[59] This follows on from the Court's decision in *Firma Feryn*, in which a firm was found to have discriminated when it stated publicly that it was recruiting, but did not want to hire 'immigrants' because customers would be reluctant to allow them into their homes.[60] If an argument along these lines were to be accepted, discrimination law would do little to tackle prejudices in wider society. However, the more recent case of *WABE* suggests that customer preferences may not be wholly irrelevant.[61] There, the employer was allowed to rely on an argument that customers of its nursery preferred their children to be cared for by workers who did not wear any visible religious symbols as part of its argument on objective justification. As Barnard explains, this was regarded as a 'legitimate' customer preference, in contrast to that in *Bougnaoui*.[62] It remains to be seen how the boundary between legitimate and illegitimate customer preferences will be drawn in future cases. One factor of possible importance in *WABE* is that parents have a right recognised in both the Charter and the ECHR to determine whether or not their children receive a religious education and, if so, of what kind.[63]

But the most common argument offered by employers in support of their dress codes is that they want their workforce to present a 'neutral' image, without religious or other symbols, to the wider world. In *Achbita*, the Court of Justice was very sympathetic to the employer's position on this issue, stating that 'the desire to display, in relations with both public and private sector customers, a policy of political, philosophical or religious neutrality must be considered legitimate'.[64] The Court reinforced its position by referring to Article 16 of the Charter, the employer's freedom to run a business.[65] It placed few conditions on the neutrality policy, other than that it should be 'genuinely pursued in a consistent and systematic manner'[66] and applied only to workers who came into contact with customers.[67] In *WABE*, the Court refined

---

[56] Above n 21, [73].
[57] *Achbita*, above n 30; *LF*, above n 22.
[58] Above n 3.
[59] Case C-188/15 *Bougnaoui v Micropole SA* EU:C:2017:204, [2017] 3 CMLR 22.
[60] Case C-54/07 *Centrum voor Gelijkheid van Kansen en voor Racismebestrijding v Firma Feryn NV* EU:C:2008:397, [2008] ECR I-5187.
[61] Above n 21, [65].
[62] Above n 59.
[63] EU Charter of Fundamental Rights, Article 14; ECHR, Protocol No 1, Article 2.
[64] Above n 30, [37].
[65] ibid [38].
[66] ibid [40].
[67] ibid [38].

its position somewhat, so that the mere assertion by the employer of a desire to appear neutral is no longer sufficient in itself. The Court identified three further criteria:

> … first, that that policy meets a genuine need on the part of that employer, which it is for that employer to demonstrate, taking into consideration, inter alia, the legitimate wishes of those customers or users and the adverse consequences that that employer would suffer in the absence of that policy, given the nature of its activities and the context in which they are carried out; secondly, that that difference of treatment is appropriate for the purpose of ensuring that the employer's policy of neutrality is properly applied, which entails that that policy is pursued in a consistent and systematic manner; and, thirdly, that the prohibition in question is limited to what is strictly necessary having regard to the actual scale and severity of the adverse consequences that the employer is seeking to avoid by adopting that prohibition.[68]

Under this approach, it is necessary for the employer to demonstrate that its business will be harmed, for example, by internal conflict within the workplace or by (legitimate) adverse reactions from customers, unless it adopts the neutrality policy. It remains to be seen how this will be applied in subsequent cases.

The ECtHR's approach is similar – neutrality is generally accepted as a legitimate aim – but it is worth noting a significant contextual difference. While the EU case law has tended to concern private employers, much of the ECtHR's case law has developed in relation to the public sector. As noted above, some, but by no means all, signatory states have a strong principle of state secularism, which is used to justify banning the wearing of religious clothing and symbols by public sector employees, such as civil servants or teachers. Although the point is clearly open to debate, the Court accepts that secularism is motivated by a desire to reassure all citizens that they will be treated equally when they access public services, and that states enjoy a wide margin of appreciation in adopting and implementing such an approach.[69] Thus, in the leading case of *Ebrahimian*, the Court accepted that it was a proportionate means of achieving a legitimate aim to ban a Muslim nurse in a public hospital from wearing a headscarf.[70] The Court has considered the situation of private employers much less frequently. In *Eweida*, the Court found that the employer had acted disproportionately in refusing to permit a religious symbol to be worn – perhaps suggesting greater scrutiny of private firms – but the facts were unusual.[71] The employer's policy permitted some items of religious clothing, such as turbans and headscarves, so there was a discriminatory element in its refusal to permit a cross to be worn, and in any event, the employer had eventually changed its mind and allowed the applicant to wear her cross.

There are relatively few domestic cases on dress codes. In *Mandla*, the House of Lords held that a school had discriminated against a Sikh boy by refusing to admit him if he continued to wear a turban in breach of its uniform policy.[72] The policy could not be justified because its objective was discriminatory: to ban visible symbols of a person's ethnic origins. Although the context is different, there is a marked contrast here with the Court of Justice's treatment of neutrality policies in the workplace. In *Azmi*, a school's policy requiring the claimant language teacher to have her face uncovered when speaking to children in the classroom (but not at other times) was objectively justified because of the need to be able to communicate effectively with the children.[73] Both of these cases predate *Eweida*, and any case nowadays would, of course, fall to be decided in accordance with the principles laid down in that case, but they seem consistent

---

[68] Above n 21, [70].
[69] *SAS v France* (2015) 60 EHRR 11.
[70] *Ebrahimian v France*, App No 64846/11, 26 November 2015.
[71] Above n 3.
[72] *Mandla v Dowell Lee* [1983] 2 AC 548.
[73] *Azmi v Kirklees MBC* [2007] ICR 1154.

with the idea that a specific, practical justification needs to be found if a discriminatory dress code is to be justified.

Any argument in favour of a dress code – health and safety or effective communication, for example – can be challenged on the facts, and there is always a suspicion that a lack of understanding of others' traditions may motivate some apparently neutral concerns. For example, the argument that face coverings impede communication would probably carry much less weight in a society in which they were commonplace. But the most challenging issue around dress codes is clearly the idea of 'neutrality'. As Barnard points out, an employer could be 'neutral' as between different beliefs either by banning all manifestations of belief, or by allowing all manifestations of belief.[74] Either of these strategies could demonstrate to customers that the employer did not support one set of beliefs over another, and that customers of all beliefs or none were equally welcome to use its services. However, a significant challenge for both the CJEU and the ECtHR is the deep constitutional commitment to secularism in some states, which is perhaps harder for those from other cultural contexts to appreciate.

5. 'Conscientious Objection' to Providing a Particular Service

In some circumstances, a worker may object to the performance of a particular work task because of their religious beliefs. In general terms, the courts have not been sympathetic to these types of claim because they involve interference with the rights and freedoms of others, though there are a few specific statutory exceptions, for example, for medical professionals.

In the ECHR context, the appropriate framework for analysis is set out in the *Ladele* and *McFarlane* cases, heard with *Eweida*.[75] Ms Ladele was a registrar who refused to conduct civil partnership ceremonies for gay couples, and Mr McFarlane was a relationship counsellor who refused to work with gay couples, both on grounds of their religious beliefs. In both cases, the employers (one public sector and one private sector) had policies requiring that their services should be offered to all without discrimination. The Court found that although both applicants had suffered serious consequences because they had lost their jobs, the employers' policies were designed to uphold the rights of others and were not disproportionate.

In medical settings, disputes often arise around contraception and abortion. In *Pichon and Sajous v France*, the applicant pharmacists refused to sell contraceptives prescribed by a doctor because of their religious views.[76] They were convicted of an offence under consumer law. The ECtHR declared the case inadmissible, holding that the applicants could not 'give precedence to their religious beliefs and impose them on others as justification for their refusal to sell such products, since they can manifest those beliefs in many ways outside the professional sphere'.[77] However, in relation to abortion, states may choose to create a right of conscientious objection by statute. In the UK, the Abortion Act 1967 provides for this in s 4, subject to an exception for emergency situations in which the patient's life is in danger or there is a risk of 'grave permanent injury' to their physical or mental health.[78] Guidance issued by the General Medical Council

---

[74] Barnard, above n 42, 339–40.
[75] Above n 3.
[76] *Pichon and Sajous v France*, App No 49853/99, 2 October 2001.
[77] ibid 4.
[78] See also Human Fertilisation and Embryology Act 1990, s 38. The ECtHR recently declared inadmissible a case which would have provided it with an opportunity to clarify its position on conscientious objection to abortion: *Grimmark v Sweden* [2020] IRLR 554. See W Brzozowski, 'The Midwife's Tale: Conscientious Objection to Abortion after *Grimmark* and *Steen*' (2021) 10 *Oxford Journal of Law and Religion* 298.

(GMC) on a doctor's right to refuse to provide a particular treatment more generally emphasises the importance of ensuring that the patient can access the medical care they are seeking from another source, and not leaving them with nowhere else to turn.[79]

A worker's unwillingness to undertake a particular work task on religious grounds can often be dealt with by arranging for another worker to cover for them. This approach had been adopted in Ms Ladele's workplace, until her colleagues had begun to object. But this is an 'accommodation' approach and it is not required by the law. An employer is generally within its rights to insist that workers perform all work tasks regardless of religious objections.

6. Expressing Religious Views

The law also allows employers to order workers not to express religious or other views at work, again because of the risk that this may interfere with the rights and freedoms of others. A difficulty here, which we also explored in chapter 16, is in determining the boundaries of this principle, for example, where the worker expresses their beliefs publicly on social media, or where the worker's beliefs might result – but have not yet resulted – in problems in the workplace.

In some cases, it is tolerably clear that the claimant's expression of religious views at work was inappropriate because it interfered with their relationships with work colleagues or with their job performance.[80] For example, in the domestic case of *Wasteney*, the claimant was an evangelical Christian who had tried to encourage a more junior Muslim colleague to attend church events.[81] The colleague found the claimant's approaches unwanted and intimidating. The EAT held that the employer's imposition of a disciplinary sanction was not discriminatory on religious grounds because it was connected not with the claimant's beliefs but with her inappropriate behaviour towards a colleague. In the ECtHR case of *Pitkevich v Russia*, the applicant was a judge who had expressed her religious views in court, prayed during hearings and offered favourable outcomes to litigants who joined her church.[82] Her claim that her Article 10 rights had been violated was dismissed as manifestly ill-founded because she had acted improperly as a judge and breached her duty of impartiality. The Court is generally supportive of the idea that the state should be able to restrict the religious and other expressive rights of civil servants and other public officials in order to present an image of neutrality, an idea discussed above in the context of dress codes.

More complex questions arise where the employee expresses their religious beliefs outside work, particularly when the beliefs are controversial in some way, but does not seek to express or act on them in the workplace. The employer may nevertheless be concerned about the reaction of its customers or the impact on its reputation. In *Smith v Trafford Housing*, the claimant expressed his opposition on social media to a proposal he had read in a news report that churches would be obliged by law to solemnise the marriages of gay couples.[83] His employer disciplined him for a breach of its code of conduct, on the basis that his posts might bring it into disrepute and make colleagues and customers feel uncomfortable. The High Court upheld his claim for breach

---

[79] GMC, *Good Medical Practice* (2024), para 21; *Personal Beliefs and Medical Practice* (2013).
[80] For an interesting argument that there may be scope for proselytising at work where it does not interfere with work tasks and is not unwanted by the recipient, see A Hambler, 'Is there "No Place in the Work Context" for Religious Proselytism?' (2022) 51 *ILJ* 346.
[81] *Wasteney v East London NHS Foundation Trust* [2016] ICR 643.
[82] *Pitkevich v Russia*, App No 47936/99, 8 February 2001.
[83] *Smith v Trafford Housing* [2012] EWHC 3221 (Ch), [2013] IRLR 86.

of contract, holding that the posts were made in a private capacity and could not reasonably be regarded as liable to bring the employer into disrepute. Nor could the employer's code of conduct be construed as applying to the claimant's expression in non-work contexts. While this appears to carve out a space for the free expression of religious views, it is worth noting that the decision was closely tied to the correct construction of the employer's policy. The courts should not be too quick to allow an employer to restrict the expression of religious views outside work by means of a code of conduct or other contractual mechanism; otherwise it would be hard to see how an employee's rights were being protected at all.[84]

Most of the cases in this area have been framed as an argument that the employer's attempt to restrict the employee's speech outside work is either directly discriminatory (because it targets particular views) or indirectly discriminatory (because it is facially neutral but has a disparate impact on the employee because of the particular views they hold). As noted above, a finding that the employer's actions were directly discriminatory would normally preclude any possibility of justification in domestic law. However, the courts have sought to render the Equality Act 2010 compatible with Article 9 by drawing a distinction between acceptable and 'objectionable' manifestations of religion or belief. In *Page v NHS Trust Development Authority*, the claimant was a magistrate and a non-executive director of an NHS Trust who held the view, based on his religious beliefs, that children should be raised by a male and female parent.[85] He was removed as a magistrate after refusing to authorise adoptions by same-sex couples, and then gave a number of media interviews in which he expressed his views. He was suspended and ultimately removed from his role with the NHS Trust, which believed that his actions would discourage gay people from using its services. The Court of Appeal held that the employer's actions did not constitute direct discrimination on grounds of religion or belief because they were based not on the claimant's beliefs as such, but on his objectionable manifestation: his repeated expression of them in the national media without any reference to the employer.[86] From an indirect discrimination perspective, the employer could readily justify its actions because of the serious concern that the claimant's interviews would deter service users, thereby preventing the employer from effectively carrying out its core function. Similarly, in *Higgs*, the employer school dismissed a Christian administrator for her social media posts criticising the sex education curriculum.[87] The EAT remitted the case to the tribunal to determine whether the employer had acted on the basis of the claimant's beliefs (which would be unlawful) or on the basis of her 'objectionable' manifestation of those beliefs, which would be justified under Article 9 and would therefore fall outside the protection of domestic equality law.

As Bell rightly points out, it is increasingly difficult for people to accept the idea that a person with a controversial religious or other belief might be capable of holding that belief, but not acting on it in the workplace, for example, by discriminating against people who do not conform to the moral standards laid down by their religion.[88] To some extent at least, this may be fuelled by the argument often made by believers in other contexts, and noted above, that it is not possible to have a 'public/private divide' in matters of faith. For this reason, it seems likely that employers will continue to be faced with calls to take action against employees who express controversial religious beliefs, even in private. There is some suggestion from the ECtHR in the *Redfearn* case

---

[84] For a similar problem in relation to Article 8, see *Barbulescu v Romania* [2017] IRLR 1032.
[85] *Page v NHS Trust Development Authority* [2021] EWCA Civ 255, [2021] ICR 941.
[86] See also *Higgs v Farmor's School* [2023] EAT 89, [2023] ICR 1072, remitting to the tribunal on the proportionality question.
[87] ibid.
[88] Bell, above n 2, 77.

(which arose in the context of Article 11) that an employer might be justified in taking action against an employee with views which were discriminatory, even though there were no complaints about his work.[89] However, if this approach were to be developed and applied to religious beliefs, the scope for working people to express controversial beliefs would be severely curtailed. The reminder in *Higgs* that the freedom to manifest beliefs includes unpopular or offensive beliefs is important, but the boundary between legitimate and objectionable manifestations of such beliefs may prove particularly challenging for courts (and employers) to draw.[90]

7. Religious Organisations as Employers

So far, we have focused on the conflicts which may arise when working people wish to manifest their beliefs in the workplace. For religious organisations themselves, a different set of problems arises. They may want to ensure that their own employees share their religious beliefs, have particular characteristics and, often, conform to a set of religiously-motivated moral standards. The law allows some scope for this, usually through the mechanism of a 'genuine occupational requirement' (GOR). Religious organisations may make it a GOR that employees in leadership roles, such as priests in a church, share their religious beliefs and have particular characteristics: being an unmarried man, for example. But religious organisations often employ people in other roles, such as cleaners or maintenance workers, or run other institutions, such as hospitals or schools, with a wide range of different kinds of employees. On the whole, the law does not allow religious organisations to impose special requirements on these 'ordinary' employees, particularly when such requirements would discriminate on another ground or infringe those employees' other rights, for example, under Article 8 or Article 10.

In EU law, religious organisations may avail themselves of the general exception for 'genuine occupational requirements' under Article 4(1) ETD to discriminate on grounds such as gender when making appointments to positions of religious significance in the organisation. Moreover, the ETD makes special provision for religious organisations in Article 4(2), allowing Member States to legislate to the effect that:

> … in the case of occupational activities within churches and other public or private organisations the ethos of which is based on religion or belief, a difference of treatment based on a person's religion or belief shall not constitute discrimination where, by reason of the nature of these activities or of the context in which they are carried out, a person's religion or belief constitute a genuine, legitimate and justified occupational requirement, having regard to the organisation's ethos.

In *Egenberger*, the Court made it clear that it was not normally appropriate for courts to make any judgment about the legitimacy of the organisation's ethos in itself, but it was appropriate to review the organisation's reliance on the 'genuine occupational requirement' (GOR) provision in the light of its ethos.[91] In particular, it was necessary to determine whether the GOR was genuine and proportionate[92] in the light of the activities to be carried out by the worker to whom it was being applied:

> Such a link may follow either from the nature of the activity, for example where it involves taking part in the determination of the ethos of the church or organisation in question or contributing to its mission of

---

[89] *Redfearn v United Kingdom* (2013) 57 EHRR 2, [44]–[45].
[90] Above n 86, [94].
[91] Case C-414/16 *Egenberger v Evangelisches Werk fur Diakonie und Entwicklung eV* EU:C:2018:257, [2019] 1 CMLR 9.
[92] ibid [68]: proportionality is not expressly mentioned in Article 4(2) but the Court finds that it is applicable.

proclamation, or else from the circumstances in which the activity is to be carried out, such as the need to ensure a credible presentation of the church or organisation to the outside world.[93]

This is clearly intended to ensure that religious organisations do not apply the GOR too broadly to workers who are not central to its mission or employed in public-facing roles.

The UK approach is set out in Sch 9 to the Equality Act 2010. This provides for the concept of a GOR in general terms, but then makes two specific provisions for religious GORs. The first, in para 3, allows a person 'with an ethos based on religion or belief' to apply a GOR requiring a worker to be of a particular religion or belief. This is similar to the provision in EU law, discussed above. The second, in para 2, allows for the application of discriminatory GORs (on grounds of marital status or sexual orientation, for example) where 'the employment is for the purposes of an organised religion'[94] and either 'the requirement is applied so as to comply with the doctrines of the religion'[95] or 'because of the nature or context of the employment, the requirement is applied so as to avoid conflicting with the strongly held religious convictions of a significant number of the religion's followers'.[96] This is a more precise version of the general GOR in Article 4(1) ETD.

However, it is worth noting that, if the employer does not assert that a GOR is in operation, and simply takes action against a worker based on its religiously-motivated disapproval of their private life, the employer may well be found to have discriminated on another ground. For example, in *Gan Menachem Hendon Ltd v De Groen*, the employer was found to have discriminated directly on grounds of sex when it took action against a worker who was living with her boyfriend, in contravention of the employer's religious principles.[97] Similarly, in *O'Neill v Governors of St Thomas More School*, the claimant teacher in a Catholic school was dismissed when it became apparent that she had had a relationship with a priest and was pregnant.[98] This amounted to direct discrimination because of her pregnancy, and it was not relevant that the school governors' decision to dismiss her was because of their religiously-motivated disapproval.

Under the ECHR, religious organisations have rights under Article 9, but corporations or legal persons of any kind do not.[99] The Court regards religious organisations as having a substantial degree of autonomy to determine their own beliefs and practices. It expects the state to remain neutral in religious disputes and will not generally intervene in internal matters itself.[100] This means that, for example, a dispute about whether a person is qualified for a leadership role in a faith organisation, such as the priesthood in a church, will be declared inadmissible, even though this could also be seen as an employment issue.[101] If a person gets into a dispute with the religious group to which they belong, their Article 9 rights can be safeguarded by leaving the group.[102]

However, the Court has developed a relatively large body of case law dealing with other types of employee of faith-based organisations. The leading cases are *Fernández Martínez v Spain*[103] and *Schüth v Germany*.[104] These cases establish two important principles. First, although religious organisations can demand a higher degree of 'loyalty' from their employees than other types of

---

[93] ibid [63].
[94] Equality Act 2010, Sch 9, para 2(1).
[95] ibid para 2(5). For application, see eg *Pemberton v Inwood* [2018] EWCA Civ 564, [2018] ICR 1291.
[96] ibid para 2(6).
[97] *Gan Menachem Hendon Ltd v De Groen* [2019] ICR 1023.
[98] *O'Neill v Governors of St Thomas More Roman Catholic Voluntary Aided Upper School* [1997] ICR 33.
[99] *X v Switzerland*, App No 7865/17, 1 January 1978.
[100] eg *Miroļubovs v Latvia*, App No 798/05, 15 September 2009.
[101] eg *Karlsson v Sweden*, App No 12356/86, 8 September 1988.
[102] ibid.
[103] *Fernández Martínez v Spain* (2015) 60 EHRR 3.
[104] *Schüth v Germany* (2011) 52 EHRR 32.

employer, this depends on the nature of the job in question.[105] In *Fernández Martínez*, for example, it was accepted that this heightened duty of loyalty was owed by a person with responsibility for the religious education of children,[106] but in *Schüth*, the Court doubted whether the same was true of a music director within a church and criticised the national courts for accepting the church's assertion on the point without scrutiny.[107] Second, it is crucial that the national court (within a margin of appreciation) balances the rights of the religious organisation against the rights of the person affected. These might include (among other examples) Article 10 rights to freedom of expression, where the individual has publicly expressed a dissenting view, or Article 8 rights to respect for private and family life, where the individual's personal choices conflict with the organisation's teaching. Again, in *Fernández Martínez*, no violation was found where the applicant knew that his public advocacy for a change to the Catholic Church's rules on celibacy for priests would put him at odds with his superiors.[108] But in *Schüth*, where the music director had been dismissed for divorcing his wife and moving in with a new partner, the Court found a violation of Article 8.[109] Although he had signed a contract undertaking to respect church teachings, the Court found that this was excessive given the non-central nature of his role. It also took into account the fact that he had merely failed to comply with church teachings in his personal life, rather than taking any public stance against them, and that it was difficult for him to get another job given his highly specialist skills as a church musician.

8. Conclusion

As we have seen, religion occupies a complex position in people's lives, in which it is (at one and the same time) a deeply private and personal matter for the individual, but with the potential for manifestations of belief in non-private times and spaces, including in the workplace. These manifestations can cut across a variety of core employer prerogatives, such as the power to decide when a person works, what tasks they should perform, what they should wear to work and how they should conduct themselves in interactions with colleagues and customers. Courts interpreting and applying the right to freedom of religion are faced with a complex task of ensuring that employers do not discriminate against particular religious groups or apply blunt policies with no sensitivity to their workers' religious needs, whilst at the same time ensuring that workers themselves do not unreasonably seek to impose their views on others or exempt themselves from key parts of their jobs. The proportionality test plays a crucial role in this area, and must be applied with care and sensitivity on both sides.

---

[105] *Fernández Martínez*, above n 103, [131].
[106] ibid [135].
[107] *Schüth*, above n 104, [69], [71].
[108] *Fernández Martínez*, above n 103, [136]–[142].
[109] *Schüth*, above n 104.

18

The Right to Protection against Unjustified Dismissal

1.	Why is Protection against Unjustified Dismissal Important?	6.	Justified Grounds of Dismissal for Reasons of Business Reorganisation
2.	The Missing Right	7.	Fair Procedure Prior to Termination of Employment
3.	The Right to Work		
4.	The Right to Respect for Private Life	8.	Exclusions
5.	Justified Grounds of Dismissal for Fault Under the ILO Convention	9.	Conclusion

1. Why is Protection against Unjustified Dismissal Important?

'An employee has the right not to be unfairly dismissed by his employer.' Enacted in the United Kingdom (UK) by s 94(1) of the Employment Rights Act 1996 (ERA 1996), this right provides a vital protection for employees against unfair disciplinary action. The law requires an employer to state a reason for dismissal that a court or tribunal regards as a fair ground for dismissal in all the circumstances. If it is decided that the dismissal was unfair, the normal remedy is compensation for the loss caused by the dismissal, such as loss of wages during a period of unemployment. Why is this right an important part of the protections for employees provided by employment law?

One benefit to employees is that the right may assist them and their dependants in the event of a sudden loss of income resulting from a dismissal. An award of compensation for unfair dismissal should provide compensation for the loss of income until such time as it would be reasonable for the employee to find another job. But that compensatory purpose is also served by other legal mechanisms. In most countries, employers are normally required to give reasonable notice of dismissal or pay wages in lieu. The right to reasonable notice either gives an employee warning of the need to find another job before the current position is terminated or provides a continuation of income even though the employee is dismissed summarily. In addition, many countries require a severance payment to be made by the employer that rises according to the number of years of service for the employer. Often such a payment is required regardless of the circumstances of the termination of the employment, but in the UK this source of compensation can only be obtained by successfully claiming either unfair dismissal (the basic award)[1] or that the dismissal was for the reason of redundancy (a redundancy payment).[2] Finally, the compensatory

---

[1] ERA 1996, s 119.
[2] ERA 1996, s 135.

role of the law can also be achieved through the social security system, where welfare payments for unemployed workers in many countries are regarded as a kind of social insurance against economic hardship. In the UK, the emphasis has switched from insurance against unemployment to the provision of an incentive to look for work through the 'jobseeker's allowance' and the 'welfare to work' activation policies.

A more distinctive benefit provided by the right to protection against unfair dismissal concerns the protection of the dignity of the employee. Contracts of employment grant employers the power and authority to direct the work performed by their employees according to the needs of production. This power is usually necessary for the efficient operation of the organisation. Directions and instructions by managers need to be backed up by the possibility for employers to impose disciplinary sanctions in the event of disobedience. Dismissal is the most severe sanction available. Evidently this command structure creates a risk that the exercise of this disciplinary power may be misused or abused. An employer might decide to dismiss an employee for a trivial matter, or in response to a false allegation, or for some capricious ground. Although employers may not often make such decisions because of the costs of recruiting and training new staff, it clearly happens. Sometimes these abuses of disciplinary power may be challenged using the law of discrimination and the right to be treated as an equal in UK law. Under close examination, weak reasons for a dismissal may reveal a discriminatory prejudice on the basis of sex, race, or some other protected characteristic. But the right to protection against unfair dismissal provides a more general protection against inadequate or misconceived reasons for a dismissal by an employer.

In general, the law of contract does not control the termination of contractual relationships by examining the reasons for the termination. At most, the law requires compensation for any breach of contract, but no more. Accordingly, the common law of the contract of employment merely requires the employer to pay compensation for wages owed and for a period of reasonable notice in accordance with the express and implied terms of the contract. Similarly, if I decide to cancel my supermarket delivery order, provided the cancellation is done before the agreed deadline, the supermarket has no legal right to challenge my decision. It cannot require me to justify why I have switched supermarkets or decided to go to the farmers' market instead. But the protection of the right against unjustified dismissal does require an employer to justify the dismissal of an employee with a reason that is regarded as valid and adequate. Why is the contract of employment different from almost every other kind of contract by requiring a justification for termination of the contract? There are at least three important reasons for according employees this additional protection.

First, a right not to be unfairly dismissed provides an opportunity to challenge misuses of managerial power. It is a safeguard against arbitrary or misconceived dismissals. The existence of the law provides employers with an incentive to make accurate and well-founded disciplinary decisions. In the long run, only justifiable dismissals will be conducive to the efficient operation of the business. If an employer develops a reputation for arbitrary disciplinary decisions, employees will quit to find more secure employment, with the consequence that it will be hard for the employer to recruit and retain experienced and productive staff.

Second, a right not to be unfairly dismissed protects the dignity and self-respect of employees. In employment relationships, if employees are continually subject to arbitrary and unfair demands by managers, which are backed up by the threat of dismissal, the system seems calculated to make employees feel that they are of inferior worth to others. The necessary subordination to the demands of efficient production becomes a system of oppression and domination. Furthermore, if the employee is dismissed unreasonably, the employee is likely to experience an attack on their dignity or self-worth. If the employer tells an employee that they are worthless or falsely accuses another of misconduct such as stealing from their employer, those attacks on an employee's self-respect and reputation signify disrespect for the dignity of that employee. Similar unjust accusations by government, the police, and other powerful organisations would be subject in law to detailed procedural safeguards and a heavy burden of proof because it is understood that a liberal society must protect the dignity of its members. Similarly, to protect the dignity of employees against the misuses of disciplinary authority, both private and public employers have to be made subject to legal controls that provide safeguards for the dignity and self-respect of their employees.

Third, a right not to be unfairly dismissed facilitates the autonomy of employees by enhancing job security. In this context, autonomy means the freedom and capacity for individuals to plan their lives independently in ways that they believe will be fulfilling and give their lives a purpose. For most people, a job is an important part of their lives in these respects. Not only does it provide the necessary income to support themselves and their dependants, but it also provides the opportunity to pursue a meaningful life and to forge relationships with others. Although many jobs may not be especially fulfilling, most people find some purpose in their lives through work. Certainly, most people experience more fulfilling lives if they have work rather being unemployed and stuck at home. Many employees are lucky enough to have a career in a job that they view as both a vocation and a way of bringing meaning to their lives. Protection against unfair dismissal enables employees to plan their lives around their jobs and to form goals for what they regard as a fulfilling career. The degree of job security provided by protections against unjustified dismissal is conducive to employees developing aspirations, careers, and a sense of fulfilment in their lives.

2. The Missing Right

These justifications for a right to protection against unjustified dismissal in terms of dignity and autonomy resonate with the normal justifications put forward for protection of human rights. What is perhaps surprising, therefore, is the noticeable absence of an express right to protection against unjustifiable dismissal in many international declarations and conventions on human rights. There is no express mention of such a right, for instance, in the Universal Declaration of Human Rights or in the International Covenant on Economic, Social and Cultural Rights. It was also missing from the European Social Charter 1961, but was included in the Revised European Social Charter 1996, Article 24.[3] The right is also acknowledged in Article 30 of the Charter of Fundamental Rights of the European Union, but is not given independent force and direct applicability in Member States: 'Every worker has the right to protection against unjustified dismissal, in accordance with Union law and national laws and practices.'[4]

What explains this paucity of express declarations of a right to protection against unjustifiable dismissal? The main explanation is likely to be found in firm opposition from employers and

---

[3] See M Schmitt, 'Article 24: The Right to Protection in Cases of Termination of Employment' in N Bruun, K Lörcher, I Schömann and S Clauwaert (eds), *The European Social Charter and the Employment Relation* (Oxford, Hart Publishing/Bloomsbury, 2017). The text of Article 24 is the same as Article 4 of the ILO Convention 158 on Termination of Employment (1982), discussed below.

[4] Case T-107/11 P *ETF v Schuerings* EU:T:2013:624, [100]: 'Article 30 of the [C]harter ... does not lay down any specific obligations.' D Leczykiewicz, 'Effectiveness of EU Law Before National Courts: Direct Effect, Effective Judicial Protection, and State Liability' in A Arnull and D Chalmers (eds), *Oxford Handbook of European Union Law* (Oxford, Oxford University Press, 2015) 212. There was no mention of the right in the earlier non-binding Community Charter of the Fundamental Social Rights of Workers, 10 December 1989.

sympathetic governments.[5] They argue that such a right will impose substantial costs on employers in carrying out dismissals and defending their decisions before courts and tribunals. They doubt that there will be any off-setting benefits to employers from improved disciplinary decisions because they are sceptical that employers make rash and erroneous dismissals. More deeply, there is a resistance to any kind of judicial supervision over how a business is managed. While some labour regulation such as minimum wage laws and maximum hours laws can be justified as protecting employers against unscrupulous competitors, a law against unfair dismissal is directed against managerial decisions of a particular employer. Many employers view management as a private matter, which, in the absence of criminal conduct, is none of the law's business. Managers are answerable to shareholders and other bodies to whom they report, and not to the public in general or the state. Laws against unfair dismissal represent a deep penetration into managerial control over the operation of the business to assess its fairness according to broad moral standards rather than what appears to managers to be efficient or necessary.

As well as resistance from employers, a second reason for the absence of explicit declarations of a fundamental right to protection against unjustified dismissal may be the presence of the influential International Labour Organization (ILO) Convention No 158 Concerning Termination of Employment at the Initiative of the Employer (1982).[6] This Convention sets out in detail what should be included in a national law that protects against unfair dismissal. Article 4 includes the key provision that:

> The employment of a worker shall not be terminated unless there is a valid reason for such termination connected with the capacity or conduct of the worker or based on the operational requirements of the undertaking, establishment or service.

The presence of this labour standard may explain to some extent the absence of pressure for protection of a right through conventions on human rights. Very few countries have in fact ratified this ILO Convention. A Committee of the ILO reported in 2016 that the Convention applied in 20 per cent of countries, most of them very small, so that it was only applicable to 9 per cent of the world's working population.[7] The Committee noted, however, that there was a high level of compliance in practice with the requirements of the Convention even in the absence of ratification.[8] The UK is one of those many countries that has not ratified the Convention, but in practice domestic law complies with most of its requirements. Since the ILO Convention has served as a model for national laws giving protection against unjust dismissal, in the discussion below its provisions provide the main subject matter for an examination of what the right requires. Because the Revised European Social Charter replicates Article 4 of the ILO Convention, we can also draw on interpretations of the Charter by the European Committee of Social Rights to clarify the requirements of the standards.

There may be a third reason why there has been an absence of express references to the right to protection against unjustified dismissal in international conventions on human rights. From time to time, it has been suggested that protection against arbitrary and unfair dismissal is an

---

[5] eg the opposition of employers' representatives to any strengthening of the ILO regime: International Labour Organization, International Labour Standards Department, *Final report Tripartite Meeting of Experts to Examine the Termination of Employment Convention, 1982 (No 158), and the Termination of Employment Recommendation, 1982 (No 166)* (Geneva, 18–21 April 2011) TMEE/C.158-R.166/2011/2.

[6] A detailed discussion of all the provisions of the Convention and the associated recommendation is found in: International Labour Conference, 82nd Session 1995, III (Part 4B) Report of the Committee of Experts, General Survey on the Termination of Employment Convention (No 158) and Recommendation (No 166), 1982.

[7] ILO, Tripartite Meeting of Experts, above n 5.

[8] The ILO publishes a digest that provides a summary of the law of unfair dismissal in most countries: https://eplex.ilo.org/?p_lang=en.

implied aspect of the right to work, a right that is present in most international conventions since the Universal Declaration of Human Rights. In addition, a limited right to protection against unjustified dismissal has been evolving under the European Convention on Human Rights (ECHR) through interpretations of the right to respect for private life. In this chapter, we will examine these implicit dimensions of the right to work and the right to respect for private life before engaging directly with the standards established in the ILO Convention.

3. The Right to Work

The UN Human Rights Council has adopted the view that the right to work, which is included in the Universal Declaration of Human Rights, requires this protection. The Council:

> Emphasizes that the right to work entails, inter alia, the right not to be deprived of work arbitrarily and unfairly, and that States, in accordance with the relevant obligations in relation to the right to work, are required to put in place measures ensuring the protection of workers against unlawful dismissal.[9]

This connection between the right to work and protection against unfair termination of employment has also been asserted by the UN Committee on Economic, Social and Cultural Rights (CESCR),[10] and the ILO Committee of Experts on the Application of Conventions and Recommendations (CEACR).[11] The European Committee of Social Rights (ECSR) has also directly linked the right to work and job security, especially in connection with discrimination in employment.[12] In an influential lecture, Sir Bob Hepple argued that the right to work included 'a right to remain continuously employed, including the right to be reinstated in the event of unjustified termination'.[13]

This claim that the right to protection against unjustifiable dismissal is implicit in the right to work is, however, open to doubt. In the absence of high levels of unemployment, a dismissed employee can usually obtain another job. Normally, therefore, a dismissal does not interfere with the right to work. Dismissal does interfere with job security, but it is questionable whether the right to work includes a requirement that an employee should enjoy long-term employment.[14]

In some cases, however, a dismissal does interfere with the right to work.[15] If the effect of the dismissal is to prevent an individual from pursuing their chosen career, this is an interference with the right to freely choose a profession or career. This effect of deprivation of a career may occur, for instance, if the employee is dismissed for serious misconduct or incompetence in performing the job. Examples might include a surgeon dismissed wrongly for professional misconduct,[16] a banker dismissed wrongly for money laundering,[17] and a youth worker wrongly dismissed for reasons concerned with safeguarding children.[18] To protect the right to work in such cases, it

---

[9] United Nations, Human Rights Council, Thirty-first session, 22 March 2016, *Realization of the right to work*, A/HRC/31/L.32, para 8.
[10] CESCR, The Right to Work – General Comment No 18, adopted on 24 November 2005, E/C 12/GC/18 (6.02.2006) §§11 and 35.
[11] ILC, 59th Session, 1974, Record of Proceedings, 527.
[12] ECSR Conclusions XVI-1 (2002), Austria; Conclusions 2008, Azerbaijan.
[13] B Hepple, 'A Right to Work' (1981) 10 *Industrial Law Journal* 65, 73.
[14] On the meaning of the right to work, see chapter 8.
[15] H Collins, 'Progress towards the Right to Work in the United Kingdom' in V Mantouvalou (ed), *The Right to Work: Legal and Philosophical Perspectives* (Oxford, Hart Publishing, 2015) 227, 242–246.
[16] *Edwards v Chesterfield Royal Hospital NHS Foundation Trust* [2011] UKSC 58, [2012] ICR 201.
[17] *Mahmoud v Bank of Credit and Commerce International SA* [1998] AC 20, HL.
[18] *Botham v Ministry of Defence* [2011] UKSC 58, [2012] ICR 201.

is necessary to ensure that the employer is able to justify the allegations of serious misconduct or incompetence. Furthermore, if the employer is unable to justify those allegations, to protect the right to work it will be necessary for the employer to rectify the situation either by reinstating the employee, or by including in letters of recommendation statements to the effect that the employee is satisfactory and allegations to the contrary were mistaken. When an employer objected to having to include statements that vindicated the reputation of a dismissed employee on the ground that such an order from a labour arbitrator violated the employer's constitutional right to freedom of expression, the Canadian Supreme Court held that the right to work, as recognised in international human rights documents, justified such an interference with the right to freedom of expression.[19] Finally, unjustifiable dismissals that interfere with the right to work should be sanctioned with compensation that adequately addresses the loss not merely of a job, but of a long-term career. Unfortunately, the courts in the UK have steadfastly resisted awards of substantial damages to compensate such losses.[20]

Another context when dismissal interferes with the right to work concerns cases of discrimination. If the evidence of discrimination demonstrates that an employee with a protected characteristic was dismissed for that reason, protection against dismissal also protects that person's right to work. For example, if a woman is dismissed because she is not regarded as being fit for a post such as a security guard because she is a woman, that instance of dismissal on grounds of sex discrimination is also an interference with that woman's right to work because she is unable to pursue her chosen career or occupation.[21]

4. The Right to Respect for Private Life[22]

Under the ECHR, the ECtHR has developed protection for dismissed employees. For the most part, these cases concern the interference with one of the Convention rights such as freedom of expression or freedom of association, which are discussed in other chapters. In those cases, the employer's reason for dismissal amounts to an unjustifiable interfere with a Convention right. There is another line of cases, however, where the Court accepted that the adverse consequences of dismissal on a person's life were sufficiently grave to amount to an interference with private life contrary to Article 8(1) of the ECHR. Unless the employer can justify the dismissal on grounds falling within Article 8(2), the dismissal will be declared to be a violation of a Convention right and the state will be under a positive obligation to enact laws to prevent such dismissals from occurring.

The ECtHR has held that dismissals from a job may have severely deleterious consequences for a worker's private life, not only in material terms of causing poverty and economic insecurity, but also in psychological terms of ruining a person's hopes of a career, expectations of fulfilment through work, undermining personal relationships at home and at work, and obstructing life plans in general. What is important to notice is that these destabilising adverse consequences to private life may arise whatever the employer's reason for making a dismissal. There may be devastating consequences for an employee's personal life whether the dismissal is justified by the

---

[19] *Slaight Communication Incorporated v Ron Davidson*, 4 May 1989, [1989] 1 SCR 1038, Supreme Court of Canada.
[20] *Edwards v Chesterfield*, above n 16.
[21] *Emel Boyraz v Turkey* [2014] ECHR 1344, [2015] IRLR 164.
[22] This section draws substantially on H Collins, 'An Emerging Human Right to Protection against Unjustified Dismissal' (2020) 50 *Industrial Law Journal* 36.

employer on grounds of misconduct, incompetence, redundancy, financial exigency, or any kinds of capricious or arbitrary grounds, including giving no reason at all. If serious adverse consequences to a worker's personal life are caused by a dismissal, whatever the reason for the dismissal, Article 8 is likely to be engaged. The potential scope of the regulation of dismissals by the ECHR is therefore greatly expanded from the 'reasons-based' approach, which examines whether the reason of the dismissal violates the ECHR, to a broader 'consequences-based' approach, which examines the consequences of a dismissal on a person's life, and may include dismissals for any kind of reason.

The first sign of this broader use of Article 8 by the ECtHR arose in *Sidabras and Dziautas v Lithuania*.[23] The applicants had been dismissed from their public sector jobs in accordance with a new law that prohibited the employment of 'former KGB officers' not only in the public sector but also in law firms, banks, communications organisations, and educational institutions. The ECtHR decided the case by combining Article 8 with Article 14, the provision that requires all the Convention rights to be protected and applied without discrimination. The Court held that the prevention of the applicants from obtaining a wide and indeterminate range of private sector jobs fell 'within the ambit' of Article 8, and though the legislation pursued the legitimate aim of national security, it was a disproportionate discriminatory measure against former officers in the security services, contrary to Article 14 read in conjunction with Article 8. As the Court observed, the ban on seeking employment affected to an extremely significant degree the opportunities for the applicants to pursue various professional activities, so they were prevented from 'leading a normal personal life'.[24]

That decision was followed by several cases of judges dismissed from office such as *Oleksandr Volkov v Ukraine*, which supported the broad proposition that 'dismissal from office has been found to interfere with the right to respect for private life'.[25] The ECtHR brought the case under Article 8 by pointing to a broad range of adverse consequences of the dismissal for the ordinary private life of the applicant:

> The dismissal of the applicant from the post of judge affected a wide range of his relationships with other persons, including relationships of a professional nature. Likewise, it had an impact on his 'inner circle' as the loss of his job must have had tangible consequences for the material well-being of the applicant and his family. Moreover, the reason for the applicant's dismissal, namely breach of the judicial oath, suggests that his professional reputation was affected.[26]

Dismissals of people in any line of work might have similar adverse consequences for a person's private life. This ground for the application of Article 8 therefore opened up the possibility of a broad protection against unjustified dismissal on the basis of a consequences-based approach.

In many cases, however, the reasons-based approach to Article 8 could be blended with a consequences-based consideration of the impact of the dismissal on private life. In *Fernández Martinez v Spain*,[27] the applicant, a Catholic priest, had married and had five children. He became a teacher of religious education in schools. Spanish law provided that the state should only employ teachers of religious education who had been approved by the Church authorities. Following an interview given by the applicant to the press in which he explained why priests

---

[23] *Sidabras and Dziautas v Lithuania* [2004] ECHR 395. See V Mantouvalou, 'Work and Private Life: Sidabras and Dziautas v Lithuania' (2005) 30 *European Law Review* 573.
[24] *Sidabras*, ibid [49].
[25] *Oleksandr Volkov v Ukraine* [2011] ECHR 1871 [165], relying on, though extending, the earlier unreported decision in *Özpınar v Turkey*, App No 20999/04, 19 October 2010, [43]–[48].
[26] *Oleksandr Volkov v Ukraine* [2011] ECHR 1871, [166].
[27] *Fernández Martinez v Spain* [2014] ECHR 615 (Grand Chamber).

should marry, the pope withdrew his status as a priest. Consequently, the applicant was dismissed from his post because he was not approved by the Church. The applicant's claim for unfair dismissal under Spanish law was unsuccessful owing to his lack of the requisite approval by the Church. The majority of the ECtHR held that Article 8 was applicable because the dismissal and exclusion from the applicant's professional life as a teacher of religious education at age 60 were serious consequences that occurred on account of events mainly relating to personal choices he had made in his private and family life.[28] This reasoning blends a consequences-based approach that emphasises the applicant's permanent exclusion from a chosen profession with a reasons-based approach that links the motive for the dismissal to his private family life. The majority concluded, however, that in upholding the fairness of the dismissal, the Spanish courts had acted within the margin of appreciation when assessing the proportionality of the dismissal, taking into account the need to respect the Catholic church.[29]

The possible application of Article 8 to dismissals solely on the basis of adverse consequences for a person's ordinary private life was confirmed in the Grand Chamber's decision in *Denisov v Ukraine*.[30] In this case, after a long and distinguished career as a judge, while the applicant was taking a long summer holiday, he was removed from his office of president of a Court of Appeal, though he retained his office as a judge, on the ground of 'significant shortcomings, omissions and errors, and grave violation of the foundation of the organisation and administration of justice'. His application to the ECtHR succeeded under Article 6, because the applicant had not had the opportunity to challenge his removal from office before an independent and impartial tribunal. When considering the application of Article 8(1) to the dismissal, the Court approved and applied a consequences-based approach, making it clear from its analysis of prior decisions and the general principles to be drawn from them that the adverse effects of a dismissal on personal life provide an independent ground for invoking Article 8. In particular, the Court referred to three kinds of possible adverse consequences that might justify the application of Article 8(1): '(i) impact on the individual's "inner circle", in particular where there are serious material consequences; (ii) the individual's opportunities "to establish and develop relationships with others", and (iii) the impact on the individual's reputation'.[31]

Whilst a dismissal in itself may not count as a material loss that is sufficient to damage family life in a way that engages Article 8, this ground for invoking the protection of this Convention right is potentially broad since damage to family life or relationships in the 'inner circle' caused by material hardship could in principle result from any reason given by an employer for dismissal. A severe degree of material harm could arise, for instance, in cases of economic dismissal or redundancy. In *Wandsworth v Vining*, the UK Court of Appeal acknowledged this possibility and agreed that 'it would be unwise to lay down a rule that the circumstances of a redundancy can never engage Article 8'.[32] In that case, the local authority had closed down its parks police force and dismissed all its constables on the ground of redundancy. The applicants' claim for unfair dismissal and other kinds of compensation was apparently blocked by a statutory exclusion of the police. The applicants argued that if Article 8 was engaged, the statutory exclusion of the police should be narrowly interpreted to permit these claims. The Court of Appeal held that the evidence of damage to family life or personal development was insufficient. They rejected the argument that the relative difficulty of finding new employment for the applicants who were

---

[28] ibid [113].
[29] ibid [151].
[30] *Denisov v Ukraine* [2018] ECHR 1061.
[31] ibid [107].
[32] *Wandsworth Borough Council v Vining and Francis* [2017] EWCA Civ 1092, [2018] ICR 499, [49].

aged 52 and 60 respectively was sufficient in itself, or when combined with evidence of other kinds of damage to personal life, to engage Article 8.[33] The result might have been different if the applicants had been able to demonstrate particular personal harm resulting from the economic dismissal. For example, in France, in cases of economic dismissal, under section L 1233-5 of the Code du Travail,[34] an employer is expected to take into account the family sizes of employees, taking note in particular of single parents, and whether or not an employee is likely to experience special difficulties in obtaining a new job, especially those with disabilities or the elderly; and in cases of assignments to a different location in the same company, the employer should seek to avoid upsets in the familial or social life of the employee.[35] These considerations are apparently designed to take into account the consequences-based factors that might trigger the application of Article 8.

Having confirmed the breadth of the consequences-based approach to the interpretation of Article 8, the Grand Chamber in *Denisov v Ukraine* added a crucial proviso that had not been stressed as much before. 'In cases where the Court employs the consequence-based approach, the analysis of the seriousness of the impugned measure's effects occupies an important place.'[36] In fact, it occupies two important places. First, severe damage to private life is essential for the purpose of establishing proof of the consequences-based approach to Article 8. Second, significant detriment is necessary to pass the test of admissibility under the Convention for a full hearing at the ECtHR.[37] If the court decides that a violation of a Convention right has not caused serious detriment, the case will be declared inadmissible. The Grand Chamber offered guidance as to how courts should assess the severity of alleged damage to private life:

> An applicant's suffering is to be assessed by comparing his or her life before and after the measure in question. The Court further considers that in determining the seriousness of the consequences in employment-related cases it is appropriate to assess the subjective perceptions claimed by the applicant against the background of the objective circumstances existing in the particular case. This analysis would have to cover both the material and non-material impact of the alleged measure.[38]

The applicant, Denisov, was unable to show sufficient evidence of serious harmful effects such as significant loss of income, damage to family life, or major injury to reputation leading to loss of professional or personal opportunities, so the ECtHR held that the case based upon Article 8 was inadmissible. In contrast, the requirement of 'significant disadvantage' is very likely to be met in cases where a dismissal has effectively prevented someone from pursuing a career or a vocation,[39] as in the example of the secret blacklisting of union members,[40] or where the reason for the dismissal is tainted by discrimination and a denial of respect for the individual.[41]

---

[33] ibid.
[34] As modified by Ordonnance n° 2017-1718 du 20 décembre 2017, Article. 1.
[35] J-E Ray and J Rojot, 'Worker Privacy in France' (1995) 17 *Comparative Labour Law and Policy Journal* 61, 63.
[36] *Denisov v Ukraine* [2018] ECHR 1061.
[37] ECHR, Article 35(3)(b): '[The Court shall declare an application inadmissible] if the applicant has not suffered a significant disadvantage, unless respect for human rights as defined in the Convention and the Protocols thereto requires an examination of the application on the merits and provided that no case may be rejected on this ground which has not been duly considered by a domestic tribunal'. (entered into force 1 June 2010). Cf D Shelton, 'Significantly Disadvantaged? Shrinking Access to the European Court of Human Rights' (2016) 16 *Human Rights Law Review* 303.
[38] *Denisov v Ukraine*, above n 36, [117].
[39] *Bigaeva v Greece* [2011] ECHR 2164; *Schüth v Germany*, App No 1620/03, 23 September 2010.
[40] *Brough v UK*, App No 52962/11, Admissibility Decision of 30 August 2016; *Smith v UK*, App No 54357/15, Admissibility Decision of 28 March 2017. For discussion of the *Brough* decision, see K Ewing and J Hendy, 'Article 11(3) of the European Convention on Human Rights' (2017) *European Human Rights Law Review* 356 at 373 ff. See also V Mantouvalou, 'Labour Rights, Human Rights and Criminal Wrongs' in A Bogg et al (eds) *Criminality at Work*, (Oxford, Oxford University Press, 2020) 10, 218.
[41] *Özpınar v Turkey*, above n 25; *IB v Greece* [2013] ECHR 908.

Cases may arise under the consequences-based approach where the damage to private life is a significant disadvantage, but Article 8 will not be applied because of the fault of the applicant. For example, a dismissal for serious misconduct such as fraud or theft may severely damage a person's reputation and make it hard for them to obtain similar employment again. If the misconduct is proven, however, it is said that it is not the dismissal that caused the harm but rather the employee's misconduct, so the employee was the author of their own misfortune.[42]

What happens if the misconduct cannot be proven beyond reasonable doubt and the employee maintains their innocence? Provided the employer takes all reasonable steps to investigate the case and continues to believe on reasonable grounds that the employee is guilty of misconduct, the English Court of Appeal in *Turner v East Midlands Trains Ltd*[43] has held that Article 8 does not apply. In that case, the employee's job as a senior train conductor involved issuing tickets from a computerised ticket machine. Sometimes the machine produced a faulty ticket that ought not to be given to a customer, but if it was, the conductor had the opportunity to retain the customer's payment. A statistical analysis revealed that the claimant had printed vastly more faulty tickets than her colleagues. After a disciplinary procedure where there was no further evidence and the claimant maintained her innocence, she was dismissed. The Court of Appeal accepted that the damage to her reputation resulting from a dismissal might engage Article 8, but concluded that, provided the employer had followed a properly conducted and fair disciplinary process, the claimant would be regarded as the author of her own misfortune. On the question of what kind of disciplinary process was required when Article 8 was engaged, the Court of Appeal insisted that the normal requirement under the domestic law of unfair dismissal in the ERA 1996, s 98(4) was sufficient. The question is simply whether a reasonable employer could have acted as the employer did, taking into account the potential adverse consequences to the employee.

It seems correct that the band of reasonable responses test of fairness is appropriate to determine the fairness of the disciplinary procedure used by the employer to determine whether the misconduct was proven. But it seems wrong to draw from this decision the broader conclusion that when the issue of justification for interference with all Convention rights is considered, the band of reasonable responses test is no different from the test of proportionality used by the ECtHR. On the contrary, because the ECtHR recognises that dismissal is a severe sanction, the question of whether it was necessary for the employer's legitimate purpose requires a higher threshold than the question whether other reasonable employers would have dismissed in those circumstances.

5. Justified Grounds of Dismissal for Fault under the ILO Convention

Although the scope of control over unjustified dismissals is extensive under the ECHR, it differs from the approach established in the ILO Convention 158 on Termination of Employment (1982), and its partial replication in the Revised European Social Charter 1996, Article 24. Both Article 24 and Article 4 of the ILO Convention focus on the same double requirement for an employer to give reasons for dismissal and for those reasons to be valid reasons connected with the capacity or conduct of the employee or the organisational requirements of the business. The Convention further specifies in Articles 5 and 6 that certain reasons are forbidden as invalid: dismissal for membership of a trade union, discrimination on grounds of race and sex and other

---

[42] *Sidabras v Lithuania*, above n 23, [49]; *Kyriakides v Cyprus*, App No 39058/05, 16 October 2008.
[43] *Turner v East Midlands Trains Ltd* [2012] EWCA Civ 1470, [2013] ICR 525.

protected characteristics, dismissal for the filing of a legal complaint, and dismissal for temporary absence through maternity leave, sickness, or personal injury.

The reason for focusing on the employer's reason for dismissal in these international standards is in part to make it clear that laws that merely require an employer to pay compensation on termination of employment do not comply with the international standard, because they fail to investigate the justice of the dismissal and vindicate employees in cases of unfairness. A further reason for detailed assessment of the reasons for dismissal is to try to ensure, as explained in the Recommendation that accompanies the ILO Convention as an aid to its interpretation,[44] that only reasons that serve a legitimate purpose and are proportionate are likely to count as valid reasons for dismissal.

In recent years, perhaps the most controversial issue has been whether dismissal of older workers when they reach pensionable age is a valid reason for dismissal. The ECSR takes the view that merely reaching a national retirement age is not a valid reason for dismissal under Article 24.[45] What is needed in addition is that the selected age is a proportionate measure in pursuit of a legitimate aim such as creating opportunities for younger workers in the labour market. That interpretation appears to match the approach of the EU Directive on age discrimination.[46]

Both the ESC and the ILO Convention also insist that employees who wish to contest the fairness of their dismissals should have access to a court, a tribunal, or an established legal mechanism such as labour arbitration.[47] If the relevant institution finds the dismissal to be unjustified, it should order reinstatement, or if that is not legally possible or practicable, 'order payment of adequate compensation or such other relief as may be deemed appropriate'.[48] Although the ILO Convention does not specify what amounts to adequate compensation, it includes but is not exhausted by wages during a reasonable notice period,[49] and an award that reflects the number of years of service prior to dismissal.[50] The compensation payable in lieu of notice should correspond exactly to the wages due during that notice period.[51] Apart from a rather short minimum notice period,[52] the UK law of unfair dismissal broadly complies with these requirements: the basic award reflects the number of years of service,[53] and the 'just and equitable award' of compensation has the potential to amount to adequate compensation.[54]

6. Justified Grounds of Dismissal for Reasons of Business Reorganisation

The ILO Convention 158 deals separately with dismissals for economic reasons. Operational requirements of the undertaking, establishment or service are likely to provide valid reasons

---

[44] Termination of Employment Recommendation, 1982 (No 166).
[45] Malta, Conclusions (2020) 2020_def_MLT_24_EN.
[46] Council Directive 2000/78 on employment equality; *Seldon v Clarkson Wright and Jakes* [2012] UKSC 16, [2012] IRLR 590.
[47] ILO Convention No 158 Concerning Termination of Employment at the Initiative of the Employer (1982), Article 8.
[48] ibid Article 10.
[49] ibid Article 11.
[50] ibid Article 12.
[51] *Blantyre Netting Co v Chidzulo* (MSCA Civil Appeal 17 of 1995) [1996] MWSC 1 (Malawi).
[52] ERA 1996, s 86.
[53] ERA 1996, s 119.
[54] ERA 1996, s 123.

for dismissal. Similarly, under the law of the UK, dismissals for reasons of redundancy are not in general unfair dismissals, though the employer is required to compensate the employee the modest amount of a statutory redundancy payment.

Article 9(3) of the ILO Convention requires that in cases of dismissals for organisational reasons, a court or tribunal or other dispute mechanism such as arbitration under a collective agreement that has jurisdiction over dismissals 'shall be empowered to determine whether the termination was indeed for these reasons'. This requirement is not replicated under UK law, because in the absence of obviously misleading claims about the need for redundancies, employment tribunals will not challenge an employer's assessment of whether dismissals were required for economic reasons. In some cases, however, tribunals will assess whether the selection criteria for those employees who are going to be dismissed were fair and applied correctly.[55]

A distinctive requirement for dismissals for reasons of business reorganisation is that workers' representatives have to be consulted. Under Article 13 of the ILO Convention 158, the employer is required to:

(a) provide the workers' representatives concerned in good time with relevant information including the reasons for the terminations contemplated, the number and categories of workers likely to be affected and the period over which the terminations are intended to be carried out;
(b) give, in accordance with national law and practice, the workers' representatives concerned, as early as possible, an opportunity for consultation on measures to be taken to avert or to minimise the terminations and measures to mitigate the adverse effects of any terminations on the workers concerned such as finding alternative employment.

The Convention admits the possibility of limiting this requirement of worker consultation to cases in which the number of workers whose termination of employment is contemplated is at least a specified number or percentage of the workforce. A similar limitation can be applied to the further duty placed on an employer to notify the competent public authority of collective dismissals at a time prior to making them.[56]

UK law complies with these ILO and ESC standards regarding collective consultation as a result of legislation that implements the EU Collective Redundancies Directive.[57] The Trade Union and Labour Relations (Consolidation) Act 1992 (TULRCA 1992), s 188(1) provides that:

Where an employer is proposing to dismiss as redundant 20 or more employees at one establishment within a period of 90 days or less, the employer shall consult about the dismissals all the persons who are appropriate representatives of any of the employees who may be affected by the proposed dismissals or may be affected by measures taken in connection with those dismissals.

This requirement of collective consultation was held in *Wandsworth v Vining*[58] to be sufficiently analogous to collective bargaining as to fall within the requirement under Article 11 ECHR, as recognised by the Grand Chamber in *Demir and Baykara v Turkey*.[59] The right to collective consultation over redundancies is therefore an aspect of the human right to be a member of a trade

---

[55] *Williams v Compair Maxam Ltd* [1982] ICR 156, EAT.
[56] ILO Convention 158, above n 47, Art 13.
[57] Council Directive 98/59/EC of 20 July 1998.
[58] *Wandsworth v Vining*, above n 32.
[59] *Demir and Baykara v Turkey* [2008] ECHR 1345; see chapter 6.

union and for it to represent its members. The right to consultation is also guaranteed by the EU Charter of Fundamental Rights, Article 27:

> Workers or their representatives must, at the appropriate levels, be guaranteed information and consultation in good time in the cases and under the conditions provided for by community law and national laws and practices.

The CJEU has held that Article 27 does not confer on individuals a directly enforceable right and so cannot be invoked in a dispute between private parties to disapply restrictions on consultation contained in national law that are incompatible with the Collective Redundancies Directive.[60]

7. Fair Procedure Prior to Termination of Employment

The ILO Convention 158 requires an employer to follow a fair procedure prior to dismissal. Article 7 provides:

> The employment of a worker shall not be terminated for reasons related to the worker's conduct or performance before he is provided an opportunity to defend himself against the allegations made, unless the employer cannot reasonably be expected to provide this opportunity.

The ILO Recommendation that assists in the interpretation of the Convention provides more detail about the requirements of a fair procedure.[61] Termination for misconduct that would only justify dismissal if repeated should not be a ground for dismissal unless the worker has received a prior written warning. In cases of unsatisfactory performance, termination should not occur unless the employee has been given appropriate instructions and a written warning. When defending themselves at a hearing prior to dismissal, an employee is entitled to be assisted by another person. In general, the UK law of unfair dismissal complies with these requirements by holding that a failure to follow the ACAS Code of Disciplinary Procedure,[62] which sets out a more detailed list of procedural steps, will normally result in a finding of unfair dismissal.[63]

It is a controversial question whether the employer's disciplinary procedure prior to a dismissal is also governed by the right to a fair trial protected in Article 6 of the ECHR. So far, the additional protections of Article 6 such as access to legal representation have been confined to tribunal and court hearings and not applied to an employer's internal disciplinary procedure.[64] In *KMC v Hungary*,[65] the government dismissed a civil servant without giving any reasons, which effectively prevented any legal challenge. The ECtHR held that this denial of access to a court was a violation of Article 6 ECHR. That conclusion was supported by reference to Article 24 ESC, which expressly requires judicial oversight of the justice of a dismissal. In a concurring opinion, Judge Pinto de Albuquerque suggested that Article 6 should be interpreted more broadly by reference to both Article 24 ESC and Article 4 of the ILO Convention, so that it would require employers not only to provide reasons for a dismissal, but also to put forward the approved kinds of valid

---

[60] Case C-176/12 *Association de Médiation Sociale v Hichem Laboubi* ECLI:EU:C:2014:2, [2014] ICR 411.
[61] Recommendation 166, above n 44, Articles 7–12.
[62] ACAS Code of Practice 1, *Code of Practice on Disciplinary and Grievance Procedures* (2015), issued under TULRCA 1992, s 199.
[63] *Polkey v A.E.Dayton Services Ltd* [1988] ICR 142, HL.
[64] *R (on the application of G) v Governors of X School* [2011] UKSC 30; A Sanders, 'A "Right" to Legal Representation (in the Workplace) during Disciplinary Proceedings?' (2010) 39 *ILJ* 166.
[65] *KMC v Hungary* [2012] ECHR 1563.

reasons such as misconduct, lack of capability, and the economic needs of the business. Claiming that the requirement to give valid reasons for dismissal was part of a European consensus on protection in cases of termination of employment, he maintained that this requirement of Article 6 applied even to those contracting states such as Hungary (and the UK) which had not undertaken the obligations under Article 24 ESC. Summing up, the judge stated (using underlining for emphasis):

> the right to protection in the event of termination of employment has a minimum content in European human rights law, consisting of four core requirements: a formal written notice of termination of employment given to the employee, a pre-termination opportunity to respond given to the employee, a valid reason for termination, and an appeal to an independent body.

Even if Article 6 ECHR does not apply to the disciplinary procedures of employers prior to dismissal, the absence of a fair procedure will make it far harder for an employer to justify a dismissal that interferes with a Convention right. An inadequate procedure must cast doubt on whether the employer is pursuing a legitimate aim. Nor is dismissal likely to be an appropriate sanction if the disciplinary procedure was cursory and unfair.

8. Exclusions

One of the most contested elements of the protection against unjustified dismissal concerns exclusions from the scope of the right. Article 2 of the ILO Convention 158 acknowledges that it is appropriate and necessary for states that have ratified the Convention to exclude various categories of workers. These include the self-employed, those workers on fixed term contracts, those serving a period of probation (or qualifying period), casual and temporary workers, and those employed by small undertakings.[66] These permitted exclusions create the risk that states will legislate to exclude large swathes of the working population from protection against unfair dismissal. Since the exclusions are stated in broad terms without any precise limits, their application leads to controversial decisions.

For example, France adopted legislation in 2005 enabling enterprises with fewer than 20 employees to employ workers without providing the protection against unjustified dismissal required under the Convention during their first two years of employment. The law's objective was to facilitate the employment of workers in small and medium size enterprises (SMEs). The Court of Cassation held that the ILO Convention was directly applicable under French law (which takes a unitary view of international law) and that two years could not be considered as a reasonable period under Article 2(2)(b).[67] The legislation was abrogated in 2008.[68] Subsequently, the Court of Cassation held that a one year probationary period was also excessive, but upheld a collectively agreed six months probationary period as compatible with international standards.[69] The ECSR in its reports on compliance with Article 24 has taken the even more robust position that a six-month probationary period during which termination at will is permitted is contrary

---

[66] ILO Convention 158, above n 3, Article 2(1), 2(2) and 2(5).
[67] Cour de cassation, Social Chamber, *M Samzun v Ms de Wee*, 1 July 2008, Appeal No F 07-44.124.
[68] ILO Tripartite report, above n 5, para 47.
[69] Cour de cassation, Social Chamber, 4 June 2009, Appeal No. 08-41.359. The Cour de Cassation treats ILO Convention 158 as a matter of public order, so that in the case of a contract of employment expressly governed by Irish law but performed entirely in France, it held that the one year probation period was unlawful and permitted a claim for unfair dismissal under French law: Supreme Court, Social Chamber, 26 March 2013, Appeal No 11-25580.

to the Convention.[70] On any of these views, the law of dismissal in the UK, which has a two years qualifying period for all employees, must be in violation of the standard in the ILO Convention and Article 24 ESC. Together with Cyprus and Tunisia, the UK has the longest qualifying period before protection against unfair dismissal is available.[71]

It must also be questioned whether the exclusions permitted by Article 2 of the ILO Convention can be maintained in cases where there is interference with ECHR rights including the consequences-based approach to Article 8. For instance, qualifying periods before protection against unjustified dismissal seem inconsistent with the need to protect human rights. In the UK, this point is often acknowledged by granting the entitlement to protection from unfair dismissal on the first day of employment in cases of reasons-based interferences with Convention rights,[72] but this protection is not extended to the consequences-based protection provided by Article 8.

9. Conclusion

In recent decades, a fundamental right to protection against unjustified dismissal has increasingly been acknowledged in conventions on social and labour rights. The ECtHR has also provided substantial protection for such a right through interpretations of Article 8 ECHR. Most European countries, including the UK, broadly comply with those standards either through legal rights or equivalent protections through national level collective agreements. Employers have resisted this control over their disciplinary powers and questioned whether such a human right exists. Yet this right to protection against unjustified dismissal matches closely the usual justifications of human rights. It protects individuals against abuses of power by a dominant force, in this case an employer rather than the state. And like other human rights, the purpose of this protection is ultimately for the sake of human dignity and personal autonomy.

---

[70] ESRC, Article 24, Malta, Conclusions (2020) 2020_def_MLT_24_EN.
[71] https://eplex.ilo.org/probationary-trial-period/.
[72] ERA 1996, s 108(3).

19

Human Rights as the Justification for Labour Law

1.	The Implicit Agenda	6.	Should All Labour Rights be Regarded as Human Rights?
2.	The Formal Qualities of Human Rights	7.	Public and Private Law
3.	Human Rights or Fundamental Rights?	8.	Subordination in Employment
		9.	Radical Critics of Human Rights
4.	Two Conceptions of the Interests Protected by Human Rights	10.	The Moral Justification of Labour Law
5.	Are Labour Rights Human Rights?		

1. The Implicit Agenda

This book has an implicit agenda: to present employment law (or labour law or work law) as grounded in the protection of human rights. This agenda is both interpretive and justificatory. As an interpretation of the law, it is claimed that the idea of human rights provides principles that account for the content of existing employment laws and labour standards. The protection of human rights explains why labour law protects and prioritises certain interests but not others. As a justificatory endeavour, this book claims that the moral value of human rights supplies the principal normative foundations for the existence of labour laws. It justifies this branch of the law by demonstrating that it performs a vital moral role in securing human rights. This justificatory or normative dimension may also be used to criticise the law, usually on account of its failure to protect human rights at work properly in some respect.

The preceding chapters of this book are concerned primarily with the interpretive aspect of this agenda. In the context of the employment relation and the workplace, they examine the legal implications of acknowledging and enforcing protections for human rights such as freedom of expression or freedom of association. Some chapters had to engage with the additional question of whether the proposed human right exists or has the shape and content that would account for employment law. This further problem arises both where the meaning of a right appears vague, such as the right to fair pay or the right to work, and where the right is not explicitly acknowledged in most authoritative texts on human rights, such as the right to strike or the right to protection against unjustified dismissal.

This interpretive task is valuable because it offers a sustained account of employment law that differs from three traditional explanations. The first traditional explanation accounts for labour law as a necessary regulatory corrective to persistent market failure. In particular, the weaker bargaining power of workers tends to lead to unfair and exploitative market transactions. Labour law can remedy this inequality of bargaining power either through direct interventions, such as the imposition of a mandatory minimum wage, or indirectly by supporting workers in increasing their bargaining power through collective organisation. A second traditional interpretation of labour law is that it is concerned to make society more equal and just. By supporting workers' collective organisations, the law both helps workers to improve their standard of living and to have a greater say in the direction their lives will take. A third traditional explanation is often summarised by the slogan 'Labour is not a Commodity' that we find in the International Labour Organization (ILO) Declaration of Philadelphia of 1944. Although the precise implications of this principle are contested, the general idea is that workers should be treated like human beings, not things or mere instruments of their employers. This principle requires workers to be treated with respect and due recognition for their contribution to the productive organisation and to society.

An interpretation of employment law based on human rights is closest to this third account of labour law. Indeed, human rights may be a modern way of expressing the insight that workers should not be treated as if they were mere things. Yet an account in terms of human rights is plainly far more extensive in its detailed explanation of what is required to treat a worker as a human being. A list of protected human rights provides a much richer account of what is needed to treat workers with respect and dignity. It should also be noted that human rights arguments provide support for collective organisation and organised challenges to exploitative labour conditions, so they are not substantially inconsistent with traditional justifications, but rather emphasise a different starting point.

Although the preceding chapters have focused on developing an interpretation of labour law as grounded in human rights, this final chapter is devoted to the justificatory or normative dimension of the agenda of this book. Here the task is to explain why the justification for labour law as an articulation of human rights in the context of work is coherent and morally compelling.

Why is such a justification needed? One reason for seeking a moral justification for labour law in terms of human rights is a concern that traditional justifications for labour law in terms of welfare or social justice are no longer widely regarded as adequate and convincing.[1] Such justifications have been undermined by assertions that employment law causes inefficiency and damages employment opportunities. Similarly, whereas once the principles of labour law were regarded as helping everyone, since nearly everyone was a worker for most of their lives, today the law is frequently presented as serving special interest groups that seek to gain an unfair share of wealth. Even terms like 'worker' and 'labour' are often regarded as anachronistic.[2] Although such arguments rarely withstand close inspection, they have succeeded in raising questions about the need for employment laws.

When this scepticism is combined with pressures arising from intensified global competition between national and regional economies, it encourages a political agenda designed to minimise costs to business by the elimination of employment law altogether. As was recognised at the Versailles Peace Treaty of 1919 after the First World War and shortly after the Russian revolution, a regulatory race to the bottom driven by intense international competition undermines labour laws and damages the living standards of ordinary working people. In the long term, the abandonment of good labour standards undermines social cohesion and destabilises states. The

---

[1] M Weiss, 'Re-Inventing Labour Law?' in G Davidov and B Langille (eds), *The Idea of Labour Law* (Oxford, OUP, 2011) 43; B Langille, 'Labour Law's Theory of Justice' in Davidov and Langille, ibid 101; A Hyde, 'The Idea of the Idea of Labour Law: A Parable' in Davidov and Langille, ibid 88. Of course, many labour lawyers stick to the traditional justifications for the subject, albeit with some adaptation to modern labour market conditions: eg G Davidov, 'Re-Matching Labour Laws with Their Purpose' in Davidov and Langille, ibid 179.

[2] H Arthurs, 'Labour Law after Labour' in Davidov and Langille, ibid 13, 22.

response of the international community was to create a new body, the International Labour Office, later renamed the International Labour Organization, tasked with developing mandatory minimum labour standards that would prevent the regulatory race to the bottom. Following the Second World War, these universal labour standards were reformulated as human rights in the Universal Declaration of Human Rights.[3]

A new justification for labour law that is grounded in human rights seeks to establish fresh and comprehensive foundations for the subject using the concepts that are regarded as presenting powerful moral reasons for action. Indeed, human rights are usually regarded as being 'trumps',[4] or as providing peremptory reasons for action.[5] The state and perhaps others have duties to respect and comply with those rights. The appeal to human rights also addresses the issue of globalisation and deregulation, for these rights are universal and mandatory, requiring compliance by all states that participate in the international community.

To perform this task of providing a robust justification of labour law, a theory of human rights must explain why the rights have such a peremptory quality that usually overrides other considerations. At the same time, these rights have to be sufficiently concrete and detailed to provide credible foundations for a body of law that resembles current labour law systems.[6] The rights cannot be confined to issues such as the prohibition of slavery and forced labour, but must ground a full range of labour laws including worker representation, decent work, fair wages, protection of periods of rest, and the health and safety of workers. In elaborating the case for justifying employment law as protecting and respecting human rights, several issues need to be addressed.

Inevitably, the first question is what are human rights? Why do they have this strong moral imperative? Answers to those questions are hotly disputed and have an important bearing on the justificatory ambitions of this book. In particular, we should consider the challenge that many labour rights are conventionally classified as social and economic rights, which are often not regarded as human rights as such, but rather as aspirations for social justice and peace, not urgent moral imperatives like other human rights. Finally, we need to rebut some of the criticisms advanced by supporters of high labour standards against attempts to justify this branch of the law based on the protection of labour rights as human rights.

2. The Formal Qualities of Human Rights

What are human rights? One starting-point for an answer to that question is to refer to authoritative statements of human rights, such as the Universal Declaration of Human Rights of the United Nations or the European Convention on Human Rights of the Council of Europe. Those documents list many rights that are described as human rights. But they do not explain what makes those interests deserving of the label of being human rights (and not others). Furthermore, the content of these lists is often politically controversial, with some participants trying to minimise the content of human rights to essential liberties, while others seek to expand the category in order to promote progressive political ambitions such as greater equality and respect for others in society. These lists of rights should not be regarded as determinative of what should

---

[3] H Collins, 'Theories of Rights as Justifications for Labour Law' in Davidov and Langille, ibid 137, 143.
[4] RM Dworkin, *Taking Rights Seriously* (Cambridge, Mass, Harvard University Press, 1977), Introduction and ch 12.
[5] J Raz, *Practical Reason and Norms* (London, Hutchinson, 1975); J Raz, *The Morality of Freedom* (Oxford, Oxford University Press, 1986) 192.
[6] Collins (n 3) 154.

be regarded as a human right.[7] Instead, a philosophical theory is required to provide a justified conception of human rights.[8]

Although the idea of human rights took off in political discussions after 1945, similar notions, often described as natural rights, have long antecedents stretching back to the 17th century. In that natural law tradition, which sought to identify the key features of a moral social order (often presumed to be given by divine inspiration), natural rights shared four formal characteristics.

These fundamental rights are urgent and weighty claims for the protection of vital interests of individuals, such as a right to life or the freedom from slavery. Normally the protection of such weighty interests overrides all other considerations such as efficiency or collective goals. In other words, aims of the society as a whole, such as wealth maximisation or territorial defence, though usually valuable, are rarely if ever of sufficient weight to override the protection of human rights. For instance, torturing people to gather information about the plans of the enemy is not permitted under human rights law.

Second, the rights should apply universally to all people simply by virtue of being human. Unfortunately, it was not until the 20th century that all racial and sex-based exclusions from the enjoyment of rights were firmly rejected. Although universally available, many rights are only applicable to individuals who find themselves in particular situations such as being on trial, imprisoned, or workers who seek to form a political party or a trade union. Rights are only universal in the sense that they apply to everyone who finds themselves in a relevant situation.[9]

Third, these rights should be timeless in the sense that the protected interests are ones that everyone would value throughout history. Of course, as economic and social conditions change, the precise way in which those interests require protection alters. For instance, in agrarian societies, the interests in food and shelter were typically met by granting peasants the right to farm land and build shelter there. In today's industrial and post-industrial societies, subsistence usually depends on being able to work and gain an income from employment to purchase food and shelter through the market. The vital human interest in subsistence remains constant even though its mode of acquisition changes.

Finally, human rights are distinctive because the core of each right requires an essential minimum of the interest to be protected vigorously, as the ECtHR regularly says in its case law.[10] Some rights such as freedom from slavery or torture are presented as absolute rights, with no possible exceptions.[11] Other rights permit justified exceptions. On this line of thinking, many rights have a core of meanings, but at the penumbra of the abstract concepts there is uncertainty about their scope. In all these cases, however, there is a core of the right that must be protected even if in broader and less certain applications of the right some qualifications may be permitted. This last feature also recognises that sometimes the interests protected by human rights conflict. In such cases, human rights law insists that the protection of one right cannot be achieved at the

---

[7] For discussion of different approaches to labour rights as human rights, see further V Mantouvalou, 'Are Labour Rights Human Rights?' (2012) 3 *European Labour Law Journal* 151.

[8] See J Atkinson, 'Human Rights as Foundations for Labour Law' in H Collins, G Lester and V Mantouvalou (eds), *Philosophical Foundations of Labour Law* (Oxford, Oxford University Press, 2018) 122.

[9] Mantouvalou, above n 7.

[10] See, for instance, 'Relating to Certain Aspects of the Laws on the Use of Languages in Education in Belgium' v Belgium [1968] ECHR 3; *Baka v Hungary* [2016] ECHR 568, [120].

[11] See Article 3 of the ECHR on the prohibition of torture, inhuman and degrading treatment, and Article 4 ECHR on the prohibition of slavery and servitude.

cost of completely sacrificing another. Where a balance between human rights is required, the interference with each right must be kept to a minimum and be proportionate to the aims being sought.[12]

3. Human Rights or Fundamental Rights?

Not every kind of right satisfies these formal criteria. Human rights are moral rights that everyone has simply by virtue of being a human being. We have a right to life, to liberty, and freedom from slavery and so forth because these moral rights are regarded as essential dimensions of being human. Many rights enshrined in constitutions of states may have the same qualities as human rights, but other constitutional rights may be regarded as fundamental or important, but not of the same moral force as human rights. For instance, constitutional rights may be confined to citizens of the state rather than being universally applicable, or they may be heavily qualified by considerations of public policy.

It is certainly possible to justify a scheme of fundamental or constitutional rights without invoking a naturalistic theory of human rights. For instance, rights such as freedom of speech might be protected as vital safeguards of liberty, autonomy, and democracy by the hypothetical social contracts of liberal theories of justice, as in the work of John Rawls.[13] Similarly, certain rights may be vigorously protected as a technique for enhancing 'capabilities' or the freedom to pursue a life that one has reason to value.[14] More pragmatically, as in the case of the Magna Carta, rights such as property and inheritance rights may have been legally recognised as mandatory rights in the past to resolve conflicts between powerful groups. In all these theories and examples, the rights contained in constitutions and charters such as freedom of speech or the right to the peaceful enjoyment of property are not justified as moral rights that everyone has by virtue of being human, but rather they have the status of fundamental mandatory rights because they have been constitutionalised in order to obtain instrumental benefits such as freedom, social order, democracy, and well-being.[15]

The same argument might be used to provide the foundations for labour rights as fundamental constitutional rights.[16] Instead of mirroring pre-existing moral rights, labour rights in international conventions or national constitutions might be regarded as fundamental rights that have been generally recognised because of the valuable instrumental purposes that they serve, such as the avoidance of exploitation, oppression, restrictions on liberty, dangers to health and safety, and the destruction of dignity. From a historical point of view, as we have noted, the idea of labour

---

[12] On 'double proportionality' see *Re S (Identity: Restrictions on Publication)* [2004] UKHL 47, [2005] 1 AC 593, [17] (Lord Steyn); H Collins, 'On the Incompatibility of Human Rights Discourse and Private Law' in H-W Micklitz, *Constitutionalisation of European Private Law* (Oxford, Oxford University Press, 214) 26, 49. For theoretical analysis and critique of the test of proportionality, see G Letsas, 'Proportionality as Fittingness: The Moral Dimension of Proportionality' (2018) 71 *Current Legal Problems* 53. See also S Tsakyrakis, 'Proportionality: An Assault on Human Rights?' (2009) 7 *International Journal of Constitutional Law* 468.

[13] J Rawls, *A Theory of Justice* (Oxford, Oxford University Press, 1972).

[14] AK Sen, *Development as Freedom* (Oxford, Oxford University Press, 1999); AK Sen, *The Idea of Justice* (London, Penguin Group, 2009); B Langille (ed), *The Capability Approach to Labour Law* (Oxford, Oxford University Press, 2019).

[15] L Murphy, 'The Artificial Morality of Private Law: The Persistence of an Illusion' (2020) 70 *The University of Toronto Law Journal* 453.

[16] S Besson, 'In What Sense Are Economic Rights Human Rights? Departing From Their Naturalistic Reading in International Human Rights Law' in J Queralt and B Van der Vossen (eds), *Economic Liberties and Human Rights* (New York, Routledge, 2019) ch 3.

rights started as fundamental standards that were justified at the time of the Versailles Treaty of 1919 because of their contribution to peace, stability, and welfare.

Although this account of labour rights as standards that are regarded as instrumentally useful for workers can provide a coherent justification of labour law, it may not attach the same weight to labour rights as they would attain if they were human rights. Its attraction as a justification for labour law is the flexibility that labour rights do not have to comply with the four formal qualities of human rights.[17] Its demerit is that fundamental rights based on instrumental concerns lack the moral imperative that makes human rights such weighty considerations. Where rights are fundamental because of the instrumental purposes that they serve, it is always possible to argue that the rights should be qualified for the sake of other important public policies or that some people, such as migrant workers, should not have those rights because that exclusion will be conducive to the general welfare of citizens. Such an argument would not be possible if employment rights were human rights, because the core of the rights would have to be respected universally regardless of instrumental considerations concerning the labour market.

Historically, labour rights have always been politically controversial. They always seem vulnerable to challenges from powerful interest groups such as employers. It seems a dangerous line of argument, therefore, to admit that labour rights are simply conventions or fundamental rights developed because they serve instrumental purposes, for then governments will feel entitled to reduce or abolish the fundamental right if they take a different view of the instrumental benefits of observing the right. The persistent arguments about the existence of a right to strike or a right to protection against unjustified dismissal illustrate how fundamental rights are vulnerable to evisceration by governments relying on policy considerations such as reducing costs to business. If labour rights are to provide universal guarantees of just conditions of work, ideally they should satisfy the formal characteristics of human rights.

4. Two Conceptions of the Interests Protected by Human Rights

Although the four formal features of human rights are widely accepted, there is much less agreement about the content of the vital human interests protected by human rights. It is possible to draw a contrast between two principal conceptions of those protected interests.

One conception views the interests protected by human rights as primarily concerned with the liberty of the individual. The rights protect what is regarded as distinctively human about our species in comparison with other forms of life. At its core, this liberal or republican conception uses human rights to articulate necessary protections for individuals to lead an autonomous life in the sense of being able to pursue their own conception of the good life. In some scholarship, human rights protect this choice of a path through life.[18] As well as human rights to liberty and freedom from coercion, an individual needs to enjoy other freedoms such as freedom of expression, freedom of religion, a right to educational opportunities, and protection against coercive disapproval by others of how one chooses to lead one's life (the right to respect for private life). Even if it is conceded that an autonomous life is impossible without a minimum material standard of life, such as food and shelter, those rights are only to the basic necessities of life. This

---

[17] Collins (n 3) 137.
[18] J Griffin, *On Human Rights* (Oxford, Oxford University Press, 2008).

conception of the interests protected by human rights predominates in the text of the European Convention on Human Rights and the scope of many other international conventions of human rights.

A contrasting conception of human rights takes a much broader view of the needs and interests that are protected by human rights. As well as fundamental freedoms and civil liberties, the interests protected include what is needed to lead a dignified and respected life as a member of a community. Here the concept of dignity extends beyond freedom from coercion and subordination to the enjoyment of the necessary economic and social conditions to permit an individual to pursue a worthwhile life according to the standards of that community.[19] The state is under a duty to promote everyone's capability to pursue the kind of life they have reason to choose.[20] This conception of human rights includes social, economic, and cultural rights. It is also linked to ideas of social justice, because it is especially concerned that the rights and the capabilities that they protect should be enjoyed by everyone to a significant degree, not just a wealthy and powerful elite.[21]

Some of those social and economic rights are recognised in the Universal Declaration of Human Rights. As well as the rights discussed in this book, such as the right to work and the right to fair pay, a social welfare system is viewed as a human right in Article 25(1):

> Everyone has the right to a standard of living adequate for the health and well-being of himself and of his family, including food, clothing, housing and medical care and necessary social services, and the right to security in the event of unemployment, sickness, disability, widowhood, old age or other lack of livelihood in circumstances beyond his control.

Similarly, the Charter of Fundamental Rights of the European Union contains social and economic rights as well as civil and political rights. It includes, for instance, the right to collective bargaining and strike action, the right to protection against unjust dismissal, and the right to fair and just working conditions.

It is sometimes objected, however, that these social and economic rights are different in kind from human rights properly so called. It is said that they have different formal qualities from human rights. The obligation placed on states is the progressive achievement of social and economic rights, not a strict obligation to respect those rights. It has also been argued that social and economic rights are different because they require the state to use resources raised through taxation to implement them such as paying for public schools, whereas civil and political rights merely impose negative constraints on governments not to do things. But that contrast about the use of resources is not always well-founded. For example, the right to a fair trial requires considerable expenditure on a criminal justice system. A society that respects human rights must have an expensive system of government that observes the rule of law and has elaborate systems of checks and balances. It is also argued that because of the features mentioned already, social and economic rights cannot be justiciable in courts.[22] If someone claims that they have been denied a right to housing or to education, it is asked, how can a court adjudicate over whether the state should have devoted more resources to that human interest as opposed to others? Although respect for the decisions about expenditures of democratically elected governments is important, that constraint does not prevent adjudication on the issue of whether the core of the right has been denied.[23] If there are no schools at all, or if there are only schools for boys, this is a

---

[19] N Rao, 'Three Concepts of Dignity in Constitutional Law' (2011) 86 *Notre Dame Law Review* 183.
[20] MC Nussbaum, 'Capabilities and Human Rights' (1997) 66 *Fordham Law Review* 273.
[21] S Fredman, *Human Rights Transformed* (Oxford, Oxford University Press, 2008).
[22] C Gearty and V Mantouvalou, *Debating Social Rights* (Oxford, Hart Publishing, 2011).
[23] eg *Republic of South Africa v Grootboom*, Case No CCT 11/00, 2000 (11) BCLR 1169 (right to housing).

denial of the right to education, even if the reason for the lack of schools is partly a matter of resources.

Even if the formal differences between civil and political rights, on the one hand, and social and economic rights on the other are not as sharp as has often been asserted, it might still be argued that social and economic rights are less morally weighty and compelling than the typical liberal and republican rights. If they are less important from a moral point of view, that would explain why often they are treated differently in legal instruments and why they are often regarded as non-justiciable in courts. Many have challenged this claim that social and economic rights are less morally vital to human life than other kinds of human rights.

5. Are Labour Rights Human Rights?

Waldron, for instance, has argued, firstly, that social and economic rights are indispensable for people to benefit from the protection of civil liberties and to achieve a life of dignity. Basic needs such as subsistence, shelter, clothing, and good health must be met if the civil liberties so cherished in the liberal tradition are to be worth having at all.[24] This argument for making those basic needs into human rights of equal stature appears to be that since those social and economic interests are necessary for the enjoyment of other human rights, they need to be guaranteed as forcibly as other human rights and freedoms.

Waldron argued, secondly, that 'a moral theory of individual dignity is plainly inadequate' if it does not take issues such as death, disease, malnutrition, and economic despair into account. The best way to give those interests the weight they deserve is to treat them as human rights based on respect for human dignity.[25] The conclusion of this analysis is that in a society concerned deeply about the dignity and autonomy of individuals, ultimately social and economic rights are just the other side of the coin from civil and political liberties.

Even though scholars make a compelling case for the recognition of some social and economic rights as human rights, it still needs to be considered whether that extended set of protected economic interests includes labour rights. Can the same reasons that are given for regarding some social and economic rights as human rights apply to labour rights?

The argument that having food to eat and somewhere to live are essential preconditions for enjoying any human rights is persuasive. But are labour rights similarly essential to the enjoyment of other rights? Are rights, such as a right to fair working conditions, a right to work, a right to be a member of a trade union, or a right to strike similarly necessary preconditions for the enjoyment of civil and political rights? Some of the labour rights discussed in this book qualify under that test of necessity, such as the right against forced labour and slavery, because victims of those practices are unlikely to have access to other human rights. Similarly, the right to work seems likely to qualify as a necessary precondition for the enjoyment of other rights in contemporary society where material welfare including sustenance and shelter usually depends on being able to obtain employment. It seems less convincing, however, to argue that other labour rights, such as fair working conditions and the right to be a member of a trade union, are necessary conditions for the enjoyment of other human rights. Good working conditions and the protection of organised labour will certainly help workers to have access to and to enjoy their civil and political

---

[24] J Waldron, *Liberal Rights* (Cambridge, Cambridge University Press, 1993) 8. Cf H Shue, *Basic Rights: Subsistence, Affluence, and US Foreign Policy* (Princeton NJ, Princeton University Press, 1980).
[25] J Waldron, ibid 11.

rights, but they may still have access to a minimum set of civil and political rights even if they toil under poor labour conditions.

Gilabert insists that some labour rights are essential for the enjoyment of other human rights.[26] This argument is made with respect to the labour rights included in Articles 23 and 24 of the Universal Declaration of Human Rights (UDHR). Article 23 begins with the protection of the right to work. Why is work so valuable that it deserves to be treated as a human right? Gilabert points out that work is valuable for several reasons: (1) access to material goods, (2) to develop our productive abilities, (3) to socialise with others, (4) to contribute to the well-being of others by producing goods and services, and (5) as a vital contribution to our sense of self-esteem and self-respect. These are important interests. But these interests will only be achieved if the job fulfils those interests by, for instance, being paid a living wage and not being subject to oppressive and dangerous working conditions. Once it is accepted that the right to work is an essential condition for the enjoyment of other human rights, the argument is that the work performed must have certain qualities for it to enable the enjoyment of those rights. Those additional features of work such as fair working conditions are a necessary part of the right to work, which itself is an essential pre-condition for the enjoyment of other rights. It is unclear, however, whether this argument can be extended to other labour rights beyond those listed in the UDHR, such as the right to fair pay or the right to protection against unjustified dismissal.

A second line of argument was presented above, which perhaps offers a more promising case for regarding all labour rights as human rights. Here the contention is that social and economic rights including labour rights are derived from and form an important and valuable part of the protection for the abstract values that inspire all human rights instruments, namely individual dignity and autonomy. The liberal and republican rights protected in international conventions, such as freedom of expression, freedom of religion, and the right to respect for private life, can all be justified as forming necessary features of individuals having the opportunity to live a life of dignity and to choose their path in life. Equally, those who live in abject poverty, suffering from disease and malnutrition, are unable to live a life of dignity and autonomy. For that reason, basic social and economic rights to health and sustenance are essential features of the system of human rights aimed at protecting dignity and autonomy. Can the same argument be made with respect to labour rights?

Atkinson tackles this question of whether some labour rights might be justifiable under a more elaborate account of the liberal and republican conception of human rights inspired by the values of dignity and autonomy.[27] He focuses on the right to work. Although this right is not regarded as a human right by some liberal and republican philosophers, Atkinson argues that it can be derived from the foundational abstract rights of autonomy and dignity. In addition to being a source of income and material welfare, work provides opportunities for self-respect, self-fulfilment, and recognition of one's worth from others, all of which contribute to dignity. Furthermore, having the right to work in the sense of being able to freely choose a career to pursue or a vocation is clearly a vital aspect of autonomy, for otherwise barriers to entry to types of jobs such as being a lawyer, a doctor, or a horse trainer inevitably restrict a person's autonomy. Once the right to work is recognised as being derived from the abstract values of dignity and autonomy, it is evident that the significance of work in most people's lives requires us to regard the right to work as a human right. Furthermore, the right to work needs to be further protected by additional rights such as protection against unjustifiable discrimination on the basis of criteria such as sex and race. Atkinson extends this argument that labour rights can be derived from the abstract values of dignity

---

[26] P Gilabert, 'Labor Human Rights and Human Dignity' (2016) 42 *Philosophy and Social Criticism* 171.
[27] Atkinson (n 8) 132.

and autonomy that provide the foundation for the liberal and republican conception of human rights. He gives the examples of workplace health and safety regulations as necessary to protect the right to life and to protect the autonomy of individuals. Similarly, restrictions on working time are needed to enable people to have some opportunities in their leisure time to pursue valuable options such as having a family or enjoying cultural events.

6. Should All Labour Rights be Regarded as Human Rights?

The conclusion that all labour rights are derived from the abstract values underlying human rights raises the question of whether *all* labour rights are properly regarded as human rights. It is not in question that detailed labour standards are important for the well-being of workers and represent an important moral standard that should normally be followed by governments and employers. The issue is rather whether all labour rights have the degree of moral weight and an intrinsic and inseparable link to the protection of liberty and dignity of the individual that they deserve to be protected by the stringent entitlements of human rights. Or should we distinguish between, on the one hand, some essential labour standards, such as the right to form and join trade unions, the right to strike and freedom from slavery, servitude, forced and compulsory labour that are properly regarded as human rights, from, on the other hand, other labour standards, which though important and valuable, are better regarded as morally valuable standards that should normally be followed if resources permit and there are no countervailing policy considerations?[28]

Such a distinction seems to be at the root of the initiative of the ILO to promulgate its Declaration on Fundamental Principles and Rights at Work.[29] ILO Conventions promulgate labour standards that the member states may choose to follow or ratify as they wish. In addition to that mechanism for guiding labour market regulation, the ILO resolved that membership of the ILO requires states

> to respect, to promote and to realize, in good faith and in accordance with the Constitution, the principles concerning the fundamental rights which are the subject of those Conventions, namely:
> (a) freedom of association and the effective recognition of the right to collective bargaining;
> (b) the elimination of all forms of forced or compulsory labour;
> (c) the effective abolition of child labour;
> (d) the elimination of discrimination in respect of employment and occupation; and
> (e) a safe and healthy working environment.

This initiative from the ILO has attracted opposing criticisms. On the one hand, it can be said that the ILO will focus its attention on this relatively narrow agenda of five rights and not pursue as vigorously as it should the development and application of labour standards which are essential for social justice everywhere.[30] On the other hand, it can be argued that the invocation of the idea of human rights and a focus on core principles is necessary to ensure that all states pay attention to the key values represented by the ILO, especially the UK and the great powers such as the USA

---

[28] Mantouvalou (n 7) 169–72.
[29] ILO Declaration on Fundamental Principles and Rights at Work and its Follow-up Adopted at the 86th Session of the International Labour Conference (1998) and amended at the 110th Session (2022).
[30] P Alston, '"Core Labour Standards" and the Transformation of the International Labour Rights Regime' (2004) 15 *European Journal of International Law* 457; P Alston (ed), *Labour Rights as Human Rights* (Oxford, Oxford University Press, 2005).

and China, which typically ignore any conventions and recommendations of the ILO.[31] From our point of view, there is a strong case for a much more elaborate range of labour rights than that included in the ILO Declaration on Fundamental Principles and Rights at Work, as it has been argued throughout this book.

It seems unsatisfactory to accept such a limited list of labour rights as human rights. It has been argued that all labour rights contained in ILO Conventions and Recommendations contribute to the promotion and protection of human rights.[32] Our view is that the core ideas at stake in the various rights that have been set out in this book should be acknowledged as human rights. Detailed descriptions and derivations of those rights may be more contested and open to question. For instance, although the right to work should be acknowledged as a human right, some of the more detailed rights that are said to be derived from the right to work may not be justifiable in any straightforward manner. It has been claimed that the right to work includes within its meaning the right to protection against unjustifiable dismissal. This is not a logical entailment, though, because it is possible to continue to work after a dismissal, albeit for a different employer. Yet protection of job security may be derived from the right work, especially in circumstances where loss of a job often has further repercussions for the pursuit of a career or vocation.

Similarly, the right to a paid holiday listed in Article 24 UDHR is sometimes criticised as a human right because it does not seem to protect a vital human interest.[33] It is wrong to think that this right does not concern an interest worthy of protection as a human right. Every human being needs a period of rest from work from time to time, partly for reasons of health, but also to make time for other important ways to achieve personal fulfilment, such as having a personal life and a family, enjoying culture, and having fun. In a world where most people depend on paid work for the fulfilment of their material needs, such as food and shelter, it is necessary before they take time off from a job that they earn sufficient to pay for those essential material needs. That result can be achieved by paying a living wage or providing paid holidays. The core of this human right is the opportunity to rest and to form a worthwhile balance between work and other aspects of life as a human being. The precise expression of how this period of rest can be achieved is, however, open to different interpretations according to the local economic conditions. The solution of a paid holiday makes sense in a market system where rates of pay barely provide enough on which to survive from one day to the next.

In the previous chapters of this book, we described core labour rights to be protected as human rights, and further considered the possibility of derivations from the core and the extent of the penumbra of protection. Although those descriptions of the full extent of the rights can be contested, that debate should not cast doubt on the validity of regarding the core of each right as a human right.

7. Public and Private Law

Even if this argument for justifying a substantial number of labour rights as human rights is accepted, there may still be objections to their implementation in ordinary employment relations.

---

[31] BA Langille, 'Core Labour Rights – The True Story (Reply to Alston)' (2005) 16 *European Journal of International Law* 409.
[32] N Valticos, 'International Labour Standards and Human Rights: Approaching the Year 2000' (1998) 37 *International Labour Review* 135.
[33] M Cranston, *What Are Human Rights?* (London, The Bodley Head, 1973) 66–67.

The criticism is that human rights govern the relationship between the citizen and the state. The government of the state must recognise and respect human rights of its citizens and those present in its territory. But that duty placed on states does not apply to private sector employers. Their legal obligations are fixed primarily by the terms of contracts on which they hire workers. Provided they comply with those terms by paying the agreed wages etc, and do not breach other mandatory legal duties such as criminal law, private sector employers should be regarded as complying with all the applicable law. In other words, there is a sharp distinction between public law, which governs the state, and private law, which provides the legal framework for contractual relations such as employment. Human rights belong to public law. Therefore, they only apply to the state and not to private sector employers.

This separation between public and private law is justified further by drawing a distinction between two kinds of justice. For society as a whole, we achieve social justice by establishing a fair distribution of wealth and power among all citizens. A just society requires a state to respect everyone's human rights. But in relations between private citizens such as contracts, there is a different standard of justice that can be described as interpersonal justice or relational justice. This dimension of justice is concerned with what is fair between two individuals. For instance, they might be required to keep their promise to perform a contract because that is required by the principles of interpersonal justice, even though performance of a particular contract, such as work for exploitative rates of pay, might harm social justice by adding to the wealth of the rich whilst not helping the poorest.

Just societies must uphold both the demands of social justice in society as a whole and the requirements of the principles of interpersonal justice between individuals. A problem with the application of human rights to contractual relations such as employment is that sometimes they challenge and undermine the principles of interpersonal justice. In determining the law applicable to contractual relations such as employment, it is usually regarded as important to prioritise the principles of interpersonal justice. The terms of contracts should be upheld, even if they might interfere with the interests of workers that are described as human rights or human rights. For instance, if a person takes a job that requires working on Sunday, they cannot complain later that the working hours interfere with their right to manifest a religion by going to church on Sundays. The use of human rights to override terms of contracts that have been agreed would undermine the importance of observing the principles of interpersonal justice and the social institutions it supports, such as a flourishing labour market.

This rejection of labour rights as human rights on the ground that it would disrupt the institutions supported by private law by imposing inappropriate public law standards such as human rights makes an important point. The law would certainly be confusing if workers could always sue their employer simply on the ground that they believe there has been an interference with their human rights even though the interference is warranted by the contract of employment. But making human rights directly enforceable by employees against their private sector employers regardless of their contractual relations is not necessarily what is required by treating labour rights as human rights.

Human rights are often only indirectly enforceable against private sector employers (and arguably public sector institutions acting in a market capacity such as entering contracts). In general, workers cannot simply launch a legal claim that an employer is interfering with their human rights. Instead, the human rights are protected indirectly ('indirect horizontal effect') through interpretations of the laws that already govern the legal relation between employer and employee. Initially, the contract may be interpreted in a way that restricts the extent to which the employer can lawfully interfere with a human right. For instance, it may be a term of the contract that employees should not write messages with content that might offend other employees, but that term might be confined to emails at work and not postings on social media at weekends in order to provide an interpretation of the contract that does not unjustifiably interfere with freedom of expression and the right to respect for private life.[34] Similarly, additional terms may be implied into contracts of employment that serve the purpose of protecting human rights such as implied terms to protect the health and safety of workers.[35] In the second place, statutory employment rights such as laws against discrimination or unfair dismissal can be interpreted by courts in ways that protect human rights. The criteria of unfairness that found a claim for discrimination or dismissal can be interpreted on the basis of human rights, so that these statutory rights can be used indirectly to protect a worker's interest in human rights. While it may be necessary and appropriate to grant directly enforceable human rights in some instances such as modern slavery or sex and race discrimination, in most cases where employers unjustifiably interfere with workers' human rights, it is possible to protect the human right indirectly through an appropriate interpretation of the terms of the contract or relevant statutory entitlements.

The risk entailed by only protecting human rights at work indirectly is that the laws governing contracts and the statutes conferring private rights may not provide the opportunities for courts to interpret them in ways that secure the protection of labour rights. In the absence of a law against unjustifiable dismissal, for instance, it is hard for private sector employees to complain about infringements of their human rights that have in effect forced them out of a job. The solution to this problem developed under the aegis of the Council of Europe is to regard many human rights protected under the ECHR as imposing positive duties on states. States must not only refrain from interfering with those human rights and fundamental freedoms themselves, but they also have a positive duty to develop and enact laws that protect the enjoyment of those human rights throughout society. It is not enough, for instance, for a state to refrain from preventing workers from becoming members of a trade union. It is necessary under the positive obligation for the state to enact laws that protect workers against anti-union discrimination by employers, whether private or public sector, for without such protection, the rights would not be adequately protected in practice. If the state fails to enact such laws that provide adequate protection for the enjoyment of human rights whatever the source of the interference with those rights, it will be found to be in violation of the ECHR. The Council of Europe expects states that fail to comply with their positive obligations to amend their laws or face repeated claims for compensation by wronged individuals.

8. Subordination in Employment

If it is accepted that the correct relationship between human rights and institutions of private law such as contracts is one in which human rights are indirectly effective through interpretations of private law, that opens up the possibility that every contract, every personal relationship, and every proprietary interest should be subject to the influence of human rights. Occasionally we do observe the introduction of human rights into such contexts, such as development of the right to respect for privacy in the law of tort based on the right to respect for private life.[36] For the most

---

[34] *Smith v Trafford Housing Trust* [2012] EWHC 3221 (Ch), [2013] IRLR 86. See chapter 2 above.
[35] H Collins and V Mantouvalou, 'Human Rights and the Contract of Employment' in Mark Freedland (Gen ed), *The Contract of Employment* (Oxford, Oxford University Press, 2016) 188; J Atkinson, 'Implied Terms and Human Rights in the Contract of Employment' (2019) 48 *Industrial Law Journal* 515.
[36] *Campbell v MGN Ltd* [2004] UKHL 22, [2004] 2 AC 457.

part, however, the application of human rights indirectly to the interpretation of the relevant rules of private law and statutory protections makes no difference to the outcome. The relevant rights have already been taken into account in the formation of the law. In most disputes in private law, human rights are not perceived to be either relevant or enlightening.

Matters are different in employment law. Why is that? The principal answer is that the contract of employment contains an inherent threat to the enjoyment of human rights. The structure of the contract confers authority on an employer to direct the workers to perform work that serves the purposes of the business.[37] All workers are therefore treated under the contract as instruments of the employer. They are in a subordinate position to the employer. This subordination is not imposed by force or threats of force. It is constructed from the terms of a consensual contract. It is conducive to efficient production by minimising transaction costs. Nevertheless, once this subordinate relation has been created, it poses an inherent threat to the liberty, dignity and the treatment of the worker as an equal, a person worthy of respect. This threat is not just the risk that a few employers might abuse their position and power over their workforce, though that risk certainly materialises. The problem is rather that the institution of the contract of employment creates a power relation of hierarchy, an authority relation, that runs deeply against the grain of respect for human rights.

Employers therefore present a similar systematic risk to the enjoyment of rights as is posed by the state itself. Just as human rights were created to provide citizens with legal protections against the misuse of their power by government authorities, so too human rights are needed to protect employees against similar misuses of authority by employers. Most employees experience considerable constraints on their liberty. These arise not only from the requirement to attend work and perform tasks throughout the contracted hours, but also constraints arising from rules promulgated by the employer about such matters as dress codes, statements on social media, and freedom of expression generally. The employment relation also jars with the liberal concept of being treated as an equal, for though there is formal equality in entering into the contract, the terms are almost exclusively directed to the protection of the interests of the employer, and most workers understand that they should be subservient and deferential to their managers if they want to succeed. The employment relation is also inherently opposed to respect for private life, for the workplace rules will often discourage the formation of personal relationships and chatting with colleagues, and furthermore in many cases those rules will place limits on what employees can do in their leisure time, such as joining associations, enjoying non-heterosexual relationships, and enjoying an alternative lifestyle. The main source of all these interferences with the enjoyment of human rights by workers is the relation of subordination at the heart of the employment relation. This element of subordination is necessary for employment relations to function efficiently. But the values protected by human rights need to be predominant in employment law in order to prevent labour from being treated no better than a commodity or a machine.

9. Radical Critics of Human Rights

Since the 19th century, going back at least to Karl Marx, scepticism has been voiced by those sympathetic to the interests of the working class about the instrumental benefits of the agenda of justifying and claiming labour rights as fundamental or natural rights. Whilst this book does

---

[37] H Collins, 'Is the Contract of Employment Illiberal?' in Collins, Lester and Mantouvalou (n 8) 48.

not accept those criticisms of labour rights in their entirety, it is important to be alert to the concerns that have been voiced by progressives and guard against the perceived dangers of grounding labour law in human rights. Three main challenges need to be addressed.

The first criticism is that the agenda of protecting human rights diverts attention from the more important goal of promoting social justice in society. If the progressive aim is to achieve greater equality in the distribution of wealth and power, legal claims to protect human rights will only help at the margins. Greater equality only results from actions based on collective solidarity. These may be political actions such as forming political parties and pursuing social democratic goals through legislation and government. They may also be trade union actions, where organisation and collective bargaining can materially improve the well-being of disadvantaged workers. These collective endeavours often create substantial material improvements for the working class. But the human rights claimed by workers can be dismissed by governments and judges as mere rhetoric. Furthermore, even when those rights are justiciable in courts, a victory does not transform society, but merely secures a benefit for one successful claimant.

If the point of this first challenge is that human rights law is not exclusively focused on distributive justice in society, this criticism is well-founded. It is not a body of law devoted principally to egalitarian measures such as progressive taxation and redistribution through welfare benefits. Yet human rights do offer universal protections that can ameliorate the position of the most disadvantaged in many fields of life. They can be protected against exploitation through extended definitions of the prohibition of slavery, servitude, forced and compulsory labour, the right to fair pay and just working conditions. Freedom of association and freedom of expression are also necessary preconditions for solidaristic political action and collective bargaining. These rights serve valuable purposes that contribute to social justice. Moreover, traditional justifications for labour law that viewed one of its vital purposes as contributing to social justice never claimed that this was the sole purpose of labour law. Arguably, human rights provide the justification and foundations for an appropriate role for labour law as a contribution to social justice in society.

A second criticism of justifications for labour law in terms of human rights argues that the language of human rights is excessively individualistic.[38] The language of rights views society as composed of atomistic, self-interested individuals, who do not recognise that they necessarily form part of an interdependent community or society. Constant talk about individual rights also tends to depoliticise discussions about exploitative labour conditions and turn them into arguments about the meaning of words in documents drafted generations before. Although these aspects of rights may exist, it can be argued that the criticism presents a false contrast between the individualism of rights and the collectivism of politics and community movements. For instance, political associations and organised labour need a legal framework of rights in order to flourish and influence society. Freedom of association, freedom of speech, and freedom to protest and take industrial action are vital foundations for any effective action. Often fundamental rights function as a necessary instrument for the achievement of community goals. It is a mistake to view rights, especially labour rights, as always ends in themselves rather than necessary pre-conditions for the achievement of social justice or the enhancement of capabilities to build communities and to pursue our projects with others.[39] It may also be a mistake to view human and labour rights as individualistic, as Robin West has argued.[40]

---

[38] M Koskenniemi, 'The Effect of Rights on Political Culture' in P Alston (ed), *The EU and Human Rights* (Oxford, Oxford University Press, 1999) 99; J Youngdahl, 'Solidarity First: Labor Rights are not the Same as Human Rights' (2009) 18 *New Labor Forum* 31.
[39] R West, 'Rights, Capabilities, and the Good Society' (2000–2001) 69 *Fordham Law Review* 1901, 1912.
[40] R West, *Re-imagining Justice* (Aldershot, Ashgate, 2003) 86.

A third criticism made of the agenda of justifying labour law as an articulation of human rights is that it concedes too much ground to employers and owners of capital. Employers have powerful rights too. They have the right to property, which gives them control over the means of production and access to paid work. They can exercise their property rights to exclude pickets and union organisers trying to communicate with workers. Having the right to freedom of expression, they can use their wealth to control the media and political discourse as well as running anti-union campaigns. Through the right to privacy, employers can protect their reputation by, for example, dismissing any employee whom they think is harming their image through speech or activities. Constitutional protections of human rights can be used to challenge the legal validity of ordinary employment laws because they interfere with the freedom of employers to manage their business and fix the terms of their contracts.[41] Furthermore, whereas employers as a single corporate entity can use their coordinated resources to take full advantage of rights to protect their interests, organisations of workers can often only be effective if the interests of individuals are sacrificed for the general good.[42] In short, human rights in the context of employment relations seem calculated to protect vigorously the power of the owners of capital against workers. For this reason, they may not appear to many as fertile ground on which to develop an effective system of labour law.

This third criticism, as presented here, overstates the problem, but we certainly should be alert to the fact that employers (unlike states) have human rights as well. The effect of employers having those rights is that most of employment law can be understood as a balance struck between competing rights and interests. That balancing exercise is not necessarily a problem, provided that it is remembered that the role of labour rights is precisely to challenge the dominance of the rights of employers in the ordinary law of contract and property. If we are to protect the core of labour rights, they must qualify or derogate the rights of employers to a significant extent.

10. The Moral Justification of Labour Law

This chapter has defended the agenda of this book that it is possible to justify the existence and content of a system of employment law by regarding its rules and principles as being grounded in respect for human rights. This is not the only possible justification for employment law, and there are some laws that are probably better explained by alternative values such as competitiveness, egalitarianism, or principles of interpersonal justice, such as good faith. Even so, we hope that we have established that an account and justification of employment law as grounded in human rights is compelling. The justification of labour rights as human rights seems especially important today as traditional justifications for labour law are questioned and political leaders appear to advocate the dismantling of most of employment law for reasons of wealth maximisation and liberty. They may dismiss employment law as just so much red tape, but its fundamental purpose is best understood as the morally compelling task of the protection of human rights at work.

---

[41] eg *Lochner v New York* 198 US 45 (1905) S Ct US.
[42] C Offe, 'Two Logics of Collective Action' in C Offe, *Disorganised Capitalism* (J Keane, ed), (Cambridge, Polity Press, 1985) 170.

Index

abuse of power, 11–12, 255, 296–97, 323
academic freedom, 257–59
Acquired Rights Directive (ARD), 21, 44
   business restructuring, 101–3
Adequate Minimum Wages Directive, 20, 23, 45
   collective bargaining, 89, 91, 100, 106–8
   right to fair pay, 172
African Charter of Human and Peoples' Rights, 141
age discrimination, 22, 59–61, 305
agency workers, 31, 33–34, 39, 76, 179, 254
agricultural work, 153–54
   Agricultural Wages Boards
      collective bargaining regime, 94
   Seasonal Workers visa, 154–56
artificial intelligence, threat of, 10–11, 104
assimilated law, 22–23
   UK General Data Protection Regulation, 225
automation, threat of, 10–11
autonomy, 314, 317–19
   collective solidarity versus individual autonomy, 4, 68
      trade union autonomy, 81–85, 108, 124
   freedom of expression, 242–43, 245, 259, 261–62, 272, 275–76, 277
   protections against unfair dismissal, 297, 309
   religious organisations as employers, 293
   right to private life
      at work, 228
      away from work, 233–36, 240, 241
   right to work, importance of, 134
   trade union autonomy, 81–85
   working time
      'opt-out', 187
   see also right to respect for private and family life

balancing rights, 9–10, 15–16, 313–14, 325
   age discrimination
      intergenerational balance, 60
   employee/employer balance of power, 21, 47, 115
   freedom of expression, 271–72
   right to private life at work, 221–22
   right to private life away from work, 233–36, 240
   right to strike, 115, 121, 128–29, 130–31
   work-life balance, 194–96, 219, 233–36, 240, 320
   workplace monitoring and surveillance, 217–18
   freedom of expression, 250–51, 254, 262, 270–71
      employer's reputation, 271–72
   illegality doctrine, 39–40
   trade union autonomy and individual rights, 67, 83–84, 85
   see also conflicting rights; proportionality

begging:
   criminalisation, 140–41
   right to work, 140–41
blacklisting, 66–67, 75–77, 85, 144, 303
breach of contract:
   compensation, 296
   freedom of expression, relationship with, 243–47, 258
   unfair dismissal, 262, 268–69
   right to strike, 122
      complete withdrawal of labour, 116–17
      go slow/work to rule, 118
      inducing breach of contract, 123–24
      partial performance, 118
      repudiatory breach of contract, 116–17
   unfair dismissal, 262, 268–69, 296
Brexit:
   assimilated law, 22–23
   Seasonal Workers visa, 154–56
business restructuring:
   economic reasons for dismissal, 305–6
      worker consultation requirement, 306–7

Central Arbitration Committee (CAC):
   recognition of trade unions, 95–98
Charter of Fundamental Rights of the EU (EUCFR), 3, 20–23
   academic freedom, 257–58
   Court of Justice of the EU, 9
   freedom of/manifestation of religion
      neutrality policy, 284
   freedom to run a business (Art. 16), 21, 103, 282, 284, 287–88
   information and consultation, 91, 99, 307
   labour migration, 152
   limitations, 21
   paid annual leave, 191
   political belief, 282
   protection from unjustified dismissal (Art. 30), 29, 297
   right to engage in work (Art. 15), 60
   right to fair and just working conditions (Art. 31), 29
   right to work, 133, 138–39
   Solidarity Chapter, 29
   welfare-to-work schemes, 149–50
   workers voice, 91, 99–100
   see also EU law
child labour:
   Ethical Trading Initiative, 203
   ILO Declaration on Fundamental Principles and Rights at Work, 24, 25–26, 201–2, 319

climate crisis, threat of, 11, 104, 265, 281
closed shop arrangements, 67
    compulsory union membership, 6, 68, 77–81, 85, 144
        freedom of association, 81–82
        freedom of contract, 83–84
        human rights, 79–83
        individual autonomy, 82–83
collective bargaining, 2–3, 11
    business restructuring
        economic reasons for dismissal, 306–7
    EU law, 67–68, 106–8
    individual offers, 98–99
    international law, 25, 68
    right to fair pay, 166, 167, 168–69
    UK law, 98–99
collective laissez-faire concept, 2–3
    human rights as a threat to, 5–6
collective trade union rights:
    individual civil and political rights, relationship with, 5–6
Collective Redundancies Directive (CRD), 44
    business restructuring, 101–3, 306–7
Committee of Experts on the Application of Conventions and Recommendations (CEACR), 24–25
    right to work and unfair dismissal, 299
Committee on Economic, Social and Cultural Rights (CESCR):
    forced or compulsory labour
        prison labour, 144–45
    right to work, 136
        occupations freely chosen or accepted, 144
        protection from unjustified dismissal, relationship with, 299–300
Committee on Freedom of Association (CFA), 25, 69–70, 90
Community Charter of the Fundamental Social Rights of Workers, 3, 79–81, 91, 191
Conference Committee on the Application of Standards (CCAS), 25
conflicting ideologies:
    individual and collective freedoms, 66–67, 109, 243–47, 261–62
conflicting rights, 269
    contracts of employment
        employment protections versus human rights protections, 33–35
    dismissal, 234–36, 238
    freedom of association, 66–67
    freedom of expression
        contractual terms, 243–47
        ideological conflicts with employers, 243–47, 261–62, 271–72
        outside work, 271–72
        trade union activities, 249
    freedom to manifest a religion
        conscientious objection, 289–90
        dress codes, 286–89
        expressing religious views at work, 290–92
        working hours, 285–86
    religious beliefs versus opinions, 280, 281–82
    religious organisations as employers, 292–94

right to strike
    core versus essential rights, 121
    freedom of establishment, 22
    right versus immunity, 131–32
    trade union closed shops, 66–67, 83
    workplace surveillance, 217–19
        domestic workers, 224
conscientious objection:
    non-discrimination, relationship with, 289–90
    medical setting
        abortion, 289–90
contracts of employment, 30–31
    employee/independent contractor ambiguities, 32–33
    employment protections versus human rights protections, 33–35
    employment status tests, 31–33
    exclusions, 31, 33–34
    freedom of expression, relationship with, 243–47
    mutuality of obligation, 34
    statutory definition, 32
    under-inclusiveness, 31–32
Convention on the Elimination of All Forms of Discrimination against Women (CEDAW), 49–50, 54–55
corporate governance:
    worker voice, 89
Corporate Sustainability Due Diligence Directive (CSDDD), 205–6, 208–9, 212–13
Council of Europe:
    European Convention on Human Rights, 16–17
        see also European Convention on Human Rights
    European Social Charter, 17–18
        see also European Social Charter
    fundamental rights of workers, 3
    separation of rights, 18
Court of Appeal:
    contract, presence or lack of, 31, 33–34
    illegality doctrine, 159
    employment relationships, 31, 33–34, 36–38
    freedom of association, 97, 103, 126
        procedural requirements, 124–25
    indirect discrimination and group disadvantage, 52, 291
    interpretation of domestic legislation, 14–15, 36–38
    unfair dismissal, 245, 251–52, 270, 285–86
        right to respect for private life, 302–4
Court of Justice of the EU (CJEU):
    age discrimination, 59, 60–61
    autonomous concept of 'worker', 43, 44
    judges, 45
    collective redundancies, 102–3
    dress codes, 286–89
    equal pay, 178
    equality in the workplace, 55–56, 283
        age discrimination, 59, 60–61
    EUCFR, 9
    fair pay, 107
    freedom of/manifestation of religion
        neutrality policy, 284, 287–88
    freedom of establishment, 129
    information and consultation, 91, 106, 307
    neutrality policy, 284
    paid annual leave, 191–93
    political belief, 282

right to strike, 129–30
rights reasoning, 21–23
supremacy of EU law, 9, 21
working time, 46, 184, 188–89
see also Charter of Fundamental Rights of the EU; EU law
criminal convictions:
  begging, 140–41
  criminal records checks, 226
  data protection, 226
  Disclosure and Barring Service, 226
  discrimination, 51
  private life (activities outside work), 238–40
  sex work, 139–40
  trade union exclusion, 83

damages:
  defamation, 248–59
  due diligence failures, 208
  right to strike, 116, 127, 128
    breach of contract, 117
  wrongful dismissal, 42, 71, 255, 300
data protection:
  criminal convictions, 226
  platform workers, 226–27
  workplace monitoring and surveillance of employees, 225
  guidance, 225–26
Data Protection Act (DPA) 1998, 76
Data Protection Act (DPA) 2018, 225
  workplace monitoring and surveillance of employees, 225
  guidance, 225–26
declarations of incompatibility, 9–10, 74, 120–21
democracy at work, 109
  right to voice at work, 86–88
    dual channel representation, 88
    process, 88
    process versus outcome, 89
    single channel representation, 88
    subject, 88–89
    workplace autocracy, 86–88
  see also workers' voice
dignity, 1, 4–5, 87, 228, 311, 314–15, 316, 317–19, 323
  freedom of belief, 265–66, 281
  human trafficking, 162
  living wage, 167–68, 170–71
  protections against unfair dismissal, 296–97, 309
  right to fair pay, 167–68, 170–71, 182
  right to work, 133–34, 136, 139–41
  welfare conditionality, 147, 149–50
direct discrimination, 49
  dress codes, 286–87
  free movement rights, 143
  prohibition of discrimination (ECHR Art. 14), 51–52
  religion or belief, 264, 266, 283–84
    display of religious symbols, 286–87
    expression of religious views in the workplace, 290–92
  right to fair pay, 179
  right to organise, 71
disability discrimination, 49–50, 61
  reasonable accommodation, 62–63, 138, 196, 284–85

disclosure obligations:
  multi-national companies, regulation of, 204–5
discrimination, 13–14, 25–26
  age discrimination, 22, 59–61, 305
  disability discrimination, 49–50, 61
    reasonable accommodation, 62–63, 138, 196, 284–85
  prohibition of discrimination (ECHR Art. 14), 50
    direct versus indirect discrimination, 51–52
    disability discrimination, 61–63
    employment status, relationship with, 38–39
    expansion of scope, 53–54
    'group disadvantage' requirement, 52
    justification, 51–52
    unlimited scope, 50–51
  women's rights
    domestic work, 56–57
    international law, 54–56
    sex work, 56
    unpaid work at home, 57–59
  see also Convention on the Elimination of All Forms of Discrimination against Women
dismissal, *see* protection from unjustified dismissal; termination; unfair dismissal
domestic labour:
  domestic servitude, 161
  human trafficking, 157–58
  Overseas Domestic Worker visas, 151–52, 156–58
  private life (at work), 224–25
  private life at work, 224–25
  slavery, servitude and forced labour, 7, 161
  workplace surveillance and monitoring, 224
dress codes, 52, 279–80, 284–85, 286–89, 290, 323
due diligence obligations:
  Corporate Sustainability Due Diligence Directive, 205–6, 208–9, 212–13
  human rights due diligence, 204, 212–13
  multinational companies, regulation of, 205–6, 209

employer/employee relationship, 2, 28–29, 36–38
  agency workers, 31, 33–34, 39, 76, 179, 254
  'autonomous' concept of worker, 43
  cross-border employment relationships, *see* supply chains
  data protection, 225–27
  gig workers, 97–98
  ILO Employment Relationship Recommendation 198, 36, 37
  migrant workers, 158–59
  paid annual leave, 191–93
  platform workers, 46–47
  protected industrial action, 97–98, 119–20
  working time, 196–98
  workplace monitoring and surveillance, 216–19, 225
  zero-hour contracts, 39, 148–50
  see also private life (activities outside work), private life (at work)
Employer Insolvency Directive:
  business restructuring, 101–3
Employment Appeal Tribunal (EAT), 14
  freedom of expression, 269–70, 276
  manifestations of belief, 283–84
  philosophical beliefs, 265–66, 281–82

religious beliefs, 265–66, 281–82, 290–91
rest breaks, 188
trade union membership, 72
unfair dismissal, 244–45, 146–47
whistleblowing protections, 39
employment rights and human rights protections, 3, 310–12
  criticisms of human rights in employment law context, 323–24
    diversion of attention from social justice, 324
    individualism of language of human rights, 324
    weight of rights in favour of employers, 324
  human rights concept
    core minimum must be protected, 313–14
    fundamental nature and protection of vital interests, 312–13
    timelessness, 313
    universality, 313
  moral justification of labour law, 325–26
  see also discrimination; equal pay; redundancy; working time
Employment Rights Act (ERA) 1992:
  disclosure and public interest, 255–56
Employment Rights Act (ERA) 1996, 13, 14
  academic freedom, 257–58
  interpretation, 15
  reasonable responses test, 275
  unfair dismissal
    fairness test, 268
    protections against, 296, 304
    qualifying period of employment, 274
    right to private life, 230–32
    whistle-blowing, 254
Employment Rights Act (ERA) 2004:
  collective bargaining, 98–99
  right to organise, 71
  use of trade union services, 74
  workers' voice, 98–99
employment status:
  contracts of employment, 31–33
  freedom of association (ECHR Art. 11), relationship with, 35–38
  unfair dismissal, 41–42
  illegality doctrine, relationship with, 39–41
  personal scope of employment rights, relationship with, 28–29
    contracts of employment, 30–31
    employee versus independent contractor, 30
    general employment protections, 29–30
  prohibition of discrimination (ECHR Art. 14), relationship with, 38–39
employment tribunals, 14
  see also Employment Appeals Tribunal
entitlement to paid leave, 22, 185, 192, 193–96
equal pay, 3, 54, 167–68, 178
  TFEU, 43
  Treaty of Rome, 20
  see also fair wages; right to fair pay
Equal Treatment Directive (ETD):
  genuine occupational requirements, 292–93
  religion and belief, 282, 283
equality, 11, 48–50
  see also discrimination; prohibition of discrimination; women's rights

Equality Act 2010, 13–14, 14, 63–64, 262, 291
  access to employment, 144
  employer liability
    sub-contracted workers, 179
  equal pay provisions, 178
  genuine occupational requirements, 293
  protection against discrimination, 49
    protected characteristics, 50–51
  reasonable adjustments/accommodation, 62
  religious beliefs, 264, 267–68, 281, 283
  unfair dismissal, 42
essential services:
  right to strike, 112, 113–14, 122–23, 126–28
Ethical Trading Initiative (ETI), 202
  child labour, 203
  freedom of association, 203
EU law, 3, 20
  assimilated law, as, 22–23
  CJEU, 21–23
  collective bargaining, 106–8
  employment law, 20
  EUCFR, 20–21
  see also Charter of Fundamental Rights of the EU
  workers voice, 106–8
  see also individual Directives
European Committee of Social Rights (ECSR), 17–18
  closed shops, 79–81
  forced or compulsory labour, 138
  human trafficking, 224–25
  living wage, 171–72
  prison labour, 144–46
  right to work, 137–38, 142
    age discrimination, 305
    protection from unjustified dismissal, relationship with, 299–300, 308–9
  standard of living, 171–72
  unjustified dismissal
    qualifying period of employment, 308–9
    right to work, relationship with, 299–300, 308–9
  welfare-to-work schemes, 149–50
European Convention on Human Rights (ECHR), 3
  academic freedom, 257–59
  background, 16–17
  collective bargaining, 68
  ECtHR interpretation, 8
    integrated approach, 8–9, 18–19
  forced or compulsory labour
    prison labour, 145
  freedom of assembly and association (Art. 11), 14, 17, 29
    closed shops, 80–81
    employment status, relationship with, 35–38
    trade union recognition, 93–94
    unfair dismissal, 41–42
    see also freedom of association
  freedom of expression (Art. 10), 14, 17
    abuse, 247–48
    academic freedom, 257–59
    contractual terms, conflicts with, 243–47
    performance of work, 242–43
    trade union activities, 248–52
    unfair dismissal, 41–42, 268–71
    whistle-blowing, 252–57

Index

'valuable' speech, 247–48
see also freedom of expression (in the workplace); freedom of expression (outside work)
freedom of thought, conscience and religion (Art. 9), 14, 279–80, 282–83, 294
   conscientious objection, 289
   dress codes, 288–89
   expression of religious views, 290, 291–92
   prohibition of abuse of rights, relationship with, 281–82
   religion and other beliefs, 280–81
   religious organisations as employers, 293–94
   working hours, 285
   see also freedom of thought, conscience and religion
Human Rights Act, relationship with, 13–14
indirect horizontal effect, 14–15
prison labour, 145–46
prohibition of abuse of rights (Art. 17)
   freedom of thought, conscience and religion, relationship with, 281–82
prohibition of discrimination (Art. 14), 50
   direct versus indirect discrimination, 51–52
   disability discrimination, 61–63
   employment status, relationship with, 38–39
   expansion of scope, 53–54
   'group disadvantage' requirement, 52
   justification, 51–52
   unlimited scope, 50–51
   see also prohibition of discrimination
prohibition of slavery and forced labour (Art. 4), 7, 14, 17
   welfare-to-work schemes, 147–48
   see also modern slavery
right to a fair trial (Art. 6), 14, 143, 307, 316
right to education (Prot. 1, Art. 2), 281
right to life (Art. 2), 7, 17, 227, 313
right to peaceful enjoyment of your property (Prot. 1, Art. 1), 314
right to respect for private and family life (Art. 8), 7, 14, 17, 231–32
   data protection and criminal convictions, 226
   disability discrimination, 61–63
   protection from unjustified dismissal, relationship with, 300–4
   see also right to respect for private and family life
state responsibilities, 7
workers' voice, 68
European Court of Human Rights (ECtHR), 8
   freedom of/manifestation of religion
     neutrality policy, 284, 288
   interpretation of ECHR, 8
   integrated approach, 8–9, 18–19
   margin of appreciation, 9, 19, 64, 76, 246
   manifestation of beliefs, 282, 288, 293–94
   private life at work, 221–22
   private life away from work, 236–37
   right to strike, 115–16, 118, 121, 131–32
   trade union recognition and collective bargaining, 92–95, 97, 99, 109
   unfair dismissal, 302
   prison labour, 146
European Social Charter (ESC), 1
   background, 17–18
   collective bargaining, 67–68

dismissal
   duty to provide valid reasons for dismissal, 304–5
   freedom of association, 67–68
   information and consultation, 91
   living wage, 170
   prison labour, 144–45, 146
   reporting obligations, 17–18
   right of migrant workers to protection and assistance (Art. 19), 17
   right to benefit from social welfare services (Art. 14), 17
   right to collective bargaining (Art. 6), 67, 114
   right to just conditions of work (Art. 2), 17
   right to organise (Art. 5), 17, 67
   right to organise, 71–72
   right to work (Art. 1), 17, 137–38
   workers voice, 91
European Trade Union Confederation (ETUC), 55, 100, 104
European Works Councils (EWC), 92, 103–6
expectation of privacy, 216–19, 221, 223, 231–32

fair wages, 166
   bonuses and bonus caps, 181
   equal pay for women, 178
   excessive inequalities, 180–82
   fairness concept, 175–76
     desert, 176–77
     recognition, 177
   horizontal comparisons, 177–79
   indirect discrimination, 179
   market rates for pay, 180–81
   pay differentials, 180–81
   vertical comparisons, 180–82
   see also right to fair pay
fixed term contracts:
   employment law protections, 30–31
     protection from unjustified dismissal, 308
   older workers, 22
   social dialogue, 100–1
Fixed-term Work Directive, 100–1
flexible working, 58–59, 183, 185–86
   employers' duties, 196
   parents, 195–96
   right to request, 196–98
forced or compulsory labour, 25–26, 138, 146, 160, 319
   prison labour, 144–45
   see also modern slavery
freedom of association, 67–68, 85
   blacklisting, 66–67, 75–77
   closed shop, 79–81
   Committee on Freedom of Association, 25
   ECHR Art. 11, 14, 17, 29, 67, 68, 85
   employment status, relationship with, 35–38
   right to organise, 69, 70–71
   trade union recognition, 93–94
   unfair dismissal, 41–42
   freedom of expression overlap, 248–49
   ILO, 25, 68
   negative freedom of association, 77–79
   see also right to organise
freedom of contract, 78, 82, 83–85, 111, 166
freedom of establishment, 22, 103, 129–30

freedom of expression (in the workplace):
  abuse, 247–48
  academic freedom, 257–59
  contractual terms, conflicts with, 243–47
  ECHR Art. 10, 14, 17
  performance of work, 242–43
  religious views, 290–92
  trade union activities, 248–52
  unfair dismissal, 41–42
  whistle-blowing, 252–57
  'valuable' speech, 247–48
freedom of expression (outside work), 277–78
  freedom of belief, relationship with, 264
    conduct connected to belief, 266
    proportionality, 266–68
    scope of protected belief, 265–66
  hate speech, 275–77
  ideological conflicts with employers, 261–62
  legitimate interests of employers
    business interests, 271
    employers' reputation, 271–73
  offensive speech, 275–77
  political speech, 273–75
  social media, 262–64
  unfair dismissal, 268–71
freedom of movement:
  direct discrimination, 143
  right to strike, relationship with, 129–31
  ECHR Prot. 4, Art. 2
  EU law, 152
    right to strike, 129–31
    right to work, 143
freedom of thought, conscience and religion
    (ECHR Art. 9), 14, 279–80, 282–83, 294
  conscientious objection, 289
  dress codes, 288–89
  expression of religious views, 290, 291–92
  freedom of expression, relationship with, 264
    conduct connected to belief, 266
    proportionality, 266–68
    scope of protected belief, 265–66
  prohibition of abuse of rights, relationship with, 281–82
  religion and other beliefs, 280–81
  religious organisations as employers, 293–94
  working hours, 285
freedom to run a business (EUCFR Art. 16), 21, 103, 282, 284, 287–88

General Data Protection Regulation (EU):
  workplace monitoring and surveillance of employees, 225–27
General Data Protection Regulation (UK):
  workplace monitoring and surveillance of employees, 225–27
genuine occupational requirement (GOR), 283–84, 287, 292–94

hate speech, 275–77, 278
human rights conceptualised:
  core minimum must be protected, 313–14
  criticisms of human rights in employment law context, 323–24
    diversion of attention from social justice, 324
    individualism of language of human rights, 324
    weight of rights in favour of employers, 324
  dignity, protection of, 316
  fundamental nature and protection of vital interests, 312–13
  fundamental rights compared, 314–15
  interests protected by human rights, 315–16
  labour rights and human rights, 317–20
  liberty, protection of, 315–16
  public and private law divide, 320–32
    enjoyment of rights, threat to, 322–23
  social and economic versus civil and political, 316–17
  timelessness, 313
  universality, 313
Human Rights Act (HRA) 1998, 3, 4, 9–10, 13–14
  collective redundancies, 103
  compatibility with ECHR, 15–16, 73–74
  declarations of incompatibility, 73–74
  freedom of association, 36–38, 72, 73–74
  indirect horizontal effect of ECHR, 14–15
  interpretation of the law
    compliance with ECHR, 15–16, 41, 72–73
  right to strike, 120, 122, 131
  trade union rights, 36–38, 72
  unfair dismissal, 120
    freedom of expression, 268
    manifestation of belief, 283
    right to private life, 230–31
    standard of reasonableness, 15
human rights due diligence (HRDD):
  UN Human Rights Council, 204
  draft binding instrument, 212–13
human trafficking, 5, 11–12, 26, 160–62
  domestic workers, 157–58
  human trafficking for sexual exploitation, 7, 56, 162
  illegality doctrine, 39–40, 159
  Modern Slavery Act, 163–64, 204–5
  Overseas Workers visa, 157–58
  undocumented workers, 158–60

illegality doctrine, 39–41
  human trafficking, 39–40, 159
  undocumented workers, 158
ILO Convention 158 on Termination of Employment (1982), 253, 298, 304–5
  business restructuring, 305–7
  fair termination procedures, 307–8
ILO Declaration on Fundamental Principles and Rights at Work, 311, 319–20
  child labour, 24, 25–26, 201–2, 319
  collective bargaining, 67–68, 89–90
  ethical standards, 201–2, 211
  forced and compulsory labour, 160
  freedom of association, 67–68
importance of human rights at work, 11–12
in-work poverty, 148–49
independent contractors:
  employee rights compared, 30–31
  living wage, 173–74
indirect discrimination:
  dress codes, 286–87
  personality testing, 228

religion or belief, 283–84
  expression of religious views in the workplace, 290–92
indirect horizontal effect of ECHR, 7, 14–15, 321–22
individual versus human rights, 5–6
  closed shop arrangements, 67
    individual autonomy, 82–83
  collective bargaining, 2–3, 11
    individual offers, 98–99
  collective solidarity versus individual autonomy, 4, 68
    trade union autonomy, 81–85, 108, 124
  collective trade union rights
    individual civil and political rights, relationship with, 5–6
  right to strike, 110
    individual strikers' rights, 116–22
industrial action, *see* right to strike; trade unions
industrial autonomy, 2
Industrial Relations Act 1971, 3
information and consultation, 11
  business restructuring
    economic reasons for dismissal, 306–7
  duty to consult, 103–6
  EU law, 11, 20, 46, 91–92, 99–100, 106, 107, 109
  European Works Councils, 103–6
  ILO, 89–90
  Information and Consultation Directive, 11, 46, 106
  platform workers, 107
injunctions:
  right to strike, 128–29
integrated approach to interpretation of human rights, 8–9, 18–19, 27, 68, 70, 80–81, 82, 93–94, 114–15
International Court of Justice (ICJ), 8, 25, 114
International Covenant on Civil and Political Rights (ICCPR):
  due diligence obligations, 205–6
  prohibition of discrimination, 139
  prohibition of slavery, servitude, forced and compulsory labour, 147–48
International Covenant on Economic, Social and Cultural Rights (ICESCR), 1, 8
  due diligence obligations, 205–6
  living wage, 170
  paid leave, 191
  prison labour, 144
  reasonable working hours, 184, 186–87
  right to work, 135–37
    prison labour, 144
    welfare-to-work schemes, 149
International Labour Conference (ILC), 24–25
International Labour Office, 1, 311–12
  see also International Labour Organization
International Labour Organization (ILO), 23
  child labour, 24, 25–26, 201–2, 319
  collective bargaining, 25, 68
  discrimination, 25–26
  enforcement challenges, 27
  forced or compulsory labour, 25–26, 146, 319
  form and technique of instruments, 26–27
  freedom of association, 25, 68
  human trafficking, 26
  ILO Committee on Freedom of Association, 25, 69–70, 90

ILO Convention 158 on Termination of Employment (1982)
  business restructuring, 305–7
  duty to provide valid reasons for dismissal, 304–5
  economic reasons for dismissal, 305–7
  fair termination procedures, 307–8
ILO Declaration on Fundamental Principles and Rights at Work, 24, 25–26, 201–2, 319
ILO Governing Body, 24–25, 114
information and consultation, 89–90
key challenges, 26–27
living wage, 170
multinational companies, regulation of, 201
  ILO Declaration, 201–2, 205
  disclosure obligations, 205
prison labour, 145, 146
standard-setting, 24, 25–26
supervisory and enforcement mechanisms, 24
  complaints of violations, 25
  reporting requirements, 24–25
trade union rights, protection of, 6
  closed shop, 78, 79
tripartite nature, 24
workers voice, 25, 68, 89–90

justification for labour rights as human rights, 4–5, 11–12, 311, 324–25

labour exploitation:
  forced and compulsory labour, *see* forced and compulsory labour
  human trafficking, *see also* human trafficking
  modern slavery, *see* modern slavery
  servitude, *see* servitude
  undocumented workers, *see* undocumented workers
labour migration, *see* migrant workers
labour rights as human rights, 4
  instrumental approach, 4–5, 314–15
  justification, 4–5, 11–12, 311, 324–25
  normative approach, 5, 218, 310–11
  positivist approach, 4
legal history of labour law, 2–3, 16–18, 310–12
  labour rights and human rights, 4–5, 310–12, 314–15, 324
legitimate purposes:
  age of compulsory retirement, 60–61
  dismissal, 304–5
  right to strike, 123
living wage:
  calculation of minimum standard, 171–73
  decency and dignity, 170–71
  exclusions
    education and training, 174
    family members, 173
    independent contractors, 173–74
    prisoners/detainees, 175
    young workers, 174
  pensions, 173
  right to fair pay, 167, 170–75

margin of appreciation, 9, 19, 64, 76, 246
  manifestation of beliefs, 282, 288, 293–94
  private life at work, 221–22
  private life away from work, 236–37

right to strike, 115–16, 118, 121, 131–32
  trade union recognition and collective bargaining, 92–95, 97, 99, 109
  unfair dismissal, 302
maternity leave and pay, 3, 13–14, 185, 193–95, 304–5
  Convention on the Elimination of All Forms of Discrimination against Women, 54–55
migrant workers, 11, 151–52, 315
  agricultural work, 154–56
  domestic workers, 156–58
  employment rights, 63
  exploitation, 11–12
  labour migration schemes, 152–53, 154, 165
  modern slavery, 160–63
  prohibition of discrimination (ECHR Art. 14), 64
  protection and assistance (ESC Art. 19), 17
  right to respect for private and family life (ECHR Art. 8), 64–65
  undocumented workers, 7, 158–60
  unequal treatment, challenging, 63–64
  vulnerability of, 152–53
  see also forced and compulsory labour; modern slavery; servitude
minimum service levels:
  right to strike, 113–16, 126–28
minimum wages, 3
  prohibition of discrimination (ECHR Art. 14), 59–60
  see also national minimum wage; right to fair pay
modern slavery, 160
  domestic workers, 224
  ECHR Art. 4, 7, 11–12, 138, 145–46, 160–63
    conditionality of welfare benefits, 147–48
  illegality doctrine, 39
  Modern Slavery Act (MSA) 2015, 163
    criticisms, 163–64
    disclosure obligations, 204–5
  servitude compared, 160–61
  sexual exploitation, 162–63
  slavery, servitude, forced and compulsory labour, 160–61
  undocumented workers, 161–62
monitoring of employees, 214–15
multinational companies (MNCs), 199–201, 213
  home state regulation, 204, 209
    civil liability for human rights abuses, 206–9
    disclosure obligations, 204–5
    due diligence obligations, 205–6
  international initiatives, 209–10
    OECD guidelines, 210
    UN Guiding Principles, 210–12
    UN HRC draft binding instruments, 212–13
  self-regulation, 201–3

national living wage, 172–73, 174
national minimum wage:
  age discrimination, 59–60
  apprenticeships, 174
  fair pay, 171–73
  main employer liability, 179
  prison labour, 175
natural justice, law and rights, 84–85, 313, 314, 323–24
negative and positive obligations, 6–8, 133, 211

neutrality policy:
  freedom of/manifestation of religion, 284, 287–89, 290
    CJEU, 287–88
    ECtHR, 288
non-discrimination, see prohibition on discrimination

offensive speech, 275–77
Organisation for Economic Co-operation and Development (OECD):
  Guidelines for Multinational Enterprises on Responsible Business Conduct, 210
  multinational companies, regulation of, 201
  disclosure obligations, 205
Overseas Domestic Worker (ODW) visas, 151–52, 156–58

paid annual leave, 9, 22–23, 184–85, 191–93
parental leave, 53, 55–56, 58–59, 100–1, 185, 193–95
Parental Leave Directive, 100–1
Part-time Work Directive, 45, 100–1
paternity leave, 58–59, 184–85, 194
pensions:
  age discrimination, 53, 60
  prison labour, 146
  right to equal treatment, 53, 60
  right to fair pay, 173
personal scope of employment rights, 47
  employment status, relationship with, 28–29
    contracts of employment, 30–31
    employee versus independent contractor, 30
    general employment protections, 29–30
  EU law, 42–43
    autonomous concept of worker, 43–44
    Directives, 44–46
  limitations, 29
  statutory protections, 29–31
    exclusions, 31
  universal entitlement of human rights, relationship with, 28–29
philosophical belief, discrimination on the grounds of:
  freedom of expression outside work, 264
    conduct connected to belief, 266
    proportionality, 266–68
    scope of protected belief, 265–66
Platform Work Directive, 46–47
political speech, 264, 273–75
political strikes:
  right to strike, 111, 113–14, 123
positive obligations, 6–8, 133, 211
posted workers, 129–30
precarious workers, 11–12, 29, 30–35, 111, 148–50
  collective bargaining, 106–7
  employer monitoring, 214–15, 228
  leave arrangements, 195
  migrant workers, 152–53, 158
  undocumented workers, 158–60
  welfare conditionality, 147–48
  working hours
    reasonable working hours, 189
    reliable working hours, 197–98
Pregnant Workers Directive (PrWD), 44, 193–94
prison labour, 144–46
  compulsion to work, 145

prisoners:
 living wage, 175
 pensions, 146
private life (activities outside work), 229, 241
 contextual dependence, 233–36
 criminal convictions, 238–40
 dismissal, 230–32
 public versus private space, 232–33
 reconceptualization of privacy, 240–41
 reputation of a business, impact on, 240
 right to private life, 230–32
 sexual intimacy, 236–38
 see also right to respect for private and family life
private life (at work):
 blood or urine testing, 227–28
 domestic workers, 224–25
 excessive surveillance and monitoring of employees, 214–15
  ECtHR guidance, 217–18
  employee right to privacy, 223
  monitoring productivity, 223
  non-covert surveillance of lectures and teaching, 218–19
  phone tapping, 216
  prior notification, 219
  reasonable expectation of privacy, 216–17
 genetic testing, 227–28
 personal/professional life boundaries, 219
  cloud storage, 220
  personal devices used for work, 220–22
 personality testing, 228
 random drugs and alcohol tests, 227–28
 right to respect for private and family life (ECHR Art. 8), 215–16
  data protection and criminal convictions, 226
 working from home, 222–23
 see also right to respect for private and family life
private versus public sector employment:
 right to strike, 121
probation, see qualifying periods of employment
procedural conditions:
 right to strike, 111, 122, 124–26
prohibition of abuse of rights (ECHR Art. 17):
 freedom of expression, relationship with, 277
 freedom of thought, conscience and religion, relationship with, 281–82
prohibition of discrimination:
 conscientious objection, relationship with, 289–90
 ECHR Art. 14, 50
  age discrimination, 59–61
  direct versus indirect discrimination, 51–52
  disability discrimination, 61–63
  employment status, relationship with, 38–39
  expansion of scope, 53–54
  'group disadvantage' requirement, 52
  justification, 51–52
  migrant workers, 63–65
  right to work, 59–61
  unlimited scope, 50–51
 equality laws, 283
 EUCFR (Art. 21), 282
 International Covenant on Civil and Political Rights, 139
 religion and religious beliefs
 women, positive rights for, 54
  Convention on the Elimination of All Forms of Discrimination against Women, 54–56
  domestic work, 56–57
  sex work, 56
  unpaid work at home, 57–59
prohibition of slavery and forced labour (ECHR Art. 4), 7, 11–12, 138, 145–46, 160–63
 conditionality of welfare benefits, 147–48
 see also modern slavery
proportionality, 12, 28–29
 dismissal, justification for, 42, 239
 freedom of expression, 246–47, 266–68
 freedom of religion or belief, 264, 266–68, 284
  dress codes, 288
  working hours, 286
 genuine occupational requirements, 292–93
 illegality doctrine, 40, 42
 non-discrimination, 38–39, 51–52
  margin of appreciation, 64, 221, 237
 offensive or hate speech, 275–76
 philosophical belief, discrimination on the grounds of, 266–68
 right to private life, 221, 228, 234–35, 237
  unlawful dismissal, 239, 241
 right to strike, 112, 129–30
 unlawful dismissal
  freedom of expression, 246, 248, 250–52, 259, 269–71
  right to private life, 239, 241
 whistle-blowing, 253–54
 working hours, 196
protected characteristics, 11, 49, 50–52, 59, 144, 264, 267–68, 279, 281–82, 296, 300, 304–5
protected disclosures:
 reasonable belief of public interest, 255, 257
 unfair dismissal, 254–55
 see also whistle-blowing
protection against unfair deductions from wages, 3, 117, 118, 120, 122, 166, 255
protection from unjustified dismissal:
 EUCFR Art. 30, 29, 297
 exclusions, 308–9
 ILO protection, 298
  see also ILO Convention 158 on Termination of Employment
 importance of, 295–96
  autonomy of employees, 297
  dignity and self-respect of employees, 296–97
  misuse of managerial power, 296
  resistance from employers, 297–98
 right to respect for private and family life (ECHR Art. 8), relationship with, 300–4
 right to strike, 119–20
  protections from other detriments, 120–22
 right to work, relationship with, 298–99, 299–300
 see also unfair dismissal
public interest:
 freedom of expression, 247–48, 250, 275
 protected disclosures, 255
 whistle-blowing, 252–57
public policy, 39–40, 314–15

qualifying periods of employment:
　unfair dismissal, 41–42, 274, 308–9

race discrimination, 3, 13–14
reasonable accommodation:
　disability discrimination, 62–63, 138, 196, 284–85
　religion or belief, 284–85
redundancy payments, 3, 59, 296, 305–6
　see also dismissal
regulation of hours of work, see working time
regulation of multinational companies, see multinational companies
religious beliefs defined, 280–81
　belief versus opinions, 281–82
　see also freedom of thought, conscience and religion
religious organisations as employers, 292–94
reporting obligations, 17–18, 24, 204–6, 208
retirement:
　compulsory retirement age, 60–61
　pensions
　　age discrimination, 53, 60
　　prison labour, 146
　　right to equal treatment, 53, 60
　　right to fair pay, 173
right of migrant workers to protection and assistance (ESC Art. 19), 17
right to a fair trial (ECHR Art. 6), 14
right to benefit from social welfare services (ESC Art. 14), 17
right to collective bargaining (ESC Art. 6), 67
right to engage in work (EUCFR Art. 15), 60
right to education (ECHR Prot. 1, Art. 2), 281, 315–17
right to fair and just working conditions (EUCFR Art. 31), 29, 46, 191
right to fair pay, 166
　collective bargaining, 167, 168–69
　fairness concept, 175–76
　　desert, 176–77
　　recognition, 177
　labour rights and standards, 167
　legal history, 166–68
　living wage, 167, 170–75
　relative wages within organisations, 167, 175–82
right to just conditions of work (ESC Art. 2), 17
right to life (ECHR Art. 2), 7, 17, 227, 313
right to organise, 17, 67, 68–71
　TULRCA, 71–72, 85
　protection of union activities, 73–74
　remedies, 74–75
　right to organise, 71–72
　trade union membership, 3, 71–72, 72–73
　use of trade union services, 74
　see also freedom of association
right to respect for private and family life (ECHR Art. 8), 7, 14, 17
　compulsory retirement, 60–61
　data protection and criminal convictions, 226
　disability discrimination, 61–63
　migrant workers, 64–65
　private life and activities outside work, 229, 241
　　contextual dependence, 233–36
　　criminal convictions, 238–40
　　dismissal, 230–32
　　public versus private space, 232–33
　reconceptualization of privacy, 240–41
　reputation of a business, impact on, 240
　right to private life, 230–32
　sexual intimacy, 236–38
private life at work, 215–16
　blood or urine testing, 227–28
　data protection and criminal convictions, 226
　domestic workers, 224–25
　ECtHR guidance, 217–18
　employee right to privacy, 223
　excessive surveillance and monitoring of employees, 214–19, 223
　genetic testing, 227–28
　monitoring productivity, 223
　non-covert surveillance of lectures and teaching, 218–19
　personal devices used for work, 220–22
　personal/professional life boundaries, 219–22
　personality testing, 228
　phone tapping, 216
　prior notification, 219
　random drugs and alcohol tests, 227–28
　reasonable expectation of privacy, 216–17
　right to respect for private and family life (ECHR Art. 8), 215–16, 226, 231–32
　working from home, 222–23
　protection from unjustified dismissal, relationship with, 300–4
　social media use, 263–64
　see also private life (activities outside work); private life (at work)
right to strike, 110
　collective bargaining, see collective bargaining
　common law
　　complete withdrawal of labour, 116–17
　　go slow/work to rule, 118
　　partial performance, 118
　　repudiatory breach of contract, 116–17
　core versus essential rights, 121
　damages, 128
　essential services, 126–28
　freedom of assembly and association (ECHR Art. 11), 115–16, 117–18
　freedom of expression (ECHR Art. 10), 113, 114–15
　EU law
　　free movement, impact of, 129–31
　ILO, 113–14
　individual strikers' rights, 116–22
　injunctions, 128–29
　legitimate purposes, 123
　liberty argument, 111
　margin of appreciation, 115–16
　moral and political foundations, 110–12
　minimum service levels, 126–28
　political strikes, 123
　private versus public sector employment, 121
　procedural conditions, 124–26
　protection from unfair dismissal, 119–20
　protections from detriments, 120–22
　purposive dimension, 110–11
　radical view of, 111–12
　restrictions, 112
　right to bargain collectively (ESC Art. 6), 67, 114
　right versus immunity, 131–32

rights at collective level, 122–29
secondary action, 121, 123
social democratic justification, 111
statutory protections
  detriment short of dismissal, 120–22
  unfair dismissal, 119–20
trade disputes, 123
right to work, 133–39
  age discrimination, 59–61
  begging, 140–41
  employer controls, 144
  protection from unjustified dismissal, relationship with, 298–99, 299–300
  restrictions to types of work
    bankrupt persons, 142
    free movement of workers, relationship with, 143
    misconduct, 143
    previous employment, based on, 141–42
  sex work, 139–40
  unjustified interferences with right to work, 141–43
  welfare-to-work schemes, 148–50
rule of law, 111–12, 253–54, 316

Seasonal Workers visa:
  agricultural work, 153–56
secondary action:
  right to strike, 113, 115, 121, 123
self-employment:
  collective bargaining, 106–7
  employment status, 30, 32, 39
  equal pay law, 43–44
  living wage, 173–74
  platform workers, 46–47
  protections and rights, 43–44
    unjustified dismissal, 308
  see also independent contractors
servitude:
  domestic servitude, 161
  modern slavery compared, 160–61
sex discrimination, 3, 13–14
sex work, 49–50, 56
  criminalisation, 139–40
  right to work, 139–40
  women's rights, 56
sexual intimacy:
  right to private life, 236–38
small undertakings:
  unfair dismissal, 308–9
social media:
  freedom of expression, 262–64
Solidarity Chapter of EUCFR, 29
supremacy doctrine, 9, 21
supply chains, 204, 209, 213
  civil liability for human rights abuses, 206–9
  disclosure obligations, 204–5
  due diligence obligations, 205–6
  ethical standards, 201–2, 203
  Ethical Trading Initiative code, 203
  European Works Councils, 104
  labour exploitation, 200
    regulation, 200–1
  UN Global Company, 201–3

surveillance and monitoring of employees, 214–15
  balancing rights, 217–19
  data protection issues, 225–27
  domestic workers, 224
  private life (at work)
    excessive surveillance and monitoring of employees, 214–19, 223

technological developments, threat of, 10–11, 214–15
termination, 11
  duty to provide valid reasons for dismissal, 304–5
  economic reasons for dismissal
    business restructuring, 306–7
    operational requirements, 305–6
  fair procedure prior to dismissal
  ideological conflicts, 234–36
  ILO Convention 158 on Termination of Employment (1982), 304–5
    business restructuring, 305–7
    fair termination procedures, 307–8
  right to private life, 230–32
  see also unfair dismissal
terms and conditions of employment, 2
  freedom of association, 202, 203
  freedom of expression, 247–48
  right to bargain collectively, 29, 87–88, 99–100
  right to fair pay, 179
  strike action, 110, 115, 123, 129
  trade union membership
    closed shop arrangements, 77–78
time off, 3, 11, 320
  entitlement to paid leave, 22, 185, 192, 193–96
  family purposes, 184–85, 193–96
  maternity leave and pay, 3, 13–14, 185, 193–95, 304–5
    Convention on the Elimination of All Forms of Discrimination against Women, 54–55
  paid annual leave, 9, 22–23, 184–85, 191–93
  parental leave, 53, 55–56, 58–59, 100–1, 185, 193–95
  paternity leave, 58–59, 184–85, 194
trade disputes, 79
  right to strike, 123
Trade Union and Labour Relations (Consolidation) Act (TULRCA) 1992, 13, 14, 85
  business restructuring, 102–3
  freedom of expression, 250–51
  protection of union activities, 73–74
  remedies, 74–75
  right to organise, 71–72
  right to strike
    core versus essential rights, 121
    damages, 128
    essential services, 126–28
    individual strikers' rights, 116–22
    injunctions, 128–29
    legitimate purposes, 123
    minimum service levels, 126–28
    political strikes, 123
    private versus public sector employment, 121
    procedural conditions, 124–26
    protection from unfair dismissal, 119–20
    protections from detriments, 120–22
    rights at collective level, 122–29
    secondary action, 121, 123
    trade disputes, 123

secondary strike action, 121
trade union membership, 3, 71–72, 72–73
  closed shop, 78–79
trade union recognition, 95–98
use of trade union services, 74
trade unions:
  autonomy, 81–82
  collective bargaining, 2
  collective trade union rights
    individual civil and political rights, relationship with, 5–6
  exclusion from membership, 83–84
  freedom of expression
    democratic importance, 249
    EU law, 249–50
    freedom of association overlap, 248–49
    freedom to challenge and criticise employers, 249
    UK statutory protections, 250–51
  membership, 3, 71–72, 72–73
    closed shop, 77–81
  trade union discipline, 84–85
  trade union recognition
    ECHR, 93–94
    TULRCA, 95–98
  victimisation of trade union representatives, 251–52
Transparent and Predictable Working Conditions Directive, 23, 197–98
Treaty on the Functioning of the European Union (TFEU):
  equal pay for men and women, 43
  EU's legislative competence, 100, 107
  freedom of establishment, 103
  free movement of workers, 143
  information and consultation, 100
    social dialogue, 100–1
  social dialogue, 100–1
  worker voice mechanisms, 100

UK Independent Mechanism (UKIM):
  disability discrimination, 61
UK Supreme Court (UKSC), 14
  collective bargaining, 98–99
  Disclosure and Barring Service, 226
  equal treatment
    benefits and non-working households, 58
    migrant workers, 64
    women, 58
  illegality doctrine, 39–40
  religious discrimination, 34–35
  right to strike
    declaration of incompatibility, 73–74
    detriment short of dismissal, 120–22
  right to work
    restrictions on types of work, 143
  status of gig economy workers, 32–33, 34, 37
    working hours, 186, 189
  termination of employment because of off-duty conduct, 240–41
  trade union recognition, 97–98
  undocumented workers, 158–59
  welfare conditionality, 148
  whistleblowing protections, 32, 38–39

UN Convention on the Rights of Persons with Disabilities (CRPD), 61–63
UN Global Compact, 201–3, 211
UN Guiding Principles on Business and Human Rights, 208, 210–12
UN Human Rights Committee (HRC):
  compliance with ICCPR, 139
UN Human Rights Council:
  draft binding instruments, 212–13
  right to work, 299–300
  UN Guiding Principles on Business and Human Rights, 210–12
undocumented workers, 151–52, 157–58, 158–60, 161–62, 165
unfair deductions from wages, 3, 117, 118, 120, 122, 166, 255
unfair dismissal:
  autonomy of employees, 297
  dignity and self-respect of employees, 296–97
  freedom of expression outside work, 268–71
  misuse of managerial power, 296
  protected disclosures, 255
  protection from unjustified dismissal, 295–97
    EUCFR Art. 30, 29, 297
    importance of, 295–97
  see also protection from unjustified dismissal
  qualifying periods of employment, 41–42
  right to strike
    detriment short of dismissal, 120–22
    unfair dismissal, 119–20
  standard of reasonableness, 15
  see also protection from unjustified dismissal
union security arrangements:
  closed shops, 77–78
unionisation of workers, 3, 68–69, 86–87, 96
Universal Declaration of Human Rights (UDHR), 1, 8, 48, 318
  due diligence obligations, 205–6
  right to a paid holiday, 320
  right to fair pay, 175
    living wage, 170–71
  right to work, 135
  trade union membership, 167–68
  working hours, 184
universality of human rights, 29, 48–50
unjustified dismissal, see unfair dismissal

vulnerable workers, 2, 11
  employment status, 29–35
    excluded workers, 35–42
  migrant workers, 152–53
    agricultural work, 153–54
    seasonal work, 153–55
  prison labour, 144–46
  sex work, 49–50, 56, 139–41
  slavery, servitude, forced and compulsory labour, 160–64
  undocumented workers, 158–60
  women
    domestic workers, 56–57, 156–58
    sex work, 49–50, 56, 139–41

wages, 11
    equal pay, 3, 54, 167–68, 178
        TFEU, 43
        Treaty of Rome, 20
    fair wages, 166
        bonuses and bonus caps, 181
        desert, 176–77
        equal pay for women, 178
        excessive inequalities, 180–82
        fairness concept, 175–77
        horizontal comparisons, 177–79
        indirect discrimination, 179
        market rates for pay, 180–81
        pay differentials, 180–81
        recognition, 177
        vertical comparisons, 180–82
    right to fair pay, 166
        collective bargaining, 167, 168–69
        fairness concept, 175–77
        desert, 176–77
        recognition, 177
        labour rights and standards, 167
        legal history, 166–68
        living wage, 167, 170–75
        relative wages within organisations, 167, 175–82
welfare-to-work schemes (welfare conditionality), 146–47
    prohibition of forced and compulsory labour, 147–48
    right to work, 148–50
whistle-blowing, 252–53
    confidentiality and loyalty, 255–57
    human rights basis, 253–55
    public interest, 255
women:
    vulnerable workers, 2, 11
        domestic workers, 56–57, 156–58
        sex work, 49–50, 56, 139–41
    see also Convention on the Elimination of All Forms of Discrimination against Women; women's rights
women's rights:
    domestic work, 56–57
    international law, 54–56
    sex work, 56
    unpaid work at home, 57–59
    see also Convention on the Elimination of All Forms of Discrimination against Women
workers voice, 86–88
    collective bargaining, 2–3, 11, 25, 67–68, 98–99, 106–8
    dual channel representation, 88
    information and consultation, 11, 46, 91–92
        duty to consult, 103–6
        European Works Councils, 103–6
        ILO, 89–90
        Information and Consultation Directive, 11, 46, 106
    process versus outcome, 89
    process, 88
    protection of, 89–92
    single channel representation, 88
    subject, 88–89
workers with protected characteristics, see protected characteristics
working conditions, 4, 155
    prison labour, 145–46
    Adequate Minimum Wages Directive, 107
    ILO, 26, 56–57
    right to fair and just working conditions (EUCFR Art. 31), 29
    right to just conditions of work (ESC Art. 2), 17, 135, 137
    Transparent and Predictable Working Conditions Directive, 23, 197–98
        due diligence obligations, 204–5
    see also workplace surveillance and monitoring of employees
working time, 11, 183–86
    entitlement to paid leave, 195–96
    flexible working
        employers' duties, 196
        right to request, 196–97
    maternity leave, 193–94
    paid annual leave, 191–93
    parental leave, 194–95
    paternity leave, 194
    precarious workers and more reliable working hours, 197–98
    religion or belief, 285–86
    weekly working time, 186–90
Working Time Directive (WTD), 22, 44, 46
workplace autocracy, 86–89
workplace surveillance and monitoring of employees, 214–15
    balancing rights, 217–19
    data protection issues, 225–27
    domestic workers, 224
    private life (at work)
        excessive surveillance and monitoring of employees, 214–19, 223

young persons:
    age discrimination, 59
    living wage, 174

zero-hour contracts, 39, 148–50